Cournot oligopoly

T0318346

From *Econometrica,* 1933, courtesy of Claire Friedland and George J. Stigler.

Cournot oligopoly

Characterization and applications

Edited by
Andrew F. Daughety
UNIVERSITY OF IOWA

The right of the
University of Cambridge
to print and sell
all manner of books
was granted by
Henry VIII in 1534.
The University has printed
and published continuously
since 1584.

Cambridge University Press

Cambridge
New York   New Rochelle   Melbourne   Sydney

CAMBRIDGE UNIVERSITY PRESS
Cambridge, New York, Melbourne, Madrid, Cape Town, Singapore, São Paulo

Cambridge University Press
The Edinburgh Building, Cambridge CB2 2RU, UK

Published in the United States of America by Cambridge University Press, New York

www.cambridge.org
Information on this title: www.cambridge.org/9780521361767

First published 1988
This digitally printed first paperback version 2005

A catalogue record for this publication is available from the British Library

Library of Congress Cataloguing in Publication data
Cournot oligopoly.
Bibliography: p.
1. Oligopolies.   2. Cournot, A. A. (Antoine Augustin),
1801–1877 – Contributions in economics.   I. Daughety,
Andrew F.
HD2757.3.C68   1988   338.8′2   88–7261

ISBN-13 978-0-521-36176-7 hardback
ISBN-10 0-521-36176-1 hardback

ISBN-13 978-0-521-02284-2 paperback
ISBN-10 0-521-02284-3 paperback

Contents

Preface   vii

v

Preface

Fifty years ago, in an address to the Cournot Memorial session of the Econometric society, A. J. Nichol observed that if ever there was an apt illustration of Carnegie's dictum that "It does not pay to pioneer," then Cournot's life and work would be it. His work was essentially ignored (especially by his countrymen) for many years. What survives in most economists' minds today is Cournot's model of duopoly. And this, too, if one consults the treatment in most current microeconomics texts, seems to linger on as an image of the past, a traditional topic for inclusion in a chapter on imperfect competition, sandwiched somewhere between monopoly and the bibliography, or neatly tucked away as an example of an application of game theory. So why dust off this musty topic now?

A peek at the extended bibliography and the papers in this volume should make the reason for reconsidering Cournot clear: There has been a veritable explosion of Cournot-based models of strategic behavior over the last two decades, and the end is not in sight. In recognition of this, this volume is a celebration of the publication of Augustin Cournot's model of noncooperative behavior and an examination of its relevance and importance to economic theory and analysis 150 years after its first appearance. The introduction examines the Cournot model and its relationship to many of the classical and recent analyses of market behavior. A few special papers of older vintage are included (Cournot's chapter on oligopoly, a translation of Bertrand's review, and Nash's generalization of the Cournot solution) but the book consists mainly of recently published papers that either examine the Cournot model itself or apply it to provide a deeper understanding of economic theory and behavior. Eight papers concerned with existence, the versatility of noncooperative models of behavior, the rationality and reasonableness of such behavior, and the variety and interrelatedness of modeling options are collected in a section entitled "Applications." Eight other papers focus on applications, using Cournot's model to analyze theoretical models of perfect and imperfect competition and observed structure and behavior in firms and markets. These sixteen papers are a sample of recent work in economic theory and

vii

analysis, reflecting a revival of interest in Cournot's model largely due to increased emphasis on aspects of imperfect competition and strategic behavior in various economic models. All papers were faithfully reproduced, which means that typos in the papers were also left intact as long as they did not cause serious misunderstanding of the material; those that might were corrected. The introduction, part overviews, and the extended bibliography of over 300 references provide links to the existing literature on oligopolistic behavior.

Not surprisingly, there are a number of people to thank. This book grew out of a conversation with Xavier Vives. Also, this volume would be very short without the papers that have been reprinted; I thank the publishers and the authors for permission to include their works in this volume. Jim Friedman and Mort Kamien provided a wealth of historical observations and insights; with Jennifer Reinganum they also provided productive comments on various versions of the introductory chapter. Support by the National Science Foundation via two grants (SES-8218684 and IST-8610360) and by the Department of Decision Sciences of The Wharton School, University of Pennsylvania, where this project originated while I was a visitor there, is also gratefully acknowledged. Mark Knez of Wharton and Suresh Mutuswami of Iowa provided diligent help on the extended bibliography. I want especially to thank Colin Day, formerly of Cambridge University Press, now with The University of Michigan Press, who shepherded this book from concept to contract to production schedule. Last, but most important, I want to thank my wife, Ginny, and our children, Sam and Kassie, who gave constant support and encouragement and put up with untold numbers of nights and weekends given over to a word processor.

PART I

Introduction

Introduction, purpose, and overview

ANDREW F. DAUGHETY

> Cournot's genius must give new mental activity to everyone who passes
> through his hands.　　　　　　　　　　　　　　　– Alfred Marshall
> 　　　　　　　　　　　　　　　　　　　　　Preface to First Edition of
> 　　　　　　　　　　　　　　　　　　　　　*Principles of Economics*

The analysis of strategic choice by noncooperative agents has come a long
way since Augustin Cournot first developed a model of such behavior in
his 1838 work, *Researches into the Mathematical Principles of the Theory
of Wealth.*[1] The current volume is a celebration of the publication of
Cournot's model of multiagent behavior and an examination of its relevance and importance to economic theory and analysis 150 years after its
first appearance.[2] The contents of this volume will encompass both old
and new. It includes contributions by Cournot, Bertrand, and Nash as
well as recent papers that focus on the properties and uses of Cournot's

Support by NSF grants SES-8218684 and IST-8610360, and by the Department of Decision
　　Sciences, The Wharton School, University of Pennsylvania, is gratefully acknowledged,
　　as are fruitful discussions with, and suggestions from, James Friedman, Mort Kamien,
　　Jennifer Reinganum, and a host of others. Mark Knez and Suresh Mutuswami provided
　　diligent help on the Extended Bibliography that appears at the end.
Departments of Economics and Management Sciences, The University of Iowa.

[1] Cournot appears to be the first to have formally modeled non-cooperative behavior by
　agents. Everybody, however, seems to have a predecessor. James Waldgrave appears to
　be the first to have computed a mixed strategy Nash equilibrium for a normal form of a
　two-person zero-sum card game in 1713; see "Waldgrave's Comments: Excerpt from
　Montmort's Letter to Nicholas Bernoulli," and the preface to the letter by Harold Kuhn,
　in Baumol and Goldfeld [1968]. I am indebted to Stephen Salant for bringing this exam-
　ple to my attention.

[2] Cournot's book covered many areas of economics and exerted a significant influence on
　the development of economic theory in the nineteenth century. For example, he devel-
　oped the mathematical and graphical representation of a demand function; see Fry and
　Ekelund [1971] and Rhodes [1978]. Our current basic model of monopoly is that which
　Cournot developed in his fifth chapter (see Hicks [1935]). More generally, Marshall, in
　the preface to his first edition, attributes his realization of the importance of balanc-
　ing marginal effects not to Jevons but to Cournot (and, to a lesser degree, von Thunen);
　see Blaug [1962]. Fisher [1898, 1938] credits Cournot as the founder of mathematical
　economics.

model of competition among the few. These papers reflect a revival of interest in Cournot's model due largely to increased emphasis by economists on capturing elements of imperfect competition and strategic behavior (for a sample of other recent articles, see the Extended Bibliography at the end of this chapter). This expansion of interest is not limited to microeconomics; recent work in macroeconomics has also started to feature imperfect competition as an integral part of the analysis. The reason for this renaissance is clear: Cournot developed the basic model of non-cooperative behavior by agents and it is to variations on this model that economists turn when imperfect competition is analyzed.

The purpose of this chapter is twofold. First, it will provide a unified framework for considering the Cournot model and some of its many variations and revisions that have developed over time (including the models of Bertrand, Edgeworth, Stackelberg, and Chamberlin). This will be accomplished by providing and contrasting the associated extensive form games for each model. For example, Bertrand's model involves the addition of another agent (Cournot's model involves two agents, Bertrand's involves three) and is, in an important sense, the ancestor of modern models of consumer search. Stackelberg's model can be viewed as a refinement of Cournot's model (specifically, that information sets for players are singletons). By employing both the extensive form and the more traditional normal form representations, a more complete image of Cournot's contribution to oligopoly theory emerges. Second, this approach will provide a basis for examining the varieties of characterizations of Cournot's model in section three and the applications to be presented in section four.

Three parts (Background, Characterization, and Applications) follow this introductory chapter. Each is preceded by a brief overview for the part, discussing the papers in the part and, with this chapter, providing linkage to the extant literature.

Part two of the volume provides three important source documents: (1) Cournot's chapter wherein he develops his model of oligopoly; (2) James Friedman's translation of Bertrand's review of Cournot's book; this review is the source of the Bertrand model (Many recent papers refer to Bertrand's review, but heretofore scholars have not had access to a useful English translation of the original article; thus this translation fills a significant gap in the literature.); (3) Nash's paper on noncooperative games, which generalized Cournot's basic model of simultaneous noncooperative behavior.

Part three focuses on the Cournot model itself and consists of three subsections of papers addressing the following classical issues:

Introduction, purpose, and overview

1. Under what conditions does the static Cournot solution exist? More generally, if noncooperative models are internally consistent, why should we use them to predict the behavior of groups of agents when cooperation can lead to higher returns to all agents? Is collusion possible in a model of noncooperative behavior? What outcomes occur if firms play a repeated Cournot game: specifically, how can repetition lead to collusion or competition?
2. Is the model consistent with modern notions of rational expectations behavior? Is the behavior predicted by the model observed?
3. Can games in prices yield the Cournot outcome? How are price and quantity games related? Are prices or quantities the "appropriate" decision variables in models of oligopolies? More precisely, what might influence the selection of strategic variable(s)?

Finally, the fourth part of the book focuses on applications of Cournot's model. There are literally hundreds of recent applications from which to choose. The selection reflects a strategy that emphasizes two themes: using Cournot's model to highlight and better understand theories of perfect and imperfect competition and using Cournot's model to examine and understand "real world" (albeit economic) phenomena.

Cournot oligopoly

Cournot's chapter on oligopoly[3] (reproduced in Part II) provides four contributions, not all of which have been equally well received:

1. The Cournot *model* of simultaneous, noncooperative behavior by agents;
2. The Cournot *analysis* of a quantity game among oligopolists;
3. The Cournot *story* of disequilibrium behavior by agents;
4. The Cournot *characterization* of best response behavior.

This list attempts to separate *how* things are examined (items 1 and 4) from *what* things are examined (items 2 and 3). Cournot's great contribution concerns the *how* more than the *what*. This chapter examines these four contributions in detail and uses them both to lay out the Cournot model and to link it with other representations of strategic behavior by a group of agents. Before examining the aforementioned topics in detail, an overview of what they refer to is undoubtedly worthwhile.

---

[3] Friedman [1977, 1983], Jacquemin [1987], and Shapiro [forthcoming] provide reviews of the general oligopoly literature. See also the recent symposium on Strategic Behavior and Competition in the June, 1986 issue of the *Journal of Economic Theory*. Finally, Dixit [1986] provides an extensive review of comparative statics for oligopoly models.

The Cournot model of simultaneous noncooperative behavior by agents will be the starting point. As will be shown, this is the basic building block of oligopoly models, including every one of the traditional models (that is, Bertrand, Edgeworth, Stackelberg, Chamberlin, and so forth). Cournot's model is essentially the direct predecessor of Nash's equilibrium point. Cournot's model of simultaneous choice by agents can be applied in a variety of contexts and leads to a variety of outcomes. For our purposes, the Cournot model involves agents making simultaneous optimal choices for themselves wherein they must conjecture what the other agents will also choose. Significantly, strategies cannot in any way be contingent upon any other agent's actions. Correct conjectures by all parties leads to an equilibrium as an outcome.

The phrase "Cournot analysis" refers to the particular example of oligopolistic behavior by firms to which Cournot applied his model, namely firms making quantity choices in a setting involving an aggregate demand function to represent consumers. Though it is not uncommon for economists to think of Cournot's model as applying only to a situation wherein duopolists incur zero costs, his chapter actually addresses models involving n firms and nonconstant, nonidentical costs of production.

The Cournot story of disequilibrium behavior is the familiar one of each firm observing the other's output and then choosing a new production level, assuming that the other firm will stay at its observed output level. Cournot used this version of pseudo-dynamic behavior to explain why the proposed static solution should be thought of as the reasonable outcome to predict. Fellner [1949] characterized the outcome of Cournot's analysis as involving the oligopolists being "right for the wrong reasons." This story of turn-taking provides a model of disequilibrium adjustment and has led to an extensive literature on the "stability" of the Cournot solution (see Okuguchi [1976]). In general, the standard story strains credulity, with firms never learning that other firms do adjust.

Finally, the Cournot story, along with the first order conditions for Cournot's analysis, led Cournot to the notion of a "reaction function." Since the model involves a static setting, this is an unfortunate choice of words to describe an alternative representation of static noncooperative behavior, but it reflects the confusion between the story and the model, which Cournot fostered by his exposition. In the static setting a reaction function is a decision rule which gives the optimal decision for the agent as a function of the conjectured action to be taken by the other agent(s); significantly, some alternative decision processes lead to the same decision rule (this point will be explored shortly).

6

Introduction, purpose, and overview

The Cournot model

The Cournot model is a simultaneous move, single-shot game wherein the strategy space for each player is the same as that for every other player. In particular, this means that consumers are not agents in the game, since consumers pick levels of a good to purchase *and* which firm to purchase the good from. As we shall see below, this demarcates the Cournot game from the Bertrand game. Furthermore, all agents make their choices in ignorance of the choices made by any other agent. Actions are chosen simultaneously, not sequentially.[4]

For convenience, let us consider a two-firm model wherein firm i ($i = 1, 2$) chooses strategy x_i (for example, quantity or price) in a strategy space $X = [0, \bar{x}]$, $\bar{x} > 0$, and receives reward $\pi_i(x_1, x_2)$.[5] Figure 1 represents the Cournot model of the two-firm decision problem in extensive form. Numbered squares represent the firms making decisions about which strategy to follow. The range of choices for, say, firm 1 is indicated in the figure by the curved double-headed arrows on the branches emanating from the square labeled "1" in the diagram; the curved arrow indicates that there are an infinite number of branches emanating from this square, with the two most extreme ones depicted. This is also true for firm 2. Note that there are (implicitly) an infinite number of squares labeled "2" in the diagram, with the two associated with the extreme choices by firm 1 of 0 and $\bar{x}$ depicted. The dashed line linking the two extreme (that is, left and right) squares for firm 2 represents the information set for firm 2. This reflects the assumption that firms pick strategies simultaneously and in ignorance of each other's actions.[6] Consumers are not represented in the game as strategic players. Rather they appear only in the payoffs for the two firms (via the demand function).

[4] In contrast, in the Stackelberg model actions are chosen sequentially and thus some agents (those who wait) are informed about the choices made by other agents. In some settings this works to the advantage of those who moved first and in some settings this works to the advantage of those who became informed by waiting to move second (see Gal-Or [1987]). We will return to this issue shortly.

[5] The bound $\bar{x}$ is assumed for convenience of exposition (especially with respect to the diagrams). It is decidedly not the purpose of this chapter to provide a general model or to emphasize necessary and/or sufficient conditions. Rather, the focus is on making the underlying story clear and intuitive. For instance, we will assume appropriate restrictions are in force (that is, continuity, concavity, differentiability, etc.) as necessary, without further comment. For a more careful treatment of some of the technical requirements, see the papers by Nash, Novshek, and Vives in this volume.

[6] Technically, the extensive form always indicates a sequence of play. In this case though firm 2 "goes second," he has no information about what firm 1 has chosen to do and thus must conjecture exactly as he would have, had he chosen simultaneously with firm 1. With this minor abuse of this technical consideration we proceed as indicated.

7

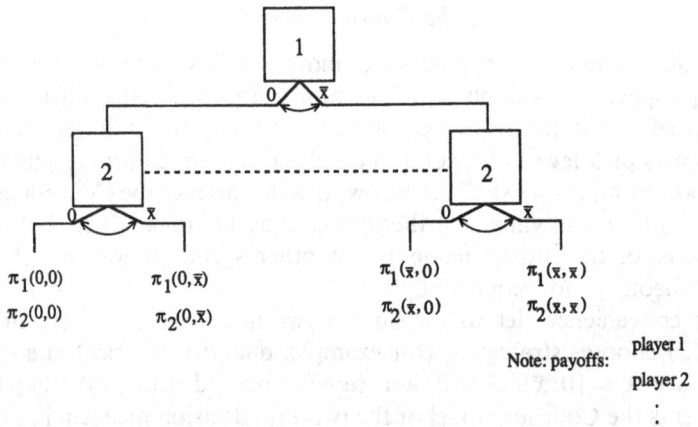

Figure 1. The Cournot model.

The Cournot equilibrium is the Nash equilibrium[7] of the Cournot model; that is, we are interested in vectors $x^C \in X^2$ such that[8]

$$\pi_1(x_1^C, x_2^C) \geq \pi_1(x_1, x_2^C), \quad \forall x_1 \in X, \tag{1}$$

$$\pi_2(x_1^C, x_2^C) \geq \pi_2(x_1^C, x_2), \quad \forall x_2 \in X. \tag{2}$$

Cournot expressed this in terms of derivatives $(\partial_j \pi_i \equiv \partial \pi_i / \partial x_j)$:

$$\partial_i \pi_i(x_1^C, x_2^C) = 0, \quad i = 1, 2, \tag{3}$$

[see his equations (1) and (2)]. The Cournot–Nash equilibrium involves agents making optimizing decisions based on conjectures about the strategies that will be employed by the other agents. In the Cournot model agents' strategies are simple one-time decisions, while in a more dynamic setting a Nash strategy could reflect planned play in a game which depends upon the actions of others over the course of the game. In both cases, however, strategies must be chosen before actual play begins, and are thus based upon conjectures about what the other agents will choose as their strategies. Thus, each agent solves a payoff maximization prob-

---

[7] It may seem circular to employ a Nash equilibrium to define the Cournot equilibrium, but as should become clear, this provides a convenient unification, especially since the Nash equilibrium is a generalization of the Cournot equilibrium (for example, agents other than firms are allowed).

[8] Since our main interest involves multiagent interaction and our main tool of exposition will employ calculus, we will focus on interior solutions. Needless to say, this glosses over the interesting issue of entry deterrence (and exit) in general.

lem wherein the strategies of the other agents appear as parameters in the optimization model. The Berge Maximum Theorem (Berge [1963]) tells us that each agent can be viewed, under appropriate restrictions on pay-off functions and strategy spaces, as employing a solution function that varies with the parameters of the problem. In particular, if π_i is strictly concave in x_i for each value of x_j, then the solutions to (3) can, as a vector, be represented by a continuous function $\phi: X^2 \to X^2$ with $x_i = \phi_i(x_j)$, $i, j = 1, 2$, $j \neq i$. Thus, a third way to express the Cournot equilibrium is in terms of the ϕ-functions:

$$x_i^C = \phi_i(x_j^C), \quad i, j = 1, 2, \quad j \neq i. \tag{4}$$

Equivalently, the Cournot solution is a fixed point of the function ϕ.[9]

Historically, the ϕ-functions have been referred to as *reaction functions,* or *best response functions,* or *best reply functions,* all unfortunate terms since moves are made simultaneously in this game, and the words "reaction," "response," and "reply" suggest sequential movement. Cournot discussed the solution to (3) in terms of sequential reactions along the curves described by the ϕ-functions, thereby providing what was referred to earlier as the Cournot story.

In the current context we will view a ϕ-function as providing a *conjecture dependent* optimal choice rule; given a conjecture by an agent about the actions to be taken by the other agents, the appropriate ϕ-function indicates an optimal choice for the one-shot simultaneous game. If both agents make correct conjectures and use their choice rules then the resulting choices (which are "best responses" to their conjectures) will form a Nash equilibrium.

Now the question becomes: How to make conjectures? Clearly there are many ways to make conjectures. Cournot's story involved firms actually making observations, forming conjectures that the other agents would not adjust their observed choices, and then using their choice rules sequentially. Cournot tells a story of each producer observing the output level the other firm has chosen and adjusting his choice of output level in response. His motivation was to provide a stability rationale for his proposed solution. Clearly, the story involves a dynamic setting wherein agents ignore the effect their current choices have on future choices by all agents. This is a disequilibrium adjustment story, wherein, under appropriate conditions, agents end up at equilibrium. The story is unacceptable for three reasons. First, this is a dynamic "rationalization" for a solution to a static problem. If one really has a dynamic analysis in mind, then the dynamics should be explicitly modeled. Second, even if

---

[9] See Friedman [1986] for details and for the relationship between fixed points of best-reply mappings and Nash equilibria.

we accept this in an "as if" analysis, with the static outcome reflecting some sort of eventual steady state of the dynamic process of interest, agents appear to assume that the other agents' choices will not respond to their choices, though they can readily predict that they themselves would react. Thus all agents make best responses to choices and not to choice rules; choices by others are taken as fixed. Third, even if agents were so naïve, extrapolation of this procedure to more than two agents also strains credulity: Cournot's procedure would have each agent adjust once every n periods in an n-player setting, and sit blithely by for the other $n-1$ periods.[10]

An alternative, purely static, method for constructing conjectures comes from the decision process of the agents and leads back to the exact same Cournot choices. Assume that all information is common knowledge. Moreover, assume that payoffs are strictly concave in own-strategy. If this fails, multiple equilibria can occur and players may then incur coordination failures (that is, agents may use equilibrium strategies, but not all may choose to play a strategy from the same equilibrium). If agents assume that each other agent will maximize payoffs *and* that this will provide the forecasting mechanism that each will use for the other, then, say, agent i proceeds to solve an infinite regress problem wherein i chooses a strategy to maximize i's payoff, using a model of j (specifically, j's payoff function) to forecast what j is likely to do, which in turn is dependent upon a model by i *of j* of what agent i will do, and so on. Common knowledge of payoffs and of the joint employment of this particular forecasting procedure means that the infinite regress can be consistently solved by all agents. The restriction that all players use the proposed forecasting process and that this is common knowledge is important, since failure for this to hold can mean that playing Nash strategies can be pathological (see Bernheim [1984] and Pearce [1984]).[11] The quantity decision version of this story is provided in Daughety [1985, reprinted in this volume]. The important point for the issue at hand is that this amounts to each agent choosing a best response to the decision process for the other agent, while assuming that the other agent is doing likewise, a mutually consistent assumption. This can be shown (under mild conditions on the infinite regress process so that it yields a fixed-point

---

[10] An alternative interpretation is that all firms move together, jointly observe, and then move again, etc. This eliminates the third objection, but not the first two.

[11] Bernheim [1984] and Pearce [1984] show that rationality is not sufficient to imply that outcomes of games will be Nash equilibria. Recently, Brandenburger and Dekel [1987] have shown that all rationalizable outcomes are refinements of various notions of correlated equilibria, a generalization of mixed strategy Nash equilibrium. Thus, in an appropriately defined sense, rationality does lead to playing strategies that form an equilibrium.

problem) to yield the system of equations (3). Thus, not only is the Cournot equilibrium the result of best responses to conjectured actions, it is also the result of best responses to decision rules. Note that breaking this symmetry yields other outcomes; for example, having one agent make best responses to conjectures while the other makes best responses to rules can yield the Stackelberg solution, as will be seen below.

Cournot's analysis of oligopoly

In Cournot's analysis of a duopoly, the strategies for the firms are output levels of a homogeneous good (some later writers have interpreted this to be production capacities). Let q_i denote the output level for firm i, and assume that firm i incurs marginal and average cost of production c_i. The vector of outputs is $\mathbf{q} = (q_1, q_2)$. Since we will also want to use functions to provide quantities and prices at certain points, a potential for confusion due to notation arises which must be balanced with the cost of using more and more complex (and less suggestive) notation. To avoid this, I will use the convention that any symbol in a mathematical expression that is immediately followed by a left parenthesis is supposed to represent a function of the arguments following the left parenthesis, while vectors will be unsubscripted and in boldface. Thus, $\mathbf{q}$ is a vector and $q(\cdot)$ is a function.

The upper bound on the strategy space $X \equiv Q = [0, \bar{q}]$ will be taken to reflect maximum aggregate consumer demand. More precisely, we model consumers as follows. Assume that there is a continuum of identical consumers, each of whom can be represented by a demand function[12] $d(p)$, p a scalar for the product in question and such that there are finite positive numbers $\bar{p}$ and $\bar{d}$ such that $d(\bar{p}) = 0$ and $d(0) = \bar{d}$. The assumption of a continuum of identical consumers is used to enforce the role of consumers as pure price takers, without bargaining power, and at the same time provides a representative consumer (thereby allowing for simple extensive form game trees). Moreover, assume that these demand functions can be aggregated into a "nice" aggregate demand function $q(p)$, with inverse $p(q)$, with all the usual desirable properties, where again there are finite positive scalars $\bar{p}$ and $\bar{q}$ such that $q(\bar{p}) = 0$ and $q(0) = \bar{q}$. Note that $\bar{q}$ is the upper bound of Q.

Thus, for any vector $(q_1, q_2) \in Q^2$, firm i's reward is its profit

$$\Pi_i^Q(q_1, q_2) = p(q_1 + q_2)q_i - c_i q_i, \quad i = 1, 2,$$

and the Cournot equilibrium, $\mathbf{q}^C = (q_1^C, q_2^C)$, is the solution to the system of equations:

---

[12] Let $\rho(d)$ denote the inverse demand function with corresponding properties.

$$\partial_i \Pi_i^Q(q_1, q_2) = p(q_1 + q_2) + \partial_i p(q_1 + q_2)q_i - c_i = 0, \quad i = 1, 2. \tag{5}$$

Alternatively $\mathbf{q}^C$ satisfies equations (1) and (2) above as $\mathbf{x}^C$.

In terms of decision rules, solving (5) yields the functions φ_1 and φ_2, where $q_i = \varphi_i(q_j)$, $i, j = 1, 2$, $j \neq i$. Second-order conditions and concavity of the demand function mean that the choice rules are downward-sloping and have a fractional (absolute) slope at any point: $\partial_j \varphi_i \in (-1, 0)$. This yields the familiar geometry displayed in Figure 2, a version of which appears in Cournot's treatment of oligopoly (see Figure 1.2 in Cournot's chapter in Part II). The intersection of the two curves is the Cournot equilibrium.

Figure 2 indicates the isoprofit lines that form the decision curves. The slope of the curves reflects the fact that the two agents produce goods that are substitutes for each other. Note also that the existence of fixed costs would induce discontinuities in the response functions, reflecting the choice to shut down rather than incur variable costs in excess of revenue. Dixit [1979] uses such discontinuities to examine entry-forestalling behavior.

Szidarovszky and Yakowitz [1977] show that concave demand and convex costs are sufficient to guarantee existence. McManus [1962] showed that considerably weaker conditions on demand were possible in the case of symmetric costs. Specifically, as long as the reaction functions only had jumps "up" (for example, due to nonconcavity of the demand function) then a symmetric Cournot equilibrium exists (see also Roberts and Sonnenschein [1976]). Unfortunately, even slightly nonidentical costs can result in nonexistence (see example 2 in Novshek's 1985 paper, reprinted in this volume). Novshek provides a significantly relaxed set of sufficient conditions that ensure existence of an n-firm Cournot equilibrium in the case of homogeneous goods with quantity as the decision variable. Interestingly, the main restriction is on revenue; the restrictions on the cost functions are very weak. Specifically, Novshek requires that cost functions be nondecreasing and lower semicontinuous[13] and that individual agent marginal revenue declines as aggregate output for all other agents increases (for inverse demand positive). The weakness of the restrictions on the cost functions is especially noteworthy, since by allowing firm technologies to reflect economies of scale, this theorem provides existence for exactly the environment that models of oligopoly were supposed to address.[14]

---

[13] Thus, the cost functions are continuous from the left, allowing for jumps such as would occur if there were avoidable setup costs in a production process.

[14] Necessary and sufficient conditions for uniqueness of a Cournot equilibrium in the homogeneous goods case are provided by Kolstad and Mathiesen [1987]; see also Szidarovszky

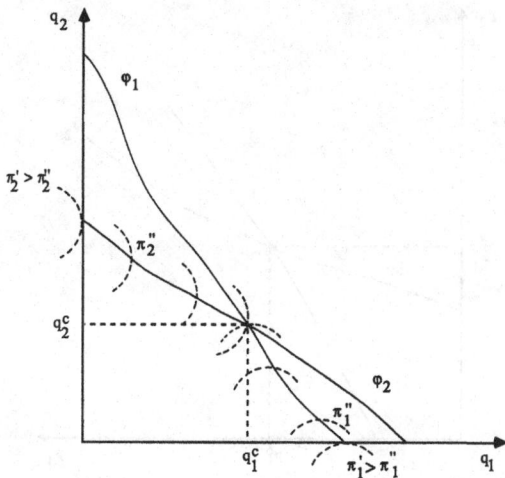

Figure 2. Decision rules in quantities.

Differentiated products and the Cournot model

One could just as easily apply the Cournot model to the differentiated product problem.[15] Let $q_i(p_1, p_2)$, $i = 1, 2$, be the aggregate demand functions for the two firms dependent upon their prices. Further, assume that there are prices $\bar{p}_1$ and $\bar{p}_2$ such that $q_1(\bar{p}_1, \infty) = 0$ and $q_2(\infty, \bar{p}_2) = 0$. Now let $\bar{p} = \max(\bar{p}_1, \bar{p}_2)$, and let $X \equiv P = [0, \bar{p}]$. Finally, let $\Pi_i^P(p_1, p_2) = p_i q_i(p_1, p_2) - c_i q_i(p_1, p_2)$ be firm i's profit. Then, in a manner similar to the previous analysis, $\mathbf{p}^C = (p_1^C, p_2^C) \in P^2$ would be a Cournot equilibrium in prices if $\mathbf{p}^C$ satisfied equations (1) and (2) with $x_i = p_i$ and $\pi_i = \Pi_i^P$. Again, under appropriate conditions, the necessary optimality condition equivalent to (3), namely $\partial_i \Pi_i^P(p_1, p_2) = 0$, yields decision rules $\Psi_i(\cdot)$, $i = 1, 2$. If the goods are substitutes, as is typically assumed, then increasing conjectures by firm i about firm j's price will yield higher posted prices by firm i, as indicated in Figure 3. Again, the Cournot equilibrium occurs where the decision rules cross, where $p_i^C = \Psi_i(p_j^C)$, $i, j = 1, 2$, $j \neq i$.

With some further effort, this basic model provides a model of monopolistic competition, yielding the results that Chamberlin [1933] first

and Yakowitz [1982]. Algorithms for computing oligopoly market equilibria have been developed by Harker [1984] and Murphy et al. [1982].

[15] This has been referred to recently as the Bertrand model, because of the presence of prices. Earlier usage was to refer to this as Cournot in prices. As we shall see, Bertrand's contribution was the introduction of search by consumers as active agents in the game. Thus, I will stick to the older language.

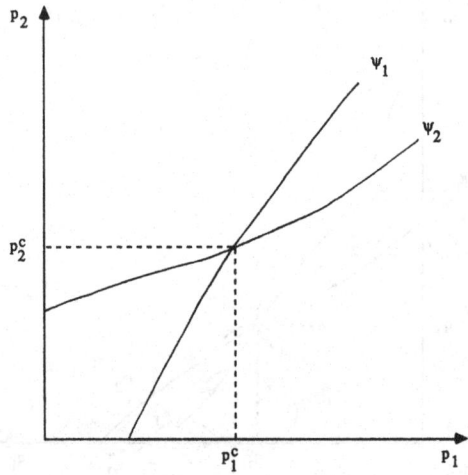

Figure 3. Decision rules in prices.

attempted to provide. Hart [1985] uses a model with firms playing Cournot in prices, with entry, and with special restrictions on consumer preferences to produce Chamberlinian results. Specifically, Hart defines monopolistic competition as having four characteristics:

1. many firms producing differentiated commodities
2. each firm negligible in terms of impact on other firms
3. free entry leading to zero profits for firms in the industry
4. each firm facing a downward sloping demand curve.

Hart's restriction on consumer preferences is that consumers only like a finite subset of the brands produced and that for each consumer every combination of the finite set is equally likely to be preferred by that consumer (for an imperfect information version of this consumer, see Wolinsky [1986]). This rules out neighboring goods effects, which means that a change in the action of one firm is spread out evenly over all other firms, thereby providing (2) above when the number of firms is large. Hart then defines ϵ-equilibria (wherein profits may be slightly positive with a finite number of firms) and then shows that we can always get arbitrarily close to a zero profit (that is, "true"), monopolistically competitive equilibrium with an ϵ-monopolistically competitive equilibrium.

Finally, as is well known, the basic Cournot model applied to differentiated products is readily generalized to allow for less restrictive assumptions about cost functions and demand functions (see Friedman [1977]).

14

Introduction, purpose, and overview

In general, however, conditions for existence are currently much more restrictive in the heterogeneous goods case than in the homogeneous goods case.

Cournot outcomes under prices and quantities

Figure 1 therefore readily represents quantity decisions for homogeneous goods and price decisions for heterogeneous goods. There is a strong relationship between the outcomes of the Cournot model in the two settings. Note that in general, in both applications of the Cournot model, price exceeds marginal cost and firms make excess profits.

$$p(q_1^C + q_2^C) - c_i = -[\partial_i p(q_1^C + q_2^C)]q_i^C \quad i = 1, 2 \qquad \text{homogeneous goods}$$

$$p_i^C - c_i = -[\partial_i q_i(p_1^C, p_2^C)]^{-1} q_i(p_1^C, p_2^C) \quad i = 1, 2 \quad \text{heterogeneous goods}$$

With demand downward-sloping in own price and optimal strategies in the interior of their respective strategy spaces, price exceeds marginal cost.

Moreover, as Cournot pointed out, aggregate profits are generally less than if the firms *inter*dependently chose the monopoly quantity (M_i) or the monopoly price (p_i^M).

$$\max(\Pi_1^Q(M_1, 0), \Pi_2^Q(0, M_2)) \geq \sum_i \Pi_i^Q(q_1^C, q_2^C) \qquad \text{homogeneous goods}$$

$$\max(\Pi_1^P(p_1^M, \infty), \Pi_2^P(\infty, p_2^M)) \geq \sum_i \Pi_i^P(p_1^C, p_2^C) \qquad \text{heterogeneous goods}$$

The Cournot outcome is a vector $\theta \in Q^2 \times P^2 \times \mathcal{R}^2$ of quantities, prices, and profits, which depends upon whether the decision variables involve quantities:

$$\theta^Q = (q_1^{QC}, q_2^{QC}, p_1^{QC}, p_2^{QC}, \Pi_1^{QC}, \Pi_2^{QC}) \quad \begin{cases} q_i^{QC} \equiv q_i^C, \\ p_i^{QC} \equiv p(q_1^C + q_2^C) \\ \Pi_i^{QC} \equiv \Pi_i^Q(q_1^C, q_2^C) \end{cases}$$

or prices:

$$\theta^P = (q_1^{PC}, q_2^{PC}, p_1^{PC}, p_2^{PC}, \Pi_1^{PC}, \Pi_2^{PC}) \quad \begin{cases} p_i^{PC} \equiv p_i^C, \\ q_i^{PC} \equiv q_i(p_1^C, p_2^C) \\ \Pi_i^{PC} \equiv \Pi_i^P(p_1^C, p_2^C). \end{cases}$$

Thus, in both cases the Cournot outcome involves price in excess of marginal cost and aggregate profits below the cartel profit. Extension to the n-firm case is straightforward.

Vives ([1985, reprinted in this volume]; see also Cheng [1985], Hathaway and Rickard [1979], and Singh and Vives [1984])[16] has examined quantity and price setting in a differentiated goods model, thereby providing a direct means for examining the welfare and profit implications of choice of strategic variable, via the use of a very convenient duality[17] that exists between the Cournot-in-quantities and the Cournot-in-prices models. To see this, consider the following demand functions:

$$p_i = \alpha_i - \beta_i q_i - \gamma q_j, \quad \alpha_i, \beta_i > 0, \quad \beta_i \beta_j - \gamma^2 > 0, \quad i, j = 1, 2, \ i \neq j,$$

which comes from a consumer's surplus maximization problem with the indicated parameters providing a quadratic utility function in the two quantities (for details, see the Vives paper). Commodities are substitutes, independent, or complements as γ is >0, $=0$, or <0. Solving for the quantities yields the inverse demand functions $q_i = a_i - b_i p_i + c p_j$, where $a_i = (\alpha_i \beta_j - \alpha_j \gamma)/\delta$, $b_i = \beta_j/\delta$, $c = \gamma/\delta$ and $\delta = \beta_1 \beta_2 - \gamma^2$. The label duality becomes evident when we write down the Cournot-in-quantities and the Cournot-in-prices models:

Cournot-in-quantities   Cournot-in-prices

$$\max_{q_i}(\alpha_i - \beta_i q_i - \gamma q_j)q_i \quad \max_{p_i}(a_i - b_i p_i + c p_j)p_i$$

Label matchings:
(duality) $\alpha_i \Leftrightarrow a_i, \quad \beta_i \Leftrightarrow b_i, \quad \gamma \Leftrightarrow -c, \quad q_i \Leftrightarrow p_i.$

In particular, since γ corresponds to $-c$, but c is of the same sign as γ, Cournot-in-quantities for substitutes (complements) corresponds to Cournot-in-prices for complements (substitutes). As an example, this means that optimal choice rules in price space for goods that are complementary will be downward sloping (since the optimal choice rules for substitutes in quantity space are downward sloping; see Figure 2) while optimal choice rules for complements will be upward sloping in quantity

---

[16] Vives refers to Cournot in prices as Bertrand, which provides an efficiency of language when comparing with a Cournot in quantities reexpressed in prices via a change of variables transformation.

[17] To be precise, the duality used in Vives and the related papers is a *label* duality, as opposed to an *optimization* duality. In a label duality two problems are related ("dual") if one is obtained from the other by switching symbols for variable and/or parameters. Examples include DeMorgan's laws in set theory, or the relationship between mechanical and electrical oscillatory systems (via their differential equations). Characterizing the solution to one model and then switching symbols (or labels) helps us characterize the solution to the other. The solutions, however, need not be related in any precise manner. An optimization duality further exploits the underlying space described by the two dual problems. Examples are primal and dual linear programs wherein values of the shadow prices in a primal solution are the optimal dual variable values. Similarly, modern production and cost theory rests on an optimization duality.

Introduction, purpose, and overview

space (since optimal choice rules for substitutes are upward sloping in price space; see Figure 3). This matching accounts for the now standard result in the literature that by switching from Cournot-in-quantities to Cournot-in-prices, model outcomes change. This happens in the information sharing literature, in the literature on the effects of mergers, and in the literature on delegation, as well as countless other examples of multi-stage games wherein the second stage involves choices in either prices or quantities.

Moreover, Vives has shown that, for constant marginal cost and for general demand structures, consumers will prefer outcome θ^P to θ^Q. Singh and Vives [1984] also examine a two-stage game wherein firms can choose whether to play in prices or quantities; firms choose quantities. Klemperer and Meyer [1986, reprinted in this volume] examine a one-stage game wherein firms can choose prices or quantities and where there are exogenous demand shocks. Here firms strictly prefer prices or quantities depending upon the slope of the marginal cost function, the curvature of the demand function, and the nature of the uncertainty itself, while without uncertainty multiple Nash equilibria in both decision variables exist.[18]

The interplay between price and quantity choices becomes even richer when the opportunity for firms to share private information is considered.[19] Consider the following generic two-stage problem. In stage two firms individually receive some information (about the state of industry demand or the state of their own costs) and then pick output (or price). In stage one firms have a common prior on the information they will receive private signals about in stage two and must decide whether, and to what degree, to share their information with the others. Papers by Ponssard [1979], Novshek and Sonnenschein [1982], Clarke [1983], Fried [1984], Vives [1984, reprinted in this volume], Li [1985], Gal-Or [1986, reprinted in this volume], and Shapiro [1986] have employed variations of this two-stage game to examine the incentives for competitors to share information. The answer depends upon the nature of the strategies (quantities versus prices), the nature of the goods (substitutes versus complements), and the nature of the information (common attributes such as the intercept of industry demand versus private attributes such as marginal costs). Let the "base case" be quantity competition, substitute goods,

[18] For a dynamic model of quantity and price choice, see Benoit and Krishna [1987]. Friedman [1987] provides a model of simultaneous price and quality choice in a differentiated product setting with general contingent demand.
[19] There is also an interesting interplay between the nature of the good (substitutes versus complements) and the nature of the strategic interaction; see Bulow, et al. [1985]. This can then be extended to provide conditions for choice of Stackelberg roles; see Dowrick [1986] and McAndrews [1987].

17

and information about the demand intercept. In this case firms do not want to share information. Now vary one of the three provisos and the results are reversed. The trade-off here is between the advantage of more information versus the effect of correlating firm actions.[20]

None of the foregoing has directly addressed a classical criticism of Cournot's analysis: his treatment of price competition with homogeneous goods, to which we turn next.

The Bertrand model and analysis

Cournot did not live to see the publication of what has become one of the profession's most famous "referee reports," Joseph Bertrand's 1883 review of Cournot's book.[21] In his review Bertrand attacks Cournot's theory of oligopoly on two fronts. First, Bertrand chastises Cournot for not assuming that the two duopolists collude and set a monopoly price. Actually, Cournot carefully discusses this possibility (see page 63 of this volume):

We say *each independently,* and this restriction is very essential, as will soon appear; for if they should come to an agreement so as to obtain for each the greatest possible income, the results would be entirely different, and would not differ, so far as consumers are concerned, from those obtained in treating of a monopoly.

Moreover, we now know that the key to this issue is repeated interactions and the ability to provide credible threats of reprisal for deviation from the collusive outcome (see Stigler [1964]). The interesting aspect of this is that in many settings, collusive outcomes are achievable by noncooperative behavior (as examples, see Friedman [1971, reprinted in this volume], Radner [1980, reprinted in this volume], Green and Porter [1984], and Abreu, Pearce, and Stacchetti [1986]), thereby extending the power of the model of noncooperative behavior initially proposed by Cournot in a static setting. We will return to this issue later in this chapter.

Bertrand's other criticism of this chapter of Cournot's book is the one for which he is best known. He asserted that if one changed the model by using price as the decision variable rather than quantity, the purported oligopoly results obtained by Cournot would melt away (along with the

[20] In the one-shot game the value of correlating actions depends upon whether decision rules are rising or falling in conjectures. Note that in a repeated game, knowing that every agent is equally well informed contributes a third consideration: defections from a collusive agreement are more appropriately attributed to bad behavior than to conflicting information and therefore the credibility of retaliation under conditions of randomly fluctuating demand is strengthened if information is shared. This suggests that sharing is more likely to hold in repeated settings.

[21] It was not the first review, however. Actually, an earlier review by R. de Fontenay appeared in 1864 (see Nichol [1938]). Bertrand's review also covered Walras' *Théorie mathématique de la richesse sociale.*

excess profits), a phenomenon that has been repeated many times since 1883 to the chagrin of many a seminar speaker.

In order to understand the relationship between the Bertrand and Cournot models, we shall extend the extensive form analysis applied earlier by recasting the Bertrand model as an extensive form game and comparing it with variations on the Cournot model. It will be shown that the real difference between Bertrand and Cournot is not so much the choice of strategic variable used in the analysis, but of who the participants are in the game, when they make their choices, and what they know when they make those choices.

More precisely, when the normal form representation of the two approaches is employed, a subtle shift in the modeling of consumer demand occurs; this shift is, in large part, responsible for the differences in outcomes. This modeling shift becomes apparent when one examines the extensive form game. The Cournot model is a simultaneous move game amongst firms, but the Bertrand model involves a sequential game wherein firms simultaneously choose prices followed by consumers choosing where to buy and how much to purchase, with full information about each firm's posted price. The Bertrand model represents a radical and important departure from the Cournot model, wherein strategic consumers have been added to the game. The introduction of consumers as strategic agents in the Cournot model also eliminates the Cournot outcome, by enforcing a collusive solution. The Cournot outcome relies on nonstrategic consumers while the Bertrand outcome relies on the introduction of specially constrained strategic consumers (in particular, consumers with no individual bargaining power, but strength in numbers).

In order to provide a precise comparison, representative consumers must be introduced in both the Cournot and Bertrand extensive forms. To do this, recall that the representative consumer was characterized by demand function $d(p)$, with inverse demand function $\rho(d)$. Using this, recall the traditional versions of the Cournot and Bertrand analyses, which employ a normal form representation of the problem. For convenience, assume that $c = 0$. [This also avoids Edgeworth's result that without constant marginal costs, pure strategies fail to exist in the price strategy game (Edgeworth [1925]). Mixed strategies do exist in such a model; see Allen and Hellwig [1986] and Dasgupta and Maskin [1986].]

For the Cournot case, the payoff[22] for firm i is its profit, namely

---

[22] It may seem peculiar to be making decisions for an infinitesimal consumer rather than with an aggregate demand curve. Since consumers are identical and marginal costs are constant, however, solving at one level is equivalent to solving at the other. Thus the models to come, where consumers are introduced as strategic players, are consistent with this basic model.

$$\Pi_i^Q(d_1, d_2) = \rho(d_1 + d_2)d_i,$$

where d_i is the (per consumer) output level for firm i. Since the firms are identical, the Cournot–Nash equilibrium is the vector $\mathbf{d}^C = (\xi^C, \xi^C)$ such that firm i chooses to produce $d_i = \xi^C$ and firm j chooses to produce $d_j = \xi^C$. Under very reasonable conditions on the demand function, $\rho(\xi^C + \xi^C)\xi^C$ is positive for $i = 1, 2$, and thus firms enjoy excess profits.

In the standard Bertrand analysis firms produce homogeneous goods and pick prices. Typically, firm i is viewed as facing the following demand curve:

$$D^i(p_1, p_2) = \begin{cases} 0 & \text{if } p_i > p_j \\ \frac{1}{2}d(p_i) & \text{if } p_i = p_j \\ d(p_i) & \text{if } p_i < p_j, \end{cases} \tag{6}$$

meaning that if i's price was below j's price then i got the whole market, while if they charged the same price they split the market. Clearly, the Nash equilibrium involves both firms setting price at marginal cost (that is, zero). In contrast with the Cournot case, firms here make zero profits.

The Cournot game with consumers as players

Now consider Figure 4. The only difference between this figure and Figure 1 is that a third agent has been explicitly added to the game: the representative consumer, depicted in the figure by a circle. Note that the consumer must choose which firm to buy from (and how much to buy), and does so simultaneously with the other players in keeping with the simultaneity requirement of the Cournot model. This makes the consumer a strategic player in a very weak sense: he cannot bargain (recall the continuum assumption) but he can choose which firm to buy from and his choice is important because all other consumers in the economy will choose in precisely the same manner as the representative consumer. Thus, there is no game among the consumers and the game between the consumers and the firms is quite limited in that it avoids any opportunities to bargain.

Let r be the probability that the consumer chooses to go to firm 1; thus r takes values in the set $\Delta = [0, 1]$. In other words, since the consumer is playing simultaneously with the firms, he is modeled as using a mixed strategy; one could view this as providing the fraction of consumers who will arrive at firm 1, with the complementary fraction arriving at firm 2. The vector of strategies is (d_1, d_2, r). Payoffs are now $r\rho(d_1)d_1$ for firm 1, $(1-r)\rho(d_2)d_2$ for firm 2, and $rV[\rho(d_1)] + (1-r)V[\rho(d_2)]$ for the consumer, where $V(p)$ is the consumer's indirect utility function (suppressing other commodity prices and income).[23]

[23] V solves an appropriate set of integrability conditions.

20

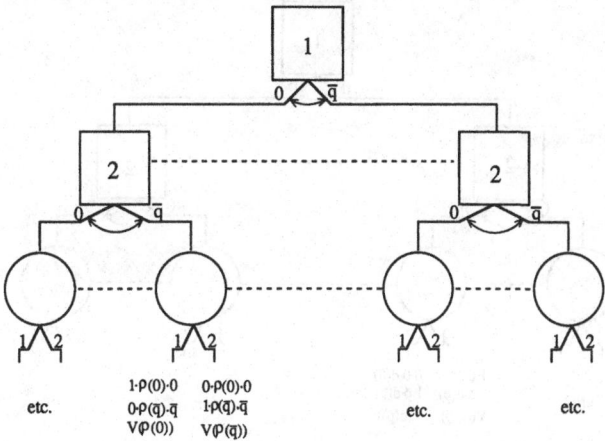

Figure 4. Cournot in quantities with simultaneous consumers.

This seemingly small adjustment has a major effect on the nature and number of equilibria. Specifically, the equilibria of interest are of the form (M, M, r), $r \in (0, 1)$, where M is the output level a monopoly would set when facing the individual consumer demand function $d(p)$; there are also two sets of degenerate equilibria $(d_1, M, 0)$, $\forall d_1 \in [0, M)$ and $(M, d_2, 1)$, $\forall d_2 \in [0, M)$. In the (M, M, r) equilibria firm 1 produces M times the fraction r of the populace, while firm 2 produces M times $(1 - r)$ of the populace, understanding that the market clearing price is the monopoly price. Thus, as each customer arrives at firm i, the firm produces M and charges the customer $\rho(M)$.

Clearly then, for the Cournot model to generate the Cournot outcome, consumers *cannot* be simultaneous strategic players with the firms; the only strategic players are the firms. This also holds true if we substitute prices for quantities. As before, let firm i's strategy be its price p_i, which takes values in the set $P = [0, \bar{p}]$. The payoff associated with the strategy vector (p_1, p_2, r) is, for firm one, $r p_1 d(p_1)$, for firm 2, $(1 - r) p_2 d(p_2)$, and for the consumer, $r V(p_1) + (1 - r) V(p_2)$.[24] This is illustrated by the game tree in Figure 5. Again, the Nash equilibria involve monopoly pricing by one or both firms. Observe that product differentiation is *not* required here and that simply substituting prices for quantities does not necessarily imply the Bertrand outcome. This observation is important

---

[24] Here the integrability conditions must yield a V which may depend upon the attributes of the product, since the outputs of the two firms may be differentiated.

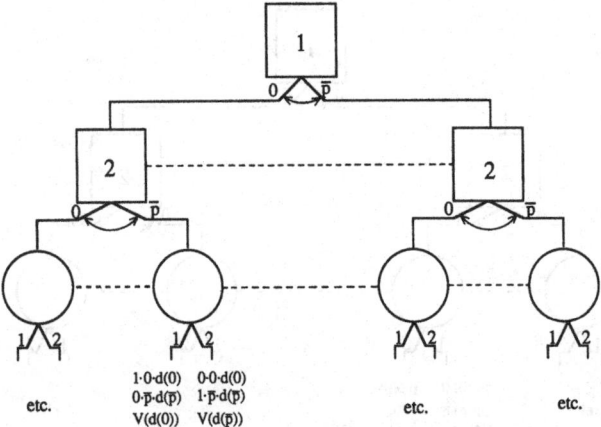

1-0-d(0) 0-0-d(0)
0-p̄-d(p̄) 1-p̄-d(p̄)
V(d(0)) V(d(p̄))

etc.   etc.   etc.

Figure 5. Cournot in prices with simultaneous consumers.

since it is usually believed that the difference between the Cournot and Bertrand models is that one uses quantities and the other uses prices. Instead, as we shall see, slight modification of Figure 5 yields the Bertrand outcome.

The Bertrand game

In the above two models consumers were not able to search over the firms, but had to choose a strategy without observation of the firm's choices. This meant that firms should have posted their monopoly price. In Bertrand's review the classical story of consumers choosing which firm to go to based on *observed* price is provided: "In fact, whatever jointly determined price were adopted, if only one of the competitors lowers his, he gains, disregarding all unimportant exceptions, all the sales, and he will double his returns if his competitor allows him to do so." (See the translation of this review in this volume, p. 77.) Bertrand is introducing the consumer as an active participant in the game and providing the consumer with considerable power via the assumption that consumers *costlessly* search over the firms to find the lowest price; only thus can firms with lower prices realize increased sales.

Figure 6 illustrates a game whose equilibrium is the Bertrand outcome, for firms to price at marginal cost. The only difference between Figure 6 and Figure 5 is the information set for the consumer: the consumer can be viewed as going *after* the firms, with full knowledge of the prices each

22

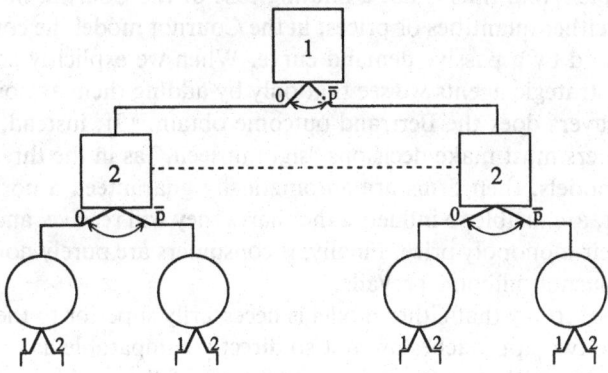

--- same payoffs as in Figure 5 ---

Figure 6. The Bertrand model.

firm will charge (thus, this is a search model with *zero* search costs). In this case the consumer uses a mixed strategy that is a function of the prices; understanding this, firms move first and choose the prices to post. The consumer's strategy is:

$$r(p_1, p_2) \begin{cases} = 1 & \text{if } p_1 < p_2 \\ \in (0, 1) & \text{if } p_1 = p_2 \\ = 0 & \text{if } p_1 > p_2. \end{cases}$$

With this strategy the Nash equilibrium is as in the normal form version, for each firm to set price equal to marginal cost and for the consumer to randomly choose which firm to visit (recall that in the normal form version, the market split was arbitrarily set at half for each firm).

In other words, the Cournot and Bertrand models treat consumers very differently. In the Cournot model consumers are strictly nonstrategic agents. Note that the consumer is powerful in the Bertrand model because he or she goes second and actively (and costlessly) searches over firms.[25] This attribute "sneaks" into the normal form analysis when demand functions such as that specified in (6) are used. Such a model implicitly adds an active strategic agent with extraordinary search power

---

[25] Note also that the consumer is powerful because he is strictly representative of the entire mass of consumers. Differentiating consumers might eliminate the Bertrand outcome (and might even result in monopoly or Cournot pricing); reducing the number of consumers and allowing bargaining might once again push price back toward competitive levels.

to the problem and thus is not a limiting case of the Cournot model expressed in either quantities or prices; in the Cournot model the consumer is represented by a passive demand curve. When we explicitly add consumers as strategic agents we see that only by adding them as nonsimultaneous players does the Bertrand outcome obtain.[26] If, instead, strategic consumers must make decisions "sight unseen," as in the three-agent Cournot models, then firms are automatically guaranteed a portion of the market, are unable to influence the shares they will receive, and therefore set their monopoly price. Finally, if consumers are purely nonstrategic, the Cournot outcome prevails.

This is not to say that either model is necessarily superior to the other. Rather, the two approaches are not so directly comparable as is usually assumed because they treat an important part of the analysis (the consumer) quite differently.[27] Moreover, as one would expect, it is the institutional setting of the problem to be analyzed that determines not only whether to use quantities or prices as strategies, but who the players are, what they know, and when they can make what choices.

To emphasize this point, consider the following examples. First, a classic example of the difference between the Cournot model and the Bertrand model is Hotelling's 1929 model of location and pricing decisions for duopolists facing a continuum of consumers in a linear market. Hotelling makes it quite clear that he wants to resurrect Cournot's noncompetitive duopoly results, which had been attacked by both Bertrand and Edgeworth. He provides a two-stage procedure wherein for fixed locations (the notion of product differentiation employed) price functions are developed, and then optimal locations are found. Hotelling found that the two firms move to the center of the market and that price exceeds marginal cost. Unfortunately, Hotelling's model is an example of the extensive form game shown in Figure 6. As he states, "No customer has any preference for either seller except on the ground of price plus transportation cost" ([1929], p. 46); he has injected price-searching consumers. As D'Aspremont, et al. [1979] show, Hotelling's minimum differentiation equilibrium with price above marginal cost fails to exist, and the equilibrium that does exist (after introducing increasing marginal costs of search via quadratic transport costs) involves product differentiation.

Kreps and Scheinkman [1983] have examined a two-stage game wherein first quantity decisions are made and then firms choose prices, resulting

---

[26] On the other hand, if we further allow firms to revise their prices and to restrict the manner in which they do so, we obtain the monopoly outcome; this will be made more precise shortly.

[27] There is a nice duality between two of Cournot's chapters, his chapters on oligopoly and complementary monopoly; see Sonnenschein [1968].

in the Cournot outcome. Davidson and Deneckere [1986] have shown that this result is pathological in the sense that, as the representation of contingent demand changes, so too does the outcome. In general, however, the basic result stands that the two-stage game in homogeneous products leads to price above marginal cost.[28]

Thus, we see that knowing whether prices or quantities are used need not be very informative about what results obtain. As indicated earlier, all else equal, the choice of prices and/or quantities as the strategic variable(s) can affect the existence and efficiency of the outcome. More generally, however, it is the strategies the agents can employ, the information they have, and the restrictions on behavior and choice they face, that determine the results of the interaction.

The Cournot structure in other models of competition

Stackelberg leadership

The common element in the foregoing discussion was that firms made simultaneous decisions about what action to take based upon conjectures about what competitors would do. Now consider a modification of Figure 1 wherein agent (firm) two can observe agent one's decision before making a decision; this is illustrated in Figure 7, which is the extensive form representation of the Stackelberg model (Stackelberg [1934]).

Note the only difference between Figures 1 and 7: The information set for agent two is always a singleton; the agent always knows precisely where in the tree he is. Knowing this, agent one uses agent two's optimal choice rule $\phi_2(x_1)$ in its optimization problem. Thus the first order conditions that describe the equilibrium (under suitable sufficient conditions) are as follows:

$$\partial_1 \pi_1(x_1, \phi_2(x_1)) + \partial_2 \pi_1(x_1, \phi_2(x_1)) \cdot \partial_1 \phi_2(x_1) = 0 \qquad (7)$$

$$\partial_2 \pi_2(x_1, x_2) = 0 \qquad (\text{i.e., } x_2 = \phi_2(x_1)). \qquad (8)$$

The asymmetry in Figure 7 is reflected in Eqs. (7) and (8); agent two chooses a best response with respect to agent one's *observed* decision, while agent one chooses a best response to agent two's decision rule.

Making choices in quantities[29] with goods that are substitutes provides a well-known output-space geometry, especially when attention is restricted

---

[28] Tune the dial and get another station: Friedman [1987] uses a differentiated products model with very general contingent demand to show that simultaneous price and quantity choice can lead to nonexistence, while sequencing the choices (that is, a two-stage game) leads to Cournot solutions (in the first stage variable).

[29] When the Stackelberg model is expressed in prices it is called the price leader model; for the linear case, see Kamien [1987].

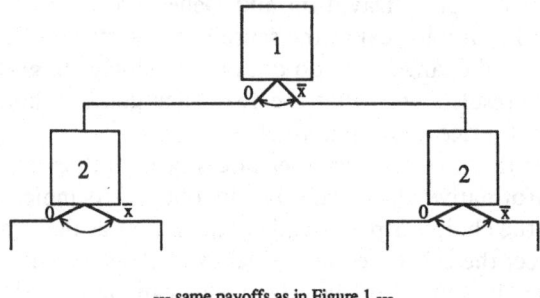

--- same payoffs as in Figure 1 ---

Figure 7. The Stackelberg variant of Cournot's model.

to the case of linear demand $(p(q_1+q_2)=a-b(q_1+q_2),\ a>0,\ b>0)$ and constant (and equal) marginal cost c; this is illustrated in Figure 8. Here point C is the Cournot solution and the S_i are the Stackelberg solutions, wherein firm i is the first mover (leader) and firm j is the second mover (follower). The point designated PC is the "perfectly competitive" solution wherein each firm makes zero profits. The points on the axes labeled M are the monopoly outputs and the line joining these two points provides the possible set of output combinations that would yield maximal *joint* profits. Where this hyperplane crosses the 45° line is the "equal shares" cartel solution.

The resulting geometry is suggestive, though it is important to remember that it is for a highly restricted case. If both firms play their monopoly outputs, PC results. If one plays its monopoly output and the other plays a best response, a Stackelberg solution results. If both play their Stackelberg follower output, the equal shares collusive solution results. Moreover, note that aggregate output is higher (and price is lower) at S_i than at C. Here the Nash equilibrium in quantities is unique. Saloner [1987] has shown that the uniqueness of this outcome depends upon the restriction of production opportunities occurring in one period; if firms can produce in two periods then many solutions are subgame perfect. In particular, any outcome on the outer envelope of the response functions between S_1 and S_2 is a subgame perfect Nash equilibrium.[30]

---

[30] On the other hand, Fershtman and Kamien [1987] look at Cournot solutions as asymptotic limits of a dynamic model wherein prices adjust with a lag, and the lag is allowed to shrink. (Here production and sales occur in a "period," in contrast with the multiperiod production of Saloner.) They find that open loop strategies (that is, output rate paths through time that firms commit themselves to at the beginning of the game)

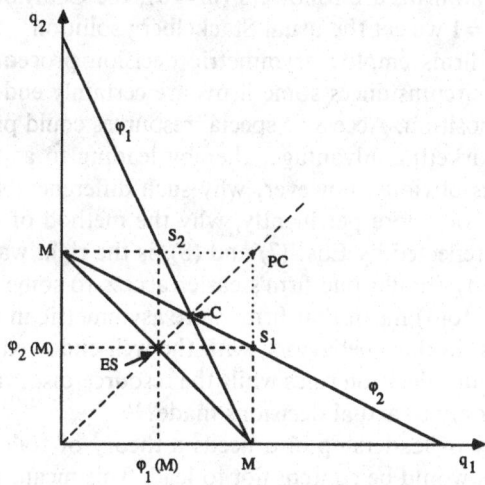

Figure 8. Traditional output space geometry.

The Cournot model also allows us to extend the standard one-leader treatment of the Stackelberg model to a multileader solution as follows.[31] Assume there are n firms with m "leaders" and $n-m$ "followers." Each of the followers takes the aggregate output of the leaders as given, makes conjectures about the outputs of all other followers, and produces an output based on its φ-function. Knowing this, each leader takes the response functions for the followers, makes conjectures about the outputs for the other leaders, and computes a best response output to produce. Thus, the followers "play Cournot" against all other firms while the leaders "play Cournot" against the other leaders only. The extensive form game is a direct extension of Figure 7: replace agent one with an m-agent simultaneous move (that is, Cournot) game, and replace each decision node for agent two by an $(n-m)$-agent simultaneous move (Cournot) game. This model involves consistent employment of asymmetric behavior in that no leaders or followers are misjudging what any other player is doing. When all firms are leaders ($m = n$) the Cournot solution obtains;

have the Cournot static solution as their asymptotic limit. On the other hand, if firms use closed loop strategies (i.e., output rate strategies that depend upon time and observed price), then the asymptotic limit is between the Cournot and competitive outcomes. Closed loop strategies are subgame perfect, while the open loop strategies are not.

[31] This is based on Sherali [1984].

similarly when all firms are followers ($m = 0$), the Cournot solution obtains. When $m = 1$ we get the usual Stackelberg solution.

Why should firms employ asymmetric decision procedures to begin with? In some circumstances some firms are certainly endowed with an advantageous position. Access to special resources could provide a technological or marketing advantage, thereby leading to asymmetric outcomes. It is less obvious, however, why such differences should persist in the long run or, more pertinently, why the method of capturing the asymmetry, as reflected by Eqs. (7) and (8), is the right way to do it. In other words, why should one firm's easier access to some input market (often the story told) mean that firms were asymmetric in their *decision process* (that is, in their behavior), with the well-endowed making optimal choices against decision rules while the resource-disadvantaged made best responses only to actual decisions made?[32]

A real theory of leadership also needs a theory of followership, that is, of why firms would be content not to lead. This means that an asymmetric organization of the firms should itself be a Nash equilibrium in some larger game (for some recent efforts, see Dowrick [1986], Sadanand [1982], Daughety [1984], Golding [1984], Kambhu [1984], and McAndrews [1987]). Since the focus of this book is Cournot, a review of this literature would take us too far afield. It is worth reiterating, however, that we usually assume that agents are very resourceful, especially in the long run. Thus, any observation of asymmetric behavior should suggest that both parties to the equilibrium derive benefits; in particular, if the seemingly disadvantaged party does not find it advantageous to defect, this suggests that, from its viewpoint, followership is optimal.[33]

Models that generate collusive and competitive outcomes

In this section we will consider how adjustments in the Cournot model can lead to collusive or perfectly competitive outcomes. Specifically we will focus on three examples based on results in the recent literature.

1. If firms can revise prices and restrict the manner in which revision is employed, then the cartel price can be a Nash equilibrium.

[32] There may be other strategies that a low-cost player might pursue vis-à-vis a high-cost competitor, such as driving him out of the market (or at least trying to); see Milgrom and Roberts [1982] and Friedman [1983] for analyses of the related notion of limit pricing by a monopolist against an entrant.

[33] Scherer [1980] provides a nice example of followers disciplining a leader (U.S. Steel) for leader actions that were not beneficial to the followers. It should also be clear that this sort of reasoning starts to cross the line into variations on collusive behavior.

Furthermore, if they can make commitments, then competition can be reduced.

2. If the simple one-shot Cournot model is repeated, collusive outcomes can be obtained in finite and infinite horizon settings, and with imperfect information on demand.
3. If the number of firms becomes large, perfectly competitive outcomes can obtain and considerations of information sharing may become irrelevant.

We will examine these in turn.

First, let us examine a modification of the Bertrand model involving "most-favored-consumer" or "meet competition" pricing policies (see Cooper [1986], Salop [1986], Golding and Slutsky [1986], and P'ng and Hirshleifer [1986]). In a most-favored-consumer clause a firm commits itself to compensate a current purchaser for any future price reductions that it might make. Alternatively, and this is the focus of Figure 9, a firm commits itself to "meet competition" in the sense that it will match any other firm's price, should it be lower.[34] In Figure 9, the Bertrand game in Figure 6 is modified by allowing firms to revise prices downward upon observing a competitor's price.

Thus, for example, if firm one posts price p' and firm two posts $p'' < p'$, firm one can choose to stay with p' or revise its price to p'', understanding that consumers go last with full information on posted prices. In this case firm two has no second move, since revision occurs only if a competitor has posted a lower price, and revision is to *meet* competition. The effect of adopting such a policy is that now all possible price pairs (involving equal prices) are Nash equilibria. In particular, each firm choosing $p_i = p^M$, and the consumer randomizing over where to buy, is a Nash equilibrium. Thus, even though consumers get to go last and have zero search costs, they end up being powerless. Here firms were able to eliminate the need to simultaneously commit themselves on price, and substituted a commitment on pricing policy. Note, however, that this depends crucially on firms (including entrants) committing to meet, not *beat,* competition.[35]

Other forms of commitments can also help firms reduce competition and reap higher profits. Vickers [1985, reprinted in this volume] studies delegation and managerial incentives. He shows that since the outcome of a game depends upon the objectives of all the players, owners can

---

[34] The firm could provide the following guarantee: "Buy at this price from me and if you find a lower price anywhere else, I'll refund the difference."

[35] In particular, see the discussion of Salop's paper which raises a number of caveats on this approach.

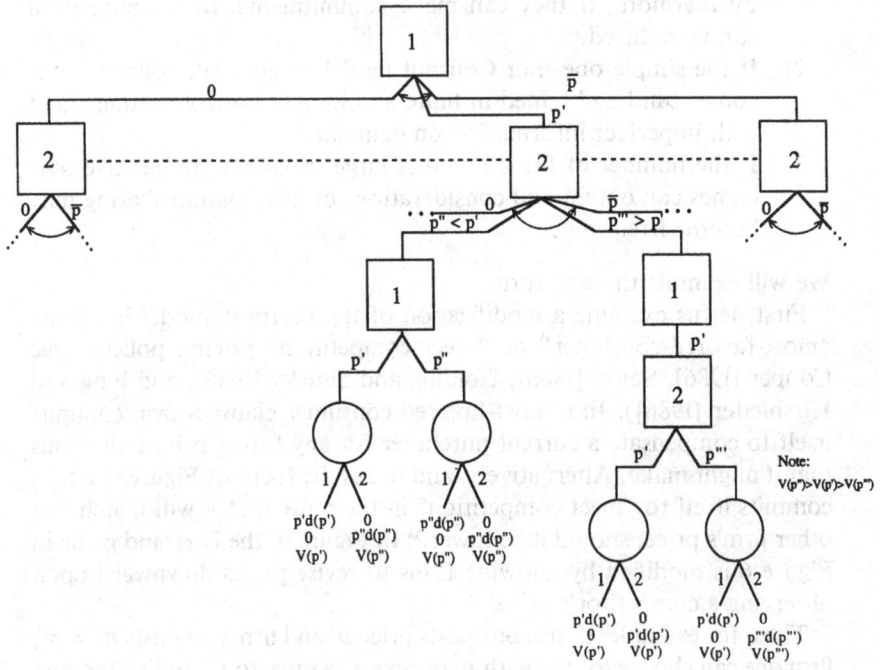

Figure 9. Price revision.

find it profitable to contract with managers to maximize something other than profits. Specifically, the game involves owners picking managers and providing them with a managerial objective function which is a weighted combination of profits and sales; managers then compete in a Cournot quantity game. The result is that the profit-maximizing weight on sales is nonzero. Thus owners should hire managers and contract to reward them for the weighted combination of sales and profits; this will yield maximum profits. Other papers considering the role of delegation in reducing competition include Sklivas [1987], Fershtman and Judd [1987], Fershtman, Judd, and Kalai [1987], and Gal-Or [1987].

The delegation example is one of a number of recent papers wherein a two-stage game is analyzed with an opportunity for commitment (via capital purchases, advertising, R&D expenditure, information transfer, product choice, etc.) in the first stage followed by some variant of a Cournot second stage (see Shapiro [forthcoming] and Fudenberg and Tirole [1986] for a review of these models). Brander and Lewis [1986, reprinted in this volume] use financial structure to provide a link between the debt/equity considerations of a firm and strategic behavior in the product market. They show that firms have an incentive to use their financial structure to influence their product markets, since shareholders and bondholders are asymmetrically affected by random shocks to profits (debtholders are residual claimants in bad states of the world wherein the firm goes bankrupt, whereas shareholders are residual claimants in good states of the world). The result is that the level of debt, and the effect of uncertainty on marginal profits, influence the optimal level of output in the product market. A perfect competitor or a monopolist would end up choosing to hold no debt, but this will not be true in general for oligopolies, due to the effect on product markets.

Next, let us consider the repeated interaction of oligopolists. The basic rule of thumb is that collusive outcomes can be supported as Nash equilibria under a number of scenarios (see Fudenberg and Maskin [1986]). For example, games involving repetition over a finite or infinite horizon admit the employment of trigger strategies wherein each agent plays a specified (usually collusive) strategy as long as some criterion is met (for example, everyone else has done likewise in the preceding period), but otherwise reverts to a predetermined alternative strategy if the criterion is not met.[36] As a specific example, in the infinitely repeated Prisoner's Dilemma game, a grim strategy involves playing cooperatively on the first move and then playing what the other agent played the previous period, with the proviso that if the other agent ever defects from the cooperative outcome, the strategy then specifies playing the defect strategy forever. Trigger strategies were first suggested in Luce and Raiffa [1957] in the context of the Prisoner's Dilemma game, and first formally discussed by Friedman [1971, reprinted in this volume] as a means of linking cooperative and noncooperative game theory. Variations on trigger strategies have been applied and expanded in a number of papers in settings with infinite or finite horizons and perfect or imperfect observation of competitor actions (see Radner [1980, reprinted in this volume], Porter [1983a], Green and Porter [1984], Friedman [1985]; for strategies using optimal punishments see Benoit and Krishna [1985] and Abreu, Pearce, and Stacchetti [1986]; also see Kreps, et al. [1982] and Fudenberg and Maskin [1986] for related general results involving incomplete information games).[37]

---

[36] For the strategies to be subgame perfect, punishments must be prescribed for defectors, and for defectors from the punishments, etc. In the finite horizon cases multiple equilibria, incomplete information, bounded rationality, and the ability to hire agents and specify their reward structure all have been used to effect such strategies.

[37] Trigger strategies need not only entail discontinuous responses to defection. Friedman and Samuelson [1988] examine trigger response to defections wherein the response is contingent on the degree of defection (essentially a marriage of trigger strategies and reaction curves).

Trigger strategies may have been employed in past examples of collusion in the "real world": Porter [1983b, reprinted in this volume] examines the behavior of the Joint Executive Committee railroad cartel between the years 1880 and 1886. Price wars are often taken as evidence of the failure of a cartel. Instead, Porter shows (as discussed in Green and Porter [1984]) that periodic price wars may reflect the operation of trigger strategies to maintain a cartel. In a world of perfect information one should never observe the triggering of a response to a defection because firms would not find it optimal to defect. However, in a world of imperfect information, defections might be hard to separate from general swings in demand due to uncertainty. This makes retaliation for defection more difficult, however, and thereby tends to reduce the credibility of the retaliation and increase the incentive to cheat (see Stigler [1964]). Green and Porter provide a trigger strategy involving a finite horizon reversion to a punishment (wherein all firms produce their Cournot output levels; this is called Cournot reversion) triggered by a sufficient fluctuation in demand. To make such punishment credible firms must be prepared to suffer through a period of reversion that might, in truth, have been triggered by a random drop in demand (and not secret price cutting). This is necessitated by the inability of firms to separate the effect of secret price cutting from other sources of demand shocks simply by observation of demand conditions and the need to make the threat of reversion a credible response to defection from the collusive outcome.

Radner's paper in this volume presents an especially interesting example employing Cournot reversion in a finite horizon setting. He considers an n-firm homogeneous goods industry with firms choosing quantity strategies. When the Cournot equilibrium is unique, it is the T-period solution for profit-maximizing firms. In contrast, an infinite horizon solution involves a trigger strategy wherein all agents produce their collusive output until and unless an agent defects; if this occurs, all produce their Cournot output forevermore. Thus, for all finite horizon cases, firms play Cournot and forgo the returns to collusion, while in the infinite horizon case they collude. Radner shows that the previously described trigger strategies form a perfect ϵ-equilibrium in the *finite* horizon setting, for any $\epsilon > 0$, where profits incurred may be ϵ below optimal.[38] Moreover, he links the persistence of a cartel solution to the number of agents and the length of the horizon, showing that if the number of agents is not

---

[38] In other words, this can be viewed as a bounded rationality argument. See Rubinstein [1986] for an alternative approach in the context of the Prisoner's Dilemma.

Introduction, purpose, and overview

large then collusion persists, while if the number of agents grows without limit, the solution approaches a competitive outcome.[39]

This last observation leads to the third point above. One way to view Cournot's model of competition among the few is as a preliminary to a model of "unlimited competition" that would yield perfectly competitive outcomes; he discusses this in Chapter Eight of his book. Radner's paper contributes a finite horizon, partial equilibrium example of perfect competition by noncooperative agents. Novshek and Sonnenschein [1978, reprinted in this volume] provide a static general equilibrium treatment of this notion, wherein firms with ∪-shaped costs are modeled as Cournot players.[40] The key idea (also employed in Novshek [1980]) is that a sequence of economies involving firms with progressively smaller minimum efficient scales of production is employed so that firms take into account their individual effects on price, but in the limit the firms are arbitrarily small in comparison with their markets and thus their influence on price disappears.[41] This means that the Cournot model provides a means of generating Walrasian outcomes without recourse to price-taking firms.

What if firms have private information, as discussed earlier? What does entry imply? Palfrey [1985, reprinted in this volume] examines a model with identical (constant marginal cost) firms with private information about their cost functions and about the industry demand function intercept. He shows that in the limit, price will equal actual marginal cost and aggregate market outcomes will be determined by the actual costs and demand.[42] Thus, the Cournot game aggregates all the firms' private information; the result is as if firms shared all their information.

Finally, contrast this with what happens when the number of firms shrinks. Salant et al. [1983, reprinted in this volume] use a Cournot model with constant marginal costs and linear demand to examine industries wherein there are mergers of firms. At first blush one might think that merged firms must always do better since they could always replicate their premerger choices; this need not hold, however. The merged firm must

---

[39] Novshek [1980] examines the static free entry, partial equilibrium model wherein firms have nonconstant marginal costs; see also Green [1980] and Lambson [1984] on large dynamic markets.

[40] Ruffin [1971] focused on constant marginal costs.

[41] For a very nice summarization of their 1978 paper and related research over the past decade, see Novshek and Sonnenschein [1987]. Also see the April, 1980 symposium issue of the *Journal of Economic Theory*, "Noncooperative Approaches to the Theory of Perfect Competition."

[42] There are only a finite number of possible values that the uncertain parameters can take (that is, a finite state space) and a finite number of possible signals. A necessary condition is that, in the aggregate, the vectors of posterior estimates of the parameters generated by the signals must span a space of the dimension of the number of states.

ANDREW F. DAUGHETY

still choose strategies in a noncooperative, competitive setting. Salant, et al. show that their quantity model predicts losses from exogenously constructed mergers (that is, in a model wherein industry structure is not endogenously determined), and that such results are reasonably robust to model formulation. Is this result outlandish? Perhaps not: Scherer [1980], using a multination study of mergers, finds that average gains from mergers were either negative or zero. On the other hand, Perry and Porter [1985] show that the Salant, et al. results change when the cost functions are modified and Deneckere and Davidson [1985] once again demonstrate the now familiar effect of reliance on strategic variable, showing that the results can be reversed if we study Cournot in prices rather than Cournot in quantities. More generally, however, these theoretical results echo the observation made in the earlier discussions of price/quantity decisions and of Stackelberg models: A model of endogenous industry structure and strategic variable choice is clearly called for.

Efforts to unify static oligopoly models: conjectural variations

A holy grail for some economists has been the notion of a unified model of oligopoly. An early effort at this for static models by Bowley [1924] and Frisch [1933] involved modifying the optimality conditions (3) to parametrically generate a range of potential oligopoly solutions. Again, let $\pi_i(x_1, x_2)$ be firm i's profit and now totally differentiate this function with respect to x_i.

$$d\pi_i(x_1, x_2)/dx_i = \partial_i \pi_i(x_1, x_2) + \partial_j \pi_i(x_1, x_2) \cdot \partial_i x_j \quad i = 1, 2, \ j \neq i. \quad (9)$$

The last part of the second term in (9) is called the "conjectural variation" and is supposed to represent i's conjecture about how j might respond to a small adjustment in i's output. As Fellner [1949] stated, "...producers do not believe that the output of their rivals is fixed and independent of their own output. Instead, they believe that the output of their rivals depends on their own output *in some fashion.*"

Mechanically, by varying the assumed values of this term, one can generate a variety of oligopoly solutions. For example, the first-order condition for the quantity model (5) now becomes:

$$d\Pi_i^Q(q_1, q_2)/dq_i = p(q_1+q_2) + \partial_i p(q_1+q_2)q_i - c_i + \partial_j p(q_1+q_2)q_i \cdot \partial_i q_j$$
$$= 0.$$

In general, $\partial_i p(q_1+q_2) = \partial_j p(q_1+q_2)$ and therefore $\partial_i q_j = -1, 0$ or 1 yields (respectively):

34

1. "perfect competition," since the derivatives on the right-hand-side cancel
2. the Cournot solution, since the last term vanishes
3. (for equal marginal costs) joint profit maximization.

In Figure 8 this represents movement along the 45° line from *PC* to the equal shares solution. Conceptually, other values of the conjectural variation term will provide alternative oligopoly outcomes between perfect competition (−1) and perfect collusion (+1). Moreover, conjectural variations need not be symmetric, or even constant.

Are some values of the conjectural variation (CV) more reasonable than others? There are two answers to this question. First, one could presumably use industry data to estimate the CV. Iwata [1974] in an early effort used the Japanese plate glass industry, Gollop and Roberts [1979] use the coffee roasting industry, and Appelbaum [1982] examines the U.S. rubber, textile, electrical machinery, and tobacco industries (see Bresnahan [forthcoming] for a review of the empirical literature using CVs). Alternatively, one might impose a theoreticaly motivated restriction on the CV, such as requiring that it be correct in equilibrium. A number of papers pursued this approach (see Laitner [1980], Bresnahan [1981], Perry [1982], and Kamien and Schwartz [1983]). The restriction is called consistency. A consistent conjectural variation (CCV) is the slope of the appropriate reaction function; a consistent conjectures equilibrium (CCE) is an equilibrium with CCVs. In other words, in equilibrium, my conjecture about how you might adjust to small changes in my output should be correct: my CV for you and the slope of your ϕ-function (at the equilibrium output level) should be the same.

If we apply this restriction in the case of linear demand and constant and equal marginal cost it can be shown that the CCE involves pricing at marginal cost. Thus, in Figure 8 the unique CCE is the point label *PC*, where each firm produces *M*. Note in particular that the Cournot equilibrium is not a CCE, suggesting that it violates basic notions of rational expectations: agents are seemingly making incorrect conjectures about each other in equilibrium.

Figure 8 indicates, however, why the CCE is *not* an equilibrium. At *PC* the profits for both firms are zero. In the orthant "south and west" of *PC* both firms enjoy positive profits. Thus, for each firm, any output choice in the interval between 0 and *M* strictly dominates the strategy "produce *M*." Either firm can improve by cutting its output; (M, M) is not an equilibrium in the quantity game. Something more fundamental is wrong here, since rationality of the conjectural variation leads to an irrational outcome: Both agents are playing strictly dominated strategies and they both know it. Interestingly, in a series of laboratory experiments to test the CCE against the Cournot equilibrium, Holt [1985, reprinted in this volume] found that subjects rejected the CCE and played the Cournot strategy, making positive profits. What is it that they know that we don't know? ("If you're so smart, why aren't you rich?")

The problem stems from Bowley's notion of the conjectural variation itself. Daughety [1985, reprinted in this volume] used an infinite regress model to provide an endogenous means of forming conjectures by agents about each other's actions and about each other's conjectures. Thus endogenously determined conjectural variations are also defined. These turn out to be different from Bowley's notion, but intimately related. In particular, Bowley's CV is an infinite product of these endogenously determined CVs, implying two results. First, under some mild restrictions so the infinite regress problems have solutions, the endogenously determined CVs are shown to have exactly the slopes of the ϕ-functions, and thus are "consistent" as defined above (recall from a much earlier discussion that the solution to the infinite regress turned out to be the Cournot solution; now we see that the Cournot solution *is* consistent). Second, the endogenously determined CVs are (negative) fractions, and the Bowley CV is therefore an infinite product of fractions: it will be zero *by construction*. Thus, the Cournot model is not a model of zero conjectural variations meaning that one player *assumes* that the other would not adjust; this way of thinking mixes static and dynamic behavior. Rather it is a model of zero Bowley conjectural variations which occurs because the infinite stream of endogenously determined conjectures and conjectural variations is correct.

Does this mean that conjectural variation models have no value? Though the static approach pioneered by Bowley seems to be fundamentally flawed, at least in the presence of some variant of a rationality restriction, some caution in rejecting the entire area is clearly called for here. First, dynamic models wherein dynamic conjectures can arise might be quite reasonable (see Smithies and Savage [1940] and Riordan [1985]). Second, static CV models might be able to summarize more complex dynamic models. In this case, however, we are still left with the difficulties raised above (see Makowski [1983]) since such representations of complex processes may not be robust to reasonable rationality restrictions (such as not employing dominated strategies, a criterion that the static CCE fails as indicated earlier).

Summary

Figure 10 summarizes the main linkages between the Cournot model and some of the other standard models in oligopoly theory explored above. Under homogeneous goods, simultaneous choices in quantities yield

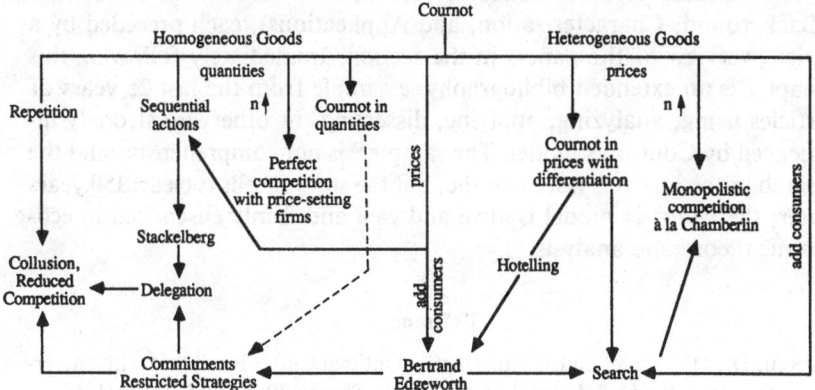

Figure 10. Cournot and oligopoly theory.

1. the standard results labeled "Cournot in quantities"
2. perfect competition as the number of firms increases without limit
3. collusion via repetition.

Altering the information sets yields Stackelberg equilibria. If choices are made in prices, then adding consumers yields the Bertrand and Edgeworth models for constant and increasing marginal costs respectively. The Bertrand/Edgeworth models provide the basic models for search by consumers for the minimal price; positive search costs can be viewed as initially entailing information sets for consumers which are not singletons (in contrast with those in Figure 5), but which can be resolved by consumers at a cost. Thus, by allowing consumers a sequence of costly choices they can refine their knowledge of where they are in the tree. On the other hand, restrictions on strategy spaces (such as the meet competition example) or the use of commitments allow firms to reduce competition and can yield collusive outcomes. The Stackelberg model expressed in prices (for either homogeneous or heterogeneous goods) yields models of price leadership.

When the goods are heterogeneous the basic model is "Cournot in prices" (though, of course, this model could be expressed in quantities, too). Adding consumers and eliminating product differentiation can again yield the Bertrand/Edgeworth model. This happened in the Hotelling case, where consumers searched for the minimum cost firm and thus location at the center of the market yielded the Bertrand result. Increasing the number of firms without limit yields a model of monopolistic competition à la Hart.

37

As indicated earlier, the rest of the volume contains three sections (Background, Characterization, and Applications), each preceded by a brief overview of the papers in the section. Immediately following this chapter is an extended bibliography, a sample from the last 25 years of articles using, analyzing, applying, dissecting, or otherwise strongly influenced by Cournot's model. The sample[43] is not comprehensive and the search procedure was not scientific, but the story it tells is clear: 150 years later, the Cournot model is alive and well and firmly ensconced in economic theory and analysis.

References

Abreu, D., D. Pearce, and E. Stacchetti, "Optimal Cartel Equilibria with Imperfect Monitoring," *Journal of Economic Theory* 39, 1, 1986, pp. 251–69.

Allen, B. and M. Hellwig, "Bertrand-Edgeworth Oligopoly in Large Markets," *Review of Economic Studies* 53, 1986, pp. 175–204.

Appelbaum, E., "The Estimation of the Degree of Oligopoly Power," *Journal of Econometrics* 19, 1982, pp. 287–99.

Aspremont, C. d', J. Gabszewicz, and J-F. Thisse, "On Hotelling's Stability in Competition," *Econometrica* 47, 5, 1979, pp. 1145–50.

Baumol, W. and S. Goldfeld, *Precursors in Mathematical Economics: An Anthology,* Number 19 in the *Series of Reprints of Scarce Works in Political Economy,* London School of Economics and Political Science, London, 1968.

Benoit, J. P. and V. Krishna, "Finitely Repeated Games," *Econometrica* 53, 4, 1985, pp. 905–22.

———, "Dynamic Duopoly: Prices and Quantities," *Review of Economic Studies* 54 (January 1987), pp. 23–35.

Berge, C., *Topological Spaces,* translated by E. M. Patterson, Oliver and Boyd Ltd., Edinburgh, 1963; originally published as "Espaces Topologiques, fonctions multivoques," Dunod, Paris, 1959.

Bernheim, B. D., "Rationalizable Strategic Behavior," *Econometrica* 52, 4, 1984, pp. 1007–28.

Blaug, M., *Economic Theory in Retrospect,* Richard D. Irwin, Homewood, IL, 1962.

Bowley, A. L., *The Mathematical Groundwork of Economics,* Oxford University Press, Oxford, 1924.

Brandenburger, A. and E. Dekel, "Rationalizability and Correlated Equilibria," *Econometrica* 55, 6, 1987, pp. 1391–1402.

[43] The main journals sampled were *Econometrica, The Rand Journal of Economics* (and its predecessor *The Bell Journal of Economics*), *The Review of Economic Studies,* and the *Journal of Economic Theory.* To a lesser extent *The American Economic Review, The Quarterly Journal of Economics,* the *Journal of Political Economy,* and the *International Economic Review* were also sampled.

Introduction, purpose, and overview

Brander, J. A. and T. R. Lewis, "Oligopoly and Financial Structure: The Limited Liability Effect," *American Economic Review* 76, 5, 1986, pp. 956-70.

Bresnahan, T. F., "Duopoly Models with Consistent Conjectures," *American Economic Review* 71, 5, 1981, pp. 934-45.

———, "Empirical Studies of Industries with Market Power," in the *Handbook of Industrial Organization,* eds. R. Schmalensee and R. Willig, forthcoming.

Bulow, J., J. D. Geanakoplos, and P. D. Klemperer, "Multimarket Oligopoly: Strategic Substitutes and Complements," *Journal of Political Economy* 93, 3, 1985, pp. 488-511.

Chamberlin, E. H., *The Theory of Monopolistic Competition,* Harvard University Press, Cambridge, 1933.

Cheng, L., "Comparing Bertrand and Cournot Equilibria: a Geometric Approach," *Rand Journal of Economics* 16, 1, 1985, pp. 146-52.

Clarke, R., "Collusion and the Incentives for Information Sharing," *Bell Journal of Economics* 14, 2, 1983, pp. 383-94.

Cooper, T., "Most-Favoured-Customer Pricing and Tacit Collusion," *Rand Journal of Economics* 17, 3, 1986, pp. 377-88.

Cournot, A., *Researches into the Mathematical Principles of the Theory of Wealth,* Nathaniel T. Bacon, trans., Macmillan, New York, 1897; reprinted with notes by Irving Fisher, Macmillan, New York, 1927; reprinted, Augustus M. Kelley, New York, 1960; originally "Recherches sur les principes mathématiques de la théorie des Richesses," L. Hachette, Paris, 1838.

Dasgupta, P. and E. Maskin, "The Existence of Equilibrium in Discontinuous Economic Games, II: Applications," *Review of Economic Studies* 53, 1986, pp. 27-41.

Daughety, A. F., "Endogenously Determined Industrial Organization," Working Paper, Department of Economics, The University of Iowa, November 1984.

———, "Reconsidering Cournot: The Cournot Equilibrium Is Consistent," *Rand Journal of Economics* 16, 3, 1985, pp. 368-79.

Davidson, C. and R. Deneckere, "Long-Run Competition in Capacity, Short-Run Competition in Price, and the Cournot Model," *Rand Journal of Economics* 17, 3, 1986, pp. 404-15.

Deneckere, R. and C. Davidson, "Incentives to Form Coalitions with Bertrand Competition," *Rand Journal of Economics* 16, 4, 1985, pp. 473-86.

Dixit, A., "A Model of Duopoly Suggesting a Theory of Entry Barriers," *Bell Journal of Economics* 10, 2, 1979, pp. 20-32.

———, "Comparative Statics for Oligopoly," *International Economic Review* 27, 1986, pp. 107-22.

Dowrick, S., "Von Stackelberg and Cournot Duopoly: Choosing Roles," *Rand Journal of Economics* 17, 2, 1986, pp. 251-60.

Edgeworth, F. Y., "The Pure Theory of Monopoly," in *Papers Relating to Political Economy,* Vol. 1, Macmillan, London, 1925, pp. 111-42.

Fellner, W., *Competition Among the Few,* Knopf, New York, 1949; reprinted by Augustus M. Kelley, New York, 1965.

Fershtman, C. and K. Judd, "Equilibrium Incentives in Oligopoly," *American Economic Review,* 77, 5, 1987, pp. 927–40.

Fershtman, C., K. Judd, and E. Kalai, "Cooperation Through Delegation," Working Paper, Center for Mathematical Studies in Economics and Management Sciences, Northwestern University, 1987.

Fershtman, C. and M. Kamien, "Dynamic Duopolistic Competition with Sticky Prices," *Econometrica* 55, 5, 1987, pp. 1151–64.

Fisher, I., "Cournot and Mathematical Economics," *Quarterly Journal of Economics* 12, 1898, pp. 119–38.

———, "Cournot Forty Years Ago," *Econometrica* 6, 3, 1938, pp. 198–202.

Fried, D., "Incentives for Information Production and Disclosure in a Duopolistic Environment," *Quarterly Journal of Economics* 99, 2, 1984, pp. 367–81.

Friedman, J. W., "A Non-cooperative Equilibrium for Supergames," *Review of Economic Studies* 38, 1, 1971, 1–12.

———, *Oligopoly and the Theory of Games,* North-Holland, Amsterdam, 1977.

———, *Oligopoly Theory,* Cambridge University Press, New York, 1983.

———, "Limit Pricing Entry Prevention when Complete Information Is Lacking," *Journal of Economic Dynamics and Control* 5, 1983, pp. 187–99.

———, "Cooperative Equilibria in Finite Horizon Noncooperative Supergames," *Journal of Economic Theory* 35, 1985, pp. 390–8.

———, *Game Theory with Applications to Economics,* Oxford University Press, New York, 1986.

———, "On the Strategic Importance of Prices versus Quantities," Working Paper, Department of Economics, University of North Carolina, 1987.

Friedman, J. W. and L. Samuelson, "Subgame Perfect Equilibrium with Continuous Reaction Functions," Working Paper, Department of Economics, University of North Carolina, 1988.

Frisch, R., "Monopoly-Polypoly – The Concept of Force in the Economy," trans. W. Beckerman, reprinted in *International Economic Papers* 1, 1951, pp. 23–36; originally published as "Monopole-Polypole – La notion de force dans l'économie," in *Festschrift til Harald Westergaard, Supplement to National-økonomisk Tidsskrift,* 1933.

Fry, C. L. and R. B. Ekelund Jr., "Cournot's Demand Theory: A Reassessment," *History of Political Economy* 3, 1971, pp. 190–7.

Fudenberg, D. and E. Maskin, "The Folk Theorem in Repeated Games with Discounting and with Incomplete Information," *Econometrica* 54, 3, 1986, pp. 533–54.

Fudenberg, D. and J. Tirole, *Dynamic Models of Oligopoly,* Harwood Academic Publishers, Chur, Switzerland, 1986.

Gal-Or, E., "Information Transmission – Cournot and Bertrand Equilibria," *Review of Economic Studies* 53, 1, 1986, pp. 85–92.

———, "First Mover Disadvantages with Private Information," *Review of Economic Studies,* 54, pp. 279–92.

———, "Excessive Retailing at the Bertrand Equilibria," Working Paper, Graduate School of Business, University of Pittsburgh, 1987.

Introduction, purpose, and overview

Golding, E. L., "The Decision to Play a Cournot or Stackelberg Game when Market Demand Is Imperfectly Known," Working Paper, Department of Economics, University of Florida, November 1984.

Golding, E. L. and S. Slutsky, "The Effects of 'We Won't Be Undersold' Policies in Markets with Consumer Search," Working Paper, Department of Economics, University of Florida, 1986.

Gollop, F. M. and M. J. Roberts, "Firm Interdependence in Oligopolistic Markets," *Journal of Econometrics* 10, 1979, pp. 313–31.

Green, E. "Noncooperative Price Taking in Large, Dynamic Markets," *Journal of Economic Theory* 22, 2, 1980, pp. 155–82.

Green, E. and R. Porter, "Noncooperative Collusion Under Imperfect Price Information," *Econometrica* 52, 1, 1984, pp. 87–100.

Harker, P. T., "A Variational Inequality Approach to the Determination of Oligopolistic Market Equilibrium," *Mathematical Programming* 30, 1, 1984, pp. 105–11.

Hart, O. D., "Monopolistic Competition in the Spirit of Chamberlin: A General Model," *Review of Economic Studies* 52, 4, 1985, pp. 529–46.

Hathaway, N. J. and J. A. Rickard, "Equilibria of Price-Setting and Quantity-Setting Duopolies," *Economics Letters* 3, 1979, pp. 133–7.

Hicks, J. R., "Annual Survey of Economic Theory: The Theory of Monopoly," *Econometrica* 3, 1935, pp. 1–20.

Holt, C. A., "An Experimental Test of the Consistent-Conjectures Hypothesis," *American Economic Review* 75, 3, 1985, pp. 314–25.

Hotelling, H., "Stability in Competition," *Economic Journal,* 39, 1929, pp. 41–57.

Jacquemin, A., *The New Industrial Organization,* trans. F. Mehta, MIT Press, Cambridge, 1987.

Kambhu, J., "Uncertainty and Endogenous Stackelberg Equilibrium," Working Paper, Department of Economics, Columbia University, January 1984.

Kamien, M. I., "Notes on Cournot's Theory of Oligopoly," mimeo, Northwestern University, 1987.

Kamien, M. I. and N. L. Schwartz, "Conjectural Variations," *Canadian Journal of Economics* 16, 1983, pp. 191–211.

Klemperer, P. and M. Meyer, "Price Competition vs. Quantity Competition: The Role of Uncertainty," *Rand Journal of Economics* 17, 4, 1986, pp. 618–38.

Kolstad, C. D. and L. Mathiesen, "Necessary and Sufficient Conditions for Uniqueness of a Cournot Equilibrium," *Review of Economic Studies,* 54, 1987, pp. 681–90.

Kreps, D. M., P. Milgrom, J. Roberts, and R. Wilson, "Rational Cooperation in the Finitely Repeated Prisoner's Dilemma," *Journal of Economic Theory,* 27, 1982, pp. 245–52.

Kreps, D. M. and J. A. Scheinkman, "Quantity Precommitment and Bertrand Competition Yield Cournot Outcomes," *Bell Journal of Economics* 14, 2, 1983, pp. 326–37.

Laitner, J., "'Rational' Duopoly Equilibria," *Quarterly Journal of Economics* 95, 4, 1980, pp. 641–62.

Lambson, V. "Self-Enforcing Collusion in Large Dynamic Markets," *Journal of Economic Theory* 34, 2, 1984, pp. 282–91.

Li, L., "Cournot Oligopoly with Information Sharing," *Rand Journal of Economics* 16, 4, 1985, pp. 521–36.

Luce, R. D. and H. Raiffa, *Games and Decisions,* Wiley, New York, 1957.

Makowski, L. "'Rational Conjectures' Aren't Rational, 'Reasonable Conjectures' Aren't Reasonable," Economic Theory Discussion Paper No. 66, Cambridge University, 1983.

McAndrews, J., "Strategic Role Complementarity," Working Paper, Department of Economics, The University of Iowa, November 1987.

McManus, M., "Equilibrium, Number and Size in Cournot Oligopoly," *Yorkshire Bulletin of Economic and Social Research* 16, 1964, pp. 68–75.

Milgrom, P. and J. Roberts, "Limit Pricing and Entry Under Incomplete Information," *Econometrica* 50, 2, 1982, pp. 443–59.

Murphy, F. H., H. D. Sherali, and A. L. Soyster, "A Mathematical Programming Approach for Determining Oligopolistic Market Equilibrium," *Mathematical Programming* 24, 1, 1982, pp. 92–106.

Nichol, A. J., "Tragedies in the Life of Cournot," *Econometrica* 6, 3, 1938, pp. 193–7.

Novshek, W., "Cournot Equilibrium with Free Entry," *Review of Economic Studies* 47, 1980, pp. 473–86.

———, "On the Existence of Cournot Equilibrium," *Review of Economic Studies* 52, 1, 1985, pp. 85–98.

Novshek, W. and H. Sonnenschein, "Cournot and Walras Equilibria," *Journal of Economic Theory* 19, 2, 1978, pp. 223–66.

———, "Fulfilled Expectations Cournot Duopoly with Information Acquisition and Release," *Bell Journal of Economics* 13, 1, 1982, pp. 214–8.

———, "General Equilibrium with Free Entry," *Journal of Economic Literature* 25, 3, 1987, pp. 1281–306.

Okuguchi, K., *Expectations and Stability in Oligopoly Models,* Springer-Verlag, Berlin, 1976.

Palfrey, T., "Uncertainty Resolution, Private Information Aggregation and the Cournot Competitive Limit," *Review of Economic Studies* 52, 1, 1985, pp. 69–83.

Pearce, D. G., "Rationalizable Strategic Behavior and the Problem of Perfection," *Econometrica* 52, 4, 1984, pp. 1029–50.

Perry, M., "Oligopoly and Consistent Conjectural Variations," *Bell Journal of Economics,* 13, 1, 1982, pp. 197–205.

Perry, M. and R. Porter, "Oligopoly and the Incentive for Horizontal Merger," *American Economic Review* 75, 1, 1985, pp. 219–27.

Ponssard, J. P., "The Strategic Role of Information on the Demand Function in an Oligopolistic Market," *Management Science* 25, 3, 1979, pp. 243–50.

Porter, R. "Optimal Cartel Trigger Price Strategies," *Journal of Economic Theory* 29, 2, 1983a, pp. 313–38.

———, "A Study of Cartel Stability: The Joint Economic Committee: 1880-1886," *Bell Journal of Economics* 14, 2, 1983b, pp. 301-14.

P'ng, I. P. L. and D. Hirshleifer, "Price Discrimination Through Offers to Match Price," Working Paper No. 151, Center for Marketing Studies, Graduate School of Management, University of California, Los Angeles, 1986.

Radner, R. "Collusive Behavior in Noncooperative Epsilon-Equilibria of Oligopolies with Long but Finite Lines," *Journal of Economic Theory* 22, 2, 1980, pp. 136-54.

Rhodes, G. F. Jr., "A Note Interpreting Cournot's Economics by His General Epistemology," *History of Political Economy* 10, 2, 1978, pp. 315-21.

Roberts, J. and H. Sonnenschein, "On the Existence of Cournot Equilibrium without Concave Profit Functions," *Journal of Economic Theory* 13, 1976, pp. 112-17.

Rubinstein, A., "Finite Automata Play the Repeated Prisoner's Dilemma Game," *Journal of Economic Theory* 39, 1, 1986, pp. 83-96.

Ruffin, R., "Cournot Oligopoly and Competitive Behavior," *Review of Economic Studies* 38, 1971, pp. 493-502.

Sadanand, V., "Cournot or Stackelberg?" Working Paper, California Institute of Technology, 1982.

Salant, S. W., S. Switzer, and R. J. Reynolds, "Losses from Horizontal Merger: The Effects of an Exogenous Change in Industry Structure on Cournot-Nash Equilibrium," *Quarterly Journal of Economics* 98, 2, 1983, pp. 185-99.

Saloner, G., "Cournot Duopoly with Two Production Periods," *Journal of Economic Theory,* 42, 1987, pp. 183-7.

Salop, S., "Practices that (Credibly) Facilitate Oligopoly Co-ordination," in *New Developments in the Analysis of Market Structure,* eds., J. E. Stiglitz and G. F. Mathewson, Cambridge, MIT Press, 1986, pp. 265-90.

Scherer, F. M., *Industrial Market Structure and Economic Performance,* 2d ed., Chicago, Rand McNally, 1980.

Shapiro, C., "Exchange of Cost Information in Oligopoly," *Review of Economic Studies* 53, 1986, pp. 433-46.

———, "Theories of Oligopoly Behavior," in the *Handbook of Industrial Organization,* eds., R. Schmalensee and R. Willig, forthcoming.

Sherali, H. D., "A Multiple Leader Stackelberg Model and Analysis," *Operations Research* 32, 2, 1984, pp. 390-404.

Singh, N. and X. Vives, "Price and Quantity Competition in a Differentiated Duopoly," *Rand Journal of Economics* 15, 4, 1984, pp. 546-54.

Sklivas, S. D., "The Strategic Choice of Managerial Incentives," *Rand Journal of Economics* 18, 3, 1987, pp. 452-60.

Smithies, A. and L. J. Savage, "A Dynamic Problem in Duopoly," *Econometrica* 8, 2, 1940, pp. 130-43.

Sonnenschein, H., "The Dual of Duopoly Is Complementary Monopoly: or, Two of Cournot's Theories Are One," *Journal of Political Economy* 76, 2, 1968, pp. 316-18.

Stackelberg, H. von, *Marktform und Gleichgewicht,* Springer, Vienna, 1934.

Stigler, G. J., "A Theory of Oligopoly," *Journal of Political Economy* 72, 1, 1964, pp. 44–61.

Szidarovszky, F. and S. Yakowitz, "A New Proof of the Existence and Uniqueness of the Cournot Equilibrium," *International Economic Review* 18, 1977, pp. 787–9.

———, "Contributions to Cournot Oligopoly Theory," *Journal of Economic Theory* 28, 1, 1982, pp. 51–70.

Vickers, J., "Delegation and the Theory of the Firm," *Economic Journal Supplement* 95, 1985, pp. 138–47.

Vives, X., "Duopoly Information Equilibrium: Cournot and Bertrand," *Journal of Economic Theory* 34, 1, 1984, pp. 71–94.

———, "On the Efficiency of Bertrand and Cournot Equilibria with Product Differentiation," *Journal of Economic Theory* 36, 1, 1985, pp. 166–75.

Wolinsky, A., "Prices as Signals of Product Quality," *Review of Economic Studies* 50, 1986, pp. 647–58.

Extended bibliography

Abreu, D., "Extremal Equilibria of Oligopolistic Supergames," *Journal of Economic Theory* 39, 1, 1986, 191-225.

Abreu, D., D. Pearce, and E. Stacchetti, "Optimal Cartel Equilibria with Imperfect Monitoring," *Journal of Economic Theory* 39, 1, 1986, 251-69.

Alger, D., "Laboratory Tests of Equilibrium Predictions with Disequilibrium Data," *Review of Economic Studies* 54 (January 1987), 105-45.

Allen, B. and M. Hellwig, "Bertrand–Edgeworth Oligopoly in Large Markets," *Review of Economic Studies* 53, 1986, 175-204.

Al-Nowaihi, A. and P. Levine, "The Stability of the Cournot Oligopoly Model: A Reassessment," *Journal of Economic Theory* 35, 2, 1985, 307-21.

Arvan, L., "Some Examples of Dynamic Cournot Duopoly with Inventory," *Rand Journal of Economics* 16 (Winter, 1985), 569-78.

———, "Sunk Capacity Costs, Long-Run Fixed Costs, and Entry Deterrence under Complete and Incomplete Information," *Rand Journal of Economics* 17, 1, 1986, 105-21.

Aspremont, C. d' and L. Gerard-Valet, "Stackelberg Solvable Games and Preplay Communication," *Journal of Economic Theory*, 23, 2, 1980, 201-17.

Aspremont, C. d', J. Gabszewicz, and J.-F. Thisse, "On Hotelling's Stability in Competition," *Econometrica* 47, 5, 1979, 1145-50.

Baily, M., "Research and Development Costs and Returns: The U.S. Pharmaceutical Industry," *Journal of Political Economy* 80, 1, 1972, 70-85.

Bamon, R. and J. Fraysse, "Existence of Cournot Equilibrium in Large Markets," *Econometrica* 53, 3, 1985, pp. 587-98.

Benoit, J. P., "Financially Constrained Entry in a Game with Incomplete Information," *Rand Journal of Economics* 15, 4, 1984, 490-9.

———, "Innovation and Imitation in a Duopoly," *Review of Economic Studies* 52, 1985, 99-106.

Benoit, J. P. and V. Krishna, "Dynamic Duopoly: Prices and Quantities," *Review of Economic Studies* 54 (January 1987), 23-35.

Bergstrom, T. and H. Varian, "When Are Nash Equilibria Independent of the Distribution of Agents' Characteristics?" *Review of Economic Studies* 52, 1985, 715-18.

Bernheim, B. D., "Rationalizable Strategic Behavior," *Econometrica* 52, 4, 1984, 1007-28.

45

———, "Strategic Deterrence of Sequential Entry into an Industry," *Rand Journal of Economics* 15, 1, 1984, 1–11.

Bernheim, B. D. and M. D. Whinston, "Common Marketing Agency as a Device for Facilitating Collusion," *Rand Journal of Economics* 16, 2, 1985, 269–81.

———, "Coalition-Proof Nash Equilibria. II. Applications," *Journal of Economic Theory* 42, 1, 1987, 13–29.

Bhattacharya, G., "Learning and the Behavior of Potential Entrants," *Rand Journal of Economics* 15, 2, 1984, 281–9.

Bhattacharya, S. and D. Mookherjee, "Portfolio Choice in Research and Development," *Rand Journal of Economics* 17, 4, 1986, 594–605.

Bishop, R. L., "The Stability of the Cournot Oligopoly Solution: Further Comment," *Review of Economic Studies* 29, 1962, 332–6.

Bonanno, G. and C. Zeeman, "Limited Knowledge of Demand and Oligopoly Equilibria," *Journal of Economic Theory* 35, 2, 1985, 276–83.

Borenstein, S., "Price Discrimination in Free-Entry Markets," *Rand Journal of Economics* 16, 3, 1985, 380–97.

Brander, J. and B. Spencer, "Strategic Commitment with R&D: The Symmetric Case," *Bell Journal of Economics* 14, 1, 1983, 225–35.

Brander, J. A. and J. Eaton, "Product Line Rivalry," *American Economic Review* 74, 3, 1984, 323–34.

Brander, J. A. and T. R. Lewis, "Oligopoly and Financial Structure: The Limited Liability Effect," *American Economic Review* 76 (December 1986), 956–70.

Bresnahan, T. F., "Duopoly Models with Consistent Conjectures," *American Economic Review* 71 (December 1981), 934–45.

Brock, W. and J. Scheinkman, "Price Setting Supergames with Capacity Constraints," *Review of Economic Studies* LII, 1985, 371–82.

Bryant, J., "Competitive Equilibrium with Price-Setting Firms and Stochastic Demand," *International Economic Review* 21, 3, 1980, 619–26.

Bucovetsky, S., "Price Dispersion and Stockpiling by Consumers," *Review of Economic Studies* L, 1983, 443–65.

Bucovetsky, S. and J. Chilton, "Concurrent Renting and Selling in a Durable-Goods Monopoly under Threat of Entry," *Rand Journal of Economics* 17, 2, 1986, 261–75.

Bulow, J., J. D. Geanakoplos, and P. D. Klemperer, "Multimarket Oligopoly: Strategic Substitutes and Complements," *Journal of Political Economy* 93, (June 1985), 488–511.

Burns, M., "Predatory Pricing and the Acquisition Cost of Competitors," *Journal of Political Economy* 94, 2, 1986, 266–94.

Carlson, J. and R. McAfee, "Discrete Equilibrium Price Dispersion," *Journal of Political Economy* 91, 3, 1983, 480–93.

Caves, R., M. Fortunato, and P. Ghemawat, "The Decline of Dominant Firms, 1905–1929," *Quarterly Journal of Economics* 99, 3, 1984, 523–46.

Cheng, L., "Comparing Bertrand and Cournot Equilibria: A Geometric Approach," *Rand Journal of Economics* 16 (Spring 1985), 146–52.

Extended bibliography

Clarke, R., "Collusion and the Incentives for Information Sharing," *Bell Journal of Economics* 14 (Autumn 1983), 383–94.

Clemhout, S., G. Leitman, and H. Y. Wan, Jr., "A Differential Game Model of Duopoly," *Econometrica* 39, 6, 1971, 911–38.

Conlisk, J., "Competitive Approximation of a Cournot Market," *Review of Economic Studies* 50 (October 1983), 597–607.

Cooper, T., "Most-favoured-customer Pricing and Tacit Collusion," *Rand Journal of Economics* 17, 3, 1986, 377–88.

Cyert, R. M. and M. H. Degroot, "Multiperiod Decision Models with Alternating Choice as a Solution to the Duopoly Problem," *Quarterly Journal of Economics* 84 (August 1970), 410–29.

———, "Interfirm Learning and the Kinked Demand Curve," *Journal of Economic Theory* 3, 1971, 272–87.

———, "Bayesian Analysis and Duopoly Theory," *Journal of Political Economy* 78 (September/October 1970), 1168–84.

Dahlby, B. and D. West, "Price Dispersion in an Automobile Insurance Market," *Journal of Political Economy* 94, 2, 1986, 418–38.

Dana, R. and L. Montrucchio, "Dynamic Complexity in Duopoly Games," *Journal of Economic Theory* 40, 1, 1986, 40–56.

Dansby, R. E. and R. D. Willig, "Industry Performance Gradient Indexes," *American Economic Review* 69, 3, 1979, 249–60.

Dasgupta, P. and J. Stiglitz, "Uncertainty, Industrial Structure, and the Speed of R&D," *Bell Journal of Economics* 11 (Spring 1980), 1–28.

Dasgupta, P. and E. Maskin, "The Existence of Equilibrium in Discontinuous Economic Games, I: Theory, *Review of Economic Studies* 53 (January 1986), 1–26.

———, "The Existence of Equilibrium in Discontinuous Economic Games, II: Applications," *Review of Economic Studies* 53 (January 1986), 27–41.

Daughety, A., "Regulation and Industrial Organization," *Journal of Political Economy,* 92, 5, 1984, 932–53.

———, "Reconsidering Cournot: The Cournot Equilibrium Is Consistent," *Rand Journal of Economics* 16, 3, 1985, 368–79.

Davidson, C. and R. Deneckere, "Long-Run Competition in Capacity, Short-Run Competition in Price, and the Cournot Model," *Rand Journal of Economics* 17 (Autumn 1986), 404–15.

Decanio, S., "Delivered Pricing and Multiple Basing-Point Equilibria: A Reevaluation," *Quarterly Journal of Ecomonics* 99, 2, 1984, 329–49.

Demange, G. "Free Entry and Stability in a Cournot Model," *Journal of Economic Theory* 40, 2, 1986, 283–303.

Deneckere, R. and C. Davidson, "Incentives to Form Coalitions with Bertrand Competition," *Rand Journal of Economics* 16, 4, 1985, 473–86.

DePalma, A., V. Glinsburgh, Y. Papageorgio, and J.-F. Thisse, "The Principle of Minimum Differentiation Holds under Sufficient Heterogeneity," *Econometrica* 53, 4, 1985, 767–81.

Deshmukh, S. and S. Chikte, "Dynamic Pricing with Stochastic Entry," *Review of Economic Studies* XLIII, 1976, 91–7.

Dixit, A., "A Model of Duopoly Suggesting a Theory of Entry Barriers," *Bell Journal of Economics* 10 (Spring 1979), 20-32.

———, "Comparative Statics for Oligopoly," *International Economic Review* 27 (February 1986), 107-22.

Dixit, A. and V. Norman, "Advertising and Welfare," *Bell Journal of Economics* 9, 1, 1978, 1-17.

Dolbear, F. T., L. B. Lave, G. Bownan, A. Lieberman, E. Prescott, F. Rueter, and R. Sherman, "Collusion in Oligopoly: An Experiment on the Effect of Numbers and Information," *Quarterly Journal of Economics* 82 (May 1968), 240-59.

Douglas, E. "Price Variation Duopoly with Differentiated Products: A Note," *Journal of Economic Theory* 6, 5, 1973, 618-20.

Dowrick, S., "von Stackelberg and Cournot Duopoly: Choosing Roles," *Rand Journal of Economics* 17, 2, 1986, 251-60.

Dubey, P., A. Mas-Colell, and M. Shubik, "Efficiency Properties of Strategic Market Games: An Axiomatic Approach," *Journal of Economic Theory* 22 (April 1980), 339-62.

Eaton, B. and R. Lipsey, "A Comment on Location and Industrial Efficiency with Free Entry," *Quarterly Journal of Economics* 93, 3, 1979, 447-50.

———, "Exit Barriers Are Entry Barriers: The Durability of Capital as a Barrier to Entry," *Bell Journal of Economics* 11, 2, 1980, 721-9.

———, "Capital, Commitment and Entry Equilibrium," *Bell Journal of Economics* 12, 2, 1981, 593-604.

Eaton, B. and M. Wooders, "Sophisticated Entry in a Model of Spatial Competition," *Rand Journal of Economics* 16, 2, 1985, 282-97.

Eaton, B. C. and R. Ware, "A Theory of Market Structure with Sequential Entry," *Rand Journal of Economics* 18 (Spring 1987), 1-16.

Eaton, J. and H. Kierzkowski, "Oligopolistic Competition, Product Variety, Entry Deterrence and Technology Transfer," *Rand Journal of Economics* 15, 1, 1984, 99-107.

Eaton, J. and G. M. Grossman, "Optimal Trade and Industrial Policy Under Oligopoly," *Quarterly Journal of Economics* 101 (May 1986), 386-406.

Economides, N., "Nash Equilibrium in Duopoly with Products Defined by Two Characteristics," *Rand Journal of Economics* 17, 3, 1986, 431-9.

Encaoua, D. and A. Jacquemin, "Degree of Monopoly, Indices of Concentration and Threat of Entry," *International Economic Review* 21, 1, 1980, 87-105.

Farrell, J., "Moral Hazard as an Entry Barrier," *Rand Journal of Economics* 17, 3, 1986, 440-9.

Fershtman, C. and M. Kamien, "Dynamic Duopolistic Competition with Sticky Prices," *Econometrica* 55, 5, 1987, 1151-64.

Fershtman, C. and E. Muller, "Capital Accumulation Games of Infinite Duration," *Journal of Economic Theory* 33, 2, 1984, 322-39.

———, "Capital Investments and Price Agreements in Semi-Collusive Markets," *Rand Journal of Economics* 17, 2, 1986, 214-26.

Fisher, F. M., "The Stability of the Cournot Oligopoly Solution: the Effects of

Extended bibliography

Speeds of Adjustment and Increasing Marginal Costs," *Review of Economic Studies* 28 (February 1961), 125-35.

———, "Stability and Competitive Equilibrium in Two Models of Search and Individual Price Adjustment," *Journal of Economic Theory* 6, 1973, 446-70.

Fisher, F. and J. McGowan, "Advertising and Welfare: Comment," *Bell Journal of Economics* 10, 2, 1979, 726-7.

Flaherty, M., "Dynamic Limit Pricing, Barriers to Entry and Rational Firms," *Journal of Economic Theory* 23, 2, 1980, 160-82.

Frank, C., "Entry in a Cournot Market," *Review of Economic Studies* 32, 1965, 245-50.

Frank C. and R. Quandt, "On the Existence of Cournot Equilibrium," *International Economic Review* 4, 1, 1963, 92-6.

———, "Static Cournot Equilibrium: Reply," *International Economic Review* 5, 3, 1964, 337-8.

Fried, D., "Incentives for Information Production and Disclosure in a Duopolistic Environment," *Quarterly Journal of Economics* 99, 2, 1984, 367-81.

Friedman, J. W., "Reaction Functions and the Theory of Duopoly," *Review of Economic Studies* 35, 1968, 257-72.

———, "On Experimental Research in Oligopoly," *Review of Economic Studies* 36, 1969, 399-416.

———, "A Noncooperative View of Oligopoly," *International Economic Review* 12, 1, 1971, 106-22.

———, "A Non-Cooperative Equilibrium for Supergames," *Review of Economic Studies* 38, 1, 1971, 1-12.

———, "On Reaction Function Equilibria," *International Economic Review* 14 (October 1973), 721-33.

———, "Non-Cooperative Equilibria in Time Dependent Supergames," *Econometrica* 42 (March 1974), 221-37.

———, "Reaction Functions as Nash Equilibria," *Review of Economic Studies* 43, 1976, 83-90.

———, "Noncooperative Equilibria for Exit Supergames," *International Economic Review* 20, 1, 1979, 147-56.

———, "Advertising and Oligopolistic Equilibrium," *Bell Journal of Economics* 14, 2, 1983, 464-73.

———, "Cooperative Equilibria in Finite Horizon Noncooperative Supergames," *Journal of Economic Theory* 35, 1985, pp. 390-8.

Fudenberg, D. and J. Tirole, "Learning-by-Doing and Market Performance," *Bell Journal of Economics* 14, 2, 1983, 522-30.

———, "Capital as a Commitment: Strategic Investment to Deter Mobility," *Journal of Economic Theory* 31, 2, 1983, 227-50.

———, "Preemption and Rent Equalization in the Adoption of New Technology," *Review of Economic Studies* 52, 1985, 383-401.

———, "A 'Signal-Jamming' Theory of Predation," *Rand Journal of Economics* 17, 3, 1986, 366-76.

Furth, D., "Stability and Instability in Oligopoly," *Journal of Economic Theory* 40, 2, 1986, 147–228.

Gabszewicz, J. and J.-F. Thisse, "Price Competition, Quality and Income Disparities," *Journal of Economic Theory* 20, 2, 1979, 340–59.

———, "Entry (and Exit) in a Differentiated Industry," *Journal of Economic Theory* 22, 2, 1980, 327–38.

Gabszewicz, J. and J. Vial, "Oligopoly, A La Cournot in a General Equilibrium Analysis," *Journal of Economic Theory* 4, 1972, 381–400.

Gallini, N. and R. Winter, "Licensing in the Theory of Innovation," *Rand Journal of Economics* 16, 2, 1985, 237–52.

Gal-Or, E., "Quality and Quantity Competition," *Bell Journal of Economics* 14, 2, 1983, 590–600.

———, "Price Dispersion with Uncertain Demand," *International Economic Review* 25, 2, 1984, 441–57.

———, "Information Sharing in Oligopoly," *Econometrica* 53, 2, 1985, 329–44.

———, "Differentiated Industries without Entry Barriers," *Journal of Economic Theory* 37, 2, 1985, 310–39.

———, "Information Transmission – Cournot and Bertrand Equilibria," *Review of Economic Studies* 53, 1, 1986, 85–92.

Gannon, C., "Product Differentiation and Locational Competition in Spatial Markets," *International Economic Review* 18, 2, 1977, 293–321.

Gaskins, D. "Dynamic Limit Pricing: Optimal Pricing Under Threat of Entry," *Journal of Economic Theory* 3, 1971, 306–22.

Gee, J., "A Model of Location and Industrial Efficiency with Free Entry," *Quarterly Journal of Economics* 90, 4, 1976, 557–74.

———, "Location and Industrial Location with Free Entry: A Reply," *Quarterly Journal of Economics* 93, 3, 1979, 451–4.

Gehrig, W., "On the Complete Solution of the Linear Cournot Oligopoly Model," *Review of Economic Studies* 48 (October 1981), 667–70,

Gelman, J. and S. Salop, "Judo Economics: Capacity Limitation and Coupon Competition," *Bell Journal of Economics* 14, 2, 1983, 315–25.

Gerard-Varet, L. and H. Moulin, "Correlation and Duopoly," *Journal of Economic Theory* 19, 1, 1978, 124–49.

Ghemanat, P. and B. Nalebuff, "Exit," *Rand Journal of Economics* 16, 2, 1985, 184–94.

Gilbert, R., "Dominant Firm Pricing Policy in a Market for an Exhaustible Resource," *Bell Journal of Economics* 9, 2, 1978, 385–95.

Gilbert, R. and S. Goldman, "Potential Competition and the Monopoly Price of an Exhaustible Resource," *Journal of Economic Theory* 17, 2, 1978, 319–31.

Gilbert, R. and R. Harris, "Competition with Lumpy Investment," *Rand Journal of Economics* 15, 2, 1984, 197–212.

Gilbert, R. and X. Vives, "Entry Deterrence and the Free Rider Problem," *Review of Economic Studies* 53, 1986, 71–83.

Gisser, M., "Price Leadership and Dynamic Aspects of Oligopoly in U.S. Manufacturing," *Journal of Political Economy* 92, 6, 1984, 1035–48.

Extended bibliography

Green, E. "Noncooperative Price Taking in Large, Dynamic Markets," *Journal of Economic Theory* 22, 2, 1980, 155-82.

Green, E. and R. Porter, "Noncooperative Collusion Under Imperfect Price Information," *Econometrica* 52, 1, 1984, 87-100.

Greenhut, M. L. and H. Ohta, "Vertical Integration of Successive Oligopolists," *American Economic Review* 69 (March 1979), 137-41.

Greenhut, J., M. Greenhut, and S. Y. Li, "Spatial Pricing Patterns in the United States," *Quarterly Journal of Economics* 94, 2, 1980, 329-50.

Grossman, G. and C. Shapiro, "Informative Advertising with Differentiated Products," *Review of Economic Studies* 51, 1984, 63-81.

Grossman, S., "Nash Equilibrium and the Industrial Organization of Markets with Large Fixed Costs," *Econometrica* 49, 5, 1981, 1149-72.

Guasch, J. and A. Weiss, "Erratum: Adverse Selection by Markets and the Advantage of Being Late," *Quarterly Journal of Economics* 95, 1, 1980, 201.

Hadar, J., "Stability of Oligopoly with Product Differentiation," *Review of Economic Studies* XXXIII, 1966, 57-60.

Hahn, F. H., "The Stability of the Cournot Oligopoly Solution," *Review of Economic Studies* 29, 1962, 329-31.

Harrington, J. E., "Noncooperative Behavior by a Cartel as an Entry-Deterring Signal," *Rand Journal of Economics* 15, 3, 1984, 426-33.

———, "Limit Pricing When the Potential Entrant Is Uncertain of Its Cost Function," *Econometrica* 54, 2, 1986, 429-37.

Heal, G., "Spatial Structure in the Retail Trade: A Study in Product Differentiation with Increasing Returns," *Bell Journal of Economics* 11, 2, 1980, 565-83.

Heinkel, R., "Uncertain Product Quality: The Market for Lemons with an Imperfect Testing Technology," *Bell Journal of Economics* 12 (Autumn 1981), 625-36.

Hoggatt, A. C., "Response of Paid Student Subjects to Differential Behavior of Robots in Bifurcated Duopoly Games," *Review of Economic Studies* 36 (October 1969), 417-32.

Holt, Charles A., "An Experimental Test of the Consistent-Conjectures Hypothesis," *American Economic Review* 75 (June 1985), 314-25.

Holthausen, D., "Kinky Demand, Risk Aversion, and Price Leadership," *International Economic Review* 20, 2, 1979, 341-48.

Horowitz, I., "Research Inclinations of a Cournot Oligopolist," *Review of Economic Studies* XXX, 1963, 128-30.

Horstmann, I., G. MacDonald, and A. Slivinski, "Patents as Information Transfer Mechanisms: To Patent or (Maybe) Not to Patent," *Journal of Political Economy* 93, 5, 1985, 837-58.

Hosomatsu, Y., "A Note on the Stability Conditions in Cournot's Dynamic Market Solution when Neither the Actual Market Demand Function nor the Production Levels of Rivals Are Known," *Review of Economic Studies* XXXVI, 1969, 117-21.

Howrey, E. and R. Quandt, "The Dynamics of the Number of Firms in an Industry," *Review of Economic Studies* XXXV, 1968, 349-53.

51

Ireland, N., "Concentration and the Growth of Market Demand: A Comment on Gaskins Limit Price Model," *Journal of Economic Theory* 5, 1972, 303–5.

———, "Dual Equilibria and Discontinuous Response in Monopolistic Competition with Two Classes of Consumers," *Rand Journal of Economics* 15, 3, 1984, 377–84.

Issac, R. M. and V. Smith, "In Search of Predatory Pricing," *Journal of Political Economy* 93, 2, 1985, 320–45.

Iwata, G., "Measurement of Conjectural Variations in Oligopoly," *Econometrica* 42, 5, 1974, 947–66.

Jones, M., "Note on Oligopoly: Rival Behavior and Efficiency," *Bell Journal of Economics* 11, 2, 1980, 709–14.

Joskow, P. L., "Firm Decision Making Processes and Oligopoly Theory," *American Economic Review* 65 (May 1975), 270–9.

Jovanovic, B., "Entry with Private Information," *Bell Journal of Economics* 12, 2, 1981, 649–60.

Judd, K., "Credible Spatial Preemption," *Rand Journal of Economics* 16, 2, 1985, 153–66.

Judd, K. and B. Petersen, "Dynamic Limit Pricing and Internal Finance," *Journal of Economic Theory* 39, 2, 1986, 368–99.

Just, R. E. and W. S. Chern, "Tomatoes, Technology and Oligopsony," *Bell Journal of Economics* 11 (Autumn 1980), 584–602.

Kalai, E. "Strategic Behavior and Competition: An Overview," *Journal of Economic Theory* 39, 1, 1986, 1–13.

Kamien, M. I. and N. L. Schwartz, "Limit Pricing and Uncertain Entry," *Econometrica* 39, 3, 1971, 441–54.

———, "Timing of Innovations Under Rivalry," *Econometrica* 40 (January 1972), 43–60.

———, "Cournot Oligopoly with Uncertain Entry," *Review of Economic Studies* 42, 1975, 125–31.

———, "The Degree of Rivalry for Maximum Innovative Activity," *Quarterly Journal of Economics* 90, 2, 1976, 245–60.

Kamien, M. I., and Y. Tauman, "Fees versus Royalties and the Private Value of a Patent," *Quarterly Journal of Economics* 101, 3, 1986, 471–92.

Katz, M. L., "An Analysis of Cooperative Research and Development," *Rand Journal of Economics* 17, 4, 1986, 527–43.

Katz, M. L. and C. Shapiro, "On the Licensing of Innovations," *Rand Journal of Economics* 16 (Winter 1985), 504–20.

Kirman, A. and M. Sobel, "Dynamic Oligopoly with Inventories," *Econometrica* 42, 2, 1974, 279–87.

Klemperer, P. and M. Meyer, "Price Competition vs. Quantity Competition: The Role of Uncertainty," *Rand Journal of Economics* 17, 4, 1986, 618–38.

Klette, T. and D. deMeza, "Is the Market Biased Against Risky R&D?" *Rand Journal of Economics* 17, 1, 1986, 133–9.

Koenker, R. and M. Perry, "Product Differentiation, Monopolistic Competition, and Public Policy," *Bell Journal of Economics* 12, 1, 1981, 217–31.

Extended bibliography

Kolstad, C. D. and L. Mathiesen, "Necessary and Sufficient Conditions for Uniqueness of a Cournot Equilibrium," *Review of Economic Studies* 54, 1987, 681–90.

Kreps, D. and R. Wilson, "Reputation and Imperfect Information," *Journal of Economic Theory* 27, 1982, 253–79.

Kreps, D. M. and J. A. Scheinkman, "Quantity Precommitment and Bertrand Competition Yield Cournot Outcomes," *Bell Journal of Economics* 14 (Autumn 1983), 326–37.

Laffont, J.-J. and M. Moreaux, "The Non-Existence of a Free Entry Cournot Equilibrium in Labor-Managed Economies," *Econometrica* 51, 2, 1983, 455–62.

Laitner, J., "'Rational' Duopoly Equilibria," *Quarterly Journal of Economics* 95, 4, 1980, 641–62.

Lambson, V., "Self-Enforcing Collusion in Large Dynamic Markets," *Journal of Economic Theory* 34, 2, 1984, 282–91.

Lane, W., "Product Differentiation in a Market with Endogenous Sequential Entry," *Bell Journal of Economics* 11, 1, 1980, 237–60.

Lederer, P. and A. Hurter, Jr., "Competition of Firms: Discriminatory Pricing and Location," *Econometrica* 54, 3, 1986, 623–40.

Lee, L. F. and R. Porter, "Switching Regression Models with Imperfect Sample Separation Information with an Application on Cartel Stability," *Econometrica* 52 (March 1984), 391–418.

Lee, T. and L. Wilde, "Market Structure and Innovation: A Reformulation," *Quarterly Journal of Economics* 94 (March 1980), 429–36.

Lee, W., "Oligopoly and Entry," *Journal of Economic Theory* 11, 1975, 35–54.

Levhari, D. and L. Mirman, "The Great Fish War: An Example Using a Dynamic Cournot–Nash Solution," *Bell Journal of Economics* 11, 1, 1980, 322–34.

Levitan, R. and M. Shubik, "Price Duopoly and Capacity Constraints," *International Economic Review* 13, 1, 1972, 111–22.

———, "Price Variation Duopoly with Differentiated Products and Random Demand," *Journal of Economic Theory* 3, 1971, 23–39.

Lewis, T. and R. Schmalensee, "On Oligopolistic Markets for Nonrenewable Natural Resources," *Quarterly Journal of Economics* 95, 3, 1980, 475–92.

———, "Cartel Deception in Non-renewable Resource Markets," *Bell Journal of Economics* 13, 1, 1982, 263–71.

Li, L., "Cournot Oligopoly with Information Sharing," *Rand Journal of Economics* 16, 4, 1985, 521–36.

Loury, G. C., "Market Structure and Innovation," *Quarterly Journal of Economics* 93, 3, 1979, 395–410.

———, "A Theory of 'Oil'igopoly: Cournot Equilibrium in Exhaustible Resource Markets with Fixed Supplies," *International Economic Review* 27 (June 1986), 285–301.

Lustgarten, S. and S. Thomadakis, "Valuation Response to New Information: A Test of Resource Mobility and Market Structure," *Journal of Political Economy* 88, 5, 1980, 977–93.

53

Macleod, W., "On Adjustment Costs and the Stability of Equilibria," *Review of Economic Studies* 52, 1985, 575–91.

MacMinn, R., "Search and Market Equilibrium," *Journal of Political Economy* 88, 2, 1980, 308–27.

Manas, M., "A Linear Oligopoly Game," *Econometrica* 40, 5, 1972, 917–22.

Mankin, N. and M. Whinston, "Free Entry and Social Inefficiency," *Rand Journal of Economics* 17, 1, 1986, 48–58.

Marschak, T. and R. Selten, "Restabilizing Responses, Inertia Supergames and Oligopolistic Equilibria," *Quarterly Journal of Economics* 92, 1, 1978, 71–93.

Mas-Colell, A., "Walrasian Equilibria as Limits of Non-Cooperative Equilibria. Part I: Mixed Strategies," *Journal of Economic Theory* 30, 1, 1983, 153–70.

———, "Noncooperative Approaches to the Theory of Perfect Competition: Presentation," *Journal of Economic Theory* 22, 2, 1980, 121–35.

Matthews, S. and L. Mirman, "Equilibrium Limit Pricing: The Effects of Private Information and Stochastic Demand," *Econometrica* 51, 4, 1983, 981–96.

Matthews, S. and A. Postelwaite, "Quality Testing and Disclosure," *Rand Journal of Economics* 16, 3, 1985, 328–40.

McManus, M., "Dynamic Cournot-Type Oligopoly Models: A Correction," *Review of Economic Studies* XXIX, 1962, 337–9.

———, "A Note on Static Cournot Equilibrium," *International Economic Review* 5, 3, 1964, 335–36.

———, "Static Cournot Equilibrium: Rejoinder," *International Economic Review* 5, 3, 1964, 339–40.

Milgrom, P. and J. Roberts, "Limit Pricing and Entry Under Incomplete Information," *Econometrica* 50, 2, 1982, 443–59.

———, "Predation, Reputation and Entry Deference," *Journal of Economic Theory* 27, 1982, 280–312.

———, "Price and Advertising Signals of Product Quality," *Journal of Political Economy* 94, 4, 1986, 796–820.

Moorthy, S. K., "Cournot Competition in a Differentiated Oligopoly," *Journal of Economic Theory* 36 (June 1985), 86–109.

Nakao, T., "Product Quality and Market Structure," *Bell Journal of Economics* 13 (Spring 1982), 133–42.

Nelson, P., "Information and Consumer Behavior," *Journal of Political Economy* 78, 2, 1970, 311–29.

———, "Advertising as Information," *Journal of Political Economy* 81, 4, 1974, 729–54.

Neudecker, H., "Cournot's Dynamic Solution and Hosomatsu's Lemma: An Alternative Proof," *Review of Economic Studies* 37 (July 1970), 447–8.

Newberg, D., "Stochastic Limit Pricing," *Bell Journal of Economics* 9, 1, 1978, 260–9.

Nishimura, K. and J. Friedman, "Existence of Nash Equilibrium in *n*-Person Games without Quasi-Concavity," *International Economic Review* 22, 3, 1981, 637–48.

Norman, G., "Spatial Pricing with Differentiated Products," *Quarterly Journal of Economics* 98, 2, 1983, 291–310.

Novshek, W., "Cournot Equilibrium with Free Entry," *Review of Economic Studies* 47 (April 1980), 473–86.

———, "Finding All *n*-Firm Cournot Equilibria," *International Economic Review* 25, 1, 1984, 61–70.

———, "On the Existence of Cournot Equilibrium," *Review of Economic Studies* 52 (January 1985), 85–98.

———, "Perfectly Competitive Markets as the Limits of Cournot Markets," *Journal of Economic Theory* 35, 1, 1985, 72–82.

Novshek, W. and H. Sonnenschein, "Cournot and Walras Equilibria," *Journal of Economic Theory* 19, 2, 1978, 223–66.

———, "Fulfilled Expectations Cournot Duopoly with Information Acquisition and Release," *Bell Journal of Economics* 13, 1, 1982, 214–18.

———, "Walrasian Equilibria as Limits of Non-cooperative Equilibria. Part II: Pure Strategies," *Journal of Economic Theory* 30, 1, 1983, 171–87.

Nti, K. and M. Shubik, "Noncooperative Oligopoly with Entry," *Journal of Economic Theory* 24, 2, 1981, 187–204.

O'Hara, D., "Location of Firms within a Square Central Business District," *Journal of Political Economy* 85, 6, 1977, 1189–207.

Okuguchi, K., "The Stability of the Cournot Oligopoly Solution: A Further Generalization," *Review of Economic Studies* 31 (April 1964), 143–6.

———, "Adaptive Expectations in an Oligopoly Model," *Review of Economic Studies* 37 (April 1970), 233–7.

———, "Quasi-Competitiveness and Cournot Oligopoly," *Review of Economic Studies* 40, 1973, 145–8.

Okuno, M., A. Postlewaite, and J. Roberts, "Oligopoly and Competition in Large Markets," *American Economic Review* 70 (March 1980), 22–31.

Omon, T. and G. Yarrow, "Product Diversification, Entry Prevention, and Limit Pricing," *Bell Journal of Economics* 13, 1, 1982, 242–8.

Osborne, D. K., "The Duopoly Game: Output Variations," *American Economic Review* 61 (September 1971), 538–60.

Osborne, M. and C. Pitchik, "Price Competition in a Capacity Constrained Duopoly," *Journal of Economic Theory* 38, 2, 1986, 238–60.

Palfrey, T. R., "Risk Advantages and Information Acquisition," *Bell Journal of Economics* 13 (Spring 1982), 219–24.

———, "Uncertainty Resolution, Private Information Aggregation and the Cournot Competitive Limit," *Review of Economic Studies* 52, 1985, 69–83.

Peles, Y., "A Note on Equilibrium in Monopolistic Competition," *Journal of Political Economy* 82, 3, 1974, 626–30.

Perrakis, S. and G. Warskett, "Capacity and Entry under Demand Uncertainty," *Review of Economic Studies* 50, 1983, 495–511.

Perry, M. "Oligopoly and Consistent Conjectural Variations," *Bell Journal of Economics* 13, 1, 1982, 197–205.

Perry, M. and R. Groff, "Trademark Licensing in a Monopolistically Competitive Industry," *Rand Journal of Economics* 17, 2, 1986, 189–200.

Perry, M. and R. Porter, "Oligopoly and the Incentive for Horizontal Merger," *American Economic Review* 75, 1, 1985, 219–27.

Peters, M., "Restrictions on Price Advertising," *Journal of Political Economy* 92, 3, 1984, 472–85.

———, "Bertrand Equilibrium with Capacity Constraints and Restricted Mobility," *Econometrica* 52, 5, 1117–27.

———, "Immobility, Rationing and Pricing Competition," *Review of Economic Studies* LII, 1985, 593–604.

Peters, M. and R. Winter, "Research and Development with Publicly Observed Outcomes," *Journal of Economic Theory* 40, 2, 1986, 349–63.

Phlips, L., "Intertemporal Price Discrimination and Sticky Prices," *Quarterly Journal of Economics* 94, 3, 1980, 525–42.

Porter, R., "Optimal Cartel Trigger Price Strategies," *Journal of Economic Theory* 29, 2, 1983, 313–38.

———, "A Study of Cartel Stability: The Joint Economic Committee: 1880–1886," *Bell Journal of Economics* 14 (Autumn 1983), 301–14.

Pratt, J., D. Wise, and R. Zeckhauser, "Price Differences in Almost Competitive Markets," *Quarterly Journal of Economics* 93, 2, 1979, 189–212.

Prescott, E., "Market Structure and Monopoly Profits," *Journal of Economic Theory* 6, 1973, 546–57.

Prescott, E. and M. Visscher, "Sequential Location among Firms with Foresight," *Bell Journal of Economics* 8, 2, 1977, 378–93.

Primeaux, W. and M. Bomball, "A Re-examination of the Kinky Oligopoly Demand Curve," *Journal of Political Economy* 82, 4, 1974, 851–62.

Quirmbach, H., "The Diffusion of New Technology and the Market for an Innovation," *Rand Journal of Economics* 17, 1, 1986, 33–47.

Radner, R., "Collusive Behavior in Noncooperative Epsilon-Equilibria of Oligopolies with Long but Finite Lines," *Journal of Economic Theory* 22, 2, 1980, 136–54.

Reinganum, J. F., "A Simple Model of Equilibrium Price Dispersion," *Journal of Political Economy* 87, 4, 1979, 851–8.

———, "Dynamic Games of Innovation," *Journal of Economic Theory* 25, 1, 1981, 21–41.

———, "Market Structure and the Diffusion of New Technology," *Bell Journal of Economics* 12, 2, 1981, 618–24.

———, "On the Diffusion of New Technology: A Game Theoretic Approach," *Review of Economic Studies* 48, 1981, 395–405.

———, "Market Structure and the Diffusion of New Technology," *Bell Journal of Economics* 12, 2, 1981, 618–24.

———, "Strategic Search Theory," *International Economic Review* 23, 1, 1982, 1–17.

———, "A Dynamic Game of R&D: Patent Protection and Competitive Behavior," *Econometrica* 50, 3, 1982, 671–88.

———, "Technology Adoption under Imperfect Information," *Bell Journal of Economics* 14, 1, 1983, 57–69.

Extended bibliography

——, "Nash Equilibrium Search for the Best Alternative," *Journal of Economic Theory* 30, 1, 1983, 139–52.

Rickard, J. and I. Murray, "The Dynamics of Some Duopoly Games Involving the Market Share and Nichol Strategies," *Journal of Economic Theory* 17, 1, 1978, 51–65.

Riley, J., "Competition with Hidden Knowledge," *Journal of Political Economy* 93, 5, 1985, 958–76.

Riordan, M. H., "Imperfect Information and Dynamic Conjectural Variations," *Rand Journal of Economics* 16 (Spring 1985), 41–50.

Roberts, J. and H. Sonnenschein, "On the Existence of Cournot Equilibrium without Concave Profit Functions," *Journal of Economic Theory* 13, 1976, 112–17.

——, "On the Foundations of the Theory of Monopolistic Competition," *Econometrica* 45 (January 1977), 101–13.

Roemer, J., "A Cournot Duopoly Problem," *International Economic Review* 11 (October 1970), 548–52.

Rogerson, W., "A Note on the Incentive for a Monopolist to Increase Fixed Costs as a Barrier to Entry," *Quarterly Journal of Economics* 99, 2, 1984, 399–402.

Rosenthal, R., "A Dynamic Model of Duopoly with Customer Loyalties," *Journal of Economic Theory* 27, 1, 1986, 69–76.

——, "A Model in Which an Increase in the Number of Sellers Leads to a Higher Price," *Econometrica* 48, 6, 1980, 1575–79.

——, "A Dynamic Oligopoly Game with Lags in Demand: More on the Monotonicity of Price in the Number of Sellers," *International Economic Review* 23, 2, 1982, 353–60.

Rothschild, M., "Models of Market Organization with Imperfect Information: A Survey," *Journal of Political Economy* 81, 6, 1973, 1283–308.

Ruff, L., "Research and Technological Progress in a Cournot Economy," *Journal of Economic Theory* 1, 1969, 397–415.

Ruffin, R., "Cournot Oligopoly and Competitive Behavior," *Review of Economic Studies* 38, 1971, 493–502.

Rust, J., "When Is It Optimal to Kill Off the Market for Used Durable Goods?" *Econometrica* 54, 1, 1986, 65–86.

Sakai, Y., "The Value of Information in a Simple Duopoly Model," *Journal of Economic Theory* 36, 1, 1985, 36–54.

Salant, S., "Exhaustible Resources and Industrial Structure: A Nash-Cournot Approach to the World Oil Market," *Journal of Political Economy* 84, 5, 1976, 1079–93.

Salant, S., S. Switzer, and R. Reynolds, "Losses from Horizontal Merger: The Effects of an Exogenous Change in Industry Structure on Cournot-Nash Equilibrium," *Quarterly Journal of Economics* 98, 2, 1983, 185–200.

Saloner, G., "Cournot Duopoly with Two Production Periods," *Journal of Economic Theory* 42, 1987, pp. 183–7.

Salop, S., "Monopolistic Competition with Outside Goods," *Bell Journal of Economics* 10, 1, 1979, 141–56.

Sanghvi, A., "Stochastic Reaction Functions in 2×2 Duopoly," *Journal of Economic Theory* 18, 2, 1978, 362–7.

Sato, R. and K. Nagatani, "The Stability of Oligopoly with Conjectural Variations," *Review of Economic Studies,* XXXIV, 1967, 409–16.

Satterthwaite, M., "Consumer Information, Equilibrium Industry Price, and the Number of Sellers," *Bell Journal of Economics* 10, 2, 1979, 483–502.

Scharfstein, D., "A Policy to Prevent Rational Test-Market Predation," *Rand Journal of Economics* 15, 2, 1984, 229–43.

Scherer, F. M., "Research and Development Resource Allocation under Rivalry," *Quarterly Journal of Economics* 81 (August 1967), 359–94.

Schmalensee, R., "A Model of Promotional Competition in Oligopoly," *Review of Economic Studies* 43, 1976, 493–507.

———, "Comparative Static Properties of Regulated Airline Duopolies," *Bell Journal of Economics* 8, 2, 1977, 565–76.

———, "Entry Deterrence in the Ready-to-Eat Breakfast Cereal Industry," *Bell Journal of Economics* 9, 2, 1978, 305–27.

———, "A Model of Advertising and Product Quality," *Journal of Political Economy* 86, 3, 1978, 485–503.

———, "Economies of Scale and Barriers to Entry," *Journal of Political Economy* 89, 6, 1981, 1228–38.

———, "Advertising and Entry Deterrence: An Exploratory Model," *Journal of Political Economy* 91, 4, 1983, 636–53.

Scotchmer, S., "Two-Tier Pricing of Shared Facilities in a Free-Entry Equilibrium," *Rand Journal of Economics* 16, 4, 1985, 456–72.

Seade, J., "The Stability of Cournot Revisited," *Journal of Economic Theory* 23, 1, 1980, 15–27.

———, "On the Effects of Entry," *Econometrica* 48, 2, 1980, 479–88.

Shaked, A. and J. Sutton, "Natural Oligopolies," *Econometrica* 51, 5, 1983, 1469–83.

Shapiro, C., "Exchange of Cost Information in Oligopoly," *Review of Economic Studies* LIII, 1986, 433–46.

Shapiro, L., "Decentralized Dynamics in Duopoly with Pareto Optimal Outcomes," *Bell Journal of Economics* 11, 2, 1980, 730–44.

Shilony, Y., "Mixed Pricing in Oligopoly," *Journal of Economic Theory* 14, 1977, 373–8.

Shitovitz, Benyamin, "Oligopoly in Markets with a Continuum of Traders," *Econometrica* 41 (May 1973), 467–501.

Simon, J., C. Puig, and J. Aschoff, "A Duopoly Simulation and Richer Theory: An End to Cournot," *Review of Economic Studies* XL, 1973, 353–66.

Singh, N. and X. Vives, "Price and Quantity Competition in a Differentiated Duopoly," *Rand Journal of Economics* 15, 4, 1984, 546–54.

Sklivas, S. D., "The Strategic Choice of Managerial Incentives," *Rand Journal of Economics* 18, 3, 1987, 452–60.

Smallwood, D. and J. Conlisk, "Product Quality in Markets where Consumers Are Imperfectly Informed," *Quarterly Journal of Economics* 93, 1, 1979, 1–24.

Extended bibliography

Smiley, R. and S. Ravid, "The Importance of Being First: Learning Price and Strategy," *Quarterly Journal of Economics* 98, 2, 1983, 353-62.

Sonnenschein, H., "The Dual of Duopoly Is Complementary Monopoly: Or, Two of Cournot's Theories Are One," *Journal of Political Economy* 76 (March/ April 1968), 316-18.

Spatt, C. S. and F. Sterbenz, "Learning, Pre-emption and the Degree of Rivalry," *Rand Journal of Economics* 16, 1, 1985, 84-92.

Spence, A. M., "Entry, Capacity, Investment and Oligopolistic Pricing," *Bell Journal of Economics* 8, 2, 1977, 534-44.

———, "Investment Strategy and Growth in a New Market," *Bell Journal of Economics* 10, 1, 1979, 1-19.

———, "Cost Reduction, Competition, and Industry Performance," *Econometrica* 52 (January 1984), 101-21.

Spencer, B. A. and J. A. Brander, "International R&D Rivalry and Industrial Strategy," *Review of Economic Studies* 50 (October 1983), 707-22.

Spiller, P. and E. Favaro, "The Effects of Entry Regulation on Oligopolistic Interaction: The Uruguayan Banking Sector," *Rand Journal of Economics* 15, 2, 1984, 244-54.

Srivastava, S., "Pure Strategy Nash Equilibria with Continuous Objections," *Journal of Economic Theory* 36, 1, 1985, 26-35.

Stahl, K., "Location and Spatial Pricing Theory with Nonconvex Transportation Cost Schedules," *Bell Journal of Economics* 13, 2, 1982, 575-82.

Stanford, W., "Subgame Perfect Reaction Function Equilibria in Discounted Duopoly Supergames are Trivial," *Journal of Economic Theory* 39, 1, 1986, 226-32.

———, "On Continuous Reaction Functions Equilibria in Duopoly Supergames with Mean Payoffs," *Journal of Economic Theory* 39, 1, 1986, 233-50.

Stewart, M., "Noncooperative Oligopoly and Preemptive Innovation without Winner-Take-All," *Quarterly Journal of Economics* 98, 4, 1983, 681-94.

Suppes, P. and J. Carlsmith, "Experimental Analysis of a Duopoly Situation from the Viewpoint of Mathematical Learning Theory," *International Economic Review* 3, 1, 1962, 60-78.

Szidarovszky, F. and S. Yakowitz, "A New Proof of the Existence and Uniqueness of the Cournot Equilibrium," *International Economic Review* 18 (October 1977), 787-9.

———, "Contributions to Cournot Oligopoly Theory," *Journal of Economic Theory* 28, 1, 1982, 51-70.

Telser, L., "A Theory of Innovations and Its Effects," *Bell Journal of Economics* 13, 1, 1982, 69-92.

Theocharis, R. D., "On the Stability of the Cournot Solution on the Oligopoly Problem," *Review of Economic Studies* 27 (February 1960), 133-4.

Ushio, Y., "Approximate Efficiency of Cournot Equilibria in Large Markets," *Review of Economic Studies* 52, 1985, 547-56.

———, "Cournot Equilibrium with Free Entry: The Case of Decreasing Average Cost Functions," *Review of Economic Studies* 50, 1983, 347-54.

Viton, P., "On Competition and Product Differentiation in Urban Transportation: The San Francisco Bay Area," *Bell Journal of Economics* 12, 2, 1981, 362–79.

Vives, X., "Duopoly Information Equilibrium: Cournot and Bertrand," *Journal of Economic Theory* 34, 1, 1984, 71–94.

——, "On the Efficiency of Bertrand and Cournot Equilibria with Product Differentiation," *Journal of Economic Theory* 36, 1, 1985, 166–75.

von Weizsacker, C., "A Welfare Analysis of Barriers to Entry," *Bell Journal of Economics* 11, 2, 1980, 399–420.

Wenders, J., "Collusion and Entry," *Journal of Political Economy* 79, 6, 1971, 1258–77.

Wolinsky, A., "Prices as Signals of Product Quality," *Review of Economic Studies* 50, 1983, 647–58.

PART II

Background

Overview

Three papers comprise this section. First, Chapter Seven of Cournot's book, "Of the Competition of Producers," is reproduced. In this chapter Cournot provides the first model of independent multiagent choice, initially analyzing two duopolists under constant marginal cost production; this is later extended to n firms and nonconstant marginal cost. As Fisher [1898] points out (and as is still true today), much of the main body of Cournot's book contains contributions to economic theory (see also the discussion in the Introduction) that few economists credit Cournot for. Cournot was the first to introduce aggregate demand and supply curves, and to provide the notion of diminishing returns (see Fisher [1898]). His original work on monopoly provides the basic model still in use today (Hicks [1935]).

Nathanial T. Bacon, brother-in-law of Irving Fisher's wife, translated Cournot's 1838 work into English in 1897. Fisher [1898] initially believed that Cournot had been grossly careless in the preparation of his manuscript, but it later transpired that Cournot was partially blind during this period (Nichol [1938], Fisher [1938]). Further reflections on Cournot's contributions and life may be found in the papers of Fisher and Nichol.

Cournot was a mathematician and, given the level of mathematics of most 19th-century economists, it is probably not surprising that at some point his work would be reviewed by another mathematician, in this case Joseph Bertrand, a name identified in mathematics with areas such as probability theory and differential geometry. His review, which also covered Walras's *Théorie mathématique de la richesse sociale,* first appeared in 1883 and became an oft-referenced source. It somehow eluded English translation and general availability, but has now been translated by James W. Friedman and follows the Cournot chapter here.

Finally, John Nash's paper on equilibrium points reintroduces Cournot's model of strategic behavior in a more generally applicable form. Nash focuses on games with a finite set of pure strategies and shows that every finite game has an equilibrium point (possibly requiring mixed strategies to be played). The really significant difference between the Nash equilibrium and the Cournot equilibrium is that Cournot's model focuses on one set of similar agents (firms) and a one-shot decision. Nash's concept is applied to finite games in general and thereby allows for a variety of potential agents and a multiperiod application. Most general game theory texts provide extensive discussions of Nash equilibria (for example, Friedman [1986], Moulin [1981], Owen [1982], and Shubik [1982]), but van Damme [1983] concentrates exclusively on the Nash equilibrium and various refinements (that is, attempts to reduce multiple Nash equilibria to a unique choice).

References

Damme, E. van, *Refinements of the Nash Equilibrium Concept,* Springer Verlag, Berlin, 1983.

Fisher, I., "Cournot and Mathematical Economics," *Quarterly Journal of Economics* 12, 1898, 119–38.

Fisher, I., "Cournot Forty Years Ago," *Econometrica* 6, 3, 1938, 198–202.

Friedman, J. W., *Game Theory with Applications to Economics,* Oxford University Press, New York, 1986.

Hicks, J. R., "Annual Survey of Economic Theory: The Theory of Monopoly," *Econometrica* 3, 1935, 1–20.

Moulin, H., *Game Theory for the Social Sciences,* New York University Press, New York, 1981.

Nichol, A. J., "Tragedies in the Life of Cournot," *Econometrica* 6, 3, 1938, 193–7.

Owen, G., *Game Theory, Second Edition,* Academic Press, New York, 1982.

Shubik, M., *Game Theory in the Social Sciences: Concepts and Solutions,* MIT Press, Cambridge, 1982.

CHAPTER 1

Of the competition of producers

AUGUSTIN COURNOT

43

Every one has a vague idea of the effects of competition. Theory should have attempted to render this idea more precise; and yet, for lack of regarding the question from the proper point of view, and for want of recourse to symbols (of which the use in this connection becomes indispensable), economic writers have not in the least improved on popular notions in this respect. These notions have remained as ill-defined and ill-applied in their works, as in popular language.

To make the abstract idea of monopoly comprehensible, we imagined one spring and one proprietor. Let us now imagine two proprietors and two springs of which the qualities are identical, and which, on account of their similar positions, supply the same market in competition. In this case the price is necessarily the same for each proprietor. If p is this price, $D = F(p)$ the total sales, D_1 the sales from the spring (1) and D_2 the sales from the spring (2), then $D_1 + D_2 = D$. If, to begin with, we neglect the cost of production, the respective incomes of the proprietors will be pD_1 and pD_2; and *each of them independently* will seek to make this income as large as possible.

We say *each independently,* and this restriction is very essential, as will soon appear; for if they should come to an agreement so as to obtain for each the greatest possible income, the results would be entirely different, and would not differ, so far as consumers are concerned, from those obtained in treating of a monopoly.

Instead of adopting $D = F(p)$ as before, in this case it will be convenient to adopt the inverse notation $p = f(D)$; and then the profits of proprietors (1) and (2) will be respectively expressed by

Augustin Cournot, "Of the Competition of Producers," Chapter 7 in *Researches into the Mathematical Principles of the Theory of Wealth,* 1838, translated by Nathanial T. Bacon, Macmillan, New York, 1897; reprinted with notes by Irving Fisher, Macmillan, New York, 1927; reprinted, Augustus M. Kelley, New York, 1960; originaly published as "Recherches sur les principes mathématiques de la théorie des richesses," L. Hachette, Paris, 1838.

$$D_1 \times f(D_1 + D_2), \quad \text{and} \quad D_2 \times f(D_1 + D_2),$$

i.e. by functions into each of which enter two variables, D_1 and D_2.

Proprietor (1) can have no direct influence on the determination of D_2: all that he can do, when D_2 has been determined by proprietor (2), is to choose for D_1 the value which is best for him. This he will be able to accomplish by properly adjusting his price, except as proprietor (2), who, seeing himself forced to accept his price and this value of D_1, may adopt a new value for D_2, more favourable to his interests than the preceding one.

Analytically this is equivalent to saying that D_1 will be determined in terms of D_2 by the condition

$$\frac{d[D_1 f(D_1 + D_2)]}{dD_1} = 0,$$

and that D_2 will be determined in terms of D_1 by the analogous condition

$$\frac{d[D_2 f(D_1 + D_2)]}{dD_2} = 0,$$

whence it follows that the final values of D_1 and D_2, and consequently of D and of p, will be determined by the system of equations

$$f(D_1 + D_2) + D_1 f'(D_1 + D_2) = 0, \tag{1}$$

$$f(D_1 + D_2) + D_2 f'(D_1 + D_2) = 0. \tag{2}$$

Let us suppose the curve $m_1 n_1$ (Figure 2) to be the plot of equation (1), and the curve $m_2 n_2$ that of equation (2), the variables D_1 and D_2 being represented by rectangular coordinates. If proprietor (1) should adopt for D_1 a value represented by ox_1, proprietor (2) would adopt for D_2 the value oy_1, which, for the supposed value of D_1, would give him the greatest profit. But then, for the same reason, producer (1) ought to adopt for D_1 the value ox_{11}, which gives the maximum profit when D_2 has the value oy_1. This would bring producer (2) to the value oy_{11} for D_2, and so forth; from which it is evident that an equilibrium can only be established where the coordinates ox and oy of the point of intersection i represent the values of D_1 and D_2. The same construction repeated on a point of the figure on the other side of the point i leads to symmetrical results.

The state of equilibrium corresponding to the system of values ox and oy is therefore *stable*; *i.e.* if either of the producers, misled as to his true interest, leaves it temporarily, he will be brought back to it by a series of reactions, constantly declining in amplitude, and of which the dotted lines of the figure give a representation by their arrangement in steps.

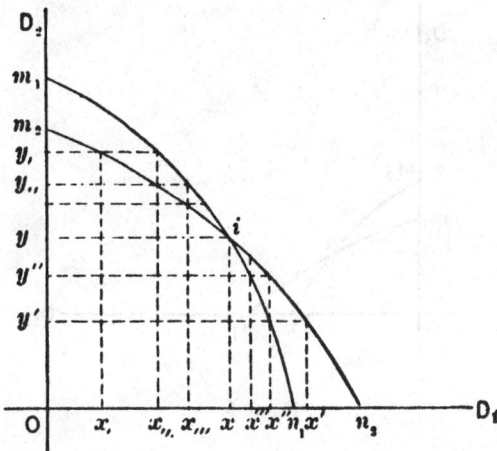

Figure 2.

The preceding construction assumes that $om_1 > om_2$ and $on_1 < on_2$: the results would be diametrically opposite if these inequalities should change sign, and if the curves $m_1 n_1$ and $m_2 n_2$ should assume the disposition represented by Figure 3. The coordinates of the point i, where the two curves intersect, would then cease to correspond to a state of stable equilibrium. But it is easy to prove that such a disposition of the curves is inadmissible. In fact, if $D_1 = 0$, equations (1) and (2) reduce, the first to

$$f(D_2) = 0,$$

and the second to

$$f(D_2) + D_2 f'(D_2) = 0.$$

The value of D_2 derived from the first would correspond to $p = 0$; the value of D_2 derived from the second corresponds to a value of p which would make the product pD_2 a maximum. Therefore the first root is necessarily greater than the second, or $om_1 > om_2$, and for the same reason $on_2 > on_1$.

44

From equations (1) and (2) we derive first $D_1 = D_2$ (which ought to be the case, as the springs are supposed to be similar and similarly situated), and then by addition:

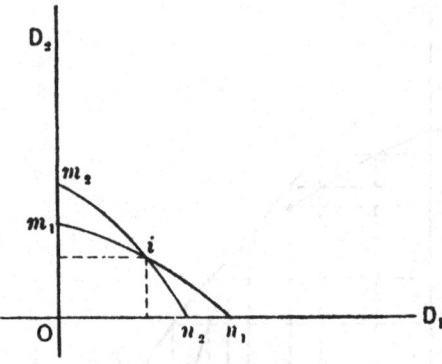

Figure 3.

$$2f(D) + Df'(D) = 0,$$

an equation which can be transformed into

$$D + 2p \frac{dD}{dp} = 0, \tag{3}$$

whereas, if the two springs had belonged to the same property, or if the two proprietors *had come to an understanding,* the value of p would have been determined by the equation

$$D + p \frac{dD}{dp} = 0, \tag{4}$$

and would have rendered the total income DP a *maximum,* and consequently would have assigned to each of the producers a greater income than what they can obtain with the value of p derived from equation (3).

Why is it then that, for want of an understanding, the producers do not stop, as in the case of a monopoly or of an association, at the value of p derived from equation (4), which would really give them the greatest income?

The reason is that, producer (1) having fixed his production at what it should be according to equation (4) and the condition $D_1 = D_2$, the other will be able to fix his own production at a higher or lower rate with a *temporary benefit.* To be sure, he will soon be punished for his mistake, because he will force the first producer to adopt a new scale of production which will react unfavourably on producer (2) himself. But these successive reactions, far from bringing both producers nearer to the original

66

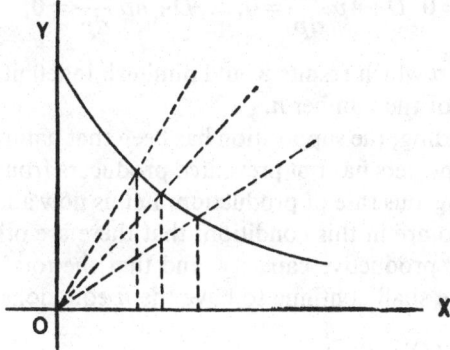

Figure 4.

condition [of monopoly], will separate them further and further from it. In other words, this condition is not one of stable equilibrium; and, although the most favourable for both producers, it can only be maintained by means of a formal engagement; for in the moral sphere men cannot be supposed to be free from error and lack of forethought any more than in the physical world bodies can be considered perfectly rigid, or supports perfectly solid, etc.

45

The root of equation (3) is graphically determined by the intersection of the line $y = 2x$ with the curve $y = -F(x)/F'(x)$; while that of equation (4) is graphically shown by the intersection of the same curve with the line $y = x$. But, if it is possible to assign a real and positive value to the function $y = -F(x)/F'(x)$ for every real and positive value of x, then the abscissa x of the first point of intersection will be smaller than that of the second, as is sufficiently proved simply by the plot of Figure 4. It is easily proved also that the condition for this result is always realized by the very nature of the law of demand. In consequence the root of equation (3) is always smaller than that of equation (4); or (as every one believes without any analysis) the result of competition is to reduce prices.

46

If there were $3, 4, \ldots, n$ producers in competition, all their conditions being the same, equation (3) would be successively replaced by the following:

67

$$D+3p\frac{dD}{dp}=0,\ D+4p\frac{dD}{dp}=0,...,D+np\frac{dD}{dp}=0;$$

and the value of p which results would diminish indefinitely with the indefinite increase of the number n.

In all the preceding, the supposition has been that natural limitation of their productive powers has not prevented producers from choosing each the most advantageous rate of production. Let us now admit, besides the n producers, who are in this condition, that there are others who reach the limit of their productive capacity, and that the total production of this class is Δ; we shall continue to have the n equations

$$\left.\begin{aligned} f(D)+D_1 f'(D)&=0,\\ f(D)+D_2 f'(D)&=0,\\ \vdots\\ f(D)+D_n f'(D)&=0, \end{aligned}\right\} \tag{5}$$

which will give $D_1=D_2=\cdots=D_n$, and by addition,

$$nf(D)+nD_1 f'(D)=0.$$

But $D=nD_1+\Delta$, whence

$$nf(D)+(D-\Delta)f'(D)=0,$$

or

$$D-\Delta+np\frac{dD}{dp}=0.$$

This last equation will now replace equation (3) and determine the value of p and consequently of D.

47

Each producer being subject to a cost of production expressed by the functions $\phi_1(D_1),\phi_2(D_2),...,\phi_n(D_n)$, the equations of (5) will become

$$\left.\begin{aligned} f(D)+D_1 f'(D)-\phi_1'(D_1)&=0,\\ f(D)+D_2 f'(D)-\phi_2'(D_2)&=0,\\ \vdots\\ f(D)+D_n f'(D)-\phi_n'(D_n)&=0. \end{aligned}\right\} \tag{6}$$

If any two of these equations are combined by subtraction, for instance if the second is subtracted from the first, we shall obtain

$$D_1 - D_2 = \frac{1}{f'(D)} [\phi_1'(D_1) - \phi_2'(D_2)]$$

$$= \frac{dD}{dp} [\phi_1'(D_1) - \phi_2'(D_2)].$$

As dD/dp is essentially negative, we shall therefore have at the same time

$$D_1 \gtreqless D_2, \quad \text{and} \quad \phi_1'(D_1) \lesseqgtr \phi_2'(D_2).$$

Thus the production of plant A will be greater than that of plant B, whenever it will require greater expense to increase the production of B than to increase the production of A by the same amount.

For a concrete example, let us imagine the case of a number of coal mines supplying the same market in competition one with another, and that, in a state of stable equilibrium, mine A markets annually 20,000 hectoliters and mine B, 15,000. We can be sure that a greater addition to the cost would be necessary to produce and bring to market from mine B an additional 1000 hectoliters than to produce the same increase of 1000 hectoliters in the yield of mine A.

This does not make it impossible that the costs at mine A should exceed those at mine B at a lower limit of production. For instance, if the production of each were reduced to 10,000 hectoliters, the costs of production at B might be smaller than at A.

48

By addition of equations (6), we obtain

$$nf(D) + Df'(D) - \sum \phi_n'(D_n) = 0,$$

or

$$D + \frac{dD}{dp} [np - \sum \phi_n'(D_n)] = 0. \tag{7}$$

If we compare this equation with the one which would determine the value of p in case all the plants were dependent on a monopolist, viz.

$$D + \frac{dD}{dp} [p - \phi'(D)] = 0, \tag{8}$$

we shall recognize that on the one hand substitution of the term np for the term p tends to diminish the value of p; but on the other hand substitution of the term $\sum \phi_n'(D_n)$ for the term $\phi'(D)$ tends to increase it, for the reason that we shall always have

$$\sum \phi_n'(D_n) > \phi'(D);$$

and, in fact, not only is the sum of the terms $\phi_n'(D_n)$ greater than $\phi'(D)$, but even the average of these terms is greater than $\phi'(D)$, *i.e.* we shall have the inequality

$$\frac{\sum \phi_n'(D_n)}{n} > \phi'(D).$$

To satisfy one's self of this, it is only necessary to consider that any capitalist, holding a monopoly of productive property, would operate by preference the plants of which the operation is the least costly, leaving the others idle if necessary; while the least favoured competitor will not make up his mind to close his works so long as he can obtain any profit from them, however modest. Consequently, for a given value of p, or for the same total production, the costs will always be greater for competing producers than they would be under a monopoly.

It now remains to be proved that the value of p derived from equation (8) is always greater than the value of p derived from equation (7).

For this we can see at once that if in the expression $\phi'(D)$ we substitute the value $D = F(p)$, we can change $\phi'(D)$ into a function $\psi(p)$; and each of the terms which enter into the summational expression $\sum \phi_n'(D_n)$, can also be regarded as an implicit function of p, in virtue of the relation $D = F(p)$ and of the system of equations (6). In consequence the root of equation (7) will be the abscissa of the point of intersection of the curve

$$y = -\frac{F(x)}{F'(x)}, \tag{a}$$

with the curve

$$y = nx - [\psi_1(x) + \psi_2(x) + \cdots + \psi_n(x)]; \tag{b}$$

while the root of equation (8) will be the abscissa of the point of intersection of the curve (a) with one which has for its equation

$$y = x - \psi(x). \tag{b'}$$

As has been already noted, equation (a) is represented by the curve MN (Figure 5), of which the ordinates are always real and positive; we can represent equation (b) by the curve PQ, and equation (b') by the curve $P'Q'$. In consequence of the relation just proved, viz.,

$$\sum \psi_n(x) > \psi(x),$$

we find for the value $x = 0$, $OP > OP'$. It remains to be proved that the curve $P'Q'$ cuts the curve PQ at a point I situated below MN, so that the abscissa of the point Q' will be greater than that of the point Q.

70

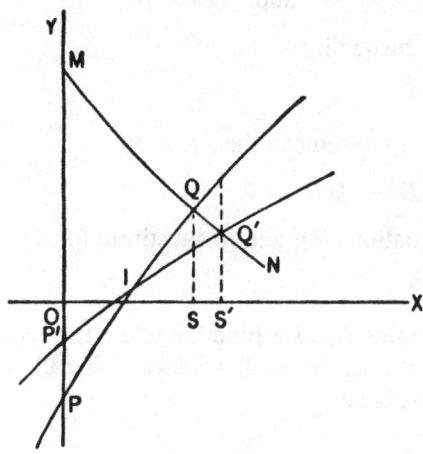

Figure 5.

This amounts to proving that at the points Q and Q', the ordinate of the curve (b) is greater than the ordinate of the curve (b') corresponding to the same abscissa.

Suppose that it were not so, and that we should have

$$x - \psi(x) > nx - [\psi_1(x) + \psi_2(x) + \cdots + \psi_n(x)],$$

or

$$(n-1)x < \psi_1(x) + \psi_2(x) + \cdots + \psi_n(x) + \psi(x).$$

$\psi(x)$ is an intermediate quantity between the greatest and smallest of the terms $\psi_1(x), \psi_2(x), \ldots, \psi_{n-1}(x), \psi_n(x)$; if we suppose that $\psi_n(x)$ denotes the smallest term of this series, the preceding inequality will involve the following inequality:

$$(n-1)x < \psi_1(x) + \psi_2(x) + \cdots + \psi_{n-1}(x).$$

Therefore x will be smaller than the average of the $n-1$ terms of which the sum forms the second member of the inequality; and among these terms there will be some which are greater than x. But this is impossible, because producer (k), for instance, will stop producing as soon as p becomes less than $\phi'_k(D_k)$ or $\psi_k(p)$.

49

Therefore if it should happen that the value of p derived from equations (6), combined with the relations

$$D_1 + D_2 + \cdots + D_n = D, \quad \text{and} \quad D = F(p),$$

should involve the inequality

$$p - \phi_k'(D_k) < 0,$$

it would be necessary to remove the equation

$$f(D) + D_k f'(D) - \phi_k'(D_k) = 0$$

from the list of equations (6), and to substitute for it

$$p - \phi_k'(D_k) = 0,$$

which would determine D_k as a function of p. The remaining equations of (6), combined with equations (9), will determine all the other unknown quantities of the problem.

CHAPTER 2

Review of Walras's *Théorie mathématique de la richesse sociale* and Cournot's *Recherches sur les principes mathématiques de la théorie des richesses*

JOSEPH BERTRAND

Théorie mathématique de la richesse sociale, by Léon Walras, professor of political economy at the academy of Lausanne, Lausanne, 1883.
Recherches sur les principes mathématiques de la théorie des richesses, by Augustin Cournot, Paris, 1838.

The title of these books seems to promise a new and secure path for the science of Adam Smith; however, the authors have received a very indifferent reception. A distinguished scholar, a skillful writer, endowed with an original and lofty intellect, Cournot was a master in the art of deduction. Mr. Walras does himself credit by being his disciple. "Mr. Cournot," he says, "is the first person to have seriously attempted the application of mathematics to political economy; he did so in a work published in 1838 which no French author has ever criticized. I have insisted," adds the learned professor of Lausanne, "upon mentioning the author of a remarkable endeavor upon which, I repeat, no judgment has been brought and to which I dare say justice has not been rendered."

This reproach, publicly addressed to Cournot's fellow countrymen, gave me a reason for re-reading a thoroughly forgotten work which, in spite of the well deserved reputation of the author, has not left a favorable impression upon all of those who have read it. "The title of my work," says Cournot in his preface, "not only announces theoretical research, it indicates that I intend to apply to it the forms and symbols of mathematical analysis." The formulas and symbols of mathematical analysis impose

Joseph Bertrand, Review of "Théorie mathématique de la richesse sociale," and "Recherches sur les principes mathématiques de la théorie des richesses," *Journal des Savants,* 1883, pp. 499–508, translation by James W. Friedman, Department of Economics, University of North Carolina, Chapel Hill, NC 27514. I am grateful to Jean Enelow for making a first, rough draft, translation. With this starting point my task was greatly eased. Jacques Crémer and Vincent Tarascio made suggestions rendering the translation more graceful and accurate. Any inaccuracies or infidelity to the original are solely my responsibility. I have followed the practice of placing Bertrand's footnote, indicated by a number, in the text where it originally appeared and placing translator's notes, indicated by letters, at the end.

precision and promise rigor; they do not inspire nor do they give the right to any leniency. The formulas are true or false, the definitions vague or precise, the arguments rigorous or nonsensical. Such is the language of mathematicians. It is also Cournot's. Several attempts preceded his; he only cites one of them: *Les principes d'économie politique* by Canard, a short work honored by the Institute and published in year X of the revolutionary calendar. "These alleged principles," says Cournot, "are so radically false and their application so erroneous that even the approval of an eminent society could not preserve the work from oblivion. It is easily understandable that works of this sort have not inclined economists such as Say and Ricardo to the use of mathematics."

Citizen Canard, although a professor of mathematics, is unaware of or forgot the elements of the calculus of functions. Knowing that the price of a commodity increases with the number of buyers, with their needs and income, and that it decreases with the number and eagerness of sellers, the translation into mathematical language is immediate for him: $B + Ax$ is, in effect, according to Canard, the model for all functions which are increasing in the variable x, and $B' - A'x$, for all decreasing functions. Such is his point of departure and the foundation of his theory.

How did he become a prize winner of the Institute? On the report of what commission? I have not been indiscreet enough to try to track it down.[1]

The problems attacked by Cournot are insoluble by reasoning alone; however, it does not enter into the learned author's plan to resort to the observation of facts. Not that he does not recognize the importance of them, but the work must be divided and his lies elsewhere. He studies laws, leaving numbers to others. His formulas, where only letters are employed, are full of unknown functions and he believed that applying himself to finding them was going beyond his purpose. True or false, their study must seem a useless hardship for practical men; they withdraw from it by shutting the book. If Cournot's theory of wealth, in spite of the author's knowledge, the merited respect associated with him, the authority of his position, and the merit of his other writings, has not been able to attract serious attention for half a century, it is because the ideas disappear under the abundance of mathematical symbols. Suppression of the

---

[1] The second class of the Institute (moral and political sciences) had proposed the following question:

In an agricultural country, does every sort of tax fall on the landowners? And, if so, do the indirect taxes fall on the same landowners with a surcharge?

Canard was awarded the prize. As winner, he answered in the negative, but in arriving at the required solution there was "a link in a series of consequences" whose falsity Cournot correctly pointed out.

Review of Théorie mathématique

symbols would reduce the book to a few pages, and almost all of them would then offer some wise observations and noteworthy assertions. Does Cournot wish to study the laws of the struggle which determines the current price of each commodity in a market, that problem so ineptly solved by Canard? He points out that, for a given commodity, the sale price being necessarily related to the flow, that by calling it p the supply can be represented by $F(p)$.[a] $F(p)$ denoting a function whose derivative is negative, the total revenue of the seller will be the product $pF(p)$. If the good cost nothing to produce, it is this product which must be maximized. Consequently, without further knowledge or research, following the rules of differential calculus, equate the derivative to zero. Thus

$$pF'(p) + F(p) = 0$$

is the equation which the seller must solve; he still must ensure that the second derivative is negative, verifying the inequality:

$$pF''(p) + 2F'(p) < 0.$$

Such is the mathematical theory of monopoly in the case of a good which costs nothing to produce and which is not burdened with any tax. Those who would like to apply it will only have to look for the function $F(p)$. The learned author wisely points out that, if he cannot satisfy all buyers, the seller must reduce the demand to equal the maximum possible amount of production by raising the price. Things being thus established, if the good is hit with a tax, what must happen? The price will most often increase. It can remain unchanged in certain cases, but the effect of the tax will never be to lower it. All these assertions by Cournot are correct, but was it necessary to use mathematics to make them clear? Let us stress this case of a mineral spring whose capacity output is less than the profit maximizing amount. When a tax is established on each liter sold, it may be in the owner's interest to raise the price above that which previously gave him the most profit by lowering the level of production. Indeed, a price increase on each liter sold affords him the same advantage as before the establishment of the tax, but the loss is no longer the same, for, on the unsold bottles, he gains what he gave to the treasury. It can happen however that the reduction in sales outweighs the double advantage of selling at a higher price and paying a lesser tax. The owner of the spring must then pay the whole tax without changing either his price or his production level.

[a] In his review Bertrand used ϕ here to denote the demand function. Cournot used ϕ for the cost function and F for demand. A little later in the review, Bertrand introduces costs and, following Cournot, uses ϕ for cost and F for demand. To avoid possible confusion, I have followed Cournot's notation.

"From this," adds Cournot, "in this case it seems that the treasury would be limited in assessing the tax only by the condition that it not entirely absorb the profit of the producer. But this conclusion would be wrong and its falsity can be proven in at least one case."

Cournot defines this case mathematically; it is the one in which the function $\phi'(D)$ is increasing with D, and where $p' - p_0 > i$, p_0 and p' being, respectively, the roots of the equations:

$$F(p) + [p - \phi'(D)]F'(p) = 0 \tag{1}$$

$$F(p) + [p - \phi'(d) - i]F'(p) = 0.$$

These symbols and functions have appeared in the preceding pages and are known to the reader; however, even a mathematician could wish for a less pedantic explanation. Without giving one, Cournot continues: "Let Δ be the capacity limit and π the value of p derived from the relation $F(p) = \Delta$, then, given the hypothesis, $\pi > p'$ and a fortiori $\pi > p_0 + i$, with i being equal to $\pi - \phi(\Delta)/\Delta$. Therefore, $\pi > p_0 + \pi - \phi(\Delta)/\Delta$ or $p_0 < \phi(\Delta)/\Delta$.

"But this last inequality certainly cannot hold if $\phi'(D)$ is, as assumed, an increasing function of D; for then, p_0 being less than π, the demand D_0 corresponding to p_0 is greater than Δ. $\phi(D_0)/D_0 > \phi(\Delta)/\Delta$ which would imply $p_0 < \phi(D_0)/D_0$.

"This value of p_0 would therefore cause the producer a loss and consequently could not be the root of equation (1)."

A translation becomes necessary.

The question is the following: Under the stated conditions for the owner of the mineral spring, could the State, using a tax on each liter of the good, appropriate all of the owner's profit without diminishing it and without causing an increase in the market price? According to one of the mathematically expressed hypotheses, the cost for each liter rises with the total amount of output. If the tax on the whole absorbs all the profits, the tax obtained on the last liters, which cost more to produce than the others, will cause the producer a loss. He will not produce them, and the goods being scarcer, the price will rise, which contradicts the hypothesis. It is therefore a contradiction to allow that one can, without diminishing production, absorb the total profit through a fixed tax. Moreover, it is not necessary that cost itself be increasing in order for the owner to try to protect himself before abandoning to the public treasury the whole of his profits by accepting diminished profit and raising price. It is difficult to understand why Cournot, declaring that one could make the proof in *at least one case,* seems to question what would happen in the others. It is in respect to the chapter from which these examples and formulas were drawn that Mr. Walras has written: "The theory of monopoly has been presented in a mathematical form, which is the clearest and most precise form, by Mr. Cournot in chapter V of his *Researches into the mathematical principles of the theory of wealth*. Unfortunately economists have not judged it worthwhile to look into this theory, and on the subject of monopoly, they are thereby reduced to a confusion of ideas which, among them, is admirably expressed in a confusion of words."

The judgment is harsh. The calculations, a passage of which we have quoted, are not clear to everyone; the results seem of little importance; I must admit they sometimes appear unacceptable.

Such is the study, made in chapter VII, of the struggle between two proprietors who own mineral springs of the same quality and have no fear of other competition. It would be in their interest to join together in partnership or at least to fix a common price so as to get from the buyers the greatest possible profit, but this solution is rejected. Cournot conjectures that one of the competitors will lower his price to attract buyers, and that the other, in order to bring them back, will lower his more. They will continue until each of them would no longer gain anything more by lowering his price. A peremptory objection arises: With this hypothesis a solution is impossible; the price reduction would have no limit. In fact, whatever jointly determined price were adopted, if only one of the competitors lowers his, he gains, disregarding all unimportant exceptions, all the sales, and he will double his returns if his competitor allows him to do so. If Cournot's formulas mask this result, it is because, through a peculiar oversight, he introduces under the names D and D' the quantities sold by the two competitors, and treating them as independent variables, he assumes that the one quantity happening to change through the will of one owner, the other would remain constant. The contrary is obviously true.

On other subjects Cournot presents abstractions in the statement of his problems whose formal statement shelters him from his responsibility as a mathematician. Is not one always free to state a problem as one likes? So it is in translating into formulas a question so complex as commercial liberty after having demonstrated mathematically that the nation which exports increases its revenue and those that receive goods diminish theirs, he adds: "We do not consider as a deduction from this real decrease of revenue the ensuing advantage for consumers who buy as a result of the price reduction that they thereby put their revenue to a more advantageous use."

Let us suppose, for example, that the price of woolen cloth falls by half in a nation which we have just declared impoverished. By trade those who wear cotton clothing in winter will be able to replace them with wool and, by thus putting their revenue to a *use more to their advantage,* diminish mortality. It is an advantage and Cournot recognizes it, but, not being able to evaluate it in his formulas, he simply warns that he will not take it into consideration. Do we have the right to reproach him anything?

Geometric representations in Mr. Walras's book often replace formulas. The arguments are more accessible, the results closer to applications, and success has been more rapid and greater. "If the state of the question were considered only in France and England," he wrote to the learned professor Stanley Jevons, who agreed with him on more than one point, "we would scarcely have more than a reputation as visionary dreamers to share, but it is otherwise elsewhere, notably in Italy, where the new method has been understood, in its meaning and in its scope, with astounding skill and swiftness."

Without broaching here the numerous important and difficult questions treated by Mr. Walras, and without my passing judgment on the conclusions which split the best judges, I wish to limit myself to discuss a principle proposed as fundamental.

Imagine a market in which the holders of good (A) appear, disposed to give some part of it in order to procure some of good (B), and where, on another side, holders of good (B) appear who wish to convert it into good (A). A certain price will be established, and m(A) will be exchanged for n(B). What elements make up this price? Mr. Walras, whom I summarize, supposes in order to solve the problem that each holder of one of the goods, without leaving anything to last minute impressions, has made before arriving at the market a precise decision for each of the cases which could arise. For more conciseness, let us replace good (B) with money and suppose that good (A) is wheat. The market brings together farmers who want the highest prices and buyers who would like the lowest. Each buyer, by assumption, will give his orders to an agent and will say to him, for example: if the price is twenty francs buy one hundred hectoliters, at twenty five francs take only sixty, at thirty francs I want only ten, and at thirty five I want none. The complete list will make known, for each price, the corresponding amount of sales. The sellers, on their side, have given their orders and, for each price, the quantity each proposes to sell is known.

The solution is quite simple: The learned professor supposes that if you join the notebooks of all the buyers, and that for each successive price, you form the sum of their demands, uniting the sellers' notebooks will furnish a similar list. These resulting lists can be replaced by curves whose abscissas are the sale prices. The point of intersection of the two curves has for abscissa the price that Mr. Walras calls the equilibrium price; that is the one that tends to establish itself.

78

Such is Mr. Walras's theorem; here is its demonstration. Suppose the curves intersect in a point whose abscissa is twenty five. If, from the beginning of the market, the price of twenty five francs per hectoliter is proposed, the quantity demanded at this price equalling by assumption that of the offers, the transactions will be easily completed with each seller finding a buyer and each buyer finding a seller. But no further sale will be possible. Above twenty five francs there will be no more buyers, nor below, any sellers. If one had at the outset a price higher than twenty five francs, after several transactions it would be realized that the offers surpassed the demands and there would be a price reduction; a lower price than twenty five francs would bring, on the contrary, a rise. In both cases price moves toward the equilibrium price.

I believe that I have summed up, without harm to its clarity, the argument of the learned Lausanne professor.

I will make an objection here. By replacing the group of buyers with a single buyer demanding at each price as many hectoliters as all the real buyers taken together, the conditions of the problem are changed. It is not permissible to replace all the buyers by a single one. To prove this by an example, suppose that two buyers have each demanded one hundred hectoliters, the first at a price of twenty francs and nothing at a higher price, the second at whatever the price may be. Suppose, moreover, that at the first price of twenty francs, the agent entrusted with all the sale orders has sold one hundred hectoliters. He is not indifferent to whether it is to the advantage of the first or of the second buyer to withdraw from the market, for the presence of one tends to lower the price and that of the other to raise it.

It must be noted that the curves representing the buyers' orders at various prices must necessarily vary for each one of them during the duration of the market without their intentions having changed. The resultant curves whose intersection solves the problem constantly change shape, and one can easily demonstrate the necessary variation of the abscissa of the point where they intersect. For example, suppose that one of the buyers has written down the following orders: at twenty francs buy one hundred hectoliters, at twenty five buy sixty, and at thirty buy fifty. The first price is twenty francs, but, on the hundred hectoliters that he asks for, only fifty can be bought. Then the price rises to thirty francs and holds. What must the agent do? Buy fifty hectoliters at thirty francs? Not at all, for fifty hectoliters at twenty francs and fifty at thirty are equivalent to one hundred at twenty five francs, and he wants only sixty at this price. The agent will have to decide by the condition that the mean price between his new purchase and the fifty hectoliters already bought correspond, on the client's notebook, to the total purchases made on his account. Each price presents a similar problem and the curve that represents the orders must be calculated and remade after each transaction. In order to obtain the equilibrium price, must a new curve be used? If the answer is yes, Mr. Walras's theorem loses its geometric character, the final result depending on the haphazard circumstances that one had claimed to have eliminated. However, how can one answer no? How can it be admitted that a newcomer in the market who would be informed of the current state of affairs does not have the right to apply these principles? One might well inquire about orders placed in the market in the preceding month in order to forecast prices.

If any doubts remain, one last argument will completely dispel them. Let us suppose that, according to the known intentions of the buyers and of the sellers, the equilibrium price calculated an hour before the opening of the market by means of the theorem discussed is twenty five francs per hectoliter. A new buyer appears: below twenty five francs he wishes to buy without limit and takes nothing at this price of *a fortiori* above. If Mr. Walras's rule is to be believed, his presence would exert no influence; in fact, it raises to infinity the curve of the demands for the points whose abscissa is below twenty five. Can such a conclusion be accepted? Supposing that a price of twenty five francs tends to be established, it will neither be the sole nor the first; the price will oscillate around it. Each time that it is below, the new buyer will appear and those who sell to him, having disposed of all or part of their merchandise, will no longer offer what they had offered at the beginning at the price of twenty five francs. I assume one of them had brought one hundred hectoliters to the market. At a price of twenty five francs he wanted to sell everything and at twenty four, give up only eighty. The price twenty four occurred, the buyer of whom we speak has taken his eighty hectoliters, and he has only twenty left to offer. For the abscissa of twenty five, the ordinate of the sellers' curve has undergone a decrease equal to or larger than eighty, while that of the purchasers has not changed. Therefore, the point of intersection of the two curves is displaced and, as one of them has an infinite ordinate when the abscissa is less than twenty five, the new intersection will occur on the other side and, even according to the rule we are contesting, the intervention of the new buyer must raise the final price.

It is not my intention to analyze Mr. Walras's book. I would find much to commend in it, also much to contradict. In conclusion, I wish to limit myself to pointing out a definition in which the learned author strays from the usual meaning of a word whose common meaning is well known. This is assuredly permitted, but on the condition that the new meaning be rigorously defined. I do not believe that condition to be fulfilled and yet the word *rareté,*[b] as Mr. Walras understands it, plays a large role in his arguments.

The ingenious author, whose explanations I shall take the liberty of abridging, assumes that the possessor of a quantity α of a given commodity gets a known utility from that possession, a known satisfaction of his needs or of his desires, and that utility grows successively with each particle acquired in such a manner that, as the quantity possessed goes from x to $x + dx$, the additional benefit to him is represented by $\phi(x)\, dx$. The possession of α is then equivalent to the integral $\int_0^\alpha \phi(x)\, dx$. The price ruled by market conditions has no necessary relation with the function ϕ, which varies from one individual to another. If p is the price of each unit bought or sold, it is clear that by paying pdx, the increase dx which, for him, represents a satisfaction measured by $\phi(x)\, dx$, the person makes a good deal if $\phi(x)$ is greater than p and a bad one if $\phi(x)$ is less than p. He will have to buy or sell a certain amount of his commodities depending on whether one or the other of these conditions is fulfilled and to cease his purchase or sale when $\phi(x) = p$ is attained. If $x = \alpha$ is the root of this equation, $\phi(\alpha)^c$ is what Mr. Walras calls *rareté* of goods for the person in question.

This definition, without mentioning the disadvantage of disposing of the meaning of a well known and common word, seems to have the serious defect of losing all significance when it is applied to businessmen, which it would be necessary to do. A wheat dealer buys millions of hectoliters and knows what they have cost him; he sells at the daily market price that he finds profitable, sometimes at a loss when he foresees a price drop in order to avoid a greater loss. He stores in a warehouse when he hopes for a higher price, and by no means is he guided only by the profits which the various uses of the stock could procure for him.

The two theories which I have just summarized both play an important role in the notable work of Mr. Walras. Giving up these theories would disturb more than one argument, but many others would remain intact. I shall abstain from engaging upon them.

[b] Walras used the word *rareté* in roughly the way that *marginal utility* is presently used; however, it is usual to use Walras's term in English translations of his work. On this see Léon Walras, *Elements of Pure Economics,* translated by William Jaffé, Irwin (Homewood, 1954), translator's note [9], page 506.

[c] At this point Bertrand identifies α as *rareté,* rather than $\phi(\alpha)$. I have made the alteration to conform with what Walras wrote, presuming a typographical or other careless error.

CHAPTER 3

Non-cooperative games

JOHN NASH

Introduction

Von Neumann and Morgenstern have developed a very fruitful theory of
two-person zero-sum games in their book *Theory of Games and Economic Behavior*. This book also contains a theory of *n*-person games of
a type which we would call cooperative. This theory is based on an analysis of the interrelationships of the various coalitions which can be formed
by the players of the game.

Our theory, in contradistinction, is based on the *absence* of coalitions
in that it is assumed that each participant acts independently, without
collaboration or communication with any of the others.

The notion of an *equilibrium point* is the basic ingredient in our theory.
This notion yields a generalization of the concept of the solution of a
two-person zero-sum game. It turns out that the set of equilibrium points
of a two-person zero-sum game is simply the set of all pairs of opposing
"good strategies."

In the immediately following sections we shall define equilibrium points
and prove that a finite non-cooperative game always has at least one equilibrium point. We shall also introduce the notions of solvability and strong
solvability of a non-cooperative game and prove a theorem on the geo-
metrical structure of the set of equilibrium points of a solvable game.

As an example of the application of our theory we include a solution
of a simplified three-person poker game.

Formal Definitions and Terminology

In this section we define the basic concepts of this paper and set up standard terminology and notation. Important definitions will be preceded
by a subtitle indicating the concept defined. The non-cooperative idea
will be implicit, rather than explicit, below.

John Nash, "Non-Cooperative Games," *Annals of Mathematics,* 54, 2, 1951, pp. 286–95.

Non-cooperative games

Finite Game:

For us an *n-person game* will be a set of n *players*, or *positions*, each with an associated finite set of *pure strategies;* and corresponding to each player, i, a *payoff function*, p_i, which maps the set of all n-tuples of pure strategies into the real numbers. When we use the term *n-tuple* we shall always mean a set of n items, with each item associated with a different player.

Mixed Strategy, s_i:

A *mixed strategy* of player i will be a collection of non-negative numbers which have unit sum and are in one to one correspondence with his pure strategies.

We write $s_i = \sum_\alpha c_{i\alpha} \pi_{i\alpha}$ with $c_{i\alpha} \geq 0$ and $\sum_\alpha c_{i\alpha} = 1$ to represent such a mixed strategy, where the $\pi_{i\alpha}$'s are the pure strategies of player i. We regard the s_i's as points in a simplex whose vertices are the $\pi_{i\alpha}$'s. This simplex may be regarded as a convex subset of a real vector space, giving us a natural process of linear combination for the mixed strategies.

We shall use the suffixes i, j, k for players and α, β, γ to indicate various pure strategies of a player. The symbols s_i, t_i, and r_i, etc. will indicate mixed strategies; $\pi_{i\alpha}$ will indicate the ith player's αth pure strategy, etc.

Payoff function, p_i:

The payoff function, p_i, used in the definition of a finite game above, has a unique extension to the n-tuples of mixed strategies which is linear in the mixed strategy of each player [n-linear]. This extension we shall also denote by p_i, writing $p_i(s_1, s_2, ..., s_n)$.

We shall write $\mathfrak{s}$ or $\mathfrak{t}$ to denote an n-tuple of mixed strategies and if $\mathfrak{s} = (s_1, s_2, ..., s_n)$ then $p_i(\mathfrak{s})$ shall mean $p_i(s_1, s_2, ..., s_n)$. Such an n-tuple, $\mathfrak{s}$, will also be regarded as a point in a vector space, the product space of the vector spaces containing the mixed strategies. And the set of all such n-tuples forms, of course, a convex polytope, the product of the simplices representing the mixed strategies.

For convenience we introduce the substitution notation $(\mathfrak{s}; t_i)$ to stand for $(s_1, s_2, ..., s_{i-1}, t_i, s_{i+1}, ..., s_n)$ where $\mathfrak{s} = (s_1, s_2, ..., s_n)$. The effect of successive substitutions $((\mathfrak{s}; t_i); r_j)$ we indicate by $(\mathfrak{s}; t_i; r_j)$, etc.

Equilibrium Point:

An n-tuple $\mathfrak{s}$ is an *equilibrium point* if and only if for every i

$$p_i(\mathfrak{s}) = \max_{\text{all } r_i\text{'s}} [p_i(\mathfrak{s}; r_i)]. \tag{1}$$

Thus an equilibrium point is an n-tuple $\mathfrak{s}$ such that each player's mixed strategy maximizes his payoff if the strategies of the others are held fixed. Thus each player's strategy is optimal against those of the others. We shall occasionally abbreviate equilibrium point by eq. pt.

83

We say that a mixed strategy s_i *uses* a pure strategy $\pi_{i\alpha}$ if $s_i = \sum_\beta c_{i\beta}\pi_{i\beta}$ and $c_{i\alpha} > 0$. If $\mathfrak{s} = (s_1, s_2, \ldots, s_n)$ and s_i uses $\pi_{i\alpha}$ we also say that $\mathfrak{s}$ uses $\pi_{i\alpha}$. From the linearity of $p_i(s_1, \ldots, s_n)$ in s_i,

$$\max_{\text{all } r_i\text{'s}}[p_i(\mathfrak{s}; r_i)] = \max_\alpha[p_i(\mathfrak{s}; \pi_{i\alpha})]. \tag{2}$$

We define $p_{i\alpha}(\mathfrak{s}) = p_i(\mathfrak{s}; \pi_{i\alpha})$. Then we obtain the following trivial necessary and sufficient condition for $\mathfrak{s}$ to be an equilibrium point:

$$p_i(\mathfrak{s}) = \max_\alpha p_{i\alpha}(\mathfrak{s}). \tag{3}$$

If $\mathfrak{s} = (s_1, s_2, \ldots, s_n)$ and $s_i = \sum_\alpha c_{i\alpha}\pi_{i\alpha}$ then $p_i(\mathfrak{s}) = \sum_\alpha c_{i\alpha}p_{i\alpha}(\mathfrak{s})$, consequently for (3) to hold we must have $c_{i\alpha} = 0$ whenever $p_{i\alpha}(\mathfrak{s}) < \max_\beta p_{i\beta}(\mathfrak{s})$, which is to say that $\mathfrak{s}$ does not use $\pi_{i\alpha}$ unless it is an optimal pure strategy for player i. So we write

$$\text{if } \pi_{i\alpha} \text{ is used in } \mathfrak{s} \text{ then } p_{i\alpha}(\mathfrak{s}) = \max_\beta p_{i\beta}(\mathfrak{s}) \tag{4}$$

as another necessary and sufficient condition for an equilibrium point.

Since a criterion (3) for an eq. pt. can be expressed by the equating of n pairs of continuous functions on the space of n-tuples $\mathfrak{s}$ the eq. pts. obviously form a closed subset of this space. Actually, this subset is formed from a number of pieces of algebraic varieties, cut out by other algebraic varieties.

Existence of equilibrium points

A proof of this existence theorem based on Kakutani's generalized fixed point theorem was published in Proc. Nat. Acad. Sci. U.S.A., 36, pp. 48–49. The proof given here is a considerable improvement over that earlier version and is based directly on the Brouwer theorem. We proceed by constructing a continuous transformation T of the space of n-tuples such that the fixed points of T are the equilibrium points of the game.

Theorem 1. *Every finite game has an equilibrium point.*

Proof. Let $\mathfrak{s}$ be an n-tuple of mixed strategies, $p_i(\mathfrak{s})$ the corresponding pay-off to player i, and $p_{i\alpha}(\mathfrak{s})$ the pay-off to player i if he changes to his αth pure strategy $\pi_{i\alpha}$ and the others continue to use their respective mixed strategies from $\mathfrak{s}$. We now define a set of continuous functions of $\mathfrak{s}$ by

$$\varphi_{i\alpha}(\mathfrak{s}) = \max(0, p_{i\alpha}(\mathfrak{s}) - p_i(\mathfrak{s}))$$

and for each component s_i of $\mathfrak{s}$ we define a modification s_i' by

Non-cooperative games

$$s_i' = \frac{s_i + \sum_\alpha \varphi_{i\alpha}(\mathfrak{s}) \pi_{i\alpha}}{1 + \sum_\alpha \varphi_{i\alpha}(\mathfrak{s})},$$

calling $\mathfrak{s}'$ the n-tuple $(s_1', s_2', s_3', \ldots, s_n')$.

We must now show that the fixed points of the mapping $T: \mathfrak{s} \to \mathfrak{s}'$ are the equilibrium points.

First consider any n-tuple $\mathfrak{s}$. In $\mathfrak{s}$ the ith player's mixed strategy s_i will use certain of his pure strategies. Some one of these strategies, say $\pi_{i\alpha}$, must be "least profitable" so that $p_{i\alpha}(\mathfrak{s}) \le p_i(\mathfrak{s})$. This will make $\varphi_{i\alpha}(\mathfrak{s}) = 0$.

Now if this n-tuple $\mathfrak{s}$ happens to be fixed under T the proportion of $\pi_{i\alpha}$ used in s_i must not be decreased by T. Hence, for all β's, $\varphi_{i\beta}(\mathfrak{s})$ must be zero to prevent the denominator of the expression defining s_i' from exceeding 1.

Thus, if $\mathfrak{s}$ is fixed under T, for any i and β $\varphi_{i\beta}(\mathfrak{s}) = 0$. This means no player can improve his pay-off by moving to a pure strategy $\pi_{i\beta}$. But this is just a criterion for an eq. pt. [see (2)].

Conversely, if $\mathfrak{s}$ is an eq. pt. it is immediate that all φ's vanish, making $\mathfrak{s}$ a fixed point under T.

Since the space of n-tuples is a cell the Brouwer fixed point theorem requires that T must have at least one fixed point $\mathfrak{s}$, which must be an equilibrium point. ∎

Symmetries of games

An *automorphism*, or *symmetry*, of a game will be a permutation of its pure strategies which satisfies certain conditions, given below.

If two strategies belong to a single player they must go into two strategies belonging to a single player. Thus if ϕ is the permutation of the pure strategies it induces a permutation ψ of the players.

Each n-tuple of pure strategies is therefore permuted into another n-tuple of pure strategies. We may call χ the induced permutation of these n-tuples. Let ξ denote an n-tuple of pure strategies and $p_i(\xi)$ the pay-off to player i when the n-tuple ξ is employed. We require that if

$$j = i^\psi \quad \text{then} \quad p_j(\xi^\chi) = p_i(\xi)$$

which completes the definition of a symmetry.

The permutation ϕ has a unique linear extension to the mixed strategies. If

$$s_i = \sum_\alpha c_{i\alpha} \pi_{i\alpha} \quad \text{we define} \quad (s_i)^\phi = \sum_\alpha c_{i\alpha} (\pi_{i\alpha})^\phi.$$

The extension of ϕ to the mixed strategies clearly generates an extension of χ to the n-tuples of mixed strategies. We shall also denote this by χ.

We define a *symmetric n-tuple* $\mathfrak{s}$ of a game by $\mathfrak{s}^\chi = \mathfrak{s}$ for all χ's.

Theorem 2. *Any finite game has a symmetric equilibrium point.*

Proof. First we note that $s_{i0} = \Sigma_\alpha \pi_{i\alpha} / \Sigma_\alpha 1$ has the property $(s_{i0})^\phi = s_{j0}$ where $j = i^\psi$, so that the n-tuple $\mathfrak{s}_0 = (s_{10}, s_{20}, \ldots, s_{n0})$ is fixed under any χ; hence any game has at least one symmetric n-tuple.

If $\mathfrak{s} = (s_1, \ldots, s_n)$ and $t = (t_1, \ldots, t_n)$ are symmetric then

$$\frac{\mathfrak{s} + t}{2} = \left(\frac{s_1 + t_1}{2}, \frac{s_2 + t_2}{2}, \ldots, \frac{s_n + t_n}{2} \right)$$

is also symmetric because $\mathfrak{s}^\chi = \mathfrak{s} \Leftrightarrow s_j = (s_i)^\phi$, where $j = i^\psi$, hence

$$\frac{s_j + t_j}{2} = \frac{(s_i)^\phi + (t_i)^\phi}{2} = \left(\frac{s_i + t_i}{2} \right)^\phi,$$

hence

$$\left(\frac{\mathfrak{s} + t}{2} \right)^\chi = \frac{\mathfrak{s} + t}{2}.$$

This shows that the set of symmetric n-tuples is a convex subset of the space of n-tuples since it is obviously closed.

Now observe that the mapping $T : \mathfrak{s} \to \mathfrak{s}'$ used in the proof of the existence theorem was intrinsically defined. Therefore, if $\mathfrak{s}_2 = T\mathfrak{s}_1$ and χ is derived from an automorphism of the game we will have $\mathfrak{s}_2^\chi = T\mathfrak{s}_1^\chi$. If $\mathfrak{s}_1$ is symmetric $\mathfrak{s}_1^\chi = \mathfrak{s}_1$ and therefore $\mathfrak{s}_2^\chi = T\mathfrak{s}_1 = \mathfrak{s}_2$. Consequently this mapping maps the set of symmetric n-tuples into itself.

Since this set is a cell there must be a symmetric fixed point $\mathfrak{s}$ which must be a symmetric equilibrium point. ∎

Solutions

We define here solutions, strong solutions, and sub-solutions. A non-cooperative game does not always have a solution, but when it does the solution is unique. Strong solutions are solutions with special properties. Sub-solutions always exist and have many of the properties of solutions, but lack uniqueness.

S_1 will denote a set of mixed strategies of player i and $\mathfrak{S}$ a set of n-tuples of mixed strategies.

Solvability:

A game is *solvable* if its set, $\mathfrak{S}$, of equilibrium points satisfies the condition

$$(t; r_i) \in \mathfrak{S} \quad \text{and} \quad \mathfrak{s} \in \mathfrak{S} \Rightarrow (\mathfrak{s}; r_i) \in \mathfrak{S} \quad \text{for all } i\text{'s.} \tag{5}$$

Non-cooperative games

This is called the *interchangeability* condition. The *solution* of a solvable game is its set, $\mathfrak{S}$, of equilibrium points.

Strong solvability:

A game is *strongly solvable* if it has a solution, $\mathfrak{S}$, such that for all i's

$$\mathfrak{s} \in \mathfrak{S} \quad \text{and} \quad p_i(\mathfrak{s}; r_i) = p_i(\mathfrak{s}) \Rightarrow (\mathfrak{s}; r_i) \in \mathfrak{S}$$

and then $\mathfrak{S}$ is called a *strong solution*.

Equilibrium strategies:

In a solvable game let S_i be the set of all mixed strategies s_i such that for some t the n-tuple $(t; s_i)$ is an equilibrium point. [s_i is the ith component of some equilibrium point.] We call S_i the set of *equilibrium strategies* of player i.

Sub-solutions:

If $\mathfrak{S}$ is a subset of the set of equilibrium points of a game and satisfies condition (1); and if $\mathfrak{S}$ is maximal relative to this property then we call $\mathfrak{S}$ a *sub-solution*.

For any sub-solution $\mathfrak{S}$ we define the ith *factor set*, S_i, as the set of all s_i's such that $\mathfrak{S}$ contains $(t; s_i)$ for some t.

Note that a sub-solution, when unique, is a solution; and its factor sets are the sets of equilibrium strategies.

Theorem 3. *A sub-solution, $\mathfrak{S}$, is the set of all n-tuples $(s_1, s_2, \ldots, s_n)$ such that each $s_i \in S_i$ where S_i is the ith factor set of $\mathfrak{S}$. Geometrically, $\mathfrak{S}$ is the product of its factor sets.*

Proof. Consider such an n-tuple $(s_1, s_2, \ldots, s_n)$. By definition $\exists t_1, t_2, \ldots, t_n$ such that for each i $(t_i; s_i) \in \mathfrak{S}$. Using the condition (5) $n-1$ times we obtain successively $(t_1; s_1) \in \mathfrak{S}$, $(t_1; s_1; s_2) \in \mathfrak{S}$, $\ldots$, $(t_1; s_1; s_2; \ldots; s_n) \in \mathfrak{S}$ and the last is simply $(s_1, s_2, \ldots, s_n) \in \mathfrak{S}$, which we needed to show. ∎

Theorem 4. *The factor sets $S_1, S_2, \ldots, S_n$ of a sub-solution are closed and convex as subsets of the mixed strategy spaces.*

Proof. It suffices to show two things:
(1) if s_i and $s_i' \in S_i$ then $s_i^* = (s_i + s_i')/2 \in S_i$; (2) if $s_i^{\#}$ is a limit point of S_i then $s_i^{\#} \in S_i$.

Let $t \in \mathfrak{S}$. Then we have $p_j(t; s_i) \geq p_j(t; s_i; r_j)$ and $p_j(t; s_i') \geq p_j(t; s_i'; r_j)$ for any r_j, by using the criterion of (1) for an eq. pt. Adding these inequalities, using the linearity of $p_j(s_1, \ldots, s_n)$ in s_i, and dividing by 2, we get $p_j(t; s_i^*) \geq p_j(t; s_i^*; r_j)$ since $s_i^* = (s_i + s_i')/2$. From this we know that $(t; s_i)$ is an eq. pt. for any $t \in \mathfrak{S}$. If the set of all such eq. pts. $(t; s_i^*)$ is

87

added to $\mathfrak{S}$ the augmented set clearly satisfies condition (5), and since $\mathfrak{S}$ was to be maximal it follows that $s_i^* \in S_i$.

To attack (2) note that the n-tuple $(t; s_i^{\#})$, where $t \in \mathfrak{S}$, will be a limit point of the set of n-tuples of the form $(t; s_i)$ where $s_i \in S_i$, since $s_i^{\#}$ is a limit point of S_i. But this set is a set of eq. pts. and hence any point in its closure is an eq. pt., since the set of all eq. pts. is closed. Therefore $(t; s_i^{\#})$ is an eq. pt. and hence $s_i^{\#} \in S_i$ from the same argument as for s_i^*. ∎

Values:

Let $\mathfrak{S}$ be the set of equilibrium points of a game. We define

$$v_i^+ = \max_{\mathfrak{s} \in \mathfrak{S}}[p_i(\mathfrak{s})], \qquad v_i^- = \min_{\mathfrak{s} \in \mathfrak{S}}[p_i(\mathfrak{s})].$$

If $v_i^+ = v_i^-$ we write $v_i = v_i^+ = v_i^-$. v_i^+ is the *upper value* to player i of the game; v_i^- the *lower value;* and v_i the *value,* if it exists.

Values will obviously have to exist if there is but one equilibrium point.

One can define *associated values* for a sub-solution by restricting $\mathfrak{S}$ to the eq. pts. in the sub-solution and then using the same defining equations as above.

A two-person zero-sum game is always solvable in the sense defined above. The sets of equilibrium strategies S_1 and S_2 are simply the sets of "good" strategies. Such a game is not generally strongly solvable; strong solutions exist only when there is a "saddle point" in *pure* strategies.

Simple examples

These are intended to illustrate the concepts defined in the paper and display special phenomena which occur in these games.

The first player has the roman letter strategies and the pay-off to the left, etc.

Ex. 1

5	$a\alpha$	-3
-4	$a\beta$	4
-5	$b\alpha$	5
3	$b\beta$	-4

Solution $\left(\dfrac{9}{16}a + \dfrac{7}{16}b, \dfrac{7}{17}\alpha + \dfrac{10}{17}\beta\right)$.

$v_1 = \dfrac{-5}{17}, \quad v_2 = +\dfrac{1}{2}.$

Ex. 2

1	$a\alpha$	1
-10	$a\beta$	10
10	$b\alpha$	-10
-1	$b\beta$	-1

Strong Solution (b, β).

$v_1 = v_2 = -1.$

Ex. 3

1	$a\alpha$	1
-10	$a\beta$	-10
-10	$b\alpha$	-10
1	$b\beta$	1

Unsolvable; equilibrium points (a, α), (b, β), and $\left(\dfrac{a}{2} + \dfrac{b}{2}, \dfrac{\alpha}{2} + \dfrac{\beta}{2}\right)$. The strategies in the last case have maxi-min and mini-max properties.

Ex. 4   1 $a\alpha$ 1   Strong solution: all pairs of mixed strategies.
         0   $a\beta$ 1
         1   $b\alpha$ 0 $v_1^+ = v_2^+ = 1,\ v_1^- = v_2^- = 0.$
         0   $b\beta$ 0

Ex. 5   1 $a\alpha$ 2   Unsolvable; eq. pts. (a, α), (b, β) and
        −1 $a\beta$ −4 $\left(\dfrac{1}{4}a + \dfrac{3}{4}b,\ \dfrac{3}{8}\alpha + \dfrac{5}{8}\beta\right).$ However, empirical
        −4 $b\alpha$ −1
         2   $b\beta$ 1   tests show a tendency toward (a, α).

Ex. 6   1 $a\alpha$ 1   Eq. pts.: (a, α) and (b, β), with (b, β) an
         0   $a\beta$ 0   example of instability.
         0   $b\alpha$ 0
         0   $b\beta$ 0

Geometrical form of solutions

In the two-person zero-sum case it has been shown that the set of "good" strategies of a player is a convex polyhedral subset of his strategy space. We shall obtain the same result for a player's set of equilibrium strategies in any solvable game.

Theorem 5. *The sets* $S_1, S_2, \dots, S_n$ *of equilibrium strategies in a solvable game are polyhedral convex subsets of the respective mixed strategy spaces.*

Proof. An n-tuple $\mathfrak{s}$ will be an equilibrium point if and only if for every i,

$$p_i(\mathfrak{s}) = \max_{\alpha} p_{i\alpha}(\mathfrak{s}) \tag{6}$$

which is condition (3). An equivalent condition is for every i and α

$$p_i(\mathfrak{s}) - p_{i\alpha}(\mathfrak{s}) \geq 0. \tag{7}$$

Let us now consider the form of the set S_j of equilibrium strategies, s_j, of player j. Let $\mathfrak{t}$ be any equilibrium point, then $(\mathfrak{t}; s_j)$ will be an equilibrium point if and only if $s_j \in S_j$, from Theorem 2. We now apply conditions (2) to $(\mathfrak{t}; s_j)$, obtaining

$$s_j \in S_j \Leftrightarrow \text{for all } i, \alpha \qquad p_i(\mathfrak{t}; s_j) - p_{i\alpha}(\mathfrak{t}; s_j) \geq 0. \tag{8}$$

Since p_i is n-linear and $\mathfrak{t}$ is constant these are a set of linear inequalities of the form $F_{i\alpha}(s_j) \geq 0$. Each such inequality is either satisfied for all s_j or for those lying on and to one side of some hyperplane passing through the strategy simplex. Therefore, the complete set [which is finite] of conditions will all be satisfied simultaneously on some convex polyhedral subset of player j's strategy simplex. [Intersection of half-spaces.] ∎

As a corollary we may conclude that S_j is the convex closure of a finite set of mixed strategies [vertices].

Dominance and contradiction methods

We say that s_i' dominates s_i if $p_i(\mathfrak{t}; s_i') > p_i(\mathfrak{t}; s_i)$ for every $\mathfrak{t}$.

This amounts to saying that s_i' gives player i a higher pay-off than s_i no matter what the strategies of the other players are. To see whether a strategy s_i' dominates s_i it suffices to consider only pure strategies for the other players because of the n-linearity of p_i.

It is obvious from the definitions that *no equilibrium point can involve a dominated strategy s_i.*

The domination of one mixed strategy by another will always entail other dominations. For suppose s_i' dominates s_i and t_i uses all of the pure strategies which have a higher coefficient in s_i than in s_i'. Then for a small enough ρ

$$t_i' = t_i + \rho(s_i' - s_i)$$

is a mixed strategy; and t_i dominates t_i' by linearity.

One can prove a few properties of the set of undominated strategies. It is simply connected and is formed by the union of some collection of faces of the strategy simplex.

The information obtained by discovering dominances for one player may be of relevance to the others, insofar as the elimination of classes of mixed strategies as possible components of an equilibrium point is concerned. For the t's whose components are all undominated are all that need be considered and thus eliminating some of the strategies of one player may make possible the elimination of a new class of strategies for another player.

Another procedure which may be used in locating equilibrium points is the contradiction-type analysis. Here one assumes that an equilibrium point exists having component strategies lying within certain regions of the strategy spaces and proceeds to deduce further conditions which must be satisfied if the hypothesis is true. This sort of reasoning may be carried through several stages to eventually obtain a contradiction indicating that there is no equilibrium point satisfying the initial hypothesis.

A three-man poker game

As an example of the application of our theory to a more or less realistic case we include the simplified poker game given below. The rules are as follows:

(a) The deck is large, with equally many *high* and *low* cards, and a hand consists of one card.
(b) Two chips are used to ante, open, or call.
(c) The players play in rotation and the game ends after all have passed or after one player has opened and the others have had a chance to call.
(d) If no one bets the antes are retrieved.
(e) Otherwise the pot is divided equally among the highest hands which have bet.

We find it more satisfactory to treat the game in terms of quantities we call "behavior parameters" than in the normal form of *Theory of Games and Economic Behavior*. In the normal form of representation two mixed strategies of a player may be equivalent in the sense that each makes the individual choose each available course of action in each particular situation requiring action on his part with the same frequency. That is, they represent the same behavior pattern on the part of the individual.

Behavior parameters give the probabilities of taking each of the various possible actions in each of the various possible situations which may arise. Thus they describe behavior patterns.

In terms of behavior parameters the strategies of the players may be represented as follows, assuming that since there is no point in passing with a *high* card at one's last opportunity to bet this will not be done. The Greek letters are the probabilities of the various acts.

	First Moves	Second Moves
I	α Open on *high* β Open on *low*	κ Call III on *low* λ Call II on *low* μ Call II and III on *low*
II	γ Call I on *low* δ Open on *high* ϵ Open on *low*	ν Call III on *low* ξ Call III and I on *low*
III	ζ Call I and II on *low* η Open on *low* θ Call I on *low* ι Call II on *low*	Player III never gets a second move

We locate all possible equilibrium points by first showing that most of the Greek parameters must vanish. By dominance mainly with a little contradiction-type analysis β is eliminated and with it go γ, ζ, and θ by dominance. Then contradictions eliminate μ, ξ, ι, λ, κ, and ν in that order. This leaves us with α, δ, ϵ, and η. Contradiction analysis shows that none of these can be zero or one and thus we obtain a system of simultaneous algebraic equations. The equations happen to have but one solution with the variables in the range $(0, 1)$. We get

$$\alpha = \frac{21 - \sqrt{321}}{10}, \qquad \eta = \frac{5\alpha + 1}{4}, \qquad \delta = \frac{5 - 2\alpha}{5 + \alpha}, \qquad \epsilon = \frac{4\alpha - 1}{\alpha + 5}.$$

These yield $\alpha = .308$, $\eta = .635$, $\delta = .826$, and $\epsilon = .044$. Since there is only one equilibrium point the game has values; these are

$$v_1 = -.147 = -\frac{(1 + 17\alpha)}{8(5 + \alpha)}, \qquad v_2 = -.096 = -\frac{1 - 2\alpha}{4},$$

and

$$v_3 = .243 = \frac{79}{40}\left(\frac{1 - \alpha}{5 + \alpha}\right).$$

A more complete investigation of this poker game is published in Annals of Mathematics Study No. 24, *Contributions to the Theory of Games*. There the solution is studied as the ratio of ante to bet varies, and the potentialities of coalitions are investigated.

Applications

The study of n-person games for which the accepted ethics of fair play imply non-cooperative playing is, of course, an obvious direction in which to apply this theory. And poker is the most obvious target. The analysis of a more realistic poker game than our very simple model should be quite an interesting affair.

The complexity of the mathematical work needed for a complete investigation increases rather rapidly, however, with increasing complexity of the game; so that analysis of a game much more complex than the example given here might only be feasible using approximate computational methods.

A less obvious type of application is to the study of cooperative games. By a cooperative game we mean a situation involving a set of players, pure strategies, and pay-offs as usual; but with the assumption that the players can and will collaborate as they do in the von Neumann and Morgenstern theory. This means the players may communicate and form coalitions which will be enforced by an umpire. It is unnecessarily restrictive, however, to assume any transferability or even comparability of the

Non-cooperative games

pay-offs [which should be in utility units] to different players. Any desired transferability can be put into the game itself instead of assuming it possible in the extra-game collaboration.

The writer has developed a "dynamical" approach to the study of cooperative games based upon reduction to non-cooperative form. One proceeds by constructing a model of the pre-play negotiation so that the steps of negotiation become moves in a larger non-cooperative game [which will have an infinity of pure strategies] describing the total situation.

This larger game is then treated in terms of the theory of this paper [extended to infinite games] and if values are obtained they are taken as the values of the cooperative game. Thus the problem of analyzing a cooperative game becomes the problem of obtaining a suitable, and convincing, non-cooperative model for the negotiation.

The writer has, by such a treatment, obtained values for all finite two-person cooperative games, and some special n-person games.

Acknowledgments

Drs. Tucker, Gale, and Kuhn gave valuable criticism and suggestions for improving the exposition of the material in this paper. David Gale suggested the investigation of symmetric games. The solution of the Poker model was a joint project undertaken by Lloyd S. Shapley and the author. Finally, the author was sustained financially by the Atomic Energy Commission in the period 1949–50 during which this work was done.

Bibliography

1. J. von Neumann, O. Morgenstern, *Theory of Games and Economic Behavior,* Princeton University Press, 1944.
2. J. F. Nash, Jr., *Equilibrium Points in N-Person Games,* Proc. Nat. Acad. Sci. U.S.A. 36 (1950) 48–9.
3. J. F. Nash, L. S. Shapley, *A Simple Three-Person Poker Game,* Annals of Mathematics Study No. 24, Princeton University Press, 1950.
4. John Nash, "Two Person Cooperative Games," to appear in *Econometrica.*
5. H. W. Kuhn, *Extensive Games,* Proc. Nat. Acad. Sci. U.S.A., 36 (1950) 570–6.

PART III

Examining Cournot's model

Overview

The eight papers in this part deal with various aspects of Cournot's model and analysis and thus focus on the model itself, as opposed to applications of the model. The first three papers explore the basic notion of non-cooperative behavior embodied in Cournot's model and focus around two themes: existence and versatility. Novshek's paper provides existence. As discussed in the Introduction, this paper is especially appealing in that it specifically admits cost functions which are conceptually consistent with long-run oligopoly behavior, in stark contrast with the earlier existence literature which usually employed an assumption (such as convexity of all cost functions) that eliminated or severely restricted scale economies.

The versatility of the noncooperative model of multiagent behavior is best seen by considering collusion. At least since Adam Smith many economists have harbored the deep suspicion that, given the opportunity, firms in an industry will collude. The problem for the firms, of course, is how to make the collusion stick. For many years collusion was viewed as requiring individually irrational behavior on the part of the participants: short of enforcement via government intervention, individual maximizing behavior on the part of the agents should lead to defections from the collusive solution. Specifically, at least one firm would find it advantageous to expand output and cut price.

More generally, the strategies for firms that would support a collusive outcome do not form a Nash equilibrium in the one-shot game, since they do not reflect individual maximizing behavior. Thus, some economists countered that worries about collusion were unfounded: collusive behavior carried its own seeds of destruction.

From this viewpoint of modeling multiagent strategic behavior, the sword cuts both ways. On the one hand we could tell ourselves that if we really believe in such a version of noncooperative behavior, we need not worry about collusion. On the other hand, the problem might lie with the models: Where there is a will there is a way, and where there is money there is usually the will, and if noncooperative models rule out mutually advantageous cooperative outcomes then perhaps it is the models that are naive and not the agents!

Noncooperative models *are* quite versatile. They do allow for cooperative outcomes under appropriately defined conditions. Stigler [1964] observed that firms engage in repeated interactions with each other, and that retaliation for defection was therefore a possibility. During the last twenty-five years an enormous number of papers have employed variations on this observation to show that cooperative outcomes are achievable via noncooperative play. This section includes two pioneering works in this area. The Radner and Friedman papers show how cooperative outcomes can arise from properly defined noncooperative behavior. Both papers employ trigger strategies, but they deal with significantly different settings requiring different approaches. Radner deals with a quantity oligopoly operating over a finite horizon while Friedman examines a repeated game over an infinite horizon. Radner's approach relies upon a version of bounded rationality (pure maximizing behavior over a finite horizon, coupled with the fact that the stage game has a unique equilibrium, would result in no cooperative outcomes being supported as Nash equilibria). Friedman examines the infinite horizon discounted game, using Cournot reversion as described in the Introduction. In both cases conditions are provided wherein cooperative outcomes are supported by noncooperative equilibrium strategies.

The papers by Novshek, Radner, and Friedman emphasize the internal consistency and breadth of applicability of noncooperative models in general and the Cournot model in particular. The next two papers focus on a second topic raised for this section in the introductory chapter: given that we represent multiagent behavior via a noncooperative equilibrium, does not the Cournot model reflect irrational conjectures about each other on the part of the players? As discussed in the Introduction, this is a variant on the Bowley/Frisch theme that Cournot play reflects a zero conjectural variation (CV) and that Cournot players are always surprised to learn that all the other players are also making strategic choices and would react to changes made by any agent in the game. This interpretation of Cournot's model was placed in its sharpest perspective by the recent literature on consistent conjectures equilibria (CCE) (see Laitner [1980], Bresnahan [1981], Perry [1982], and Kamien and Schwartz [1983]) which examined noncooperative oligopoly solutions with the added requirement that a firm's CV(s) should equal the appropriate reaction function slope(s), at least in equilibrium. This is the starting point for the next two papers. The first paper employs a special version of rationalizability (see Bernheim [1984] and Pearce [1984] on rationalizability, and

Brandenburger and Dekel [1987] on why all such outcomes are, properly defined, equilibria) to show that the CCE is not rationalizable (it employs dominated strategies) because restricting the Bowley/Frisch CV is the wrong procedure, and leads to "irrational" results. The second paper indicates that players already know this. Here Holt uses experimental methods to test the CCE concept and finds that players reject the CCE (and generally play Nash) when the CCE is sufficiently separated from the Nash equilibrium. For reviews of the use of experimental methods, see Friedman [1969], Plott [1982], and Smith [1982]; also see Dolbear, et al. [1968], Fouraker and Siegel [1963], Friedman [1967], and Hoggatt [1969] for other examples of specific studies.

The last three papers focus around the third issue, choice of strategic variable. As indicated in the Introduction, this discussion has historically tended to concentrate on the choice of price or quantity as "the" strategic variable. The three papers by Kreps and Scheinkman, Vives, and Klemperer and Meyer refocus the issue. First, timing of decisions and information reception are as important as the specification of decision variables; this is the lesson of Kreps and Scheinkman. Their exact result has been modified and extended (in this specific context, see Davidson and Deneckere [1986], Friedman [1987], and Benoit and Krishna [1987], and more generally see Fudenberg and Tirole [1986]), but the basic story is that the choice of strategic variable is but one part of the analysis of oligopolistic interaction.

The final two papers focus on the implications of choice of variable and how those implications feed back to influence the structuring of the game, since, to a great degree, the players of the game usually attempt to make the rules. Vives's paper focuses on the effect of such choices on competition and welfare. This paper, with Singh and Vives [1984] and Cheng [1985], is an example of a growing body of papers specifically exploring the duality between the price and quantity versions of a differentiated products Cournot model. More generally this approach contributes to our understanding of how characteristics of agents' choice rules influence the nature of the solution. The expanded story concerns the slopes and manipulability of the best reply functions. For example, choice rule slopes are changing when we bounce between prices and quantities or between attributes of the goods such as whether they are substitutes or complements (see Bulow et al. [1985], Judd [1985], and Fudenberg and Tirole [1986]). By adding stages to the game and expanding the set of strategic variables (to include capacities, advertising outlays, opportunities to share information, managerial incentives, etc.) we allow the slopes and positions of the optimal choice rules to be manipulated, thereby further affecting the degree of competition between the agents. This

97

will be seen as a primary organizing theme for some of the applications in Part IV.

The Klemperer and Meyer paper examines a one-stage game with endogenous price/quantity variable choice, and focuses on the role of uncertainty in providing a specific prediction of choice of strategic variable. This paper is thus one of a handful of efforts at endogenizing attributes of the game to be played. It provides a nice example of the effect structural characteristics such as demand, technology, and the nature of uncertainty have on this endogenously determined choice of strategic variable.

References

Benoit, J. P. and V. Krishna, "Dynamic Duopoly: Prices and Quantities," *Review of Economic Studies* 54, 1, 1987, 23–35.

Bernheim, B. D., "Rationalizable Strategic Behavior," *Econometrica* 52, 4, 1984, 1007–28.

Brandenburger, A. and E. Dekel, "Rationalizability and Correlated Equilibria," *Econometrica* 55, 6, 1987, 1391–1402.

Bresnahan, T. F., "Duopoly Models with Consistent Conjectures," *American Economic Review* 71, 5, 1981, 934–45.

Bulow, J., J. D. Geanakoplos, and P. D. Klemperer, "Multimarket Oligopoly: Strategic Substitutes and Complements," *Journal of Political Economy* 93, 3, 1985, 488–511.

Cheng, L., "Comparing Bertrand and Cournot Equilibria: A Geometric Approach," *Rand Journal of Economics* 16, 1, 1985, 146–52.

Davidson, C. and R. Deneckere, "Long-Run Competition in Capacity, Short-Run Competition in Price, and the Cournot Model," *Rand Journal of Economics* 17, 3, 1986, 404–15.

Dolbear, F. T., L. B. Lave, G. Bownan, A. Lieberman, E. Prescott, F. Rueter, and R. Sherman, "Collusion in Oligopoly: An Experiment on the Effect of Numbers and Information," *Quarterly Journal of Economics* 82, 1968, 240–59.

Fouraker, L. E. and S. Siegel, *Bargaining Behavior,* McGraw-Hill, New York, 1963.

Friedman, J. W., "An Experimental Study of Cooperative Duopoly," *Econometrica* 35, 3–4, 1967, 379–97.

———, "On Experimental Research in Oligopoly," *Review of Economic Studies* 36, 1969, 399–416.

———, "On the Strategic Importance of Prices versus Quantities," Working Paper, Department of Economics, University of North Carolina, 1987.

Fudenberg, D. and J. Tirole, *Dynamic Models of Oligopoly,* Harwood Academic Publishers, Chur, Switzerland, 1986.

Hoggatt, A. C., "Response of Paid Student Subjects to Differential Behavior of Robots in Bifurcated Duopoly Games," *Review of Economic Studies* 36, 1969, 417–32.

Judd, K., "Credible Spatial Preemption," *Rand Journal of Economics* 16, 2, 1985, 153–66.

Kamien, M. I. and N. L. Schwartz, "Conjectural Variations," *Canadian Journal of Economics* 16, 1983, 191–211.

Laitner, J., " 'Rational' Duopoly Equilibria," *Quarterly Journal of Economics* 95, 4, 1980, 641–62.

Pearce, D. G., "Rationalizable Strategic Behavior and the Problem of Perfection," *Econometrica* 52, 4, 1984, 1029–50.

Perry, M., "Oligopoly and Consistent Conjectural Variations," *Bell Journal of Economics* 13, 1, 1982, 197–205.

Plott, C., "Industrial Organization Theory and Experimental Economics," *Journal of Economic Literature* 20, 4, 1982, 1485–527.

Singh, N. and X. Vives, "Price and Quantity Competition in a Differentiated Duopoly," *Rand Journal of Economics* 15, 4, 1984, 546–54.

Smith, V. L., "Microeconomic Systems as an Experimental Science," *American Economic Review* 72, 5, 1982, 923–55.

Stigler, G. J., "A Theory of Oligopoly," *Journal of Political Economy* 72, 1, 1964, 44–61.

EXISTENCE AND VERSATILITY

CHAPTER 4

On the existence of Cournot equilibrium

WILLIAM NOVSHEK

This paper examines the existence of n-firm Cournot equilibrium in a market for a single homogeneous commodity. It proves that if each firm's marginal revenue declines as the aggregate output of other firms increases (which is implied by concave inverse demand) then a Cournot equilibrium exists, without assuming that firms have nondecreasing marginal cost or identical technologies. Also, if the marginal revenue condition fails at a "potential optimal output," there is a set of firms such that no Cournot equilibrium exists. The paper also contains an example of nonexistence with two nonidentical firms, each with constant returns to scale production.

1. Introduction

Cournot equilibrium is commonly used as a solution concept in oligopoly models, but the conditions under which a Cournot equilibrium can be expected to exist are not well understood. The nature of each firm's technology, whether all firms have identical technologies, and restrictions on the market inverse demand vary from model to model, and are all important for the existence of Cournot equilibrium. This paper examines the question of existence of (pure strategy) Cournot equilibrium in a single market for a homogeneous good. In this context there are two known types of existence theorems. The first type allows general (downward sloping) inverse demand and shows the existence of Cournot equilibrium when there are n identical firms with convex technologies (nondecreasing marginal cost and no avoidable fixed costs). See McManus [1962, 1964] and Roberts and Sonnenschein [1976]. The second type shows the existence of Cournot equilibrium in markets with n not necessarily identical firms when each firm's profit function is concave. Sometimes the concavity of profit functions is an explicit assumption (see Frank and Quandt [1963]), other times assumptions on the inverse demand and cost functions which imply concave profit functions are used (for example, inverse demand is

Stanford University, Stanford CA.
William Novshek, "On the Existence of Cournot Equilibrium," *Review of Economic Studies* 52, 1, 1985, 85–98.

103

assumed to be concave over the range where it is positive and all firms have convex cost functions in Szidarovszky and Yakowitz [1977]).[1]

The main result of the paper is a new existence theorem for n-firm Cournot equilibrium. With only minimal assumptions on cost functions, and without requiring identical firms or convex technologies we show that a commonly imposed assumption on inverse demand is sufficient to guarantee the existence of an n-firm Cournot equilibrium. The condition is equivalent to the condition that (throughout the relevant region) each firm's marginal revenue is declining in the aggregate output of other firms. Since each firm's cost function is assumed to depend on its own output, but not on the output of any other firm, this marginal revenue condition is also equivalent to the condition that (throughout the relevant region) the cross partial of the firm's profit function with respect to its own output and any other firm's output is non-positive. These assumptions on marginal revenue or profit functions are commonly imposed in the industrial organization literature and in the literature concerning the stability or comparative static properties of Cournot equilibrium (see for example Ruffin [1971] and Okuguchi [1973]). The new existence theorem shows that this literature can drop essentially all of the common assumptions imposed on the cost functions of the firms (for example, convexity of cost functions) and still obtain existence of equilibrium with only the marginal revenue condition. Assumptions on cost functions need only be introduced if needed in the subsequent stability of comparative static analysis.

The marginal revenue condition is implied by concave inverse demand, another common assumption in this literature. Thus the new existence theorem shows it is possible to drop the explicit or implicit assumptions on the cost functions needed in the second, previous type of existence theorem (using concave profit functions).

We also provide two examples of nonexistence of Cournot equilibrium to help delineate the conditions under which equilibrium can be expected to exist. The first example is of a well-known type, and it shows that general demand and identical firms with nonconvex technologies can lead to nonexistence of equilibrium. The second example does not seem to be well known. It shows that with general demand and convex technologies, if firms are not identical then equilibrium may not exist.

In a remark we also examine the extent to which the assumptions of the new existence theorem can be weakened. The only really substantial

---

[1] Kim Border brought to my attention a paper by Nishimura and Friedman (1981) in which they prove a third type of existence theorem for Cournot equilibrium. They have an assumption on the derived reaction correspondence which does not have a natural counterpart in terms of the primitive inverse demand and cost functions. Their assumption requires that for any $(y_1, y_2, ..., y_n)$ which is not an equilibrium, for at least one firm j,

assumption, the marginal revenue condition, is not a necessary condition for existence of equilibrium since the condition may fail at an "irrelevant point." For example, suppose the marginal revenue condition fails at output y for a single firm when the total output of the $n-1$ other firms is Y. This is irrelevant if the total revenue the single firm obtains at y is less than the total revenue it could obtain at some smaller output, given output Y by others. Since revenue is larger at the smaller output, and (for any cost function satisfying the standard assumption that total cost is nondecreasing in output) cost is no larger at the smaller output, profit is also larger at the smaller output. Thus when the total output of the $n-1$ other firms is Y, output y for the remaining firm is irrelevant: it is dominated by a smaller output no matter what the cost function is. In this case we will say that given Y, y is not a "potential optimal output." We show that if, for some inverse demand function, the marginal revenue condition fails at some point which is a "potential optimal output" then there exists an integer n, and n firms with cost functions satisfying the assumptions of the theorem, such that the market with these n firms and the given inverse demand function has no pure strategy Cournot equilibrium.

In terms of the three most commonly used factors (whether each firm's technology is convex, whether all firms have identical technologies, and whether inverse demand is concave) the results on existence of Cournot equilibrium can be summarized as follows: concavity of inverse demand is enough by itself to guarantee existence of Cournot equilibrium; identical firms and convex technology together guarantee existence of Cournot equilibrium; and without concavity of inverse demand (actually, the marginal revenue condition), if firms are either not identical or technologies are not convex, equilibrium may not exist.

In Section 2 we state versions of the previous existence theorems. In Section 3 we present our two examples of nonexistence. Section 4 contains the new existence theorem. Section 5 contains remarks on weakening the assumptions of the theorem, on extension of the existence theorem to endogenous n (i.e. the case of an unlimited number of potential firms), and on the use of the theorem to prove a very general version of the limit results in Novshek (1980).

2. Previous existence results

Consider the market for a single homogeneous good with inverse demand function $P(\cdot)$ and n firms. Firm $f \in \{1, 2, \ldots, n\}$ has cost function $C_f(\cdot)$.

either all optimal responses to Y by firm j are strictly greater than y_j for all Y sufficiently near $\sum_{i \neq j} y_i$, or they are all strictly less than y_j. In this paper we are concerned with assumptions on the basic elements of the model, inverse demand and cost functions, and their relationship to the existence question.

Definition. $(y_1, y_2, \ldots, y_n) \in \mathbb{R}^n_+$ is a Cournot equilibrium if

$$P\left(\sum_{j=1}^{n} y_j\right)y_f - C_f(y_f) \geq P\left(\sum_{j=1}^{n} y_j - y_f + y\right)y - C_f(y)$$

for all $y \geq 0$, for all $f \in \{1, 2, \ldots, n\}$.

In order to state the first result we need two technical definitions.

Definition. A function $P: (0, \infty) \to \mathbb{R}_+$ is upper-semi-continuous if for all $Z > 0$, for all $\epsilon > 0$ there exists a $\delta > 0$ such that $|X - Z| < \delta$ implies $P(X) < P(Z) + \epsilon$.

Definition. A cost function $C: \mathbb{R}_+ \to \mathbb{R}_+$ has nondecreasing incremental cost if for any $y > y' \geq 0$ and $x > 0$,

$$C(y + x) - C(y) \geq C(y' + x) - C(y').$$

Note that nondecreasing incremental cost implies the cost function is continuous at zero, so $C(0)$ is sunk cost. Then the relevant cost function, $C^*(y) = C(y) - C(0)$, has nondecreasing average cost.

Theorem 1 (McManus [1964]). *Given a market for a single homogeneous good with inverse demand $P(\cdot)$ and n identical firms, each with cost function $C(\cdot)$, if*

    (1)   *$P: (0, \infty) \to \mathbb{R}_+$ is a nonincreasing, upper-semi-continuous function and total revenue, $ZP(Z)$, is bounded, and*

    (2)   *$C: \mathbb{R}_+ \to \mathbb{R}_+$ is continuous and monotonically increasing, with nondecreasing incremental cost,*

then an n-firm Cournot equilibrium exists.

McManus showed that all jumps in the reaction correspondence, $r(Y) := \{y \in \mathbb{R}_+ \mid P(Y + y)y - C(y) \geq P(Y + x)x - C(x) \text{ for all } x \in \mathbb{R}_+\}$, must be jumps up, so the line $y = Y/(n+1)$ must intersect the graph of the reaction correspondence, yielding a symmetric n-firm equilibrium.

As noted in the introduction, the second type of existence theorem takes various forms. For comparison we state it as follows:

Theorem 2 (Szidarovszky and Yakowitz [1977]). *Given a market for a single homogeneous good with inverse demand $P(\cdot)$ and n firms with cost functions $C_1, C_2, \ldots, C_n$, if*

    (1)   *$P: \mathbb{R}_+ \to \mathbb{R}_+$ is nonincreasing and is twice continuously differentiable and concave on the interval where it has positive value (so $P(Z) > 0$ implies $P'(Z) \leq 0$ and $P''(Z) \leq 0$), and*

The existence of Cournot equilibrium

(2) *for all* $f \in \{1, 2, \ldots, n\}$, $C_f : \mathbb{R}_+ \to \mathbb{R}_+$ *is nondecreasing, twice continuously differentiable, and convex (so* $C_f'(y) \geq 0$ *and* $C_f''(y) \geq 0$ *for all* y)

then there exists an n-firm Cournot equilibrium.

The proof of Theorem 2 follows from the observation that, in the relevant region, each firm's profit function is concave in its own output, so a standard existence theorem for concave games can be applied.

3. Examples of nonexistence

Our first example of nonexistence has an inverse demand function which is not everywhere concave, and identical firms with nonconvex cost functions. The possibility of nonexistence under these conditions is well known.

Example 1. Inverse demand is

$$P(Z) = \begin{cases} 100 - 4Z & Z \in [0, 0 \cdot 25] \\ 527 - 1712Z & Z \in (0 \cdot 25, 0 \cdot 3] \\ 14 - 2Z & Z \in (0 \cdot 3, 7] \\ 0 & Z \in (7, \infty) \end{cases}$$

and all firms have identical cost functions with decreasing average cost:

$$C(y) = \begin{cases} 0 & y = 0 \\ 10 + y & y > 0 \end{cases}$$

The reaction correspondence is then

$$r(Y) = \begin{cases} \left\{ \dfrac{1}{4} - Y \right\} & Y \in \left[0, \dfrac{\sqrt{33,516} - 183}{2} \right) \\[2ex] \left\{ \dfrac{1}{4} - Y, \dfrac{13}{4} - \dfrac{Y}{2} \right\} & Y = \dfrac{\sqrt{33,516} - 183}{2} \\[2ex] \left\{ \dfrac{13}{4} - \dfrac{Y}{2} \right\} & Y \in \left(\dfrac{\sqrt{33,516} - 183}{2}, \dfrac{13}{2} - 2\sqrt{5} \right) \\[2ex] \{\sqrt{5}, 0\} & Y = \dfrac{13}{2} - 2\sqrt{5} \\[2ex] \{0\} & Y \in \left(\dfrac{13}{2} - 2\sqrt{5}, \infty \right). \end{cases}$$

For $n \geq 2$ there is no *n*-firm equilibrium in this example: each active firm produces more than all other firms combined [i.e. for all Y, all nonzero

107

elements of $r(Y)$ exceed Y] so at most one firm can be active. But if only one firm is active it produces the monopoly output, which is not viable with $n \geq 2$, since $0 \notin r(\frac{1}{4})$. This example can be easily modified to show nonexistence with $\cup$-shaped average cost.

We now turn to cases in which firms have different technologies. Again inverse demand is not everywhere concave but the two firms have convex cost functions (constant marginal cost with no fixed cost) which are different. The possibility of nonexistence under these conditions seems not to be well known.

Example 2. Inverse demand is

$$P(Z) = \begin{cases} 2-Z & Z \in [0, 0.99] \\ \dfrac{8219}{8119} - \dfrac{19}{8119}Z & Z \in \left(0.99, \dfrac{100}{19}\right] \\ \dfrac{10,019}{19} - 100Z & Z \in \left(\dfrac{100}{19}, \dfrac{100 \cdot 19}{19}\right] \\ 0 & Z \in \left(\dfrac{100 \cdot 19}{19}, \infty\right). \end{cases}$$

There are two firms with constant marginal cost and no fixed costs, but firm 1 has marginal cost 881/800 while firm 2 has marginal cost 381/400.

The first firm's reaction correspondence is

$$r_1(Y) = \begin{cases} \left\{\dfrac{719}{1600} - \dfrac{Y}{2}\right\} & Y \in \left[0, \dfrac{719}{800}\right] \\ \{0\} & Y \in \left(\dfrac{719}{800}, \infty\right) \end{cases}$$

while the second firm's reaction correspondence is

$$r_2(Y) = \begin{cases} \left\{\dfrac{419}{800} - \dfrac{Y}{2}\right\} & Y \in \left[0, \dfrac{21}{400}\right) \\ \left\{\dfrac{398}{300}, \dfrac{100}{19} - \dfrac{21}{400}\right\} & Y = \dfrac{21}{400} \\ \left\{\dfrac{100}{19} - Y\right\} & Y \in \left(\dfrac{21}{400}, \dfrac{3,999,639}{760,000}\right] \\ \left\{\dfrac{8,000,722}{3,040,000} - \dfrac{Y}{2}\right\} & Y \in \left(\dfrac{3,999,639}{760,000}, \dfrac{8,000,722}{1,520,000}\right] \\ \{0\} & Y \in \left(\dfrac{8,000,722}{1,520,000}, \infty\right). \end{cases}$$

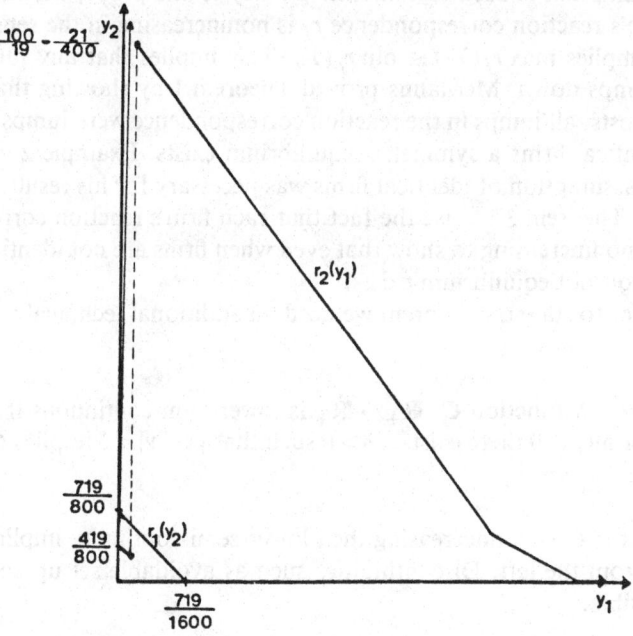

Figure 1. Reaction correspondences for Example 2.

From Figure 1 we see there is no equilibrium. This example can be easily modified to strictly increasing average cost, or strictly decreasing average cost, or ∪-shaped average cost.

4. Existence theorem

The new existence theorem improves Theorem 2 by removing the requirement that firms have convex cost functions and weakening the assumption that inverse demand be concave. The remaining assumption on cost functions is quite minimal, and is needed to guarantee that each firm's reaction correspondence is nonempty valued. The only restrictive assumption is the (commonly used) requirement that a firm's marginal revenue be everywhere (in the relevant region) a declining function of the aggregate output of others; i.e. for all nonnegative y and Y with $P(y+Y) > 0$, for revenue $yP(Y+y)$,

$$\frac{\partial^2 \{yP(Y+y)\}}{\partial Y \partial y} = P'(Y+y) + yP''(Y+y) \le 0.$$

109

This assumption is used to establish the key to the proof, the fact that each firm's reaction correspondence r_f is nonincreasing in the sense that $Y' > Y$ implies max $r_f(Y') \leq$ min $r_f(Y)$. This implies that any jumps in r_f are jumps down. McManus proved Theorem 1 by showing that with convex costs, all jumps in the reaction correspondence were jumps up, so with identical firms a symmetric equilibrium exists. Example 2 showed that the assumption of identical firms was necessary for his result. In the proof of Theorem 3 we use the fact that each firm's reaction correspondence is nonincreasing to show that even when firms are not identical, an n-firm Cournot equilibrium exists.

In order to state the theorem we need an additional technical assumption.

Definition. A function $C: \mathbb{R}_+ \to \mathbb{R}_+$ is lower-semi-continuous if for all $y \geq 0$, for all $\epsilon > 0$ there exists a $\delta > 0$ such that $|x - y| < \delta$ implies $C(x) > C(y) - \epsilon$.

Note that if C is nondecreasing then lower-semi-continuity implies continuity from the left. Discontinuities such as avoidable set up costs are still possible.

Theorem 3. *Given a market for a single homogeneous good with inverse demand $P(\cdot)$ and n firms with cost functions $C_1, C_2, ..., C_n$, if*

    (1) $P: \mathbb{R}_+ \to \mathbb{R}_+$ *is continuous,*

    (2)   *there exists $Z' < \infty$ such that $P(Z') = 0$ and P is twice continuously differentiable and strictly decreasing on $[0, Z')$,*

    (3)   *for all $Z \in [0, Z')$, $P'(Z) + ZP''(Z) \leq 0$, and*

    (4)   *for all $f \in \{1, 2, ..., n\}$, $C_f: \mathbb{R}_+ \to \mathbb{R}_+$ is a nondecreasing, lower-semi-continuous function,*

then there exists an n-firm Cournot equilibrium.

Note that given assumption (2), assumption (3) is equivalent to the assumption that for all nonnegative Y and y with $Y + y < Z'$,

$$P'(Y+y) + yP''(Y+y) \leq 0,$$

so each firm's marginal revenue is decreasing in the aggregate output of other firms. Assumption (3) is also equivalent to the assumption that each firm's profit function has non-positive cross partials with respect to its own and other firms' outputs. The profit function version of the assumption follows from the observation that firm i's cost is independent of other firms' output, so only the revenue side appears in the profit cross partial, making it identical to the derivative of marginal revenue with respect to the aggregate output of other firms.

The proof is relatively long and complicated. The main idea of the proof is to use the fact that, under the assumption, reaction correspondences are nonincreasing to "construct" an equilibrium. Rather than use the reaction correspondence r_f we use a "backward reaction mapping," $b_f(Q)$, which gives the optimal outputs for firm f which are consistent with aggregate output Q for all n firms [i.e. $q \in b_f(Q)$ if and only if $q \in r_f(Q-q)$]. The advantage of this mapping is that in equilibrium all firms face the same aggregate output Q, so Q^* is an equilibrium if and only if $Q^* \in \Sigma_{f=1}^n b_f(Q^*)$. The difficult part of the proof is making a selection from the correspondence $b_f(Q)$ in such a way that the (generally necessary) discontinuities in the selection do not cause problems. The selection made for firm f at Q depends on the selection made for all firms for all $Q' > Q$.

Proof. Let the assumptions of Theorem 3 hold. First observe the properties of each firm's reaction correspondence. For any $Y < Z'$, for any firm, all optimal responses to Y are less than $Z' - Y$ since the response $y = (Z' - Y)/2$ generates strictly positive revenue [compared to zero revenue for outputs greater than or equal to $Z' - Y$ because $P(Z') = 0$] at lower cost (because all cost functions are nondecreasing). For $Y < Z'$, the reaction correspondence is thus $r_f(Y) := \{y \in [0, Z'] \mid P(Y+y)y - C_f(y) \geq P(Y+x)x - C_f(x)$ for all $x \in [0, Z']\}$.

For convenience we define $r_f(Z') := \{0\}$. Note zero is always an optimal response to Z', but other responses are also optimal if $C_f(y) = C_f(0)$ for some $y > 0$. These other responses are clearly not interesting. By our assumptions, each r_f is a nonempty valued, upper-hemi-continuous correspondence on $[0, Z']$.

Next observe that each reaction correspondence is nonincreasing: if $Y < Y' < Z'$ and $y < y' = \max r_f(Y')$ then

$$P(Y+y')y' - P(Y+y)y = \int_y^{y'} [P(Y+x) + xP'(Y+x)] \, dx$$

$$\geq \int_y^{y'} [P(Y'+x) + xP'(Y'+x)] \, dx$$

$$= P(Y'+y')y' - P(Y'+y)y$$

$$\geq C_f(y') - C_f(y)$$

where the first weak inequality follows from assumptions (2) and (3) and our initial note, and the second weak inequality follows from $y' \in r_f(Y')$.

111

Thus $y \notin r_f(Y)$, and r_f is nonincreasing in the sense that $Y' > Y$ implies $\max r_f(Y') \leq \min r_f(Y)$. Each r_f has at most countably many discontinuities, and all jumps are jumps down.

Next, for each f, use r_f to define the convex valued correspondence s_f by $s_f(Y) := $ convex hull of $r_f(Y)$ for $Y \in [0, Z']$. Then s_f is also nonincreasing in the sense above, and for each $y \in [0, \max r_f(0)]$, the set of Y with $y \in s_f(Y)$ is a nonempty, closed interval.

Now define the upper-hemi-continuous, possibly empty valued "backward reaction correspondence" b_f by

$$b_f(Q) := \{q \mid \text{there exists } Y \in [0, Z'] \text{ such that } q \in r_f(Y) \text{ and } Y + q = Q\}$$

$$= \{q \mid q \in r_f(Q - q)\}$$

(see Novshek [1984a] for a detailed discussion of this correspondence). Similarly define the correspondence h_f by

$$h_f(Q) := \{q \mid \text{there exists } Y \in [0, Z'] \text{ such that } q \in s_f(Y) \text{ and } Y + q = Q\}.$$

Consider the properties of b_f and h_f. First, note that

$$b_f(Z') = h_f(Z') = \{0\} \quad \text{for all } f.$$

The graph of h_f can be continuously parameterized as $(Q_f^*(t), q_f^*(t))$ for $t \in [0, 1]$ such that $(Q_f^*(0), q_f^*(0)) = (Z', 0)$, $q_f^*(t) \in h_f(Q_f^*(t))$ for all t, $q_f^*(t)$ is nondecreasing in t, and $(Q_f^*(1), q_f^*(1)) = (\max r_f(0), \max r_f(0))$. Thus larger q_f values are associated with larger t values. Vertical jumps in r_f correspond to "jumps" along a 45 degree line for b_f (if $y, y' \in r_f(Y)$ and $y \neq y'$ then $y \in b_f(Y + y)$ but $y' \in b_f(Y + y')$). The only difference between b_f and h_f is that these "45 degree jumps" have been filled in with a line segment in the graph of h_f. For each q, the set of Q with $q \in b_f(Q)$ is a closed interval, possibly empty. See Figure 2. Note the points Q_1 and Q_2 at which branches of b_f disappear as Q increases. By the definition of b_f, $(q_1, q_2, \ldots, q_n)$ is a Cournot equilibrium if and only if $q_f \in b_f(\Sigma_{j=1}^n q_j)$ for all f.

The points at which branches of the correspondence b_f disappear as Q increases (such as (Q_1, q_1) in Figure 2) play an important role in the proof. We first prove the result for the case in which the union over all f of these points is a finite set. Then we explain the modifications needed for the case in which this set is infinite.

Let T_f be the set of points at which a branch of b_f disappears as Q increases, let $T = \bigcup_{f=1}^n T_f$, and let T' be the set of Q values such that $(Q, q) \in T$ for some q. Until stated otherwise, we assume T is finite. Then T' is also finite. Let $T' = \{Q_1, \ldots, Q_k\}$ where $Q_1 > Q_2 > \cdots > Q_k$. Since $b_f(Z') = \{0\}$ for all f, $Z' > Q_1$. Starting at Z', we will decrease Q, assigning

112

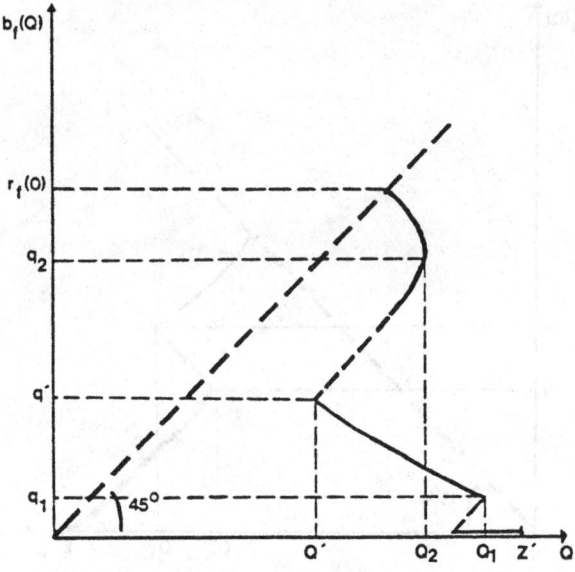

Figure 2.

some $q_f(Q) \in b_f(Q)$ to each firm at each Q until we reach an equilibrium at $Q^* = \Sigma_{f=1}^n q_f(Q^*)$.

At $Q = Z'$, $b_f(Q) = \{0\}$ so $q_f(Z') = 0$ and $\Sigma_{f=1}^n q_f(Z') = 0 < Z'$. In (Q_1, Z'), for each f, $q_f(Q)$ is assigned so that it is continuous and non-increasing on $(Q_1, Z']$. This is well defined because the graph of each h_f can be continuously parameterized as discussed earlier. Then $\Sigma_{f=1}^n q_f(Q)$ is continuous and nonincreasing on (Q_1, Z'). If at any $Q \in (Q_1, Z']$, $\Sigma_{f=1}^n q_f(Q) = Q$ we have an equilibrium. If not, for each f let $q_f = \lim_{Q \to Q_1, Q > Q_1} q_f(Q)$. If $\Sigma_{f=1}^n q_f = Q_1$ we have an equilibrium (since the b_f are upper-hemi-continuous). Otherwise $\Sigma_{f=1}^n q_f < Q_1$.

If $\Sigma_{f=1}^n q_f < Q_1$, let

$$F_1 = \{ f \mid (Q_1, q) \in T_f \text{ for some } q \} \neq \emptyset.$$

Let $\{f_1, f_2, \ldots, f_m\} = F_1$ where $f_1 < f_2 < \cdots < f_m$. For $f \neq F_1$ set $q_f(Q_1) = q_f$, so $q_f(\cdot)$ is continuous from the right. We now introduce discontinuities into $q_f(\cdot)$ for some $f \in F_1$ as follows. Let $q_{f_1}(Q_1) = \max\{q \mid q = q_{f_1}$ or both $(Q_1, q) \in T_{f_1}$ and $q_{f_1} \leq q \leq Q_1 - \Sigma_{f \notin F_1} q_f(Q_1) - \Sigma_{j=2}^m q_{f_j}\}$ i.e. $q_{f_1}(Q_1)$ jumps to the largest point of a discontinuity in b_{f_1} which does not lead to a sum of individual actions exceeding Q_1. If

113

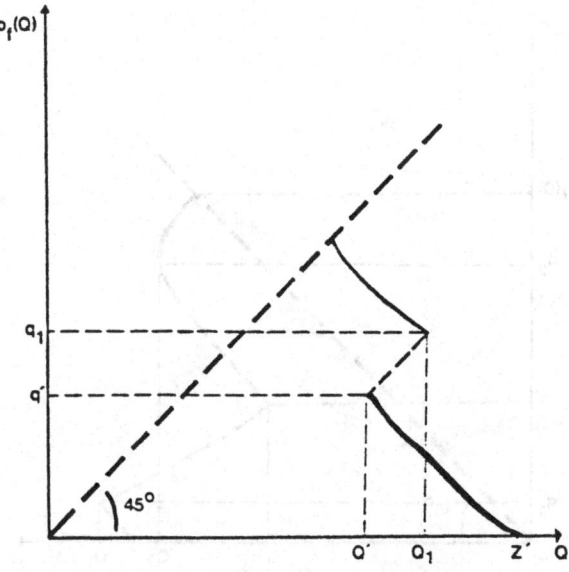

Figure 3.

$$\sum_{f \notin F_1} q_f(Q_1) + q_{f_1}(Q_1) + \sum_{j=2}^{m} q_{f_j} = Q_1$$

we have an equilibrium. If not, the sum is less than Q_1 and we repeat the process for f_2 (using $q_{f_1}(Q_1)$ as the value assigned to f_1), etc., until either the sum equals Q_1, in which case we have an equilibrium, or $q_{f_1}(Q_1)$ is assigned for all $j = 1, 2, \ldots, m$, and $\sum_{f=1}^{n} q_f(Q_1) < Q_1$.

In (Q_2, Q_1), for each f, $q_f(Q)$ is assigned so that it is continuous and nonincreasing on $(Q_2, Q_1]$. This is again well defined by the properties of b_f, and $\sum_{f=1}^{n} q_f(Q)$ is continuous and nonincreasing on $(Q_2, Q_1]$. If at any $Q \in (Q_2, Q_1]$, $\sum_{f=1}^{n} q_f(Q) = Q$ we have an equilibrium. If not, for each f let $q_f = \lim_{Q \to Q_2, Q > Q_2} q_f(Q)$. If $\sum_{f=1}^{n} q_f = Q_2$ we have an equilibrium. Otherwise $\sum_{f=1}^{n} q_f < Q_2$ and we define $q_f(Q_2)$ using the same procedure used at Q_1 to define $q_f(Q_1)$.

Continue the process of defining $q_f(Q)$ for all f until we get an equilibrium or it cannot continue, as at (Q', q') in Figure 2. We cannot reach points such as this if all continuous branches of b_f are nonincreasing in Q as in Figure 3. [This is the case if no r_f ever has slope less than negative one, such as when $C_f''(y) \geq P'(Y+y)$ for all Y and y.] In Figure 3 we could not reach (Q', q') since $\sum_{i \neq f} q_i(Q') + q' < Q'$ implies

114

$$\sum_{i \neq f} q_i(Q_1) + q_1 \leq \sum_{i \neq f} q_i(Q') + q_1$$

$$= \sum_{i \neq f} q_i(Q') + q' + (q_1 - q')$$

$$= \sum_{i \neq f} q_i(Q') + q' + (Q_1 - Q') < Q_1$$

so $q_f(Q_1) = q_1$ and $q_f(Q) > q_1 > q'$ for all $Q < Q_1$. This argument holds in general. If all continuous branches of each b_j are nonincreasing then it is not possible to reach a $Q' \notin T'$ at which some selection $q_f(Q)$ must be discontinuous. All the discontinuities would be as introduced in our previous discussion. Then the procedure would have to end at an equilibrium since the only other point at which it cannot continue is at some firm's monopoly output, which is an equilibrium.

Thus to reach an end of the process before reaching an equilibrium some firm must have a branch of b_f which increases as Q increases. Pick one firm, say j, for which the process of decreasing Q cannot continue. Now *increase* Q maintaining all other firms on their previously determined selections, $q_f(Q)$. Recall $q_f(Q)$ is nonincreasing in Q (it is nonincreasing where continuous and all jumps are jumps down). We will define a new selection, $q_j^*(Q)$, for firm j. This selection will be continuous and *nondecreasing* but it will be a selection from h_j not b_j. For example it could follow a "45 degree jump" such as the increasing dotted segment beginning at (Q', q') in Figure 2. By the properties of h_j, q_j^* is well defined. Note $Q - (\sum_{f \neq j} q_f(Q) + q_j^*(Q))$ cannot change sign along a "45 degree jump" since it starts out positive (otherwise we have already found an equilibrium) and $Q - q_j^*(Q)$ is constant along a "45 degree jump" while $-\sum_{f \neq j} q_f(Q)$ is nondecreasing. Thus the first Q at which $Q = \sum_{f \neq j} q_f(Q) + q_j^*(Q)$ must be such that $q_j^*(Q) \in b_j(Q) \subset h_j(Q)$.

At the starting point for defining $q_j^*(Q)$, $Q - (\sum_{f \neq j} q_f(Q) + q_j^*(Q))$ was positive. As Q increases, all the jumps in each $q_f(\cdot)$ are jumps down, while $q_j^*(\cdot)$ is continuous. At the end of the continuous, nondecreasing branch of h_j (the last point at which a q_j^* satisfying the required properties can be defined), $Q - (\sum_{f \neq j} q_f(Q) + q_j^*(Q))$ is negative by the procedure used to define the original $q_j(Q)$ at such a point from T'. Thus we must reach a Q^* at which $Q^* = \sum_{f \neq j} q_f(Q^*) + q_j^*(Q^*)$, and as argued above, it must be true that at the smallest such Q^*, $q_j(Q^*) \in b_j(Q^*) \subset h_j(Q^*)$. Since $q_f(Q^*) \in b_f(Q^*)$ for $f \neq j$, we have an n-firm Cournot equilibrium.

Now consider the case in which T is infinite. Two possibilities must be dealt with: there may be some Q such that for infinitely many q, $(Q, q) \in T$, or there may be infinitely many Q in T'. In the first case, it may be necessary to replace "maximum" with "supremum" in the step used to

115

define $q_{f_j}(Q)$ at a Q value corresponding to the end of infinitely many branches of b_{f_j}, but this creates no problem since b_{f_j} is upper-hemi-continuous. In the second case, we must explain how to continue the process of defining the q_f when Q is a limit point of T'. If q_f has been defined on $[Q', Z']$ for all f, then either (a) $(q_1(Q'), ..., q_n(Q'))$ is an equilibrium, or (b) q_f need not be defined for any $Q < Q'$ since we have reached a point from which Q should be increased with only one q_f being replaced with a continuous, nondecreasing q_f^* as in the last step of the proof for T finite, or (c) there is a "branch" of b_f which is "continuous from the left" at $(Q', q_f(Q'))$. In the case of the continuous "branch," the "branch" may consist of infinitely many actual branches, but the jumps between branches become arbitrarily small as $(Q', q_f(Q'))$ is approached. If $\sum_{f=1}^{n} q_f(Q') < Q'$ then for some $\epsilon > 0$, for $Q \in [Q' - \epsilon, Q')$, q_f can be defined as the maximum of the b_f values in the "branch." Then q_f may have infinitely many jumps in $[Q' - \epsilon, Q')$, but is continuous at Q', and $\sum_{f=1}^{n} q_f(Q) < Q$ for Q near Q'. Thus the process of defining q_f can be continued at limit points of T' when necessary. This completes the extension of the result to T infinite. ∎

5. Remarks

5.1. Can the assumptions of Theorem 3 be significantly weakened? The first thing to note is that the marginal revenue condition is the only really substantial assumption. The assumptions about cost functions are either basic economic assumptions (nondecreasing cost) or necessary to guarantee that each firm's reaction correspondence is nonempty valued (lower-semi-continuous cost). The other assumptions on inverse demand can't be weakened significantly without being inconsistent with the marginal revenue condition. To be consistent with the marginal revenue condition (or its nondifferentiable analog) P cannot be increasing or have jumps up, and any jumps down must be jumps to zero (Theorem 3 can easily be extended to the case of a single jump to zero for the inverse demand). Inverse demand is assumed twice continuously differentiable to use the differentiable version of the marginal revenue condition. Finally, if we assume that monopoly revenue is not maximized at infinite output $(\lim_{Z \to \infty} ZP(Z) < \sup_Z ZP(Z))$ then the marginal revenue condition implies that there is some Z' such that $P(Z') = 0$. Thus the only significant assumption is the marginal revenue condition.

The marginal revenue condition is not a necessary condition for the existence of Cournot equilibrium because it can fail at an irrelevant point. However, if it fails at a "potential optimal output" then a counterexample can be constructed. Recall a "potential optimal output" y (in response to aggregate output Y by other firms) is an output at which total revenue exceeds the total revenue at all smaller outputs (in response to Y). Since all cost functions are nondecreasing, any output failing this condition could not be an optimal response for a firm with any cost function. Counterexamples to a general existence theorem when the marginal revenue condition fails at a "potential optimal output" are constructed in the proof of the following result.

Theorem 4. *Given an inverse demand function P such that*

(1) *$P: \mathbb{R}_+ \to \mathbb{R}_+$ is continuous,*

(2) *there exists $Z' < \infty$ such that $P(Z') = 0$ and P is twice continuously differentiable and strictly decreasing on $[0, Z')$, and*

(3) *there exist nonnegative y and Y such that $y + Y < Z'$, $P'(Y+y) + yP''(Y+y) > 0$, and $P(Y+y)y > P(Y+y')y'$ for all $y' \in [0, y)$*

there exists an integer n and n cost functions $C_1, \ldots, C_n$, satisfying

(4) *for all $f \in \{1, 2, \ldots, n\}$, $C_f: \mathbb{R}_+ \to \mathbb{R}_+$ is a nondecreasing, lower-semi-continuous function,*

such that the market with inverse demand P and n firms with cost functions $C_1, \ldots, C_n$ does not have a Cournot equilibrium.

Conditions (1), (2), and (4) of Theorems 3 and 4 are identical. Condition (3) of Theorem 4 requires that Condition (3) of Theorem 3 fail at a "potential optimal output." Theorem 3 shows that if an inverse demand function satisfies conditions (1), (2), and (3) of that theorem then for any integer n, and any n cost functions satisfying condition (4), an n-firm Cournot equilibrium exists. In the proof of Theorem 4 we will construct an example to show that if an inverse demand function satisfies conditions (1) and (2) of Theorem 3 but fails condition (3) of Theorem 3 at a "potential optimal output" then there exists an integer n and n cost functions satisfying condition (4) of Theorem 3 such that there is no n-firm Cournot equilibrium.

Proof. Assume the conditions of the Theorem hold. Then we can find strictly positive y^* and Y^* such that

$$P(Y^*+y^*) > 0, \qquad P'(Y^*+y^*) + y^*P''(Y^*+y^*) > 0,$$

$$P(Y^*+y^*) + y^*P'(Y^*+y^*) > 0, \quad \text{and} \quad P(Y^*+y^*)y^* > P(Y^*+y')y'$$

for all $y' \in [0, y^*)$. We will sketch the construction of the required example.

117

The first firm has no set up cost, and marginal cost which is constant and near zero on $[0, y^* - \delta]$, continuous and linear on $[y^* - \delta, y^* + \delta)$ with $C_1'(y^*) = P(Y^* + y^*) + y^* P'(Y^* + y^*)$, and very large and nondecreasing on $[y^* + \delta, \infty)$. By choice of sufficiently small δ, this generates a firm with a corresponding $b_1(\cdot)$ which, in a neighborhood of $Y^* + y^*$, is single valued and strictly increasing with slope very small and strictly positive.

All other firms are identical, with marginal cost constant and near zero on $[0, \epsilon)$ and extremely large on (ϵ, ∞). These firms have a set up cost so that there are two optimal responses to aggregate output $Y^* + y^* - \epsilon$ by other firms, zero and ϵ. By choice of ϵ sufficiently small, these firms all have corresponding b_f which are $\{\epsilon\}$ on $[0, Y^* + y^* - \epsilon)$, $\{0, \epsilon\}$ on $[Y^* + y^* - \epsilon, Y^* + y^*]$, and $\{0\}$ on $(Y^* + y^*, \infty)$.

With $\delta < Y^*$,

$$\sum_{f=1}^{n} b_f(Q) = b_1(Q) \le y^* + \delta < Q \quad \text{for} \quad Q \in (Y^* + y^*, \infty).$$

Choosing n very large,

$$\sum_{f=1}^{n} b_f(Q) \ge (n-1)\epsilon > Y^* + y^* > Q \quad \text{for} \quad Q \in [\epsilon, Y^* + y^* - \epsilon).$$

Thus if an equilibrium exists, Q^* must be in $[Y^* + y^* - \epsilon, Y^* + y^*]$. Let $[Y^*/\epsilon]$ be the greatest integer less or equal to Y^*/ϵ. If ϵ is chosen very small and such that the fractional part of Y^*/ϵ (i.e. $Y^*/\epsilon - [Y^*/\epsilon]$) is very near one (relative to the slope of b_1 near $Y^* + y^*$) then $b_1(Q) + ([Y^*/\epsilon] + 1)\epsilon > Q$ for all $Q \in [Y^* + y^* - \epsilon, Y^* + y^*]$ while $b_1(Q) + [Y^*/\epsilon]\epsilon < Q$ for all $Q \in [Y^* + y^* - \epsilon, Y^* + y^*]$. Thus for appropriately chosen small δ and ϵ there is no equilibrium. ∎

Why do these counterexamples work? First of all, some reaction correspondence just have a discontinuity to prevent application of a standard fixed point theorem to show existence of an equilibrium. However, the key feature distinguishing the proof of Theorem 3 from the counterexamples of Theorem 4 or Examples 1 and 2 is whether any reaction correspondence is increasing (all these cases have discontinuities). Theorem 3 showed discontinuities create no problem as long as all reaction correspondences are nonincreasing. In all the counterexamples some firm's increasing reaction correspondence combined with its own or some other firm's discontinuity to prevent existence of equilibrium. Only in the special case with identical firms with convex cost functions are increasing reaction correspondences and discontinuities compatible with a general existence result. Without the flexibility to allow firms to have different cost functions, it is not possible to create a counterexample for that case.

The existence of Cournot equilibrium

Note that the counterexamples constructed in the proof of Theorem 4 had $n-1$ identical firms with convex variable cost and an avoidable set up cost and one other firm with convex total cost.

5.2. We now consider the extension of the theorem to exogenous determination of n. For some types of cost functions it is already the case that in equilibrium some firms will be inactive (when n is sufficiently large), so n is endogenous in those cases. However, Theorem 3 cannot be extended to $n = \infty$ without additional conditions. First, note that equilibrium does not exist for $n = \infty$ under the conditions of Theorem 1 - identical firms with convex cost, whether or not inverse demand is concave. This is easily seen using the "backward mapping" b_j. In this case, for large Q, $b_j(Q) = \{0\}$ but as Q declines b_j continuously increases (at least initially). If Q' is the smallest output at which $b_j(Q) = \{0\}$ then $\sum_{j=1}^{\infty} b_j(Q') = 0 < Q'$ but for all $\epsilon > 0$, $\sum_{j=1}^{\infty} b_j(Q' - \epsilon) = \infty > Q'$. Because average cost is minimized at infinitesimal outputs, if any firm is active then *all* firms are active. For any exogenous n this creates no problem. However, for $n = \infty$ there is no equilibrium. The continuity of b_j near Q' prevents the extension of the existence result to endogenous n.

This same problem can occur with ∪-shaped (or always declining) average cost if average cost is flat enough relative to inverse demand. It cannot occur if there are avoidable set up costs (or the average cost of small outputs is sufficiently large relative to inverse demand) since b_j will discontinuously jump to zero. Then we can show the existence of an equilibrium for $n = \infty$ in which all but a finite number of firms are inactive.

Nonexistence of equilibrium for $n = \infty$ can also occur when firms are not identical. For example, if all cost functions are different, and convex (or with average cost sufficiently flat relative to inverse demand) then it is still possible that there is a Q' such that for each b_j, Q' is the smallest output at which $b_j(Q) = \{0\}$ and b_j is continuous near Q'. Again $\sum_{j=1}^{\infty} b_j(Q' - \epsilon) = \infty$ for all $\epsilon > 0$ is possible while $\sum_{j=1}^{\infty} b_j(Q') = 0$. A similar problem can occur when the b_j discontinuously jump to zero. For example, if for $j = 1, 2, \ldots$ firm j has reaction correspondence $r_j(Y) = 1/(j+1)$ for $Y \leq 2 - 1/(j+1)^2$ and $r_j(Y) = 0$ for $Y \geq 2 - 1/(j+1)^2$ then $\sum_{j=1}^{\infty} b_j(Q) = \infty$ for $Q < 2$ but $\sum_{j=1}^{\infty} b_j(2) = 0$. The problem is that the firms are not "different enough." In all these examples some point (Q, q) is a cluster point for significant points in the graphs of the different b_j (points at which b_j first became zero, etc.). If firms are "different enough" then no such cluster points exist, and the existence result can be extended to endogenous determination of the number of active firms with $n = \infty$.

Thus in order to extend the existence result to $n = \infty$ and endogenous determination of the number of active firms it is sufficient to either assume

119

identical firms with sufficiently strongly increasing returns to scale for small outputs, or to assume that firms have sufficiently different cost functions.

5.3. If we consider a sequence of Markets M_k which converge to a perfectly competitive limit market M with infinitesimal firms, we can ask (1) for k large does M_k have a Cournot equilibrium and (2) how do the Cournot equilibria of M_k compare to the competitive equilibria of M? For a special case in which firms were identical within each M_k, and the markets were related in a very strong way, Novshek (1980) shows that with downward sloping inverse demand and U-shaped average cost, (1) for large k, M_k has a Cournot equilibrium and (2) the Cournot equilibria of M_k converge to the competitive equilibria of M. Using Theorem 3 this result can be considerably generalized: for downward sloping inverse demand, as long as the markets M_k converge to M in an appropriate sense, (1) for large k, M_k has a Cournot equilibrium and (2) the Cournot equilibria converge to the competitive equilibrium of M. (When firms are identical and have convex cost functions, this result requires that the measure of available firms in M be finite. As discussed above, this need not rule out endogenous determination of the number of active firms in other cases.) General results of this type are contained in Novshek (1984b). The existence question, (1), is also addressed in Bamon and Fraysse (1985). In their paper, Bamon and Fraysse independently prove a fixed point theorem which is similar to, but weaker than, Theorem 3. Their result directly assumes that reaction correspondences have at most one jump, which is down, and have slope everywhere greater than negative one. These assumptions are natural consequences of the assumptions they place on cost functions in their sequence of markets framework, though they may not hold in a single market.

First version received September 1983; final version accepted June 1984 (Eds.).

This research was supported by National Science Foundation Grant SES 79-25690 at the Institute for Mathematical Studies in the Social Sciences, Stanford University. I am grateful to participants in the USC Economic Theory seminar and the UCLA Mathematical Economics Theory Workshop for their comments. Comments by Kevin Roberts and a referee also helped to clarify the presentation of the results. All errors are my own.

References

Bamon, R. and Fraysse, J. (1985), "Existence of Cournot Equilibrium in Large Markets," *Econometrica* (forthcoming).

Frank, C. R., Jr. and Quandt, R. E. (1963), "On the Existence of Cournot Equilibrium," *International Economic Review* 5.

The existence of Cournot equilibrium

McManus, M. (1962), "Numbers and Size in Cournot Oligopoly," *Yorkshire Bulletin of Social and Economic Research* 14.

———, (1964), "Equilibrium, Numbers and Size in Cournot Oligopoly," *Yorkshire Bulletin of Social and Economic Research* 16.

Nishimura, K. and Friedman, J. (1981), "Existence of Nash Equilibrium in n Person Games without Quasi-concavity," *International Economic Review* 22.

Novshek, W. (1980), "Cournot Equilibrium with Free Entry," *Review of Economic Studies* 47.

———, (1984*a*), "Finding All n-firm Cournot Equilibria," *International Economic Review* 25.

———, (1984*b*), "Perfectly Competitive Markets as the Limits of Cournot Markets," *Journal of Economic Theory* 34.

Okuguchi, K. (1973), "Quasi-Competitiveness and Cournot Oligopoly," *Review of Economic Studies* 40.

Roberts, J. and Sonnenschein, H. (1976), "On the Existence of Cournot Equilibrium without Concave Profit Functions," *Journal of Economic Theory* 13.

Ruffin, R. J. (1971), "Cournot Oligopoly and Competitive Behaviour," *Review of Economic Studies* 38.

Szidarovszky, F. and Yakowitz, S. (1977), "A New Proof of the Existence and Uniqueness of the Cournot Equilibrium," *International Economic Review* 18.

CHAPTER 5

Collusive behavior in noncooperative epsilon-equilibria of oligopolies with long but finite lives

ROY RADNER

In a game of a finite number of repetitions of a Cournot-type model of an industry, if firms are satisfied to get close to (but not necessarily achieve) their optimal responses to other firms' sequential strategies, then in the resulting non-cooperative "equilibria" of the sequential market game, (1) if the lifetime of the industry is large compared to the number of firms, there are equilibria corresponding to any given duration of the cartel, whereas (2) if the number of firms is large compared to the industry's lifetime, all equilibria will be close (in some sense) to the competitive equilibrium.

1. Introduction

In 1838 Augustin Cournot introduced his model of market equilibrium, which has become known in modern game theory as a noncooperative (or Nash) equilibrium [1]. Cournot's model was intended to describe an industry with a fixed number of firms with convex cost functions, producing a homogeneous product, in which each firm's action was to choose an output (or rate of output), and in which the market price was determined by the total industry output and the market demand function. A Cournot–Nash equilibrium is a combination of outputs, one for each firm, such that no firm can increase its profit by changing its output alone.

Cournot thought of his model as describing "competition" among firms; this corresponds to what we call today the "noncooperative" character of the equilibrium. He showed that, if the number of firms is regarded as a parameter of the market, a larger number of firms would lead to a larger industry output and a lower price (in equilibrium), and that as the number of firms increased without limit, the corresponding equilibria would converge to the situation he called "unlimited competition," in which marginal cost equaled price.

If there are at least two firms, then they can make more profit than in the Cournot–Nash equilibrium (CNE) by forming a cartel in which the

Bell Laboratories, Murray Hill, NJ 07974.
Roy Radner, "Collusive Behavior in Noncooperative Epsilon-Equilibria of Oligopolies with Long but Finite Lives," *Journal of Economic Theory* 22, 2, 1980, 136–54.

total industry output is chosen to maximize total industry profit, and this profit is shared equally among the firms. This corresponds to what would be called a cooperative solution of the game.

What determines whether there will be a cooperative rather than a noncooperative outcome in the market situation? If the market situation were repeated a number of periods, then, even in the absence of some institution (such as regulation) to enforce cooperation, it would seem that the firms would have opportunities to signal their willingness to cooperate. Furthermore, the larger the number of periods, the greater would be the relative loss due to defection from the cartel and a reversion to the CNE outputs and profits. On the other hand, the larger the number of firms, the greater would be the difficulty of holding the cartel together, at least according to conventional wisdom.

If the market situation is repeated, say T times, then this gives rise to a game in which the strategies available to the players (firms) are sequential. A sequential strategy is a sequence of functions, one for each period, each of which determines the output in that period as a function of the outputs of all firms in the previous periods. One can show that every perfect Cournot–Nash equilibrium of the T-period game results in each firm producing its one-period CNE output in each period.[1] (For this result, one assumes that each firm's objective is to maximize its average, or total discounted, profit over the T periods.) I should emphasize that this property of T-period perfect CNE's is satisfied for any finite T, no matter how large. On the other hand, one can show that if T is infinite, and each firm's objective is to maximize its long-run-average profit, then there is a perfect CNE of the (infinite-period) game that results in indefinite survival of the cartel.[2] The result for infinite T goes part of the way towards confirming our intuition about the determinants of cooperation, but has the unsatisfactory feature that the infinite case is not well approximated by the case of large but finite T. Another unsatisfactory feature of the result is that it holds for any number of firms, no matter how large.

In this paper I explore the consequences of weakening the strict rationality of the Cournot–Nash equilibrium concept, so that each player is satisfied to get close to (but not necessarily achieve) his best response to the other players' strategies. Formally, an *epsilon-equilibrium* is a combination of strategies, one for each player, such that each player's strategy

---

[1] A perfect equilibrium of a sequential game is defined in Section 3. As will be seen there, the restriction that the equilibrium be perfect excludes equilibria based on unconvincing threats. The statement in the text is no longer correct if one eliminates the condition that equilibria be perfect.

[2] This is a special case of a more general theorem on perfect equilibria of infinite supergames, due to Aumann and Shapley (unpublished) and Rubinstein [5, 6].

is within epsilon in utility (e.g., average profit) of the maximum possible against the other players' strategies. I shall show that, for any fixed positive epsilon, any given number of firms, and any integer k, there is an integer T_0 such that, for all T exceeding T_0, there is a perfect epsilon-equilibrium of the T-period game in which the cartel lasts exactly k periods. In choosing T_0, it is sufficient to make $(T_0 - k)$ larger than some number that depends on epsilon and the number of firms. In particular, one can (approximately) achieve any desired fraction, k/T, by taking T large enough.

The effect on perfect epsilon-equilibria of varying the number of firms depends on the relationship between the industry demand function and the number of firms. (The latter is a parameter of the game.) Suppose first that, as we compare markets with different numbers of firms, the demand price is the same function of the *average* industry output *per firm;* call this the *replication case.* This would be the situation that would obtain if, when we doubled the number of firms, we also duplicated the population of consumers. In the replication case, one can show that, for every fixed positive epsilon and T, as the number of firms increases without limit all perfect epsilon-equilibria approach competitive equilibrium (Cournot's "unlimited competition") in the following sense. For every positive ϵ, T, and N (>1), there is a number $B(\epsilon, T, N)$ such that, in every perfect ϵ-equilibrium of the T-period game, each firm's output and total industry output at each date are all within $B(\epsilon, T, N)$ of their corresponding one-period CNE values. The bounds $B(\epsilon, T, N)$ can be chosen so that, (1) for every ϵ and T, the ratios $B(\epsilon, T, N)/N^{1/2}$ are uniformly bounded in N, and (2) for every T and N, $B(\epsilon, T, N)$ approaches zero as ϵ approaches zero. One can further show that, for fixed ϵ and T, as N increases without limit, at every date (1) average output per firm approaches the competitive equilibrium output per firm, (2) market price approaches marginal cost, and (3) every firm's relative share of total industry output approaches zero. Finally, under the same conditions, the difference between each firm's profit and its one-period CNE profit is uniformly bounded in N, and approaches zero as ϵ approaches zero.

Leaving the replication case, suppose now that the industry demand function is fixed as we compare markets with different numbers of firms; call this the *fixed-demand* case. In this case, one can show that, for any fixed number of periods, T, there is a number B (depending on epsilon and T) such that, in all perfect epsilon-equilibria of the T-period game, the outputs and profits of all firms, total industry output and profit, and market price are all within B of their corresponding one-period CNE values, *uniformly in the number of firms.* Furthermore, the bound B tends to zero as epsilon tends to zero, with T fixed. This implies that, in the fixed-demand case, for any fixed number of periods and *small* epsilon, all perfect epsilon-equilibria are "close" to competitive equilibrium in terms of outputs, profits, and prices, for a sufficiently large number of firms.

Note that the effect of increasing the number of firms on reducing the possibilities for cooperation is observed in the replication case, but not in the fixed-demand case. In both cases, reducing epsilon reduces the possibilities for cooperation (i.e., keeps all perfect epsilon-equilibria closer to the CNE), and increasing the number of firms brings the CNE closer, of course, to the competitive equilibrium. Thus, for the replication case, one can paraphrase the results of this paper as follows: if firms are satisfied to get close to (but not necessarily achieve) their optimal responses to other firms' strategies, then in the resulting noncooperative "equilibria" of the sequential market game, (1) if the lifetime of the industry is large compared to the number of firms, there are equilibria corresponding to any given duration of the cartel, whereas (2) if the number of firms is large compared to the lifetime of the industry, all equilibria will be close (in some sense) to the competitive equilibrium.

Although the replication case is the one of central interest here, I shall use the fixed demand case (Section 5) as a stepping-stone in the analysis of the replication case (Section 6).

As will be seen below, several alternative definitions of perfect epsilon-equilibria may be reasonably considered. I shall begin the analysis with the simplest one (Section 4). A more satisfactory definition is introduced in Section 7. An important behavioral implication of this second definition is that cooperation will tend to break down as the industry approaches the horizon T. In Section 8, I discuss some alternative interpretations of epsilon.

The entire analysis in the present paper is carried out only for a special model, in which the market demand function is linear, and all firms have the same linear homogeneous cost function (average and marginal costs are equal and constant). However, the analysis can be extended easily to the case in which each firm has a fixed (setup) cost of production, and in which there is free entry. In this case, the number of firms in the industry is endogenous.[3] This extension will be discussed in a forthcoming paper.

2. The one-period Cournot game

Consider an industry producing a single homogeneous product, with N firms. The cost to a single firm of producing a quantity Q is γQ. If firm

---

[3] For this situation, Cournot–Nash equilibria in the one-period game have been studied by Novshek [2] and by Novshek and Sonnenschein [3].

j produces quantity Q_j, the market-clearing price P is determined by the industry demand function

$$P = \alpha - \beta \sum_{j=1}^{N} Q_j, \tag{2.1}$$

if this is positive; otherwise it is zero. The profit to firm i is therefore

$$PQ_i - \gamma Q_i = \left(\alpha - \beta \sum_{j=1}^{N} Q_j\right) Q_i - \gamma Q_i$$

$$= \left(\alpha - \gamma - \beta \sum_{j \neq i} Q_j\right) Q_i - \beta Q_i^2.$$

Assume that $\alpha > \gamma$, and define

$$Q_i' \equiv \sum_{j \neq i} Q_j, \quad \delta \equiv \alpha - \gamma; \tag{2.2}$$

then firm i's profit can be expressed as

$$p(Q_i, Q_i') \equiv (\delta - \beta Q_i') Q_i - \beta Q_i^2. \tag{2.3}$$

Equations (2) and (3) define a game with N players, in which the pure strategy of player i is a nonnegative number Q_i, and his utility is $p(Q_i, Q_i')$.

It is easily verified that, given Q_i', the Q_i that maximizes i's profit is

$$r(Q_i') \quad \begin{array}{ll} \equiv \dfrac{\delta - \beta Q_i'}{2\beta}, & \text{if } \textit{this is nonnegative,} \\[2mm] \equiv 0, & \textit{otherwise.} \end{array} \tag{2.4}$$

I shall call $r(Q_i')$ firm i's *best response* to Q_i'. If the best response is positive, firm i's corresponding maximum profit is

$$g(Q_i') = \frac{(\delta - \beta Q_i')^2}{4\beta}; \tag{2.5}$$

otherwise it is zero. A *Cournot–Nash equilibrium* (CNE) is an N-tuple (Q_i) of outputs such that, for each i, Q_i is the best response to $\sum_{j \neq i} Q_j$. In other words, a CNE is a solution (Q_i) of

$$r\left(\sum_{j \neq i} Q_j\right) = Q_i, \quad i = i, \dots, N.$$

It is easily verified that the unique CNE is given by

$$Q_i = Q_N^* \equiv \frac{\delta}{(N+1)\beta}, \quad i = 1, \dots, N, \tag{2.6}$$

and the corresponding CNE profit per firm is

126

$$\frac{\delta^2}{\beta(N+1)^2}. \tag{2.7}$$

Note that the total industry CNE output is

$$\frac{N\delta}{(N+1)\beta}, \tag{2.8}$$

and the total industry CNE profit is

$$\frac{N\delta^2}{(N+1)^2\beta}. \tag{2.9}$$

Therefore, as N increases without bound, total CNE industry output approaches δ/β, total industry CNE profit approaches zero, and CNE price approaches $\alpha - \delta = \gamma$ (i.e., marginal cost), all of which conditions characterize a competitive equilibrium.

If the industry acts as a cartel to maximize total industry profit then the cartel output is $(\delta/2\beta)$, and the corresponding cartel profit is $(\delta^2/4\beta)$. If the cartel output and profit were divided equally among the firms, then the corresponding cartel output per firm would be

$$\hat{Q}_N \equiv \frac{\delta}{2\beta N}, \tag{2.10}$$

and the cartel profit per firm would be

$$\frac{\delta^2}{4\beta N}. \tag{2.11}$$

Note that if $N > 1$, then the cartel profit per firm is strictly greater than the CNE profit per firm, so that (from the point of view of the firms) the CNE is not Pareto optimal.

If the capacities of the firms are sufficiently large, then no coalition of fewer than N firms can guarantee itself more than a zero profit. That is to say, for any output of the coalition, there is an output of the other firms such that the coalition's profit is not greater than zero. Hence in this case, the core is the set of all nonnegative allocations of the cartel profit among the firms.[4] Given the symmetry among the firms, the equal division of the cartel profits is a "reasonable" target for cooperation, and in any case is the one to which attention will be given in this paper.

In what follows, I shall simplify the formulas by taking $\beta = 1$ and $\delta = 1$, unless notice is given to the contrary. This normalization will not entail any essential loss of generality.

---

[4] For a characterization of the core with arbitrary capacities, see Radner [4].

3. The several-period Cournot game

Consider now a sequential, *T-period,* game in which the one-period game is repeated T times (T finite). The resulting utility to a firm is assumed to be the average of the T one-period profits. Let Q_{it} denote the output of firm i at date t ($1 \le t \le T$), i.e., during the ith one-period game. A pure strategy for firm i is a sequence of functions, σ_{it}, one for each date t; the function for date t determines i's output at t as a function of the outputs of all firms at all previous dates. A Cournot–Nash equilibrium of the T-period game is a combination of strategies, one for each firm, such that each firm's strategy is a best response to the combination of the other firms' strategies.

The concept of *perfect* equilibrium of the T-period game has been introduced by Selten (1975) to rule out equilibria in which players use threats that are not credible. For every data t, let H_t denote the *history* of all the firms' outputs through t, i.e., the array of outputs Q_{ik}, $i=1,...,N$, $k=1,...,t$. For any sequential strategy σ_i for firm i, any date t and any history H_{t-1} let $\sigma_i[t, H_{t-1}]$ denote the *continuation* of σ_i from date t on, given the history H_{t-1}. A strategy combination (σ_i) is a *perfect* CNE if, for every date t and history H_{t-1}, the strategy combination $(\sigma_i[t, H_{t-1}])$ is a CNE of the sequential game corresponding to the remaining dates $t,...,T$. Note that in the definition of a perfect CNE one must test, for each t, whether the combination of continuations is a CNE for *all* possible histories H_{t-1}, not just the history that would be produced by the strategy combination (σ_i).

It is easy to verify that in every perfect CNE of the T-period game, each firm produces output Q^* at each date, where Q^* is given by (2.6). This can be seen by "working backwards," since at the end of period t the firms face a $(T-t)$-period game. The resulting utility to each firm is, from (2.7), $1/(N+1)^2$. (Recall that $\beta = \delta = 1$.)

On the other hand, if each firm were to produce its cartel output $\hat{Q}$ at each date [see (2.10)], then the resulting utility to each player would be $1/4N$. Since there are several periods, the firms have the opportunity to react differently to cooperative and noncooperative moves by the other firms. For example, consider the following strategy: firm i produces output $\hat{Q}$ in each period as long as every other firm has been doing the same; thereafter firm i produces Q^* in each period. Call this strategy C_T. Formally, define D_i as follows:

$$D_i \begin{aligned} &= \infty, \quad \text{if } Q_{jt} = \hat{Q} \text{ for all } t \text{ and all } j \ne i, \\ &= \min\{t: Q_{jt} \ne \hat{Q} \text{ for some } j \ne i\}, \quad \text{otherwise.} \end{aligned} \tag{3.1}$$

The pure strategy C_T is defined by:

$$Q_{it} \begin{array}{ll} = \hat{Q} & \text{if } t \le D_i, \\ = Q^* & \text{if } t > D_i. \end{array}$$

(3.2)

More generally, for any integer k between 0 and T define the pure strategy C_k by:

$$Q_{it} \begin{array}{ll} = \hat{Q} & \text{if } t \le \min(D_i, k), \\ = Q^* & \text{if } t > \min(D_i, k). \end{array}$$

(3.3)

Note that if i uses the strategy C_0, then he always produces the CNE output Q^*.

The strategy C_k is a special case of a slightly more general class, which I shall call *trigger strategies of order k*. Let D_i be defined again as in (3.1) and let Q^D be some output. If $D_i \ge k$, then

$$Q_{it} \begin{array}{ll} = \hat{Q} & \text{if } 5 \le k, \\ = Q^D & \text{if } t = k+1, \\ = Q^* & \text{if } t \ge k+2. \end{array}$$

(3.4)

If $D_i \le k$, then

$$Q_{it} \begin{array}{ll} = \hat{Q} & \text{if } t \le D_i, \\ = Q^* & \text{if } t > D_i. \end{array}$$

(3.5)

One might call Q^D the *defection output*, which i uses once only if all other firms have stayed with the cartel for (at least) k periods.

Suppose now that all firms other than i use the same trigger strategy of order $k > 0$, with some defection output $Q^D > \hat{Q}$. I shall show that i's best response is a trigger strategy of order $(k-1)$, with a defection output equal to

$$\tilde{Q} \equiv r[(N-1)\hat{Q}] = \frac{N+1}{4N}.$$

(3.6)

Note that $\tilde{Q}$ is the best *one-period* response to a total output of $(N-1)\hat{Q}$ by all the other firms, and yields a one-period profit of

$$\frac{(N+1)^2}{16N^2}.$$

(3.7)

To prove this, first observe that if at some date t any firm i produces an output different from $\hat{Q}$, then at all subsequent dates all firms other than

129

i will produce Q^*, and it will be optimal for firm i to do the same. Hence firm i's best response has the property that

$$Q_{jt} \neq \hat{Q} \quad \text{for some } j \text{ implies}$$
$$Q_{it'} = Q^* \quad \text{for all } t' > t. \tag{3.8}$$

It follows that firm i's best response to the given trigger strategies of order k is a trigger strategy of some order n. It is straightforward to verify that if $n < k$ then the optimal defection output is $\tilde{Q}$, with resulting *total* profit

$$\frac{n}{4N} + \frac{(N+1)^2}{16N^2} + \frac{T-n-1}{(N+1)^2}. \tag{3.9}$$

If $n = k$, then the optimal defection output is $r[(N-1)Q\tilde{Q}^D]$, and the corresponding total profit is

$$\frac{k}{4N} + g[(N+1)Q^D] + \frac{T-k-1}{(N+1)^2}. \tag{3.10}$$

Finally, if $n > k$, then i's defection output is irrelevant and the corresponding profit is

$$\frac{k}{4N} + p[\hat{Q}, (N-1)Q^D] + \frac{T-k-1}{(N+1)^2}. \tag{3.11}$$

In (3.10) and (3.11), if $k = T$, then it is to be understood that the final term in the equation is zero. Since $Q^D > \hat{Q}$;

$$\left(\frac{N+1}{4N}\right)^2 = g[(N-1)\hat{Q}] > g[(N-1)Q^D] \geq p[\hat{Q}, (N-1)Q^D].$$

Hence since (3.9) is increasing in n, it follows that i's optimal response has $n = (k-1)$. This completes the proof that i's *optimal response to a trigger strategy of order $k > 0$ with defection output $Q^D > \hat{Q}$ is a trigger strategy of order $k-1$ with defection output $\tilde{Q}$. The resulting average profit for i is

$$\left(\frac{1}{T}\right)\left[\frac{k-1}{4N} + \left(\frac{N+1}{4N}\right)^2 + \frac{T-k}{(N+1)^2}\right]. \tag{3.12}$$

Note that neither i's optimal response nor his resulting average profit depend on the other firms' defection output.

In particular, if all firms $j(\neq i)$ use the trigger strategy C_T, then i's best response gives him an average profit of

$$\frac{1}{T}\left[\frac{T-1}{4N} + \left(\frac{N+1}{4N}\right)^2\right], \tag{3.13}$$

whereas if *all* firms use C_T, then every firm's average profit is $(1/4N)$, which is the cartel profit (per firm). The difference between (3.13) and the cartel profit per firm is

$$\left(\frac{1}{T}\right)\left(\frac{N-1}{4N}\right)^2. \tag{3.14}$$

Hence, as T increases without limit, the advantage to any one firm of defecting from the cartel one period before the end of the game approaches zero.

4. Epsilon-equilibria

In the previous section it was noted that, in the T-period game, all perfect Cournot–Nash equilibria have the property that each firm produces the one-period CNE output in each period. On the other hand, the advantage to any one firm of defecting from the cartel approaches zero as T gets large, provided the other firms use trigger strategies of order T.

These considerations suggest a weakened form of the Cournot–Nash equilibrium concept. For any positive number ϵ, an *ϵ-equilibrium* is an N-tuple of strategies, one for each firm, such that each firm's average profit is within ϵ of the maximum average profit it could obtain against the other firms' strategies. In this and the following sections I shall explore some of the properties of epsilon-equilibria in the T-period Cournot game. I do not, however, have a complete characterization of epsilon-equilibria in this game.

The first candidate for an epsilon-equilibrium is the situation in which each firm uses the trigger strategy C_k (with defection output Q^*). From (3.10) and (3.12) we see that the difference in average profit between the best response and C_k, for an individual firm, is

$$\left(\frac{1}{T}\right)\left[\left(\frac{N+1}{4N}\right)^2 - \frac{1}{4N}\right] = \left(\frac{1}{T}\right)\left(\frac{N-1}{4N}\right)^2. \tag{4.1}$$

Hence the N-tuple (C_k) is an ϵ-equilibrium with $k > 0$ if and only if

$$\left(\frac{1}{T}\right)\left(\frac{N-1}{4N}\right)^2 \leq \epsilon \quad \text{or} \quad T \geq \left(\frac{1}{\epsilon}\right)\left(\frac{N-1}{4N}\right)^2. \tag{4.2}$$

Note that (4.2) is independent of k, so that either (C_k) is an ϵ-equilibrium for all $k = 1, \ldots, T$, or for none. Note, too, that for fixed ϵ, (4.2) is satisfied uniformly in N for sufficiently large T. Of course, (C_0) is a Cournot–Nash equilibrium, so it is an ϵ-equilibrium for all ϵ.

The concept of perfect CNE can be extended to epsilon-equilibria as follows. A strategy combination (σ_i) is a *perfect ϵ-equilibrium* if for every date t, every history H_{t-1}, and every firm i, the continuation of i's strategy

131

from date t on, given the history H_{t-1}, is within ϵ of being the best response to the corresponding continuations of the other firms' strategies. In this definition, the utility of a continuation of a strategy is the average of the profits in *all* T periods. (For an alternative definition, see Section 7.)

It is easy to verify that (4.2) is a necessary and sufficient condition for the combination (C_k) of trigger strategies to be a perfect ϵ-equilibrium. Hence, *for any $\epsilon > 0$ there is a T_ϵ such that, for all $T \geq T_\epsilon$ and all $k = 0, \ldots, T$, there is a perfect ϵ-equilibrium in which each firm produces its cartel output for exactly k periods.* Furthermore, one can take T_ϵ to be independent of the number of firms.

An examination of (3.9)–(3.11) shows that one can get similar results for N-tuples of trigger strategies that use defection outputs other than Q^*, and even for N-tuples of trigger strategies that differ among firms in both the orders of the trigger strategies and the defection outputs. No attempt will be made here to characterize all such perfect epsilon-equilibria, but it is clear that for fixed ϵ, the larger T is the larger, in some sense, is the set of perfect ϵ-equilibria.

In the rest of this paper, all epsilon-equilibria are to be understood as perfect, unless specific notice is given to the contrary.

5. Large number of firms: the fixed-demand case

In the last section I considered how the set of (perfect) ϵ-equilibria varied with T, the number of periods, with the number of firms fixed. In this section I consider the effect of increasing N, the number of firms, with the horizon, T, fixed. I first analyze the case in which the total industry demand function remains fixed as the number of firms varies. The results for this case will be used to analyze the more interesting, but slightly more complicated, replication case (Section 6).

To begin the analysis of the fixed-demand case, first observe that, by (4.2), for fixed T, there is no (C_k) ϵ-equilibrium ($k \geq 1$) for ϵ sufficiently small.

I shall prove, in addition, a result that is in some ways stronger. Roughly speaking, I shall show that if ϵ is small then all ϵ-equilibria are close to the CNE, *uniformly in N.* To be precise I shall show: for every $\epsilon > 0$ and $T \geq 1$ there is a number $B(\epsilon, T)$ such that for every $N > 1$ and every ϵ-equilibrium the following are all bounded by $B(\epsilon, T)$:

$$|Q_{it} - Q_N^*|, \quad \left| \sum_{i=1}^{N} Q_{it} - NQ_N^* \right|,$$

$$\left| p\left(Q_{it}, \sum_{j \neq i} Q_{jt} \right) - \frac{1}{(N+1)^2} \right|, \tag{5.1}$$

for $i = 1, \ldots, N$, $t = 1, \ldots, T$. In addition, for every T

$$\lim_{\epsilon \to 0} B(\epsilon, T) = 0. \tag{5.2}$$

The first line of (5.1) is the difference between firm i's output in period t and CNE output; the second line is the difference between total industry output in period t and industry CNE output; and the third line is the difference between firm i's profit in period t and CNE profit per firm. It follows that, for any positive number d, and any horizon T, there is a positive ϵ such that, for all N and all ϵ-equilibria of the T-period game with N firms, industry outputs and market prices in all periods $t = 1, \ldots, T$ will be within d of their corresponding one-period CNE values (note that ϵ does not depend on N). In particular, as N increases without limit, the corresponding one-period CNE values will converge to their respective competitive equilibrium values, and hence any corresponding sequence of ϵ-equilibria will approach the "neighborhood" of competitive equilibrium defined by the distance d, with respect to total industry output and price.

To prove (5.1) and (5.2), I shall first do the one-period case, and then make an induction on T. For the one-period case, an ϵ-equilibrium is an N-tuple $(Q_1, \ldots, Q_N)$ satisfying

$$p\left(Q_i, \sum_{j \neq i} Q_j\right) \geq g\left(\sum_{j \neq i} Q_j\right) - \epsilon, \quad i = 1, \ldots, N. \tag{5.3}$$

Define new variables x_i and x_i' by

$$x_i \equiv Q_i - Q_N^* = Q_i - \frac{1}{N+1},$$

$$x_i' \equiv \sum_{j \neq i} x_j. \tag{5.4}$$

Using (2.3) and (2.5) one easily verifies that (5.3) is equivalent to

$$(x_i + (x_i'/2))^2 \leq \epsilon, \quad i = 1, \ldots, N,$$

or to

$$|x_i + x.| \leq 2h, \quad i = 1, \ldots, N,$$

where $\tag{5.5}$

$$x. \equiv \sum_{j=1}^{N} x_j, \quad h \equiv (\epsilon)^{1/2}.$$

Summing the inequalities (5.5) one gets

$$|x.| \leq \frac{2Nh}{N+1}; \tag{5.6}$$

this and (5.5) imply

$$|x_i| \leq \frac{2(2N+1)h}{N+1},$$ (5.7)

$$|x_i'| \leq \frac{2(3N+1)h}{N+1}.$$ (5.8)

Lemma. *If* $|x| \leq b$ *and* $|x'| \leq b$, *then*

$$|p[Q_N^* + x, (N-1)Q_N^* + x'] - p[Q_N^*, (N-1)Q_N^*]| \leq \frac{b}{N+1} + 2b^2.$$

(5.9)

Proof. The inequality can be verified using (2.3), (2.6), and (2.7). ∎

Note that the right-hand sides of inequalities (5.6)–(5.8) are all dominated by $6h$. Hence, by the lemma, one can take

$$B(\epsilon, 1) = \max\left[6h, \frac{6h}{N+1} + 2(6h)^2 \right].$$ (5.10)

For ϵ sufficiently small ($(\epsilon)^{1/2} \leq 1/18$), the right side of (5.10) is $6h = 6(\epsilon)^{1/2}$.

Now make the induction hypothesis that the main result is true for any number of periods up to and including T. Fix ϵ, and consider any $(T+1)$-period ϵ-equilibrium. Given the initial outputs Q_{i1}, $i = 1, \ldots, N$, the remaining T-period strategies constitute, *a fortiori*, a T-period, ϵ'-equilibrium, where

$$\epsilon' \equiv \frac{(T+1)\epsilon}{T}.$$ (5.11)

Let i be any particular firm, which will remain fixed for the time being, let $Q = Q_{i1}$ be i's output in period 1, and let S denote the strategy that i follows during periods 2 through $(T+1)$. Given the strategies of the other firms, one may denote i's average profit as

$$\frac{p(Q, Q')}{T+1} + V(Q, S) \equiv \pi(Q, S),$$ (5.12)

where Q' is the total output in period one of all the firms other than i.

The induction hypothesis is that all of the quantities in (5.1), for $i = 1, \ldots, N$ and $t = 2, \ldots, T+1$, are bounded by $b \equiv B(\epsilon', T)$. Actually, I shall strengthen the induction hypothesis to add the following inequalities:

$$\left| \sum_{j \neq i} Q_{jt} - (N-1)Q_N^* \right| \leq b, \quad i = 1, \ldots, N, \ t = 2, \ldots, T+1.$$ (5.13)

134

The definition of epsilon-equilibrium implies that

$$\pi(Q, S) \geq M - \epsilon,$$

where   (5.14)

$$M \equiv \max_{q,s} \pi(q, s).$$

[In the definition of M, (q, s) ranges over all $(T+1)$-period strategies for firm i, holding constant the ϵ-equilibrium strategies of the other firms.] This last is equivalent to

$$\frac{p(Q, Q')}{T+1} + V(Q, S) \geq M - \epsilon,$$

or

$$p(Q, Q') \geq (T+1)[M - \epsilon - V(Q, S)].$$ (5.15)

By the induction hypothesis,

$$\frac{(T+1)V(Q, S)}{T} - \frac{1}{(N+1)^2} \leq b.$$ (5.16)

To get a bound on M, note that

$$(T+1)M \geq g(Q') + Tm,$$

where

$$m \equiv \max_{x} \min_{Y} \{ p(X, Y) : |Y - (N-1)Q_N^*| \leq b \}.$$ (5.17)

One easily verifies that

$$m = g[(N-1)Q_N^* + b] = \frac{1}{(N+1)^2} - \frac{b}{(N+1)} + \frac{b^2}{4}.$$ (5.18)

Putting together (5.15)–(5.18), one has

$$p(Q, Q^*) \geq g(Q') - \epsilon'',$$

where

$$\epsilon'' \equiv \frac{T(N+2)b}{(N+1)} + (T+1)\epsilon.$$ (5.19)

The inequality (5.19) holds for all firms i. In other words, in a $(T+1)$-period ϵ-equilibrium, the first-period outputs constitute a one-period ϵ''-equilibrium, where ϵ'' is given by (5.19) and

$$b = B\left[\frac{(T+1)}{T}\epsilon, T\right].$$ (5.20)

Hence, by the one-period case, the quantities in (5.1) and (5.13), with $t = 1$, are all bounded by

$$b' \equiv 6(\epsilon'')^{1/2} = 6\left[\frac{T(N+2)b}{(N+1)} + (T+1)\epsilon\right]^{1/2}, \tag{5.21}$$

provided that $\epsilon''^{1/2} \leq 1/18$. If we take

$$B(\epsilon, T+1) = \max\{b', B(\epsilon, T)\}, \tag{5.22}$$

then the induction step is completed, as far as the inequalities (5.1) and (5.13) are concerned. Furthermore, (5.20)–(5.22) determine a recursion formula for the bounds $B(\epsilon, T)$, which with the formulas (5.5) and (5.10) for $B(\epsilon, 1)$ prove (5.2), i.e., that $B(\epsilon, T)$ tends to zero as ϵ tends to zero, for fixed T.

6. Large numbers of firms: the replication case

In the replication case, the demand function depends on the number of firms, so that corresponding to (2.1) we have

$$P = \alpha - \frac{\beta_1 Q}{N}, \tag{6.1}$$

where Q is the total industry output, P is the demand price, and β_1 is a parameter that is independent of N, the number of firms. One may motivate this formulation in terms of replicating an industry. Consider an industry with 1 firm and a given population of M potential buyers, whose demand function is given by

$$Q = \frac{\alpha - P}{\beta_1}. \tag{6.2}$$

The N-fold replication of this industry is made up of N firms, together with a population of NM potential buyers with the same per capita demand at any price as the original population. The resulting demand function is then

$$\frac{Q}{N} = \frac{\alpha - P}{\beta_1}.$$

which is equivalent to (6.1). Without essential loss of generality, I shall take $\beta_1 = 1$ and $\delta = \alpha - \gamma = 1$.

Corresponding to the formulas of Section 2, one has the following formulas, obtained by everywhere replacing β by $1/N$. Firm i's profit function is

$$p(Q_i, Q_i') = \left(1 - \frac{Q_i'}{N}\right)Q_i - \frac{Q_i^2}{N}. \tag{6.3}$$

Its optimal response to Q_i' is

$$r(Q_i') \quad \begin{aligned} &= \frac{N-Q_i'}{2N}, \quad \text{if this is positive,} \\ &= 0, \qquad \text{otherwise,} \end{aligned} \tag{6.4}$$

and its corresponding profit is

$$g(Q_i') = \frac{(N-Q_i')^2}{4N}, \tag{6.5}$$

if this is nonnegative, and zero otherwise.

The one-period CNE output and profit per firm are given by

$$Q_N^* = \frac{N}{N+1}, \tag{6.6}$$

$$g[(N-1)Q_N^*] = \frac{N}{(N+1)^2}. \tag{6.7}$$

The one-period cartel output and profit per firm are

$$\hat{Q}_N = \tfrac{1}{2}, \tag{6.8}$$

$$p[\hat{Q}_N, (N-1)\hat{Q}_N] = \tfrac{1}{4}. \tag{6.9}$$

Firm i's best response if each other firm produces the cartel output is

$$r[(N-1)\hat{Q}_N] = \frac{N+1}{4N}, \tag{6.10}$$

with corresponding profit

$$g[(N-1)\hat{Q}_N] = \frac{(N+1)^2}{16N}. \tag{6.11}$$

Turning to the T-period game, one easily verifies that the strategy combination in which each firm has the trigger strategy C_k (cf. Section 4) is an ϵ-equilibrium if and only if

$$T \geq \left(\frac{N}{2}\right)\left(\frac{N-1}{4N}\right)^2; \tag{6.12}$$

compare this with (4.2). Hence, as in the fixed-demand case, for every ϵ and N, every (C_k) strategy combination is an ϵ-equilibrium for all sufficiently large T. However, in this case one gets the result that, for fixed ϵ and T, no (C_k) strategy combination ($k > 0$) is an ϵ-equilibrium for sufficiently large N. In other words, *for any fixed ϵ and number of periods, the cartel cannot survive at all if the number of firms is large enough.*

Corresponding to the rest of the analysis in Section 5, one has the following results. For every ϵ, T, and $N(>1)$, there is a number $B(\epsilon, T, N)$ such that, in every ϵ-equilibrium, the following quantities are bounded by $B(\epsilon, T, N)$:

$$|Q_{it} - Q_N^*|,$$

$$\left| \sum_j q_{it} - NQ_N^* \right|, \tag{6.13}$$

for $i = 1, \ldots, N$ and $t = 1, \ldots, T$; the bounds $B(\epsilon, T, N)$ may be chosen so that, for every ϵ and T,

$$\frac{B(\epsilon, T, N)}{N^{1/2}} \text{ is uniformly bounded in } N, \tag{6.14}$$

and for every T and N,

$$\lim_{\epsilon \to 0} B(\epsilon, T, N) = 0. \tag{6.15}$$

It follows from (6.6) that average output per firm approaches 1, and market price approaches $1 - \alpha = \gamma$ (marginal cost) as N increases without limit. In addition, in every period every firm i's *relative* share of total industry output, which is

$$\frac{Q_{it}}{\sum_j Q_{jt}} = \frac{(1/N)Q_{it}}{(1/N) \sum_j Q_{jt}},$$

converges to zero as N gets large. Finally, one can show that, in every period, every firm i's profit is within

$$\frac{B(\epsilon, T, N)}{N+1} + \frac{2[B(\epsilon, T, N)]^2}{N} \tag{6.16}$$

of the one-period CNE profit, which is $N/(N+1)^2$, and this bound is uniformly bounded in N, and goes to zero with ϵ.

Thus, in these various ways, for large N, ϵ-equilibria are close to competitive equilibrium.

I shall omit the proof of these results, which parallels the argument in Section 5. The key facts are that, for the one-period case, Eqs. (5.5)–(5.8) are still valid, but with

$$h = (N\epsilon)^{1/2}, \tag{6.17}$$

and in the Lemma of Section 5, the right side of (5.9) must be replaced by

$$\frac{b}{N+1} + \frac{2b^2}{N}, \tag{6.18}$$

138

which is less than b for

$$b < \frac{N^2}{2(N+1)}. \tag{6.19}$$

In particular, for the one-period case one can take

$$B(\epsilon, 1, N) = (N\epsilon)^{1/2}, \tag{6.20}$$

provided that

$$(\epsilon)^{1/2} \le \frac{N}{12(N+1)}, \tag{6.21}$$

7. An alternative definition of perfect epsilon-equilibrium

As an alternative to the definition of perfect epsilon-equilibrium given in Section 4, one can take the utility of the continuation of a strategy to be the average of the profits in the remaining periods, rather than the average of the profits in all T periods.[5] This change leads to a definition of perfect epsilon-equilibrium that is more restrictive, in the sense that, for every positive epsilon, the set of perfect epsilon-equilibria is smaller. Results analogous to those of Sections 5 and 6 can be derived for this definition; I omit the details. However, the results in Section 4, on trigger strategies, are changed in an interesting way. For a fixed positive epsilon, and a fixed number of firms, the combination (C_k) of trigger strategies is a perfect epsilon-equilibrium for all sufficiently large horizons T and all k not too close to T, namely, if and only if

$$T - k \ge \left(\frac{1}{\epsilon}\right)\left(\frac{N-1}{4N}\right)^2 - 1.$$

Thus, for this alternative definition of epsilon-equilibrium, *a cartel held together by trigger strategies will break down as the industry approaches the horizon T.*

8. Interpretations of epsilon

Why should a firm be satisfied with a less-than-optimal response to the strategies of other firms? One type of answer refers to the various costs of discovering and using alternative strategies, and alludes to the possibility that a truly optimal response might be more costly to discover and use than some alternative, "nearly optimal" strategy. In this interpretation, the "epsilon" for a particular firm represents a judgment of the firm that

[5] This alternative was suggested to me by Sanford Grossman and Robert Rosenthal.

the additional benefits from improving its strategy would be outweighed by the additional costs. (In the present analysis, all firms were assumed to have the same epsilon, but this simplification is not strictly needed for the results.) It would be consistent with the spirit of the model for this judgment to be in part subjective, rather than necessarily based on some precise calculation of benefits and costs.

A second interpretation of epsilon might be based on the supposition that the firms realize that strict optimization of each firm's response to the other firms' strategies would lead to a breakdown of the cartel. This approach is intuitively appealing, but I am not aware of any satisfactory formal model of rational behavior on which it could be based.

Recall that, in the model of the present paper, it is assumed that each firm uses the criterion of average profit per period to compare strategies; thus epsilon is measured in "dollars per period." This scale of measurement would be consistent with the cost-of-decision interpretation of epsilon-equilibrium. In a more general treatment, epsilon would be measured in units of utility. However, epsilon-equilibria would not be invariant under transformations of the utility functions of the firms that change the unit of measurement of utility. For example, if the preferences of a firm were scaled in terms of a von Neumann–Morgenstern utility function, then epsilon-equilibria would not be invariant under all transformations of the utility function that leave the firm's preferences invariant. A solution to this last problem would be to adopt a "canonical" utility representation for each firm, and then to interpret epsilon with reference to those canonical utility functions. This would be equivalent, for each firm, to interpreting epsilon as a given *percentage* of the difference in utility between two reference profits. Within this framework, the interpretation of the results of the present paper is straightforward, with the proviso that, for those situations in which the number of firms increases without limit, some condition of "similarity" of the epsilons of the different firms would have to be satisfied (as would naturally occur in the replication case).

Acknowledgments

I am grateful to R. Rosenthal, C. Futia, and A. Mas-Colell for helpful discussions of this problem. Preliminary versions of this paper were presented at the North American regional meeting of the Econometric Society, Boulder, CO, June 1978, and at the IMSSS, Stanford University, July 1978.

References

1. A. Cournot, "Researches into the Mathematical Principles of the Theory of Wealth," Nathaniel T. Bacon, trans., Macmillan, New York/London, 1897;

reprinted with notes by Irving Fisher, Macmillan, 1927; reprinted, Richard D. Irwin, Inc., Homewood, Ill., 1963; originally published as "Recherches sur les principes mathématiques de la théorie des Richesses," Hachette, Paris, 1838.

2. W. Novshek, "Nash–Cournot Equilibrium with Entry," Discussion Paper No. 303, Center for Math. Studies in Econ. and Man. Sci., Northwestern University, August 1977.
3. W. Novshek and H. Sonnenschein, Cournot and Walras equilibrium, *J. Econ. Theory* 19 (1978), 223–266.
4. R. Radner, Notes on the core of a cartel, unpublished lecture notes, Dept. of Econ., University of California, Berkeley, 1977.
5. A. Rubinstein, "Equilibrium in Supergames," Research Memorandum No. 25, Center for Research in Math. Economics and Game Theory, The Hebrew University, Jerusalem, May 1977.
6. A. Rubinstein, Equilibrium in supergames with the overtaking criterion, *J. Econ. Theory* 21 (1979), 1–9.
7. R. Selten, Re-examination of the perfectness concept for equilibrium points in extensive games, *Int. J. Game Theory* 4 (1975), 25–55.

CHAPTER 6

A non-cooperative equilibrium
for supergames

JAMES W. FRIEDMAN

I. Introduction

John Nash has contributed to game theory and economics two solution concepts for nonconstant sum games. One, the non-cooperative solution [9], is a generalization of the minimax theorem for two person zero sum games and of the Cournot solution; and the other, the cooperative solution [10], is completely new. It is the purpose of this paper to present a non-cooperative equilibrium concept, applicable to supergames, which fits the Nash (non-cooperative) definition and also has some features resembling the Nash cooperative solution. "Supergame" describes the playing of an infinite sequence of "ordinary games" over time.[1] Oligopoly may profitably be viewed as a supergame. In each time period the players are in a game, and they know they will be in similar games with the same other players in future periods.

The most novel element of the present paper is in the introduction of a completely new concept of solution for non-cooperative supergames. In addition to proposing this solution, a proof of its existence is given. It is also argued that the usual notions of "threat" which are found in the literature of game theory make no sense in non-cooperative supergames. There is something analogous to threat, called "temptation," which does have an intuitive appeal and is related to the solution which is proposed.

In section II the ordinary game will be described, the non-cooperative equilibrium defined and its existence established. Section III contains a description of supergames and supergame strategies. In section IV a definition and discussion of a non-cooperative equilibrium for supergames is given. This equilibrium shares some of the attributes of the

University of Rochester.

James W. Friedman, "A Non-Cooperative Equilibrium for Supergames," *Review of Economic Studies*, 38, 1, 1971, pp. 1–12.

The author gratefully acknowledges the support of the National Science Foundation in the research reported here.

[1] Some discussion of early work on supergames may be found in Luce and Raiffa [8], and some interesting developments in cooperative supergames, by Aumann, is begun in [1].

Non-cooperative equilibrium for supergames

Nash–Harsanyi [10, 6] cooperative solution, and is very much in the spirit of the solution proposed several years ago by Professor Robert L. Bishop in the *American Economic Review* [2]. In section V existence will be proved, in section VI some assumptions will be relaxed, and in section VII economic applications will be discussed.

II. The game and the Nash non-cooperative equilibrium

An "ordinary game" is a game in which each player has a set of strategies which is a compact, convex subset of a Euclidean space of finite dimension, there are a finite number of players and the payoff to each player is a function of the chosen strategies of all players. In this section, the ordinary game will be described in detail. A proposition, due originally to Nash [9], will be proved. It establishes the existence of a non-cooperative equilibrium for the ordinary game. Although this result was previously known, it is included for completeness. A game is said to be "non-cooperative" if it is not possible for the players to form coalitions or make agreements.

Denote the strategy of the ith player by s_i, a vector in r_i-dimensional Euclidean space, R^{r_i}. The strategy set of the ith player is taken to be a compact, convex subset of R^{r_i}, denoted S_i. There is a fixed, finite number of players, n, and the strategy set of the game S, is $S_1 \times \cdots \times S_n$, the Cartesian product of the individual strategy sets. A vector of strategies, one for each player, is denoted $s = (s_1, \ldots, s_n)$ and $\bar{s}_i$ denotes the strategy vector $(s_1, \ldots, s_{i-1}, s_{i+1}, \ldots, s_n)$. Thus $\bar{s}_i$ consists of the strategy choices of all players except the ith, and $s = (\bar{s}_i, s_i)$.

Payoff to the ith player is a real valued function of strategy, s, and is denoted $\pi_i(s)$. A vector of payoffs, associated with a given vector of strategies, may be denoted

$$\pi(s) = (\pi_1(s), \ldots, \pi_n(s)) \in R^n.$$

Assumptions made on the strategy space S and the payoff functions are:

A1 S_i is compact and convex $(i = 1, \ldots, n)$;
A2   The payoff functions, $\pi_i(s)$, are continuous and bounded on S, for all i;
A3   The payoff functions $\pi_i(s) = \pi_i(\bar{s}_i, s_i)$ are quasi-concave functions of s_i, for all i.

A point in the payoff space $(\pi_1(s^*), \ldots, \pi_n(s^*)) = \pi(s^*)$ is said to be "Pareto optimal" if

JAMES W. FRIEDMAN

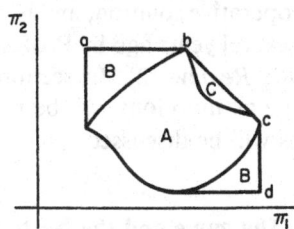

Figure 1.

(i) $s^* \in S$ and

(ii) there is no $s \in S$ for which $\pi_i(s) > \pi_i(s^*)$ $(i = 1, \ldots, n)$.

Denote by H, the set of attainable payoffs: $H = \{\pi(s) \mid s \in S\}$. Denote by $H^* \subset H$, the set of Pareto optimal payoffs.

A4   If $\pi' \leq \pi''$ (i.e., $\pi_i' \leq \pi_i''$, $i = 1, \ldots, n$) and $\pi', \pi'' \in H$, then $\pi \in H$ where $\pi' \leq \pi \leq \pi''$;

A5 H^* is concave.

Most of the assumptions above are both reasonable and clear. The least so is A4, which will be discussed in section VI. Figure 1 illustrates the meaning of certain of the assumptions. Region "A" is an arbitrary compact set. Compactness is required by A1 and A2. By A4, the regions denoted "B" are added, and by A5, region "C" is added. H^* is the heavy outer boundary *abcd*. Assumptions A4 and A5 mean that sets $H(\pi') = \{\pi \mid \pi > \pi', \pi \in H\}$ are convex, and for any $\pi \in H$ any non-negatively sloped ray through π will intersect H^* at exactly one point. This property will prove convenient in sections IV and V.

It remains in this section to define "non-cooperative equilibrium," and prove its existence for ordinary games of the sort under study in this section. s^* is a non-cooperative equilibrium strategy vector if $s^* \in S$ and

$$\pi_i(s^*) = \max_{s_i \in S_i} \pi_i(\bar{s}_i^*, s_i), \quad i = 1, \ldots, n.$$

Proposition 1. *Any game satisfying A1, A2, and A3 has a non-coopera-tive equilibrium.*

Proof.[2] Define $\mu(s) = \mu_1(\bar{s}_1) \times \mu_2(\bar{s}_2) \times \cdots \times \mu_n(\bar{s}_n)$ as follows:

$$\mu_i(\bar{s}_i) = \left\{ t_i \mid t_i \in S_i, \pi_i(\bar{s}_i, t_i) = \max_{s_i \in S_i} \pi_i(\bar{s}_i, s_i) \right\}, \quad (i = 1, \ldots, n), \ s \in S;$$

[2] This proposition is an easy generalization of the Nash [9] theorem, which deals with S_i which are finite sets of pure strategies, together with all mixed strategies attainable

144

Non-cooperative equilibrium for supergames

$\mu_i(\bar{s}_i)$ is clearly compact and convex. As $\mu_i(\bar{s}_i) \subset S_i$, it is bounded. That $\mu_i(\bar{s}_i)$ is closed follows from the continuity of π_i, and convexity follows from the quasi-concavity of π_i in s_i. As this holds for all i, the sets $\mu(s) = \mu_i(\bar{s}_i) \times \mu_2(\bar{s}_2) \times \cdots \times \mu_n(\bar{s}_n)$ are compact, convex and subsets of S.

If it can be shown that the correspondence $\mu: S \to S$ is upper semi-continuous, the Kakutani [7] fixed point theorem may be applied. A fixed point of μ is a non-cooperative equilibrium. Let $\bar{s}_i^l \in \bar{S}_i$, $l = 1, 2, \ldots$, be a sequence of strategies converging to $\bar{s}_i^0$. $\mu_i(\bar{s}_i)$ is upper semi-continuous if, when

(a) $s_i^l \in \mu_i(\bar{s}_i^l)$, $l = 1, 2, \ldots$, and
(b) $\lim_{l \to \infty} \bar{s}_i^l = \bar{s}_i^0$ and $\lim_{l \to \infty} s_i^l = s_i^0$ then
(c) $s_1^0 \in \mu_i(\bar{s}_i^0)$.

Assume a sequence as described in (a) and (b), but assume (c) is false (i.e., $s_i^0 \notin \mu_i(\bar{s}_i^0)$). If $s_i^0 \notin \mu_i(\bar{s}_i^0)$, then $\pi_i(\bar{s}_i^0, s_i^0) < \pi_i(\bar{s}_i^0, s_i')$ for $s_i' \in \mu_i(\bar{s}_i^0)$. Say $\pi_i(\bar{s}_i^0, s_i') - \pi_i(\bar{s}_i^0, s_i^0) = \epsilon > 0$. Now consider $\pi_i(\bar{s}_i^l, s_i^l)$. By the continuity of π_i, it is possible to choose an arbitrary $\delta > 0$ such that for $0 \geq \mathcal{L}(\delta)$ ($\mathcal{L}(\delta)$, finite),

$$\pi_i(\bar{s}_i^0, s_i') - \delta < \pi_i(\bar{s}_i^l, s_i^l) < \pi_i(\bar{s}_i^0, s_i') + \delta.$$

Choosing $\delta < \epsilon$ leads to a contradiction; hence, $s_i^0 \in \mu_i(\bar{s}_i^0)$ and μ_i is upper semi-continuous. As this holds for all i, μ is upper semi-continuous and has a fixed point. Let such a fixed point be $s^* \in \mu(s^*)$. By the definition of the μ_i,

$$\max_{s_i \in S_i} \pi_i(\bar{s}_i^*, s_i) = \mu_i(s^*), \quad i = 1, \ldots, n,$$

therefore s^* is a non-cooperative equilibrium strategy vector and $\pi(s^*)$ a non-cooperative equilibrium payoff vector. ∎

It may be noted in passing that when the payoff functions are profit functions, the players are firms and the strategies are prices or quantities, the game is a (single period) oligopoly. The non-cooperative equilibrium becomes the same as the "Cournot solution" [3]. In this instance S_i is merely the interval of prices (or quantities) among which the firm is allowed to choose. Frank and Quandt [5] proved the existence of the Cournot equilibrium for a quantity model. Their result is, of course, a special case of Proposition 1, above, and, *a fortiori*, a special case of the theorem of Debreu [4].

from them. The proposition is, on the other hand, a special case of a theorem of Debreu [4], which, so far as the author is aware, is the most general statement of existence of non-cooperative equilibria in finite strategy spaces.

145

Before proceeding to the next section, a final characteristic of the pay-off space will be noted: let $\rho = (\rho_1, \ldots, \rho_n)$ be a vector such that $\rho_i \geq 0$, $i = 1, \ldots, n$ and $\sum_{i=1}^{n} \rho_i = 1$. If k is a scalar, then the points $\pi(s) + k\rho$ $(-\infty < k < \infty)$ form a ray through $\pi(s)$ having non-negative slope. By A4, for any ρ there is a unique $k(\rho) \geq 0$ such that

$$\pi(s) + k(\rho) \cdot \rho \in H^*$$

for any $s \in S$. In particular, this property holds when s is a non-cooperative equilibrium.

III. Supergames and supergame strategies

The games of the preceding section have been dealt with in the "normal" form – the form in which there is a payoff function for each player giving his payoff as a function of a strategy vector, $\pi_i(s)$. It is convenient now to define "supergame" in extensive form; i.e., in the form in which each "move" is described. An "ordinary" game may be termed a "finite" game because the strategy sets of the players are compact and reside in a finite space.

Now consider a sequence of ordinary games with strategy sets $S_{i1}, S_{i2}, \ldots,$ $S_{it}, \ldots$ and payoff functions $\pi_{it}(s_t)$ $(s_t \in S_t)$; $t = 1, \ldots$; $i = 1, \ldots, n$. The tth game has $S_{1t} \times \cdots \times S_{nt} = S_{nt} = S_t$ as its strategy set and $\pi_{it}(s_t)$ $(i = 1, \ldots, n)$ as its payoff functions. A "supergame" is a game in which the tth move $(t = 1, \ldots)$ is the playing of the tth ordinary game in the sequence. At each move a payoff is received and, if the strategy sequence $s_1, \ldots, s_t, \ldots$ is played, the payoff to the ith player in the supergame is

$$\sum_{t=1}^{\infty} \alpha_{it} \pi_{it}(s_t),$$

where α_{it} is the discount parameter of the ith player in the tth time period. It is obvious that a "supergame" in which the number of moves is finite is merely a finite game; hence, attention will be restricted to supergames as defined above, which have a countably infinite number of moves.

The general definition of a supergame strategy for the ith player is as follows:

$$s_{it} = f_{it}(s_1, \ldots, s_{t-1}), \quad t = 2, 3, \ldots,$$

$$= s_{i1}, \quad t = 1.$$

f_{it} $(t = 2, 3, \ldots)$ is a sequence of functions which map all preceding ordinary game strategies of all players into the present (tth) ordinary game

146

strategy of the ith player. As there is no past information available in the initial period, there must be a particular initial move. Then $(s_{i1}, f_{i2}, f_{i3}, \ldots)$ is a supergame strategy for the ith player. Existence of non-cooperative equilibria in the supergame is no problem. Indeed the problem is the reverse; it is easy to show existence of a large number. The principal task of this paper is to choose among these in a particular way and single out certain equilibria as being of special interest.

IV. Equilibrium strategies in the supergame

This section is devoted to describing a very large class of supergame strategies, to showing when members of this class are non-cooperative equilibria and to introducing a new solution concept.

The exposition will be simplified by using four additional assumptions: (A6) all constituent games of the supergame are identical, (A7) the discount parameters are the same in all periods, (A8) the ordinary game has only one non-cooperative equilibrium, and (A9) the non-cooperative equilibrium is not Pareto optimal. All of these assumptions may be removed with only minor effect on the results. This will be done in section VI.

Denote by σ_i a supergame strategy for the ith player, and denote the non-cooperative equilibrium of the ordinary game by s^c. The "Cournot strategy" is denoted σ^c and is defined by $\sigma_i^c = (s_i^c, s_i^c, \ldots)$, $(i = 1, \ldots, n)$. The Cournot strategy is the repeated choice of the non-cooperative equilibrium of the ordinary game. It is immediate that

$$\sigma^c = (\sigma_1^c, \ldots, \sigma_n^c)$$

is a non-cooperative equilibrium in the supergame. Should any single player in any periods choose moves other than s_i^c he will (by definition of s^c) reduce his payoff in those periods and leave unaffected his payoff in the periods when he still chooses s_i^c.

Now a new class of non-cooperative equilibrium supergame strategies will be specified and discussed.

Let

$$B = \{s \mid s \in S, \pi_i(s) > \pi_i(s^c), \ i = 1, \ldots, n\}.$$

B consists of all ordinary game strategies which dominate the ordinary game non-cooperative equilibrium. Let $s' \in B$. Now define a strategy for the ith player, σ_i', as follows:

$s_{i1} = s_i'$,

$s_{it} = s_i'$ if $s_{j\tau} = s_j'$ $j \neq i$, $\tau = 1, \ldots, t-1$, $t = 2, 3, \ldots$,

$s_{it} = s_i^c$ otherwise.

147

Thus, the ith player chooses s_i' in period 1 and will continue to choose s_i' indefinitely, unless someone else chooses something other than s_j' $(j \neq i)$. If any player in any period chooses $s_j \neq s_j'$ $(j \neq i)$, then in each succeeding period the ith player chooses s_i^c. The supergame strategy vector $\sigma' = (\sigma_1', \ldots, \sigma_n')$ is a non-cooperative equilibrium if:

$$\sum_{\tau=0}^{\infty} \alpha_i^{\tau} \pi_i(s') > \pi_i(\bar{s}_i', t_i) + \sum_{\tau=1}^{\infty} \alpha_i^{\tau} \pi_i(s^c), \quad i = 1, \ldots, n,$$

or

$$\frac{\alpha_i}{1 - \alpha_i} [\pi_i(s') - \pi_i(s^c)] > \pi_i(\bar{s}_i', t_i) - \pi_i(s'), \quad i = 1, \ldots, n,$$

where $t_i \in S_i$ and $\pi_i(\bar{s}_i', t_i) = \max_{s_i \in S_i} \pi_i(\bar{s}_i', s_i)$.

To see whether σ_i' is the best strategy for the ith player, given $\bar{\sigma}_i'$, consider his alternatives. One is to choose σ_i', which results in using s_i' in every period, while all other players will choose s_j' $(j \neq i)$ and the discounted payoff stream will be

$$\sum_{\tau=0}^{\infty} \alpha_i^{\tau} \pi_i(s') = \frac{\pi_i(s')}{1 - \alpha_i}.$$

Another is to choose $s_{i1} = t_i$, and $s_{it} = s_i^c$ $(t > 1)$. t_i will yield the maximum possible payoff in period 1 (given the other players will choose s_j' $(j \neq i)$). After period 1 all other players will revert to the Cournot strategy, so the payoff maximizing choice after period 1 is $s_{it} = s_i^c$. Any other strategy is weakly dominated by one of the two just described, when the other players are using σ_j' $(j \neq i)$.

Which strategy to adopt simply depends upon which discounted profit stream is the larger. I.e., if the gain in the first period of maximizing against $\bar{s}_j'[\pi_i(\bar{s}_i', t_i) - \pi_i(s')]$ is less than the discounted loss from being at the Cournot point in all succeeding periods

$$\left(\frac{\alpha_i}{1 - \alpha_i} [\pi_i(s') - \pi_i(s^c)] \right),$$

then σ_i' is the strategy which maximizes discounted payoff for the ith player, given that the strategy choices of the other players are $(\sigma_j', j \neq i)$.

As the discount parameter approaches one from below (discount rate falls to zero), the discounted loss from being at the Cournot point goes to infinity, while the single period gain from choosing t_i is finite and unchanging. So for any $s' \in B$ there is a lower bound for α_i, $\alpha_i(s')$, (such that $\alpha_i(s') < 1$) and if $s' \in B$ and $\alpha_i > \alpha_i(s')$, then σ_i' is optimal against $\bar{\sigma}_i'$. If these conditions hold for $i = 1, \ldots, n$, then $(\sigma_1', \ldots, \sigma_n')$ is a non-cooperative equilibrium.

148

Non-cooperative equilibrium for supergames

Certain of the $s \in B$ are of special interest. There is a subset $B^* \subset B$ of move vectors which give rise to Pareto optimal payoff vectors:

$s^* \in B^*$ if

(a) $s^* \in B$ and

(b) $\pi(s^*) \in H^*$.

In considering a move vector (i.e. an ordinary game strategy vector), $s^* \in B^*$, why might a player cease choosing s_i^* if he has reason to believe the others will continue choosing s_j^* $(j \neq i)$? Clearly, he may feel a temptation to choose t_i (which maximizes the single period payoff against $\bar{s}_i^*$) because of the extra payoff which may be gained in the short run $[\pi_i(\bar{s}_i^*, t_i) - \pi_i(s^*)]$. Because the players should never, in the long run, receive less than $\pi(s^c)$ per period and because they may follow strategies which send them to π^c under some circumstances, it is intuitively appealing to measure the temptation associated with s^* in relation to $\pi_i(s^*) - \pi_i(s^c)$. Associated with the equilibrium proposed in this paper is the equilibrium move vector, s^*, which satisfies:

$$s^* \in B^*, \tag{1}$$

$$\frac{\pi_i(\bar{s}_i^*, t_i) - \pi_i(s^c)}{\pi_i(s^*) - \pi_i(s^c)} = \frac{\pi_j(\bar{s}_j^*, t_j) - \pi_j(s^c)}{\pi_j(s^*) - \pi_j(s^c)}, \quad i, j = 1, \dots, n. \tag{2}$$

This point is Pareto optimal and leaves each player equally tempted (in the sense of the preceding paragraph) to maximize against $\bar{s}_i^*$. An alternative way of expressing (2) is

$$\frac{\pi_i(\bar{s}_i^*, t_i) - \pi_i(s^*)}{\pi_i(s^*) - \pi_i(s^c)} = \frac{\pi_j(\bar{s}_j^*, t_j) - \pi_j(s^*)}{\pi_j(s^*) - \pi_j(s^c)}, \quad i, j = 1, \dots, n. \tag{2'}$$

Thus, if

$$\frac{\alpha_i}{1 - \alpha_i} > \frac{\pi_i(\bar{s}^*, t_i) - \pi_i(s^*)}{\pi_i(s^*) - \pi_i(s^c)}, \quad (i = 1, \dots, n),$$

then the strategies $\sigma^* = (\sigma_1^*, \dots, \sigma_n^*)$ form a non-cooperative equilibrium, where σ_i^* is defined by

$s_{i1} = s_i^*$,

$s_{it} = s_i^*$ if $s_{j\tau} = s_j^*$ $(j \neq i)$, $\tau = 1, \dots, t-1$, $t > 1$,

$s_{it} = s_i^c$ otherwise.

It should be emphasized that σ^*, in addition to being a non-cooperative equilibrium, is Pareto optimal. s^c, the non-cooperative equilibrium of the basic game need not be Pareto optimal, and, as students of oligopoly

149

theory are aware, its oligopoly counterpart, the Cournot solution, is generally *not*. It remains to show that ordinary game strategies satisfying (1) and (2) above do, in fact, exist. Before turning to that task, some comments will be made concerning properties of this concept of solution.

It is natural to ask if the proposed solution possesses any appealing properties and also whether one might expect a cooperative solution to emerge (such as the Nash–Harsanyi [10, 6] even though the game is noncooperative. While the Nash–Harsanyi solution applies to ordinary games, one could propose the sequence of Nash–Harsanyi solutions of the ordinary games as the solution of the supergame. The main reason for rejecting this, and other, cooperative solutions is that they rely on features of games which are peculiar to cooperative games and absent in non-cooperative. These revolve about the notion of "threat."

It is often part of a cooperative game that the players name threat strategies and then, if they fail to come to agreement, they are forced to carry out these threat strategies. If he were not forced, a player would do better in the absence of agreement to maximize against the strategies he expects the others to use. Applying this reasoning to all players, one would expect them to choose the non-cooperative equilibrium – if they were not forced to carry out threats. This undermines the credibility of the threats.

Now consider the cooperative game from another vantage point. When a single player (or a subset forming a coalition) calculates the best payoff he can get by himself, he does so on the assumption that all other players will band together and adopt a strategy aimed at minimizing his payoff. Even in a cooperative game, this may appear an unduly costly way for the others to act; however, as a threat to coerce the player into an agreement with all other players, it has some appeal. By contrast, in the non-cooperative game coalitions are ruled out, players cannot talk and bargain with one another; hence, it is foolish to think other players wish to minimize one's own payoff. Each will want to maximize his own payoff and will not really care about payoffs to others. In other words, threats are out of place in non-cooperative games because they cannot be clearly and effectively voiced, and because they are not credible. They need not be carried out and there is no incentive to do so.

The notion of "temptation" in the supergame is slightly analogous to threat. If a player can increase his single period profit for a period or so, he may be tempted to do so, but the other players are, in response, likely to revert to a "safe" position. This is a position in which no one has any temptation to move for the sake of short term gain.

There are certain properties which one might like an equilibrium to possess:

$\alpha 1$.   The solution should be unique, and always exist;

$\alpha 2$.   The solution should be independent of irrelevant alternatives;

$\alpha 3$.   The solution should be Pareto optimal;

$\alpha 4$.   The solution should be symmetric;

$\alpha 5$.   The solution should be invariant to a positive linear transformation of a payoff function;

$\alpha 6$.   The solution should be a non-cooperative equilibrium.

The Nash cooperative solution satisfies $\alpha 2$–$\alpha 5$. The solution proposed here satisfies $\alpha 3$–$\alpha 6$. Properties $\alpha 3$ and $\alpha 6$ are obviously fulfilled, as is $\alpha 5$ [note that equation (2) is free of origin and scale]. The meaning of $\alpha 4$ is that the solution should not depend on who is called player 1, who player 2, etc. That $\alpha 1$ is not met is obvious already, as existence depends on the discount parameter not being too small. It will be seen that if the α_i are sufficiently near one, an equilibrium must exist. Neither the present equilibrium nor the Nash-Harsanyi need be unique (except for the $N-H$ when $n = 2$).

The irrelevant alternatives assumption, $\alpha 2$, deserves special mention. Its meaning is that if you enlarge the set of available strategies, S, to a set $A \supset S$, then one of two conditions will hold: (i) the solution to the enlarged game will be the same as in the smaller game, or (ii) the solution will be a point, $y \in A$, which was not previously available ($y \notin S$). In other words the addition of new strategies cannot affect the solution unless one of the new strategies is the new solution. Thus the solution depends only on local properties of the payoff surface in the neighbourhood of the solution. This is very restrictive.

With the solution concept presented here one can well imagine $\alpha 2$ being violated. For example, enlarge the move space from S to $A = A_1 \times \cdots \times A_n$. Conceivably one or more players find that, while the old solution, $s^* \in S$, is still Pareto optimal (and s^c is still the only single period non-cooperative equilibrium), the t_i do not satisfy

$$\max_{s_i \in A_i} \pi_i(\bar{s}_i^*, s_i) = \pi_i(\bar{s}_i^*, t_i).$$

Should this happen, the point, y^*, which is the new equilibrium, might be in S, although the associated t_i will not all be in S.[3] It is good that the solution offered in this paper is not restricted by $\alpha 2$.

---

[3] Strictly speaking, this is necessarily true if the original equilibrium s^* is unique. If s^* and y^* are both equilibria of the smaller game, it is possible that enlarging the move space eliminates s^*, leaves y^* unaffected and creates no new equilibrium points. This still violates $\alpha 2$.

V. Existence of equilibrium

The existence proof is based upon a fixed point argument which, while it guarantees existence, does not guarantee uniqueness. The fixed point argument will be used to show that points s^* exist such that

$$\frac{\pi_i(\bar{s}_i^*, t_i) - \pi_i(s^*)}{\pi_i(s^*) - \pi_i(s^c)} = \frac{\pi_j(\bar{s}_j^*, t_j) - \pi_j(s^*)}{\pi_j(s^*) - \pi_j(s^c)}, \quad (i, j = 1, \ldots, n).$$

A point s^* has n points $(\bar{s}_i^*, t_i)$ associated with it. The t_i are determined by

$$\pi_i(\bar{s}_i^*, t_i) = \max_{s_i \in S_i} \pi_i(\bar{s}_i^*, s_i).$$

In fact $\bar{s}_i^* \in \bar{S}_i$ is mapped into π_i. Denote this mapping ϕ_i. A preliminary result will now be proved.

Proposition 2. *The mappings ϕ_i are continuous, for all i.*

Without loss of generality, the proposition may be proved with specific reference to ϕ_1. Let $\bar{s}_1^0$ be any point in $\bar{S}_1$ and let $s_1^0 \in S_1$ be chosen so that $\pi_1(\bar{s}_1^0, s_1^0) = \phi_1(\bar{s}_1^0)$. Let $\bar{s}_1^l$ $(l = 1, 2, \ldots)$ be a sequence of points in $\bar{S}_1$ such that $\bar{s}_1^l \to \bar{s}_1^0$ as $l \to \infty$. By definition of ϕ_1, there is a s_1^l associated with $\bar{s}^l$ such that $\pi_1(\bar{s}_1^l, s_1^l) = \phi_1(\bar{s}_1^l)$, $(l = 1, 2, 3, \ldots)$. It must now be shown that

$$\lim_{l \to \infty} \phi_1(\bar{s}_1^l) = \phi_1(\bar{s}_1^0).$$

Clearly $\lim_{l \to \infty} \phi_1(\bar{s}_1^l) \geq \lim_{l \to \infty} \pi_1(\bar{s}_1^l, s_1^0)$. But $\lim_{l \to \infty} \pi_1(\bar{s}_1^l, s_1^0) = \pi_1(\bar{s}_1^0, s_1^0) = \phi_1(\bar{s}_1^0)$ by continuity of π_1. But if $\lim_{l \to \infty} \phi_1(\bar{s}_1^l) > \phi_1(\bar{s}_1^0)$, there would be a value of $\bar{s}_1 = \lim_{l \to \infty} s_1^l$ such that $\pi_1(\bar{s}_1^0, \bar{s}_1) > \pi_1(\bar{s}_1^0, s_1^0)$, due to continuity of π_1. This, of course, contradicts the definition of ϕ_1; hence the function of ϕ_1 is continuous. The same argument may be repeated for the remaining ϕ_i. ∎

With the continuity of the ϕ_i established, it is now possible to prove the existence of a Pareto optimal move s^*, satisfying the condition

$$\frac{\pi_i(\bar{s}_i^*, t_i) - \pi_i(s^c)}{\pi_i(s^*) - \pi_i(s^c)} = \frac{\pi_j(\bar{s}_j^*, t_j) - \pi_j(s^c)}{\pi_j(s^*) - \pi_j(s^c)},$$

$$\pi_i(\bar{s}_i^*, t_i) = \phi_i(\bar{s}_i^*).$$

Proposition 3. *There exists a move $s^* \in S$ such that $\pi(s^*)$ is Pareto optimal and*

$$\frac{\phi_i(\bar{s}_i^*) - \pi_i(s^c)}{\pi_i(s^*) - \pi_i(s^c)} = \frac{\phi_j(\bar{s}_j^*) - \pi_j(s^c)}{\pi_j(s^*) - \pi_j(s^c)}, \quad (i, j = 1, \ldots, n).$$

152

Non-cooperative equilibrium for supergames

For any $\rho = (\rho_1, \ldots, \rho_n)$, $(\rho_i \geq 0, \sum \rho_i = 1)$ there is one Pareto optimal point $\pi(s_\rho)$ such that

$$\frac{\pi_i(s_\rho) - \pi_i(s^c)}{\sum_{j=1}^{n} [\pi_j(s_\rho) - \pi_j(s^c)]} = \rho_i, \quad i = 1, \ldots, n.$$

The condition of Pareto optimality ensures that this mapping from points on the unit simplex, ρ, to certain Pareto optimal profit vectors (i.e. from the unit simplex to points in the closure of B^*) is one–one and onto. Now define a mapping Ω as follows:

Ω maps a point ρ on the unit simplex into δ where:

$$\delta_i = \frac{\phi_i(\bar{s}_{i\rho}) - \pi_i(s^c)}{\sum_{j=1}^{n} [\phi_j(\bar{s}_{j\rho}) - \pi_j(s^c)]} = \Omega_i(\rho), \quad i = 1, \ldots, n.$$

Clearly δ is a point on the n-dimensional unit simplex, for $\delta_i \geq 0$ because

$$\phi_i(\bar{s}_{i\rho}) \geq \pi_i(s_\rho) \geq \pi_i(s^c).$$

Continuity of the ϕ_i implies continuity of Ω; therefore the Brouwer fixed point theorem may be applied. Any point, $s^* = s_\rho$, such that $\rho = \Omega(\rho)$, satisfies the conditions of the proposition. ∎

While existence is assured, uniqueness is not. Furthermore, existence of a point s^* does not, by itself, assure existence of an equilibrium strategy vector $(\sigma_i^*, \ldots, \sigma_n^*)$, satisfying (1) and (2). This depends, additionally, on the discount rates of the players, $(1 - \alpha_i)/\alpha_i$, not being too large. In particular, existence is assured if

$$\frac{1 - \alpha_i}{\alpha_i} < \frac{\pi_i(s^*) - \pi_i(s^c)}{\phi_i(\bar{s}_i^*) - \pi_i(s^c)}.$$

Thus, the following proposition is established:

Proposition 4. *If A1–A9 are true, then a supergame strategy, σ^*, which satisfies (1) and (2) exists and is, in addition, a non-cooperative equilibrium when*

$$\frac{1 - \alpha_i}{\alpha_i} < \frac{\pi_i(s^*) - \pi_i(s^c)}{\phi_i(\bar{s}_i^*) - \pi_i(s^c)}, \quad i = 1, \ldots, n.$$

When σ^* is a non-cooperative equilibrium it might be called the "balanced temptation solution," for its characteristic (apart from being both Pareto optimal and a non-cooperative equilibrium) is that the ratio of short term gain from maximizing against $\bar{s}_i^*$ to the loss per period of having done so is identical for all players. I.e.:

153

JAMES W. FRIEDMAN

$$\frac{\pi_i(\bar{s}_i^*, t_i) - \pi_i(s^*)}{\pi_i(s^*) - \pi_i(s^c)} = \frac{\pi_j(\bar{s}_j^*, t_j) - \pi_j(s^*)}{\pi_j(s^*) - \pi_j(s^c)} \quad \text{for all } i \text{ and } j.$$

An equivalent statement is that σ^* is defined so that $\alpha_i(s^*) = \alpha_j(s^*)$, for all i and j. That is, the discount parameter which makes the ith player indifferent between choosing σ_i^* and choosing $(t_i, s_i^c, s_i^c, \ldots)$ against the σ_j^* is the same for all players.

VI. The relaxation of assumptions

The first assumptions to be dropped are those made at the beginning of section IV: (A6), all constituent games of the supergame are identical; (A7), the discount parameters are the same in all periods; (A8), the basic game has only one non-cooperative equilibrium; and (A9) the non-cooperative equilibrium is not Pareto optimal.

Taking (A9) first, it is immediate that if $\pi(s^c) \in H^*$, then it is the only element of H^*. By default, the supergame equilibrium strategy would be for each player to always choose s_i^c $(i = 1, \ldots, n)$. Relaxing the remaining assumptions, let S_{it} be the strategy set of the ith player in the ordinary game of period t, let $C_t \subset S_t = S_{it} \times \cdots \times S_{nt}$ be the set of non-cooperative equilibria of the ordinary game of period t, and let α_{it} be the present value of the discount parameter of the ith firm in period t. That is, if the one period discount rates are $r_{i1}, \ldots, r_{it}, \ldots$, then

$$\alpha_{it} = \prod_{\tau=1}^{t-1} \frac{1}{1 + r_{i\tau}} = \frac{\alpha_{i, t-1}}{1 - r_{i, t}}, \quad t = 2, 3, \ldots;$$

$$\alpha_{i1} = 1.$$

If $C = C_1 \times C_2 \times \cdots$, then $c = (c_1, c_2, \ldots) \in C$ is an infinite sequence of ordinary game non-cooperative equilibria, where c_t is a non-cooperative equilibrium in the game described by (S_t, π_t). Proposition 3 proves a result about ordinary games: if $c_t \in C_t$, then the set of points $p_t \in P_t(c_t)$ such that

$$\frac{\phi_{it}(\bar{p}_{it}) - \pi_{it}(c_t)}{\pi_{it}(p_t) - \pi_{it}(c_t)} = \frac{\phi_{jt}(\bar{p}_{jt}) - \pi_{jt}(c_t)}{\pi_{jt}(p_t) - \pi_{jt}(c_t)}, \quad i, j = 1, \ldots, n; \ t = 1, 2, \ldots, \tag{3}$$

$$\pi_t(p_t) \in H_t^*, \pi_t(p_t) \geq \pi_t(c_t), \quad t = 1, 2, \ldots, \tag{4}$$

is not empty. The symbols π_{it} and ϕ_{it} are defined as before, except that they are in relation to the game of the ith period.

Let t_{it} be defined as follows:

$$\pi_{it}(\bar{p}_{it}, t_{it}) = \max_{s_{it} \in S_{it}} \pi_i(\bar{p}_{it}, s_{it}).$$

154

Non-cooperative equilibrium for supergames

Let $p \in P(c) = P_1(c_1) \times \cdots \times P_t(c_t) \times \cdots$ be a sequence of points satisfying conditions (3) and (4), above. In relation to a given $c \in C$ and $p \in P(c)$, the supergame strategy $\sigma_i(c, p)$ is defined for the ith player:

$$s_{i1} = p_{i1}, \tag{5}$$

$$s_{it} = p_{it} \quad \text{if} \quad s_{j\tau} = p_{j\tau}, \quad j = 1, \ldots, n; \quad \tau = 1, \ldots, t-1, \quad t \geq 2, \tag{6}$$

$$s_{it} = c_{it} \quad \text{otherwise.} \tag{7}$$

$\sigma(c, p) = [\sigma_1(c, p), \ldots, \sigma_n(c, p)]$ is a non-cooperative equilibrium for the supergame if:

$$\sum_{\tau=t}^{\infty} \alpha_{i\tau} \pi_{it}(p_t) > \alpha_{it} \pi_{it}(\bar{p}_{it}, t_{it}) + \sum_{\tau=t+1}^{\infty} \alpha_{i\tau} \pi_{i\tau}(c_\tau), \quad i = 1, \ldots, n, \quad t = 1, 2, \ldots. \tag{8}$$

If these conditions are met, the actual moves chosen will be p ($= p_1$, $p_2, \ldots$). Here it must be true that no player in any period finds it more profitable to maximize against $\bar{p}_{it}$ and see the future moves be $c_{t+1}, \ldots$. Of course, this was true previously; however, when the same game is repeated in each period and discount rates are invariant over time, it is either never profitable to choose t_i, or most profitable to do so in the first period of the supergame.

If $p_t = c_t$ for all but a finite number of time periods, σ cannot be an equilibrium, and, if that were true for all $c \in C$, the only supergame non-cooperative equilibria would be strategies in which basic game non-cooperative equilibria were repeated.

Thus Proposition 4 is now extended to supergames, satisfying only A1–A5:

Proposition 5. *If A1–A5 are true, then a supergame strategy satisfying (3)–(7) exists and is a non-cooperative equilibrium for the supergame if (8) is satisfied.*

A4 might be weakened to say that for given $c_t \in C_t$ and $(\rho_1, \ldots, \rho_n)$ exactly one member of the family of vectors $[k(\rho_1, \ldots, \rho_n) + \pi_t(c_t)]$, $\rho_i \geq 0$, $i = 1, \ldots, n$, $\sum \rho_i = 1$, $k \geq 0$ coincides with a point on the payoff possibility frontier. Thus a surface such as is found in Figure 2 would be possible. Proposition 3 is still valid. There will be at least one point on the profit frontier, in the segment from a to b, which will map into itself. Such a point provides the basis for a non-cooperative equilibrium which satisfies axioms $\alpha4$–$\alpha6$. Pareto optimality cannot be guaranteed. Now two possibilities emerge. (*a*) Do not require Pareto optimality of the solution, merely require that it lie on the frontier. (*b*) If the solution found by (*a*),

155

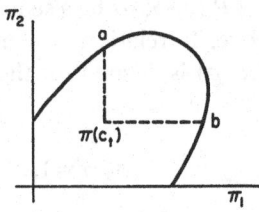

Figure 2.

preceding, is not Pareto optimal, substitute for it the nearest Pareto optimal point which has a larger payoff to each player.

VII. Comments on economic applications

A promising area of application for the equilibrium concept developed here is to the theory of oligopoly. With the game interpreted as an oligopoly, the Cournot, or ordinary game non-cooperative, equilibrium is not a Pareto optimal point. Considerable dissatisfaction has been voiced over the years with this equilibrium as a viable outcome in oligopoly. Even though out and out explicit collusion is difficult in a nation having antitrust legislation, because agreements are not legally binding and even meetings to attempt agreement may be illegal; still it seems unsatisfactory for firms to achieve only the profits of the Cournot point when each firm must realize more can be simultaneously obtained by each.

This line of argument often leads to something called "tacit collusion" under which firms are presumed to act as if they colluded. How they do this is not entirely clear, though one explanation is that their market moves are interpretable as messages. They converse in a code, as it were. Another explanation is that the "tacit collusion" is spontaneous. Everyone is so aware of the shortsightedness of Cournot behaviour that they simply behave better.

Yet, despite these misgivings, the Cournot solution has never been entirely in disrepute. It remains, neither wholeheartedly accepted, nor firmly rejected. No doubt this is because no acceptable alternative has been proposed, and because a non-cooperative equilibrium possesses attractive properties which are hard to entirely forgo.

The equilibrium presented here is a sort of reconciliation. It provides an equilibrium which is both Pareto optimal and a non-cooperative equilibrium. Thus, it is possible to see the firm as selfish, willing to make any alteration in its behaviour which will increase its (discounted) profits, and, at the same time, all firms are jointly earning a Pareto optimal vector of profits. They are neither forgoing profit, nor behaving in a way which exposes firms to being "double-crossed."

In the preceding section, it was found that there may be many basic game non-cooperative equilibria and, for each such point, many Pareto optimal points which could form part of a supergame non-cooperative equilibrium. Were this so, it would be impossible to choose one supergame equilibrium and regard it as a "natural" game solution, i.e., a particular set of strategies one should expect the players to adopt. It is possible, however, that in application to oligopoly, the additional knowledge of the structure of the game may be such as to guarantee existence of only one equilibrium. A unique equilibrium would be a natural solution. Likewise, the difficulty that Proposition 3 could lead to a point on the profit frontier which is not Pareto optimal may turn out impossible in oligopoly models.

References

1. Aumann, R. J. "Acceptable Points in General Cooperative n-person Games," *Contributions to the Theory of Games IV*, Annals of Mathematics Study 40 (Princeton University Press, 1959), 287–324.
2. Bishop, R. L. "Duopoly: Collusion or Warfare," *American Economic Review* (1960), 933–61.
3. Cournot, A. *Researches into the Mathematical Principles of the Theory of Wealth,* trans. by N. T. Bacon (Kelley, New York, 1960).
4. Debreu, G. "A Social Equilibrium Existence Theorem," *Proceedings of the National Academy of Science* (1952), 886–93.
5. Frank, C. R. and Quandt, R. E. "On the Existence of Cournot Equilibrium," International Economic Review (1963), 92–6.
6. Harsanyi, J. C. "A Simplified Bargaining Model for the n-Person Cooperative Game," *International Economic Review* (1963), 194–220.
7. Kakutani, S. "A Generalization of Brouwer's Fixed Point Theorem," *Duke Mathematical Journal* (1941), 457–59.
8. Luce, R. D. and Raiffa, H. *Games and Decisions* (Wiley, New York, 1957).
9. Nash, J. "Noncooperative Games," *Annals of Mathematics,* 54 (1951), 286–95.
10. Nash, J. "Two Person Cooperative Games," *Econometrica* (1953), 128–40.

RATIONALITY OF CONJECTURES AND OBSERVATION OF BEHAVIOR

CHAPTER 7

Reconsidering Cournot: the Cournot equilibrium is consistent

ANDREW F. DAUGHETY

This article uses an infinite-regress model of firm-level decisions to find a rational expectations equilibrium for a duopoly and to relate concepts of conjectural variations and consistency to the Cournot equilibrium. The model derives a conjectural variation instead of assuming it. In particular, the Cournot equilibrium is shown to be consistent in the usual sense of the literature. The conflict between notions of consistent conjectures and the Cournot equilibrium results from a compounding problem inherent in the earlier models. We extend these results to the n-firm problem. Alternatively, the article can be viewed as providing a purely static model that generates the Cournot equilibrium without reference to conjectures or quasi dynamics.

1. Introduction

Recently, the use of the Cournot model as a valid equilibrium solution in noncooperative oligopoly settings has been questioned in a variety of articles using the concept of a consistent conjectural variation (see, e.g., Laitner (1980), Bresnahan (1981), Kamien and Schwartz (1983), Perry (1982), and Kalai and Stanford (1982). A *conjectural variation* is a conjecture by one firm about how the other firm will adjust its decision variable with respect to potential adjustments in the first firm's action. A *consistent conjectural variation* is a conjectural variation that is correct: predicted change (locally) in the relevant decision variable (output or price) on the part of one's competitor is what actually occurs. A *consistent conjectures equilibrium* is a consistent conjectural variation equilibrium, in the sense that no individual change in a decision variable is profitable. As Bresnahan (1981, p. 935) observes, "One might view this as a kind of rational

University of Iowa.
Andrew F. Daughety, "Reconsidering Cournot: The Cournot Equilibrium Is Consistent," *Rand Journal of Economics* 16, 3, 1985, pp. 368–79.
This work was partly supported by NSF Grant SES-8218684. Special thanks are due to Jan Aaftink, Michael Balch, Ben Eden, Robert Forsythe, Charles Holt, Peter Huang, John Kennan, Steve Landsburg, Leonard Mirman, David Malueg, Guillermo Owen, Thomas Pogue, Ray Riezman, Stephen Salant, and Sam Wu for stimulating conversations and ideas.

expectations oligopoly theory." The standard result is that the Cournot equilibrium is, in general, not a consistent conjectures equilibrium.

The consistent conjectures equilibrium is not, however, an equilibrium in the full sense of the term: there are actions each firm can take that can guarantee higher profits. To see this consider the surprising result that symmetric firms, choosing output levels, facing linear demand, and subject to constant marginal costs, produce outputs so that price equals marginal cost if they employ consistent conjectural variations (Bresnahan, 1981, p. 937). In other words the consistent conjectures equilibrium in this case is the perfect competition outcome with zero profits. Now let us assume that each of the players (firms) has read the consistent conjectural variations literature and knows this result. Notice that a firm could individually choose *not* to act in the consistent conjectural variations sense, e.g., to play Cournot.

What will happen? If only one firm chooses to play Cournot while the other plays consistent conjectural variations, the result is the von Stackelberg outcome with positive profits for *both* players. If we assume symmetry of good reading habits, we get the Cournot outcome! In other words, since it is individually rational to choose to take an action which guarantees positive profits as a von Stackelberg follower rather than zero profits as a consistent conjectural variations player, the consistent conjectures equilibrium is not an equilibrium outcome.

Recent experimental evidence also suggests that the consistent conjectures equilibrium is not a good general predictor of equilibrium. Holt (1982) has constructed a series of duopoly experiments involving symmetric firms operating with zero marginal costs and facing linear industry demand. In the experiments the consistent conjectures equilibrium involved positive profits (all profits were increased by a positive amount) to encourage player participation. In general (a few of the duopoly pairs achieved a collusive outcome) the consistent conjectures equilibrium did not occur; the Cournot equilibrium, in fact, obtained. Moreover, Holt (1982) indicates that previous studies supporting the consistent conjectures equilibrium may have suffered from insufficient separation of that equilibrium and Cournot equilibria.[1]

The heart of the problem is the notion of a conjectural variation. This notion is *ad hoc* inasmuch as none of the models using a conjectural variation explains how it is formed or whence it came. Moreover, as we shall demonstrate, the operationalization of the concept of a conjectural variation as a derivative of the rival firm's output with respect to "own" output

[1] Holt's results are marred by the existence of multiple consistent conjectures equilibria and multiple Cournot equilibria. It is still true, however, that the consistent conjectures equilibria are, as a group, separated from the Cournot equilibria (taken as a group).

is incorrect, independent of how firms make decisions about output levels. Rather, a conjectural variation will be the change in the conjectured output of the rival in response to an "own" conjecture of a rival's conjecture about "own" output. Using optimal conjectures will result in the new conjectural variation's being consistent. This will also lead to a characterization of the standard conjectural variation in terms of compoundings of optimal conjectural variations, and thus will relate the standard Cournot model to the model presented in this article.

In what follows we view a firm as solving an infinite regress problem: firm i chooses an output level to maximize profits subject to a model representing its adversary (j), which is (in turn) subject to a model of its adversary's model of i, and so on. This provides a purely static model. There is no "initial" versus "final" position in this model: both positions are the same since there will be one (and only one) move. We define a rational duopoly equilibrium and show that that equilibrium exists if and only if the Cournot equilibrium exists and the rational duopoly equilibrium *is* the Cournot equilibrium. Next, we derive a conjectural variation from the structure of the infinite regress problem, and show that it is a consistent conjectural variation. We then relate the standard conjectural variation to that of the infinite regress model by embedding the infinite regress model in the standard model. Finally, we examine the n-firm problem and extend the rational duopoly equilibrium to cover the general case.

2. A rational expectations duopoly model

Consider a two-firm industry producing a single homogeneous good. Each firm produces output $x_i \in R_+$ under cost function $c_i: R_+ \to R_+$. The inverse demand function for industry output is $p: R_+ \to R_+$, where industry output is $x_i + x_j$. Cost and demand functions are common knowledge, as is the individual goal of profit maximization by each firm.

To choose an output level, each firm must forecast what the other firm will do. Thus, each firm conjectures a model of the other firm, and in particular, each firm maximizes profits and assumes this to be true of the other. Since they each do this, they each realize that the other firm is also doing this. Moreover, firm i's model of j clearly requires a model of what i believes j believes will be i's output. This goes on forever, forming an infinite regress: i maximizes its profits subject to a model of j that is subject to i's model of j's model of i that in turn is subject to i's model of j's model of i's model of j, etc.

Let $\pi(u, w, k) = p(u+w)u - c_k(u)$ be the profit function for firm k facing industry (inverse) demand curve $p(\cdot)$, choosing output level u,

163

using a cost function $c_k(\cdot)$, and predicting that its adversary will produce w. Moreover, assume that $p(\cdot)$ is concave and $c_k(\cdot)$ is convex, and thus · $\pi(\cdot, w, k)$ is strictly concave. In what follows, the decision variable is always the first variable in the π-function.

To structure the modeling of conjectures, let us use the following notation:

$$(lk) \equiv \text{that } l \text{ assumes that } k \text{ assumes,}$$

and

$$(lk)^n = \underbrace{lk...lk.}_{n \text{ times}}$$

Thus, the statement "that i assumes that j assumes about i" will be written as $(ij)i$ while the statement "that i assumes that j assumes that i assumes that j assumes that i assumes about j" can be written as $i(ji)^2j$. Note that the above formalization always places the final object of thought (the letter following the word "about") outside of the parentheses as the last term. Note also that there are generically two types of statements for firm i: (1) $(ij)^ni$, $n \geq 0$ (statements about i itself) and (2) $i(ji)^nj$, $n \geq 0$ (statements about j from i's viewpoint). Finally, the notation $\{k\}$ will denote "statement k," which will be an *admissible* sequence of i's and j's, where admissible means that no two neighboring *elements* in the sequence are the same [i.e., ijj is not admissible, while $ijij = (ij)(ij)$ is].

Firm i's decision problem is to find $x^i \in R_+^\infty$, with $x^i = (x_i, x_{ij}, ...)$, that solves the following ("am" stands for "argument that maximizes," x is the decision variable "dummy," and the variable to the left of the equal sign is the variable being optimized):

$$x_i = \text{am}_x \pi(x, x_{ij}, i) \tag{1}$$

subject to

$$x_{ij} = \text{am}_x \pi(x, x_{iji}, j)$$

subject to

$$x_{iji} = \text{am}_x \pi(x, x_{ijij}, i)$$

subject to

$$x_{ijij} = \text{am}_x \pi(x, x_{ijiji}, j)$$
$$\vdots$$

etc.

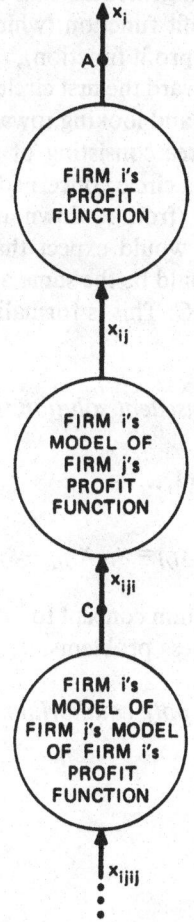

Figure 1. An infinite-regress model.

Firm i's solution to (1) (the infinite dimensional vector x^i) provides the optimal output level for firm i (x_i), what firm i believes firm j will produce (x_{ij}), what firm i believes firm j believes firm i will produce (x_{iji}), etc. There is a corresponding problem to (1) for firm j, with firm j finding $x^j \in R_+^\infty$, $x^j = (x_j, x_{ji}, x_{jij}, \dots)$. (In what follows all vectors are row vectors.)

Figure 1 represents the model in system (1). The first circle contains firm i's profit function; it uses the value of x_{ij} produced by the infinite stream of circles below it and generates x_i as a result. The second circle contains i's model of j's profit function (which, owing to the common knowledge assumption, is j's profit function), and so on. Note that standing at point A and looking toward the first circle is "observationally equivalent" to standing at point C and looking toward the third circle: in both cases the observer views a tree consisting of an infinitely repeating sequence of a finite collection (a circle concerned with i and one with j) of circles. Since these two trees (from A down and from C down) are observationally equivalent, we would expect that the solution associated with the tree starting at A would be the same as the solution at C, i.e., if we deleted everything above C. This is formalized by requiring the solution to be consistent.

Definition 1. $x^i \in R_+^\infty$ is a *consistent solution* to problem (1) for i if

$$\left. \begin{array}{l} x_{(ij)^n i} = x_{(ij)^{n-1} i} \\ x_{i(ji)^n j} = x_{i(ji)^{n-1} j} \end{array} \right\} \quad n = 1, \dots.$$

A solution x^i is consistent if $x_{iji} = x_i$, $x_{ijij} = x_j$, $x_{ijiji} = x_{iji}$, etc.

We now define the equilibrium concept to be used, on the basis of both i and j's solving infinite regress problems.

Definition 2. A *rational duopoly equilibrium* is a pair of consistent solutions

$$(x^{i^*}, x^{j^*}) \in R_+^\infty x R_+^\infty$$

such that:

$$x^{i^*} = (x_i^*, x^{j^*}) \tag{2}$$

$$x^{j^*} = (x_j^*, x^{i^*}). \tag{3}$$

Equations (2) and (3) state that firm i should correctly anticipate what firm j will do and *vice versa*; in this way decisions are best responses to correct conjectures.[2] Thus, $x_{ij}^* = x_j^*$ (what i thinks j will do is what firm j does), and $x_{ji}^* = x_i^*$ (what firm j thinks i will do is what it does). Moreover, $x_{iji}^* = x_{ji}^*$ (what i thinks j thinks i will do is what j thinks i will do), and so forth. This leads immediately to the first result under the assumption that a rational duopoly equilibrium exists.

---

[2] Bernheim (1984) and Pearce (1984) have considered models with best-response conjectures.

Reconsidering Cournot

Theorem 1. *All rational duopoly equilibria are Cournot equilibria.*

Proof. (x_i^*, x_j^*) is the Cournot equilibrium since

$$x_i^* = \text{am}_x \pi(x, x_j^*, i),$$

$$x_j^* = \text{am}_x \pi(x, x_i^*, j).$$

The rational duopoly equilibrium involves a pair of vectors that are individually consistent and mutually consistent, i.e., $x_{iji}^* = x_{ji}^*$, $x_{ji}^* = x_i^*$, etc. This continues on in this way to yield the following:

$$x^{i^*} = (x_i^*, x_j^*, x_i^*, x_j^*, \dots)$$

$$x^{j^*} = (x_j^*, x_i^*, x_j^*, x_i^*, \dots).$$

This reflects the intuition that in equilibrium, complex statements about what i thinks j thinks i thinks, etc., should be correct. Thus, using the previous notation for statements, in equilibrium we should have (where "=" means "is equivalent to"):

$$(ij)^n i = i \qquad (ji)^n j = j, \qquad n \geq 0$$

$$i(ji)^n j = j \qquad j(ij)^n i = i, \qquad n \geq 0.$$

Moreover, a Cournot equilibrium is a rational duopoly equilibrium, as can be seen from the definition. Thus, Cournot equilibria and rational duopoly equilibria are the *same*; if one exists, so does the other [for sufficient conditions for the existence of the Cournot equilibrium, see Friedman (1977) or Szidarovszky and Yakowitz (1977) among others]. In particular, the assumption of a concave demand function and convex cost functions is not necessary for this equivalence of rational duopoly and Cournot equilibria: this equivalence comes from the use of the definition of consistency as a constraint on the solutions to (1).

There is a second way[3] to think about system (1): as an example of successive approximations. To see this consider a finite truncation of (1), i.e., stopping at the optimization model giving $x_{(ij)^n}$, using an arbitrary value for $x_{(ij)^n i}$, where n is finite. The resulting value for x_i (represented as $\tilde{x}_i$) is a function of the arbitrary value for $x_{(ij)^n i}$. By letting $n \to \infty$, $\tilde{x}_i$ can be made arbitrarily close to the consistent solution to (1). This follows by using the mapping $S: R_+ \to R_+$, defined as

$$S(y) = \text{am}_u \pi(u, \tilde{v}, i)$$

subject to

---

[3] This observation is due to Stephen Salant.

167

$$\tilde{v} = \text{am}_v \pi(v, y, j),$$

and by observing that the truncated version of (1) is simply the algorithm

$$x_{(ij)^{k-1}i} = S(x_{(ij)^k i}), \quad k = n, \dots, 1.$$

We can readily show that, given the assumptions on the demand and cost functions, S is a contraction mapping. Thus, x_i can be obtained (or approximated to within an arbitrary bound) by iterating S from an arbitrary starting point with the method of successive approximations (Luenberger, 1969). Moreover, given the assumptions on the demand and cost functions, this means that not only does the rational duopoly equilibrium exist, but also it is unique [owing to the result on Cournot equilibria by Szidarovszky and Yakowitz (1977)]. ∎

3. Application to the standard example

Consider a simple, standard example:[4] the linear demand, linear cost case where $p(x_i + x_j) = a - b(x_i + x_j)$ and $c_k(x_k) = c_k x_k$ with $a, b, c_k > 0$ and $k = i, j$. Thus, i and j need not be symmetric. Moreover, assume $a \geq 2 \max(c_i, c_j)$, so that a solution exists. System (1) produces the following (infinite) set of equations as first-order conditions:

$$x_i = \frac{a - c_i}{2b} - \frac{x_{ij}}{2}$$

$$x_{ij} = \frac{a - c_j}{2b} - \frac{x_{iji}}{2}$$

$$x_{iji} = \frac{a - c_i}{2b} - \frac{x_{ijij}}{2}$$

$$\vdots \tag{4}$$

If we restrict ourselves in (4) to consistent solutions, these equations yield the following:

$$x_i^* = \frac{a - 2c_i + c_j}{3b}$$

$$x_{ij}^* = \frac{a - 2c_j + c_i}{3b}$$

$$x_{iji}^* = \frac{a - 2c_i + c_j}{3b}$$

$$\vdots$$

---

[4] Cyert and DeGroot (1970) also consider this example under the further assumption of symmetric (zero-cost) firms.

Thus, if j solves its version of (4) enforcing consistency of the solution, then the pair of solutions is:

$$x^{i^*} = \frac{a-2c_i+c_j}{3b}, \frac{a-2c_j+c_i}{3b}, \frac{1-2c_i+c_j}{3b}, \ldots$$

$$x^{j^*} = \frac{a-2c_j+c_i}{3b}, \frac{a-2c_i+c_j}{3b}, \frac{a-2c_j+c_i}{3b}, \ldots,$$

which is the rational duopoly equilibrium, and (x_i^*, x_j^*) is the Cournot equilibrium. Note that if each firm acts in this manner, equilibrium is *immediate*.[5] In other words, the infinite regress provides the output vector that is a Nash equilibrium. Thus, unlike the traditional stories associated with the Cournot model, the infinite regress model provides a purely static model (i.e., noniterative) that generates the Cournot solution.

4. Conjectures and consistency

Fellner (1949, p. 71) in his discussion of conjectural variation models states:

It is assumed that the producers do not believe that the output of their rivals is fixed and independent of their own output. Instead, they believe that the output of their rivals depends on their own output *in some fashion.* . . . The assumed change in the output of a rival per (small) unit change of the "own" output is usually termed conjectural variation.

Unfortunately, this notion usually is translated into something analogous to $\partial x_j / \partial x_i$ despite the fact that the model is a static one with simultaneous production (production must be simultaneous since each firm conjectures about the other). On the other hand, the use of a derivative such as $\partial x_j / \partial x_i$ suggests a sequential procedure, since x_j is what j will actually do and x_i is what i will actually do. The conjectural variation in this sense is calling for predictions of change in one firm's actions as a function of a change in the other firm's actions. Thus, the use of $\partial x_j / \partial x_i$ is logically inconsistent with the use of a static model and simultaneous production [see Friedman (1977) for a discussion of the problems with turn-taking static stories].

The infinite-regress model, however, is a static model with simultaneous production and logically consistent conjecturing. To see this note that "the output of their rivals" in the case of firm i is precisely captured

---

[5] If both firms do not act in this manner (assuming noncooperative behavior), then this suggests the presence of incomplete or imperfect (or both) information. A second source of disparity might be lack of common knowledge about demand and cost.

by x_{ij}, which is i's conjecture of what j will produce. This variable is in turn sensitive not to what i will produce, but to what i believes j believes i will produce. This is true since i knows that what j will do cannot be affected by what i does, but is affected by what j thinks i will do. The variable x_{iji} is what i thinks j thinks i will do and thus the correct representation of the conjectural variation is $\partial x_{ij}/\partial x_{iji}$.

Returning to the simple linear demand, linear cost model, equation system (4) implies:

$$\frac{\partial x_{ij}}{\partial x_{iji}} = -\frac{1}{2},$$

which is the slope of the Cournot reaction function. Thus, the conjectural variation ($\partial x_{ij}/\partial x_{iji}$) is consistent, and so too is the equilibrium, (x_i^*, x_j^*).

More generally, let $\pi(\cdot, w, k)$ be strictly concave, continuous in w, and twice differentiable. Then the first-order conditions for (1) is an infinite system of equations which can be written as

$$x_i = \psi_i(x_{ij})$$
$$x_{ij} = \psi_{ij}(x_{iji})$$
$$x_{iji} = \psi_{iji}(x_{ijij}),$$
$$\vdots$$

where $\psi_{\{k\}}(w) = \mathrm{am}_x \pi(x, w, l)$ and l is the object of statement k, i.e., the last letter in $\{k\}$. The assumptions on $p(\cdot)$ and $c_i(\cdot)$ will guarantee that when $\psi_{\{k\}} > 0$, it is monotone decreasing in w with slope[6] in the open interval $(-1, 0)$.

In general,

$$\psi'_{\{k\}} \equiv \frac{\partial x_{\{k\}}}{\partial w} \quad \forall_{\{k\}},$$

and therefore ψ'_{ij} is the conjectural variation as discussed earlier. On the other hand, $\psi_{\{k\}}$ is clearly the Cournot reaction function associated with statement k. In particular, ψ_{ij} is the reaction function for firm j that

---

[6] It is straightforward to show that, by differentiating the first-order conditions, $d\psi_{\{k\}}/dw = \pi_{12}/\pi_{11}$, where $\pi_{11} = \partial^2\pi(u, w, l)/\partial u^2$ and $\pi_{12} = \partial^2\pi(u, w, l)/\partial w\,\partial u$. Thus, $\psi'_{\{k\}} \in (-1, 0)$ is the requirement that $\pi_{11} < \pi_{12} < 0$. A sufficient condition is that p is concave and c_l convex, as stated in the model's assumptions. Note that the property that $\psi'_{\{k\}} \in (-1, 0)$ also guarantees that the mapping used in the earlier successive approximations discussion (i.e., S) is a contraction (Luenberger, 1969). Moreover, the requirement that $\pi_{11} < \pi_{12} < 0$ implies stability of the Cournot equilibrium in the standard model (Friedman, 1977). Finally, note also that the above argument is valid for $\psi_{\{k\}} > 0$ (Kreps and Scheinkman, 1983). We assume this in what follows.

provides the best response for firm j, given what firm i will produce. Therefore, $\partial x_{ij}/\partial x_{iji}$ is a consistent conjectural variation, and therefore in equilibrium (x_i^*, x_j^*) is a consistent conjectures equilibrium. This is summarized in Theorem 2.

Theorem 2. *Let $p(u+w)$ be concave and $c_k(u)$ be convex, both twice differentiable in u for all w and for all $k = i, j$. If (x^{i*}, x^{j*}) is a rational duopoly equilibrium, then both firms have consistent conjectural variations and (x_i^*, x_j^*) is a consistent conjectural equilibrium.*

Why the standard model has a zero variation. This produces a perplexing situation. The standard model for the Cournot duopoly involves a zero variation $(\partial x_j/\partial x_i = 0)$, while the infinite regress model involves a nonzero conjectural variation $(\psi_{ij}' < 0)$. Since the standard model can also generate the Cournot solution, what is the relationship between the two variations?

To see the relationship, consider (1), the infinite regress problem. Truncating (1) at the first constraint results in the standard problem:

$$x_i = \mathrm{am}_x \pi(x, x_{ij}, i). \tag{5}$$

Let $\pi_1 = \partial \pi(x, x_{ij}, i)/\partial x$ and $\pi_2 = \partial \pi(x, x_{ij}, i)/\partial x_{ij}$. The first-order condition for (5) is

$$\pi_1 + \pi_2 \frac{\partial x_{ij}}{\partial x_i} = 0.$$

Now consider the following sequence of problems that are equivalent (see the Appendix) to (1) when consistent solutions are required:

$$
\left.
\begin{aligned}
x_i &= \mathrm{am}_x \pi(x, x_{ij}, i) \\
\text{subject to} \quad & \\
x_{ij} &= \mathrm{am}_x \pi(x, x_i, j)
\end{aligned}
\right\} \tag{6.0}
$$

$$
\left.
\begin{aligned}
x_i &= \mathrm{am}_x \pi(x, x_{ij}, i) \\
\text{subject to} \quad & \\
x_{ij} &= \mathrm{am}_x \pi(x, x_{iji}, j) \\
\text{subject to} \quad & \\
x_{iji} &= \mathrm{am}_x \pi(x, x_{ijij}, i) \\
\text{subject to} \quad & \\
x_{ijij} &= \mathrm{am}_x \pi(x, x_i, j) \\
&\vdots
\end{aligned}
\right\} \tag{6.1}
$$

$$x_i = \text{am}_x \pi(x, x_{iji}, i)$$

subject to

$$\vdots \quad x_{ij} = \text{am}_x \pi(x, x_{iji}, j) \qquad\qquad (6.n)$$

$$\vdots$$

subject to

$$x_{i(ji)^n j} = \text{am}_x \pi(x, x_i, j).$$

Each line in a problem will be called a "level."

Generically, problem $(6.k)$ has $2(k+1)$ levels involving a first level expressing firm i's problem, followed by $2k+1$ constraints, where the last constraint involves x_i as the variable in the second position of the π function (i.e., in place of $x_{(ij)(k+1)i}$). The above problems are all equivalent to (1) (restricted to be consistent) owing to the clear symmetry exhibited by (1): all even levels have the same form in (1) as do all odd levels. Problems (6.0)–$(6.n)$ require the computation of fixed points [for $(6.k)$ the vector is of dimension $2(k+1)$]. Problem (1) has a consistent solution if and only if the $(6.k)$ problems have a (common) fixed point (again, see the Appendix).

By consecutively substituting levels into earlier levels, we can express a first-order condition for the generic problem $(6.k)$ in a similar form to the first-order condition for (5). Let $AV(t)$ be the *aggregate variation* and define it as

$$AV(t) = \prod_{n=0}^{t} \frac{\partial x_{i(ji)^n j}}{\partial x_{(ij)^{n+1}i}} \cdot \frac{\partial x_{(ij)^{n+1}i}}{\partial x_{i(ij)^{n+1}j}}.$$

Thus, for example, $AV(0) = (\partial x_{ij}/\partial x_{iji})(\partial x_{iji}/\partial x_{ijij})$. The first-order conditions for (6.0) are therefore

$$\pi_1 + \pi_2 \frac{\partial x_{ij}}{\partial x_i} = 0,$$

while for $6.k$ $(1 \le k \le n)$ they are

$$\pi_1 + \pi_2 AV(k-1) \cdot \frac{\partial x_{i(ji)^k j}}{\partial x_i} = 0.$$

Let $\overline{AV} = \lim_{t=\infty} AV(t)$. Then the first-order condition for (1) is:

$$\pi_1 + \pi_2 \overline{AV} = 0. \qquad\qquad (7)$$

Therefore, (5) is equivalent to (1) if $\partial x_{ij}/\partial x_i = \overline{AV}$. Since $\overline{AV}$ involves an infinite product of negative fractions, i.e.,

$$\overline{AV} = \psi_i' \cdot \psi_{ij}' \cdot \psi_{iji}' \dots,$$

then clearly $\overline{AV} = 0$. Thus, the infinite regress model has a consistent, nonzero conjectural variation (ψ'_{ij}) and collapses to the standard (aggregate) variation term which can be viewed as a compounding of variations from the infinite regress model. This leads to an aggregate variation of zero. It is important to observe, however, that consistency should concern the conjectural variation and not the aggregate variation.

5. Implications for more than two firms: existence of the rational oligopoly equilibrium

We provide the extension of the notation to accommodate n firms in the Appendix. The important symmetry among the firms is in terms of the decision process they each follow, not the cost functions. Common knowledge of all cost functions and the demand functions means that tree T_i representing firm i's infinite regress process can be found as a subtree in tree T_j (representing firm j's infinite regress process) and *vice versa*. This provides a ready extension of the definition of a rational duopoly equilibrium to the oligopoly case.

Definition 3. A *rational oligopoly equilibrium* involving n firms is a vector of consistent solutions $(x^{1*}, x^{2*}, \dots, x^{n*}) \in R_+^\infty \times R_+^\infty \cdots \times R_+^\infty$ (n-fold) such that

$$x(T_{ij}) = x^{j*} \equiv x(T_j), \quad i = 1, \dots, n, \quad j = 1, \dots, n, \quad i \neq j.$$

The definition is the extension of the earlier definition requiring infinitely correct conjectures in equilibrium. Thus, x^*_{ij} (the first element in $x(T_{ij})$ and the second element in $x(T_i)$) is required to be the first element in $x(T_j)$, which is x^*_j: what i thinks j will do is what j chooses to do. This is required to hold over all trees T_i and T_{ij}: each firm's subtree involving another firm is equated to that firm's tree.

The obvious extension of Theorem 1 therefore holds for the n-firm case. Moreover, given the above definition and the discussion in the Appendix (along with the assumptions that all firms have complete and perfect information and maximize profits, and that this is common knowledge), it is clear that a rational oligopoly equilibrium exists if and only if a Cournot equilibrium exists, and it is the Cournot equilibrium. Thus, the conditions for the existence of the rational oligopoly equilibrium are precisely the same as those for the existence of the Cournot equilibrium.

6. Conclusions

Therefore, the rational duopoly (oligopoly) equilibrium is, in general, a Cournot equilibrium and *vice versa*. This equilibrium is consistent in the

173

sense of Bresnahan (1981) and others in that the infinite regress model allows a precise definition of the notion of a conjectural variation, and we have shown that this conjectural variation is consistent. Moreover, the term in the standard model usually referred to as a conjectural variation is seen to be a compounding of an infinite sequence of variations at the various levels of the infinite regress model. The result is that the aggregate variation is zero. This provides the link between the standard Cournot model and the infinite regress model.

In the standard consistent conjectures equilibrium analysis, players are penalized for making (what appear to be) good conjectures: they are led to the zero-profit outcome, when poorer conjecturing would have resulted in positive profits. As has been shown, the problem comes from the *ad hoc* nature of the conjectural variation in such models. In the analysis presented above, the conjectural variation falls out as a natural aspect of the model. Moreover, the conjectural variation is consistent. Finally, the resulting equilibrium is individually rational, in that no individual actions (including deeper thought or better conjecturing) can improve a player's fortunes.

Appendix

The relationship between infinite regress problems and finite fixed-point problems. Consider an n-firm problem. Firm i's output is x_i under cost function $c_i: R_+ \to R_+$. Again, inverse industry demand is represented by $p: R_+ \to R_+$. Firm i's profits are

$$\pi(u, w, i) = p\left(u + \sum_j w_j\right)u - c_i(u),$$

where $w = (w_1, ..., w_{n-1})$ is the $(n-1)$ vector of predicted rival outputs. The infinite regress problem for firm i is represented by the tree in Figure A1a which we denote T_i, with node i the *root* of the tree T_i. In this figure $1 \le k_1 < \cdots < k_{n-1} \le n$ are integers such that $k_j \ne i$, $j = 1, ..., n-1$, and similarly

$$1 \le l_1 < \cdots < l_{n-1} \le n, \quad l_j \ne k_1, \; j = 1, ..., n-1;$$

$$1 \le m_1 < \cdots < m_{n-1} \le n, \quad m_j \ne k_{n-1}, \; j = 1, ..., n-1.$$

To illustrate, if $n = 3$, then T_1, the tree for firm 1, is as in Figure A1b.

In general, for tree T_i observe that (starting from the top) each node in the tree is labelled with a unique sequence of indexes, i.e., an *admissible* statement. Each "parent" node has $n-1$ offspring (the nodes with arcs pointed *into* the parent). The statement on an offspring consists of the

174

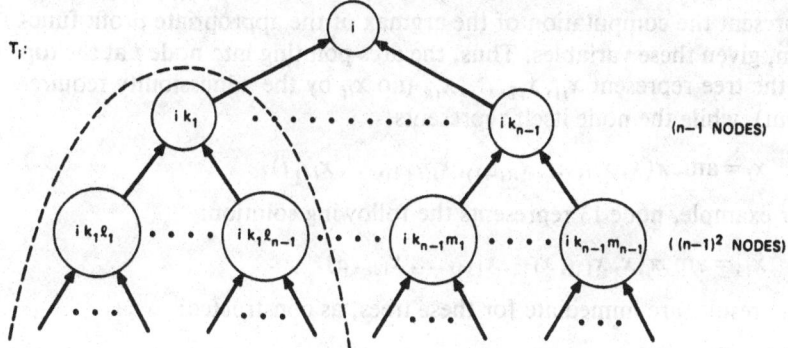

Figure A1a. The infinite-regress problem for firm i.

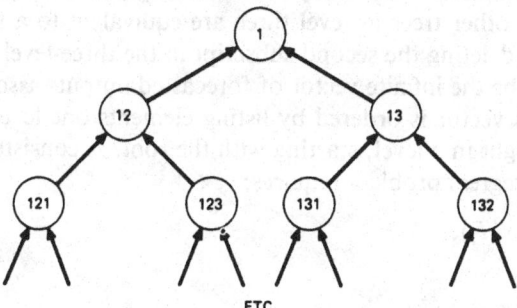

ETC.

Figure A1b. The infinite-regress problem when $n = 3$.

concatenation of the statement on the parent and a last element. Thus, if $n = 3$, the offspring of x_i would be x_{ij} and x_{ik}, where $j \neq i$, $j \neq k$, $k \neq i$.

The direction of the arrows reflects that the *offspring trees* (i.e., an offspring and all its descendants) provides the forecast for the associated offspring variable. Let $T_{\{k\}}$ be the offspring tree with root node labelled $\{k\}$. Thus, T_i is the tree shown (in the general case), while T_{ik1} is the offspring tree within the dotted line. Let l be the level of an offspring tree. The level is found by adding the number of subscripts in the statement labelling the root of the tree. Thus, tree T_{i21} (assuming $i \neq 2$) is a tree at level 3. There are therefore $(n-1)^{l-1}$ trees with roots at level l.

This tree represents the infinite regress problem if arcs in the tree represent output variables with subscript list equal to the label in the node

175

from which the arc *emanates* (i.e., nonarrow head of arc), and the nodes represent the computation of the argmax of the appropriate profit function, given these variables. Thus, the arcs pointing into node i at the top of the tree represent $x_{i1}, x_{i2}, ..., x_{in}$ (no x_{ii} by the admissibility requirement), while the node itself represents

$$x_i = \text{am}_x \pi(x, x_{i1}, ..., x_{i(i-1)}, x_{i(i+1)}, ..., x_{in}, i).$$

For example, node 13 represents the following solution:

$$x_{13} = \text{am}_x \pi(x, x_{131}, x_{132}, x_{134}, ..., x_{13n}, 3).$$

Two results are immediate for these trees, as constructed:

(i) $T_{iji} = T_i$
(ii) $T_{ijk} = T_{ik}, \ k \neq i.$

In other words, any tree at level three with a subscript list beginning and ending with the letter i is exactly the same (e.g., same x values) as T_i. Moreover, all other trees at level three are equivalent to a tree at level two found by deleting the second subscript in the three-level tree label.

Let $x(T_{\{k\}})$ be the infinite vector of forecasted outputs associated with tree $T_{\{k\}}$. This vector is ordered by listing elements one level at a time, from left to right in a level, starting with the root. A consistent solution to i's infinite regress problem requires:

$$x(T_{iji}) = x(T_i),$$

and

$$x(T_{ijk}) = x(T_{ik}), \quad i \neq k.$$

In the two-firm example considered in the text, the tree T_i is as illustrated in Figure A2. Therefore, in the consistent solution $x_i = x_{iji} = x_{ijiji} = \cdots$ and $x_{ij} = x_{ijij} = \cdots$.

Moreover, the above observation indicates why the infinite regress problem with consistency enforced is equivalent to the finite fixed-point problem. Consider the three-firm problem. The infinite regress model for firm i is

$$x_i = \text{am}_x \pi(x, x_{ij}, x_{ik}, i)$$

subject to

$$x_{ij} = \text{am}_x \pi(x, x_{iji}, x_{ijk}, j)$$

$$x_{ik} = \text{am}_x \pi(x, x_{iki}, x_{ikj}, k),$$

and so on, where each of the level-two problems has constraints, etc. Using the tree results and enforcing consistency of the solution, we obtain

Figure A2. The infinite-regress model for the two-firm example.

$$x_i = \operatorname*{am}_x \pi(x, x_{ij}, x_{ik}, i)$$

subject to

$$x_{ij} = \operatorname*{am}_x \pi(x, x_i, x_{ik}, j)$$

$$x_{ik} = \operatorname*{am}_x \pi(x, x_i, x_{ij}, k),$$

where the restrictions $x(T_{iji}) = x(T_i)$, $x(T_{iki}) = x(T_i)$, $x(T_{ijk}) = x(T_{ik})$, and $x(T_{ikj}) = x(T_{ij})$ were used. Therefore, any n-firm complete information infinite regress problem can be converted to a problem of finding a fixed point in R^n, given consistency is required. Furthermore, this means that the rational oligopoly equilibrium exists if and only if the Cournot equilibrium exists, since the tree for the rational oligopoly equilibrium can be converted to a fixed-point problem which has a solution only if the Cournot equilibrium exists [see problem (6.0) above].

References

Bernheim, B. D. "Rationalizable Strategic Behavior," *Econometrica,* Vol. 52 (July 1984), pp. 1007–28.

Bresnahan, T. F. "Duopoly Models with Consistent Conjectures." *American Economic Review,* Vol. 71 (December 1981), pp. 934–45.

Cyert, R. M. and DeGroot, M. H. "Bayesian Analysis and Duopoly Theory." *Journal of Political Economy,* Vol. 78 (September/October 1970), pp. 1168–84.

Fellner, W. *Competition among the Few.* New York: Augustus M. Kelley, 1965 (reprint of 1949 ed.).

Friedman, J. W. *Oligopoly and the Theory of Games.* Amsterdam: North Holland, 1977.

177

Holt, C. A., Jr. "An Experimental Test of the Consistent-Conjectures Hypothesis." Working Paper, Department of Economics, University of Minnesota, June 1982.

Kalai, E. and Stanford, W. "Duopoly, Conjectural Variations and Supergames." Discussion Paper 525, Center for Mathematical Studies in Economics and Management Sciences, Northwestern University, May 1982.

Kamien, M. I. and Schwartz, N. L. "Conjectural Variations." *Canadian Journal of Economics,* Vol. 16 (May 1983), pp. 191–211.

Kreps, D. M. and Scheinkman, J. A. "Quantity Precommitment and Bertrand Competition Yield Cournot Outcomes." *Bell Journal of Economics,* Vol. 14 (Autumn 1983), pp. 326–37.

Laitner, J. "'Rational' Duopoly Equilibria." *Quarterly Journal of Economics,* Vol. 95 (December 1980), pp. 641–62.

Luenberger, D. G. *Optimization by Vector Space Methods.* New York: John Wiley and Sons, 1969.

Pearce, D. G. "Rationalizable Strategic Behavior and the Problem of Perfection." *Econometrica,* Vol. 52 (July 1984), pp. 1029–50.

Perry, M. K. "Oligopoly and Consistent Conjectural Variations." *Bell Journal of Economics,* Vol. 13 (Spring 1982), pp. 197–205.

Szidarovszky, F. and Yakowitz, S. "A New Proof of the Existence and Uniqueness of the Cournot Equilibrium." *International Economic Review,* Vol. 18 (October 1977), p. 787–9.

CHAPTER 8

An experimental test of the consistent-conjectures hypothesis

CHARLES A. HOLT

A common way of analyzing multiperiod oligopoly models without dynamic interactions in the payoff structure is to compute a Nash equilibrium for each period taken separately. Many economists believe that behavior in a repeated market game cannot be predicted accurately with a period-by-period sequence of such "static" Nash equilibria, but an explicitly dynamic analysis can be extremely difficult unless the class of feasible dynamic strategies is restricted.[1]

There is an embarrassing multiplicity of alternative oligopoly "solutions" that are computationally less complex than game-theoretic approaches to multiperiod games. Many of these alternative solutions can be classified as conjectural variations models in which firms are assumed to conjecture that changes in their own decisions will induce reactions by other firms. These reactions are typically assumed to be characterized by functions that are locally linear. Almost any configuration of decisions can be an equilibrium for some conjectured reaction functions, so these models have little empirical content unless the reaction functions themselves are determined endogenously.

Department of Economics, University of Virginia, Charlottesville, VA 22901. This research was funded by the National Science Foundation. Laura Cohen, Brad Hauck, and Anne Villamil assisted in administering the experiments. Peggy Claytor assisted in the preparation of this manuscript. I am grateful to Dan Alger, Alfonso Novales, Robert Porter, Roger Sherman, and Joel Slemrod for comments on an earlier draft.

Charles A. Holt, "An Experimental Test of the Consistent-Conjectures Hypothesis," *American Economic Review* 75, 3, 1985, pp. 314–25.

[1] James Friedman (1977) discusses the existence of Nash equilibria in a general class of reaction function strategies, but one cannot actually compute nondegenerate equilibrium reaction functions for even the simplest quadratic payoff structures. More severe restrictions on the strategy spaces can produce results. For example, Richard Cyert and Morris DeGroot (1970) use backward induction to compute Nash equilibrium sequences of outputs for a finite horizon duopoly model in which firms make output decisions in alternate periods. Friedman's "balanced temptation equilibrium" is a Nash equilibrium for a super-game in which firms choose contingent strategies that specify an equilibrium output level and a commitment to a permanent switch to the firm's static Cournot output if another firm increases its output above its equilibrium level. Edward Green and Robert Porter (1984) have analyzed a stochastic generalization of this balanced temptation equilibrium.

Timothy Bresnahan (1981) has proposed a consistency condition that can often be used to determine specific conjectured reactions. Martin Perry provides a clear explanation of this consistency condition in the context of a duopoly in which firms' decisions are output quantities:

Each firm's first-order condition defines its profit-maximizing output as a reaction function on (1) the output of the other firm and (2) the conjectural variation about the other firm's response. Thus a conjectural variation by one firm about the other firm's response is consistent if it is equivalent to the derivative of the other firm's reaction function with respect to the first firm's output at equilibrium.

[1982, p. 197]

Many economists have found this notion of consistency to be appealing; Perry cites a large number of recent working papers on the theoretical properties of consistent-conjectures equilibria.

Although not explicitly dynamic, the consistent-conjectures equilibrium (CCE) approach initially seemed plausible to me because it predicts deviations from a static Nash equilibrium that are qualitatively consistent with the data reported in several published laboratory experiments with student subjects. These experiments, however, were not designed to provide a clear distinction between the CCE and other equilibrium concepts. This paper reports the results of an experiment designed specifically to test the consistent-conjectures hypothesis.

In Section I, the computation of a consistent-conjectures equilibrium is explained in the parametric context that is used to construct the experiment. Section II contains a discussion of how the payoff structures used in the previous laboratory experiments must be modified to permit a good test of the consistent-conjectures hypothesis. In Section III, I report the results of an experiment in which the theoretical predictions of the static Nash and consistent-conjectures equilibria are quite different. The data are clearly inconsistent with the CCE hypothesis. A related experiment is discussed in Section IV, and Section V contains a conclusion.

I. The consistent-conjectures hypothesis

The notion of a consistent-conjectures equilibrium is easily explained for a homogeneous-product duopoly in which variable costs are zero and industry demand is linear: $p = A - B(x_1 + x_2)$, where $A > 0$, $B > 0$, p denotes price, and x_i denotes the output of firm i. The profit function for firm i is $x_i(A - Bx_1 - Bx_2)$.

The first-order condition for the profit-maximization problem for firm i is

$$A - Bx_j - 2Bx_i - Bx_i\lambda_j = 0, \quad (i = 1, 2; \ j \neq i), \tag{1}$$

where $\lambda_j \equiv dx_j/dx_i$. The conjectural variation λ_j is assumed to be a constant.[2]

The two equilibrium outputs cannot be determined from the two equations in (1) unless the λ_j conjectural-variation parameters can be determined. To do this, Bresnahan uses a consistency condition that the actual profit-maximizing reaction of the ith firm's output to a change in x_j must be equal to the λ_i conjecture that characterizes the beliefs of firm j. Suppose that x_j changes by an amount of dx_j. Then Bresnahan computes the ith firm's profit-maximizing response to this change by totally differentiating equation (1) to obtain

$$-B\,dx_j - 2B\,dx_i - B\lambda_j\,dx_i = 0, \quad (i = 1, 2; \; j \neq i). \tag{2}$$

Dividing (2) by dx_j and using the definition of λ_i, one can express (2) as

$$-B - 2B\lambda_i - B\lambda_j\lambda_i = 0, \quad (i = 1, 2; \; j \neq i). \tag{3}$$

It follows from the two equations in (3) that $\lambda_i = \lambda_j = -1$. Then (1) implies that $x_i + x_j = A/B$, so price and profits are zero for the consistent-conjectures equilibrium in this example.[3] Note that the industry output equals A/B, but the consistent-conjectures equilibrium outputs need not be equal in this example. This is because the graphs of the reaction functions that satisfy the consistency requirement in the example are overlapping straight lines.

The consistent-conjectures equilibrium concept can be applied when decision variables are prices and there are more than two firms. When the demand is linear, the product is homogeneous, and all firms have identical constant average costs, Morton Kamien and Nancy Schwartz (1983) show that the *CCE* price equals average cost and profits are zero

---

[2] Bresnahan shows that the consistent conjectural variations will be constants when the profit function is quadratic.

[3] The *CCE* is a pair of outputs, x_1 and x_2; each firm knows the other's output with certainty and each firm calculates that a deviation will be unprofitable given the conjectured reaction of the other. The word "conjecture" itself connotes uncertainty, so it is natural to consider whether the derivation of the *CCE* in the text is affected by such uncertainty. Suppose that firm i is uncertain about the jth firm's reaction, and let the ith firm's conjectures about the other firm's reaction be represented by a random variable $\tilde{\lambda}_j$ with expected value λ_j. Also, $U_i(\cdot)$ indicates a utility function for firm i, and $E_i\{\cdot\}$ indicates an expectation with respect to the ith firm's subjective distribution for $\tilde{\lambda}_j$. The first-order necessary condition for the maximization of expected utility is

$$E_i\{U_i'(Ax_i - Bx_ix_j - Bx_i^2)[A - Bx_j - 2Bx_i - Bx_i\tilde{\lambda}_j]\} = 0.$$

Note that the random variable $\tilde{\lambda}_j$ appears only in the square brackets in the first-order condition. This is because the only uncertainty for firm i in this analysis is about the jth firm's reaction to a change in x_i. It follows from this observation and an assumption that $U_i'(\cdot) > 0$ that the necessary condition above reduces to equation (1) in the text with $\lambda_j = E_i\{\tilde{\lambda}_j\}$.

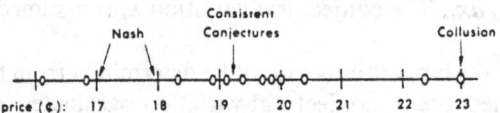

Figure 1. Price averages for the 12 duopoly experiments with complete information reported in Dolbear et al.

regardless of the number of firms and regardless of whether the decision variables are prices or quantities. The predicted "competitive" result in all cases other than monopoly in this context is the basis of the design of the experiment discussed in Section III.

II. Evidence from previous experiments

The first question that should be addressed is whether the popular static Nash equilibrium approach can explain behavior in multiperiod market experiments. F. Trenery Dolbear et al. (1968) reported data showing that behavior in multiperiod duopoly experiments deviates systematically from a static Nash equilibrium. Their subjects were students who chose prices simultaneously at the beginning of each "period." I will only discuss the "complete information" experiments in which subjects were given a pay-off table that relates price choices to payoffs in pennies.[4] The subject's price choice determined a row in the table, and the average of the prices of the subject's competitors determined a column. The payoff entries in the table were computed with a quadratic profit function that resulted from a demand function with some product differentiation. Payoffs were rounded off to the nearest penny, and as a result, there were two symmetric Nash equilibria *in prices* at common prices of 17 or 18. If subjects had been able to collude, they could have maximized their joint profit by raising prices to 23. However, subjects were not able to communicate.

In each market experiment, the subjects made simultaneous price decisions 15 times, but they were not told the number of repetitions in advance. The average price for each experiment was obtained by averaging all prices for periods 8 through 12. There were 12 duopoly experiments with complete information, and the average price in each experiment is represented by a large dot on the horizontal price scale in Figure 1. The

[4] Dolbear et al. also considered an "incomplete information" condition. The average level of price choices was approximately the same under each information condition, but there was less dispersion in the incomplete information experiments. Their paper provides an interesting analysis of the effects of information and the number of sellers on the degree of tacit collusion.

average price across all 12 experiments was 19.5, and Dolbear et al. concluded that these data indicate some tacit collusion in the sense that average prices and profits exceed the levels determined by a static Nash equilibrium in prices. Using the parameter values for the Dolbear et al. profit function, my earlier paper (1980) calculated the consistent-conjectures equilibrium price to be 19.2 in this context, and this is quite close to the observed price average.

Of course, these experiments were not designed to test the consistent-conjectures equilibrium, and there are several obvious ways in which the experiments do not provide a satisfactory test of this equilibrium concept. First, the subjects were required to make integer-valued price choices, but the *CCE* price was not an integer. Second, there is not much difference between the static Nash and the *CCE* prices. (This problem was even more severe for the oligopoly experiments with four subjects.) Finally, the word "competitors" in the subjects' payoff table may have suggested a particular type of behavior.[5]

Next, consider the previous section's quantity-choice model with a linear market-demand function and a common, constant average cost. The symmetric, static Nash (Cournot) equilibrium when strategies are output *quantities* will result in a price that is greater than average cost and less than the price resulting from perfect collusion. In contrast, the consistent-conjectures equilibrium in this context will result in competitive outputs that drive price down to average cost and profits to zero. Therefore, homogeneous-product oligopoly experiments with quantity-setting subjects and constant average costs may provide a good opportunity to discriminate between the static Nash and the consistent-conjectures theories.

Lawrence Fouraker and Sidney Siegel (1963) reported the results of some complete-information duopoly and triopoly experiments with these characteristics. The columns in their payoff table corresponded to a subject's own output choices, which were integers between 8 and 32. The row was determined by the "Quantity produced by my competition," and this quantity could be between 8 and 64. Outputs between 33 and 64 were actually possible in the triopoly experiments because the "competition" consisted of two other subjects. For a duopoly, the collusive industry output

---

[5] Roger Sherman warned me about using suggestive words, but I made the same mistake myself. In one of my pilot experiments, the term "oligopoly game" appeared on the receipt form to be completed by subjects at the end of the experimental session. This form was passed out at the beginning of the experiment, and one of the subjects who noticed the oligopoly phrase later remarked that the phrase "gave it away." He remembered seeing an assertion in a textbook that oligopolists would collude to maximize joint profit. This subject was in the only duopoly pair (out of four pairs) that was able to reach the collusive output combination in the first market experiment. All data from this pilot experiment were disregarded, and the wording of the receipt form was changed.

was 30 (15 per subject), the theoretical Nash/Cournot industry output was 40 (20 per subject), and the competitive industry output was 60 (30 per subject). As indicated in the previous section, 60 is the output predicted by the *CCE* in this context. Fouraker and Siegel do not seem to have noticed that the rounding off of payoffs to the nearest half-penny resulted in two symmetric Nash equilibria: one at an industry output of 40 and another at an industry output of 44.[6]

There were 16 complete-information duopoly experiments in this series (Experiment 10). Instead of averaging, Fouraker and Siegel used the subjects' decisions in the twenty-first period as an indicator of equilibrium behavior. The period-21 industry outputs were scattered fairly uniformly over the range from the collusive industry output (30) to the competitive (and *CCE*) industry output (60).[7]

The failure of outputs to rise to the *CCE* level in many markets may have been due to the fact that the profit was zero because price equaled average cost at this level. Subjects were told in the instructions that if they follow instructions and make "appropriate decisions," they "may earn an appreciable amount of money... but poor choices will result in small or no profit to you." Thus there is a possibility that the wording of the instructions made it less likely that the *CCE* result with zero profits would be observed. In my own experiments, subjects often appear to be frustrated after periods of very low profits, and such periods are usually followed by large output reductions that raise profits considerably.

There is, for me, a more compelling reason to expect that the outputs of 30 per duopolist would not be frequently observed in the Fouraker-Siegel duopoly experiments. Note that each subject is restricted to choose an output that is less than or equal to 32. The payoff table used by Fouraker and Siegel shows profits for values of the output of the "competition" between 8 and 64. In my opinion, each subject in the duopoly experiments was likely to realize that the outputs from 33 to 64 were irrelevant and, of course, no outputs above 32 were ever observed. If the output of the competition is less than 33, then it is a property of their table that any output below 28 will guarantee the subject a positive profit, regardless of what the competitor does. This truncation of the relevant payoff table caused by exogenous limits on output choices implies that the *CCE* profit of zero can be strictly dominated.[8] In particular, if both

---

[6] See the profit table in their appendix IV.

[7] The industry outputs in period 21 were 25, 30, 30, 32, 33, 38, 39, 40, 40, 44, 45, 49, 50, 55, 59, and 60.

[8] This is a serious limitation of the Fouraker–Siegel experiments because the main objective of these experiments seemed to have been to determine the proportions of duopoly pairs which could be best classified as either collusive, Cournot, or competitive. The

subjects were choosing outputs of 30 and earning no profit, then either one could cut output to 15 and earn at least 7.5 cents per period because the other seller's output cannot exceed 32.

This truncation argument does not apply in the triopoly experiments because the competition consists of two subjects, and there is no output decision a subject can make that will ensure a positive profit when each of the other two sellers chooses an output of 32. In fact, behavior in the triopoly experiments did seem to be much more competitive. The static Nash-equilibrium industry output for the triopoly was either 45 or 48.[9] The competitive and *CCE* output was 60, and the actual outputs in period 21 for the 11 triopoly markets were 40, 44, 46, 47, 51, 58, 59, 59, 62, 63, and 70. The median industry output of 58 is quite close to the *CCE* prediction of 60. An industry output of 58 with an approximately symmetric output configuration would result in earnings of only $.02 per subject per period in 1960 dollars.

III. An experimental test of the consistent-conjectures hypothesis

It follows from the above discussion that an experiment designed to test the consistent-conjectures hypothesis should have the following characteristics: (a) potentially suggestive words such as "competitors" should not appear in the instructions and payoff tables, (b) the *CCE* decisions should be integers, (c) the profit per hour per subject at the *CCE* should be reasonable, and (d) there should be no decision a subject can make that ensures a profit that will always exceed the *CCE* profit level.

A. The payoff structure

Bresnahan's original analysis of the *CCE* was for a duopoly in which firms' decision variables are quantities. As indicated in the previous section, models with quantity-setting duopolists are convenient because it is easy to choose market parameters that yield very distinct predictions for the Cournot and the consistent-conjectures equilibria. The experiment reported in this section involved subjects who chose output quantities.[10]

competitive or "rivalistic" outputs of 30 probably did not have a chance. In a different context, James Murphy (1966) has shown that truncation of the payoff table can have a major effect on experimental results.

[9] The output of 45 was implied by the profit-function parameters, but outputs of 16 for each subject constituted a Nash equilibrium for the payoff table that was used.

[10] In modeling *actual* market situations, the choice of how to model firms' strategies (as output quantities, prices, or something else) is very important. The specification of strategies is not arbitrary. In some markets, firms choose catalogue prices independently and

Subjects' profits depend on these output choices, and the Profit Table (Table 1) was computed from equation (1) with $A = 12$ and $B = 1/2$. In addition, \$.45 was added to each of the resulting profit entries. A calculus argument can be used to show that the outputs in a symmetric, collusive equilibrium are 6 per subject and the static Nash/Cournot outputs in a symmetric, collusive equilibrium are 8 per subject. Outputs are integer valued in the experiment, but this does not affect the collusive and Nash equilibria. For example, if both subjects choose outputs of 8, then a unilateral, integer-valued deviation will not increase a subject's profit given the Cournot conjecture. Because of the rounding off of profits to the nearest penny, there are also two asymmetric Nash equilibrium configurations: one with outputs of 7 and 9 and another with outputs of 6 and 10. In all cases, however, the industry output is 16 in a Nash equilibrium.

It follows from the calculations in Section I that the consistent conjecture is -1 in this context, and any combination of outputs that sum to 24 constitutes a *CCE*. These output combinations lie on the diagonal with \$.45 profits in the Profit Table. Starting on the diagonal, if one subject increases or decreases output by an integer amount, the other subject is conjectured to make an equal output change in the opposite direction. Thus the new output pair would again be on the \$.45 profit diagonal, so the deviation would not increase the subject's profit, given the consistent conjecture.

The collusive industry output of 12 yields earnings of \$.81 per subject, the static Nash/Cournot industry output of 16 yields earnings of \$.77 per subject in the symmetric case, and the *CCE* industry output of 24 yields earnings of \$.45 per subject. The experiment was not designed to distinguish noncooperative and collusive behavior, but neither of these modes of behavior yields outputs and profits that are close to those implied by the consistent-conjectures hypothesis in this context.[11] The high output

Footnote 10 *(cont.)*
then produce to order. Firms in such markets choose prices independently, but quantities may depend on rivals' prices, so the appropriate decision variable is price. In other markets, key production decisions are made independently in advance, but the price at which a firm's output can be sold depends on other's quantities. Those who use models with quantity-setting firms are presumably considering this type of market. Bresnahan's exposition is for quantity decisions, and it is appropriate to conduct an experimental test of the *CCE* with quantity decisions even if one believes that models with quantity-setting firms are unreasonable for most markets. A useful equilibrium concept should have the property that it yields good predictions for both specifications of decision variables, price and quantity.

[11] An increase in the A parameter will increase the spread between the Cournot and collusive output decisions, but this will increase profits and make the experiments more expensive to run. The use of a fixed cost to lower all profit entries is not possible because

Table 1. *Profit table*

Other Seller's Choice	Your output																		
	22	21	20	19	18	17	16	15	14	13	12	11	10	9	8	7	6	5	4
22	-175	-155	-135	-117	-99	-83	-67	-53	-39	-27	-15	-5	5	13	21	27	33	37	41
21	-164	-144	-125	-107	-90	-74	-59	-45	-32	-20	-9	1	10	18	25	31	36	40	43
20	-153	-134	-115	-98	-81	-66	-51	-38	-25	-14	-3	6	15	22	29	34	39	42	45
19	-142	-123	-105	-88	-72	-57	-43	-30	-18	-7	3	12	20	27	33	38	42	45	47
18	-131	-113	-95	-79	-63	-49	-35	-23	-11	-1	9	17	25	31	37	41	45	47	49
17	-120	-102	-85	-69	-54	-40	-27	-15	-4	6	15	23	30	36	41	45	48	50	51
16	-109	-92	-75	-60	-45	-32	-19	-8	3	12	21	28	35	40	45	48	51	52	53
15	-98	-81	-65	-50	-36	-23	-11	0	10	19	27	34	40	45	49	52	54	55	55
14	-87	-71	-55	-41	-27	-15	-3	7	17	25	33	39	45	49	53	55	57	57	57
13	-76	-60	-45	-31	-18	-6	5	15	24	32	39	45	50	54	57	59	60	60	59
12	-65	-50	-35	-22	-9	2	13	22	31	38	45	51	55	58	61	62	63	62	61
11	-54	-39	-25	-12	0	11	21	30	38	45	51	56	60	63	65	66	66	65	63
10	-43	-29	-15	-3	9	19	29	37	45	51	57	61	65	67	69	69	69	67	65
9	-32	-18	-5	7	18	28	37	45	52	58	63	67	70	72	73	73	72	70	67
8	-21	-8	5	16	27	36	45	52	59	64	69	72	75	76	77	76	75	72	69
7	-10	3	15	26	36	45	53	60	66	71	75	78	80	81	81	80	78	75	71
6	1	13	25	35	45	53	61	67	73	77	81	83	85	85	85	83	81	77	73
5	12	24	35	45	54	62	69	75	80	84	87	89	90	90	89	87	84	80	75
4	23	34	45	54	63	70	77	82	87	90	93	94	95	94	93	90	87	82	77

Shown in pennies.

levels (13 to 22) were included so that no output decision would guarantee a profit that exceeds the *CCE* level of $.45 per period.

The $.45 can be thought of as a normal rate of return when price equals average cost and economic profits are zero. Subjects were also given an initial stake of $.50 to cover any early losses. The announcement used to solicit subjects stated: "Although earnings cannot be predicted precisely, they will average about $6 per hour." The experiments were run at a pace of about 13 periods per hour, so the $.50 stake and the *CCE* profit of $.45 per period would result in earnings of about $6 per hour.

B. Subjects and procedures

The subjects were students in introductory and intermediate economics classes at the University of Minnesota. The instructors in these classes had not discussed experimental economics or formal oligopoly theory. The subjects had no previous experience with economics experiments.

Subjects were given about 10 minutes to read the instructions, which are available from the author on request. An additional paragraph in the instructions was read aloud by one of the people conducting the experiments. The purpose of this additional paragraph was to convince the subjects that the "other seller" in "a nearby room" was actually a person (not a computer).

The subjects were also given a Decision Sheet that revealed the "position number" of the other seller in that subject's market. The other sellers were seated in a separate room. First there was a "trial period," in which subjects marked their "output choices" on their Decision Sheets. Then they were told the output choice of the other seller, and they were asked to use the payoff table to compute both their own and the other seller's profit. This allowed us to check the subjects' understanding of the payoff table without suggesting anything by the use of hypothetical outputs to illustrate the computation of profits. In each subsequent period, we collected the Decision Sheets, computed profits, and paid the profits earned before the beginning of the next period. Subjects in the same room were spaced so that they would not be able to see exactly how much money others were earning. Subjects were also invited to write brief "explanations" of their decisions on their Explanation Sheet.

Footnote 11 *(cont.)*
the profit at the consistent-conjectures equilibrium should be sufficiently positive. A reduction in the *B* parameter will also increase the spread between the Cournot and collusive outputs, but the resulting flatness in the payoff structure results in multiple Cournot equilibria when profits are rounded off to the nearest penny.

The consistent-conjectures hypothesis

Subjects will naturally be curious about when the experiment will end, and I think the best way to deal with this is to be explicit about the stopping rule. A random stopping rule was used to avoid end effects. Subjects were told that there would be at least 7 periods and that there was a probability of 1/6 that period 7 and each following period would be the final period. The final period was determined by a six on the throw of a die, but we used the same sequence of die throws for all subjects. The throw of the die was recorded on the Decision Sheet.

There were 24 subjects that will be labeled $S1$, $S2$, etc. There were 12 initial pairings of subjects, and all subjects participated in a "first market" that was terminated by a throw of the die after 13 periods for all pairs. In order to check for experience effects, 16 of these subjects were rematched and given a new Decision Sheet with the new position number of the other seller. A different sequence of throws of the die was used, and this "second market" was terminated after 9 periods.

C. The data

The output choices for the 24 subjects who participated in the first market are shown in Table 2, and choices for the 16 experienced subjects who participated in the second market are shown in Table 3. The final-period industry inputs $(x_1 + x_2)$ for all duopoly pairs are plotted along the market demand curve in Figure 2. There was some collusive behavior resulting in outputs of 6 per subject, and there was rivalistic behavior resulting in industry outputs greater than the static Nash/Cournot industry output of 16. Regardless of whether the first-market and second-market data are considered separately or together, the mean and median (or medians) of the final-period industry outputs are between 14 and 16. Earnings averaged about $8.50 per subject per hour.

The data are clearly inconsistent with the *CCE* prediction of an industry output of 24, in my opinion. None of the final-period industry outputs exceed 21. There was only one pair of subjects ($S7$ and $S2$ in the second market) with combined outputs that were often closer to the *CCE* level of 24 than to the static Nash/Cournot level of 16. The occasional high outputs of other subjects usually appear to be attempts to punish a rival for not reducing output. For example, subject $S3$ had been in a collusive duopoly in the first market, but $S3$ was not able to induce $S6$ to collude in the second market. Apparently frustrated, $S3$ increased output from 6 to 19 in period 4 and then returned to 6 in period 5.

A statistical analysis should begin with a consideration of why some duopoly pairs are more collusive than others. Variations in market outcomes

189

Table 2. *First-market output choices for subjects S1–S24*

Period	S1	S2	S3	S4	S5	S6	S7	S8	S9	S10	S11	S12
1	10	6	10	8	8	10	12	8	10	8	10	10
2	9	10	8	10	8	8	14	9	9	10	4	8
3	10	11	8	6	7	7	13	6	11	9	10	10
4	8	4	6	7	7	9	13	7	9	8	4	8
5	8	10	6	6	8	7	11	8	8	7	10	10
6	10	9	6	6	8	10	11	10	7	7	7	10
7	8	10	6	6	10	8	9	10	7	7	7	8
8	9	8	6	6	10	8	11	9	8	7	7	8
9	10	10	6	6	10	8	10	10	7	10	7	8
10	9	9	6	6	9	9	10	9	8	10	22	8
11	8	8	6	6	9	13	10	9	9	9	7	10
12	7	7	6	6	9	6	10	9	8	8	7	8
13	6	6	6	6	9	8	10	8	7	7	7	8

	S13	S14	S15	S16	S17	S18	S19	S20	S21	S22	S23	S24
1	8	9	7	10	8	7	9	10	6	9	8	4
2	7	8	9	13	6	8	5	9	6	8	9	5
3	6	9	6	7	8	6	9	9	6	8	7	9
4	9	8	7	9	8	9	8	8	6	8	8	13
5	8	8	7	8	8	6	6	9	8	8	11	9
6	7	8	14	6	7	9	8	9	8	8	10	8
7	8	8	8	11	8	6	10	9	8	6	9	7
8	8	8	7	5	8	8	9	8	7	6	8	7
9	8	8	6	6	8	9	7	8	6	7	7	8
10	8	8	6	5	6	10	9	8	6	6	7	8
11	8	8	6	6	8	7	8	8	6	6	8	7
12	8	8	6	6	8	6	8	8	6	6	7	8
13	8	8	6	6	8	8	8	8	6	6	8	6

Subject S1 was paired with S2, S3 with S4, etc.

may be due to variations in variables not included in the oligopoly models discussed above, variables such as individuals' willingness to experiment with output changes. Suppose that individuals' characteristics are independent drawings from some population of possible characteristics. Then it is natural to think of final-period industry outputs for either the first or second market (not both together) as being independent realizations of a random variable. In the following discussion, the 8 final-period industry outputs in the second market will be denoted by $Q_1, Q_2, ..., Q_8$, and the vector of these outputs will be denoted by $\bar{Q}$. Consider a family of hypotheses of the form: $\Pr\{Q_i < y\} \leq 1/2$ for some $y > 21$; $i = 1, ..., 8$. This

Table 3. *Second-market output choices for subjects S1–S16*

Period	S1	S4	S3	S6	S5	S8	S7	S2	S9	S12	S11	S14	S13	S16	S15	S10
1	6	6	6	9	9	12	11	8	8	10	7	7	6	10	10	8
2	6	6	6	9	9	12	11	10	9	9	7	7	8	10	8	9
3	6	6	6	9	10	9	11	10	8	9	7	7	8	6	7	8
4	6	6	19	9	9	9	11	10	8	8	7	7	6	8	6	7
5	6	6	6	8	9	8	11	9	7	8	7	7	8	9	6	7
6	6	6	7	8	8	8	11	11	7	8	7	7	8	8	7	7
7	6	6	6	8	8	8	11	10	8	8	7	7	8	8	7	7
8	6	6	8	8	7	8	11	10	8	8	7	7	8	8	7	7
9	6	6	8	10	8	7	11	10	8	8	7	7	8	8	7	7

Subject S1 was paired with S4, S3 with S6, etc.

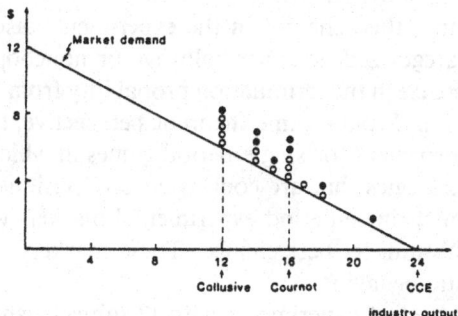

Figure 2. Final-period industry output for duopoly markets.
Note: ○ First-market duopoly output; ● second-market duopoly output.

family includes a hypothesis that the median of the industry outputs is 24, the theoretical prediction of the consistent conjectures equilibrium. Let H_y denote a particular hypothesis in this family that corresponds to a particular value of y. It can be seen from a binomial probability table that $Pr\{\bar{Q}|H_y\} \leq .0039$ because all 8 industry outputs are less than 21. However, a rejection of H_y using a classical hypothesis test would be misleading if there were no other hypothesis that is reasonable given the data observed. But there are many reasonable alternatives in this case. For example, consider a hypothesis H_{16}: $Pr\{Q_i < 16\} = 1/2$, $i = 1, ..., 8$. This hypothesis implies that a median of the distribution is 16, the theoretical prediction of the static Nash equilibrium. It follows from simple binomial probability calculations that $Pr\{\bar{Q}: H_{16}\} = .2734$, so the likelihood ratio is greater than .2734/.0039. If the posterior probabilities for H_{16} and H_y are denoted by $\Pr\{H_{16}\,|\,\bar{Q}\}$ and $\Pr\{H_y\,|\,\bar{Q}\}$, respectively, then the ratio $\Pr\{H_{16}\,|\,\bar{Q}\}/\Pr\{H_y\,|\,\bar{Q}\}$ is more than 70 times as great as the corresponding ratio of prior probabilities. A Bayesian analysis of the final-period outputs for the first-market experiments yields even stronger conclusions.

IV. A single-period duopoly experiment

The experimental design discussed above induces an infinite horizon in which the probability of termination determines the tradeoff between profit in the current period and profit in the future. In other words, the probability of termination determines the rate of which profits are discounted. If the probability of termination is low enough, subjects may be willing to make unprofitable output reductions in the hope of inducing the other seller to cut output in the future.

Roughly speaking, the behavior in the experiments discussed in Section III can be categorized as either collusive or noncooperative. I expected that an increase in the termination probability from 1/6 to 1 would result in no collusion. From a game-theoretic perspective, the static Nash equilibrium is appropriate for single-period games in which subjects are not able to use strategies that are contingent on decisions made in previous periods. Thus, single-period experimental markets would give the static Nash equilibrium its best chance. These markets may also yield even more rivalistic behavior.

I conducted one set of experiments with 12 subjects who participated in a series of 11 single-period duopoly markets with the same payoff table that was used in the multiperiod experiments. The subjects were drawn from a pool of people who had previous experience with a different series of duopoly experiments with different payoff tables. Six subjects were seated in each of two large rooms, and subjects were spaced so that they were unable to determine the "position number" of any other subject in their own room. A research assistant was present in each room at all times. The instructions for these single-period experiments are available from the author on request.

The experiment began with a trial period in which profits were computed but not paid. This was followed by 10 single-period markets. The aggregate data on individual choices for these markets are graphed in Figure 3, and data for particular subjects and their rivals are given in Table 4. The output choices are initially quite diverse, but by period 7 two-thirds of the subjects are choosing outputs of 9. This is followed by a trend toward the symmetric Nash/Cournot outputs of 8, and 7 of the

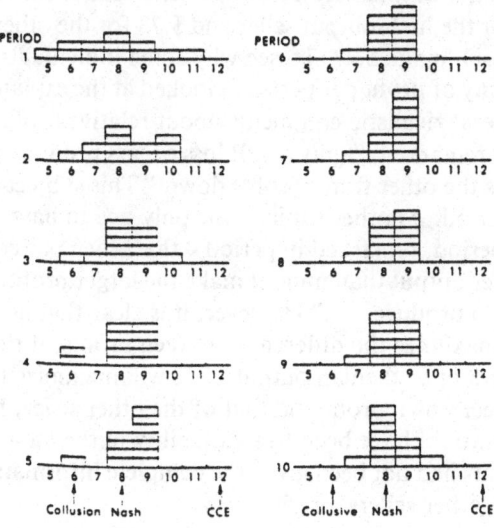

Figure 3. Frequency of individual output choices in the single-period market experiment.

Table 4. *Single-period experiments: subjects' output choices with rivals' choices shown in parentheses*

Period	S25	S26	S27	S28	S29	S30	S31	S32	S33	S34	S35	S36
Trial	7(8)	8(7)	22(10)	10(22)	5(7)	7(5)	13(7)	7(13)	6(8)	8(6)	10(5)	5(10)
1	5(10)	8(7)	9(6)	10(5)	8(6)	6(9)	11(8)	6(8)	9(7)	8(11)	7(8)	7(9)
2	6(10)	8(9)	9(7)	10(7)	8(8)	10(6)	10(8)	7(9)	9(8)	8(8)	7(10)	8(10)
3	6(7)	8(10)	9(8)	9(9)	8(9)	8(8)	10(8)	7(6)	9(9)	8(9)	8(8)	9(8)
4	6(8)	9(8)	9(9)	8(9)	8(9)	8(9)	9(8)	6(8)	9(8)	8(6)	8(6)	9(9)
5	6(9)	9(9)	9(9)	9(9)	9(9)	8(9)	9(8)	8(9)	9(8)	8(8)	8(8)	9(6)
6	7(9)	8(9)	9(7)	9(8)	9(8)	9(8)	8(9)	8(9)	9(8)	8(9)	8(9)	9(8)
7	7(8)	9(9)	9(9)	9(9)	9(9)	9(9)	9(9)	8(8)	9(9)	8(8)	8(7)	9(9)
8	7(9)	9(8)	9(9)	9(8)	9(7)	8(9)	8(8)	8(9)	9(9)	8(9)	8(8)	9(8)
9	7(8)	9(9)	9(8)	9(9)	9(8)	8(8)	8(7)	8(9)	8(9)	8(8)	8(9)	9(9)
10	7(8)	9(8)	9(8)	8(8)	9(8)	8(10)	8(9)	8(8)	8(7)	8(9)	8(9)	10(8)

12 subjects choose 8 in the final period. As expected, there was no successful collusion in the later periods of this experiment.

The frequency of rivalistic outputs of 9 in the intermediate periods is interesting. First, note that 9 is not very far from a Nash equilibrium in terms of profits. For the range of sellers' outputs in the final periods, any seller with an output of 9 could only increase profit by $.01 by switching

193

from 9 to 8. If the outputs are 9 for one seller and 8 for the other, the profit is $.76 for the high-output seller and $.73 for the other. At outputs 8 and 8, they each make $.77. To see why some individuals were willing to give up a penny of profit per period, I looked at the explanation sheets. There were several rivalistic comments about relative profits. For example, one person remarked: "Only a $.01 loss occurs producing at 9 instead of 8. This keeps the other firm's profits down." This subject did switch to 8 in the final period. Another subject, the only one to have an output of 10 in the final period, remarked in period 4 that when paired ". . . against a firm with lower output than mine, I make the larger profit, 9 is an interesting number to produce. . . ." However, it is clear that no subject's objective was to maximize the difference between profits; if the other seller produces either 8 or 9, then an output of 12 will maximize the difference between a subject's own profit and that of the other seller. In retrospect, there probably would have been less variability in the data if subjects in these experiments had not been given the complete information necessary to compute the other sellers' profit.

V. Conclusion

In this paper, I compare the theoretical predictions of the consistent-conjectures hypothesis with data for individuals' behavior in several laboratory experiments. In all experiments discussed, subjects simultaneously choose either price *or* quantity in a sequence of market periods, and subjects are given payoff tables that provide "complete information" about the relationship between decisions and profits for all participants.

My interpretation of the previously published experimental results is – the consistent-conjectures hypothesis provides a good explanation of the price choices made by subjects in the Dolbear et al. experiments, but the predictions of the consistent conjectures and static Nash equilibria are quite close. The predictions of these two equilibria are not close for the Fouraker–Siegel experiments with quantity-setting subjects. The *CCE* does not provide a good explanation of the output choices in the Fouraker–Siegel duopoly experiments, but its predictions look more reasonable in the triopoly experiments. The poor performance of the *CCE* in the duopoly case may have been because subjects' profits were zero at the *CCE* and there were other output choices a duopolist could make that would ensure a strictly positive profit.

This paper reports the results of a new set of duopoly experiments with complete information in which payoffs are positive at the *CCE*, and there is no decision that can guarantee a profit that exceeds the *CCE* profit. The consistent-conjectures equilibrium does not provide good predictions in these experiments. The data are more consistent with the Cournot equilibrium, although several duopoly pairs managed to achieve perfect collusion tacitly. Thus, there is at least one simple payoff structure (with homogeneous products, linear demand, and constant average variable costs) in which the *CCE* predictions are clearly inaccurate.

There are, however, several questions a skeptical reader may wish to consider. First, can laboratory experiments with individual decision makers be used to evaluate theories of the behavior of business firms? Many economists will give a negative answer, but I see nothing in the computation of a consistent-conjectures equilibrium that suggests that the arguments apply to business organizations but not to individuals. One obvious difference between businessmen and the student subjects is that businessmen have more experience with the markets in which they operate. But when experience has been shown to have a significant impact on behavior in experiments, the effect has been to increase the frequency of collusion.[12] Increased collusion in the experiments reported here would further skew the data away from the "competitive" *CCE* output prediction.

A second issue is whether the inaccuracy of the *CCE* prediction derived in Section I is due to something other than the inconsistency of conjectures. In particular, could it be the case that conjectures are consistent but that subjects are maximizing something other than profit? There was a slight tendency toward rivalistic behavior in the single-period experiment, so one may wish to consider an objective function R_i for the ith subject of the form: $R_i = \pi_i + w_i \pi_j$; $(i = 1, 2;\ j \neq i)$; where $\pi_i = x_i(A - Bx_1 - Bx_2)$, $-1 < w_i < 1$. If the w_i parameter is zero the subject is a profit maximizer, and as the w_i parameter approaches -1 the subject becomes very rivalistic and seeks to maximize the difference in profits. The first-order condition analogous to (1) is

$$A - Bx_j - 2Bx_i - Bx_i\lambda_j + w_i[(A - Bx_i - 2Bx_j)\lambda_j - Bx_j] = 0. \qquad (4)$$

The consistency condition analogous to (3) is

$$-B - 2B\lambda_i - B\lambda_j\lambda_i + w_i(-B - 2B\lambda_j - B\lambda_j\lambda_i) = 0, \quad (i = 1, 2;\ j \neq i). \quad (5)$$

The two equations in (5) imply that $\lambda_i = \lambda_j = -1$, so the consistent conjectures are not affected by the possible rivalistic nature of objectives. These conjectures and (3) imply that $x_i + x_j = A/B$, so the *CCE* industry output is unchanged. Thus the inaccuracy of the *CCE* predictions in this

---

[12] See Charles Plott (1982) for a discussion of the relationship between experience and collusion in laboratory experiments. Plott also has an excellent summary of the arguments for and against using laboratory experiments to test industrial organization theories.

CHARLES A. HOLT

context cannot be attributed to the possibility of nonzero values of the w_i parameters.

Finally, there is the question of the choice of the rule for ending the experiments. In experiments reported in this paper, the stopping rule was explicit, and a termination probability of 1/6 was used in the multi-period experiment. The choice of this particular termination probability was arbitrary because there is no parameter in the theoretical analysis of consistent-conjectures equilibria that corresponds to a termination probability nor is there a discount rate. The *CCE* concept is not explicitly dynamic; the timing of output deviations, initial reactions, and subsequent reactions by the deviant is not clear. As Perry points out: "The conjectural variation model is a simple static representation of the potentially complex dynamics of an oligopoly, and consistency as defined [in a *CCE*]... is the simplest adequate static condition for rational behavior in such a model" (p. 200).

The *CCE* did not provide a satisfactory representation of the dynamics in experimental markets with a termination probability of 1/6. I would expect to observe more collusion and less rivalistic behavior if the termination probability were even less than 1/6. For termination probabilities that exceed 1/6, I would expect behavior to conform more closely to the predictions of the static Cournot model. In the single-period market experiments with a termination probability of 1, the Nash/Cournot equilibrium provided accurate predictions, and there was no tendency to collude.

References

Bresnahan, Timothy F., "Duopoly Models with Consistent Conjectures," *American Economic Review,* December 1981, *71,* 934–45.
Cyert, Richard M. and DeGroot, Morris H., "Multi-period Decision Models with Alternating Choice as a Solution to the Duopoly Problem," *Quarterly Journal of Economics,* August 1970, *84,* 410–29.
Dolbear et al., F. Trenery, "Collusion in Oligopoly: An Experiment on the Effect of Numbers and Information," *Quarterly Journal of Economics,* May 1968, *82,* 240–59.
Fouraker, L. E., and Siegel, S., *Bargaining Behavior,* New York: McGraw-Hill, 1963.
Friedman, James W., *Oligopoly and the Theory of Games,* Amsterdam; New York: North-Holland, 1977.
Green, Edward J. and Porter, R. H., "Noncooperative Collusion Under Imperfect Price Information," *Econometrica,* January 1984, *52,* 87–100.
Holt, Charles A., "Equilibrium Models of Tacit Collusion in Oligopoly Experiments with Price-Setting Firms," Discussion Paper No. 80–138, Center for Economic Research, University of Minnesota, October 1980.

The consistent-conjectures hypothesis

Kamien, Morton I. and Schwartz, Nancy L., "Conjectural Variations," *Canadian Journal of Economics,* May 1983, *16*, 191–211.

Murphy, James L., "Effects of the Threat of Losses on Duopoly Bargaining," *Quarterly Journal of Economics,* May 1966, *80*, 296–313.

Perry, Martin K., "Oligopoly and Consistent Conjectural Variations," *Bell Journal of Economics,* Spring 1982, *13*, 197–205.

Plott, Charles R., "Industrial Organization Theory and Experimental Economics," *Journal of Economic Literature,* December 1982, *20*, 1485–527.

PRICES AND QUANTITIES

CHAPTER 9

Quantity precommitment and Bertrand competition yield Cournot outcomes

DAVID M. KREPS AND JOSÉ A. SCHEINKMAN

Bertrand's model of oligopoly, which gives perfectly competitive outcomes, assumes that: (1) there is competition over prices and (2) production follows the realization of demand. We show that both of these assumptions are required. More precisely, consider a two-stage oligopoly game where, first, there is simultaneous production, and, second, after production levels are made public, there is price competition. Under mild assumptions about demand, the unique equilibrium outcome is the Cournot outcome. This illustrates that solutions to oligopoly games depend on both the strategic variables employed and the context (game form) in which those variables are employed.

1. Introduction

Since Bertrand's (1883) criticism of Cournot's (1838) work, economists have come to realize that solutions to oligopoly games depend critically on the strategic variables that firms are assumed to use. Consider, for example, the simple case of a duopoly where each firm produces at a constant cost b per unit and where the demand curve is linear, $p = a - q$. Cournot (quantity) competition yields equilibrium price $p = (a + 2b)/3$, while Bertrand (price) competition yields $p = b$.

In this article, we show by example that there is more to Bertrand competition than simply "competition over prices." It is easiest to explain what we mean by reviewing the stories associated with Cournot and Bertrand. The Cournot story concerns producers who simultaneously and independently make production quantity decisions, and who *then* bring

Harvard University.
University of Chicago.
David M. Kreps and José A. Scheinkman, "Quantity Precommitment and Bertrand Competition Yield Cournot Outcomes," *Bell Journal of Economics* 14, 2, 1983, pp. 326–37.
The authors are grateful to an anonymous referee and the Editorial Board for helpful comments. Professor Kreps' research is supported by NSF Grant SES-8006407 to Stanford University and Office of Naval Research Contract N00014-77-C-0518 to Yale University. Professor Scheinkman's research is supported by NSF Grant SES-7926726 to the University of Chicago.

201

what they have produced to the market, with the market price being the price that equates the total supply with demand. The Bertrand story, on the other hand, concerns producers who simultaneously and independently name prices. Demand is allocated to the low-price producer(s), who *then* produce (up to) the demand they encounter. Any unsatisfied demand goes to the second lowest price producer(s), and so on.

There are two differences in these stories: how price is determined (by an auctioneer in Cournot and by price "competition" in Bertrand), and when production is supposed to take place. We demonstrate here that the Bertrand outcome requires both price competition and production after demand determination. Specifically, consider the following game between expected profit maximizing producers: In a first stage, producers decide independently and simultaneously how much they will produce, and this production takes place. They then bring these quantities to market, each learns how much the other produced, and they engage in Bertrand-like price competition: They simultaneously and independently name prices and demand is allocated in Bertrand fashion, with the proviso that one cannot satisfy more demand than one produced for in the first stage.

In this two-stage game, it is easy to produce one equilibrium. Let each firm choose the Cournot quantity. If each firm does so, each subsequently names the Cournot price. If, on the other hand, either chooses some quantity other than the Cournot quantity, its rival names price zero in the second stage. Since any defection in the first stage will result in one facing the demand residual from the Cournot quantity, and since the Cournot quantity is the best response to this residual demand function, this is clearly an equilibrium. What is somewhat more surprising is that (for the very special parameterization above and for a large class of other symmetric parameterizations) the Cournot outcome is the unique equilibrium outcome. Moreover, there is a perfect equilibrium that yields this outcome. (The strategies above constitute an imperfect equilibrium.) This note is devoted to the establishment of these facts.

One way to interpret this result is to see our two-stage game as a mechanism to generate Cournot-like outcomes that dispenses with the mythical auctioneer. In fact, an equivalent way of thinking about our game is as follows: *Capacities* are set in the first stage by the two producers. Demand is then determined by Bertrand-like price competition, and production takes place at zero cost, subject to capacity constraints generated by the first-stage decisions. It is easy to see that given capacities for the two producers, equilibrium behavior in the second, Bertrand-like, stage will not always lead to a price that exhausts capacity. But when those given capacities correspond to the Cournot output levels, in the second stage each firm names the Cournot price. And for the entire game, fixing capacities at the Cournot output levels is the unique equilibrium outcome. This yields a more satisfactory description of a game that generates Cournot outcomes. It is this language that we shall use subsequently.

This reinterpretation in terms of capacities suggests a variant of the game, in which both capacity creation (before price competition and realization of demand) and production (to demand) are costly. Our analysis easily generalizes to this case, and we state results for it at the end of this article.

Our intention in putting forward this example is not to give a model that accurately portrays any important duopoly. (We are both on record as contending that "reality" has more than one, and quite probably more than two, stages, and that multiperiod effects greatly change the outcomes of duopoly games.) Our intention instead is to emphasize that solutions to oligopoly games depend on both the strategic variables that firms are assumed to employ and on the context (game form) in which those variables are employed. The timing of decisions and information reception are as important as the nature of the decisions. It is witless to argue in the abstract whether Cournot or Bertrand was correct; this is an empirical question or one that is resolved only by looking at the details of the context within which the competitive interaction takes place.

2. Model formulation

We consider two identical firms facing a two-stage competitive situation. These firms produce perfectly substitutable commodities for which the market demand function is given by $P(x)$ (price as a function of quantity x) and $D(p) = P^{-1}(p)$ (demand as a function of price p).

The two-stage competition runs as follows. At the first stage, the firms simultaneously and independently *build capacity* for subsequent production. Capacity level x means that up to x units can be produced subsequently at zero cost. The cost to firm i of (initially) installing capacity level x_i is $b(x_i)$.

After this first stage, each firm learns how much capacity its opponent installed. Then the firms simultaneously and independently name prices p_i chosen from the interval $[0, P(0)]$. If $p_1 < p_2$, then firm 1 sells

$$z_1 = \min(x_1, D(p_1)) \tag{1}$$

units of the good at price p_1 (and at zero additional cost), for a net profit of $p_1 z_1 - b(x_1)$. And if $p_1 < p_2$, firm 2 sells

$$z_2 = \min(x_2, \max(0, D(p_2) - x_1)) \tag{2}$$

units at price p_2 for a net profit of $p_2 z_2 - b(x_2)$. If $p_2 < p_1$, symmetric formulas apply. Finally, if $p_2 = p_1$, then firm i sells

DAVID M. KREPS AND JOSÉ A. SCHEINKMAN

$$z_i = \min\left(x_i, \frac{D(p_i)}{2} + \max\left(0, \frac{D(p_i)}{2} - x_j\right)\right)$$

$$= \min\left(x_i, \max\left(\frac{D(p_i)}{2}, D(p_i) - x_j\right)\right) \tag{3}$$

at price p_i, for net profits equal to $p_i z_i - b(x_i)$. (In (3), and for the remainder of the article, subscript j means *not i*. Note the use of the *capacity* and *subsequent production* terminology.)

Each firm seeks to maximize the expectation of its profits, and the above structure is common knowledge between the firms. At this point the reader will notice the particular rationing rule we chose. Customers buy first from the cheapest supplier, and income effects are absent. [Alternatively, this is the rationing rule that maximizes consumer surplus. Its use is not innocuous – see Beckmann (1965) and Levitan and Shubik (1972).]

The following assumptions are made:

Assumption 1. The function $P(x)$ is strictly positive on some bounded interval $(0, X)$, on which it is twice-continuously differentiable, strictly decreasing, and concave. For $x \geq X$, $P(x) = 0$.

Assumption 2. The cost function b, with domain $[0, \infty)$ and range $[0, \infty)$, is twice-continuously differentiable, convex, and satisfies $b(0) = 0$ and $b'(0) > 0$. To avoid trivialities, $b'(0) < P(0)$ – production at some level is profitable.

3. Preliminaries: Cournot competition

Before analyzing the two-stage competition formulated above, it will be helpful to have on hand some implications of the assumptions and some facts about Cournot competition between the two firms. Imagine that the firms engage in Cournot competition with (identical) cost function c. Assume that c is (as b), twice-continuously differentiable, convex, and nondecreasing on $[0, \infty)$. Note that from Assumption 1, for every $y < D(0)$ the function $x \to xP(x+y) - c(x)$ is strictly concave on $[0, y-x]$. Define

$$r_c(y) = \underset{0 \leq x \leq X - y}{\operatorname{argmax}} \ xP(x+y) - c(x).$$

That is, $r_c(y)$ is the *optimal response function* in Cournot competition if one's rival puts y on the market. It is the solution in x of

$$P(x+y) + xP'(x+y) - c'(x) = 0. \tag{4}$$

204

Lemma 1.

(a) *For every c as above, r_c is nonincreasing in y, and r_c is continuously differentiable and strictly decreasing over the range where it is strictly positive.*

(b) *$r_c' \geq -1$, with strict inequality for y such that $r_c(y) > 0$, so that $x + r_c(x)$ is nondecreasing in x.*

(c) *If c and d are two cost functions such that $c' > d'$, then $r_c < r_d$.*

(d) *If $y > r_c(y)$, then $r_c(r_c(y)) < y$.*

Proof. (a) For any y, we have

$$P(r_c(y) + y) + r_c(y)P'(r_c(y) + y) - c'(r_c(y)) = 0.$$

Increase y in the above equation while leaving $r_c(y)$ fixed. This decreases the (positive) first term and decreases the second (it becomes more negative). Thus the concavity of $xP(x+y) - c(x)$ in x implies that, to restore equality, we must decrease $r_c(y)$. Where P is strictly positive, the decrease in $r_c(y)$ must also be strict. And the differentiability of r_c follows in the usual fashion from the smoothness of P and c.

For (b), increase y by h and decrease $r_c(y)$ by h in the equation displayed above. The first (positive) term stays the same, the second increases (becomes less negative), and the third increases. Thus the left-hand side, at $y+h$ and $r_c(y) - h$, is positive. The strict concavity of the profit function ensures, therefore, that $r_c(y+h) > r_c(y) - h$ (with the obvious qualifications about values y for which $r_c(y) = 0$).

For (c) and (d), arguments similar to (b) are easily constructed. ∎

Because of (d), the picture of duopoly Cournot competition is as in Figure 1. For every cost function c, there is unique Cournot equilibrium, with each firm bringing forward some quantity $x^*(c)$. Moreover, for c and d as in part (c) of the lemma, it is clear that $x^*(c) < x^*(d)$. In the next section, the case where c is identically zero plays an important role. To save on subscripts and arguments, we shall write $r(y)$ for $r_0(y)$ and x^* for $x^*(0)$. Also, we shall write $R(y)$ for $r(y)P(r(y)+y)$, the revenue associated with the best response to y when costs are identically zero.

{The astute reader will notice that the analysis to follow does not require the full power of Assumptions 1 and 2. All that is really required is that, for each $y > D(0)$, the functions $x \to xP(x+y) - b(x)$ and $x \to xP(x+y)$ are strictly quasi-concave [on $(0, X-y)$], and that r_b and r appear as in Figure 1. The former does require that $p \to pD(p)$ is strictly concave where it is positive, but this is not quite sufficient. In any event, we shall

205

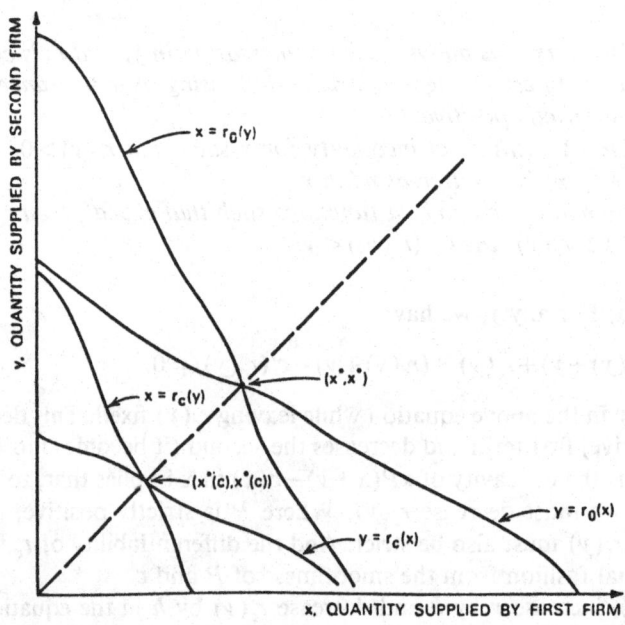

Figure 1. The picture of Cournot competition under the assumptions of the model.

continue to proceed on the basis of the assumptions given, as they do simplify the arguments that follow.}

4. The capacity-constrained subgames

Suppose that in the first stage the firms install capacities x_1 and x_2, respectively. Beginning from the point where (x_1, x_2) becomes common knowledge, we have a *proper subgame* [using the terminology of Selten (1965)]. We call this the (x_1, x_2) capacity-constrained subgame – it is simply the Edgeworth (1897) "constrained-capacity" variation on Bertrand competition. It is not *a priori* obvious that each capacity-constrained subgame has an equilibrium, as payoffs are discontinuous in actions. But it can be shown that the discontinuities are of the "right" kind. For subgames where $x_1 = x_2$, the existence of a subgame equilibrium is established by Levitan and Shubik (1972) in cases where demand is linear and marginal costs are constant. Also for the case of linear demand and constant marginal costs, Dasgupta and Maskin (1982) establish the existence of subgame equilibria for all pairs of x_1 and x_2, and their methodology

206

applies to all the cases that we consider. (We shall show how to "compute" the subgame equilibria below.)

The basic fact that we wish to establish is that for each (x_1, x_2), the associated subgame has unique expected revenues in equilibrium. (It is very probably true that each subgame has a unique equilibrium, but we do not need this and shall not attempt to show it.) Moreover, we shall give formulas for these expected revenues.

For the remainder of this section, fix a pair of capacities (x_1, x_2) and an equilibrium for the (x_1, x_2) subgame. Let $\bar{p}_i$ be the supremum of the support of the prices named by firm i; that is, $\bar{p}_i = \inf \{p: \text{firm } i \text{ names}$ less than p with probability one$\}$. And let $\underline{p}_i$ be the infimum of the support. Note that if $\min_i x_i \geq D(0)$, then, as in the usual Bertrand game with no capacity constraints, $\bar{p}_i = \underline{p}_i = 0$. And if $\min_i x_i = 0$, we have the monopoly case. Thus we are left with the case where $0 < \min_i x_i < D(0)$.

Lemma 2. *For each* i, $\underline{p}_i \geq P(x_1 + x_2)$.

Proof. By naming a price p less than $P(x_1 + x_2)$, firm i nets at most px_i. By naming $P(x_1 + x_2)$, firm i nets at worst $P(x_1 + x_2)(x_1 + x_2 - x_j) = P(x_1 + x_2)x_i$. ∎

Lemma 3. *If* $\bar{p}_1 = \bar{p}_2$ *and each is named with positive probability, then*

$$\underline{p}_i = \bar{p}_i = P(x_1 + x_2) \quad and \quad x_i \leq r(x_j), \quad for\ both\ i = 1\ and\ i = 2.$$

Proof. Suppose that $\bar{p}_1 = \bar{p}_2$ and each is charged with positive probability. Without loss of generality, assume $x_1 \geq x_2$, and suppose that $\bar{p}_1 = \bar{p}_2 > P(x_1 + x_2)$. By naming a price slightly less than $\bar{p}_1$, firm 1 strictly improves its revenues over what it gets by naming $\bar{p}_1$. (With positive probability, it sells strictly more, while the loss due to the lower price is small.) Thus $\bar{p}_1 = \bar{p}_2 \leq P(x_1 + x_2)$. By Lemma 2, we know that $\bar{p}_i = \underline{p}_i = P(x_1 + x_2)$ for $i = 1, 2$.

By naming a higher price p, firm i would obtain revenue $(D(p) - x_j)p$, or, letting $x = D(p) - x_j$, $xP(x + x_j)$. This is maximized at $x = r(x_j)$, so that were $r(x_j) < x_i$, we would not have an equilibrium. ∎

Lemma 4. *If* $x_i \leq r(x_j)$ *for* $i = 1, 2$, *than a (subgame) equilibrium is for each firm to name* $P(x_1 + x_2)$ *with probability one.*

Proof. The proof of Lemma 3 shows that naming a price greater than $P(x_1 + x_2)$ will not profit either firm in this case. (Recall that $xP(x + x_j)$ is strictly concave.) And there is no incentive to name a lower price, as each firm is selling its full capacity at the equilibrium price. ∎

Lemma 5. *Suppose that either $\bar{p}_1 > \bar{p}_2$, or that $\bar{p}_1 = \bar{p}_2$ and $\bar{p}_2$ is not named with positive probability. Then:*

(a) *$\bar{p}_1 = P(r(x_2) + x_2)$ and the equilibrium revenue of firm 1 is $R(x_2)$;*
(b) *$x_1 > r(x_2)$;*
(c) *$\underline{p}_1 = \underline{p}_2$, and neither is named with positive probability;*
(d) *$x_1 \geq x_2$; and*
(e) *the equilibrium revenue of firm 2 is uniquely determined by (x_1, x_2) and is at least $(x_2/x_1)R(x_2)$ and at most $R(x_2)$.*

Proof. For (a) and (b): Consider the function

$$\Xi(p) = p \cdot [\min(x_1, \max(0, D(p) - x_2))].$$

In words, $\Xi(p)$ is the revenue accrued by firm 1 if it names p and it is undersold by its rival. Under the hypothesis of this lemma, firm 1, by naming $\bar{p}_1$, nets precisely $\Xi(\bar{p}_1)$, as it is certain to be undersold. By naming any price $p > \bar{p}_1$, firm 1 will net precisely $\Xi(p)$. If firm 1 names a price $p < \bar{p}_1$, it will net at least $\Xi(p)$. Thus, if we have an equilibrium, $\Xi(p)$ must be maximized at $\bar{p}_1$.

We must dispose of the case $x_2 \geq D(0)$. Since (by assumption) $D(0) > \min_i x_i$, $x_2 \geq D(0)$ would imply $D(0) > x_1$. Thus, in equilibrium, firm 2 will certainly obtain strictly positive expected revenue. And, therefore, in equilibrium, $\bar{p}_2 > 0$. But then firm 1 must obtain strictly positive expected revenue. And if $x_2 \geq D(0)$, then $\Xi(\bar{p}_1) = 0$. That is, $x_2 \geq D(0)$ is incompatible with the hypothesis of this lemma.

In maximizing $\Xi(p)$, one would never choose p such that $D(p) - x_2 > x_1$ or such that $D(p) < x_2$. Thus, the relevant value of p lies in the interval $[P(x_1 + x_2), P(x_2)]$. For each p in this interval, there is a corresponding level of x, namely $x(p) = D(p) - x_2$, such that $\Xi(p) = x(p)P(x(p) + x_2)$. Note that $x(p)$ runs in the interval $[0, x_1]$. But we know that

$$\underset{x(p) \in [0, x_1]}{\text{argmax}} \ x(p)P(x(p) + x_2) = r(x_2) \wedge x_1,$$

by the strict concavity of $xP(x + x_2)$. If the capacity constraint x_1 is binding (even weakly), then $\bar{p}_1 = P(x_1 + x_2)$, and Lemma 2 implies that we are in the case of Lemma 3, thus contradicting the hypothesis of this lemma. Hence it must be the case that the constraint does not bind, or $r(x_2) < x_1$ [which is (b)], $\bar{p}_1 = P(r(x_2) + x_2)$, and the equilibrium revenue of firm 1 is $R(x_2)$ [which is (a)].

For (c): Suppose that $\underline{p}_i < \underline{p}_j$. By naming $\underline{p}_i$, firm i nets $\underline{p}_i(D(\underline{p}_i) \wedge x_i)$. Increasing this to any level $p \in (\underline{p}_i, \underline{p}_j)$ nets $p(D(p) \wedge x_i)$. Thus, we have an equilibrium only if $D(\underline{p}_i) < x_i$ and $\underline{p}_i$ is the monopoly price. [By the strict concavity of $xP(x)$, moving from $\underline{p}_i$ in the direction of the monopoly price will increase revenue on the margin.] That is, $p_i = P(r(0))$. But $p_i < \bar{p}_1 = P(r(x_2)+x_2) < P(r(0))$, which would be a contradiction. Thus $p_1 = p_2$. We denote this common value by p in the sequel. This is the first part of (c).

For the second part of (c), note first that $p > P(x_1+x_2)$. For if $p = P(x_1+x_2)$, then by naming (close to) p, firm 1 would make at most $P(x_1+x_2)x_1$. Since $x_1 > r(x_2)$ and the equilibrium revenue of firm 1 is $R(x_2)$, this is impossible.

Suppose that the firm with (weakly) less capacity named p with positive probability. Then the firm with higher capacity could, by naming a price slightly less than p, strictly increase its expected revenue. (It sells strictly more with positive probability, at a slightly lower price.) Thus, the firm with weakly less capacity names p with zero probability. Since p is the infimum of the support of the prices named by the lower capacity firm, this firm must therefore name prices arbitrarily close to *and above* p. But if its rival named p with positive probability, the smaller capacity firm would do better (since $p > P(x_1+x_2)$) to name a price just below p than it would to name a price just above p. Hence, neither firm can name p with positive probability.

For (d) and (e): By (c), the equilibrium revenue of firm i must be $p(D(p) \wedge x_i)$. We know that $p < \bar{p}_1 = P(x_2+r(x_2))$, so that $D(p) > D(P(x_2+r(x_2))) = x_2+r(x_2)$, and thus $D(p) > x_2$. Hence, firm 2 certainly gets px_2 in equilibrium. Firm 1 gets no more than px_1, so that the bounds in part (e) are established as soon as (d) is shown.

Suppose that $x_2 > x_1$. Then $D(p) > x_1$, and firm 1's equilibrium revenue is px_1. We already know that it is also $R(x_2)$, so that we would have $p = R(x_2)/x_1$, and firm 2 nets $R(x_2)x_2/x_1$. By naming price $P(r(x_1)+x_1)$ ($> p_1 = P(r(x_2)+x_2)$), firm 2 will net $R(x_1)$. We shall have a contradiction, therefore, if we show that $x_1 > r(x_2)$ implies $x_1 R(x_1) > x_2 R(x_2)$.

Let $\Theta(x) = xR(x) = xr(x)P(r(x)+x)$. We have

$$\Theta' = r(x)P(r(x)+x)+xr'(x)P(r(x)+x)+xr(x)P'(r(x)+x)(r'(x)+1)$$

$$= (r(x)-x)P(r(x)+x)+x(r'(x)+1)(P(r(x)+x)+r(x)P'(r(x)+x)).$$

The last term is zero by the definition of $r(x)$, so that we have

$$\Theta'(x) = (r(x)-x)P(r(x)+x).$$

Thus

$$x_2 R(x_2)-x_1 R(x_1) = \Theta(x_2)-\Theta(x_1) = \int_{x_1}^{x_2} (r(x)-x)P(r(x)+x)\,dx.$$

The integrand is positive for $x < x^*$ and strictly negative for $x > x^*$. We would like to show that the integral is negative, so that the worst case (in terms of our objective) is that in which $x_1 < x^*$ and x_2 is as small as possible. Since $x_1 > r(x_2)$, for every $x_1 < x^*$ the worst case is where x_2 is just a bit larger than $r^{-1}(x_1)$. We shall thus have achieved our objective (of contradicting $x_2 > x_1$, by showing that the integral above is strictly negative) if we show that for all $x < x^*$, $\Theta(x) - \Theta(r^{-1}(x)) \geq 0$.

But $\Theta(x) - \Theta(r^{-1}(x)) = xr(x)P(x+r(x)) - r^{-1}(x)xP(r^{-1}(x)+x)$. This is nonnegative if and only if $r(x)P(x+r(x)) - r^{-1}(x)P(r^{-1}(x)+x) \geq 0$, which is certainly true, since $r(x)$ is the best response to x. ∎

Lemma 6. *If $x_1 \geq x_2$ and $x_1 > r(x_2)$, there is a (mixed strategy) equilibrium for the subgame in which all the conditions and conclusions of Lemma 5 hold. Moreover, this equilibrium has the following properties. Each firm names prices according to continuous and strictly increasing distribution functions over an (coincident) interval, except that firm 1 names the uppermost price with positive probability whenever $x_1 > x_2$. And if we let $\Psi_i(p)$ be the probability distribution function for the strategy of firm i, then $\Psi_1(p) \leq \Psi_2(p)$: firm 1's strategy stochastically dominates the strategy of firm 2, with strict inequality if $x_1 > x_2$.*

Remarks. The astute reader will note that the first sentence is actually a corollary to the previous lemmas and to the (as yet unproven) assertion that every subgame has an equilibrium. The actual construction of an equilibrium is unnecessary for our later analysis, and the casual reader may wish to omit it on first reading. It is, however, of sufficient independent interest to warrant presentation. In the course of this construction, we obtain the second part of the lemma, which is also noteworthy. At first glance, it might be thought that firm 1, having the larger capacity, would profit more by underselling its rival, and therefore it would name the (stochastically) lower prices. But (as is usual with equilibrium logic) this is backwards: Each firm randomizes in a way that keeps the other firm indifferent among its strategies. Because firm 1 has the larger capacity, firm 2 is more "at risk" in terms of being undersold, and thus firm 1 must be "less aggressive."

Proof. Refer to Figure 2. There are five functions depicted there: $pD(p)$, $p(D(p)-x_2)$, $p(D(p)-x_1)$, px_1, and px_2. Note that:

(i) $px_1 = p(D(p)-x_2)$ and $px_2 = p(D(p)-x_1)$ at the same point, namely $P(x_1+x_2)$.

(ii) $px_1 = pD(p)$ at the point where $p(D(p)-x_1)$ vanishes, and similarly for 2.

(iii) The first three functions are maximized at $P(r(0))$, $P(r(x_2)+x_2)$, and $P(r(x_1)+x_1)$, respectively.

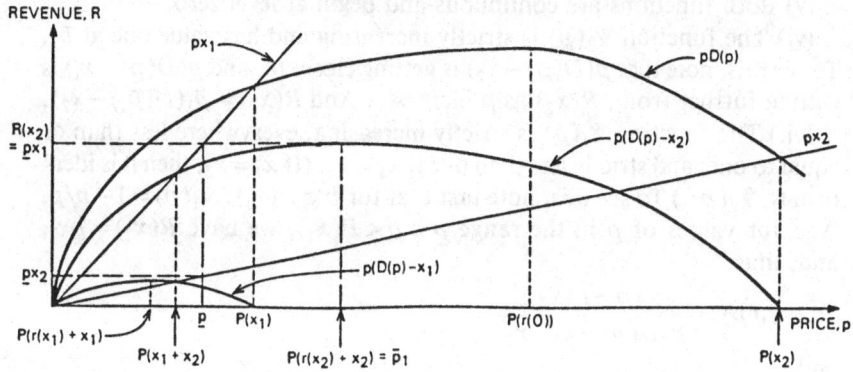

Figure 2. Determining the subgame equilibrium.

(iv) Because P is concave, the first three functions are strictly concave on the range where they are positive. And every ray from the origin of the form px crosses each of these three functions at most once. (The latter is a simple consequence of the fact that $D(p)$ is decreasing.)

Now find the value $p = P(r(x_2) + x_2)$. This is $\bar{p}_1$. Follow the horizontal dashed line back to the function $p(D(p) \wedge x_1)$. We have drawn this intersection at a point p where $D(p) > x_1$, but we have no guarantee that this will happen. In any event, the level of p at this intersection is $\underline{p}$. Follow the vertical dashed line down to the ray px_2. The height $\underline{p}x_2$ will be the equilibrium revenue of firm 2. Note that even if the first intersection occurred at a point where $x_1 > D(p)$, this second intersection would be at a level $\underline{p}$ where $D(\underline{p}) > x_2$, since $x_2 = D(p)$ at $P(x_2)$, which is to the right of $P(r(x_2) + x_2)$. Also, note that these intersections occur to the right of $P(x_1 + x_2)$, since $R(x_2) > x_1 P(x_1 + x_2)$.

Suppose that firm 1 charges a price $p \in [\underline{p}, \bar{p}_1]$. If we assume that firm 2 does not charge this price p with positive probability, then the expected revenue to firm 1 is

$$E_1(p) = \Phi_2(p) p(D(p) - x_2) + (1 - \Phi_2(p)) p(D(p) \wedge x_1),$$

where Φ_2 is the distribution function of firm 2's strategy. A similar calculation for firm 2 yields

$$E_2(p) = \Phi_1(p) p[\max(D(p) - x_1, 0)] + (1 - \Phi_1(p)) px_2.$$

(Note that for $p \in [\underline{p}, \bar{p}_1]$, we know that $D(p) - x_2 > 0$.)

Solve the equations $E_1(p) = R(x_2)$ $(= \underline{p}(D(\underline{p}) \wedge x_1))$ and $E_2(p) = \underline{p}x_2$ in $\Phi_2(p)$ and $\Phi_1(p)$, calling the solutions $\Psi_2(p)$ and $\Psi_1(p)$, respectively. Note that:

211

(v) Both functions are continuous and begin at level zero.

(vi) The function $\Psi_2(p)$ is strictly increasing and has value one at $\bar{p}_1$. To see this, note that $p(D(p)-x_2)$ is getting closer to, and $p(D(p)\wedge x_1)$ is getting further from, $R(x_2)$ as p increases. And $R(x_2) = \bar{p}_1(D(\bar{p}_1)-x_2)$.

(vii) The function $\Psi_1(p)$ is strictly increasing, everywhere less than or equal to one, and strictly less than one if $x_1 > x_2$. (If $x_1 = x_2$, then it is identical to $\Psi_2(p)$.) To see this, note first that for $p \geq P(x_1)$, $\Psi_1(p) = 1 - \underline{p}/p$. And for values of p in the range $\underline{p} \leq p < P(x_1)$, we have $R(x_2) = \underline{p}x_1$, and, thus,

$$\Psi_1(p) = \frac{(\underline{p}-p)x_2}{p(D(p)-x_1-x_2)},$$

and

$$\Psi_2(p) = \frac{(\underline{p}-p)x_1}{p(D(p)-x_1-x_2)}.$$

That is, for p between $\underline{p}$ and $P(x_1)$, $\Psi_1 = x_2\Psi_2/x_1$. Noting step (vi), the result is obvious.

(viii) $\Psi_1(p) \leq \Psi_2(p)$ for all p. This is immediate from the argument above for p in the range $\underline{p} \leq p < P(x_1)$. For $p \geq P(x_1)$, note that $pD(p)$ is receding from $R(x_2)$ more quickly than px_2 is receding from $\underline{p}x_2$ [since $p(D(p)-x_2)$ is still increasing], and $p(D(p)-x_2)$ is increasing, hence approaching $R(x_2)$ more quickly than the constant function zero is approaching px_2.

(ix) $\underline{p}x_2 \geq R(x_1)$. To see this, note first that $\underline{p}x_1 \geq R(x_2)$. Thus $\underline{p}x_2 \geq x_2R(x_2)/x_1$. To get the desired result, then, it suffices to show that $R(x_1) \leq x_2R(x_2)/x_1$, or $x_1R(x_1) \leq x_2R(x_2)$ (with strict inequality if $x_1 > x_2$.) Recall that $x_1 > x_2$. If $x_2 \geq x^*$, then the result follows easily from the formula $x_1R(x_1) - x_2R(x_2) = \int_{x_2}^{x_1}(r(x)-x)P(r(x)+x)\,dx$. If $x_2 < x^*$, then $x_2 > r(x_1)$ (since $(x_1 > r(x_2))$), and the argument from the previous lemma applies.

Putting all these points together, we see that we have an equilibrium of the desired type if firm 1 names prices according to the distribution Ψ_1, and firm 2 names them according to Ψ_2. Each firm is (by construction) indifferent among those strategies that are in the support of their (respective) distribution functions. The levels of $\bar{p}_1$ and $\underline{p}$ are selected so that firm 1 has no incentive to name a price above the first or below the second. Since firm 2 gets no more than $R(x_1)$, it has no incentive to go above $\bar{p}_1$; neither (by construction) will it gain by naming a price below $\underline{p}$. ∎

Since the construction of the equilibrium took us rather far afield of our main objective, we end this section by compiling the results established above that are important to subsequent analysis:

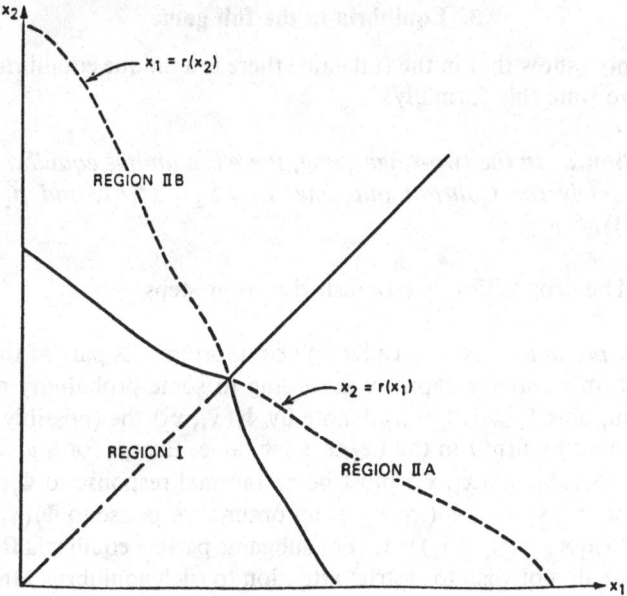

Figure 3. The different types of subgame equilibria.

Proposition 1. (Refer to Figure 3.) *In terms of the subgame equilibria, there are three regions of interest.*

(a) *If $x_i \le r(x_j)$ for both $i = 1$ and $i = 2$ (which is labeled as region I in Figure 3), the unique equilibrium has both firms naming price $P(x_1 + x_2)$ with certainty. The equilibrium revenues are, therefore, $x_i P(x_1 + x_2)$ for firm i.*

(b) *If $x_1 \ge x_2$ and $x_1 > r(x_2)$ (labeled region IIA in Figure 3), then, in equilibrium, firm 1 has expected revenue $R(x_2)$, and firm 2 has expected revenue determined by (x_1, x_2) and somewhere between $R(x_2)$ and $x_2 R(x_2)/x_1$. If $x_2 < D(0)$, the equilibrium is the randomized one constructed in Lemma 6; if $x_2 \ge D(0)$, both firms net zero and name price zero with certainty.*

(c) *If $x_2 \ge x_1$ and $x_2 > r(x_1)$ (labeled region IIB in Figure 3), then, in equilibrium, firm 2 has expected revenue $R(x_1)$, and firm 1 has expected revenue determined by (x_1, x_2) and somewhere between $R(x_1)$ and $x_1 R(x_1)/x_2$. Similar remarks apply concerning $x_1 \lesseqgtr D(0)$ as appear in (b).*

(d) *The expected revenue functions are continuous functions of x_1 and x_2.*

213

DAVID M. KREPS AND JOSÉ A. SCHEINKMAN

5. Equilibria in the full game

We can now show that in the full game there is a unique equilibrium outcome. We state this formally:

Proposition 2. *In the two-stage game, there is a unique equilibrium outcome, namely the Cournot outcome: $x_1 = x_2 = x^*(b)$, and $p_1 = p_2 = P(2x^*(b))$.*

Proof. The proposition is established in four steps.

Step 1: preliminaries. Consider any equilibrium. As part of this equilibrium firm i chooses capacity according to some probability measure μ_i with support $S_i \subseteq R$. Let us denote by $\Phi_i(x_1, x_2)$ the (possibly mixed) strategy used by firm i in the (x_1, x_2) subgame. Except for a $\mu_1 \times \mu_2$ null subset of $S_1 \times S_2$, $\Phi_i(x_1, x_2)$ must be an optimal response to $\Phi_j(x_1, x_2)$. That is, $\Omega_i = \{(x_1, x_2): \Phi_i(x_1, x_2) \text{ is an optimal response to } \Phi_j(x_1, x_2)\}$ is such that $(\mu_1 \times \mu_2)(\Omega_1 \cap \Omega_2) = 1$. (For subgame perfect equilibria $\Omega_1 \cap \Omega_2 = R^2$, but we do not wish to restrict attention to such equilibria.) In particular, if $E(x_i) = \{x_j: (x_1, x_2) \in \Omega_1 \cap \Omega_2\}$ and $\hat{X}_i = \{x_i \in S_i: \mu_j(E(x_i)) = 1\}$, then $\mu_i(\hat{X}_i) = 1$. Let π_i denote the expected profit of firm i in this equilibrium and $\pi_i(x_i)$ the expected profit when capacity x_i is built. If $X_i = \{x_i \in \hat{X}_i: \pi_i(x_i) = \pi_i\}$, then again $\mu_i(X_i) = 1$. Let $\bar{x}_i$ and $\underline{x}_i$ denote the supremum and infimum of X_i. Because the subgame equilibrium revenue functions are continuous in x_1 and x_2, and because revenues are bounded in any event, $\bar{x}_1$ and $\underline{x}_1$ must yield expected profit π_i if firm j uses its equilibrium quantity strategy μ_j and firms subsequently use subgame equilibrium price strategies.

Assume (without loss of generality) that $\bar{x}_1 \geq \bar{x}_2$.

Step 2: $\bar{x}_1 \geq r_b(\underline{x}_2)$. Suppose contrariwise that $\bar{x}_1 < r_b(\underline{x}_2)$. For every $x_1 < \bar{x}_1$, the subgame equilibrium revenue of firm 2, if it installs capacity $\underline{x}_2$, is $\underline{x}_2 P(x_1 + \underline{x}_2)$. That is,

$$\pi_2 = \int_{\underline{x}_1}^{\bar{x}_1} (\underline{x}_2 P(x_1 + \underline{x}_2) - b(\underline{x}_2)) \mu_1(dx_1).$$

If firm 2 increases its capacity slightly, to say, $x_2 + \epsilon$, where it remains true that $\bar{x}_1 < r_b(x_2 + \epsilon)$, then the worst that can happen to firm 2 (for each level of x_1) is that firm 2 will net $(\underline{x}_2 + \epsilon) P(x_1 + \underline{x}_2 + \epsilon) - b(\underline{x}_2 + \epsilon)$. Since for all $x_1 < \bar{x}_1$, $\underline{x}_2 + \epsilon < r_b(x_1)$, it follows that $(\underline{x}_2 + \epsilon) P(x_1 + \underline{x}_2 + \epsilon) - b(\underline{x}_2 + \epsilon) > \underline{x}_2 P(x_1 + \underline{x}_2) - b(\underline{x}_2)$, and this variation will raise firm 2's profits above π_2. This is a contradiction.

214

Step 3: $\bar{x}_1 \le r_b(\bar{x}_2)$. Suppose contrariwise that $\bar{x}_1 > r_b(\bar{x}_2)$. By building $\bar{x}_1$, firm 1 nets revenue (as a function of x_2) $R(x_2)$ if $\bar{x}_1 > r(x_2)$ and $\bar{x}_1 P(\bar{x}_1 + x_2)$ if $\bar{x}_1 \le r(x_2)$, assuming that a subgame equilibrium ensues. That is,

$$\pi_1 = \int_{(r^{-1}(\bar{x}_1), \bar{x}_2]} (R(x_2) - b(\bar{x}_1)) \mu_2(dx_2)$$

$$+ \int_{[\underline{x}_2, r^{-1}(\bar{x}_1)]} (\bar{x}_1 P(\bar{x}_1 + x_2) - b(\bar{x}_1)) \mu_2(dx_2). \tag{5}$$

Consider what happens to firm 1's expected profits if it lowers its capacity from $\bar{x}_1$ to just a bit less – say, to $\bar{x}_1 - \epsilon$, where $\bar{x}_1 - \epsilon > r_b(\bar{x}_2)$. Then the worst that can happen to firm 1 is that firm 2 (after installing capacity according to μ_2) names price zero. This would leave firm 1 with residual demand $D(p) - x_2$ (where $x_2 \le \bar{x}_2$). Firm 1 can still accrue revenue $R(x_2)$ if $\bar{x}_1 - \epsilon > r(x_2)$ and $(\bar{x}_1 - \epsilon)P(x_2 + \bar{x}_1 - \epsilon)$ otherwise. Thus, the expected profits of firm 1 in this variation are at least

$$\int_{[r^{-1}(\bar{x}_1 - \epsilon), \bar{x}_2]} (R(x_2) - b(\bar{x}_1 - \epsilon)) \mu_2(dx_2)$$

$$+ \int_{[\underline{x}_2, r^{-1}(\bar{x}_1 - \epsilon)]} ((\bar{x}_1 - \epsilon)P(x_2 + \bar{x}_1 - \epsilon) - b(\bar{x}_1 - \epsilon)) \mu_2(dx_2). \tag{6}$$

We shall complete this step by showing that for small enough ϵ, (6) exceeds (5), thereby contradicting the assumption.

The difference (6) minus (5) can be analyzed by breaking the integrals into three intervals: $[r^{-1}(\bar{x}_1 - \epsilon), \bar{x}_2]$, $[\underline{x}_2, r^{-1}(\bar{x}_1)]$, and $(r^{-1}(\bar{x}_1), r^{-1}(\bar{x}_1 - \epsilon))$. Over the first interval, the difference in integrands is

$$(R(x_2) - b(\bar{x}_1)) - (R(x_2) - b(\bar{x}_1 - \epsilon)) = \epsilon b'(\bar{x}_1) + o(\epsilon).$$

Note well that $b'(\bar{x}_1)$ is strictly positive. Over the second interval, the difference in integrands is

$$((\bar{x}_1 - \epsilon)P(\bar{x}_1 - \epsilon + x_2) - b(\bar{x}_1 - \epsilon)) - (\bar{x}_1 P(\bar{x}_1 + x_2) - b(\bar{x}_1))$$

$$= \epsilon(b'(\bar{x}_1) - \bar{x}_1 P'(\bar{x}_1) - P(\bar{x}_1 + x_2)) + o(\epsilon).$$

Here the term premultiplied by ϵ is strictly positive except possibly at the lower boundary (where it is nonnegative), since by step 2, $\bar{x}_1 \ge r_b(\bar{x}_2) \ge r_b(x_2)$. Over the third interval, the difference in the integrands is no more than $O(\epsilon)$, because of the continuity of $xP(x + x_2) - b(x)$. Thus as ϵ goes to zero, the integrand over the first interval will be strictly positive $O(\epsilon)$ if μ_2 puts any mass on $(r^{-1}(\bar{x}_1), \bar{x}_2]$. The integral over the second interval will be strictly positive $O(\epsilon)$ if μ_2 puts any mass on $(r_b^{-1}(\bar{x}_1), r^{-1}(\bar{x}_1)]$.

215

The integral over the third interval must be $o(\epsilon)$, since it is the integral of a term $O(\epsilon)$ integrated over a vanishing interval. The hypothesis $\bar{x}_1 > r_b(\bar{x}_2)$ implies that μ_2 puts positive mass on either $(r_b^{-1}(\bar{x}_1), r^{-1}(\bar{x}_1)]$ or on $(r^{-1}(\bar{x}_1), \bar{x}_2]$ (or both). Hence for small enough ϵ, the difference between (6) and (5) will be strictly positive. This is the desired contradiction.

Step 4. The rest is easy. Steps 2 and 3 imply that $\bar{x}_1 = r_b(\bar{x}_2) = r_b(\underline{x}_2)$, and hence that firm 2 uses a pure strategy in the first round. But then firm 1's best response in the first round is the pure strategy $r_b(x_2)$. And firm 2's strategy, which must be a best response to this, must satisfy $x_2 = r_b(x_1) = r_b(r_b(x_2))$. This implies that $x_2 = x^*(b)$, and, therefore, $x_1 = r_b(x^*(b)) = x^*(b)$. Finally, the two firms will each name price $P(2x^*(b))$ in the second round [as long as both firms produce $x^*(b)$ in the first round, which they will do with probability one]; this follows immediately from Step 1 and Proposition 1. ∎

6. The case $b \equiv 0$

When $b \equiv 0$ it is easy to check that the Cournot outcome is an equilibrium. In this case, however, there are other equilibria as well. If imperfect equilibria are counted, then one equilibrium has $x_1 = x_2 = D(0)$ (or anything larger) and $p_1 \equiv p_2 \equiv 0$. Note well that each firm names price zero regardless of what capacities are installed. This is clearly an equilibrium, but it is imperfect, because if, say, firm 1 installed a small capacity and the subgame equilibrium ensued, each would make positive profits.

There are also other perfect equilibria, although it takes a bit more work to establish them. Let $x_1 \geq D(0)$. If firm 2 installs capacity greater than $D(0)$, it will net zero profits (assuming a subgame equilibrium follows). If it installs $x_2 < D(0)$, then its profits (in a perfect equilibrium) are $\underline{p}(x_2)x_2$, where $\underline{p}(x_2) \leq p(0)$ solves the equation $\underline{p}(x_2)D(\underline{p}(x_2)) = R(x_2)$. Hence, in any perfect equilibrium where $x_1 \geq \bar{D}(0)$, x_2 must be selected to maximize $\underline{p}(x_2)x_2 = R(x_2)x_2/D(\underline{p}(x_2))$. The numerator in the last expression is increasing for $x_2 \leq x^*$ and is decreasing thereafter. (See the proof of Lemma 5.) And as $\underline{p}(x_2)$ decreases in x_2, the denominator increases in x_2. Thus, the maximizing x_2 is less than x^*. But as long as firm 2 chooses capacity less than x^*, the best revenue (in any subgame equilibrium) that firm 1 can hope to achieve is $R(x_2)$, which it achieves with any $x_1 \geq D(0)$. Thus, we have a perfect subgame equilibrium in which firm 1 chooses $x_1 \geq D(0)$ and firm 2 chooses x_2 to maximize $\underline{p}(x_2)x_2$.

7. When both capacity and production are costly

In a slightly more complicated version of this game, both capacity (which is installed before prices are named and demand is realized) and production (which takes place after demand is realized) would be costly. Assuming that each of these activities has a convex cost structure and that our assumptions on demand are met, it is easy to modify our analysis to show that the unique equilibrium outcome is the Cournot outcome computed by using the sum of the two cost functions. (This requires that capacity is costly on the margin. Otherwise, imperfect equilibria of all sorts and perfect equilibria of the sort given above will also appear.) It is notable that the cost of capacity need not be very high relative to production cost: the only requirement is that it be nonzero on the margin. Thus, situations where "most" of the cost is incurred subsequent to the realization of demand (situations that will "look" very Bertrand-like) will still give the Cournot outcome. (A reasonable conjecture, suggested to us by many colleagues, is that "noise" in the demand function will change this dramatically. Confirmation or rejection of this conjecture must await another paper.)

References

Beckmann, M. "Edgeworth–Bertrand Duopoly Revisited" in R. Henn, ed., *Operations Research-Verfahren, III,* Meisenheim: Verlag Anton Hein, 1965, pp. 55–68.

Bertrand, J. "Theorie Mathématique de la Richesse Sociale." *Journal des Savants* (1883), pp. 499–508.

Cournot, A. *Recherches sur les Principes Mathématiques de la Théorie des Richesses.* Paris: 1838 English translation: (N. Bacon, trans.), *Researches into the Mathematical Principles of the Theory of Wealth* New York: Macmillan & Company, 1897.

Dasgupta, P. and Maskin, E. "The Existence of Equilibrium in Discontinuous Economic Games, 2: Applications." Draft, London School of Economics, 1982.

Edgeworth, F. "La Teoria Pura del Monopolio." *Giornale degli Economisti,* Vol. 40 (1897), pp. 13–31. Reprinted in English as "The Pure Theory of Monopoly," in F. Edgeworth, *Papers Relating to Political Economy,* Vol. 1, London: Macmillan & Co., Ltd., 1925, pp. 111–42.

Levitan, R. and Shubik, M. "Price Duopoly and Capacity Constraints." *International Economic Review,* Vol. 13 (1972), pp. 111–22.

Selten, R. "Spieltheoretische Behandlung eines Oligopolmodells mit Nachfrageträgheit." *Zeitschrift für die gesamte Staatswissenschaft,* Vol. 121 (1965), pp. 301–24.

CHAPTER 10

On the efficiency of Bertrand and Cournot equilibria with product differentiation

XAVIER VIVES

In a differentiated products setting with n varieties it is shown, under certain regularity conditions, that if the demand structure is symmetric and Bertrand and Cournot equilibria are unique then prices and profits are larger and quantities smaller in Cournot than in Bertrand competition and, as n grows, both equilibria converge to the efficient outcome at a rate of at least $1/n$. If Bertrand reaction functions slope upwards and are continuous then, even with an asymmetric demand structure, given any Cournot equilibrium price vector one can find a Bertrand equilibrium with lower prices. In particular, if the Bertrand equilibrium is unique then it has lower prices than any Cournot equilibrium. *Journal of Economic Literature* Classification Numbers: 022, 611.   © 1985 Academic Press, Inc.

1. Introduction

It is a well-established idea that Bertrand (price) competition is more efficient than Cournot (quantity) competition. In fact with an homogenous product and constant marginal costs the Bertrand outcome involves pricing at marginal cost. This is not the case with differentiated products where margins over marginal cost are positive even in Bertrand competition. Shubik showed in a model with a linear and symmetric demand structure that the margin over marginal cost is larger in Cournot competition, and that, under certain conditions, as the number of varieties grows equilibrium prices go to marginal cost in either Bertrand or Cournot competition (see Shubik [16, Chaps. 7 and 9]). This note generalizes the first result to a general demand structure (not necessarily linear and/or symmetric) and the second to a general symmetric demand structure. We give sufficient conditions to guarantee the existence and uniqueness of

Department of Economics, University of Pennsylvania, Philadelphia, PA 19104.

Xavier Vives, "On the Efficiency of Bertrand and Cournot Equilibria with Product Differentiation," *Journal of Economic Theory* 36, 1, 1985, pp. 166–75.

I am grateful to Ray Deneckere, Andreu Mas-Colell, and Nirvikar Singh for helpful comments. This note is a revision of Sections 1 and 2 of my Dissertation Prospectus (November 1982), written under the supervision of Gerard Debreu.

both types of equilibria. These conditions are strong but otherwise usual in the oligopoly literature. Roberts and Sonnenschein [13] have shown that non-existence problems may arise with well-behaved preferences. Marginal costs are assumed constant to insure the existence of pure strategy Bertrand equilibria.[1] We follow the Chamberlinian tradition (Chamberlin [2]) and consider an industry selling differentiated substitute products in which each good is in competition with every other one.

In Section 3 the utility foundations of the demand structure are provided. It is assumed that utility is separable and linear in the numéraire (which is a standard assumption in partial equilibrium welfare analysis)[2] and some analogies with production theory are exploited. It is shown in Section 4 that if the demand structure is symmetric (and Bertrand and Cournot equilibria are unique) then prices and profits are larger and quantities smaller in Cournot than in Bertrand competition (Proposition 1). If Bertrand reaction functions are upward sloping (and continuous) then (even with an asymmetric demand structure) given any Cournot equilibrium price vector one can find a Bertrand equilibrium with lower prices (Proposition 2).[3] In particular, if the Bertrand equilibrium is unique then it has lower prices than any Cournot equilibrium. Section 5 deals with the asymptotic properties of the equilibria. It is shown that with a symmetric demand structure Cournot and Bertrand prices go to marginal cost at least at the rate $1/n$, where n is the number of goods, provided that there is a bounded demand for the industry as a whole and that inverse demands have bounded slopes. Some notation is introduced in Section 2.

2. Notation

Given a set $A \subset R^n$, int A denotes its interior and bd(A) denotes its boundary. Set theoretic union is denoted by $\bigcup$. For a function $U: R^n_+ \to R$, $DU(x)$ will denote the vector of first derivatives, $(\partial_i U(x))^n_{i=1}$ and $D^2U(x)$ the Hessian matrix of U, with entries $\partial_{ij} U(x)$; all evaluated at the point x. The vector inequality $\gg$ means strict inequality for every component. If z is a vector in R^n, z_{-i} stands for the vector derived from z by deleting the ith component.

---

[1] Mixed strategies are needed to insure existence of equilibria with price competition when marginal costs are increasing. Since a firm will not produce more than its competitive supply payoff relevant demands are contingent demands. (See Shubik [16] and Shapley [15].)

[2] See Spence [18], for example.

[3] Related results are obtained by Cheng [3], Hathaway and Rickard [9], Okuguchi [12], and Singh and Vives [17].

3. The demand structure

There are n differentiated goods in our monopolistic sector. We have a representative consumer which maximizes $\{U(x) - \sum_{i=1}^{n} p_i x_i : x \in R_+^n\}$, where p_i is the price of good i and $U(\cdot)$ is a $\mathbf{C}^3$ (differentially) strictly concave utility function on R_+^n. That is, $D^2U(x)$ is negative definite for all $x \in R_+^n$. Note that we assume $U(\cdot)$ to be differentiable at the boundary of R_+^n. Furthermore $\partial_i U(x)$ is positive in a non-empty, bounded region of R_+^n, X_i and, letting $X = \bigcap_{i=1}^{n} X_i$, $\partial_{ij} U(x) < 0$ for $x \in \text{int } X$ for any i and j (which is a reasonable assumption if the goods are substitutes). Given positive prices the solution to the maximization problem of our consumer will lie in X. The first order conditions (FOC) of the consumer problem are $\partial_i U(x) \leq p_i$ $(i = 1, \ldots, n)$, with equality if $x_i > 0$. The inverse demand system f will be a continuous function on R_+^n. For $x \in X$ prices will be strictly positive and out of X one or more prices will be zero. Consider good i. f_i restricted to int X will be of class $\mathbf{C}^2$, decreasing in all its arguments, $\partial_j f_i < 0$ for all j, and cross effects are symmetric, $\partial_j f_i = \partial_i f_j$, $j \neq i$. (All these properties follow from noting that the Jacobian of f restricted to int X is just $D^2U(\cdot)$ restricted to int X and that $\partial_{ij} U < 0$ for $x \in \text{int } X$.)

The demand system, h, is defined on R_+^n and satisfies:

(1) h is a continuous function on R_+^n.

(2) Let $P_i = \{p \in R_+^n : h_i(p) > 0\}$; then h is of class $\mathbf{C}^2$ on $R_{++}^n \setminus \bigcup_{i=1}^{n} \text{bd}(P_i)$. h_i is decreasing in its own price whenever $h_i(p) > 0$. If $h_i(p)$ and $h_j(p)$ are positive, cross effects are symmetric, $\partial_j h_i = \partial_i h_j$.

(3) $p_i \leq \partial_i U(0, \ldots, 0)$ for $p_i \in P_i$. That is, P_i is bounded along the ith axis.

Condition (1) follows by continuity and strict concavity of $U(\cdot)$. Condition (2) follows from the smoothness of $U(\cdot)$ and the FOC using the Inverse Function Theorem (extend U to a $\mathbf{C}^3$ function defined on an open set containing R_+^n). Downward sloping demand and symmetry of cross effects follow from the negative definiteness and symmetry of $D^2U(\cdot)$. Condition (3) follows from the FOC noting that $\partial_i U(h(p)) \leq \partial_i(0, \ldots, 0) < \infty$. The first inequality is true since $\partial_{ii} U$ and $\partial_{ij} U$ are negative and the second since $U(\cdot)$ is differentiable at $(0, \ldots, 0)$.

We assume, furthermore, that the goods are gross substitutes. That is, h_i is increasing in the price of firm j, $\partial_j h_i > 0$, $j \neq i$, whenever $h_i(p)$ and $h_j(p)$ are positive.[4] Note then that for $p \in \text{int } P$ the Jacobian matrix

---

[4] For $n = 2$ concavity of $U(\cdot)$ and $\partial_{12} U < 0$ imply that the goods are gross substitutes since for $p \in P$, $\partial_2 h_1 = -\partial_{12} U / \Delta$, where $\Delta = \det D^2 U$, which is positive.

of h, J_h is negative definite, since it is the inverse of $D^2 U(\cdot)$, and has positive off-diagonal entries and therefore J_h has a dominant negative diagonal in the McKenzie sense (see McKenzie [10, Theorem 2']).

The properties of our demand system, except for the symmetry of cross effects, are those assumed by J. Friedman in his treatment of demand with product differentiation (see Friedman [7]).

Example. Let $U: R_+^2 \to R$ be defined by

$$U(x) = \alpha_1 x_1 + \alpha_2 x_2 - \tfrac{1}{2}(\beta_1 x_1^2 + 2\gamma x_1 x_2 + \beta_2 x_2^2)$$

with all the parameters positive, $\beta_1 \beta_2 - \gamma^2 > 0$ and $\alpha_i \beta_j - \alpha_j \gamma > 0$, $i \neq j$, $i = 1, 2$. Then

$$X = \{x \in R_+^2 : \alpha_1 - \beta_1 x_1 - \gamma x_2 > 0, \alpha_2 - \beta_2 x_2 - \gamma x_1 > 0\},$$

the inverse demand system being

$$p_1 = \alpha_1 - \beta_1 x_1 - \gamma x_2$$

$$p_2 = \alpha_2 - \beta_2 x_2 - \gamma x_1$$

on X.

$$P = \{p \in R_+^2 : a_1 - b_1 p_1 + c p_2 > 0, a_2 - b_2 p_2 + c p_1 > 0\}$$

[where $a_1 = (\alpha_1 \beta_2 - \alpha_2 \gamma)/\Delta$, $b_1 = \beta_2/\Delta$, $c = \gamma/\Delta$, $\Delta = \beta_1 \beta_2 - \gamma^2$, and similarly for a_2 and b_2]. The direct demands on P are

$$x_1 = a_1 - b_1 p_1 + c p_2$$

$$x_2 = a_2 - b_2 p_2 + c p_1.$$

(α_1, α_2) is the maximal element of the closure of P.

Our representative consumer maximizes surplus, $CS = U(x) - \sum_{i=1}^n p_i x_i$. We can make an analogy with production theory and think that our consumer produces utils out of the consumption inputs. In that case the consumer is maximizing profits with a technology represented by $U(\cdot)$ and with the prices of utils normalized to be one. Therefore the demand system arising from this maximization will have the properties of an input demand system and consumer surplus, CS, as a function of prices will be the analog of the profit function. We know from production theory that CS will be a convex function of prices and that $\partial CS(p)/\partial p_i = -h_i(p)$ for all i.

4. Bertrand competition is more efficient than Cournot competition

Suppose that we have n firms each producing a different variety at constant marginal costs. Since $X_i(P_i)$ is bounded along the ith axis we can take the strategy space of a quantity (price) setting firm to be a compact interval. Suppose that any firm can make positive profits even when the competitors' prices equal marginal costs. This insures that in equilibrium each firm will produce a positive amount. Consider prices net of marginal cost. Profits of firm i in terms of prices are $\pi_i(p) = p_i h_i(p)$ and in terms of quantities, $\hat{\pi}_i(x) = f_i(x) x_i$. Quasiconcavity of $\pi_i(\cdot)$ with respect to p_i and of $\hat{\pi}_i(\cdot)$ with respect to x_i insures the existence of Bertrand and Cournot equilibria. Uniqueness requires stronger assumptions.

The following assumptions insure that Bertrand and Cournot best reply mappings are contractions and therefore Bertrand and Cournot equilibria exist and are unique and stable (see Friedman [7]). Let $P = \bigcap_{i=1}^{n} P_i$.

(A.1) $(1-\epsilon)\partial_{ii}\pi_i(p) + \sum_{j \neq i} |\partial_{ij}\pi_i(p)| < 0$ for all $p \in$ int P, for some $\epsilon > 0$, and

(A.2) $(1-\delta)\partial_{ii}\hat{\pi}_i(x) + \sum_{j \neq i} |\partial_{ij}\hat{\pi}_i(x)| < 0$ for all $x \in$ int X, for some $\delta > 0$.

Assumptions A.1 and A.2 are very strong, particularly the one of the quantity setting model (A.2) when the products are close to perfect substitutes. Assumption A.2 is not satisfied for an homogenous product market with downward sloping concave demand if there are more than two firms (the Cournot equilibrium is still unique though). In what follows we use A.2 only to insure the uniqueness of the Cournot equilibrium. Alternatively one could assume that inverse demand for good i depends only on x_i and on the sum of the quantities of the other firms, $\sum_{j \neq i} x_j$, and that the Cournot reaction functions have negative slope larger than -1. The uniqueness of the Cournot equilibrium is easily established then. Let p^B and p^C denote respectively Bertrand and Cournot equilibrium price vectors. Both are going to be strictly positive and will satisfy the corresponding FOC. In the Bertrand case this is $\partial_i \pi_i(p) = 0$. This equation gives implicitly the Bertrand reaction function of firm i, $p_i = R_i^B(p_{-i})$, provided $p \in P$. $R_i^B(\cdot)$ will be increasing in all its arguments (upward sloping) if $\partial_{ij}\pi_i = p_i \partial_{ij} h_i + \partial_j h_i$ is positive for all $j \neq i$. The Cournot problem for firm i in price space is to choose a price p_i to maximize

$$\pi_i(p) \text{ subject to } h_j(p) = x_j, \quad j \neq i.$$

The FOC of this problem is

$$\partial_i \pi_i - p_i [\partial_j h_i]_{j \neq i} J_{h_{-i}}^{-1} [\partial_i h_j]_{j \neq i} = 0$$

where $J_{h_{-i}}$ is the Jacobian matrix of h_{-i}. Noting that $\partial_j h_i = \partial_i h_j$ we have that at the Cournot prices p^C, $\partial_i \pi_i(p^C) < 0$ since p_i^C is positive and $J_{h_{-i}}$ is negative definite.

222

Efficiency of Bertrand and Cournot equilibria

Bertrand competition is viewed as more "competitive" than Cournot competition. An intuitive reason behind this view is that (since the goods are substitutes) in Cournot competition each firm expects the others to cut prices in response to price cuts, while in Bertrand competition the firm expects the others to maintain their prices; therefore, Cournot penalizes price cutting more. One should expect Cournot prices to be higher than Bertrand prices. This is indeed the case either if the utility function is symmetric and Bertrand and Cournot equilibria are unique or if the Bertrand reaction functions slope upwards (which is reasonable if the goods are substitutes) and the Bertrand equilibrium is unique. An immediate consequence is that consumer surplus, *CS*, is higher under Bertrand competition. Total surplus derived from an output vector x is just $U(x)$. In the symmetric case Bertrand quantities are higher than Cournot quantities and therefore total surplus is higher and firms' profits are larger under Cournot competition. If there are multiple Bertrand equilibria given any Cournot equilibrium price vector we can find a Bertrand equilibrium with lower prices. Propositions 1 and 2 state these results.

In the symmetric case the demand system will be symmetric too. Let all prices equal p and let $g(p)$ be the demand for any product. That is $g(p) = h_i(p, ..., p)$ for any i. Then since X and P are bounded there exists $\bar{p}$ and $\bar{x}$ such that $g(\bar{p}) = 0$ and $g(0) = \bar{x}$. Furthermore g is $\mathbf{C}^2$ on $(0, \bar{p})$ and $g' < 0$ since $U(\cdot)$ is a symmetric differentially strictly concave function. g would correspond to the Chamberlinian *DD* curve for "simultaneous movements in the prices of all goods." The following assumption insures that g is concave:

(A.3) $\partial_{ii} h_i(p) + \sum_{j \neq i} |\partial_{ij} h_i(p)| \leq 0$ for $p_i = q$, $q \in (0, \bar{p})$, for any i.

Proposition 1. *If $U(\cdot)$ is symmetric and A.1, A.2 and A.3 hold then prices and profits are larger and quantities smaller in Cournot than in Bertrand competition.*

Proof. The unique equilibrium (Cournot and Bertrand) will be symmetric. It is enough to consider firm 1. Let $\phi(p) = \partial_1 \pi_1(p, ..., p)$. The Bertrand price, p^B, solves $\phi(p) = 0$ (note that $\phi' < 0$ according to A.1). On the other hand we know that at the Cournot price, p^C, $\phi(p^C) < 0$. Therefore $p^C > p^B$. Note that $x^B > x^C$ since both are on g and $g' < 0$. Let $\bar{\pi}(p) = pg(p)$ and note that $\bar{\pi}$ is strictly concave in p since $g'' \leq 0$ and $g' < 0$. Consider the price a monopolist would charge, p^M. p^M solves $\bar{\pi}'(p) = 0$. At the Cournot solution $\bar{\pi}'(p^C) = p^C g'(p^C) + g(p^C)$, which is positive. To see this note that since $U(\cdot)$ is symmetric and at the Cournot solution all

223

prices equal p^C, $\partial_i h_i = \partial_1 h_1$ and $\partial_j h_i = \partial_2 h_1$ for all $i, j \neq i$. Then $\bar{\pi}'(p^C) = p^C \partial_1 h_1 + h_1 + p^C(n-1)\partial_2 h_1$ which, using the Cournot FOC, equals

$$p^C \partial_2 h_1(\partial_2 h_1 \mathbf{1}_{n-1} J_{h_{-1}}^{-1} \mathbf{1}_{n-1} + n - 1)$$

where $\mathbf{1}_{n-1}$ is an $(n-1)\times 1$ vector of ones. Inverting $J_{h_{-1}}$ one gets

$$\mathbf{1}_{n-1} J_{h_{-1}}^{-1} \mathbf{1}_{n-1} = \frac{n-1}{\partial_1 h_1 + (n-2)\partial_2 h_1}$$

and therefore

$$\partial_2 h_1 \mathbf{1}_{n-1} J_{h_{-1}}^{-1} \mathbf{1}_{n-1} + n - 1 = (n-1)\frac{\partial_1 h_1 + (n-1)\partial_2 h_1}{\partial_1 h_1 + (n-2)\partial_2 h_1},$$

which is positive since $\partial_1 h_1 + (n-1)\partial_2 h_1 = g'$ and $g' < 0$. We conclude that $\bar{\pi}'(p^C) > 0$ since $\partial_2 h_1 > 0$. Summing up, we have $\bar{\pi}'(p^M) = 0$, $\bar{\pi}'(p^C) > 0$ and $\bar{\pi}'$ strictly decreasing since $\bar{\pi}$ is strictly concave. We conclude $p^M > p^C$. Since $p^C > p^B$, this implies $\pi^C > \pi^B$. ∎

Proposition 2. *Assume, for all i, that $\pi_i(p)$ is strictly quasiconcave in p_i whenever the demand for the ith good is positive and that $R_i^B(\cdot)$ is nondecreasing in all its arguments, then given any Cournot equilibrium price vector one can find a Bertrand equilibrium with lower prices.*

Proof. Let p^C be a Cournot equilibrium price vector. We know that $\partial_i \pi_i(p^C) < 0$ for all i and that $p^C \in P$. The Bertrand reaction function of firm i, $p_i = R_i^B(p_{-i})$, is defined implicitly by $\partial_i \pi_i(p) = 0$ provided $p \in P$. It will be continuous since $\pi_i(p)$ is strictly quasiconcave in p_i. Again because of π_i's quasiconcavity, $\partial_i \pi_i(p) < 0$ means that $p_i > R_i^B(p_{-i})$. Therefore $p_i^C > R_i^B(p_{-i}^C)$ for all i. Let $R^B = (R_1^B, ..., R_n^B)$ and $p^1 = R^B(p^C)$, then $p^C \gg p^1$. Note that $p^1 \in P$ since any firm can make positive profits even when the competitors charge prices equal to marginal cost. Since R_i^B is nondecreasing for all i, $R^B(p^C) \geq R^B(p^1)$. Let $p^2 = R^B(p^1)$ and keep applying R^B to obtain a decreasing sequence p^t in P which converges since prices must be nonnegative.[5] Say p^t converges to p^*. p^* must satisfy $p^* = R^B(p^*)$, and therefore it is a Bertrand equilibrium, since $R^B(\cdot)$ is continuous. We conclude that $p^C \gg p^*$. ∎

Under the assumptions of Proposition 2 multiple Bertrand and Cournot equilibria may exist. Existence of the Bertrand equilibrium is guaranteed and there will be at least one Cournot equilibrium as long as $\hat{\pi}_i(x)$ is

[5] Similar arguments can be found in Deneckere and Davidson [5, pp. 13–14] and Spence [18, p. 221].

224

quasiconcave in x_i. Note that if there is a unique Bertrand equilibrium then it has lower prices than any Cournot equilibrium. Assumption A.1 insures the uniqueness of the Bertrand equilibrium.

5. Asymptotic results[6]

Suppose that there is a countable infinity of potential commodities. Our representative consumer has preferences over them defined by a sequence of utility functions $\{U^n\}$, $U^n: R_+^n \to R$, where each $U^n(\cdot)$ is symmetric and satisfies the assumptions of Section 2. For any given n, consider the program $\text{Max}\{U^n(x) - p\sum_{i=1}^n x_i, x \in R_+^n\}$ and let $x_i = g^n(p)$ $(i = 1, \ldots, n)$ be its solution. We know that there exist $\bar{x}_n > 0$ and $\bar{p}_n > 0$ such that $\bar{x}_n = g^n(0)$ and $g^n(\bar{p}_n) = 0$, and that g^n is downward sloping. We assume

(A.4) there exists $\bar{p} > 0$ and $k > 0$ such that $\bar{p}_n \le \bar{p}$ and $n\bar{x}_n \le k$ for all n;

(A.5) there exists $c > 0$ such that $|\partial_{ii} U^n(x, \ldots, x)| \le c$ for all i $(i = 1, \ldots, n)$, for all n and for all positive x.

Assumption A.4 means that there is a bounded demand for the varieties produced by the industry. The Chamberlinian *DD* curve for "simultaneous movements in the prices of all goods," $g^n(\cdot)$, shifts inwards as the number of varieties increase. Assumption A.5 implies that inverse demands have bounded slopes along the 45° line. This is immediate since $\partial_i f_i(x) = \partial_{ii} U(x)$. Suppose now that for any n there are unique Bertrand and Cournot equilibria (A.1 and A.2 are sufficient for this to hold). Since $U^n(\cdot)$ is symmetric the unique equilibria will be symmetric too. Denote them (p_n^B, x_n^B) and (p_n^C, x_n^C), respectively.

Proposition 3. *As n goes to infinity p_n^B and p_n^C go to marginal cost at a rate of at least $1/n$.*

Proof. (p_n^C, x_n^C) satisfy the Cournot FOC $p_n^C = x_n^C |\partial_i f_i^n(x_n^C)|$ for any i. Therefore $np_n^C = nx_n^C |\partial_i f_i^n(x_n^C)| \le kc$ from A.4 and A.5. Furthermore from Proposition 1 we know that $p_n^C > p_n^B$ and therefore $np_n^B \le kc$ also. ∎

The intuition of the result should be clear. As we put more commodities in a limited market where the absolute values of the slopes of the inverse demand functions are bounded above, the substitute goods come closer together and demand elasticities go to infinity. This holds for Bertrand or

---

[6] For asymptotic results in a Cournot homogeneous product setting see Ruffin [14] for the case of exogenous n and Novshek [11] for the free entry case.

Cournot competition. Although Bertrand is always more efficient than Cournot, the order of magnitude of their departure from efficiency is the same for both and so the rate of convergence to the efficient outcome is equal in both cases.

Examples. Let

$$U^n(x) = \alpha \sum_{i=1}^{n} x_i - \frac{1}{2}\left(\beta \sum_{i=1}^{n} x_i + 2\gamma \sum_{j \neq i} x_i x_j\right),$$

where $\beta > \gamma > 0$ and $\alpha > 0$; and let marginal costs be constant and equal to m for all firms. Then for positive demands,

$$f_i^n(x) = \alpha - \beta x_i - \gamma \sum_{j \neq i} x_j \qquad (i = 1, \ldots, n)$$

$$h_i^n(p) = a_n - b_n p_i + c_n \sum_{j \neq i} p_j \qquad (i = 1, \ldots, n),$$

where $a_n = \alpha/(\beta + (n-1)\gamma)$, $b_n = (\beta + (n-2)\gamma)/(\beta + (n-1)\gamma)(\beta - \gamma)$, and $c_n = \gamma/(\beta + (n-1)\gamma)(\beta - \gamma)$. $g^n(p) = (\alpha - p)/(\beta + (n-1)\gamma)$, $\bar{p} = \alpha$, and $\bar{x}_n = \alpha/(\beta + (n-1)\gamma)$.

It is easily checked that

$$n(p_n^C - m) \underset{n}{\to} \beta\frac{\alpha - m}{\gamma},$$

$$n(p_n^B - m) \underset{n}{\to} (\beta - \gamma)\frac{\alpha - m}{\gamma}.$$

[Note that $\partial_i f_i^n = \beta$ for all n and $\partial_i h_i^n = b_n$, which tends to $1/(\beta - \gamma)$.] Having a limited market for the monopolistic industry is not enough for our result if the slopes of the inverse demand functions are unbounded. An example by Shubik (1980) illustrates this point.

Let

$$U^n(x) = \frac{\alpha}{\beta} \sum_i x_i - \frac{1}{2\beta}\left(\sum x_i\right)^2 - \frac{n}{2\beta(1+\gamma)}\left[\sum x_i^2 - \frac{\left(\sum x_i\right)^2}{n}\right],$$

where α, β, and γ are positive constants. Then for positive demands,

$$f_i^n(x) = \frac{\alpha}{\beta} - \frac{n+\gamma}{\beta(1+\gamma)} x_i - \frac{\gamma}{\beta(1+\gamma)} \sum_{i \neq j} x_j \qquad (i = 1, \ldots, n).$$

$$h_i^n(p) = \frac{1}{n}\left(\alpha - \beta\left[p_i + \gamma\left(p_i - \frac{1}{n}\sum_i p_i\right)\right]\right) \qquad (i = 1, \ldots, n).$$

Note that $|\partial_i h_i^n| = -\beta(1 + \gamma(1 - 1/n))/n$, which goes to zero as $n \to \infty$, and that $ng^n(p) = \alpha - \beta p$, which means that we have a limited market.

226

Efficiency of Bertrand and Cournot equilibria

Certainly x_n^C and x_n^B go to zero as n goes to infinity but the corresponding prices do not go to the constant marginal cost. It is easily seen that the demand elasticity for any good does not go to infinity as n increases. We are thus in the Chamberlinian situation, where although there are many "small" firms each one of them has some market power and prices are above marginal cost.[7]

References

1. J. Bertrand, Book reviews of "Théorie mathématique de la richesse sociale" and of "Researches sur les principes mathématiques de la théorie des richesses," *J. Savants* (1983), 499–508.
2. E. H. Chamberlin, "The Theory of Monopolistic Competition," 7th ed. Harvard Univ. Press, Cambridge, Mass., 1956.
3. L. Cheng, Bertrand equilibrium is more competitive than Cournot equilibrium: The case of differentiated products, mimeo, University of Florida, 1984.
4. A. Cournot, "Researches into the Mathematical Principles of the Theory of Wealth," English edition of Cournot (1983), translated by N. T. Bacon, Kelley, New York, 1960.
5. R. Deneckere and C. Davidson, "Coalition Formation in Noncooperative Oligopoly Models," Michigan State University Working Paper Series No. 8302, 1983.
6. A. Dixit and J. Stiglitz, Monopolistic competition and optimum product diversity, *Amer. Econom. Rev.* 67 (1977), 297–308.
7. J. W. Friedman, "Oligopoly and the Theory of Games," North-Holland, Amsterdam, 1977.
8. O. Hart, "Monopolistic Competition in the Spirit of Chamberlin: (1) A General Model; (2) Special Results," ICERD discussion paper, L.S.E., 1983.
9. N. J. Hathaway and J. A. Rickard, Equilibria of price-setting and quantity setting duopolies, *Econom. Lett.* 3 (1979), 133–7.
10. L. W. McKenzie, Matrices with dominant diagonals and economic theory, 1959, in "Mathematical Methods in Social Sciences" (K. J. Arrow, S. Karlin, and K. Suppes, Eds.), Stanford Univ. Press, Stanford, Calif., 1960.
11. W. Novshek, Cournot equilibrium with free entry, *ReStuds* 47 (1980), 473–86.
12. K. Okuguchi, Price-adjusting and quantity adjusting oligopoly equilibria, undated manuscript.
13. J. Roberts and H. Sonnenschein, On the foundations of the theory of monopolistic competition, *Econometrica* 45 (1977), 101–13.
14. R. Ruffin, Cournot oligopoly and competitive behavior, *ReStuds* 38 (1971), 493–502.
15. L. S. Shapley, A duopoly model with price competition, *Econometrica* 25 (1957), 354–5.

---

[7] See Dixit and Stiglitz [6] and Hart [8] for a formalization of the Chamberlinian "large group" monopolistic competition.

16. M. Shubik (with R. Levitan), "Market Structure and Behavior," Harvard Univ. Press, Cambridge, Mass., 1971.
17. N. Singh, and X. Vives, Price and quantity competition in a differentiated duopoly, *The Rand Journal of Economics* 15, 4 (1984), 546–54.
18. M. Spence, Product selection, fixed costs and monopolistic competition, *Rev. Econom. Stud.* 43 (1976), 217–53.

CHAPTER 11

Price competition vs. quantity competition: the role of uncertainty

PAUL KLEMPERER AND MARGARET MEYER

We analyze the Nash equilibria of a one-stage game in which the nature of the strategic variables (prices or quantities) is determined endogenously. Duopolists producing differentiated products simultaneously choose either a quantity to produce or a price to charge. In the absence of exogenous uncertainty, there exist four types of equilibria with differing levels of output: (price, price), (quantity, quantity), (price, quantity), and (quantity, price). The multiplicity of equilibria stems from each firm's indifference between setting price and quantity, given its conjecture about its rival's strategy. But exogenous uncertainty about market demands, which makes firms uncertain about their residual demands, even in equilibrium, gives firms strict preferences between setting price and quantity. As a result, the number of equilibria is reduced. When uncertainty is exogenous, we analyze the effect of the slope of marginal costs, the nature of the demand disturbance, and the curvature of demand on firms' propensities to compete with price or quantity as the strategic variable. These three factors are likely to influence the nature and intensity of oligopolistic competition.

1. Introduction

Economists using games to represent oligopolistic competition debated the relative merits of models using prices or quantities as firms' strategic variables from as early as Bertrand's (1883) criticism of Cournot (1838). The extent to which firms can choose price or quantity must, of course, crucially affect the nature of competition.[1] If they have some choice,

St. Catherine's College and Institute of Economics and Statistics, Oxford.
St. John's College, Oxford.
Paul Klemperer and Margaret Meyer, "Price Competition vs. Quantity Competition: the Role of Uncertainty," *Rand Journal of Economics* 17, 4, 1986, pp. 404–15.
We have had many helpful discussions with Jim Mirrlees. We also wish to thank Ben Bernanke, Adam Brandenburger, Jeremy Bulow, Frank Hahn, and the editors and referees of this Journal for helpful comments. Financial support from the Center for Economic Policy Research at Stanford is gratefully acknowledged. This work was begun while the authors were at the Graduate School of Business, Stanford University.

[1] In an agricultural market farmers may have little choice but to pick a quantity to plant and then sell the output at the market-clearing price. A discount brokerage, on the other hand, must pick a price per share traded rather than a quantity, at least in the short run.

however, the extent to which firms want to choose price or quantity may be important.

When firms know both the market demand and, in equilibrium, other firms' choices of strategic variables, each firm is indifferent between setting price and quantity. Because the residual demand is known with certainty, each strategic variable precisely determines the other, and either can be set to ensure the monopolistic price and quantity on the residual demand curve. But when firms are uncertain about their residual demands, because shocks to market demand are unobservable or because the level or type of strategic variables chosen by other firms is unknown, each firm's choice between setting a price and setting a quantity becomes important. Setting a price and setting a quantity generally give different expected losses relative to the maximum profits that could be achieved if the residual demand were perfectly known.

Weitzman (1974) emphasized the importance of the choice between setting price and setting quantity under uncertainty. The objective function in his model was expected total surplus. In our analysis firms maximize expected profits, and we incorporate their choices between price and quantity strategies into an oligopoly model to determine the strategic variables used in equilibrium.

We present a model of a duopoly in which firms endogenously select strategic variables. Firms simultaneously choose either a quantity to produce or a price to charge. Given the types and levels of the strategic variables selected, the remaining prices and quantities are determined to clear all markets. We are interested in the Nash equilibria of this one-stage game.

In the absence of uncertainty there are four types of equilibria: (price, price), (quantity, quantity), (price, quantity), and (quantity, price). Output levels, and hence the intensity of competition, differ among these equilibria. Although each firm is indifferent between choosing price and quantity, in each equilibrium it is crucial that each firm select the strategic variable that its competitor expects. Otherwise, its competitor would face a different residual demand curve and would want to choose a different action.

When exogenous uncertainty about market demands is introduced, the duopolists are no longer indifferent between setting price and quantity. As a consequence, the number of Nash equilibria is reduced. More precisely, consider four duopoly games under uncertainty, in each of which each firm is assigned one of its two possible strategic variables, but is allowed to choose its level. Call the equilibria of these games "candidate equilibria." When we make the choice of strategic variable endogenous by enlarging firms' strategy sets, we find that not all of the candidate equilibria are Nash equilibria. In the simple models we analyze only one equilibrium remains.

We consider the determinants of equilibria in games in which strategic variables are chosen endogenously in the presence of uncertainty. After offering an illustration in Section 2, we examine in Sections 3, 4, and 5 the role of the slope of the marginal cost curve, the nature of the demand uncertainty, and the curvature of demand and show how these factors affect the duopoly equilibria by influencing a firm's preference between price and quantity under uncertainty. In the models of these three sections the duopoly equilibrium is unique. In Section 6 we present an approximate general analysis for determining an individual firm's choice between setting price and setting quantity and show how the models of the three previous sections are special cases. Section 7 contains conclusions and suggestions for extensions.

Rather than provide a complete answer to the question, "What is the 'correct' oligopoly solution concept?" – an exercise that would require including a time dimension and a theory of when firms can credibly commit to which variables and at what cost – our goal is simply to illustrate one component of the answer. We focus on how uncertainty will affect oligopolists' propensities to compete with price or with quantity as the strategic variable.

2. An illustration

Consider the case of consulting. If a consultant charges a fee per hour, he is setting a price. On the other hand, he might set a fixed fee per consultation. If he then spends less time on any one client when his office is busy than when demand is slack, so that his total work day is constant, he is, in effect, setting a quantity and adjusting price in accord with demand. In fact, many consulting firms seem to operate in the latter mode.[2]

In one international firm with both an auditing and a management consulting division, the management consulting division operates in a quantity-setting fashion, whereas the auditing division sets a price (i.e., a strictly defined fee per hour). We shall see that, because demand uncertainty in management consulting is high, the rapidly increasing marginal

---

[2] Although they often quote a fixed rate per consultant per hour, when business is slack, more hours are worked on a project than are reported, and travel time is not charged. When the office is busy, however, travel, marginally related training, and even the time spent originally negotiating the project may all be charged to the client. In some consulting firms, project managers bid for staff resources, so that the firm internally resembles an auction market in which the real price of consulting time is bid up until demand is brought into balance with the (roughly) fixed supply.

costs around full staff utilization (from close to zero to close to infinity) make fixing quantity the optimal choice for this division. In auditing, on the other hand, demand uncertainty is very low[3] so that our theory suggests that neither variable will be strongly preferred. Internal organizational factors dictate setting a price: charging a set price per hour for the hours actually worked both increases internal control and records exactly how long different tasks take, which is useful information for future audits.[4]

3. The general linear model

We analyze a differentiated products duopoly in which each firm simultaneously chooses either a quantity to produce or a price to charge. That is, each firm's strategy set is the union of all fixed quantities and all fixed prices. Given the types and levels of the two strategic variables selected, the remaining prices and quantities are determined to clear both markets. We do not model the process by which markets are cleared, just as, for example, it is not explicitly modeled in a Cournot game under uncertainty. Our interest is in characterizing the Nash equilibria of this one-stage game in which strategic variables are selected endogenously. We restrict our attention to pure-strategy equilibria.

Consider symmetric duopolists with linear marginal cost curves, $C'(q) = c_1 + c_2 q$, $c_1 > 0$, and the linear demand system,

$$p_i = \alpha - \beta q_i - \gamma q_j \tag{1a}$$

$$p_j = \alpha - \beta q_j - \gamma q_i, \tag{1b}$$

where $\alpha > c_1$, $\beta > 0$, and $\beta \geq \gamma \geq 0$. When $\gamma = \beta$, the products are perfect substitutes, whereas when $\gamma = 0$, demands are independent.

In the absence of uncertainty, if firm i conjectures that j is setting its quantity at $\bar{q}_j$, i's residual demand is $p_i = \alpha - \beta q_i - \gamma \bar{q}_j$, whereas if i conjectures that j is setting its price at $\bar{p}_j$, then i's residual demand is $p_i = \alpha(\beta - \gamma)/\beta + \gamma \bar{p}_j/\beta - q_i(\beta^2 - \gamma^2)/\beta$. This last equation is derived by solving (1b) for q_j in terms of q_i and $\bar{p}_j$ and substituting into (1a). Thus, given its conjecture about j's choice of strategic variable, i knows its residual demand exactly, and, regarding itself as a monopolist with respect to its residual demand, i identifies its profit-maximizing point (p_i^*, q_i^*). The

---

[3] Market demand is roughly fixed owing to government regulation. In addition, the large costs to clients of switching between firms keep individual firms' demands stable and predictable.

[4] It is difficult to keep different sets of books for internal and for client use. The auditing division, in contrast to the management consulting division, has built up a strong ethic that staff should accurately report the hours they work.

absence of uncertainty guarantees that i can achieve this point by setting *either* its quantity ($q_i = q_i^*$) *or* its price ($p_i = p_i^*$) appropriately, and i is thus indifferent between these two strategies. As a consequence, without uncertainty there exist four Nash equilibria that correspond to each firm's choosing either of its two possible strategic variables.[5] The equilibria are supported by each firm's choosing the strategic variable that its rival expects; although each firm sees its own choice between price and quantity as irrelevant, its choice is not irrelevant to its rival because the selection determines the residual demand curve that its rival faces.

Now suppose that both firms' demands are subject to a random shock that neither can observe at the time strategic variables are chosen.[6] In particular, let the shock be additive:

$$p_i = \alpha - \beta q_i - \gamma q_j + \epsilon \tag{2a}$$

$$p_j = \alpha - \beta q_j - \gamma q_i + \epsilon, \tag{2b}$$

where ϵ is a random variable assumed without loss of generality to have mean zero.[7] In each of the four games in which each firm is assigned one of its two possible strategic variables (price or quantity) and is allowed to choose its level, there is a unique equilibrium. Because of the linearity of the demand and marginal cost curves and the additivity of the shocks, these four "candidate equilibria" coincide with the four Nash equilibria in the game in which strategic variables are determined endogenously under certainty. Under uncertainty, however, the four candidate equilibria will not all be equilibria when firms can select which strategic variable to use, because the strategic variables assigned may not be the optimal ones to use.[8] Specifically, given its conjecture about j's choice of strategic variable ($\bar{q}_j$ or $\bar{p}_j$), i's position is that of a monopolist facing the uncertain (residual) demand given by

[5] In the case of decreasing marginal costs we assume that $c_2 > -2(\beta^2 - \gamma^2)/\beta$, so that the second-order conditions are always satisfied, and that c_1 is large enough and $|c_2|$ small enough that prices are always positive in equilibrium.

[6] Whether firms are subject to the same or different shocks is not important. When firms' demands are subject to different shocks of arbitrary correlation, the proofs become more complicated, but the results are unaffected.

[7] As specified, this system allows the possibility that a firm setting a price may sell a negative quantity, or that a firm setting a quantity may receive a negative price, in each case depending on the values of the random variables and the other firm's strategic variable. Strictly, the demand system should incorporate constraints preventing these outcomes. Henceforth, we assume for every demand system and associated pair of cost curves that the support of the noise is small enough that these constraints never affect the equilibrium.

[8] When the assumptions of linearity and of additivity of the shocks are relaxed, the set of candidate equilibria under uncertainty will not match the set of equilibria under certainty.

$$p_i = \alpha - \beta q_i - \gamma \bar{q}_j + \epsilon$$

or

$$p_i = \alpha \left(\frac{\beta - \gamma}{\beta}\right) + \frac{\gamma \bar{p}_j}{\beta} - q_i \left(\frac{\beta^2 - \gamma^2}{\beta}\right) + \left(\frac{\beta - \gamma}{\beta}\right) \epsilon.$$

Under uncertainty a monopolist is not in general indifferent between (1) choosing a quantity and then selling at the resulting market price and (2) setting a price and then producing what the market demands. In both cases the resulting price-quantity pairs will diverge from the *ex post* optimal pairs, but the two strategies will lead to different expected losses relative to the profits that would be achievable if *ex post* adjustment were feasible.[9]

We use the following lemma.

Lemma 1. *Consider a monopolist facing the uncertain demand $p = A - Bq + \theta$, where $E\theta = 0$, $E\theta^2 = \sigma^2$, $A > 0$, and $B > 0$, and having the cost function $C(q) = c_1 q + c_2(q^2/2)$, where $0 < c_1 < A$ and $c_2 > -2B$ (the latter condition ensures that the second-order conditions are satisfied). Denote the optimal set quantity $\hat{q}$ and the optimal set price $\hat{p}$. The difference in expected profits between setting $\hat{q}$ and setting $\hat{p}$ is*

$$E\Pi(\hat{q}) - E\Pi(\hat{p}) = \frac{\sigma^2 c_2}{2B^2}.$$

Hence, the monopolist strictly prefers to set quantity (price) when marginal costs slope upward (downward) and is indifferent only when marginal costs are flat.

The proof of Lemma 1 appears in the Appendix. For a graphical interpretation refer to Figure 1, which compares for a particular realization of θ the loss from setting $\hat{p}$ (dotted area) and the loss from setting $\hat{q}$ (hatched area) relative to the potential profit from setting price and quantity at their *ex post* optimal levels. Because of the linearity of demand and marginal costs, these losses are represented by similar triangles.[10] The loss from setting $\hat{p}$ exceeds the loss from setting $\hat{q}$ if the output resulting from $\hat{p}$, $q(\hat{p}, \theta)$, is farther from the monopolist's optimal output, $q^{opt}(\theta)$, than $\hat{q}$ is. Since for any θ the marginal revenue curve is twice as steep as demand,

---

[9] A monopolist would prefer to adjust both price and quantity in accord with the demand shock, but we are assuming that such *ex post* adjustment of both variables is infeasible and that one of them must be fixed *ex ante*.

[10] Linearity and additivity also ensure that $\hat{p}$ and $\hat{q}$ are equal to the *ex post* optimal price and quantity when θ takes its mean value of zero.

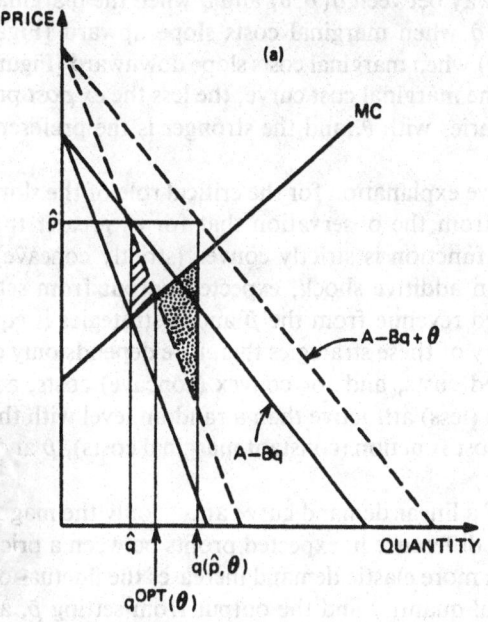

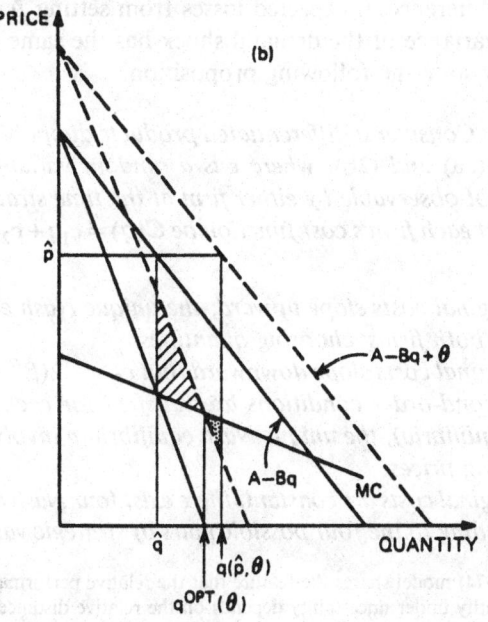

Figure 1. The slope of marginal costs.

$q^{opt}(\theta)$ is halfway between $q(\hat{p}, \theta)$ and $\hat{q}$ when the marginal cost curve is flat, closer to $\hat{q}$ when marginal costs slope upward [Figure 1(a)], and closer to $q(\hat{p}, \theta)$ when marginal costs slope downward [Figure 1(b)]. Thus, the steeper is the marginal cost curve, the less the *ex post* profit-maximizing quantity varies with θ, and the stronger is the preference for setting quantity.[11]

An alternative explanation for the critical role of the slope of marginal costs follows from the observation that for c_2 greater than (less than) zero, the cost function is strictly convex (strictly concave). With linear demand and an additive shock, expected output from setting $\hat{p}$ equals $\hat{q}$, and expected revenue from the $\hat{p}$ and $\hat{q}$ strategies is equal. The relative profitability of these strategies therefore depends only on the relative size of expected costs, and for convex (concave) costs, a fixed level of output is more (less) attractive than a random level with the same mean. With a linear cost function (constant marginal costs), $\hat{p}$ and $\hat{q}$ yield equal expected profit.

The slope of a linear demand curve affects only the magnitude and not the sign of the difference in expected profits between a price and a quantity strategy. A more elastic demand increases the fluctuations in both the *ex post* optimal quantity and the output from setting $\hat{p}$, and as a result increases the difference in expected losses from setting $\hat{p}$ and $\hat{q}$. An increase in the variance of the demand shock has the same effect.

We can now state the following proposition.

Proposition 1. *Consider a differentiated products duopoly facing the demand system (2a) and (2b), where ϵ is a random variable, with mean zero, that is not observable by either firm at the time strategic variables are chosen. Let each firm's cost function be $C(q) = c_1 q + c_2(q^2/2)$, where $0 < c_1 < \alpha$.*

(a) *If marginal costs slope upward, the unique Nash equilibrium involves both firms' choosing quantities.*

(b) *If marginal costs slope downward (but $c_2 > -2(\beta^2 - \gamma^2)/\beta$ so that the second-order conditions are satisfied for each of the candidate equilibria), the unique Nash equilibrium involves both firms' choosing prices.*

(c) *If marginal costs are constant, there exist four Nash equilibria, corresponding to the four possible pairs of strategic variable choices,*

---

[11] Weitzman's (1974) model shares the feature that the relative performance of a set price and a set quantity under uncertainty depends on the relative distances of the resulting outputs from the optimal output. But because the objective function in Weitzman's model is expected total surplus rather than expected profits, it is the sign of $c_2 - B$ that is critical.

236

Price vs. quantity competition

except if the goods are perfect substitutes, in which case only the (quantity, quantity) and (price, price) equilibria exist.

Proof. When firm j sets quantity at $\bar{q}_j$, firm i is a monopolist facing the residual demand

$$p_i = (\alpha - \gamma \bar{q}_j) - \beta q_i + \epsilon,$$

which is linear with an additive shock. When j sets price at $\bar{p}_j$, i's residual demand is

$$p_i = \alpha \left(\frac{\beta - \gamma}{\beta} \right) + \frac{\gamma \bar{p}_j}{\beta} - q_i \left(\frac{\beta^2 - \gamma^2}{\beta} \right) + \left(\frac{\beta - \gamma}{\beta} \right) \epsilon,$$

which is also linear with an additive shock. Therefore, in both cases by Lemma 1 firm i's choice of strategic variable depends only on the slope of its marginal cost curve. For c_2 greater than (less than) zero, i prefers to set a quantity (price), whichever strategic variable j chooses. By symmetry, the only Nash equilibrium entails fixed quantities (prices) when marginal costs slope upward (downward).

When marginal costs are constant and $\gamma < \beta$, Lemma 1 implies that each firm is indifferent between setting price and setting quantity, whatever action its rival chooses. Hence, all four "candidate equilibria" are Nash equilibria of the game.

For $\gamma = \beta$ (perfect substitutes), the demand system (2a) and (2b) as written is ill-specified. When we take proper account of the constraints that firms' quantities and prices can never be negative, the previous results still hold. For constant marginal costs, however, the asymmetric (price, quantity) and (quantity, price) equilibria do not exist. To show this, first observe that firm i's best response to any $\bar{p}_j > c_1$ is a price lower than $\bar{p}_j$ by an arbitrarily small amount, if $\bar{p}_j$ is less than the monopoly price. For higher $\bar{p}_j$ either a price is the unique best response or (for small uncertainty and large $\bar{p}_j$) the best price and the best quantity are equally profitable; in either case j obtains zero sales and hence zero profits.[12] Any $\bar{p}_j < c_1$ clearly involves losses. Hence, the only price that can be part of an equilibrium is c_1. If $\bar{p}_j = c_1 > 0$, i can earn expected profits of at most zero and is willing to choose either a price or a quantity. But i will not choose a quantity greater than $(\alpha + \underline{\epsilon} - c_1)/\beta$, where $\underline{\epsilon}$ is the lower bound of the support of ϵ, since to do so would risk earning negative profits. In

---

[12] The latter case arises when i can behave as a monopolist, unconstrained by j's price, and i's indifference between price and quantity then follows from Lemma 1. The former case arises if, with positive probability, the shock is so large that when i sets a quantity, j is left with positive demand.

response to $q_i \leq (\alpha + \underline{\varepsilon} - c_1)/\beta$, j would prefer to choose a price above c_1 (or a quantity), and therefore no asymmetric equilibria exist.[13] ∎

Under uncertainty, the "cost" of choosing a particular strategic variable is the loss in expected profits relative to those earned when there is optimal *ex post* adjustment of both price and quantity. That is, it is the cost of ending up at the wrong point on the (residual) demand curve. The steeper is the marginal cost curve, the larger is this cost for setting price. This result is quite robust and will emerge again in the general formulation of Section 6. For the particular oligopoly model considered in this section, whenever marginal costs are upward sloping, setting quantity is always an optimal response for both firms, so the unique Nash equilibrium involves quantities as strategic variables.

Setting price and maximum quantity

It is often argued that "price competition" is better modeled by firms' setting both prices and maximum quantities that they are willing to sell.[14] We, instead, have deliberately focused on the simplest possible model (similarly, we have not allowed a firm setting quantity to refuse to sell if prices fall excessively low), and have preserved the symmetry between price competition and quantity competition. In fact, the difference between the two representations of price competition is typically small in our model. The optimal set price is determined approximately by the intersection of expected marginal revenue with marginal cost; the optimal maximum quantity (if allowed) is where the chosen price intersects marginal cost.

Without uncertainty, therefore, the maximum-quantity constraint can never bind in a (pure-strategy) equilibrium, because the firm for which it was binding would not be at a profit-maximizing point. Thus, if we give firms the choice between (a) setting a quantity and (b) setting a price and a maximum quantity, the only possible equilibrium outcomes are those

---

[13] The nonexistence of asymmetric (price, quantity) and (quantity, price) equilibria with perfect substitutes depends on the assumption that the constant level of marginal costs is strictly positive, an assumption that we make throughout the article. If marginal costs were zero, then in response to $\bar{p}_j = 0$, i would be willing to choose a quantity large enough ($q_i \geq (\alpha + \bar{\varepsilon})/\beta$, where $\bar{\varepsilon}$ is the upper bound of the support of ϵ) that $\bar{p}_j = 0$ is an optimal response. In all of the models we consider, asymmetric equilibria exist for the case of perfect substitutes and constant marginal costs if and only if marginal costs are zero.

[14] Kreps and Scheinkman (1983) for example, present a model in which capacity commitment followed by this kind of price competition yields the same outcome as single-stage quantity competition.

corresponding to the four Nash equilibria of the simpler game. But one or more of the equilibria involving price as a strategic variable need not exist in this new game.[15]

It also follows that for a sufficiently small support of the uncertainty, the maximum-quantity constraint can never bind with positive probability.[16] Thus, the equilibria that match the equilibria of the simpler game with uncertainty are the only possible ones in the new game. Further, for the model of this section all of the equilibria in the simpler game with uncertainty survive in the new game: with increasing marginal costs the only equilibrium in the simpler game involves quantities and so remains an equilibrium, and with flat or decreasing marginal costs the quantity constraints are irrelevant, so that all the equilibria remain.

For sufficiently small uncertainty, therefore, Lemma 1 and Proposition 1 both hold when firms choose between either setting a quantity or setting a price and a maximum quantity to produce. Similarly, the subsequent results in this article all hold for a game incorporating the alternative model of price competition for sufficiently small uncertainty with the exception that, where equilibria involving prices are claimed for cases with increasing marginal costs, these may not exist.[17]

4. The nature of the uncertainty

We demonstrate in this section that firms' preferences over strategic variables, and hence the nature of the Nash equilibria in our game, are sensitive to the manner in which random disturbances affect demands. Specifically, we show that if uncertainty affects the slopes of linear demand

---

[15] The reason is that the residual demand of the competitor of the firm setting price is higher when the latter's constraint is binding than in the simpler game. The competitor may therefore prefer to reduce quantity (or raise price) from the equilibrium value of the simpler game to make its opponent's constraint binding. This behavior may upset an equilibrium of the simpler game, although it can never create a new one.

[16] If it did, one firm's marginal cost would be close to its price, and hence above its marginal revenue for all values of the shock. This would contradict the optimality of its response. With vertical marginal costs this argument does not apply, but choosing a quantity then achieves a firm's maximum possible profit for all realizations of the shock, so the equilibrium will not involve prices and maximum quantities.

[17] In some cases we can be sure that the claimed (price, price) equilibrium does exist, because the deviation that would be required of a firm to make its opponent's maximum-quantity constraint binding can be shown to be so large as to be unattractive. For example, in Proposition 2 for sufficiently small uncertainty and for marginal costs not rising excessively rapidly, driving the opponent to the point where its maximum-quantity constraint is binding requires a firm to reduce its own quantity below zero. Hence, under these conditions the claimed (price, price) equilibrium remains an equilibrium when the notion of price competition is generalized.

239

PAUL KLEMPERER AND MARGARET MEYER

curves, rather than just the intercepts, then price competition will arise for flat or not excessively rapidly rising marginal cost curves.

As in Section 3, we begin by examining the behavior of a monopolist.

Lemma 2. *Consider a monopolist facing a linear demand curve with fixed vertical intercept but random slope,*

$$p = A - \frac{Bq}{\theta},$$

where θ is a strictly positive random variable with $E\theta = 1$ and $E\theta^2 = s^2 > 1$ and where $A > 0$ and $B > 0$. Let z denote $E(1/\theta)$, which, by Jensen's inequality, is strictly greater than one. Let the cost function be $C(q) = c_1 q + c_2(q^2/2)$, where $0 < c_1 < A$ and $c_2 > -2B/s^2$. The latter condition ensures that the second-order conditions are satisfied. Denote the optimal set quantity $\hat{q}$ and the optimal set price $\hat{p}$. The difference in expected profits between setting $\hat{q}$ and setting $\hat{p}$ is

$$E\Pi(\hat{q}) - E\Pi(\hat{p}) = \frac{(A-c_1)^2}{2}\left(\frac{1}{2Bz+c_2} - \frac{1}{2B+c_2 s^2}\right).$$

Let $c_2^* = (2(z-1)/(s^2-1))B > 0$. For all c_2 less than (greater than) c_2^*, $E\Pi(\hat{q}) - E\Pi(\hat{p})$ is strictly negative (positive), and so setting a price (quantity) is strictly preferred.

The proof appears in the Appendix. The intuition is that rotation of the demand curve about the vertical intercept represents replication or shrinking of the market, with the distribution of consumers' reservation prices remaining unchanged. If marginal costs are constant, such a rotation does not alter the profit-maximizing price. Thus, setting a price is *ex post* optimal for flat marginal costs and, by continuity, is preferred to setting a quantity for slowly rising marginal costs. As in Section 3, however, as the slope of the marginal cost curve increases, the output fluctuations resulting from a set price become increasingly undesirable, because the *ex post* optimal quantity varies less and less. For a sufficiently steep marginal cost curve, setting quantity is preferred.

For another interpretation of this result, consider the dependence of price on θ for any fixed output. In Lemma 2 the price is strictly concave in θ and so has lower expected value than in Lemma 1, where the price is linear in θ. The output from setting price is linear in θ in both cases, with the same expected value. Therefore, since expected revenues from the optimal quantity and price strategies are equal in Lemma 1, the optimal quantity strategy yields strictly lower expected revenue than the optimal

240

Price vs. quantity competition

price strategy for the demand curve of Lemma 2. Against this must be set the difference in expected costs, which depends, as Section 3 showed, on the convexity or concavity of the cost curve.

For a given distribution of (multiplicative) uncertainty about the slope, the cutoff value c_2^* above which quantity is preferred is linear in the expected slope of demand. To see this, observe that multiplying the expected slope of demand and the slope of marginal costs by the same factor is equivalent to multiplying the size of the units in which we measure output and the value of the currency unit in which we measure price by that factor, and so does not alter the preference between setting price and setting quantity.

Proposition 2. *Consider a differentiated products duopoly facing the demand system,*

$$p_i = \alpha - \frac{\beta q_i}{\epsilon} - \frac{\gamma q_j}{\epsilon} \tag{3a}$$

$$p_j = \alpha - \frac{\beta q_j}{\epsilon} - \frac{\gamma q_i}{\epsilon}, \tag{3b}$$

where ϵ is a strictly positive random variable, with mean one, that is not observable by either firm at the time strategic variables are chosen. Let the cost curves be $C(q) = c_1 q + c_2 (q^2/2)$. Assume that $c_1 > 0$ and that $c_2 > -2(\beta^2 - \gamma^2)/\beta s^2$, where $s^2 = E\epsilon^2$, so that the second-order conditions are always satisfied. There exists a $\bar{c}_2 > 0$ such that for $c_2 < \bar{c}_2$ in the unique Nash equilibrium firms set prices. For all $\gamma < \beta$, $\bar{c}_2$ is strictly positive. For the case of perfect substitutes ($\gamma = \beta$), $\bar{c}_2 = 0$, and for $c_2 = 0$, the unique Nash equilibrium entails price-setting.

The proof appears in the Appendix. Note that for a given firm k the shock affects the sensitivity of the firm's price to the quantity $\beta q_k + \gamma q_m$, $m \neq k$, but does not affect the relative sensitivity of the price to the firm's own and the other firm's quantity; i.e., the degree of substitutability of the products remains unchanged.

The uncertainty in the slopes of firms' residual demands makes the analysis and intuition similar to that of Lemma 2. For the shallow marginal cost curves a firm's optimal response to either choice of strategic variable by its opponent is a set price, so for low values of c_2, there is a unique Nash equilibrium, with prices as strategic variables. Note that the cutoff value $\bar{c}_2$ below which we have a (price, price) equilibrium depends on the demand system. In particular, as the goods approach perfect substitutes, $\bar{c}_2$ approaches zero.[18] Even for perfect substitutes, however, the unique equilibrium for constant marginal costs and uncertainty about demand slopes is the (price, price) one, in contrast to Proposition 1, where both a (price, price) and a (quantity, quantity) equilibrium exist.

The models of Sections 3 and 4 have shown that the nature of competition depends in part on the nature of the uncertainty in market demands. For any demand curve, rotation about a fixed vertical intercept (i.e., $q = tg(p)$, where t varies) represents a change in the total size of a market in which the distribution of consumers' reservation prices remains unchanged. On the other hand, rotation about a fixed horizontal intercept (i.e., $p = tf(q)$) represents a particular type of change in the distribution of reservation prices, with the total size of the market remaining unchanged. A vertically additive shift of the demand function is an intermediate case. It involves a change in both the size of the market and the distribution of reservation prices. The contrast between the two extreme types of uncertainty is illustrated by the kinked demand curve of Figure 2, which has a horizontal segment at $\bar{p}$ and a vertical segment at $\bar{q}$. With marginal costs constant, uncertainty in the reservation price dictates setting the quantity $\bar{q}$ [Figure 2(a)], whereas uncertainty in the size of the market dictates setting the price $\bar{p}$ [Figure 2(b)]. Comparison of Proposition 2 with Proposition 1 shows that prices are more attractive as strategic variables when firms' uncertainty relates only to the size of the market than when the distribution of reservation prices is uncertain as well. The reason is simply that shocks that affect only the market size generate relatively little variation in the (ex post) optimal price. The variation is less, the flatter are marginal costs, and thus for not excessively rapidly rising marginal cost curves we expect to observe price competition in the presence of such shocks.[19]

5. The curvature of demand

This section explores how firms' choices between price and quantity as strategic variables are influenced by the curvature of their demands. The

[18] As the goods become better substitutes, each firm's residual demand against a set price becomes flatter so that, as in Lemma 2, the cutoff slope of marginal costs above which setting quantity is preferred falls.

[19] For constant marginal costs a monopolist prefers to set a quantity when the unobservable demand shock causes the demand curve to rotate about its intersection with the marginal cost curve. The reason is that for this type of shock, the ex post optimal quantity is constant. It follows that, for a sufficiently small level of constant marginal costs, quantity-setting is also preferred when the shock causes the demand curve to rotate about its horizontal intercept. When this type of uncertainty is incorporated into a duopoly model, the unique Nash equilibrium involves quantities as strategic variables.

Price vs. quantity competition

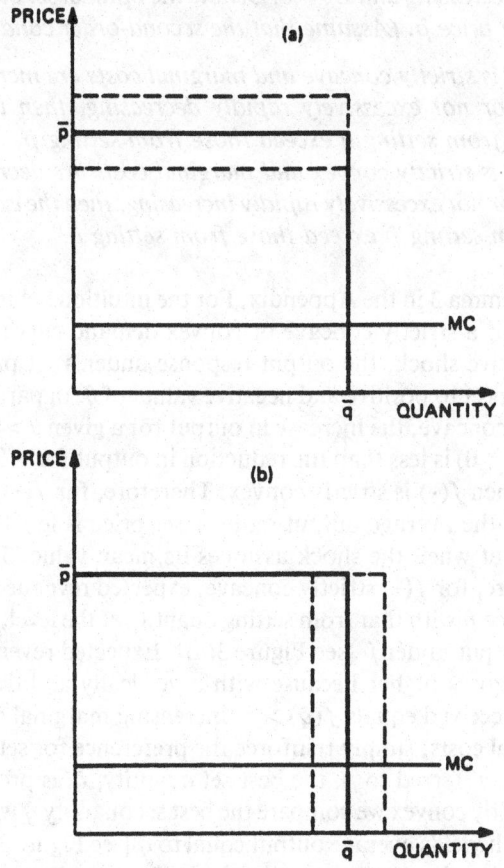

Figure 2. The nature of the uncertainty.

linear model of Section 3 showed that the slope of the demand curve affects the intensity of preference between price and quantity but not the ranking itself. The curvature of demand, on the other hand, does influence which strategic variable is preferred. It does so by introducing an asymmetry into the firm's response to positive and negative demand shocks.

As before, we first analyze the behavior of a monopolist.

Lemma 3. *Consider a monopolist facing a demand curve that is subject to a vertically additive shock,*

$$p = f(q) + \theta,$$

where $f(q)$ is decreasing and $E\theta = 0$. Denote the optimal set quantity $\hat{q}$ and the optimal set price $\hat{p}$. (Assume that the second-order conditions hold.)

(a) *If $f(\cdot)$ is strictly concave and marginal costs are increasing, constant, or not excessively rapidly decreasing, then the expected profits from setting $\hat{q}$ exceed those from setting $\hat{p}$.*

(b) *If $f(\cdot)$ is strictly convex and marginal costs are decreasing, constant, or not excessively rapidly increasing, then the expected profits from setting $\hat{p}$ exceed those from setting $\hat{q}$.*

We prove Lemma 3 in the Appendix. For the intuition behind the result, observe that for a strictly concave or convex demand curve subject to a vertically additive shock, the output response under a set price is asymmetric with respect to positive and negative values of θ. In particular, when $f(\cdot)$ is strictly concave, the increase in output for a given $\theta > 0$ (relative to the output at $\theta = 0$) is less than the reduction in output for $-\theta$, and the reverse is true when $f(\cdot)$ is strictly convex. Therefore, for $f(\cdot)$ strictly concave (convex), the average output under a set price is less than (greater than) the output when the shock assumes its mean value. To apply this fact we compare, for $f(\cdot)$ strictly concave, expected revenue from setting the optimal price $\hat{p}$ with that from setting quantity at the level, $\tilde{q} < f^{-1}(\hat{p})$, of expected output under $\hat{p}$ [see Figure 3(a)]. Expected revenue from the quantity strategy is higher because with a vertically additive shock the average price received equals $f(\tilde{q}) > \hat{p}$. Increasing marginal costs, implying convex total costs, simply reinforce the preference for setting a quantity. Since $\tilde{q}$ is preferred to $\hat{p}$, the best set quantity, $\hat{q}$, is preferred to $\hat{p}$.

For $f(\cdot)$ strictly convex we compare the best set quantity $\hat{q}$ with the price, $\tilde{p} > f(\hat{q})$, which yields average output equal to $\hat{q}$ [see Figure 3(b)]. With a vertically additive shock average price from the quantity strategy equals $f(\hat{q})$, and hence expected revenue from setting $\hat{q}$ equals $\hat{q}f(\hat{q})$, which is less than $\hat{q}\tilde{p}$, the expected revenue from setting $\tilde{p}$. Decreasing marginal costs, implying concave total costs, reinforce the preference for a variable output level. Since $\tilde{p}$ is preferred to $\hat{q}$, the best set price, $\hat{p}$, is preferred to $\hat{q}$.

For an alternative interpretation of these results, observe that the curvature of demand affects the ratio of the slope of marginal revenue, $2f'(q) + qf''(q)$, to the slope of demand, $f'(q)$. The more concave is demand, the steeper is marginal revenue relative to demand, and hence the smaller are the fluctuations in the *ex post* optimal quantity relative to the fluctuations in output under a set price. Concavity of demand therefore imparts a preference for stabilizing quantity.[20]

[20] On the cost side, the attractiveness of setting quantity depends on the slope of the marginal cost curve, whereas on the demand side, the critical factor is the slope of marginal

Price vs. quantity competition

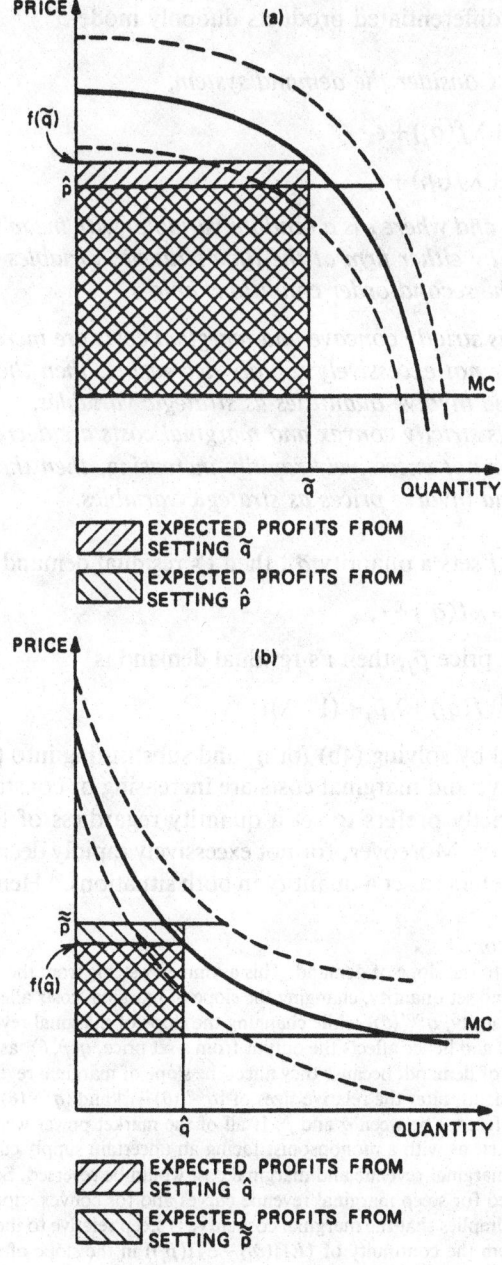

Figure 3. The curvature of demand.

245

The following proposition incorporates the effect of the curvature of demand into a differentiated products duopoly model.

Proposition 3. *Consider the demand system,*

$$p_i = f(q_i) + \lambda f(q_j) + \epsilon \tag{4a}$$

$$p_j = f(q_j) + \lambda f(q_i) + \epsilon, \tag{4b}$$

where $\lambda \in [0, 1)$ and where ϵ is a random variable, with mean zero, that is not observable by either firm at the time strategic variables are chosen. (Assume that the second-order conditions hold.)

(a) *If $f(\cdot)$ is strictly concave and marginal costs are increasing, constant, or not excessively rapidly decreasing, then the only Nash equilibria involve quantities as strategic variables.*

(b) *If $f(\cdot)$ is strictly convex and marginal costs are decreasing, constant, or not excessively rapidly increasing, then the only Nash equilibria involve prices as strategic variables.*

Proof. If firm j sets a quantity $\bar{q}_j$, then i's residual demand is

$$p_i = f(q_i) + \lambda f(\bar{q}_j) + \epsilon,$$

while if j sets a price $\bar{p}_j$, then i's residual demand is

$$p_i = (1 - \lambda^2) f(q_i) + \lambda \bar{p}_j + (1 - \lambda)\epsilon,$$

which is derived by solving (4b) for q_j and substituting into (4a). If $f(\cdot)$ is strictly concave and marginal costs are increasing or constant, then by Lemma 3, i strictly prefers to set a quantity regardless of the strategic variable j chooses. Moreover, for not excessively rapidly decreasing marginal costs, i prefers to set a quantity in both situations.[21] Hence, by sym-

Footnote 20 *(cont.)*
revenue relative to the slope of demand. This asymmetry stems from the fact that, for a given set price and set quantity, changing the slope of marginal costs affects only the *ex post* optimal quantity, $q^{opt}(\theta)$, while changing the slope of marginal revenue alters the slope of demand and hence affects the output from a set price, $q(\hat{p}, \theta)$, as well. Changes in the curvature of demand, because they affect the slope of marginal revenue relative to the slope of demand, alter the relative sizes of $|q^{opt}(\theta) - \hat{q}|$ and $|q^{opt}(\theta) - q(\hat{p}, \theta)|$ and so affect the preference between $\hat{q}$ and $\hat{p}$. If all of the market power were on the other side of the market, as with a monopsonist facing an uncertain supply curve, the asymmetric roles of marginal revenue and marginal cost would be reversed. Setting quantity would be favored for steep marginal revenue curves and for convex supply curves; the latter condition implies that the marginal cost curve is steep relative to the supply curve.
[21] This follows from the continuity of $(E\Pi(\hat{q}_i) - E\Pi(\hat{p}_i))$ in the slope of marginal costs and in the other's strategic variable when marginal costs are flat. By "continuous in the slope of marginal costs" we mean that, given any δ_1, there exists a δ_2 such that changing

metry, under these conditions, only (quantity, quantity) Nash equilibria exist. Similarly, if $f(\cdot)$ is strictly convex and marginal costs are decreasing, constant, or not excessively rapidly increasing, then by Lemma 3, i strictly prefers to set a price regardless of the strategic variable j chooses. Thus, by symmetry, under these conditions, only (price, price) Nash equilibria exist.[22] ∎

In the duopoly model consider in the proposition, each firm's residual demand has the same curvature regardless of the strategic variable the other selects, and hence each firm's preferred strategic variable is independent of the other's choice. Only one type of Nash equilibrium is therefore possible. In the presence of a vertically additive shock, concavity of the demand curve makes quantity the preferred strategic variable because of the asymmetrically large reductions in output that result from negative shocks under a set price; convexity of demand favors setting a price because of the asymmetrically large increases in output for positive shocks.

6. A general formulation

In this section we show how the effects illustrated in the three previous sections can be subsumed in an approximate general analysis of a monopolist's choice between setting price and setting quantity under demand uncertainty.

In the discussion of each of our lemmas, we saw that the ranking of the expected profits from the price and quantity strategies followed directly from the concavity or convexity of some element of the model. An alternative interpretation compared, for each value of the shock, the sizes of the deviations from the *ex post* optimal output levels under the two strategies. We now relate these two interpretations in a single formula. We exhibit a function whose local concavity or convexity provides an approximate formula for ranking price and quantity strategies. We then demonstrate that the same formula emerges from using the difference between output deviations under the two strategies to approximate the difference in their losses relative to *ex post* optimal adjustment.

Let the uncertain demand curve be $p = f(q, \theta)$, where $f(\cdot, \cdot)$ is twice continuously differentiable and $f_q < 0$ and $f_\theta > 0$ everywhere. Let $g(p, \theta)$ be defined by $f(g(p, \theta), \theta) = p$. The demand shock θ is assumed to be a

---

$C''(q)$ by not more than δ_2 at any q, but holding j's strategic variable constant, changes $(E\Pi(\hat{q}_i) - E\Pi(\hat{p}_i))$ by not more than δ_1.

[22] For $\lambda = 1$ the demand system is reasonable only if $f(\cdot)$ is linear, for which case see Proposition 1. (If $f(\cdot)$ were not linear, although $p_i = p_j$, the common price would respond to changes in q_i in a way different from that to changes in q_j.)

continuous random variable. Let the cost curve be $C(q)$. We assume it is twice continuously differentiable.

We compare a set price p^* and a set quantity q^* that for some value of the demand shock, say θ^*, both yield the *ex post* optimal point on the corresponding demand curve. There is one such pair in which p^* equals the *ex ante* optimal price $\hat{p}$ and, in general, a different pair in which q^* equals the *ex ante* optimal quantity $\hat{q}$. If the ranking of the price and quantity strategies is the same for both pairs, this is sufficient to rank $\hat{p}$ and $\hat{q}$.[23]

Define the following three functions of θ:

$$\Pi^{opt}(\theta) = \text{unconstrained maximum profit;}$$

$$\Pi^q(q^*, \theta) = f(q^*, \theta)q^* - C(q^*)$$

$$= \text{profit from setting quantity at } q^*; \tag{5a}$$

$$\Pi^p(p^*, \theta) = p^*g(p^*, \theta) - C(g(p^*, \theta))$$

$$= \text{profit from setting price at } p^*. \tag{5b}$$

By construction $\Pi^q(q^*, \theta)$ and $\Pi^p(p^*, \theta)$ are both tangent to $\Pi^{opt}(\theta)$ at θ^*, and so also tangent to each other at this point. It follows that in a neighborhood of θ^*, either $\Pi^q(q^*, \theta)$ exceeds $\Pi^p(p^*, \theta)$ everywhere or $\Pi^p(p^*, \theta)$ exceeds $\Pi^q(q^*, \theta)$ everywhere, unless the two functions coincide.

To proceed formally we work directly with the function relating $\Pi^p(p^*, \theta)$ to $\Pi^q(q^*, \theta)$. Define for all θ the function T:

$$T(\Pi^q(q^*, \theta)) = \Pi^p(p^*, \theta).$$

Differentiating with respect to θ yields

$$T'(\Pi^q(q^*, \theta)) \frac{\partial \Pi^q}{\partial \theta}(q^*, \theta) = \frac{\partial \Pi^p}{\partial \theta}(p^*, \theta). \tag{6}$$

Differentiating again with respect to θ, substituting for T' by using (6), and solving for T'', we get

$$T''(\Pi^q(q^*, \theta)) = \frac{\left[\dfrac{\partial^2 \Pi^p}{\partial \theta^2}(p^*, \theta) \dfrac{\partial \Pi^q}{\partial \theta}(q^*, \theta) - \dfrac{\partial^2 \Pi^q}{\partial \theta^2}(q^*, \theta) \dfrac{\partial \Pi^p}{\partial \theta}(p^*, \theta) \right]}{\left(\dfrac{\partial \Pi^q}{\partial \theta}(q^*, \theta) \right)^3}. \tag{7}$$

---

[23] For example, if p^* is preferred to q^* for both pairs, then $\hat{q}$ is dominated by a nonoptimal price and hence by $\hat{p}$.

Price vs. quantity competition

Since $\Pi^q(q^*, \theta)$ and $\Pi^p(p^*, \theta)$ are tangent at $\theta = \theta^*$, T is tangent to the 45°-line at the point $(\Pi^q(q^*, \theta^*), \Pi^p(p^*, \theta^*))$. It follows that if T is globally concave, profits from the quantity strategy are everywhere (weakly) larger than those from the price strategy, and therefore q^* is preferred to p^*. The reverse is true if T is globally convex.

Let us examine the sign of T'' at $\Pi^q(q^*, \theta^*)$. Since $\partial \Pi^q(q^*, \theta^*)/\partial\theta = \partial\Pi^p(p^*, \theta^*)/\partial\theta$ (because of tangency) and since $\partial\Pi^q(q^*, \theta^*)/\partial\theta > 0$ (because $f_\theta > 0$),

$$\text{sgn}[T''(\Pi^q(q^*, \theta^*))] = \text{sgn}\left[\frac{\partial^2 \Pi^p}{\partial\theta^2}(p^*, \theta^*) - \frac{\partial^2 \Pi^q}{\partial\theta^2}(q^*, \theta^*)\right].$$

Using the definitions (5a) and (5b) to evaluate the derivatives, we can write the expression in brackets on the right-hand side as

$$[p^* - C'(g(p^*, \theta^*))]g_{\theta\theta}(p^*, \theta^*) - C''(g(p^*, \theta^*))(g_\theta(p^*, \theta^*))^2 - f_{\theta\theta}(q^*, \theta^*)q^*. \tag{8}$$

Since (p^*, q^*) is the *ex post* optimal point on the demand curve $p = f(q, \theta^*)$, it satisfies the first-order condition for (*ex post*) profit maximization:

$$f(q^*, \theta^*) + q^* f_q(q^*, \theta^*) - C'(q^*) = 0,$$

or since $p^* = f(q^*, \theta^*)$ and $q^* = g(p^*, \theta^*)$,

$$p^* - C'(g(p^*, \theta^*)) = -q^* f_q(q^*, \theta^*). \tag{9}$$

Substituting (9) into (8) and replacing the derivatives of g with the appropriate derivatives of f (obtained by implicit differentiation of the identity $f(g(p, \theta), \theta) = p$), we conclude that

$$\text{sgn}[T''(\Pi^q(q^*, \theta^*))]$$
$$= \text{sgn}\{q^*[f_{qq}(q^*, \theta^*)f_\theta(q^*, \theta^*) - 2f_{q\theta}(q^*, \theta^*)f_q(q^*, \theta^*)]$$
$$- C''(q^*)f_\theta(q^*, \theta^*)\}. \tag{10}$$

Equation (10) allows identification of the factors that influence the relative size of $\Pi^q(q^*, \theta)$ and $\Pi^p(p^*, \theta)$ in the neighborhood of θ^*. Reducing the slope of the marginal cost curve (lowering C'' as in Section 3), reducing the magnitude of the demand slope as the demand curve shifts out (raising $f_{q\theta}$ as in Section 4), and increasing the convexity of demand (raising f_{qq} as in Section 5) all increase the likelihood that profits from the price strategy exceed profits from the quantity strategy.

One way to interpret (10) is to recall that, as emphasized in the discussion of each of the lemmas, the costs of setting quantity and price depend on the distances of the resulting outputs, q^* and $g(p^*, \theta)$, from the *ex*

249

post optimal output, $q^{opt}(\theta)$. We can therefore compare q^* and p^* by examining the relative sizes of $|q^{opt}(\theta) - q^*|$ and $|q^{opt}(\theta) - g(p^*, \theta)|$. The former is always larger (smaller) than the latter if $\partial[2q^{opt}(\theta) - g(p^*, \theta)]/\partial\theta$ is always positive (negative). Evaluated at (θ^*, p^*, q^*), the sign of this last expression is precisely the sign of the right-hand side of (10).

The flatter are marginal costs, the more the optimal quantity fluctuates with θ; the variation in the output resulting from a set price is, by contrast, unaffected by the slope of marginal costs. This result generalizes the conclusions of Lemmas 1 and 2 regarding the effect of c_2 in the linear model. A positive value of $f_{q\theta}$ means that demand becomes flatter as it shifts out with increases in θ and that, as a result, $q^{opt}(\theta)$ rises more rapidly with θ than if demand were simply translated vertically ($f_{q\theta} = 0$). The greater sensitivity of $q^{opt}(\theta)$ to θ makes setting a price relatively more attractive. This conclusion generalizes the contrast between the additive shock considered in Lemma 1 ($f_{q\theta} = 0$) and the rotational shock considered in Lemma 2 ($f_{q\theta} > 0$). Finally, as the demand curve becomes more convex, *ceteris paribus,* the ratio of the slope of marginal revenue to the slope of demand falls and causes the sensitivity of $q^{opt}(\theta)$ to θ to rise relative to the sensitivity of $q(\hat{p}, \theta)$ to θ. On average, $q^{opt}(\theta)$ and $q(\hat{p}, \theta)$ are relatively closer together, while $q^{opt}(\theta)$ and $\hat{q}$ are relatively farther apart, so the expected losses from setting price are reduced relative to the expected losses from setting quantity for greater convexity of demand. Conversely, for a very concave demand curve the marginal revenue curve is very steep relative to demand, so $q^{opt}(\theta)$ is very stable relative to $q(\hat{p}, \theta)$, and quantity-setting is preferred. Here we have a generalization of the result of Lemma 3.[24]

When any one of the three effects discussed in the previous paragraph is present in isolation, the local concavity or convexity of T, as determined by (10), holds globally as well. For more general environments, we can use (7) to examine the global behavior of T''.

Applying the approach of this section to identify Nash equilibria in a duopoly under uncertainty requires first calculating the candidate equilibria (for exogenously given strategic variables) and then determining for which candidate equilibria the firms' strategies remain optimal when strategic variables are endogenous. Suppose that demands are subject to a common shock and are given by

---

[24] Only for a vertically additive shock ($p = f(q, \theta) = \tilde{f}(q) + \theta$) is $f_{q\theta}$ identically zero. For a horizontal additive shock, for example, we have $f(q, \theta) = \tilde{f}(q - \theta)$, so $f_{q\theta} = -\tilde{f}''(q - \theta)$, and thus an increase in f_{qq} reduces $f_{q\theta}$. For this case the right-hand side of (10) reduces to $\tilde{f}'(q\tilde{f}'' + C'')$, which falls as $\tilde{f}''$ increases (since $\tilde{f}' < 0$). Thus, for a horizontally additive shock, greater convexity of demand increases the likelihood that setting quantity will be preferred, and greater concavity has the reverse effect. [See Figure 2(b) for an

Price vs. quantity competition

$$p_i = f(q_i, q_j, \epsilon) \tag{11a}$$

$$p_j = f(q_j, q_i, \epsilon), \tag{11b}$$

where f is twice continuously differentiable, $f_1 \leq f_2 \leq 0$ everywhere, and $f_3 > 0$ everywhere. Let each firm's cost function be $C(q)$, which we assume is twice continuously differentiable. When j sets a quantity $\bar{q}_j$, i's residual demand is

$$p_i = f(q_i, \bar{q}_j, \epsilon),$$

while when j sets a price $\bar{p}_j$, i's residual demand is

$$p_i = f(q_i, g(\bar{p}_j, q_i, \epsilon), \epsilon) \equiv F(q_i, \bar{p}_j, \epsilon),$$

where $g(\cdot, \cdot, \cdot)$ is the solution of (11b) for q_j in terms of p_j, q_i, and ϵ.

We must analyze the shape of the function T corresponding to i's residual demand curve in each candidate equilibrium. That is, using (10), we examine

$$\text{sgn}[q_i(f_{11}f_3 - 2f_{13}f_1) - C''f_3]$$

for the two candidate equilibria in which j sets quantity, and examine

$$\text{sgn}[q_i(F_{11}F_3 - 2F_{13}F_1) - C''F_3]$$

for the two candidate equilibria in which j sets price. If these expressions are all negative (positive), then by symmetry there is a unique Nash equilibrium in quantities (prices). This was the situation in the models of Sections 3, 4, and 5. In general, firm i's problem of selecting a strategic variable differs according to which candidate equilibrium we are examining. Different candidate equilibria involve different ranges of output, so the relevant value for the slope of the marginal cost curve may be different. Moreover, the shape of i's residual demand and the effect on it of the random disturbance depend on which variable j is keeping set. Thus, determining which candidate equilibria are equilibria when firms can choose which strategic variable to use often requires more specific knowledge of demand and cost conditions.

We can, however, make some generalizations. First, for sufficiently steep marginal costs the Nash equilibrium is always unique and involves quantities as strategic variables. As marginal costs become steeper, setting a quantity becomes relatively more attractive in response to both a price and a quantity strategy and eventually is preferred in both situations. Second, changes in curvature and in the effect of the uncertainty alter both of a firm's residual demand curves ($f(\cdot, \cdot, \cdot)$ and $F(\cdot, \cdot, \cdot)$) in

illustration of the latter point.] In general, therefore, comparative statics on demand curvature requires recognizing that changes in f_{qq} and in $f_{q\theta}$ are interdependent.

the same direction. That is, as f_{11} increases (decreases), *ceteris paribus*, F_{11} increases (decreases); similarly, as f_{13} rises or falls, *ceteris paribus*, F_{13} moves in the same direction. Thus, very large or very small values of f_{11} or f_{13} increase the likelihood that a firm's preferred strategic variable will be independent of the variable its rival selects and hence the likelihood that there will be a unique Nash equilibrium. Finally, as demand for each good becomes more elastic and reduces both $|f_1|$ and $|F_1|$, the fluctuations in the *ex post* optimal output and in the output under a set price increase.[25] This in turn increases the difference in expected profits from setting quantity and setting price (see Lemma 1) and so intensifies the firm's preferences over strategic variables. Greater uncertainty also strengthens these preferences. Thus, we would expect the factors we have identified – the slope of marginal costs, the nature of the demand uncertainty, and the curvature of demand – to play a larger role in determining the nature and intensity of competition in industries in which demands are relatively elastic and are affected by significant unobservable shocks.

7. Conclusion

We have shown that in an environment of uncertainty about market demands, oligopolists generally have strict preferences between setting quantity and setting price and that, as a consequence, the Bertrand and Cournot outcomes are typically not both equilibria in a game in which firms can choose which strategic variables to use. Recognizing firms' responses to uncertainty thus provides some insight into the nature of oligopolistic competition.[26]

In contrast with our approach, imposing a requirement in the spirit of Selten's (1975) concept of (trembling-hand) perfection does not eliminate any of the four types of equilibria under certainty. For each of the firms in any equilibrium it is possible to find a tremble for the opponent that makes the firm strictly prefer the strategic variable it uses in the equilibrium. There is, however, no economic rationale for the conjectured trembles. We, on the other hand, explicitly model the random effect that gives firms strict preferences over strategic variables.

In our model uncertainty arises from exogenous demand shocks. It could alternatively arise from each firm's uncertainty about its rival's behavior, owing to uncertainty about some characteristic of the rival's cost

[25] Suppose, for example, that f_1 and f_2 are both reduced by a factor of λ ($\lambda > 1$). Then $F_1 = (f_1^2 - f_2^2)/f_1$ is reduced by a factor of λ as well.

[26] In a similar spirit Daughety (1985) introduces uncertainty to choose between Cournot-Nash and Cournot-von Stackelberg equilibria by giving firms the choice between playing early or waiting to infer information about market demand and playing late.

Price vs. quantity competition

or demand function. There is thus no need for actual variation in market conditions; a lack of perfect information about the rival's behavior is sufficient to give firms strict preferences between setting prices and setting quantities.[27] Whichever the kind of uncertainty, an arbitrarily small amount can move us away from the case with four equilibria.

Three factors affect firms' preferences between quantity and price as strategic variables in the presence of uncertainty: the slope of marginal costs, the effect of the random disturbance on demand, and the curvature of demand. Each affects the relative "costs" of setting quantity and price by altering the sensitivity to the shock of the *ex post* optimal price-quantity pairs relative to the sensitivity of the price-quantity pairs resulting from the allowable strategic variables. The most compelling result concerns the slope of the marginal cost curve. When marginal costs are steep, setting quantity is preferred because the *ex post* optimal quantity is relatively stable compared with the output that would result from setting a price and producing to meet market demand. This formalizes the commonly expressed intuition that when marginal costs rise rapidly, firms will compete as Cournot players, but that when marginal costs become flatter, firms will be forced to compete on price.[28] If we enriched the model to include other costs of choosing strategic variables besides those arising from uncertainty, we would find that competition in industries with rapidly increasing marginal costs was most often through quantities, whereas competition in industries with flatter or decreasing marginal costs was most often through prices. Firms' preferences between strategic variables are stronger in industries with more elastic demands and greater uncertainty.

These results explain why the firm described in Section 2 effectively sets quantity in its management consulting division but sets price in its auditing division. They may also help explain the contrast between Eastern Airlines' competitive strategy on its shuttle routes involving New York, Boston, and Washington and the form of competition in much of the rest of the airline industry. Whereas for most routes schedules are first set and prices subsequently adjusted in response to demand fluctuations, on the shuttle routes Eastern sets a price and then provides as many planes as are necessary to

[27] In this case we look for a Bayesian Nash equilibrium in which each "type" of firm has correct conjectures about the mapping from its rival's "type" to the rival's choice of strategic variable, and chooses its own strategic variable to maximize expected profits, given these conjectures.

[28] Roughly, the intuition is that with vertical marginal cost curves the only "reasonable" supply curves or reaction curves to have, or to conjecture, are vertical ones, i.e., Cournot. Incorporating uncertainty makes this intuition rigorous by incorporating the costs that firms bear when their demand is not as expected. Another formalization of the intuition is provided by Bresnahan's (1981) consistent conjectures equilibrium, which looks more like a Cournot equilibrium as the slope of marginal cost rises.

253

meet demand. Eastern's willingness to set price and risk quantity fluctuations may reflect the comparatively low marginal cost of adding a shuttle flight.[29]

Future extensions

Recent work by Bresnahan (1982) on the identification of market power may be useful for testing our model empirically. He considers a model in which there are two sources of exogenous uncertainty that affect the slope and the intercept of market demand, and he shows that under these conditions the degree of market power, the marginal cost curve, and the demand equation are all separately identified. Suppose that we used our model to predict firms' choices of strategic variables for various industries on the basis of the estimated demand and marginal cost equations. We could then compare the implications of these choices for the degree of market power with the econometric estimates of market power.

Extension of the model to more than two firms is straightforward. In the absence of uncertainty, there are 2^n equilibria, corresponding to each firm's choosing one of its two possible strategic variables. With uncertainty the results of Propositions 1, 2, and 3 continue to hold, since under the specified conditions each firm's preferred strategic variable is independent of the strategic variables chosen by the other $n-1$ firms. The propositions also hold for firms having different levels of costs and facing different demand shocks, and can easily be generalized to incorporate other asymmetries in demand.

Our model takes firms' cost curves as exogenous and independent of their choices of strategic variables. In fact, a firm adopting a quantity strategy might experience a cost advantage relative to adopting a price strategy and having to retain a flexible production technology until the realization of demand was known. This cost advantage would, however, be reduced in a model that allowed inventories and backlogging of orders to limit the variability in production associated with a price-setting

[29] The planes are smaller, the routes are very short so that staff and equipment can return to their correct location at the end of a day at relatively low cost, and the high frequency of flights means that the expected incremental number of return flights incurred by a given extra flight is close to zero, since excess resources may build up at either end of the route. With many flights per day, a given flight reduces return costs with roughly the same probability that it increases them. With only infrequent flights, on the other hand, an extra flight almost certainly incurs a return cost.

Another reason for setting a price on the shuttle may be that the other costs of setting quantity rather than price (operating a reservation system and adjusting discounts to meet demand) are greater relative to revenues and thus greater relative to the costs arising from uncertainty. Our model has not considered these other costs. Eastern's strategy on the shuttle also differentiates its product from the products of airlines that require reservations.

strategy. More generally, inventories help to separate the production and sales decisions. They therefore reduce the effect of cost conditions on equilibrium choice of strategic variables, and so make the curvature of demand and the nature of the uncertainty relatively more important.

A more ambitious model would recognize that factors in a firm's internal structure affect the relative costs of setting a price and setting a quantity. Examples of such factors are the relationships among the firm's divisions, its reporting structures, the contracts it has with its employees, its organizational values, and its procedures and rules. In a multiperiod model the choice of both internal structure and production technology should be made before the choice of strategic variable.[30] Such a model would include fuller game-theoretic interactions, but the insights from our single-period model should still apply.[31]

A common suggestion is that price competition is best represented by each firm's choosing a price in conjunction with a maximum quantity that the firm is willing to produce (see Section 3). In Klemperer and Meyer (1985) we pursue this line in a more general framework by enlarging firms' strategy sets. In practice we think that, even in a static framework, competition is best modelled as some mixture of price and quantity competition. Our management consulting firm, for example, would typically find itself adjusting quantity as well as price in response to a demand shock. We can capture this idea by allowing firms to choose any supply schedule relating quantity to price. Setting a quantity is equivalent to choosing a vertical supply schedule, and setting a price is equivalent to choosing a horizontal supply schedule. Again there are a large number of equilibria under certainty, but they are dramatically reduced by incorporating uncertainty.

Appendix

Proofs of Lemmas 1 and 2, Proposition 2, and Lemma 3 follow.

Proof of Lemma 1. The optimal set quantity solves

---

[30] *Ceteris paribus,* a shallower short-run marginal cost of production curve will be associated with higher total costs of production than a less flexible technology, at the less flexible technology's optimal scale (Stigler, 1939). If a firm receives no new information about demand between the time it chooses its technology and the time it selects its price or quantity, this is a factor in favor of choosing an inflexible technology and subsequently setting a quantity. If, however, some information about demand is revealed between these choices (as, for example, if a single choice of technology is followed by several periods of production under different market conditions), the firm may choose a more flexible technology, which then makes price relatively more attractive in the subsequent market game.

[31] Singh and Vives (1984) and Cheng (1985) make an important start on such a model by showing that under fairly general conditions committing to set a quantity dominates committing to set a price in an environment with costless commitment and no uncertainty.

$$\max_{q} E\left(q(A - Bq + \theta) - c_1 q - c_2 \frac{q^2}{2}\right),$$

for which the first-order condition is

$$A - 2Bq - c_1 - c_2 q = 0,$$

since $E\theta = 0$. This yields

$$\hat{q} = \frac{A - c_1}{2B + c_2}.$$

Substituting for $\hat{q}$ in the objective function gives

$$E\Pi(\hat{q}) = \frac{1}{2} \frac{(A - c_1)^2}{(2B + c_2)}.$$

To find the optimal set price, invert the demand equation to obtain

$$q = \frac{A + \theta - p}{B},$$

and solve

$$\max_{p} E\left(p\left(\frac{A + \theta - p}{B}\right) - c_1\left(\frac{A + \theta - p}{B}\right) - c_2 \frac{(A + \theta - p)^2}{2B^2}\right).$$

The first-order condition is

$$\frac{A}{B} - \frac{2p}{B} + \frac{c_1}{B} + \frac{c_2(A - p)}{B^2} = 0,$$

which yields

$$\hat{p} = \frac{(A + c_1)B + c_2 A}{2B + c_2}.$$

For a given θ, the quantity resulting from setting price at $\hat{p}$ is

$$q(\hat{p}, \theta) = \frac{A - c_1}{2B + c_2} + \frac{\theta}{B},$$

and

$$E\Pi(\hat{p}) = \frac{1}{2} \frac{(A - c_1)^2}{(2B + c_2)} - \frac{\sigma^2 c_2}{2B^2}.$$

Therefore,

$$E\Pi(\hat{q}) - E\Pi(\hat{p}) = \frac{\sigma^2 c_2}{2B^2}. \quad \blacksquare$$

Proof of Lemma 2. The optimal set quantity solves

$$\max_q E\left(q\left(A - \frac{Bq}{\theta}\right) - c_1 q - c_2 \frac{q^2}{2}\right).$$

for which the first-order condition is

$$A - 2Bzq + c_1 - c_2 q = 0,$$

since $E(1/\theta) = z$. This yields

$$\hat{q} = \frac{A - c_1}{2Bz + c_2}.$$

Substituting for $\hat{q}$ in the objective function gives

$$E\Pi(\hat{q}) = \frac{1}{2} \frac{(A - c_1)^2}{(2Bz + c_2)}.$$

To derive the optimal set price, invert the demand equation to obtain

$$q = \frac{\theta(A - p)}{B}$$

and solve

$$\max_p E\left(\frac{p\theta(A - p)}{B} - \frac{c_1\theta(A - p)}{B} - \frac{c_2\theta^2(A - p)^2}{2B^2}\right).$$

The first-order condition is

$$\frac{A - 2p}{B} + \frac{c_1}{B} + \frac{c_2 s^2(A - p)}{B^2} = 0,$$

since $E\theta = 1$ and $E\theta^2 = s^2$. This yields

$$\hat{p} = \frac{(A + c_1)B + c_2 s^2 A}{2B + c_2 s^2}.$$

For a given θ, output is

$$q(\hat{p}, \theta) = \frac{(A - c_1)\theta}{(2B + c_2 s^2)},$$

and expected profits are

$$E\Pi(\hat{p}) = \frac{1}{2} \frac{(A - c_1)^2}{(2B + c_2 s^2)}.$$

Thus, we have

257

$$E\Pi(\hat{q}) - E\Pi(\hat{p}) = \frac{1}{2}(A-c_1)^2 \left(\frac{1}{2Bz+c_2} - \frac{1}{2B+c_2 s^2} \right)$$

$$= \frac{1}{2}(A-c_1)^2 \left(\frac{c_2(s^2-1)+2B(1-z)}{(2Bz+c_2)(2B+c_2 s^2)} \right).$$

The denominator is positive by the assumption that the second-order conditions are satisfied, i.e., $c_2 > -2B/s^2$. The numerator is linearly increasing in c_2, since $s^2 - 1 > 0$. Therefore, there exists a c_2^* such that for $c_2 < c_2^*$ the expression is negative, and for $c_2 > c_2^*$ the expression is positive, where c_2^* satisfies

$$c_2^*(s^2-1)+2B(1-z) = 0,$$

so

$$c_2^* = \frac{2B(z-1)}{s^2-1} > 0.$$

Note that the cutoff level c_2^* depends on the distribution of the shock and on the expected slope of demand, but not on the vertical intercepts of the demand or marginal cost curves. For a given distribution of the shock, c_2^* is linear in B. ∎

Proof of Proposition 2. When j sets quantity at $\bar{q}_j$, i's residual demand curve is

$$p_i = \left(\alpha - \frac{\gamma \bar{q}_j}{\epsilon} \right) - \frac{\beta q_i}{\epsilon}.$$

Both the slope and the intercept vary with the shock ϵ. For constant marginal costs ($c_2 = 0$), firm i's optimal set quantity in response to $\bar{q}_j$ solves

$$\max_{q_i} E \left(q_i \left(\alpha - \frac{\gamma \bar{q}_j}{\epsilon} - \frac{\beta q_i}{\epsilon} \right) - c_1 q_i \right).$$

Differentiating and rearranging yield

$$\hat{q}_i = \frac{\alpha - \gamma \bar{q}_j z - c_1}{2\beta z},$$

where $z = E(1/\epsilon)$, and so

$$E\Pi(\hat{q}_i) = \frac{(\alpha - \gamma \bar{q}_j z - c_1)^2}{4\beta z}.$$

With $c_2 = 0$ firm i's optimal set price in response to $\bar{q}_j$ solves

$$\max_{p_i} E \left((p_i - c_1) \left(\frac{\alpha \epsilon - \gamma \bar{q}_j - \epsilon p_i}{\beta} \right) \right),$$

and the solution is

$$\hat{p}_i = \frac{\alpha - \gamma\bar{q}_j + c_1}{2}.$$

$$E\Pi(\hat{p}_i) = \frac{(\alpha - \gamma\bar{q}_j - c_1)^2}{4\beta}.$$

Since $z > 1$ by Jensen's inequality and since $\gamma \geq 0$ by the assumption that the products are substitutes,

$$E\Pi(\hat{p}_i) > E\Pi(\hat{q}_i),$$

so for flat marginal costs firm i strictly prefers to set a price, whatever set quantity j has chosen. By the continuity of $(E\Pi(\hat{p}_i) - E\Pi(\hat{q}_i))$ in both c_2 and $\bar{q}_j$ and the continuity in c_1 of j's quantity, $\bar{q}_j(c_2)$, in the candidate (quantity, quantity) equilibrium, there exists a $c_2^Q > 0$ such that for $c_2 < c_2^Q$, firm i strictly prefers to set a price when j sets $\bar{q}_j(c_2)$. It follows that for $c_2 < c_2^Q$ the candidate (quantity, quantity) equilibrium is not a Nash equilibrium when strategic variables are chosen endogenously.

Now suppose that j sets price at $\bar{p}_j$. Solving equation (3b) for q_j and substituting into (3a) give i's residual demand,

$$p_i = \alpha - k_1 - \frac{q_i k_2}{\epsilon},$$

where $k_1 = \gamma(\alpha - \bar{p}_j)/\beta$ and $k_2 = (\beta^2 - \gamma^2)/\beta$. The shock affects only the slope and not the intercept of i's residual demand curve, while j's price affects only the intercept. Hence, Lemma 2 implies that for all c_2 less than $c_2^P = (2k_2(z-1)/(s^2-1)) = (2(z-1)/(s^2-1))((\beta^2-\gamma^2)/\beta)$, i strictly prefers to set a price against any set price of firm j. Similarly, j prefers to set a price against any set price of firm i. It follows that for $c_2 < c_2^P$, there exists a (price, price) Nash equilibrium and there do not exist (price, quantity) or (quantity, price) Nash equilibria. Note that $c_2^P > 0$ for imperfect substitutes ($\gamma < \beta$) and $c_2^P = 0$ for perfect substitutes ($\gamma = \beta$).

Define $\bar{c}_2 = \min\{c_2^Q, c_2^P\}$. For imperfect substitutes $\bar{c}_2 > 0$. Using the results above, we find that for $c_2 < \bar{c}_2$ the unique Nash equilibrium involves prices as strategic variables. For perfect substitutes $\bar{c}_2 = 0$. For $c_2 = 0$ the unique Nash equilibrium involves prices ($p_i = p_j = c_1$). This follows because: (i) with $\bar{p}_j = c_1$ setting $p_i = c_1$ is a best response; (ii) asymmetric (price, quantity) and (quantity, price) equilibria are ruled out by the same argument used for the corresponding case ($\gamma = \beta$, $c_2 = 0$) in Proposition 1; and (iii) setting a price is a strict best response against any quantity, as shown above. ∎

259

Proof of Lemma 3. Let the cost function be $C(q)$. Consider first the case in which $f(\cdot)$ is strictly concave and $C''(q) > 0$. Define $g(\cdot) = f^{-1}(\cdot)$. Since $f(\cdot)$ is decreasing and strictly concave, $g(\cdot)$ is strictly concave. When the firm sets the price $\hat{p}$, output satisfies $f(q) + \theta = \hat{p}$, so $q = g(\hat{p} - \theta)$, which for a sufficiently small support of θ is nonnegative for all θ. Define $\tilde{q}$ to be the expected output from setting a price $\hat{p}$: $\tilde{q} = E[g(\hat{p} - \theta)] > 0$. Define $\bar{p} = f(\tilde{q})$. Since $g(\cdot)$ is strictly concave, Jensen's inequality implies that $\tilde{q} < g(\hat{p} - E\theta) = g(\hat{p})$, and, therefore, since $f(\cdot)$ is decreasing, $\bar{p} > \hat{p}$. Now

$$E\Pi(\hat{p}) = \hat{p}E[g(\hat{p} - \theta)] - E\left[\int_0^{g(\hat{p} - \theta)} C'(q)\, dq\right]$$

$$\leq \hat{p}E[g(\hat{p} - \theta)] - \int_0^{E[g(\hat{p} - \theta)]} C'(q)\, dq \quad \text{(since } C''(q) > 0\text{)}$$

$$< \bar{p}\tilde{q} - \int_0^{\tilde{q}} C'(q)\, dq \quad \text{(from } \bar{p} > \hat{p} \text{ and the definition of } \tilde{q}\text{)}$$

$$= E[(f(\tilde{q}) + \theta)\tilde{q}] - \int_0^{\tilde{q}} C'(q)\, dq \quad \begin{array}{l}\text{(from } E\theta = 0 \\ \text{and the definition of } \bar{p}\text{)}\end{array}$$

$$= E\Pi(\tilde{q})$$

$$\leq E\Pi(\hat{q}) \quad \text{(by the definition of } \hat{q}\text{)}.$$

The difference $(E\Pi(\hat{q}) - E\Pi(\hat{p}))$ is strictly positive for $f(\cdot)$ strictly concave and $C''(q) \geq 0$, and is continuous in the slope of marginal costs. Thus, setting quantity is preferred for $f(\cdot)$ strictly concave and marginal costs not excessively rapidly decreasing [$C''(q)$ not excessively negative].

The proof for $f(\cdot)$ strictly convex and $C''(q) \leq 0$ proceeds similarly by defining $\bar{\bar{p}}$ such that $E[g(\bar{\bar{p}} - \theta)] = \hat{q}$ and by using the strict convexity of $g(\cdot)$ to show that $E\Pi(\hat{p}) \geq E\Pi(\bar{\bar{p}}) > E\Pi(\hat{q})$. Again, since the inequality $E\Pi(\hat{p}) > E\Pi(\hat{q})$ is strict, continuity implies that setting price is preferred for $f(\cdot)$ strictly convex and marginal costs not excessively rapidly increasing [$C''(q)$ not excessively positive]. ∎

References

Bertrand, J. "Theorie Mathematique de la Richesse Sociale." *Journal des Savants* (1883), pp. 499–508.

Bresnahan, T. "Duopoly Models with Consistent Conjectures." *American Economic Review,* Vol. 71 (1981), pp. 934–45.

———. "Identification of Market Power." *Economics Letters,* Vol. 10 (1982), pp. 87–92.

Price vs. quantity competition

Cheng, L. "Comparing Bertrand and Cournot Equilibria: A Geometric Approach." *Rand Journal of Economics.* Vol. 16 (1985), pp. 146–52.

Cournot, A. *Recherches sur les Principes Mathematiques de la Theorie des Richesses.* Paris, 1838.

Daughety, A. "Endogenous Information and Industrial Organization." Working Paper, College of Business Administration, University of Iowa, March 1985.

Klemperer, P. and Meyer, M. "Supply Function Equilibria under Uncertainty," Unpublished Manuscript, Stanford Graduate School of Business, 1985.

Kreps, D. and Scheinkman, J. "Quantity Precommitment and Bertrand Competition Yield Cournot Outcomes." *Bell Journal of Economics,* Vol. 14 (1983), pp. 326–37.

Selten, R. "Reexamination of the Perfectness Concept for Equilibrium Points in Extensive Games." *International Journal of Game Theory,* Vol. 4 (1975), pp. 25–55.

Singh, N. and Vives, X. "Price and Quantity Competition in a Differentiated Duopoly." *Rand Journal of Economics,* Vol. 15 (1984), pp. 546–54.

Stigler, G. "Production and Distribution in the Short Run." *Journal of Political Economy,* Vol. 47 (1939), pp. 305–27.

Weitzman, M. "Prices vs. Quantities." *Review of Economic Studies,* Vol. 41 (1974), pp. 477–91.

PART IV

Applications

Overview

This part rounds out the volume by presenting eight papers wherein the Cournot model plays a fundamental role in analyzing economic behavior. As indicated in the Introduction, there were literally hundreds of possible papers from which to choose. The organizing principle employed was to emphasize two aspects of this literature, applications of the Cournot model to provide insights about both the theoretical analyses of competitive behavior and the various observable outcomes of competitive behavior. The first five papers focus on three theoretical issues: obtaining Walrasian outcomes when firms have nonconvex technologies and some monopoly power; the incentives for competitors to implicitly correlate product market strategies via sharing of information when the ability to explicitly correlate via collusion is not possible; and the implications of strategic interaction for models that allow changes in the number of firms in an industry. The rest of the papers in this part use a Cournot model to understand seemingly contradictory behavior in the "real world." Let us consider each topic area in turn.

Papers focusing on theoretical models of competitive behavior

It is probably universally true that the first model of competitive behavior a student encounters in a course in economics is that of perfect competition. Fundamental to the exposition is an assertion that firms take prices as given, or that even if they don't they somehow act as if they do. But why should they? The answer is that they need not, and that the Cournot model provides an excellent means for producing Walrasian outcomes without all the usual perfect competition primitives. This is accomplished in the paper by Novshek and Sonnenschein wherein firms have some pricing power, technologies are characterized by ∪-shaped average cost functions, and there is free entry. Thus, rather than take perfectly competitive behavior as a primitive in a general equilibrium model, they take firms to be Cournot quantity-setters with nonconvex technologies, and explore the effect of allowing free entry. In the limit, Cournot equilibria become arbitrarily close to Walrasian equilibria and thus perfectly competitive outcomes arise from the model. This issue was of interest to Cournot (in fact some have suggested that it was the real purpose of his model of oligopoly; see Mas-Colell [1980]). More recent contributions (Novshek and Sonnenschein) include Ruffin [1971], Gabszewicz and Vial [1972], and Hart [1979]; Mas-Colell [1982], Sonnenschein [1982], and Novshek and Sonnenschein [1987] provide expositions of developments in this area.

The next three papers examine the incentives that oligopolists have to share information. The Vives and Gal-Or papers examine firms producing differentiated products. Both papers employ a label duality[1] between the Cournot-in-quantities and the Cournot-in-prices solutions (called "Cournot" and "Bertrand," respectively) to examine how the nature of the good (substitutes or complements), the nature of the strategic interaction (strategic substitutes or complements; see Bulow et al. [1985]), and the nature of the information (common, or "public," as in the case of the intercept of a demand function, versus individual, or "private," as in the case of a marginal cost of production) all affect the equilibrium choices by the oligopolists concerning whether or not to share information. The basic trade-off concerns the advantages of obtaining a more precise knowledge of the parameter in question versus the effect of correlating strategic choices. In the case of the public parameter, sharing information increases the degree of correlation, while in the private information case sharing decreases this correlation. The value of increasing or decreasing the correlation of firm strategies depends upon the nature of the good and the nature of the interaction (and therefore the slope of the optimal decision rules), thereby leading to the variety of conditions, discussed in the Introduction, under which firms will and will not share information. The third paper in this sub-group, by Palfrey, considers a homogeneous model with information on demand and provides conditions such that, asymptotically, firms are able to make decisions using all the information available

---

[1] A label duality involves replacing one set of symbols with another, thereby deriving results for two models; examples include DeMorgan's Laws for set theory. Optimization dualities typically go further and entail mathematical relationships between some of the symbols in the label sets, for example, that optimal values of the decision variables in a linear program are the optimal shadow prices in the dual linear program and vice versa. See the Introduction for a brief discussion of the label duality that is employed in the price/quantity literature.

to all players, whether agents choose to share or not: the complete sharing outcome obtains, even though firms need not have chosen to share their private information. Other papers on the topic of information sharing include Ponssard [1979], Novshek and Sonnenschein [1982], Fried [1984], Gal-Or [1985], Li [1985], and Shapiro [1986]. Recently, Li, McKelvey, and Page [1987] have considered an alternative story wherein they examine the problem of oligopolistic firms choosing to do costly research before producing rather than sharing information that is costlessly available. As one also might expect, making information costly to acquire means that even with large numbers of firms (such as in Palfrey's paper), efficient outcomes may not be achievable.

The Novshek/Sonnenschein, Vives, Gal-Or, and Palfrey papers emphasize the effect that strategic interactions have on market efficiency, and how increasing the number of firms can lead to salutary results. While small numbers of firms need not lead to unhealthy outcomes, most economists would undoubtedly expect that reductions in the number of firms are likely to lead both to reductions in overall welfare and to increases in firm profitability. The paper by Salant, Switzer, and Reynolds provides a very interesting contrast with the "large numbers" papers of Novshek and Sonnenschein and of Palfrey. In this paper mergers in a Cournot-in-quantities model are examined. Specifically, mergers can result in a lowering of profits for the resulting firm, due to the interaction of each firm's choice of output level. The firm that arises from the merger contracts output, providing an externality to the rest of the industry.[2] As usual, the results of the Cournot-in-quantities prediction (in this case, of disadvantageous merger) can be reversed by shifting to a Cournot-in-prices version (see Deneckere and Davidson [1985]), but the general observation about the interplay of market/firm structure with strategic behavior once again highlights how oligopolistic outcomes fundamentally differ from monopolistic or perfectly competitive outcomes.

Papers focusing on observed behavior

The last three papers emphasize the versatility and usefulness of Cournot's model in examining and understanding the results of strategic interaction. The paper by Vickers, which examines the decision to delegate decision-making, the paper by Porter, which examines the maintenance

---

[2] The firm in Salant, Switzer, and Reynolds acts as a unit. Recently, Kamien and Zang [1987] have considered a model involving a holding company that allows its subsidiaries to compete, finding profitable mergers in a quantity setting.

of the U.S. railroad cartel during the latter part of the 19th century, and the paper by Brander and Lewis, which links financial and product markets of oligopolistic firms, all deal with observation of behavior not properly explained by perfectly competitive models, wherein sophisticated strategic behavior (analyzed in a Cournot-based model) on the part of the agents plays a fundamental role in explaining the observations.

In Vickers's case the issue is to explain why owners might hire managers without reference to problems of effort, or competence, or span of control. Vickers shows that delegation is a means for making commitments that the original players (the owners) could not credibly make on their own. Owners can hire managers who are rewarded on some other basis than simple profitability. Interestingly, this can lead to higher profits than would have occurred if profits had been directly maximized: a profit-maximizer may be better off not choosing to maximize profits! Recent work by Sklivas [1987] and Fershtman, Judd, and Kalai [1987] has extended this observation.

In Porter's paper the Green and Porter [1984] model of collusion with imperfectly observable agent compliance (see the Introduction) is tested using data from the 1880s in what is already a classic piece of applied econometric analysis. Previous observation of price wars by firms in an industry was taken as evidence of the breakdown of cartel agreements, and of the general inability of firms to make such agreements work. Porter shows that, in fact, such observations are quite consistent with the *maintenance* of a cartel by providing continuing evidence to all members of the cartel's willingness to punish defectors. For an extensive discussion of the growing literature of empirical analyses of strategic behavior by firms, see Bresnahan [forthcoming].

Finally, the paper by Brander and Lewis represents an example of the multistage commitment models discussed in the Introduction, wherein firms can take actions that act as pre-commitments (see the Kreps and Scheinkman article in Part III and the Vickers paper in this Part). A review of the vast literature of such multiperiod games is provided by Fudenberg and Tirole [1986]. The Brander and Lewis paper uses a two-stage game to focus on the linkages between decisions regarding financial structure (debt/equity choices) and product market decisions (output choices). Previously, violations of the Modigliani and Miller theorem on the irrelevance of firm financial structure have usually involved imperfections in the financial markets themselves (such as tax-induced distortions), or have relied on some degree of firm asymmetry. By linking decisions in financial and product markets, Brander and Lewis are able to provide an output-market–based strategic motive for holding debt.

Applications

References

Bresnahan, T. F., "Empirical Studies of Industries with Market Power," in *Handbook of Industrial Organization,* ed. by R. Schmalensee and R. Willig, forthcoming.

Bulow, J., J. D. Geanakoplos, and P. D. Klemperer, "Multimarket Oligopoly: Strategic Substitutes and Complements," *Journal of Political Economy* 93, 3, 1985, pp. 488–511.

Deneckere, R. and C. Davidson, "Incentives to Form Coalitions with Bertrand Competition," *Rand Journal of Economics,* 16, 4, 1985, pp. 473–86.

Fershtman, C., K. Judd, and E. Kalai, "Cooperation Through Delegation," Working Paper, Center for Mathematical Studies in Economics and Management Sciences, Northwestern University, 1987.

Fried, D., "Incentives for Information Production and Disclosure in a Duopolistic Environment," *Quarterly Journal of Economics,* 99, 2, 1984, pp. 367–81.

Fudenberg, D. and J. Tirole, *Dynamic Models of Oligopoly,* Harwood Academic Publishers, Chur, Switzerland, 1986.

Gabszewicz, J. and J. Vial, "Oligopoly, A La Cournot in a General Equilibrium Analysis," *Journal of Economic Theory,* 4, 1972, 381–400.

Gal-Or, E. "Information Sharing in Oligopoly," *Econometrica,* 53, 2, 1985, pp. 329–43.

Green, E. and R. Porter, "Noncooperative Collusion Under Imperfect Price Information," *Econometrica,* 52, 1, 1984, pp. 87–100.

Hart, O., "Monopolistic Competition in a Large Economy with Differentiated Commodities," *Review of Economic Studies,* 46, 1, 1979, pp. 1–30.

Kamien, M. I. and I. Zang, "The Limits of Monopolization Through Acquisition," Discussion Paper No. 754, Center for Mathematical Studies in Economics and Management Sciences, Northwestern University, 1987.

Li, L., "Cournot Oligopoly with Information Sharing," *Rand Journal of Economics,* 16, 4, 1985, pp. 521–36.

Li, L., R. D. McKelvey, and T. Page, "Optimal Research for Cournot Oligopolists," *Journal of Economic Theory,* 42, 1, 1987, pp. 140–66.

Marschak, T. and R. Selten, *General Equilibrium with Price-Setting Firms,* Springer-Verlag, Berlin, 1974.

Mas-Colell, A., "The Cournotian Foundations of Walrasian Equilibrium Theory: an Exposition of Recent Theory," in *Advances in Economic Theory,* ed. by W. Hildenbrand, Cambridge University Press, Cambridge, 1982.

Novshek, W. and H. Sonnenschein, "Fulfilled Expectations Cournot Duopoly with Information Acquisition and Release," *Bell Journal of Economics,* 13, 1, 1982, pp. 214–18.

———, "General Equilibrium with Free Entry," *Journal of Economic Literature,* 25, 3, 1987, pp. 1281–306.

Ponssard, J. P., "The Strategic Role of Information on the Demand Function in an Oligopolistic Market," *Management Science,* 25, 3, 1979, pp. 243–50.

APPLICATIONS

Ruffin, R., "Cournot Oligopoly and Competitive Behavior," *Review of Economic Studies,* 38, 1971, pp. 493–502.

Shapiro, C., "Exchange of Cost Information in Oligopoly," *Review of Economic Studies,* 53, 1986, pp. 433–46.

Sklivas, S. D., "The Strategic Choice of Managerial Incentives," *The Rand Journal of Economics,* 18, 3, 1987, pp. 452–60.

Sonnenschein, H., "Recent Results on the Existence of Cournot Equilibrium when Efficient Scale Is Small Relative to Demand," in *Advances in Economic Theory,* ed. by W. Hildenbrand, Cambridge University Press, Cambridge, 1982.

ANALYZING COMPETITION

CHAPTER 12

Cournot and Walras equilibrium

WILLIAM NOVSHEK AND HUGO SONNENSCHEIN

I. Introduction

This paper unifies the two leading classical concepts of equilibrium for an economy: Walras equilibrium and Cournot equilibrium. The theory provides a fresh setting for the study of competitive markets, and leads to a description of economic equilibrium which differs in substance from the one offered by modern formal competitive theory (see, e.g., Debreu [3]).

Modern formal competitive theory does not permit free entry, hence the number of firms is fixed. Further, it is posited that firms behave in one of two ways. In one case, perfect competition is assumed: Firms act as if they have no effect on price; they maximize profit taking prices as given. In the other case, imperfect competition is assumed: Firms recognize and act on their ability to influence price. In the model we present, price and market power are determined by free entry and the size of efficient scale relative to demand. Several distinctive features of classical economic analysis occupy a central role in the development.

Specifically, we study a model in which the number of firms is determined endogenously; firms enter when it is profitable to enter, and the entry of firms is a driving force in the explanation of value. The presence of fixed costs (more precisely, the fact that the efficient scale of firms is bounded away from zero) places a limit on the number of firms which are "active" in an equilibrium. When efficient scale is small relative to the size of the market, equilibrium will be characterized by a large number of firms and small profits for each firm. In this case, firms will have very little effect on price when confined to the range in which they make non-negative profit. (We do not study the case of large efficient scale; however, in that situation, firms may make large profits and their actions may have

Northwestern University, Evanston, IL 60201 and Princeton University, Princeton, NJ 08540.

Princeton University, Princeton, NJ 08540.

William Novshek and Hugo Sonnenschein, "Cournot and Walras Equilibrium," *Journal of Economic Theory* 19, 2, 1978, pp. 223-66.

a substantial effect on price. The resulting allocations will typically lack the efficiency properties associated with perfect competition.) In contrast to modern formal theory, a change in the specification of tastes (and/or technology) will change not only the actions of firms present in the market, but typically it will alter as well the number of firms in each industry.

Price taking producer behavior obtains only as an idealization; the primitive solution concept employed is Cournot–Nash equilibrium with quantity choosing firms and entry. Firms choose a quantity action given the actions of other firms; they evaluate the profitability of their actions according to the demand function of the price-taking (consumer) sector. More precisely, prices are identified by the condition that consumer excess demand matches the aggregate action of firms. Cournot–Nash equilibrium is defined by the following two conditions: No firm in the market can increase profit by altering production, and no firm absent from the market can enter and achieve a positive profit.

There are a countable infinity of firms of a variety of basic types available; however, since efficient scale is bounded away from zero, only a finite number of them are active in an equilibrium. Since there are only a finite number of active firms, each firm is significant and affects price: Thus, isoprofit manifolds are not linear. Furthermore, profit functions are not concave. The assumption that efficient scale is bounded away from zero could be defended on grounds of realism alone. However, the need for this assumption goes deeper, and is in fact dictated by the requirement that the number of firms be endogenous and determined by the opportunities for profit. For if production becomes increasingly efficient as output converges to zero, then the size of firms will be indeterminate (arbitrarily small) and the number of firms likewise indeterminate (arbitrarily large). Nonconvex technology and free entry are intimately related. No theory of economic equilibrium which requires nonincreasing returns to scale throughout can provide a satisfactory explanation of the number of firms in a market.

Now suppose that efficient scale is very small relative to the size of the market. Assume that there are a countable infinity of firms of a variety of types available. Profit functions may not be concave and production sets are not convex; this suggests the possible nonexistence of Cournot–Nash equilibrium with entry (see, e.g., Roberts and Sonnenschein [12]). But, if an equilibrium with entry exists, it is highly likely that it will approximate a Walras equilibrium of the economy obtained by viewing there to be available, for each firm type, a continuum of price taking infinitesimal sized firms. (Formally, one replaces the given technology by a cone technology which includes all multiples of possible productions and convex combinations of such points.) Although generally loosely presented,

272

reasoning to support this belief is not uncommon in the partial equilibrium analysis of a single market. The availability of a continuum of price taking infinitesimal sized firms is formalized by a horizontal supply curve the height of which is given by minimum average cost. The perfectly competitive (Walras) output is determined by the intersection of that supply curve with the demand curve. Cournot–Nash equilibrium output cannot fall short of the perfectly competitive output by more than the cost minimizing output (efficient scale) of a single firm; otherwise, there would be entry. Thus, if the scale at which firms are most efficient becomes small relative to demand, then the deviation of Cournot–Nash output from perfectly competitive equilibrium is small. (Similar reasoning is no doubt behind a conjecture of Samuelson [14]. "As the size of the market grows relative to the size of the minimum scale at which unit costs are at their lowest, the system approaches the perfectly competitive equilibrium.") But the above argument is possibly vacuous unless one can show that the notion of Cournot–Nash equilibrium with entry is viable when efficient scale is small relative to the market. Novshek [10] provided the required argument for the case of the partial equilibrium analysis of a single market. The central achievement of this paper is to extend the analysis to the case of general economic equilibrium. We next make the preceding argument more explicit.

Consider an Arrow–Debreu private ownership economy $\mathcal{E}$ which satisfies sufficient conditions for the existence of Walras equilibrium – with one exception: Production sets are not convex. [As a leading case, consider the zero vector union a "standard" and strictly convex production possibility set which is displaced by a vector (of fixed costs) $w \leq 0$ ($\neq 0$).] If firms are infinitesimal relative to the market, and if a continuum of each type of firm is available, it is natural to consider the economy $\hat{\mathcal{E}}$ in which each firm is replaced by the smallest convex cone which contains the production possibility set of that firm. The cone so defined is viewed as an industry; and the implied industry supply curve is the counterpart of the perfectly elastic supply curve of partial equilibrium analysis. (Ownership shares are most conveniently translated into industry ownership shares; however, this is not essential.) Since $\hat{\mathcal{E}}$ has convex production sets, Walras equilibrium exists, and an equilibrium of $\hat{\mathcal{E}}$ is viewed as a Walras equilibrium of $\mathcal{E}$ in which firms both must and do take prices as given. Associated with every equilibrium is a measure of firms in each industry.

Alternatively, for each α ($0 < \alpha \leq 1$), consider the economy $\mathcal{E}(\alpha)$ obtained from the original economy $\mathcal{E}$ by replacing each firm Y by a sequence of firms, referred to as an industry, each with production set $Y(\alpha) = \alpha Y$. When $1/\alpha$ is an integer, $Y(\alpha)$ is viewed as a representation of Y in per

273

capita terms in an economy in which each consumer has been replicated $1/\alpha$ times. As α becomes small, efficient scale becomes small relative to the size of the market. As small becomes infinitesimal, i.e., as α approaches zero, it is natural to think of $\mathcal{E}(\alpha)$ as converging to $\hat{\mathcal{E}}$. This is because (in per capita terms) the sum of the production sets of each industry in $\mathcal{E}(\alpha)$ converges to the production set of the corresponding industry in $\hat{\mathcal{E}}$.

We prove that it is a generic property of economies $\mathcal{E}$ that there exists $\bar{\alpha} > 0$ such that Cournot–Nash equilibrium with free entry exists in $\mathcal{E}(\alpha)$ for all $\alpha \leq \bar{\alpha}$. The number of firms in the market is determined endogenously. Firms who choose to produce, typically have positive profit, and all firms with positive expected profit adopt pure strategies. Pure strategies are not required as a condition for equilibrium, rather they arise as a characteristic of equilibrium. Firms are permitted mixed strategies. Marginal firms are firms which maximize profit by choosing strategies of the form "produce y with probability π and stay out of the market with probability $(1-\pi)$"; by profit maximization, they must make zero expected profit. For $\alpha \leq \bar{\alpha}$ only pure and marginal firm strategies are profit maximizing in the equilibria which are exhibited; furthermore, the number of marginal firms is uniformly bounded in α. Thus, as $\alpha \rightarrow 0$, the proportion of firms which are marginal, and the aggregate output of marginal firms (per capita) converge to zero. Marginal firms arise naturally in the theory and are a proper analog of the entity which bears their name in less formal analysis. Without marginal firms, Cournot–Nash equilibrium will in general not exist and nonexistence will be "robust."

The existence theorem requires as one of its hypotheses the presence of a Walras equilibrium for $\hat{\mathcal{E}}$ at which no industry can increase profit by increasing the scale of its operation. From the present point of view, equilibria of $\hat{\mathcal{E}}$ which fail to have this property are not proper Walras equilibria. Without this property, firms of arbitrarily small size will profit from entering the industry, and upset equilibrium. Thus, a notion of downward sloping demand (DSD) arises naturally as a requirement for Walras equilibrium with entry, and equilibria which do not satisfy this condition are artifacts of a specification of the competitive model which requires that firms be infinitesimal. While it is natural to think of these equilibria as failing a "stability test," the considerations involved are in fact more basic. If α is sufficiently small, but not zero (i.e., if efficient scale is small, but not infinitesimal), then Cournot–Nash equilibria of $\mathcal{E}(\alpha)$ *cannot* exist close to a point where DSD fails. For at any proposed equilibrium of $\mathcal{E}(\alpha)$ near such a point, profits in every industry must be nonnegative, and an inactive firm can make positive profit by entering an industry in which profit increases with scale.

Cournot, Walrus equilibrium

Having settled the problem of existence, it becomes meaningful to inquire whether the set of Cournot–Nash equilibria approaches the set of (DSD) Walras equilibria as efficient scale (measured per capita) approaches zero. Two questions are distinguished. First, whether an arbitrary (DSD) Walras equilibrium of $\hat{\mathcal{E}}$ can be obtained as the limit (as $\alpha \to 0$) of a sequence of Cournot–Nash equilibria, one point in the sequence for each $\mathcal{E}(\alpha)$. Second, whether every limit of Cournot–Nash equilibria (as $\alpha \to 0$) is a DSD Walras equilibrium of $\hat{\mathcal{E}}$. Both questions are answered in the affirmative. Since the Walras equilibria of $\hat{\mathcal{E}}$ coincide with the Cournot–Nash equilibria of $\hat{\mathcal{E}}$, the preceding questions might be rephrased as pertaining to the lower and upper hemicontinuity of the Cournot–Nash correspondence at the point of infinitesimal (per capita) efficient scale. We note here that Cournot's approach of replicating firms with a fixed "demand sector" does not lead to prices which approach Walras equilibrium prices. With efficient scale bounded away from zero and nonnegative profit, prices diverge from those associated with efficient scale (competitive prices) as the number of active firms is increased. This is because the output of some firms will necessarily approach zero, and this will require prices higher than minimum average cost so that profits do not become negative. And, of course, equilibrium does not in general exist (Roberts and Sonnenschein [12]). For a partial equilibrium analysis, see Novshek, [10] and Ruffin [13].

Taken together, the existence and convergence results unify the concepts of Cournot and Walras equilibrium. For economies in which efficient scale is per capita small and entry is free, the assumption of price taking behavior (in $\hat{\mathcal{E}}$) leads to an outcome which approximates the result obtained with strategic behavior. Free entry, absent from the current formal analysis of perfect competition, is a driving force in the analysis. With free entry, as efficient scale becomes small in per capita terms, the difference between Walras equilibrium in $\hat{\mathcal{E}}$ and Cournot equilibrium becomes small. The concept of Walras equilibrium is derived from a primitive concept of strategic behavior; it is appropriate when the data of the economy indicate small (per capita) efficient scale and there is free entry. Finally, only the equilibria of $\hat{\mathcal{E}}$ which satisfy DSD are true economic equilibria. Most of this is of course very classical; what we offer is an adequate formal setting.

A word about the way in which "free entry" is to be understood. There are an infinite number of basic technologies, which for simplicity are identical in the present model. Once one technology is used, it is no longer available to others, but there are always additional (identical) technologies available. With little additional complication, we could have considered a situation in which there are an infinite number of distinct basic

275

technologies. Free entry would not mean that the technologies remain available to others once employed, but would require them to be available when not employed. This naturally leads to strictly convex production sets in $\hat{\varepsilon}$ and "scarce factor" rents.

Novshek's Theorem [10] on the existence of Cournot–Nash equilibrium with entry in a single market suggested the possibility of the general equilibrium analysis presented here. That work is surveyed in Appendix I. Prior to the completion of our paper, we had access to a manuscript by O. Hart [6]. While Hart's analysis does not include the main concern of this paper – the existence of Cournot–Nash equilibrium with entry – he does provide a convergence result which is similar in spirit to our Theorem 3, but for an economy in which firms choose the commodity they will produce from an infinite set of possible commodities. We heartily recommend this paper to the attention of the reader. Finally, we note that the interplay between significant fixed costs, the number of firms, and the variety of products actually produced, has for many years been a central ingredient of the theory of monopolistic competition. For a particularly interesting modern treatment in partial equilibrium, we recommend a paper by M. Spence [16].

The next section introduces the formal model. This is followed by Section III which presents the theorems and two sections (IV and V) devoted to their proof. Section IV is expository and is designed to introduce some of the concepts used. It is an important part of our presentation, as the formal proof involves an unusually large amount of computation. Remarks and conclusions are contained in Section VI and Section VII.

II. The model

The notion of a basic private ownership economy ε is standard.

    a. An *economy* $\varepsilon = (X_i, \omega_i, \succsim_i, Y_j, \theta_{ij})$ is:

(a1)   For each consumer $i = 1, 2, \ldots, m$, a consumption set $X_i \subset R^l$, an initial endowment vector $\omega_i \in R^l$, and a preference ordering $\succsim_i \subset X_i \times X_i$, [Whenever we speak of a collection of consumers $(X_i, \omega_i, \succsim_i)$ the following hypothesis is maintained. Desirability: for any sequence $\{p^t\} \subset \Delta_l = \{(p_1, p_2, \ldots, p_l) > 0: \ \Sigma p_r = 1\}$, if $p^t \to \bar{p} \in \bar{\Delta}_l \setminus \Delta_l$, and if for each i and t, $h^i(p^t)$ is $\succsim_i$ maximal subject to $p^{t'} x_i \le p^{t'} \omega_i$,[1] then $\|\Sigma_i h^i(p^t)\| \to \infty$];

(a2)   for each firm j or $k = 1, 2, \ldots, n$, a production set $Y_j \subset R^l$, [we maintain the hypothesis that for all j, $0 \in Y_j$ and the asymptotic

---

[1] Prime ($'$) denotes transpose.

cone (see Debreu [3, p. 22]) of Y_j contains no vectors with positive coordinates];

(a3) for each i and j a nonnegative number θ_{ij} which indicates the fraction of firm j owned by individual i. For each j, $\sum_i \theta_{ij} = 1$.

The economies $\mathcal{E}(\alpha)$ are derived from the basic economy $\mathcal{E}$ by replicating the consumer sector ($1/\alpha$ times), viewing production in per capita terms, and for each j, positing the availability of a countable infinity of each of the Y_j of $\mathcal{E}$. In the economy $\mathcal{E}(\alpha)$, we speak of the jth industry;[2] for simplicity, ownership shares in $\mathcal{E}$ are translated into industry ownership shares in $\mathcal{E}(\alpha)$.

b. For any economy $\mathcal{E} = (X_i, \omega_i, \succsim_i, Y_j, \theta_{ij})$ and any number $\alpha > 0$, the economy $\mathcal{E}(\alpha) = (X_i, \omega_i, \succsim_i, Y_{jt}(\alpha), \theta_{ijt})$ is defined by:

(b1) the m consumers are those of $\mathcal{E}$;

(b2) for each $j \leq n$ and each positive integer t,

$$Y_{jt} \in Y_{jt}(\alpha) \equiv Y_j(\alpha) \quad \text{if} \quad Y_{jt}/\alpha \in Y_j; \quad \text{and}$$

(b3) $\theta_{ijt} \equiv \theta_{ij}$ for all i, j, and t.

The economy $\hat{\mathcal{E}}$ is derived from the basic economy $\mathcal{E}$ by replacing each production set of $\mathcal{E}$ with the smallest convex cone with vertex at the origin which contains it. The economy $\hat{\mathcal{E}}$ is interpreted as the limit of $\mathcal{E}(\alpha)$ as α approaches zero, and corresponds to a view in which the actions of firms in $\mathcal{E}$ are infinitesimal in per capita terms.

c. For any economy $\mathcal{E} = (X_i, \omega_i, \succsim_i, Y_j, \theta_{ij})$, the *natural limit of* $\mathcal{E}$ is the economy $\hat{\mathcal{E}} = (X_i, \omega_i, \succsim_i, \hat{Y}_j, \theta_{ij})$ defined by:

(c1) the m consumers are exactly those of $\mathcal{E}$;

(c2) for each firm $j = 1, 2, ..., n$, $\hat{Y}_j$ is the intersection of all closed convex cones with vertex at the origin which contain Y_j; and

(c3) ownership shares are exactly those of $\mathcal{E}$.

The definition of a Walras equilibrium and a Walras allocation for economies and pure exchange economies is standard. The Walras correspondence indicates how equilibrium prices vary with initial endowments in a pure exchange economy.

d. For an economy $\mathcal{E} = (X_i, \omega_i, \succsim_i, Y_j, \theta_{ij})$, the triple $(p^*, x^*, y^*) \in R_+^l \times \Pi X_i \times \Pi Y_j$ is a *Walras equilibrium* if[3]

(d1) $p^{*\prime} x_i^* = p^{*\prime} \omega_i + \sum_j \theta_{ij} p^{*\prime} y_j$, $i = 1, 2, ..., m$;

(d2) $\sum_i x_i^* = \sum_j y_j^* + \sum_i \omega_i$;

---

[2] By industry, we mean the set of firms with identical technology. Several industries may use the same inputs to produce the same outputs.

[3] $x^{*\prime} = (x_1^{*\prime}, x_2^{*\prime}, ..., x_m^{*\prime}) \in R^{lm}$, and $y^{*\prime} = (y_1^{*\prime}, y_2^{*\prime}, ..., y_n^{*\prime}) \in R^{ln}$.

(d3) $x_i >_i x_i^*$ implies $p^{*\prime}x_i > p^{*\prime}\omega_i + \sum_j \theta_{ij} p^{*\prime}y_j$; and

(d4) $p^{*\prime}y_j > p^{*\prime}y_j^*$ implies $y_j \notin Y_j$.

If (p^*, x^*, y^*) is a Walras equilibrium for $\mathcal{E}$, then (x^*, y^*) is called a *Walras allocation.*

An exchange economy $\mathcal{E} = (X_i, \omega_i, \succsim_i)$ is an economy minus firms and profit shares (a2) and (a3) of (a). The pair $(p^*, x^*) \in R_+^l \times \Pi X_i$ is a *Walras equilibrium* for $\mathcal{E}$ if

(d5) $p^{*\prime}x_i^* = p^{*\prime}\omega_i$, $i = 1, 2, \ldots, m$;

(d6) $\sum x_i^* = \sum \omega_i$; and

(d7) $x_i >_i x_i^*$ implies $p^{*\prime}x_i > p^{*\prime}\omega_i$.

The vector p^* is called an equilibrium price and x^* is called an equilibrium allocation. For (X_i) and $(\succsim_i)$ fixed, the *Walras correspondence* W assigns to each vector $(\omega_1, \omega_2, \ldots, \omega_m)$ the equilibrium prices of $\mathcal{E} = (X_i, \omega_i, \succsim_i)$.

As mentioned in the introduction, the study of equilibrium with entry dictates the requirement that efficient scale occur away from zero output. Since we are ultimately interested in Cournot–Nash equilibria which approximate Walras equilibria of $\hat{\mathcal{E}}$, it is natural to view efficient scale relative to Walras equilibrium prices, p^* of $\hat{\mathcal{E}}$. Not only is it assumed that efficient scale occurs away from zero, but in addition that such efficiency cannot be approximated in a neighborhood of zero output. For simplicity, we add the requirement that efficient scale (relative to p^*) is uniquely attained.

e. Let (p^*, x^*, y^*) be a Walras equilibrium of $\hat{\mathcal{E}}$. We say that $\mathcal{E}$ has *efficient outputs bounded away from zero relative to p^** if for all $j \in \{1, 2, \ldots, n\}$:

(e1) $(Y_j \cap \{y: p^{*\prime}y \ge 0\}) \backslash \{0\}$ is a singleton $\gamma_j Y_j^*$ (this defines the scalar γ_j); and

(e2) for all K, $\delta \in (0, \infty)$, there exists $\epsilon > 0$, such that $p^{*\prime}y/\|y\| < -\epsilon$ for all $y \in (Y_j \cap N_l(0, K)) \backslash (N_l(\gamma_j y_j^*, \delta) \cup \{0\})$, where $N_l(a, b)$ is the ball in R^l around a with radius b.[4]

It is generic that no more than $l - 1$ industries satisfy (e1),[5] and the remaining industries are such that for all prices near p^*, all nonzero outputs

---

[4] In an abuse of notation, we use y_j to indicate a vector in R^l and a vector in R^{ln} (with all components zero except possibly $l(j-1)+1, l(j-1)+2, \ldots, l(j-1)+l$). For example, in $y + \{y_j + e_1\}$, $e_1 = (1\,0\,0 \cdots 0)' \in R^l$ is added to $y_j \in R^l$, which is then imbedded in R^{ln}, and added to $y \in R^{ln}$.

[5] Let C be the set of closed convex cones in R^l with vertex the origin and dimension greater than or equal to one, and define the metric d on C by

$$d(c_1, c_2) = h(c_1 \cap N_l(0, 1), c_2 \cap N_l(0, 1)),$$

Cournot, Walrus equilibrium

in the cones $\hat{Y}_j$ yield strictly negative profit. Since the equilibria we construct for Theorems 1 and 2 will have prices converging to p^*, these remaining industries must eventually be entirely inactive, with no profit incentive for entry. Without loss of generality, we ignore these remaining
industries, and assume that the number of industries which must be considered, n, is less than l. Of course, the set of industries which must be
considered may vary as we look at different equilibria of $\hat{\mathcal{E}}$, but it is a
generic property that the number of industries which must be considered
is less than l.

Production sets are required to have one of two forms in a neighborhood of efficient scale. Either they are finite polyhedra, or their bound-
aries are smooth manifolds. While we do not require that the manifolds
have maximal dimension $(l-1)$, we consider a formulation which rules
out (mixed) cases in which, for example, inputs can only be combined in
fixed proportion but yield varying marginal returns. While cases of this
type could be included in the analysis, their treatment increases notational complexity.

f. If there exists a cube C with center at $\gamma_j y_j^*$ such that $C \cap Y_j$ is a finite
polyhedron, then Y_j is called *locally polyhedral*, at $\gamma_j y_j^*$.

Let $S_j(y)$ be the largest subset of $\{1, 2, ..., l\}$ for which there exists a
neighborhood $N(y)$ such that the projection of the set of efficient productions of Y_j in $N(y)$ onto the $S_j(y)$ coordinate subspace is a singleton.
$L \backslash S_j(y)$ gives the co-ordinates in which production is locally variable by
the jth firm at y. If there exists a neighborhood $N(\gamma_j y_j^*)$ such that the
set of efficient productions of Y_j in $N(\gamma_j y_j^*)$ is a smooth manifold of dimension $\#(L \backslash S_j(\gamma_j y_j^*)) - 1$, then Y_j is called *smooth* at $\gamma_j y_j^*$. (We maintain the hypothesis that $1 \in L \backslash \bigcup S_j(\gamma_j y_j^*)$, where the union is taken over
j such that Y_j is smooth at $\gamma_j y_j^*$.) Y_j is *regular smooth* if $D^2 \hat{g}_j(\gamma_j y_j^*)$ is
negative definite where $\hat{g}_j$ gives the first coordinate of efficient points in
$N(\gamma_j y_j^*)$ as a function of the remaining $\#(L \backslash S_j(\gamma_j y_j^*)) - 1$ smoothly variable coordinates.[6]

A conceptual problem must be addressed prior to the definition of
Cournot–Nash equilibrium in $\mathcal{E}(\alpha)$. Suppose that several firms assert a
quantity action. In general, there will be more than one price consistent
with their actions; i.e., there may be more than one price which generates
a demand that matches the aggregate action of firms. To see this, consider the exchange economy $\hat{\mathcal{E}}$ obtained by distributing the actions of

where h is the Hausdorff metric. For each $c \in C$ let $P(c) = \{p \in R^l \backslash \{0\} \mid p'y \le 0$ for all
$y \in c$ and $p'x = 0$ for some $0 \ne x \in c\}$. Let $(c_1, c_2, ..., c_n) \in C^n$. Then the property that
$\bigcap P(c_i) = \varnothing$, $i \in I \subset \{1, 2, ..., n\}$, whenever $\#I > l-1$ is generic (i.e., the property holds
on an open dense subset of C^n).
[6] If (e1) holds, $D^2 \hat{g}(\gamma_j y_j^*)$ must be negative semidefinite.

firms in $\mathcal{E}(\alpha)$ according to profit shares (and adding these amounts to initial commodity endowments). It is clear that each equilibrium price of $\tilde{\mathcal{E}}$ generates in $\mathcal{E}(\alpha)$ a demand which balances the asserted quantity actions of the firms (Rader [11]). Unless one price is singled out, it is impossible to evaluate the actions of each firm, and so a Cournot-Nash game is not well defined. Since our methods demand that price varies smoothly with the quantity actions of firms, we develop a terminology to apply to situations in which there exists locally a twice continuously differentiable selection from an appropriate Walras correspondence. Balasko [2] has demonstrated that the existence of such a selection is generic in an appropriate space.

Prices are expressed relative to the price of the first commodity; i.e., $p_1 = 1$. We note that in noncompetitive theory the choice of numeraire typically affects the profit maximizing action of firms.[7] Our formalization requires that there is a salient commodity in which all firms measure profit.

g. Let p^* be an equilibrium price for the exchange economy $\mathcal{E} = (X_i, \omega_i, \succsim_i)$. The pair (F, p^*) is a p^* *based inverse demand function* if

(g1) F is a selection from the Walras correspondence of the exchange economy $\mathcal{E}$ with $p_1 \equiv 1$; and

(g2) F is twice continuously differentiable in a neighborhood of $\omega = (\omega_1, \omega_2, ..., \omega_m)$ and has value p^* at ω.[8]

Two notions of equilibrium for an economy $\mathcal{E}(\alpha)$ are defined. The first corresponds to a Cournot-Nash equilibrium in mixed (quantity) strategies, where payoffs are defined relative to some selection from the appropriate Walras correspondence. The second, called Cournot equilibrium, corresponds to equilibria of the above type in which optimal mixed strategies are either pure quantity strategies (typically indicating positive expected profit) or "produce y with probability π and stay out with probability $(1 - \pi)$" (indicating zero expected profit). Equilibria of the latter form, Cournot equilibria, are economically more meaningful and their existence is demonstrated in Theorem 1. Despite the fact that arbitrary

[7] Peter Hammond pointed this fact out to us. See, for example, Gabszewicz and Vial [5, pp. 398-400]. Aside from the requirement that the numeraire is a commodity which is smoothly variable for each firm, the existence theorem remains valid independent of the choice of numeraire. This is because there are only a finite number of commodities and an α which will work for each one of them.

[8] F is a function of endowments $\omega \in R^{lm}$. To determine prices we consider exchange economies where production has been distributed according to ownership shares. For convenience we will write $F(y)$ for $F((\omega_i + \sum_j \theta_{ij} y_j)_i)$, where $y = (y_1', y_2' ..., y_n') \in R^{ln}$ is the vector of productions, and $\omega = (\omega_1, \omega_2, ..., \omega_m) \in R^{lm}$ is the vector of original endowments. Throughout the analysis ω will remain fixed, while y varies.

mixed strategies are available in a Cournot equilibrium, optimizing action leads to only marginal firms and pure strategy firms.

h. Let α be a positive number. Consider an economy

$$\mathcal{E} = (X_i, \omega_i, \succeq_i, Y_j, \theta_{ij})$$

and the associated economy $\mathcal{E}(\alpha)$. A Cournot equilibrium in mixed strategies for $\mathcal{E}(\alpha)$ is a nonnegative n vector η, with integer components (η_j is the number of active firms in industry j), a function μ from $\{(j, v): j \leq n$ and $v \leq \eta_j\}$ into the set of probability measure on R^l ($\mu(j, v)(A)$ is the probability that the vth firm of type j has a production in $A \subset R^l$), and a p based inverse demand function (F, p) for the exchange economy $\tilde{\mathcal{E}} = (X_i, \omega_i + \sum_j \theta_{ij}(\sum_{v \leq \eta_j} I(y, d\mu(j, v))), \succeq_i)$[9] ($\tilde{\mathcal{E}}$ is the exchange economy with endowments determined by expected output) such that

(h1)   for all (j, v) in the domain of μ, the support of $\mu(j, v) \subset Y_j(\alpha)$ (i.e., all of a firm's actions must be in its production set);

(h2)   for all $(\bar{j}, \bar{v})$ in the domain of μ, and all probability distributions ν with support in $Y_{\bar{j}}(\alpha)$,

$$I\left(F\left(\sum_{\substack{j,v \\ v \leq \eta_j}} y_{jv}\right)' y_{\bar{j}\bar{v}}, d\mu\right) \geq I\left(F\left(\sum_{\substack{j,v \\ v \leq \eta_j}} y_{jv}\right)' y_{\bar{j}\bar{v}}, d\mu \; (\nu \text{ in } \bar{j}\bar{v})\right),$$

where μ is the product measure of the $\mu(j, v)$, ($v \leq \eta_j$, $j \leq n$), and μ (ν in $\bar{j}, \bar{v}$) is μ with the $\bar{j}, \bar{v}$ coordinate replaced by ν (i.e., each active firm is maximizing profit); and

(h3)   for all $k \leq n$, and all ν with support in $Y_k(\alpha)$,

$$I\left(F\left(\sum_{\substack{j,v \\ v \leq \eta_j + \delta_{jk}}} y_{jv}\right)' y_{k\eta_k+1}, d(\mu \times \nu)\right) \leq 0,$$

where $\mu \times \nu$ is μ with the additional coordinate (the k, $\eta_k + 1$ coordinate) ν, and $\delta_{kk} = 1$, $\delta_{jk} = 0$ if $j \neq k$ (i.e., it is not profitable for any additional firm to enter).

The probability measure ρ on R^{ln} is the *Cournot production* for $\mathcal{E}(\alpha)$ corresponding to the above Cournot equilibrium in mixed strategies if for all "μ-measurable" $A \subset R^{ln}$, $\rho(A)$ is the "μ probability" that for all j, $\sum_{v \leq \eta(j)} y_{jk}$ belongs to the projection of A onto the $(l(j-1)+1, \ldots, l(j-1)+l)$ coordinates subspace of R^{ln}. The measure ρ on R^{ln} induces a measure ξ on R^{l-1} by $\xi(P) = \rho\{y \in R^{ln}: F(y) \in \{1\} \times P\}$. The measure ξ is the *Cournot price distribution* corresponding to the above Cournot equilibrium in mixed strategies.

---

[9] $I(x, d\mu)$ is the Lebesgue–Stieltjes integral.

A *Cournot equilibrium* for $\mathcal{E}(\alpha)$ is a Cournot equilibrium in mixed strategies $(\mu, \eta, (F, p))$ such that for all j and v, either

(h4) $\mu(j, v)$ is degenerate, or
(h5) $\mu(j, v)$ is of the form "0 with probability π, $(\pi \in (0,1))$, $y_j \in Y_j(\alpha)$ with probability $(1 - \pi)$."

Firms of the type described in (h5) are referred to as *marginal firms*.[10] Since $\pi > 0$, profit maximization implies zero expected profit.

We now formalize the requirement of downward sloping demand.[11] The economy exhibits downward sloping demand at (p^*, x^*, y^*, F) if F has the property that $\lambda y_j^{*\prime} F(y^* + \lambda y_j^*) < 0$ for $\lambda \neq 0$, but small; i.e., profit of the action y_j^* decreases (from zero) as λ increases from zero, and increases (from zero) as λ decreases from zero. It is convenient at the same time to introduce a measure of the effect on the price of commodity r of a "one unit" increase in the use (output) of commodity s by industry j; for this we introduce the matrices B_j.[12] Recall that in the introduction we argued that equilibria of $\hat{\mathcal{E}}$ which fail to satisfy DSD cannot be achieved as a limit of Cournot–Nash equilibria.

i. Let $\mathcal{E} = (X_i, \omega_i, \gtrsim_i, Y_j, \theta_{ij})$ be given. Assume (p^*, x^*, y^*) is a Walras equilibrium of $\hat{\mathcal{E}}$ and (F, p^*) is a p^* based inverse demand function for the exchange economy

$$\mathcal{E}(y^*) = \left(X_i, \omega_i + \sum_j \theta_{ij} y_j^*, \gtrsim_i \right).$$

For $j \in \{1, 2, \dots, n\}$, let B_j be the $l \times l$ matrix $(\partial F / \partial y_j)(y^*)$.[13]

---

[10] A probing question by Kenneth Arrow led us to consider the possibility of marginal firms.

[11] The DSD condition only applies to the industries which are "active" in the target Walras equilibrium (p^*, x^*, y^*), i.e., those j such that there exists $0 \neq y_j \in \hat{Y}_j$ such that $p^{*\prime} y_j = 0$. As noted in the remarks after (e), all other industries are completely inactive, with no incentives for entry, for all prices near p^*, and therefore they can be ignored. (It is possible that there is a $0 \neq y_j \in \hat{Y}_j$ such that $p^{*\prime} y_j = 0$ but $y_j^* = 0$. In this case, we use y_j rather than y_j^* in the DSD condition.)

[12] The definition of B_j implicitly assumes that F is defined for certain points near y^*; later we will require that F is twice continuously differentiable in a neighborhood of y^*. If in the Walras equilibrium (p^*, x^*, y^*), all consumers do not consume a bundle in the interior of their consumption set, then the definition of $F(y)$ for some y near y^* may depend on a notion of equilibrium in which some consumers are not in their consumption sets. See remark J for a related discussion.

[13] When F is viewed as a function of endowments ω rather than production [i.e., F is written in full form $F((\omega_i + \sum_j \theta_{ij} y_j)_i)$ rather than as $F(y)$ - see footnote 8] then the rs entry of B_j is

$$\sum_{k=1}^{m} \theta_{kj} \frac{\partial F_r}{\partial \omega_{ks}} \left(\left(\omega_i + \sum_{i=1}^{n} \theta_{il} y_l^* \right)_i \right).$$

Cournot, Walrus equilibrium

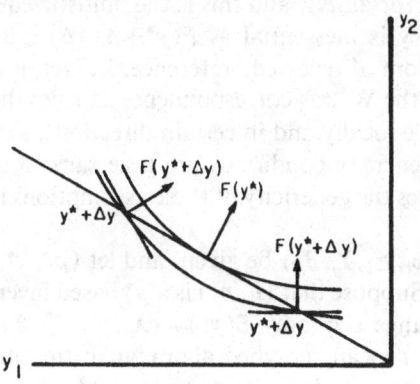

Figure 1.

The economy ϵ exhibits *downward sloping demand* (*DSD*) at (p^*, x^*, y^*, F) if $y_j^{*\prime} B_j y_j^* < 0$ for all j.[14]

It is now easy to see why a Cournot equilibrium for $\mathcal{E}(\alpha)$ (α small) cannot exist near a Walras equilibrium of $\hat{\mathcal{E}}$ at which DSD fails. At any such potential Cournot equilibrium, prices p are near p^*, so active firms of type j must have actions near $\alpha\gamma_j y_j^*$, and these firms earn nonnegative profit. If an additional firm of type j enters with action $\alpha\gamma_j y_j^*$, then the new prices are approximately $p + \alpha\gamma_j B_j y_j^*$ and the entrant earns profit (approximately) $\alpha\gamma_j y_j^{*\prime}(p + \alpha\gamma_j B_j y_j^*)$ which is strictly positive if $y_j^{*\prime} B_j y_j^* > 0$. Thus additional entry will occur, and no Cournot–Nash equilibrium with entry can exist near the Walras equilibrium at which DSD fails.[15]

We give a geometric argument (see Figure 1) that DSD is satisfied when the economy acts as a single consumer. Under the above hypothesis, there is a single Walras equilibrium production y^*, which is given by maximizing a utility function u on the production set $\hat{Y}$ (we assume strict quasiconcavity of u). Since $\hat{Y}$ exhibits constant returns to scale, $p^* y^* = 0$, where p^* is the equilibrium price vector. If the measure of firms changes, then output also changes to $y^* + \Delta y$; and so prices must change to $F(y^* + \Delta y)$ in order that this new amount will be demanded. (Both the case of more firms and less firms are considered simultaneously in the diagram.) Clearly

[14] This has a natural cost–benefit interpretation. At any Pareto optimum of $\hat{\mathcal{E}}$ which does not satisfy DSD, a planner (just as a firm) could buy resources at market prices and sell their product at a price which would more than cover cost. As such, they fail a cost–benefit test.

[15] This is formalized in Theorem 3. Note that we do not treat the case $y_j^{*\prime} B_j y_j^* = 0$, where higher order terms must be considered. Similarly, Theorem 3 shows (weak) DSD must hold (i.e., $y_j^{*\prime} B_j y_j^* \le 0$).

283

$F(y^* + \Delta y)\Delta y \leq 0$ for all Δy, and this is the finitistic equivalent of DSD. Also, the geometry is inessential as $F(y^* + \Delta y)\Delta y \leq 0$ follows directly from the weak axiom of revealed preference. In fact, it is clear that DSD will be satisfied if the Walras correspondence satisfies the weak axiom of revealed preference locally and in certain directions.

Several nondegeneracy conditions are necessary to the analysis. Appendix II establishes the genericity of these assumptions in an appropriate space.

j. Let $\mathcal{E} = (X_i, \omega_i, \gtrsim_i, Y_j, \theta_{ij})$ be given, and let (p^*, x^*, y^*) be a Walras equilibrium of $\hat{\mathcal{E}}$. Suppose that (F, p^*) is a p^* based inverse demand function for the exchange economy $\mathcal{E}(y^*) = (X_i, \omega_i + \sum_j \theta_{ij} y_j^*, \gtrsim_i)$ and that for all j, Y_j is either locally polyhedral or regular smooth at $\gamma_j y_j^*$. If Y_j is locally polyhedral at $\gamma_j y_j^*$ define G_j to be the $l \times l$ matrix of zeros. If Y_j is regular smooth at $\gamma_j y_j^*$, then $R^{L \setminus (S_j(\gamma_j y_j^*) \cup \{1\})}$ is the $\#(L \setminus S_j(\gamma_j y_j^*)) - 1$ dimensional subspace of R^l corresponding to the components other than one which are smoothly variable along the efficient production surface of Y_j near $\gamma_j y_j^*$ [see (f)]. Let $\hat{g}_j$ be as in (f)] (i.e., $\hat{g}_j$ gives the values of the first component of efficient points as a function of the other smoothly variable components). Let $\hat{G}_j := (D^2 g_j(\gamma_j y_j^*))^{-1}$ (which is negative definite) and $\hat{P}_j := I$ (the identity matrix) for $R^{L \setminus (S_j(\gamma_j y_j^*) \cup \{1\})}$. Let G_j and P_j be the corresponding matrices (filled out with zeros) for the full dimensional space R^l.

Also define $\bar{p} = p_{\setminus 1}^*$; i.e., $\bar{p}' = (p_2^*, p_3^*, \ldots, p_l^*) = (F_2(y^*), F_3(y^*), \ldots, F_l(y^*))$. The economy $\mathcal{E}$ satisfies the condition ND (nondegeneracy) at (p^*, x^*, y^*, F) provided:

(j1)

$$\begin{bmatrix} \frac{1}{\gamma_1}\begin{bmatrix} 0 & -\bar{p}' \\ 0 & I \end{bmatrix}G_1 & & 0 \\ & \ddots & \\ 0 & & \frac{1}{\gamma_n}\begin{bmatrix} 0 & -\bar{p}' \\ 0 & I \end{bmatrix}G_n \end{bmatrix}_{ln \times ln} \begin{bmatrix} B_1 B_2 \cdots B_n \\ \vdots \quad \vdots \\ B_1 B_2 \cdots B_n \end{bmatrix}_{ln \times ln} = H_1$$

does not have eigenvalue -1 (G_j and B_j are $l \times l$, I is $(l-1) \times (l-1)$).

(j2)

$$\begin{bmatrix} \frac{1}{\gamma_1}\begin{bmatrix} 0 & -\bar{p}' \\ 0 & I \end{bmatrix}G_1 - m_s\left(\frac{y_1^* y_1^{*\prime}}{y_1^{*\prime} B_1 y_1^*}\right) & & 0 \\ & \ddots & \\ 0 & & \frac{1}{\gamma_n}\begin{bmatrix} 0 & -\bar{p}' \\ 0 & I \end{bmatrix}G_n - m_s\left(\frac{y_n^* y_n^{*\prime}}{y_n^{*\prime} B_n y_n^*}\right) \end{bmatrix}_{ln \times ln} \begin{bmatrix} B_1 B_2 \cdots B_n \\ \vdots \quad \vdots \\ B_1 B_2 \cdots B_n \end{bmatrix}_{ln \times ln}$$

$$= H_2(m_s)$$

284

does not have eigenvalue -1, for a sequence of integers $m_s \to \infty$. (Only one m value is used in the proof, but its magnitude must be greater than $\bar{m}$, where $\bar{m}$ is determined by the data of the economy.)

(j3)

$$
\begin{bmatrix} y_1^{*\prime} \\ y_2^{*\prime} \\ \vdots \\ y_n^{*\prime} \end{bmatrix}_{n \times l} [B_1 B_2 \cdots B_n]_{l \times ln} \{I + H_1\}_{ln \times ln}^{-1} \begin{bmatrix} \gamma_1 y_1^* & & & 0 \\ & \gamma_2 y_2^* & & \\ & & \ddots & \\ 0 & & & \gamma_n y_n^* \end{bmatrix}_{ln \times n}
$$

has rank n.

III. Theorems

Theorem 1 is the main result of this paper. For sufficiently small α, we prove the existence of Cournot equilibrium with free entry. The number of firms in the market is determined endogenously. Firms who choose to produce typically have positive profit, and all firms with positive expected profit adopt pure strategies. The number of marginal firms is uniformly bounded.

Theorem 1. *Let* $\mathcal{E} = (X_i, \omega_i, \succsim_i, Y_j, \theta_{ij})$ *be given. Assume that* $\hat{\mathcal{E}}$ *has a Walras equilibrium* (p^*, x^*, y^*), *and that there exists a* p^* *based inverse demand function* (F, p^*) *[for the exchange economy* $\mathcal{E}(y^*) = (X_i, \omega_i + \sum_j \theta_{ij} y_j^*, \succsim_i)]$, *which exhibits downward sloping demand at* (p^*, x^*, y^*, F). *Assume* $\mathcal{E}$ *has efficient outputs bounded away from zero relative to* p^*, *and for all* j, Y_j *is either locally polyhedral or regular smooth at* $\gamma_j Y_j^*$. *Assume in addition that the nondegeneracy conditions ND are satisfied. Then, there exists* $\bar{\alpha} > 0$ *such that for all* $\alpha \leq \bar{\alpha}$ *there is a Cournot equilibrium for the economy* $\mathcal{E}(\alpha)$.

Theorem 2 is a corollary to the proof of Theorem 1. It establishes that an arbitrary (DSD) Walras equilibrium of $\hat{\mathcal{E}}$ can be obtained as the limit (as $\alpha \to 0$) of a sequence of Cournot equilibria, one point in the sequence for each $\mathcal{E}(\alpha)$. Furthermore, there exists a fixed number N such that these equilibria may be chosen so that for all $\alpha \leq \bar{\alpha}$, the number of marginal firms is less than N. It follows that as α approaches zero, the maximum of the sum of the outputs of the marginal firms in each industry becomes arbitrarily small (in euclidean norm) relative to the sum of the outputs of all firms in that industry.

This is important from a descriptive point of view because we do not want existence to rely very much on the presence of firms who move in

285

and out of the market. No such firms are necessary in the limit economy $\hat{\mathcal{E}}$. This leads us to the notion of a proper sequence of Cournot-Nash equilibria. A sequence of Cournot equilibria in mixed strategies, one for each $\mathcal{E}(\alpha_k)$, is called *proper* if the product of α_k and the number of active firms that use zero with positive probability, converges to zero. This formalizes the requirement that the firms which use zero with positive probability become a negligible part of the economy. Theorem 2 establishes that when the conditions of Theorem 1 are satisfied, there exists a proper sequence of Cournot-Nash equilibria which converge to the Walras equilibrium (p^*, x^*, y^*).

Theorem 2. *Let the conditions of Theorem 1 be satisfied. Then there exists ρ from $(0,1]$ to the set of probability measures on R^{ln} with the following property: There exists S_1, S_2, $\bar{\alpha} \in (0,\infty)$ and an integer N such that for all $\alpha \leq \bar{\alpha}$, $\rho(\alpha)$ is the Cournot production associated with some Cournot equilibrium $(\mu(\alpha), \eta(\alpha), (F(\alpha), \rho(\alpha)))$ of $\mathcal{E}(\alpha)$, and*

(2.1) *the number of marginal firms is less than N;*

(2.2) $\text{Max}_{y \in \rho \text{ support}(\alpha)} \|y^* - y\| < \alpha S_1$; *and*

(2.3) $\text{Max}_{p \in \text{support } \xi(\alpha)} \|\bar{p} - p\| < \alpha S_2$, *where $\xi(\alpha)$ is the Cournot price distribution corresponding to $(F(\alpha), \rho(\alpha))$, and $\bar{p}' = (p_2^*, p_3^*, ..., p_l^*)$.*

Theorem 3 establishes upper hemicontinuity of the Cournot equilibrium correspondence at $\alpha = 0$: Any proper sequence of Cournot equilibria with mixed strategies, one for each $\alpha_k (\alpha_k \to 0)$, for which expected output converges, converges to a DSD Walras equilibrium of $\hat{\mathcal{E}}$ [which is a Cournot equilibrium of $\mathcal{E}(0)$]. This makes precise the sense in which DSD is a necessary condition for Cournot equilibrium. Any Walras equilibrium of $\hat{\mathcal{E}}$ that does not satisfy DSD is, in the present interpretation, an artifact of the infinitesimal specification. Global analogs of (e1) and (e2) are introduced and guarantee that efficient outputs are bounded away from zero at all relevant prices.

(e1′) For all j, if $t \in$ the interior of Ω is such that $t'y \leq 0$ for all $y \in Y_j$ then there is at most one $0 \neq y(t) \in Y_j$ such that $t'y(t) = 0$.

(e2′) For all j, with t and $y(t)$ as in (e1′), given K, $\delta \in (0,\infty)$, there exists $\epsilon > 0$ such that for all $s \in N(t,\epsilon)$,

$$[\{y \in Y_j \,|\, s'y \geq 0\} \cap N(0,K)] \subset [\{0\} \cup N(y(t),\delta)].$$

(e3′) The cones $\hat{Y}_1, \hat{Y}_2, ..., \hat{Y}_n$, $-\Omega$ are positively semi-independent (see Debreu [3, p. 22]), and for each j, 0 is an exposed point of

$\hat{Y}_j$ (i.e., there exists a hyperplane of support H to $\hat{Y}_j$ through 0 for which $H \cap Y_j = \{0\}$; see Valentine [17, p. 52]).

Theorem 3. *Let* $\mathcal{E} = (X_i, \omega_i, \succsim_i, Y_j, \theta_{ij})$ *be given. Suppose that the* $Y_1, Y_2, \ldots, Y_n$ *satisfy* (e1'), (e2'), *and* (e3') *and that there exist:*

(i) $F: R^{lm} \to \{1\} \times R^{l-1}$, *a selection from the Walras correspondence for exchange economies with* $X_i, \succsim_i$ *fixed;*

(ii) *a sequence* $(\alpha_k)_{k=1}^{\infty}$ *of strictly positive reals; and*

(iii) *a function* ρ *from* $\{\alpha_1, \alpha_2, \alpha_3, \ldots\}$ *to the set of probability measures on* R^{ln}, *such that*

(iv) $\alpha_k \to 0$ *as* $k \to \infty$,

(v) *for all* k, $\rho(\alpha_k)$ *is the Cournot production associated with some Cournot equilibrium in mixed strategies* $(\mu(\alpha_k), \eta(\alpha_k), (F, p(\alpha_k))$ *of* $\mathcal{E}(\alpha_k)$; *and*

(vi) *there exists* $y^* \in R^{ln}$ *such that* $I(y, dp(\alpha_k)) \to y^*$ *as* $k \to \infty$.[16] *Then*

(3.1) *for all* $\epsilon > 0$, $\lim_{k\to\infty} \rho(\alpha_k)\{N(y^*, \epsilon)\} = 1$.

Furthermore, if F *is continuous at* y^*, *and we let* $\xi(\alpha_k)$ *denote the Cournot price distribution corresponding to* $(\rho(\alpha_k), F)$,

(3.2) *there exists* $\bar{p} \in R^{l-1}$ *such that for all* $\epsilon > 0$, $\lim_{k\to\infty} \xi(\alpha_k)\{N(\bar{p}, \epsilon)\} = 1$; *and*

(3.3) *there exists* $x^* \in R^{lm}$ *such that* $((1, \bar{p}), x^*, y^*)$, *is a Walras equilibrium of* $\hat{\mathcal{E}}$.

Finally, if the sequence of Cournot equilibria in mixed strategies is proper, if F *is twice continuously differentiable in a neighborhood of* y^*, [*more precisely in a neighborhood of* $(\omega_i + \sum_j \theta_{ij} y_j^*)_i$], *and if* B_j *is defined as in* (i) *for each* $j = 1, 2, \ldots, n$, *then*

(3.4) $y_j^{*'} B_j y_j^* \leq 0$ *for each* $j = 1, 2, \ldots, n$.

IV. Introduction to the proof of Theorem 1

The purpose of this section is to develop some of the concepts used in the proof of Theorem 1, in particular "backward mappings." Our framework is partial equilibrium: a single market with U-shaped average cost curve firms and downward sloping demand. The reader will profit from turning first to Appendix I, where that framework is explicitly introduced. Let y^* be the competitive industry output, $\alpha\gamma y^*$ be the "competitive output"

---

[16] The set of aggregate actions which are feasible is bounded, so there is always a subsequence for which $I(y, dp(\alpha_k))$ converges.

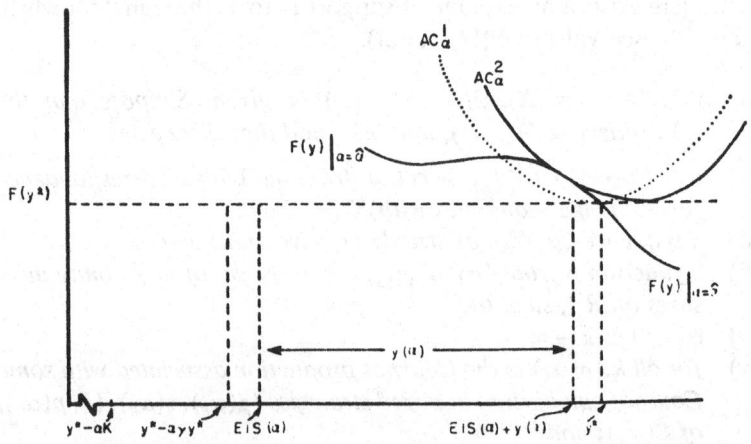

Figure 2. AC_α^1 is the average cost curve positioned with respect to residual demand when the output of other firms is $y^* - \alpha\gamma y^*$. AC_α^2 is the average cost curve positioned with respect to residual demand when the output of other firms is $EIS(\alpha)$. (Note that αK converges to zero as α converges to zero. However, in this diagram $[y^* - \alpha K, y^*]$ is independent of α and F varies with α, because the horizontal axis is relabeled as α varies. K is chosen so that all relevant outputs lie in a ball around y^* with radius αK. In partial equilibrium, any $K > \gamma y^*$ will work.)

for a firm of size α, and $EIS(\alpha)$ be the largest y for which a firm of size α has a nonzero optimal response [it can be shown that for α sufficiently small, the nonzero response is unique, call it $y(\alpha)$]. The following "residual demand" diagram (Figure 2) is standard; the average cost function AC_α^1 and demand function F are drawn relative to the action $y^* - \alpha\gamma y^*$ by other firms. We note:

1. The profit maximizing response of a single firm is less than $\alpha\gamma y^*$ and profit is strictly positive.
2. As the origin of the average cost function (equal to the aggregate action of other firms) moves to the right, maximum profit declines, and at aggregate output of others, $EIS(\alpha)$, maximum profit is zero and is achieved at both zero output and output $y(\alpha)$.
3. By adopting the convention that αK is a fixed distance on the horizontal axis, the shape of AC_α remains fixed in our diagram as α varies. For α sufficiently small, $[EIS(\alpha) - (y^* - \alpha\gamma y^*)]/\alpha$ and $[\alpha\gamma y^* - y(\alpha)]/\alpha$ are nonnegative and converge to zero, since F becomes flatter in the diagram with standard unit $\alpha\gamma y^*$.

The backward map $b(y, \alpha) [b(y, \alpha) \neq y]$ indicates what the output of other firms in the industry must have been for the nonzero action of one

288

maximizing firm to be $y - b(y, \alpha)$, yielding aggregate output y. For α small, and $y \in [EIS(\alpha), EIS(\alpha) + y(\alpha)]$, it can be shown that $b(y, \alpha)$ is a well-defined continuous function. For integers N, define the intervals $B(\alpha, N) = \{y - N(y - b(y, \alpha)) \mid y \in [EIS(\alpha), EIS(\alpha) + y(\alpha)]\}$, and note that $B(\alpha, N+1)$ is left of $B(\alpha, N)$; however, they may intersect.

If $0 \in B(\alpha, N)$ for some N, then there exists $y \in [EIS(\alpha), EIS(\alpha) + y(\alpha)]$ with $y - N(y - b(y, \alpha)) = 0$, so there is a symmetric N firm equilibrium with aggregate output y, each operating firm acting optimally and earning nonnegative profit, and no incentive for entry [since 0 is an optimal response to $y \geq EIS(\alpha)$].

If $0 \notin B(\alpha, N)$ for all N, we must introduce the backward mapping for a marginal firm. First note that a marginal firm is also profit maximizing, so the aggregate action by other firms must be $EIS(\alpha)$, where the marginal firm is indifferent between action $y(\alpha)$ and 0. For any $y \neq EIS(\alpha)$, a pure strategy strictly dominates every mixed strategy. For expected output $y \in [EIS(\alpha), EIS(\alpha) + y(\alpha)]$ the aggregate action of other firms must be $EIS(\alpha)$, with the marginal firm producing $y(\alpha)$ with probability $[y - EIS(\alpha)]/y(\alpha)$ and producing 0 with probability $1 - [y - EIS(\alpha)]/y(\alpha)$. As y varies through $[EIS(\alpha), EIS(\alpha) + y(\alpha)]$, the expected output of the marginal firm varies through $[0, y(\alpha)]$.

Let N be such that $B(\alpha, N+1) < 0 < B(\alpha, N)$. Using N regular firms and one marginal firm (and ignoring here a minor correction [which vanishes as $\alpha \to 0$] necessary because expected price is not equal to price of expected output), the total backward map from $EIS(\alpha) + y(\alpha)$ goes to $z \in B(\alpha, N+1) < 0$ since the marginal firm has the same action as a regular firm, with probability equal to 1, while the total backward map from $EIS(\alpha)$ goes to $z \in B(\alpha, N) > 0$ since the marginal firm has action 0 with probability equal to 1. The map is continuous, so there exists an equilibrium with N regular firms and one marginal firm, with expected output $y \in (EIS(\alpha), EIS(\alpha) + y(\alpha))$. In the equilibrium, all firms are profit maximizing, regular firms earn strictly positive expected profit, the marginal firm earns zero expected profit, and there is no incentive for entry. [It should be noted that in the partial equilibrium model marginal firms are not needed for small α; i.e., $O \in B(\alpha, N)$ for some N (see Appendix I).]

The essential ingredients of the above argument are: first, to surround zero by the intervals $B(\alpha, N)$ and $B(\alpha, N+1)$ [for some N], and then if necessary $(O \notin B(\alpha, N))$, to introduce marginal firms to "capture" zero. For situations in which there is more than one commodity (and/or more than one industry), the corresponding problem of surrounding and capturing zero (starting at a point of nonnegative profit and no entry) becomes more complex. The nondegeneracy assumptions (j1)–(j3) play a

289

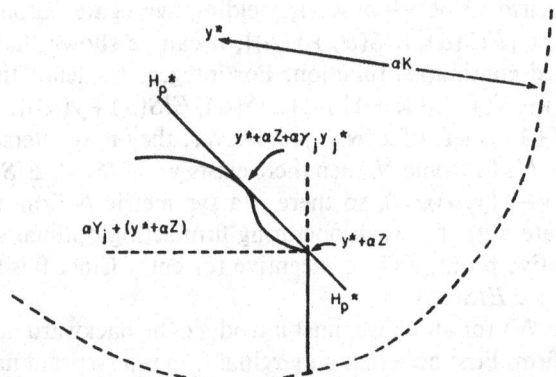

Figure 3. H_p^* is the set of actions by a firm of type j which earn zero profit when the action of other firms is $y^*+\alpha Z$ and prices are fixed at p^*.

central role in the argument. Appendix II establishes the genericity of these assumptions.

V. Proofs

The proof of Theorem 1 follows a sequence of lemmas. Let $z_j(Z, \alpha)$ denote the set of profit maximizing actions for a firm with production set $Y_j(\alpha)$ when the action of other firms is $y^*+\alpha Z$. Figure 3 is an analog of Figure 2. We have represented the production possibilities of the jth firm with $\|\alpha K\|$ a fixed distance in the diagram. If the action of "other firms" is $y^*+\alpha Z$ (for some fixed α), isoprofit manifolds are defined for the firm. Since the axes are relabeled as α varies, the relation between y^* and $y^*+\alpha Z$ remains fixed in the diagram. As α approaches zero, the actions of "other firms" approach the competitive output, and in Figure 2 (with $\|\alpha K\|$ a fixed distance), isoprofit manifolds "converge uniformly" to the isoprofit hyperplanes H_{p^*} associated with the competitive equilibrium price p^*. (The dependence of the isoprofit manifolds on α in Figure 3 is analogous to the dependence of the inverse demand function F on α in Figure 2.) In the limit, the profit maximizing actions for the jth firm are 0 and $\alpha \gamma_j y_j^*$. Lemmas 1–4 show that for α sufficiently small, the profit maximizing actions of a firm are either 0 or an efficient production in a neighborhood of $\alpha \gamma_j y_j^*$.

Lemma 1. *Assume the hypotheses of Theorem 1 are satisfied. Given $K < \infty$, there exists $M < \infty$ such that $\|x\| < M\alpha$ for all $x \in z_j(Z, \alpha)$ for all $(Z, \alpha) \in N(0, K) \times (0, 1] \subset R^{ln} \times R^1$.*

Cournot, Walras equilibrium

Proof of Lemma 1. The set of aggregate (over industries as well as firms) productions

$$S = \left[\bigcup_{\substack{\alpha \leq 1 \\ Z \in N(0, K)}} \left(Y_j(\alpha) + \left\{ \sum_t (y_t^* + \alpha Z_t) + \sum_i \omega_i \right\} \right) \right] \cap \Omega^l$$

is bounded above. By desirability [see (a1)] and the upper hemiconti-nuity of the Walras correspondence, $\{ F(y) \mid y = y_j(\alpha) + y^* + \alpha Z \in \text{Do-}$ main of F for some $(y_j(\alpha), \alpha, Z) \in Y_j(\alpha) \times (0, 1] \times N(0, K)$ such that $y_j(\alpha) + \sum_t (y_t^* + \alpha Z_t) + \sum_i \omega_i \in S\}$ is contained in a closed cone C in the in-terior of Ω^l (this set contains all prices that could result from a feasible ac-tion in $Y_j(\alpha)$ when others' actions are $y^* + \alpha Z$, $(Z, \alpha) \in N(0, K) \times (0, 1]$). Since the asymptotic cone of Y_j is contained in $-\Omega^l$, there exists $M < \infty$ such that $px < 0$ for all $p \in C \backslash \{0\}$, $x \in Y_j(1)$, $\|x\| > M$. Noting $0 \in Y_j(\alpha) = \alpha Y_j(1)$ completes the proof. ∎

Let $EY_j(\alpha)$ be the set of technologically efficient productions in $Y_j(\alpha)$:

$$EY_j(\alpha) = \{ y \in Y_j(\alpha) \mid \nexists x \in \Omega^l \backslash \{0\} \text{ such that } y + x \in Y_j(\alpha) \}.$$

Lemma 2. *Assume that the hypotheses of Theorem 1 are satisfied. Given $K < \infty$ there exists $\bar{\alpha} > 0$ such that $x \in EY_j(\alpha)$ for all $x \in z_j(Z, \alpha)$, for all $(Z, \alpha) \in N(0, K) \times (0, \bar{\alpha}]$.*

Proof of Lemma 2. The profit of a firm in the jth industry which chooses x given that the actions of other firms are $y^* + \alpha Z$ is $\Pi(x \mid Z, \alpha) = x' F(y^* + \alpha Z + x)$. By the previous lemma $\|x\| \to 0$ as $\alpha \to 0$, and by (g2) F is continuously differentiable at $y^* + \alpha Z + x$ for all α sufficiently small. Thus, $\partial \Pi / \partial x_i = F_i(y^* + \alpha Z + x) + x'((\partial F / \partial y_{ji})(y^* + \alpha Z + x))$. Since $F_i(y^*) > 0$ for all i, it follows that $\partial \Pi / \partial x_i > 0$ for α sufficiently small, and $x \in EY_j(\alpha)$ for all $x \in z_j(Z, \alpha)$. ∎

Lemma 3. *Assume that the hypotheses of Theorem 1 are satisfied. Given $K, \delta \in (0, \infty)$ there exists $\bar{\alpha} > 0$ such that $x \in N(\alpha \gamma_j y_j^*, \alpha \delta) \cup \{0\}$ for all $x \in z_j(Z, \alpha)$, $(Z, \alpha) \in N(0, K) \times (0, \bar{\alpha}]$.*

Proof of Lemma 3. By (e2) and the continuity of F in a neighborhood of y^*, there exists $\beta(M) > 0$ such that $y' F(W) / \|y\| < -\beta(M)$ for each $y \in [Y_j \cap N(0, M)] / [N(\gamma_j y_j^*, \delta) \cup \{0\}]$ and W close to y^*. Setting M equal to the M value guaranteed by Lemma 1, for α small, $(1/\alpha)x' F(\alpha Z + y^* + x) / \|(1/\alpha)x\| < -\beta(M)$ for $(1/\alpha)x \in [Y_j \cap N(0, M)] \backslash [N(\gamma_j y_j^*, \delta) \cup \{0\}]$. Not-ing that $(1/\alpha)z_j(Z, \alpha) \subset N(0, M)$ for $(Z, \alpha) \in N(0, K) \times (0, 1]$ and that zero action yields zero profit completes the proof. ∎

291

Lemma 4. *Assume that the hypotheses of Theorem 1 are satisfied and that Y_j is locally polyhedral at $\gamma_j y_j^*$. Given $K < \infty$ there exists $\bar{\alpha} > 0$ such that $z_j(Z, \alpha) \subset \{0, \alpha \gamma_j y_j^*\}$ for all $(Z, \alpha) \in N(0, K) \times (0, \bar{\alpha}]$.*

Proof of Lemma 4. Let $T_j = \{t \in R^l / \|t\| = 1$ and there exist $y_j \in Y_j$, $\lambda > 0$ such that $t = \lambda(\gamma_j y_j^* - y_j)$ and $\mu \gamma_j y_j^* + (1-\mu) y_j \in Y_j$ for all $\mu \in [0,1]\}$. If $T_j = \varnothing$, Lemma 3 yields the result. If not, there exists $\delta > 0$ such that

$$N(\gamma_j y_j^*, \delta) \cap Y_j = \{\gamma_j y_j^* - at \mid t \in T_j, a \in [0, \delta)\}.$$

By Lemma 3, $(1/\alpha) z_j(Z, \alpha) \subset (\{0\} \cup [N(\gamma_j y_j^*, \delta) \cap Y_j])$ for all $Z \in N(0, K)$, for all α sufficiently small. For any $x \in N(\gamma_j y_j^*, \delta) \cap Y_j$, $\Pi(\alpha x \mid Z, \alpha) = \alpha x' F(y^* + \alpha Z + \alpha x)$ is differentiable for α small, and $(\partial \Pi / \partial x)(\alpha x \mid Z, \alpha) = \alpha F(y^* + \alpha Z + \alpha x) + \alpha^2 [(\partial F_i / \partial y_{jk})(y^* + \alpha Z + \alpha x)]'_{ik} x$. For each $t \in T_j$, $(1/\alpha) t'(\partial \Pi / \partial x)(\alpha x \mid Z, \alpha) = t' F(y^* + \alpha Z + \alpha x) + \alpha t' [\partial F_i / \partial y_{jk}]'_{ik} x$ which is strictly positive for α sufficiently small since $t' F(y^*) > 0$ for all $t \in T_j$, and $\alpha Z + \alpha x \to 0$. Thus, for α sufficiently small, for all $Z \in N(0, K)$, $x = \gamma_j y_j^*$ maximizes $\Pi(\alpha x \mid Z, \alpha)$ over the set $x \in N(\gamma_j y_j^*, \delta) \cap Y_j$, and $z_j(Z, \alpha) \subset \{0, \alpha \gamma_j y_j^*\}$. ∎

The technique of proof involves separating out the determination of how many firms of each type are in the market from what an active firm does. From Lemmas 1–4, the aggregate action of other firms is approximately y^*, then the action of a firm which is active in equilibrium (and thus making nonnegative profit), will be approximately $\alpha \gamma_j y_j^*$. We therefore study those actions of firms which maximize profit on a neighborhood of $\alpha \gamma_j y_j^*$. As α converges to zero, the number of firms present in an equilibrium grows without bound. Although the deviation of active firms from $\alpha \gamma_j y_j^*$ becomes insignificant, the total deviation of active firms may be significant from the viewpoint of entry of new firms, and is thus important for the analysis. Lemma 5 computes the deviation of an individual firm, and Lemma 6 makes use of the significant aggregate deviation.

For each j, let $\delta_j > 0$ be such that $N(\gamma_j y_j^*, \delta_j)$ is a subset of the cube C (if Y_j is locally polyhedral at $\gamma_j y_j^*$) or the neighborhood $N(\gamma_j y_j^*)$ (if Y_j is locally regular smooth at $\gamma_j y_j^*$) which is described in (f).

Let $z_j^*(Z, \alpha)$ denote the set of profit maximizing actions in $Y_j(\alpha) \cap N(\alpha \gamma_j y_j^*, \alpha \delta_j)$ when other firms' actions are $y^* + \alpha Z$. By Lemma 3, for α sufficiently small, $z_j^*(Z, \alpha) = z_j(Z, \alpha)$ if $\Pi(x \mid Z, \alpha) > 0$ for some $x \in z_j^*(Z, \alpha)$.

Lemma 5. *Assume the hypotheses of Theorem 1 are satisfied. Given $K < \infty$ there exists $\bar{\alpha} > 0$ such that for all $(Z, \alpha) \in N(0, K) \times (0, \bar{\alpha}]$, $z_j^*(Z, \alpha)$ is a singleton and*

292

$$z_j^*(Z, \alpha) = \alpha\gamma_j y_j^* - \alpha^2 \begin{bmatrix} 0 & -\bar{p}' \\ 0 & I \end{bmatrix} G_j \begin{bmatrix} 0 & 0 \\ -\bar{p} & I \end{bmatrix} \left[\sum_t B_t Z_t + \gamma_j (B_j + B_j') y_j^* \right]$$
$$+ O(\alpha^3)^{17}$$

$(= \alpha\gamma_j y_j^*$ if Y_j is locally polyhedral at $\gamma_j y_j^*)$

and

$$\frac{\partial z_j^*(Z, \alpha)}{\partial Z_t'} = -\alpha^2 \begin{bmatrix} 0 & -\bar{p}' \\ 0 & I \end{bmatrix} G_j B_t + O(\alpha^3)$$

$(= [0]$ if Y_j is locally polyhedral at $\gamma_j y_j^*).$

[Recall $p' = (p_2^*, p_3^*, \ldots, p_l^*).]$

Proof of Lemma 5. The results for locally polyhedral Y_j follow from the proof of Lemma 3.

If Y_j is locally regular smooth at $\gamma_j y_j^*$, by Lemma 2 we can restrict attention to the smooth efficient manifold, so the profit maximization problem becomes

$$\max_{x \in P_j(R^l)} \Pi(\alpha\gamma_j y_j^* + \alpha x + \alpha g_j(x) e_1 \mid Z, \alpha),$$

where g_j gives the deviation of the first coordinate from $\gamma_j y_{j1}^*$ as a function of the deviations x of the other coordinates from $\gamma_j y_{j1}^*$ on the smooth efficient manifold of $Y_j \cap N(\gamma_j y_j^*, \delta_j)$. [$P_j$ is the projection to the space of components other than 1 which are smoothly variable].

Restricting attention to changes in x which are in $P_j(R^l)$, for α sufficiently small the profit function is differentiable, and

$$\frac{\partial \Pi}{\partial x}\Big|_{\substack{\text{restricted} \\ \text{to } P_j(R^l)}} = \alpha \left\{ P_j + \begin{bmatrix} \frac{\partial g_j(x)}{\partial x_{l \times 1}} & 0_{l \times (l-1)} \end{bmatrix} \right\}$$

$$\times \left\{ F(\ ) + \alpha \left[\frac{\partial F_i(\ )}{\partial y_{jk}} \right]_{ik}' \{\gamma_j y_j^* + x + g_j(x) e_1\} \right\},$$

where F and $\partial F_i/\partial y_{jk}$ are evaluated at $y^* + \alpha Z + \alpha\{\gamma_j y_j^* + x + g_j(x) e_1\}$ and $\partial g_j(x)/\partial x$ is *defined* to be zero for those components not variable in $P_j(R^l)$.

Since $\|x\| \to 0$ as $\alpha \to 0$ for optimal choices, $(\partial^2 \Pi/\partial x \partial x')|_{\text{restricted to } P_j(R^l)} = \alpha(\partial^2 g_j(x)/\partial x \partial x') + O(\alpha^2)$ where the s, t entry of $(\partial^2 g_j(x)/\partial x \partial x')$ is *defined* to be zero if either x_s or x_t is not variable in $P_j(R^l)$. Y_j is regular smooth at $\gamma_j y_j^*$ so $x'(\partial^2 g_j(0)/\partial x \partial x')x < 0$ for all $0 \neq x \in P_j(R^l)$.

---

[17] A function $r(\alpha)$ is $O(\alpha^n)$ if there exists $M < \infty$ such that $|r(\alpha)/\alpha^n| < M$ for small α (i.e., $r(\alpha)/\alpha^n$ is bounded as $\alpha \to 0$).

Since $(\partial^2 g_j(x)/\partial x\, \partial x')$ converges to $(\partial^2 g_j(0)/\partial x\, \partial x')$ as $x \to 0$, $z_j^*(Z, \alpha)$ is a singleton for α sufficiently small.

To find the unique profit maximizing x, set $(\partial\Pi/\partial x) = 0$, use the Taylor expansion for $F(\ )$ and $[\partial F_i(\ )/\partial y_{jk}]$ (at y^*) and $(\partial g_j(x)/\partial x)$ (at 0), note that, as defined, $(\partial g_j(0)/\partial x) = -P_j F(y^*)$ and solve to find

$$x = -\alpha G_j \begin{bmatrix} 0 & 0 \\ -\bar{p} & I \end{bmatrix} \left\{ \sum_t B_t Z_t + \gamma_j (B_j + B_j') y_j^* \right\} + O(\alpha^2).$$

(Recall $F_1 \equiv 1$ so the first row of each B_t is a zero vector.) With this evaluation of x, $g_j(x) = -F'(y^*)P_j x + O(\alpha^2)$ and the $z_j^*(Z, \alpha)$ result follows.

The $(\partial z_j^*(Z, \alpha)/\partial Z_t')$ result follows from implicit differentiation of the first order condition along with the evaluation of x above. ∎

Using the "reaction functions" of Lemma 5, it is possible to find a Cournot "equilibrium" when the number of firms of each type is fixed and allowed to be a non integer and α is small. Lemma 6 computes "equilibrium" aggregate output as a function of α and the number of operating firms of each type, which Lemma 7 shows that for α small, for certain numbers of operating firms, each firm earns positive profit (so, as noted in the discussion before Lemma 5, the "reaction function" gives the true profit maximizing action of the firm) and there is no incentive for entry.

Let $Z(v, \alpha)$, $v \in R^n$, be the normalized error from competitive output y^* in a symmetric (within industries) "equilibrium" in which there are $1/\alpha\gamma_j + v_j$ firms of type j operating and forced to maximize profit over the restricted set $Y_j(\alpha) \cap N(\alpha\gamma_j y_j^*, \alpha\delta_j)$ for $j = 1, 2, \ldots, n$ (no entry is allowed). The normalization is such that aggregate output in this "equilibrium" is $y^* + \alpha Z(v, \alpha)$. Note that $1/\alpha\gamma_j + v_j$ is not restricted to integral values.

Lemma 6. *Assume the hypotheses of Theorem 1 are satisfied. Given $K < \infty$ there exists $\bar{\alpha} > 0$ such that for all $(v, \alpha) \in N(0, K) \times (0, \bar{\alpha}] \subset R^n \times R^1$, a $Z(v, \alpha)$ exists and*

$$Z(v, \alpha) = -\{I + H_1\}^{-1} \left\{ -v_j \gamma_j y_j^* + \begin{bmatrix} 0 & -\bar{p}' \\ 0 & I \end{bmatrix} G_j \begin{bmatrix} 0 & 0 \\ -\bar{p} & I \end{bmatrix} B_j' y_j^* \right\}_j + O(\alpha)$$

where H_1 is the matrix in (j1) *(so $\{I + H_1\}$ is invertible).*

Proof of Lemma 6. Let $\varphi_j(Z, \alpha) = Z + (1/\alpha) z_j^*(Z, \alpha)$ and define $\psi_j(Z, \alpha)$ by $\varphi_j(\psi_j(Z, \alpha), \alpha) = Z$. By Lemma 5, given $K < \infty$, there exists $\bar{\alpha} > 0$ such that for all $(Z, \alpha) \in N(0, K) \times (0, \bar{\alpha}]$, $\psi_j(Z, \alpha)$ is a well-defined function and, by implicit differentiation,

$$\frac{\partial \psi_j(Z,\alpha)}{\partial Z'_t} = I + \alpha \begin{bmatrix} 0 & -\bar{p}' \\ 0 & I \end{bmatrix} G_j B_t + O(\alpha^2).$$

Using $\varphi_j(\psi_j(0,\alpha),\alpha) = 0$ and $p_j(Z,\alpha) = Z + (1/\alpha)z_j^*(Z,\alpha)$, we find

$$\psi_j(0,\alpha) = -\gamma_j y_j^* + \alpha\gamma_j \begin{bmatrix} 0 & -\bar{p}' \\ 0 & I \end{bmatrix} G_j \begin{bmatrix} 0 & 0 \\ -\bar{p} & I \end{bmatrix} B_j' y_j^* + O(\alpha^2)$$

and, for $Z \in N(0,K)$,

$$\psi_j(Z,\alpha) = Z - \gamma_j y_j^* + \alpha \begin{bmatrix} 0 & -\bar{p}' \\ 0 & I \end{bmatrix} G_j \begin{bmatrix} 0 & 0 \\ -\bar{p} & I \end{bmatrix} \left\{ \sum_t B_t Z_t + \gamma_j B_j' y_j^* \right\} + O(\alpha^2).$$

For $v \in R^n$ the backward map $\Psi(Z,v,\alpha)$ is defined by

$$\Psi(Z,v,\alpha) = Z + \frac{1}{\alpha} y^* + \sum_j \left(\frac{1}{\alpha\gamma_j} + v_j \right) [\psi_j(Z,\alpha) - Z].$$

To understand the significance of this function, note that for aggregate output in a Cournot equilibrium in pure strategies of $\mathcal{E}(\alpha)$ to be $y^* + \alpha Z$, each operating firm of type j has action $\alpha(Z - \psi_j(Z,\alpha))$ [as a result of defining $\psi_j(\cdot,\alpha)$ as the inverse of $\varphi_j(\cdot,\alpha)$]. If there are $(1/\alpha\gamma_j) + v_j$ firms of type j operating with pure strategies, their aggregate production is $(1/\alpha\gamma_j + v_j)\alpha(Z - \psi_j(Z,\alpha))$. Hence if $\Psi(Z,v,\alpha) = 0$, then $y^* + \alpha Z = \sum_j (1/\alpha\gamma_j + v_j)\alpha(Z - \psi_j(Z,\alpha))$, and the aggregate output of the $1/\alpha\gamma_j + v_j$ firms, $j = 1,2,...,n$ is exactly the aggregate output needed. Thus, the "equilibrium" error $Z(v,\alpha)$ satisfies $\Psi(Z(v,\alpha),v,\alpha) = 0$.

$$\frac{\partial \Psi(Z,v,\alpha)}{Z'} = I + \sum_j \left(\frac{1}{\alpha\gamma_j} + v_j \right) \left[\frac{\partial \psi_j(Z,\alpha)}{\partial Z'} - I \right] = I + H_1 + O(\alpha),$$

and for $(Z,v) \in N(0,K_1) \times N(0,K_2) \subset R^{ln} \times R^n$ converges uniformly to $I + H_1$ as α converges to 0 (where K_1, K_2 are any finite numbers). Also,

$$\Psi(0,v,\alpha) = \left(-v_j\gamma_j y_j^* + \begin{bmatrix} 0 & -\bar{p}' \\ 0 & I \end{bmatrix} G_j \begin{bmatrix} 0 & 0 \\ -\bar{p} & I \end{bmatrix} B_j' y_j^* \right)_j + O(\alpha)$$

so $\Psi(Z,v,\alpha) = W(0,v,\alpha) + \{I + H_1\}Z + O(\alpha)$ for $(Z,v) \in N(0,K_1) \times N(0,K_2)$, and $Z(v,\alpha) = -\{I + H_1\}^{-1}\Psi(0,v,\alpha) + O(\alpha)$. [Given the K in the statement of the lemma, an appropriate K_1 is determined by $\{Z(v,\alpha) \mid v \in N(0,K)\}$.] ∎

Lemma 7. *Assume the hypotheses of Theorem 1 are satisfied. There exist* $v^* \in R^n$, $\epsilon^* > 0$, $\bar{\alpha} > 0$ *such that*

$$\Pi(z_j^*(\psi_j(Z(v,\alpha),\alpha),\alpha),\alpha) \mid \psi_j(Z(v,\alpha),\alpha),\alpha) > 0 \quad and$$

$$\Pi(z_j^*(Z(v,\alpha),\alpha) \mid Z(v,\alpha),\alpha) < 0$$

for all $j = 1,2,...,n$, *for all* $(v,\alpha) \in \overline{N(v^*,\epsilon^*)} \times (0,\bar{\alpha}]$.

295

Proof of Lemma 7. Let

$$Z(v,0) = -\{I+H_1\}^{-1}\left(-v_j\gamma_j y_j^* + \begin{bmatrix} 0 & -\bar{p}' \\ 0 & I \end{bmatrix} G_j \begin{bmatrix} 0 & 0 \\ -\bar{p} & I \end{bmatrix} B_j' y_j^*\right)_j.$$

Then for $K < \infty$, $Z(\cdot, \alpha)$, converges uniformly to $Z(\cdot, 0)$, $\alpha Z(\cdot, \alpha)$ converges uniformly to zero, and $(1/\alpha)z_j^{*\prime}(\psi_j(Z(\cdot, \alpha), \alpha), \alpha)$ and $(1/\alpha)z_j^*(Z(\cdot, \alpha), \alpha)$ converge uniformly to $\gamma_j^* y_j$ for $v \in N(0, K)$.

The first expression for profit is

$$z_j^{*\prime}(\psi_j(Z(v, \alpha), \alpha), \alpha)F(y^* + \alpha Z(v, \alpha))$$

$$= \alpha\{Z(v, \alpha) - \psi_j(Z(v, \alpha), \alpha)\}'F(y^* + \alpha Z(v, \alpha))$$

$$= \alpha^2\gamma_j y_j^{*\prime} \sum_t B_t Z_t(v, \alpha) + O(\alpha^3) \quad \left(\text{using } F'(y^*)\begin{bmatrix} 0 & -\bar{p}' \\ 0 & I \end{bmatrix} = 0\right)$$

so $(1/\alpha^2)$ times that profit converges uniformly to

$$\gamma_j y_j^{*\prime} \sum_t B_t Z_t(v, 0).$$

The second expression for profit is

$$z_j^{*\prime}(Z(v, \alpha), \alpha)F(y^* + \alpha Z(v, \alpha) + z_j^*(Z(v, \alpha), \alpha))$$

$$= \alpha^2\gamma_j y_j^{*\prime}\left(\sum_t B_t Z_t(v, \alpha) + \gamma_j B_j y_j^*\right) + O(\alpha^3)$$

so $(1/\alpha^2)$ times that profit converges uniformly to

$$\gamma_j y_j^{*\prime}\left(\sum_t B_t Z_t(v, 0) + \gamma_j B_j y_j^*\right).$$

Thus, it suffices to show that there exists a $v^* \in R^n$ such that

$$0 < \begin{bmatrix} y_1^{*\prime} \\ \vdots \\ y_n^{*\prime} \end{bmatrix}[B_1 \cdots B_n]Z(v^*, 0) < -\begin{pmatrix} \gamma_1 y_1^{*\prime}B_1 y_1^* \\ \vdots \\ \gamma_n y_n^{*\prime}B_n y_n^* \end{pmatrix}.$$

But by (j3)

$$\begin{bmatrix} y_1^{*\prime} \\ \vdots \\ y_n^{*\prime} \end{bmatrix}[B_1 \cdots B_n]\left[\frac{\partial Z(v, 0)}{\partial v'}\right] = -\begin{bmatrix} y_1^{*\prime} \\ \vdots \\ y_n^{*\prime} \end{bmatrix}[B_1 \cdots B_n]\{I+H_1\}^{-1}$$

$$\times \begin{bmatrix} \gamma_1 y_1^* & 0 & 0 \\ & \ddots & \\ 0 & \gamma_2 y_2^* & 0 \\ & & \ddots \\ 0 & 0 & \gamma_n y_n^* \end{bmatrix}$$

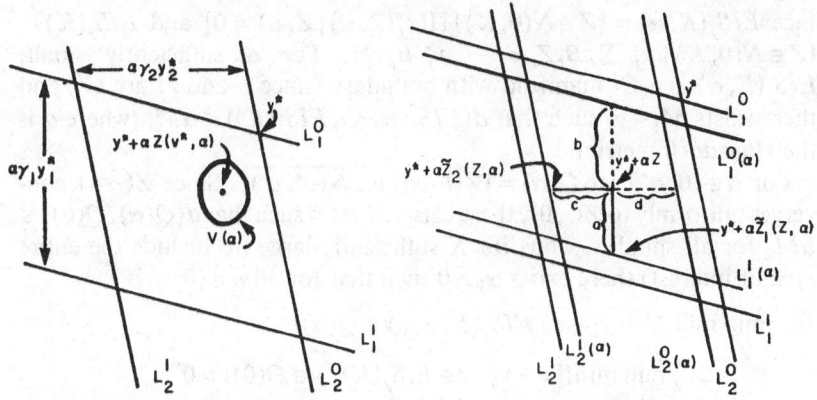

Figure 4 (left), Figure 5 (right). $L_1^0 = \{y^* + \alpha Z \mid y_1^{*\prime}(B_1 Z_1 + B_2 Z_2) = 0\}$; $L_1^i = \{y^* + \alpha Z \mid y_1^{*\prime}(B_1 Z_1 + B_2 Z_2) = -\gamma_1 y_1^{*\prime} B_1 y_1^*\} = \{y^* + \alpha Z \mid Z \in EIS_1(K)\}$; $L_2^0 = \{y^* + \alpha Z \mid y_2^{*\prime}(B_1 Z_1 + B_2 Z_2) = 0\}$; $L_2^i = \{y^* + \alpha Z \mid y_2^{*\prime}(B_1 Z_1 + B_2 Z_2) = -\gamma_2 y_2^{*\prime} B_2 y_2^*\} = \{y^* + \alpha Z \mid Z \in EIS_2(K)\}$; $V(\alpha) = \{y^* + \alpha Z(v, \alpha) \mid v \in \overline{N(v^*, \delta^*)}\}$; $L_1^i(\alpha) = \{y^* + \alpha Z \mid Z \in EIS_1(K, \alpha)\}$; $L_1^0(\alpha) = \{y^* + \alpha Z + z_1^*(Z, \alpha) \mid Z \in EIS_1(K, \alpha)\}$; $L_2^i(\alpha) = \{y^* + \alpha Z \mid Z \in EIS_2(K, \alpha)\}$; $L_2^0(\alpha) = \{y^* + \alpha Z + z_2^*(Z, \alpha) \mid Z \in EIS_2(K, \alpha)\}$; $a/(a+b) = q_1(Z, \alpha)$; $c/(c+d) = q_2(Z, \alpha)$.

has full rank, so such a v^* does exist. By the uniform convergence on compact sets and the openness of the condition just above, the $\epsilon^* > 0$ and $\bar{\alpha} > 0$ also exist. ∎

There exists $\alpha^* > 0$ such that for all $(v, \alpha) \in \overline{N(v^*, \epsilon^*)} \times (0, \alpha^*]$, the $Z(v, \alpha)$ "equilibrium" has strictly positive profit for operating firms who are therefore, by the remark before Lemma 5, at *global profit maximizing positions* $(z_j^* = z_j)$, and there is no incentive for entry *over the entire production set* $Y_j(\alpha)$. It only remains to show that there is an equilibrium with integral numbers of firms in each industry. To this end, we introduce marginal firms, and a backward map for marginal firms (see Figures 4 and 5).

As in Section IV, a marginal firm must be faced with an aggregate output of other firms which makes it indifferent between entering and staying out of the market; i.e., the output of other firms must be on the marginal firm's entry indifference surface. Given an appropriate aggregate output y, the backward map for a marginal firm gives a point Z on the entry indifference surface for that firm, and a number q between zero and one such that when the firm is faced with output Z by other firms, and is active in the market (at its optimal nonzero output) with probability q, and inactive with probability $1 - q$, then expected aggregate output is y. Lemma 8 computes the backward map for marginal firms.

WILLIAM NOVSHEK AND HUGO SONNENSCHEIN

First, for each j, for each $K < \infty$ define the entry indifference surface $EIS_j(K, \alpha) = \{Z \in N(0, K) \mid \Pi(z_j^*(Z, \alpha) \mid Z, \alpha) = 0\}$ and $EIS_j(K) = \{Z \in N(0, K) \mid y_j^{*'} \Sigma_t B_t Z_t = -\gamma_j y_j^{*'} B_j y_j^*\}$. For α sufficiently small, $EIS_j(K, \alpha)$ is a C^1 manifold with boundary (since F and z_j^* are C^1) and there exists $M_1 < \infty$ such that $d(EIS_j(K, \alpha), EIS_j(K)) \leq \alpha M_1$ (where d is the Hausdorff metric).

For $\alpha \in [0, \alpha^*]$ let $Q(\alpha) = \{Z(v, \alpha) \mid v \in \overline{N(v^*, \epsilon^*)}\}$. Since $Z(\cdot, \alpha)$ converges uniformly to $Z(\cdot, 0)$, there exists $M_2 < \infty$ such that $d(Q(\alpha), Q(0)) \leq \alpha M_2$ for all small α. Thus for K sufficiently large (to include the entire area of interest) there exists $\alpha_1 > 0$ such that for all $\alpha \in (0, \alpha_1]$,

$$\min_j \min\{\|x - y\| \mid x \in EIS_j(K, \alpha), y \in Q(\alpha)\}$$
$$> \tfrac{1}{2} \min_j \min\{\|x - y\| \mid x \in EIS_j(K), y \in Q(0)\} > 0,$$

where the last inequality follows from Lemma 7 and the definitions of $Q(0)$ and $EIS_j(K)$.

For each j, for all $Z \in Q(\alpha)$, $\alpha \in [0, \alpha_1]$, the backward map for marginal firms is defined by $\psi_j^m(Z, \alpha) = (\tilde{Z}_j(Z, \alpha), q_j(Z, \alpha)) \in EIS_j(K, \alpha) \times (0, 1)$ such that $\tilde{Z}_j(Z, \alpha) + (1/\alpha) q_j(Z, \alpha) z_j^*(\tilde{Z}_j(Z, \alpha), \alpha) = Z$ (where K is sufficiently large to include all relevant points).

Because of the properties of ψ_j and the fact that $V(\alpha)$ is bounded away from the entry indifference surface and the zero profit surface ($L_j^1(\alpha)$ and $L_j^0(\alpha)$ in Figure 5) for all j, the marginal backward map is approximately computed as follows: Find the unique point r in the intersection of the entry indifference surface $EIS_j(K, \alpha)$ and the line segment joining $y^* + \alpha Z$ and $y^* + \alpha \psi_j(Z(v, \alpha), \alpha)$, and set the probability q_j equal to the ratio of the length of the segment from $y^* + \alpha Z$ to r to the length of the (nonzero) optimal response to r, $\varphi_j((r - y^*)/\alpha, \alpha)$ (see Figures 4 and 5).

Lemma 8. *Assume the hypotheses of Theorem 1 are satisfied and v^*, ϵ^* are as in the statement of Lemma 7. Then there exists $\bar{\alpha} > 0$ such that*

$$\psi_j^m(Z(v, \alpha), \alpha) = (Z - q_j(Z(v, 0), 0) \gamma_j y_j^*, q_j(Z(v, 0), 0)) + O(\alpha)$$

for all $(v, \alpha) \in \overline{N(v^*, \epsilon^*)} \times [0, \bar{\alpha}]$, where

$$q_j(Z(v, 0), 0) = -\frac{y_j^{*'} \Sigma_t B_t Z_t(v, 0)}{\gamma_j y_j^{*'} B_j y_j^*}.$$

Proof of Lemma 8. Existence and uniqueness of $\psi_j^m(Z(v, \alpha), \alpha)$ for small α follows from the existence and uniqueness of $\psi_j(Z, \alpha)$ and the fact that $\min_j \min\{\|x - y\| \mid x \in EIS_j(K, \alpha), y \in Q(\alpha)\} > 0$ for small α. This also guarantees $q_j(Z(v, \alpha), \alpha)$ is bounded away from 0 and away from 1 for α

small and $v \in \overline{N(v^*, \epsilon^*)}$. The expression for $\psi_j^m(Z(v, \alpha), \alpha)$ follows from the properties of $z_j^*(Z, \alpha)$ and the fact that $d(EIS_j(K, \alpha), EIS_j(K)) \leq \alpha M_1$ for small α. The expression for $q_j(Z(v, 0), 0)$ follows from the form of $EIS_j(K)$ and the fact that $(1/\alpha)z_j^*(Z, \alpha)$ converges to $\gamma_j y_j^*$ as α converges to 0. ∎

Let

$$q(Z, \alpha) = \begin{pmatrix} q_1(Z, \alpha) \\ \vdots \\ q_n(Z, \alpha) \end{pmatrix}.$$

By (j3) and Lemma 8, $\{q(Z(v, \alpha), \alpha) \mid v \in \overline{N(v^*, \epsilon^*)}\}$ is the closure of a neighborhood of $q(Z(v^*, 0), 0)$ for α sufficiently small. Thus, there exists an integer $\bar{m} > 0$ and an $\bar{\alpha} > 0$ such that for all $\alpha \in (0, \bar{\alpha}]$,

$$\{\bar{m}q(Z(v, \alpha), \alpha) - v \mid v \in N(v^*, \epsilon^*)\} \supset ([-1, 1]^n + \{\bar{m}q(Z(v^*, 0), 0) - v^*\}).$$

We could use a different integer $\bar{m}_i$ for each component of q, which corresponds to having a different number of marginal firms in each industry.

Proof of Theorem 1. Let v^*, ϵ^* be as in Lemma 7, and m as in the remarks after Lemma 8. For all $\alpha > 0$, there exists a vector $\eta^*(\alpha)$ with integral components such that

$$|\eta_j^*(\alpha) - (1/\alpha\gamma_j + v_j^*) + \bar{m}q_j(Z(v^*, 0), 0)| \leq \tfrac{1}{2}$$

for all j, so there exists $\alpha^* > 0$ such that

$$\eta_j^*(\alpha) - (1/\alpha\gamma_j + \bar{v}_j(\alpha)) + \bar{m}q_j(Z(v(\alpha), \alpha), \alpha) = 0 \quad \text{for all } j,$$

for some $\bar{v}_j(\alpha) \in N(v^*, \epsilon^*)$, for all $\alpha \in (0, \alpha^*]$. (Note that

$$|\eta_j^*(\alpha) - (1/\alpha\gamma_j)| \leq |v_j^*| + \bar{m} + \tfrac{1}{2}.)$$

Now consider a backward mapping from Z with $\bar{m}$ marginal firms of each type, and $\eta_j^*(\alpha)$ pure strategy firms of type j, $j = 1, 2, ..., n$.

If $F(y)$ is not linear in y near y^* then an error is introduced because expected price is not equal to price of expected output, so the backward maps, and the entry indifference surface, etc., must be redefined to take account of the effect of the mn firms using probability distributions. However, the effect of all these changes is only $O(\alpha)$ since the support of the aggregate distribution is contained in some ball with radius αK for some $K < \infty$, and for bounded Z, $F(y^* + \alpha Z)$ is essentially linear in Z for small α.

Thus the "contribution" of the pure strategy firms is

$$\Psi(Z, \eta^*(\alpha) - (1/\alpha)\Gamma, \alpha) + O(\alpha)$$

299

where $\Gamma' = (1/\gamma_1, 1/\gamma_2, \ldots, 1/\gamma_n)$, while the "contribution" of the marginal firms is

$$-\bar{m}\begin{pmatrix} q_1\gamma_1 y_1^* \\ \vdots \\ q_n\gamma_n y_n^* \end{pmatrix} + O(\alpha).$$

The backward mapping from $Z(\bar{v}(\alpha), \alpha)$ with

$$\eta^*(\alpha) = (1/\alpha)\Gamma + \bar{v}(\alpha) - \bar{m}q(\bar{v}(\alpha), \alpha)$$

is therefore

$$\Psi(Z(\bar{v}(\alpha), \alpha), \bar{v}(\alpha) - \bar{m}q(\bar{v}(\alpha), \alpha), \alpha) - \bar{m}\begin{pmatrix} q_1(\bar{v}(\alpha), \alpha)\gamma_1 y_1^* \\ \vdots \\ q_n(\bar{v}(\alpha), \alpha)\gamma_n y_n^* \end{pmatrix} + O(\alpha)$$

(where $q_i(v, \alpha) = q_i(Z(v, \alpha), \alpha)$) which is equal to

$$Z(\bar{v}(\alpha), \alpha) + \left(-(\bar{v}_j(\alpha) - \bar{m}q_j(\bar{v}(\alpha), \alpha))\gamma_j y_j^* + \frac{1}{\gamma_j}\begin{bmatrix} 0 & -\bar{p}' \\ 0 & I \end{bmatrix} G_j \begin{bmatrix} 0 & 0 \\ -\bar{p} & I \end{bmatrix}\right.$$

$$\left.\times \left\{\sum_t B_t Z_t + \gamma_j B_j' y_j^*\right\}\right)_j - \bar{m}(q_j(\bar{v}(\alpha), \alpha)\gamma_j y_j^*)_j + O(\alpha)$$

$$= \{I + H_1\}Z(\bar{v}(\alpha), \alpha) + \left(-\bar{v}_j(\alpha)\gamma_j y_j^* + \begin{bmatrix} 0 & -\bar{p}' \\ 0 & I \end{bmatrix} G_j \begin{bmatrix} 0 & 0 \\ -\bar{p} & I \end{bmatrix} B_j' y_j^*\right)_j$$

$$+ O(\alpha)$$

$$= O(\alpha) \quad \text{by Lemma 6.}$$

If we call this backward map $\Psi_F(Z, \eta^*, \bar{m}, \alpha)$, then $\partial\Psi_F/\partial Z' = I + H_2 + O(\alpha)$, where H_2 is the matrix in (j2) (we choose $\bar{m}$ to be one of the m_s values). For α sufficiently small $\partial\Psi_F/\partial Z'$ is invertible by (j2). Since we are interested in a compact set of v values, and therefore a compact set of Z values, and the functions we consider converge uniformly on compact sets, there exists $\alpha_1 > 0$ such that the $\eta^*(\alpha)$ pure strategy and $\bar{m}n$ marginal firms are all acting optimally and generate aggregate expected output $y^* + \alpha Z(\bar{v}(\alpha), \alpha) + O(\alpha^2)$, and since $\bar{v}(\alpha) \in N(v^*, \epsilon^*)$, by Lemma 7 and the uniform convergence, there exists $\bar{\alpha} > 0$ such that for all $\alpha \in (0, \bar{\alpha}]$, there exists a true equilibrium with m marginal firms of each type and $\eta_j^*(\alpha)$ pure strategy firms of type j, $j = 1, 2, \ldots, n$. In this equilibrium

(a) there is an integral number of firms in each industry, $\bar{m} + \eta_j^*(\alpha)$;
(b) all firms, including marginal firms, are maximizing profit over all mixed strategies on their entire production set;

Cournot, Walras equilibrium

(c)   all pure strategy firms earn strictly positive expected profit, while marginal firms earn zero expected profit,

(d)   there is no incentive for entry (entrants earn strictly negative expected profit if existing firms maintain their actions);

(e)   there exists $S < \infty$ such that the support of $\rho(\alpha)$ is contained in $N(y^*, \alpha S)$ where $\rho(\alpha)$ is the Cournot production associated with the constructed Cournot equilibrium of $\mathcal{E}(\alpha)$.   ∎

Proof of Theorem 2. Let $\bar{\alpha}_0$ be the α value guaranteed by Theorem 1, and let $\rho: (0, \bar{\alpha}_0] \to$ probability measures on R^{ln} be defined by $\rho(\alpha) =$ the Cournot production associated with the Cournot equilibrium of $\mathcal{E}(\alpha)$ constructed in the proof of Theorem 1. Also, let $N = n\bar{m} + 1$ where $\bar{m}$ is as in the proof of Theorem 1. Then in each Cournot equilibrium, there are less than N marginal firms.

As noted in the proof of Theorem 1, there exists $S_1 < \infty$ such that supp $\rho(\alpha) \subset N(y^*, \alpha S_1)$ for all $\alpha \in (0, \bar{\alpha}_0]$. Since F is C^2 in a neighborhood of y^*, there exists $S_2 < \infty$ and $\bar{\alpha} \in (0, \bar{\alpha}_0]$ such that supp $\xi(\alpha) \subset N(\bar{p}, \alpha S_2)$ for all $\alpha \in (0, \bar{\alpha}]$, where $\xi(\alpha)$ is the Cournot price distribution corresponding to $(F(\alpha), \rho(\alpha))[F(\alpha) \equiv F]$.   ∎

Proof of Theorem 3. The set of feasible states is a subset of

$$\mathcal{F} = \left\{ y \in R^{ln} \mid y_j \in \hat{Y}_j, \sum_j y_j + \sum_i \omega_i \geq 0 \right\} \quad \text{for each economy } \mathcal{E}(\alpha).$$

By (e3′), there exists $\bar{K} < \infty$ such that $\mathcal{F} \subset N(0, \bar{K})$. Also by (e3′), 0 is an exposed point of $\hat{Y}_j$ so there exists x_j such that $y'x_j > 0$ for all $y \in \hat{Y}_j \setminus \{0\}$. By decomposing each $y \in \hat{Y}_j \setminus \{0\}$ into a multiple of x_j and a vector orthogonal to x_j, noting that

$$\min\left(\frac{y'x_j}{\|y\|} \,\middle|\, y \in \hat{Y}_j \setminus \{0\} \right) > 0$$

and using $\mathcal{F} \subset N(0, \bar{K})$ we see that there exists $K < \infty$ such that for any countable set A, and $\{y_a \mid a \in A\}$ where $y_a \in \bigcup_{j=1}^n \hat{Y}_j$ for each $a \in A$, $\sum_{a \in A} \|y_a\| \geq K$ implies that the corresponding economy output $y \in R^{ln}$ is not feasible.

$\mathcal{F}$ is bounded, so by desirability and the upper hemicontinuity of the Walras correspondence, the set of feasible prices is a subset of a closed cone contained in the interior of Ω, and, as in Lemma 1, there exists $M < \infty$ such that (∗) supp $\mu(\alpha_k)(j, v) \subset N(0, M\alpha_k)$ for all $0 < v \leq \eta_j(\alpha_k)$, $0 < j \leq n, k \geq 1$ (0 dominates any action outside $N(0, M\alpha_k)$, and the mixed strategies are noncooperative).

We now consider the actions of operating firms as independent (for each given k) random vectors with the same underlying probability space (with expectation operator E). Let $\bar{X}_{jv}^k$ be the random vector in R^l corresponding to the j, v firm in $\mathcal{E}(\alpha_k)$, and let $X_{jv}^k = \bar{X}_{jv}^k - E\bar{X}_{jv}^k$. Since $y^{*\prime} = (y_1^{*\prime}, y_2^{*\prime}, \ldots, y_n^{*\prime})$ and

$$E \sum_{v=1}^{\eta_j(\alpha_k)} \bar{X}_{jv}^k = \sum_{v=1}^{\eta_j(\alpha_k)} E\bar{X}_{jvi}^k \to y_j^*$$

as $k \to \infty$, in order to prove (3.1) it is sufficient to show that for all $j = 1, 2, \ldots, n$, $i = 1, 2, \ldots, l$, and $\delta > 0$,

$$\lim_{k \to \infty} \text{prob}\left\{ \left| \sum_{v=1}^{\eta_j(\alpha_k)} X_{jvi}^k \right| < \delta \right\} = 1,$$

where X_{jvi}^k is the ith component of X_{jv}^k.

By definition, X_{jv}^k induces the measure $\mu(\alpha_k)(j, v)$ on R^l, so by (*) $\text{prob}\{X_{jvi}^k \in [-M\alpha_k, M\alpha_k]\} = 1$ and therefore $\text{prob}\{|X_{jvi}^k| \le 2M\alpha_k\} = 1$.

Fix $j \in \{1, 2, \ldots, n\}$, $i \in \{1, 2, \ldots, l\}$, and $\delta > 0$, and for notational convenience let X_v^k denote X_{jvi}^k. Split the sequence $(|\sum_{v=1}^{\eta_j(\alpha_k)} X_v^k|)_k$ into two parts, depending on k: $\eta_j(\alpha_k) < (\alpha_k)^{-1/2}$; and, $\eta_j(\alpha_k) \ge (\alpha_k)^{-1/2}$. For the first part, $\text{prob}\{|\sum_{v=1}^{\eta_j(\alpha_k)} X_v^k| \le \eta_j(\alpha_k) 2M\alpha_k < 2M(\alpha_k)^{1/2}\} = 1$. For k sufficiently large, $2M(\alpha_k)^{1/2} < \delta$, and $\text{prob}\{|\sum_{v=1}^{\eta_j(\alpha_k)} X_v^k| < \delta\} = 1$.

For the second part of the sequence, by the Markov inequality [8, p. 158],

$$\text{prob}\left\{ \left| \sum_{v=1}^{\eta_j(\alpha_k)} X_v^k \right| \ge \delta \right\} \le E\left| \sum_{v=1}^{\eta_j(\alpha_k)} X_v^k \right|^r \Big/ \delta^r$$

for any $r > 0$. Let $r = 2$. The X_v^k are independent (for fixed k) with zero means, so $E|\sum_{v=1}^{\eta_j(\alpha_k)} X_v^k|^2 = \sum_{v=1}^{\eta_j(\alpha_k)} E|X_v^k|^2$. Also $\text{prob}\{|X_v^k| \le 2M\alpha_k\} = 1$ and $\text{prob}\{\sum_{v=1}^{\eta_j(\alpha_k)} |X_v^k| > 2K\} = 0$ (otherwise a state which is not feasible occurs with positive probability). Thus,

$$\sum_{v=1}^{\eta_j(\alpha_k)} E|X_v^k|^2 \le \sup\left\{ \sum_{v=1}^{\infty} |c_v|^2 : \sum_{v=1}^{\infty} |c_v| \le 2K, |c_v| \le 2M\alpha_k \quad \text{for all } v \right\}$$

$$< \left(\frac{2K}{2\alpha_k M} + 1 \right) (2M\alpha_k)^2 = \alpha_k[4KM + \alpha_k 4M^2],$$

where the second inequality follows from the fact that the sum $\sum_{v=1}^{\infty} |c_v|^2$ is maximized at a boundary solution with $|c_v| = 2M\alpha_k$ for as many v as possible. Thus, $\text{prob}\{|\sum_{v=1}^{\eta_j(\alpha_k)} X_v^k| \ge \delta\} = O(\alpha_k) \to 0$ as $k \to \infty$. This completes the proof of (3.1). ∎

Let $\bar{p}$ be defined by $F(y^*) = (1, \bar{p})$. $\xi(\alpha_k)$ is completely determined by $\rho(\alpha_k)$ and F, and (3.2) follows from (3.1) and the continuity of F at y^*.

Let x^* be the allocation in the exchange economy

$$\mathcal{E}(y^*) = (X_t, \omega_i + \Sigma_j \theta_{ij} y_j^*, \succsim_i)$$

that is an equilibrium allocation at $(1, \bar{p})$ (x^* exists by definition of F and $\bar{p}$). F is continuous at y^*, so $(1, \bar{p})$ must be supporting prices for each cone $\hat{Y}_j$ (otherwise entry would occur at some α_k, destroying the Cournot equilibrium in mixed strategies). Thus, $((1, \bar{p}), x^*, y^*)$ is a Walras equilibrium of $\hat{\mathcal{E}}$, which establishes (3.3).

To prove (3.4), suppose $y_j^{*\prime} B_j y_j^* > 0$. By (e2'), the boundedness of the set of feasible prices and (3.2), given $\delta > 0$ there exists $k_1 < \infty$ such that

$$\text{supp } \mu(\alpha_k)(j, v) \subset N(\alpha y_j((1, p^*)), \alpha\delta) \cup \{0\} \quad \text{for all } k \geq k_1.$$

The sequence is proper, so if t_k is the number of active firms in the Cournot equilibrium which use zero with positive probability, then $\alpha_k t_k \to 0$ as $k \to \infty$. Thus, for any $\epsilon > 0$, there is an $S < \infty$ such that for large k, with probability one, the aggregate action of active firms which use zero with positive probability is in $N(0, t_k \alpha_k S) \subset N(0, \epsilon/2)$. If T_{jk} is the number of active firms of type j in the Cournot equilibrium which do not use zero, then $\alpha_k T_{jk}$ is bounded (by feasibility) and, for any $\delta > 0$, for large k, the aggregate action of these firms is in $N(T_{jk} \alpha_k y_j(1, \bar{p}), T_{jk} \alpha_k \delta)$ with probability one. Combining these properties with (vi) of the theorem, we see that for any $\epsilon > 0$, for all sufficiently large k, $\rho(\alpha_k) N(y^*, \epsilon) = 1$.

For all k sufficiently large, some firm of type j must be active (by (3.1) and $y_j^* \neq 0$). For each k, let $x_k \neq 0$ be an action with positive probability for some active firm of type j, and consider an entrant using pure strategy x_k. The active firm only has actions in $N(\alpha y_j((1, p^*)), \alpha\delta) \cup \{0\}$. Conditional on the action of the active firm being 0, the entrant has nonnegative expected profit (just as the active firm does at action x_k prior to entry). Conditional on the active firm having action in $N(\alpha y_j((1, p^*)), \alpha\delta)$, the entrant's profit increases for all states with aggregate output near y^* ($y_j^{*\prime} B_j y_j^* > 0$). For any $\epsilon > 0$, for k sufficiently large, $\rho(\alpha_k) N(y^*, \epsilon) = 1$ so for ϵ, α_k sufficiently small, the increase in profit is greater than $\frac{1}{2} \alpha_k \gamma_j y_j^{*\prime} B_j (\alpha_k \gamma_j y_j^*)$. For k sufficiently large (α_k sufficiently small), the net change in expected profit has the same sign as $y_j^{*\prime} B_j y_j^*$, and entry will occur, upsetting equilibrium. This completes the proof of (3.4). ∎

VI. Remarks

A. The analysis we have presented differs substantially from standard formal treatments of competitive theory: Nonconvexity is essential, market power is endogenous, downward sloping demand is a requirement for static equilibrium, there is free entry, etc. Yet our complete dependence

303

on the results of modern competitive theory (as surveyed in Debreu [4]) should be apparent to the reader. To underscore this dependence, we list some of the ways in which the paper relates (even ties together) recent developments in competitive theory.

Theorem 1 on the existence of Cournot equilibrium with entry requires the existence of Walras equilibrium in $\hat{\mathcal{E}}$. As such the result rests on the existence of Walras equilibrium. The Pareto Optimality of Walras equilibrium translates to the approximate Pareto Optimality of Cournot Equilibrium when efficient scale is small (Theorem 3). Theorem 2, together with the result that Pareto Optima are Walras equilibria in $\hat{\mathcal{E}}$, translates to the theorem that provided efficient scale is small, any Pareto optimum which satisfies DSD is approximately a Cournot equilibrium (relative to the appropriate specification of private ownership). Also, the replication of consumers, the idea of a limit economy, convergence results, etc., borrow from a pattern well developed in the literature on limits of cores. (A natural way to obtain decreasing returns in $\hat{\mathcal{E}}$ is to exploit a measure theoretic specification of the kind used in that literature.) Theorem 2 contains a result on the "rate of convergence." The entire framework is equilibrium with endogenous uncertainty. A "differentiable" framework is for a great many reasons natural for the analysis; in addition, the possibility of a stability theory in $\hat{\mathcal{E}}$ based on the entry and exit of firms is an attractive possibility. Product differentiation with an infinity of conceivable commodities would require extensions to economies with infinite dimensional commodity spaces.

Finally, the notion of a regular economy is intimately related to the existence of a selection from the Walras correspondence, DSD is a requirement imposed on the Walras correspondence, and existence can only be guaranteed as a generic property of a class of economies.

B. The analysis could be enlarged to admit the case where industry production sets in $\hat{\mathcal{E}}$ exhibit (strictly) diminishing returns to scale. This could be modeled in one of two natural ways: diseconomies (external to the firm and internal to the industry); or a measure space of available firms in $\hat{\mathcal{E}}$ with differing efficiencies. Then, it would be possible for a firm to have a large positive profit in equilibrium (rents).

C. The limit economy $\hat{\mathcal{E}}$ is studied in greater detail in a sequel to this paper, titled "Walras Equilibrium as an Idealization of Small Efficient Scale and Free Entry." Since production in $\hat{\mathcal{E}}$ takes place in a continuum of firms, each of which reaches efficient scale at an infinitesimal level of output, the convexity of the aggregate production set $\hat{Y}$ is guaranteed by Richter's Theorem on the integral of correspondences. For any price vector p, firms may be active if they can make a nonnegative profit (and must be active if they can make a positive profit). The sum (integral) of their actions is both on the boundary of $\hat{Y}$ and is supported by p; furthermore, since some firms produce more efficiently than others, there are Ricardian rents. (Such rents disappear in the present model since all firms have access to the same technology.) Both the distribution of income among consumers as well as the amount of income which goes to each consumer depend on the ownership structure of the economy.

The existence of Walras equilibrium in $\hat{\mathcal{E}}$ follows from two arguments: (1) the standard equilibrium existence theorem (Debreu, [3]), with some minor modification, shows that there is an equilibrium with $\hat{Y}$ as the production set, and (2) profit maximization on $\hat{Y}$ is equivalent to profit maximization on the (infinite collection of) sets which are added to form $\hat{Y}$. The classical results of welfare economics apply for the present model. They follow from (2), via the standard welfare theorems (Debreu, [3]); however, the "Second Theorem" (optimal are equilibria) does not require convexity as a basic hypothesis. That assumption is replaced by the hypothesis that firms reach efficient scale at an infinitesimal level of output.

D. The assumption that consumers exhibit price-taking behavior is not necessary; what is required is that every set of quantity actions by firms yield a well defined vector of prices. For suitably smooth "F," results analogous to Theorem 1 hold. For example, suppose that in each economy $\mathcal{E}(\alpha)$, the quantity actions of firms result in an allocation in the core of the associated pure exchange economy, and let price be the implied efficiency prices. Since the cores of the exchange economies converge to the Walras equilibria of the exchange economy associated with $\hat{\mathcal{E}}$, the modified (non-price-taking) Cournot equilibria of $\mathcal{E}(\alpha)$ converge to the Walras equilibria of $\hat{\mathcal{E}}$. In connection with this point, it is appropriate to underscore the asymmetry between our treatment of consumers and producers. The present analysis is designed to explain perfectly competitive *producer* behavior and has no role in the explanation of price taking consumer behavior. The key ingredients in our explanation of perfectly competitive producer behavior are small (per capita) efficient scale and the free entry of firms. Whatever the explanation of competitive consumer behavior, it is not free entry and small efficient scale! Firms and consumers are created and exist for different purposes; they perform a different function in the allocation of resources. In contrast with standard models of Walras equilibrium, we highlight the creation of firms; this dictates the asymmetric treatment afforded consumers and producers.

305

E. Since uncertainty disappears for the equilibria exhibited in Theorem 1 as α converges to zero, the results obtained are easily extended to firms that maximize a (smooth) expected utility of income function. This admits risk aversion into the analysis.

F. As long as there are only a finite number of conceivable commodities, our analysis includes the classical case of product differentiation. For any fixed value of α, there may be many commodities which are not produced. As α converges to zero, the number of different commodities actually produced (from among the large but finite number of available commodities) may increase. For situations in which there are an infinite number of available commodities, it is necessary to consider economies $\hat{\varepsilon}$ with infinite dimensional commodity spaces (see, e.g., Hart [6] and Mas-Colell [9]).

G. With only a countable number of firms, the introduction of mixed strategies does not remove all discontinuities. The only way to remove the discontinuity associated with entry is to have a continuum of firms. Here is an outline of a simple example in which equilibrium with entry does not exist in mixed strategies for all $\alpha \geq \bar{\alpha} > 0$ (i.e., introduction of mixed strategies does not imply that equilibrium with entry exists for all α). Consider the partial equilibrium setting of Figure 1 with linear inverse demand F. Assume constant average cost $\bar{p}$ (which is greater than the competitive price $F(y^*)$) up to some positive output level. For $\bar{\alpha}$ sufficiently large, only the constant average cost portion of the cost curve is relevant. If equilibrium were to exist with a finite number of firms, then expected price must exceed $\bar{p}$ in order to insure that active firms are maximizing profit. But then entry is profitable. This can easily be turned into a general equilibrium example.

More important, arbitrary mixed strategies are not consistent with observed behavior. Thus, the fact that only pure and marginal firm strategies are profit maximizing in the equilibria of Theorem 1, even though arbitrary mixed strategies are allowed, is significant.

H. The introduction of marginal firms is essential. Restrictive assumptions are necessary to guarantee the existence of equilibrium in pure strategies for all α sufficiently small. We have substantially explored such assumptions, and existence results will be reported elsewhere.

I. A natural test of the robustness of the equilibria considered here is given by the ability of a single firm with perfect information and perfect knowledge of the behavior of other agents to increase profit by departing from the prescribed behavior. We observe that the maximum profit such a firm could obtain is less than αK, where K is a constant. Thus, the benefit which accrues to strategies which are more sophisticated than those considered here (e.g., the strategy of a firm acting as a Stackelberg leader, knowing the responses of the rest of the economy) will eventually be swamped by the costs of obtaining information (which do not depend on α). Similarly, from the point of view of cooperative action, any cartel must be sensitive to the possibility of entry if it restricts output to increase profit. Threats aside, cartels must "limit price" to prevent entry, and so the profit which accrues to a cartel is less than αL, where L is a constant. (This is discussed by Novshek [10].)[18] For this reason, we believe that the results reported here have natural extensions beyond the case of quantity choosing Cournot equilibrium.

J. Firms that recognize their effect on price do not in general maximize a weighted sum of shareholders' utilities by profit maximization. Consider a sequence of Cournot equilibria, one for each economy $\mathcal{E}(1/k)$, $k = \bar{k}, \bar{k}+1, \bar{k}+2, \ldots$, as constructed in the proof of Theorem 1, where the $\mathcal{E}(1/k)$ are viewed as "per capita" economies for k replications of each consumer type. Let $v_i(p, w)$ be an indirect utility function for consumers of type i. For large k, the equilibrium prices and wealth (p^k, w_i^k) are approximately equal to the competitive prices and wealth $(p^*, w_i^*) = (p^*, p^{*\prime}\omega_i)$. For any single firm of type j for which the tth consumer of type i has ownership share θ_{itj}^k in $\mathcal{E}(1/k)$,

$$\frac{\partial v_i}{\partial y'} \approx \frac{1}{k}\frac{\partial v_i(p^*, w_i^*)}{\partial p'}B_j + \theta_{itj}^k\frac{\partial v_i(p^*, w_i^*)}{\partial w}p^{*\prime}.$$

For $\theta_{itj}^k = (1/k)\theta_{ij}$ both terms are of the same order of magnitude so either may dominate. Whenever $\theta_{itj}^k \to 0$ as $k \to \infty$, if the firm's actions are constrained to lie in a bounded set, then the effect of a single firm on any single consumer converges to zero.

If for some itj, θ_{itj}^k is bounded away from zero, then for k sufficiently large,

$$\frac{\partial v_i}{\partial y'} \approx \theta_{itj}^k\frac{\partial v_i(p^*, w_i^*)}{\partial w}p^{*\prime},$$

and the utility maximizing solution is approximately the competitive solution which is approximately the profit maximizing solution (as seen in the proof of Theorem 1). In either case, any cost (to the firm) of learning

---

[18] Since entrants can produce as efficiently as cartel members, each cartel member faces at least the same loss as an entrant when threats are carried out.

the preferences of a consumer/owner eventually outweighs the gain from knowledge of an exact "welfare function" to be maximized by the firm.[19] The second case is related to Hart [7], which deals with a stock market model.

K. Implicit in the manner in which firms determine how much they will have to pay for an input is the assumption that in equilibria of $\hat{\mathcal{E}}$ the consumer sector consumes some of each commodity. Thus, there are neither pure inputs nor pure intermediate products. The producer sector can always obtain, from the price taking consumer sector, an additional amount of a commodity to use as an input by paying the appropriate price. This could be softened by introducing a sector of price taking firms, but such a device would be contrary to the spirit of the analysis.

L. When α is small, changes in demand lead to new equilibria in which both firms' actions and the number of active firms have changed. As $\alpha \to 0$, the change in the number of firms is dominant. This suggests the possibility of a "real time" dynamics in which the adjustment of price is determined by the rate at which firms enter. In addition, since firms recognize their effect on price, there is no contradiction in having them change the amount which they offer to the market (or even enter!) when preferences, technology, or other data of the economy change. It is only in the limit that a tension arises between price taking behavior and the need for prices to adjust in order to clear markets (see Arrow [1]).

M. Under what conditions does the Arrow–Debreu model apply? If one views industry constant returns to scale as being an idealization of small per capita efficient scale and free entry, as done here, the Arrow–Debreu model with constant returns to scale is applicable, but only if downward sloping demand is satisfied. If one views constant returns to scale for firms as empirically correct, then the Arrow–Debreu model captures formally the notion of perfect competition only in so far as we acknowledge that the technology is freely available to all users. In this case, our argument for downward sloping demand as a requirement for static equilibrium applies again, and perfectly competitive equilibria which do not satisfy the condition are simply the result of actions which are irrational

---

[19] We have assumed $\theta_{itj}^k = (1/k)\theta_{ij}$, so it is worthwhile for consumer/owners to have whole industries act collusively, in which case equilibrium (if it exists) is not in general approximately competitive. This simplifying assumption can be eliminated, but the cost is increased notational complexity. The θ_{ijt} must be specified for all ijt, and prices will depend on which firms of type j are active. However, near a Walras equilibrium of $\hat{\mathcal{E}}$, this will be only a low order effect, so under suitable conditions the proof of Theorem 1 can be modified to cover this generalization.

(and in no approximate sense rational). If we understand the Arrow–Debreu theory as appropriate for conditions of decreasing returns to scale for firms and no free entry, there is the "embarrassment" of possibly significant profit and possibly significant market power to explain. Free entry is not available to make these go away (and if it was available the model would collapse). Finally, the Arrow–Debreu model is not applicable under conditions of increasing returns to scale, since equilibrium will generally not exist.

VII. Conclusion

Theorem 1 proves the existence of Cournot equilibrium with entry. Theorems 2 and 3 unify the equilibrium concepts of Walras and Cournot by establishing that Cournot equilibria are approximated by certain Walras equilibria.

The Arrow–Debreu model is viewed as representing a "frictionless system," whose "frictions" are barriers to entry and noninfinitesimal efficient scale. When efficient scale is small (but significant) and entry is free, certain Walras equilibria serve as good approximations to Cournot equilibria with free entry. However, when there are barriers to entry, or if efficient scale is not attained at a level which is per capita small, the "frictionless" idealization is no longer appropriate. In the "frictionless system," demand determines the measure of firms which are active in each industry. Zero profit becomes a consequence of free entry, and firms take competitive prices as given because prices really are beyond their control. However, the analysis shows that the viewpoint of the Arrow–Debreu model as representing a frictionless system is only proper under conditions of downward sloping demand and when the efficient scale of firms is bounded away from zero. (Thus two cornerstones of the classical partial equilibrium diagram are introduced into formal general equilibrium analysis and play a central role.)

We present a simple proof that the perspective we have offered does "make a difference." Recall the standard line: Consider a perfectly competitive economy with one firm (two or three firms) and constant returns to scale. From the present viewpoint, it makes no sense: The number of firms is not endogenous, and perfectly competitive behavior is not a primitive solution concept; it applies if conditions are right. Finally, competitive behavior is unlikely to obtain with only one firm (two or three firms) active in equilibrium. In contrast, the formalism of the present analysis forces you to say this: Consider an economy with one industry (two or three industries), free entry, small efficient scale, and downward sloping demand. If efficient scale is small, then the production sets of each industry exhibit approximately constant returns to scale. Small efficient scale with entry dictates the result that firms have almost no effect on price when attention is restricted to the region in which they make positive profit. The addition of a demand sector determines the number of active firms in each industry. In each industry in which there is positive output, there are a large number of firms active, each of which is producing a small amount (at approximately efficient scale).

Appendix I

Partial equilibrium (Novshek, [10])

Assumptions: For the cost function $C(y)$,

(C) $C(y) = 0$ $y = 0$,

$\qquad\quad = C_0 + V(y)$ $y > 0$,

where $C_0 > 0$ and for all $y \geq 0$, $v \geq 0$, $v' > 0$, $v'' \geq 0$. Average cost is minimized uniquely at $y = 1$.

For the inverse demand function $F(Y)$,

(F) $F \in C^2([0, \infty))$ with $F' < 0$ whenever $F > 0$,

and there exists $Y^* > 0$ such that $F(Y^*) = C(1)$ (equals minimum average cost). Y^* is the competitive output.

Definitions: (II, 1) An α *size firm corresponding to* C is a firm with cost function $C_\alpha(y) = \alpha C(y/\alpha)$. For each α, C, and F, one considers a pool of available firms, each with cost function C_α, facing market inverse demand F.

(II, 2) Given C, F, and an $\alpha \in (0, \infty)$, an (α, C, F) *market equilibrium with free entry* is an integer n and a set $\{y_1, \ldots, y_n\}$ of positive outputs such that:

(a) $\{y_1, \ldots, y_n\}$ is an n firm Cournot equilibrium (without entry), i.e., for all $i = 1, \ldots, n$,

$$F\left(\sum_{j \neq i} y_j + y_i\right) y_i - C_\alpha(y_i) \geq F\left(\sum_{j \neq i} y_j + y\right) y - C_\alpha(y)$$

for all $y \geq 0$, and

(b) there is no profit incentive for additional entry, i.e.,

$$F\left(\sum_{j=1}^{n} y_j + y\right) y - C_\alpha(y) \leq 0 \quad \text{for all } y \geq 0.$$

310

Cournot, Walras equilibrium

The set of all (α, C, F) market equilibria with free entry is denoted $E(\alpha, c, F)$.

It is easily demonstrated that the Nash–Cournot equilibria exhibited converge to the competitive equilibrium Y^*; i.e., given C satisfying (C), F satisfying (F) and $\alpha \in (0, \infty)$, if n, $\{y_1, y_2, \ldots, y_n\} \in E(\alpha, C, F)$, then $\sum_{j=1}^{n} y_j \in [Y^* - \alpha, Y^*]$. This observation is made whole by the following theorem.

Theorem: *Given C satisfying* (C) *and F satisfying* (F), *there exists* $a^* > 0$ *such that for all* $\alpha \in (0, \alpha^*]$, $E(\alpha, C, F) = \varnothing$.

Appendix II

In order to show the genericity of (j1), (j2), and (j3), we use as basic G_j, y_j^*, $F(y^*)$, B_j, and θ_{ij} subject to

(a) G_j is negative semidefinite and $x'G_j x < 0$ for $x \in P_j(R^l) \setminus \{0\}$;
(b) $y_j^{*\prime} F(y^*) = 0$ for all j;
(c) $F_1(y^*) \equiv 1$;
(d) $y_j^{*\prime} B_j y_j^* < 0$ for all j;
(e) $(1, 0, 0, \ldots, 0) B_j = (0, 0, \ldots, 0)$ for all j; and
(f) $\sum_i \theta_{ij} = 1$ for all j.

The ownership shares, θ_{ij}, and the shape of production sets at competitive outputs, G_j, are clearly basic. The $F(y^*)$, y^*, and $\partial F/\partial \omega'$ are considered basic in the spirit of the result that given any prices, p, output, y, and Jacobian $[\partial y/\partial p]$, a set of consumers exist whose aggregate demand is y at prices p, and has Jacobian $[\partial y/\partial p]$ at (y, p) (Sonnenschein [15]). The B_j are used as basic rather than the $\partial F/\partial \omega$, since

$$[B_1 \cdots B_n]_{l \times ln} = \left[\frac{\partial F}{\partial \omega'}\right]_{l \times lm} \begin{bmatrix} \theta_{11} I_{l \times l} & \cdots & \theta_{1n} I_{l \times l} \\ \vdots & & \vdots \\ \theta_{m1} I_{l \times l} & \cdots & \theta_{mn} I_{l \times l} \end{bmatrix}_{lm \times ln}$$

so if $m \geq n$ and

$$\begin{bmatrix} \theta_{11} & \cdots & \theta_{1n} \\ \vdots & & \vdots \\ \theta_{m1} & \cdots & \theta_{mn} \end{bmatrix}_{m \times n}$$

has rank n (which is a generic property if $m \geq n$ since the θ_{ij} are basic) then if any $\partial F/\partial \omega'$ (with $\partial F_1/\partial \omega' = 0'$) is possible, so is any $[B_1 \cdots B_n]$ (with $(1 0 \cdots 0)_{1 \times l} [B_1 \cdots B_n]_{l \times ln} = (0 \cdots 0)_{1 \times ln}$).

When consumers are specified in terms of demand functions rather than preferences, the genericity arguments can be modified to remain valid

311

under suitable conditions. At the end of this appendix, we briefly sketch the modifications.

We only consider economies which satisfy the required differentiability assumptions, and (a)–(f). Each economy $\mathcal{E}$ in this space of economies can be represented by a vector $((G_j)_j, (y_j^*)_j, (\theta_{ij})_{i,j}, (B_j)_j, F(y^*))$, where the matrices G_j are written as vectors (row 1, row 2, ..., row l). The distance between any two economies is defined to be 1 if the number of consumers, commodities, or industries is different, or if for any industry, the set of smoothly variable commodities is different. Otherwise, the distance is defined to be the usual distance in $R^{nl^2+nl+mn+nl^2+l}$. We show that the nondegeneracy conditions hold in an open dense subset of this metric space, and are therefore generic properties. Since eigenvalues and determinants are continuous functions of the entries of the corresponding matrices, and (j1)–(j3) are open conditions, they hold in a neighborhood of an economy at which they hold. It only remains to show that (j1)–(j3) hold in a dense subset of the space.

(j1) Using the form of $\begin{bmatrix} 0 & -p' \\ 0 & I \end{bmatrix} G_j$ (the first row is a linear combination of the other rows, and row i is zero if i is not a smoothly variable component), (j1) can be transformed into an equivalent form (eliminating all components which are identically zero in $P_1(R') \times P_2(R') \times \cdots \times P_n(R')$), determinant $\{D + \tilde{G}^{-1}\} \neq 0$, where

$$\tilde{G} = \begin{bmatrix} \tilde{G}_1 & & 0 \\ & \ddots & \\ 0 & & \tilde{G}_n \end{bmatrix}$$

with $\tilde{G}_j$ the negative definitive submatrix of G_j corresponding to $P_j(R')$ (if $G_j = [0]$ then $\tilde{G}_j$ is skipped) and where D is independent of $\tilde{G}$. Since $\tilde{G}^{-1}$ has full rank, all entries of $\tilde{G}^{-1}$ can be varied, so if (j1) fails at $\mathcal{E}$, it is satisfied at a sequence of economies $\mathcal{E}_x \to \mathcal{E}$.

(j2) By (j1), the existence of $\{I + H_1\}^{-1}$ is generic. Let λ be the smallest strictly positive eigenvalue of $\{I + H_1\}^{-1}\{H_1 - H_2(1)\}$. If $H_2(m)x = -x$ then $\{I + H_1\}x = \{H_1 - H_2(m)\}x = m\{H_1 - H_2(1)\}x$ and $x = m\{I + H_1\}^{-1} \times \{H_1 - H_2(1)\}x$. When $m > (1/\lambda)$ ($m \geq 1$ if λ does not exist), then $x = m\{I + H_1\}^{-1}\{H_1 - H_2(1)\}x$ implies $x = 0$, so $H_2(m)$ does not have eigenvalue -1.

(j3) (a) It is generic that

$$N = \begin{bmatrix} y_1^{*'} & & 0 \\ & \ddots & \\ 0 & & y_n^{*'} \end{bmatrix}_{n \times ln} \begin{bmatrix} B_1 \cdots B_n \\ \vdots & \vdots \\ B_1 \cdots B_n \end{bmatrix}_{ln \times ln} \begin{bmatrix} y_1^* & & 0 \\ & \ddots & \\ 0 & & y_n^* \end{bmatrix}_{ln \times n}$$

has rank n. To see this, let

$$B_j(x) = B_j + x \begin{bmatrix} 0 & 0 \\ 0 & I \end{bmatrix}_{l+l} \quad \text{for all } j$$

(I is $(l-1)\times(l-1)$), and let $N(x)$ be the matrix corresponding to N when B is replaced by $B(x)$. Then

$$N(x) = N + x \begin{bmatrix} z_1'z_1 & \cdots & z_1'z_n \\ \vdots & & \vdots \\ z_n'z_1 & \cdots & z_n'z_n \end{bmatrix}_{n \times n},$$

where $z_j' = (y_{j2}^*, y_{j3}^* \cdots y_{jl}^*)$. The $z_1, z_2, ..., z_n \in R^{l-1}$ are generically independent since $n \le l-1$ and the y_j^* are basic, so the matrix multiplied by x has rank n generically. Expanding the determinant of $N(x)$, we find

$$\det N(x) = a_n + x a_{n-1} + x^2 a_{n-2} + \cdots + x^{n-1} a_1 + x^n a_0.$$

Let s be the largest integer such that $a_s \ne 0$ (such an s exists since $a_0 = \det([z_i'z_j]_{ij}) \ne 0$). Then $1/x^{(n-s)} \det N(x) = a_s + x a_{s-1} + \cdots + x^s a_0 \to a_s \ne 0$ as $x \to 0$. For all x sufficiently small, $\det N(x) \ne 0$ so if N does not have rank n for economy $\mathcal{E}$, $N(x)$ does for a sequence of economies $\mathcal{E}_x \to \mathcal{E}$.

(b) It is generic that

$$M = \begin{bmatrix} y_1^{*'} \\ \vdots \\ y_n^{*'} \end{bmatrix} [B_1 \cdots B_n] \{I + H_1\}^{-1} \begin{bmatrix} y_1^{*'} & & 0 \\ & \ddots & \\ 0 & & y_n^* \end{bmatrix}$$

$$= \begin{bmatrix} y_1^{*'} & & 0 \\ & \ddots & \\ 0 & & y_n^{*'} \end{bmatrix} \begin{bmatrix} B_1 \cdots B_n \\ \vdots \quad \vdots \\ B_1 \cdots B_n \end{bmatrix} \{I + H_1\}^{-1} \begin{bmatrix} y_1^* & & 0 \\ & \ddots & \\ 0 & & y_n^* \end{bmatrix}$$

has rank n. To see this, let $B(x) = B + xB\{I - xH_1 H_1\}^{-1} H_1\{I + H_1\}$, where

$$B = \begin{bmatrix} B_1 \cdots B_n \\ \vdots \quad \vdots \\ B_1 \cdots B_n \end{bmatrix}_{ln \times ln},$$

(the inverse exists for all small x), and let $M(x)$ be the matrix corresponding to M when B is replaced by $B(x)$ (note that B occurs in H_1, which becomes $H_1(x)$). Computation yields

$$B(x)\{I + H_1(x)\}^{-1} = B\{I + H_1\}^{-1}[(1-x)I + x\{I + H_1\}]$$

$$= (1-x)B\{I + H_1\}^{-1} + xB.$$

Thus $M(x) = (1-x)M + xN$ where N (the matrix from (a)) generically has rank n, and, proceeding as in (a), we see $M(x)$ has rank n for all small nonzero x. If (j3) fails for economy $\mathcal{E}$, it is satisfied for a sequence of economies $\mathcal{E}_x \to \mathcal{E}$.

We now briefly outline how, under suitable conditions, these genericity arguments can be carried out in terms of individual demand functions. Clearly only (j3) must be modified. Let the number of consumers, m, be greater than or equal to $n+l$, let $p'=(p_2, p_3, \ldots, p_l)$ $(p_1 \equiv 1)$, and let $h_i(p, w_i)$ be the ith consumer's demand, as a function of prices and wealth. Results similar to (j3) (a) and (b) can be obtained by altering the derivatives of the demand functions, evaluated at the equilibrium, prices and wealths. For any l-vector $r_i = (r_{i1}, r_{i2}, \ldots, r_{il})$, let $r^i = (r_{i2}, r_{i3}, \ldots, r_{il})'$.

First show that

$$B_j = \sum_{k=1}^{m} \theta_{kj} \begin{bmatrix} 0 \cdots 0 \\ \left[\dfrac{\partial p}{\partial \omega_k} \right] \end{bmatrix}$$

where

$$\left[\frac{\partial p}{\partial \omega_k} \right]_{(l-1) \times l}$$

$$= \left\{ \sum_{i=1}^{m} \left\{ \left[\frac{\partial h^i}{\partial p} \right] + \left(\frac{\partial h^i}{\partial w_i} \right)(\bar\omega^i)' \right\} \right\}^{-1} \left\{ \begin{bmatrix} 0 \\ \vdots \\ 0 \end{bmatrix} I \right\} - \left(\frac{\partial h^k}{\partial w_k} \right)(1, p') \right\}$$

and $\bar\omega_i = \omega_i + \sum_{j=1}^{n} \theta_{ij} y_j^*$ (for convenience call the matrix which is inverted, M).

Second, show that with suitable assumptions about the possible values of initial endowments, it is generic that $[\theta \mathcal{W}]_{m \times (n+l-1)}$ has rank $n+l-1$, where $\theta = [\theta_{ij}]_{m \times n}$ and

$$\mathcal{W} = \begin{bmatrix} (\bar\omega^1 - h^1)' \\ (\bar\omega^2 - h^2)' \\ \vdots \\ (\bar\omega^m - h^m)' \end{bmatrix}_{m \times (l-1)}$$

As in (j3), for each x there will be a different economy. Here we define new demand functions $h_i(x)$ for each x. In order to maintain the required properties of the derivatives of demand functions, we set

$$\left[\frac{\partial h^i}{\partial p}(x) \right] := \left[\frac{\partial h^i}{\partial p} \right] + \left\{ \left(\frac{\partial h^i}{\partial w_i} \right) - \left(\frac{\partial h^i}{\partial w_i}(x) \right) \right\} h^{i\prime}$$

and vary

$$\left(\frac{\partial h^i}{\partial w_i}(x) \right)$$

Cournot, Walras equilibrium

(all derivates are evaluated at equilibrium prices and wealth, which do change as x changes).

To obtain the same final result as (j3)(a), it is sufficient to find $((\partial h^i/\partial w_i)(x))$, $i = 1, 2, \ldots, m$, such that

$$\left[\left(\left(\frac{\partial h^1}{\partial w_1}(x)\right) - \left(\frac{\partial h^1}{\partial w_1}\right)\right) \cdots \left(\left(\frac{\partial h^m}{\partial w_m}(x)\right) - \left(\frac{\partial h^m}{\partial w_m}\right)\right)\right] \mathcal{W} = M(x) - M = O(x),$$

where $(M(x))^{-1} = M^{-1} + xI$. Since $\mathcal{W}$ generically has rank $l-1$ we can find $((\partial h^i/\partial w_i)(x)) \to (\partial h^i/\partial w_k)$ which satisfy the equation.

To obtain the same final result as (j3)(b), it is sufficient to find $((\partial h^i/\partial w_i)(x))$, $i = 1, 2, \ldots, m$, such that

$$\left[\left(\left(\frac{\partial h^1}{\partial w_1}(x)\right) - \left(\frac{\partial h^1}{\partial w_1}\right)\right) \cdots \left(\left(\frac{\partial h^m}{\partial w_m}(x)\right) - \left(\frac{\partial h^m}{\partial w_m}\right)\right)\right] [\theta \mathcal{W}]$$
$$= [[0]_{(l-1) \times n} S(x)_{(l-1) \times (l-1)}],$$

where $S(x)$ is a $O(x)$ matrix determined by the choice of $B(x)$ in (j3)(b). Since $[\theta \mathcal{W}]$ generically has rank $n + l - 1$, we can find $((\partial h^i/\partial w_i)(x)) \to (\partial h^i/\partial w_i)$ which satisfy the equation.

Acknowledgments

Oliver Hart, of Cambridge University, offered several detailed criticisms. Their high quality reflected his closely related research [6] and we appreciate very much his generosity. In particular, his comments led to a substantial clarification of the meaning of "free entry." John Roberts, of Northwestern University, read the manuscript, and we thank him as well for many thoughtful comments.

References

1. K. Arrow, Toward a theory of price adjustment in "The Allocation of Economic Resources: Essays in Honor of Bernard Francis Haley" (M. Abramovitz et al.), Stanford Univ. Press, Stanford, Calif. 1959.
2. Y. Balasko, Some results on uniqueness and on stability of equilibrium in general equilibrium theory, *J. Math. Econ.* 2 (1975), 95–118.
3. G. Debreu, "Theory of Value," Wiley, New York, 1959.
4. ———, Four aspects of the mathematical theory of economic equilibrium, *Proceedings of the International Congress of Mathematicians*, Vancouver, 1974.
5. J. J. Gabszewicz and J-P. Vial, Oligopoly "à la Cournot" in general equilibrium analysis, *J. Econ. Theory* 4 (1972), 381–400.
6. O. Hart, Monopolistic competition in a large economy with differentiated commodities, *Rev. Econ. Stud.* in press.
7. ———, On shareholder unanimity in large stock market economies, *Econometrica*, in press.

315

8. M. Loeve, "Probability Theory," 2nd ed. Van Nostrand, Princeton, N.J., 1960.
9. A. Mas-Colell, A model of equilibrium with differentiated commodities, *J. Math. Econ.* 2 (1975), 263-95.
10. W. Novshek, Cournot equilibrium with free entry, *Rev. Econ. Stud.*, in press.
11. J. T. Rader, Edgeworth exchange and general economic equilibrium, *Yale Econ. Essays* 4 (1964), 133-80.
12. J. Roberts and H. Sonnenschein, On the foundations of the theory of monopolistic competition, *Econometrica* 45 (1977), 101-13.
13. R. J. Ruffin, Cournot oligopoly and competitive behavior, *Rev. Econ. Stud.* 38 (1971), 493-502.
14. P. Samuelson, The monopolistic competition revolution, in "Monopolistic Competition Theory: Studies in Impact; Essays in Honor of Edward H. Chamberlin" (R. E. Kuenne, Ed.), Wiley, New York, 1968.
15. H. Sonnenschein, The utility hypothesis and market demand theory, *West. Econ. J.* 11 (1973), 404-10.
16. M. Spence, Product selection, fixed costs, and monopolistic competition, *Rev. Econ. Stud.* 43 (1976), 217-35.
17. F. A. Valentine, "Convex Sets," McGraw-Hill, New York, 1964.

CHAPTER 13

Duopoly information equilibrium:
Cournot and Bertrand

XAVIER VIVES

In a duopoly model where firms have private information about an uncertain
linear demand, it is shown that if the goods are substitutes (not) to share information is a dominant strategy for each firm in Bertrand (Cournot) competition. If
the goods are complements the result is reversed. Furthermore the following welfare results are obtained:

(i) With substitutes in Cournot equilibrium the market outcome is never optimal with respect to information sharing but it may be optimal in Bertrand competition if the products are good substitutes. With complements the market outcome
is always optimal.

(ii) Bertrand competition is more efficient than Cournot competition.

(iii) The private value of information to the firms is always positive but the
social value of information is positive in Cournot and negative in Bertrand competition. *Journal of Economic Literature* Classification Numbers: 022, 026, 611.
© 1985 Academic Press, Inc.

1. Introduction

Consider a symmetric differentiated duopoly model in which firms have
private market data about the uncertain demand. We analyze two types of
duopoly information equilibrium, Cournot and Bertrand, which emerge,
respectively, from quantity and price competition, and show that the incentives for information sharing and its welfare consequences depend
crucially on the type of competition, the nature of the goods (substitutes
or complements), and the degree of product differentiation.

Department of Economics, University of Pennsylvania, Philadelphia, PA 19104.

Xavier Vives, "Duopoly Information Equilibria: Cournot and Bertrand," *Journal of Economic Theory* 34, 1, 1984, pp. 71–94.

I am grateful to Marcus Berliant, Drew Fudenberg, Andreu Mas-Colell, Tom Palfrey, Leo
Simon, Nirvikar Singh, and participants in seminar presentations at Harvard (Business
School and Economics Department), Johns Hopkins, Pennsylvania and Wisconsin-
Madison for helpful comments on the May 1982, September 1982, and present versions
of the paper. Anonymous referees of the Journal provided useful suggestions. Domi-
nique van der Mensbrugghe took good care of the graphs. Once the manuscript of the
paper was completed some related work of Esther Gal-Or came to my attention.

317

The demand structure is linear and symmetric, and allows the goods to be substitutes, independent or complements. There is uncertainty only about the common price intercept of the demand functions. Firm i receives a signal s_i which provides an unbiased estimate of the intercept and formulates a conjecture about the behavior of its competitor which together with its beliefs about the joint distribution of the intercept and the other firm's signal given it has received s_i determines the expected profit of any action firm i may take. We assume there is a joint Normal distribution of the intercept and the signals which is common knowledge to the firms. Firms have constant and equal marginal costs and are risk neutral. In this context a Bayesian Nash equilibrium requires that firms maximize expected profit given their conjectures, and that the conjectures be right.

We suppose that there is an agency, a trade association for example, which collects market data on behalf of each firm. Firm i may allow part of its private information to be put in a common pool available to both firms. The signal a firm receives is the best estimate of the price intercept given its private information and the information in the common pool. If there is no sharing of information the error terms of the signals are independent. Pooling of information correlates them positively. A firm, when sharing market data is, at the same time, giving more information to its rival and increasing the correlation of the signals.

Since we are interested in self-enforcing pooling agreements we consider a two-stage game where first the firms, prior to the market data collection, instruct the agency how much of their private information to put in the common pool. At the second stage market research is conducted and the agency sends the signals to the firms which choose an action (quantity or price). Therefore at the second stage a Bayesian (Cournot or Bertrand) game is played. We show that the two-stage game has a unique subgame perfect equilibrium in dominant strategies at the first stage. With substitutes it involves no pooling of information in Cournot competition and complete pooling in Bertrand competition. With complements the result is reversed.

When the goods are substitutes, in Cournot competition it turns out that increases in the precision of the rival's information and increases in the correlation of the signals have adverse effects on the expected profit of the firm and we find that not to share any information is a dominant strategy. Consequently the unique subgame perfect equilibrium of the two-stage game involves no information sharing. On the other hand, in Bertrand competition the two factors mentioned above have positive effects on the expected profit of the firm and to put everything in the common pool is a dominant strategy. This is true even when a firm's information is much better than the one of its rival. When the goods are complements the situation is reversed. Since, in any case, expected profit of firm i increases with the precision of its own information, with substitutes and in Bertrand competition the firms always obtain an efficient outcome (in profit terms). This is not the case in Cournot competition, where complete pooling of information may dominate in terms of profits the no sharing arrangement if the goods are not very good substitutes and therefore the firms are in a Prisoner's Dilemma type situation since not to share any information is a dominant strategy for each firm.

Consider now a symmetric situation where firms start with the same amount of information, neglect the resource cost of information and restrict attention to the two extreme arrangements: complete pooling of information and no pooling at all. If the goods are substitutes, then in welfare terms the market outcome (the outcome of the two-stage game) is never optimal with respect to information sharing in Cournot competition since pooling always dominates no pooling in terms of expected total surplus. In Bertrand competition it may be optimal if the goods are close enough substitutes. Then pooling dominates no pooling. Otherwise no pooling is better. This contrasts with the complements case, where the market outcome is always optimal: in either Cournot or Bertrand competition it maximizes expected total surplus with respect to information sharing.

We confirm in our incomplete information setting that Bertrand competition is more efficient (in expected total surplus terms, for example) than Cournot competition although with substitute products profits may be larger in the Bertrand case if we look at the outcome of the two-stage game.

We find that the private value of information to firm i is always positive and larger or smaller in Cournot than in Bertrand competition according to whether the goods are substitutes or complements. On the other hand the social value of information is positive in Cournot and negative in Bertrand competition.

In Section 2 we survey very briefly some related literature. Section 3 describes the model without uncertainty and states some results for this case. Section 4 extends the duopoly model to an incomplete information context. Section 5 deals with the two-stage game. Section 6 examines the welfare consequences of the two extreme information sharing arrangements. Efficiency and the value of information, private and social, are considered in Section 7. Concluding remarks including extensions and policy implications of the analysis follow in the last section.

2. Relationships with the literature

Leland, in his paper about a monopoly facing an uncertain demand, states that "Although under certainty the choice of behavioral mode by a monopolistic firm is unimportant we show that it critically conditions performance under uncertainty" (Leland [8, p. 278]). This paper can be seen, in part, as an extension to a duopoly context with incomplete information of this statement.

Strategic transmission of information is dealt with in an abstract setting by Crawford and Sobel [3]. The oligopoly literature on uncertain demand and incomplete information focuses on Cournot competition with homogenous product. This is the case of the work briefly surveyed below. They also assume that demand is linear with a random intercept. Normality is assumed in all of the papers considered except the first one.

Novshek and Sonnenschein [11] consider a duopoly model with constant costs and examine the incentives for the firms to acquire and release private information. Our modeling of the signals of the firms is based on theirs.

Basar and Ho [1] consider a duopoly model with quadratic cost functions. They show existence and uniqueness of affine equilibrium strategies and that, in equilibrium, expected profits of firm i increase with the precision of its information and decrease with the precision of the rival's information.

Clarke [2] considers an n-firm oligopoly model and shows that there is never a mutual incentive for all firms in the industry to share information unless they may cooperate on strategy once information has been shared.

Harris and Lewis [6] consider a duopoly model where firms in period one decide on plant capacity before market conditions are known. In period two they choose a level of production contingent on the state of demand and their plant size. They argue that observed differences in firm size and market share may be explained by producers having access to different information at the time of their investment decisions.

Gal-Or [5] considers an oligopoly model with two stages. At the first firms observe a private signal and decide whether to reveal it to other firms and how partial this revelation will be. At the second, they choose the level of output. She shows that no information sharing is the unique Nash equilibrium of the game both when private signals are completely uncorrelated and when they are perfectly correlated.

In our model Cournot competition with a homogenous product is a particular case. Our findings for this case are consistent with those of the authors who use the Normal model.

Duopoly information equilibrium

The demand structure (with no uncertainty) we consider is a symmetric version of a duopoly model proposed by Dixit [4] the duality and welfare properties of which are analyzed in Singh and Vives [13].

3. The certainty model

In our economy we have, on the production side, a monopolistic sector with two firms, each one producing a differentiated good, and a competitive numéraire sector, and, on the consumption side, a continuum of consumers of the same type with utility function linear and separable in the numéraire good. The representative consumer maximizes $U(q_1, q_2) - \Sigma_{i=1}^2 p_i q_i$, where $q_i \geq 0$, $i = 1, 2$, are the amounts of the goods and p_i, $i = 1, 2$, their prices. U is assumed to be quadratic, (strictly) concave and symmetric in q_1 and q_2.

$$U(q_1, q_2) = \alpha(q_1 + q_2) - \tfrac{1}{2}(\beta q_1^2 + 2\gamma q_1 q_2 + \beta q_2^2) \quad \text{with } \alpha > 0, \ \beta > |\gamma| \geq 0.$$

The goods are substitutes, independent, or complements according to whether $\gamma \gtreqless 0$. When $\beta = \gamma$ the goods are perfect substitutes. When $\beta = -\gamma$, "perfect complements." γ/β goes from 1 to -1. Note that the maximization problem of the consumer may not have a solution in the perfect complements case. Inverse demands are given by

$p_1 = \alpha - \beta q_1 - \gamma q_2$ in the region of quantity space

$p_2 = \alpha - \gamma q_1 - \beta q_2$ where prices are positive.

Letting $a = \alpha/(\beta + \gamma)$, $b = \beta/(\beta^2 - \gamma^2)$, and $c = \gamma/(\beta^2 - \gamma^2)$,

$q_1 = a - bp_1 + cp_2$ in the region of price space where

$q_2 = a + cp_1 - bp_2$ quantities are positive.

Firms have constant and equal marginal costs. From now on suppose prices are net of marginal cost. The Cournot equilibrium is the Nash equilibrium in quantities and the Bertrand equilibrium the one in prices. Profits of firm i are given by $\pi_i = p_i q_i$. Notice that since π_i is symmetric in p_i and q_i and the demand structure is linear, Cournot (Bertrand) competition with substitute products is the perfect dual of Bertrand (Cournot) competition with complements and they share similar strategic properties. For example, in both cases reaction functions slope downwards (upwards). A useful corollary is that we only need to compute equilibria for one type of competition and the other follows by duality. In the Cournot case there is a unique equilibrium given by $q_i = \alpha/(2\beta + \gamma)$, $i = 1, 2$, and correspondingly a unique Bertrand equilibrium given by $p_i = a/(b - c)$, $i = 1, 2$, which equals $\alpha(\beta - \gamma)/(2\beta - \gamma)$.

321

Table 1.

	π_i	CS	TS
Cournot	$\dfrac{\beta}{(2\beta-\gamma)^2}\alpha^2$	$\dfrac{\beta+\gamma}{(2\beta+\gamma)^2}\alpha^2$	$\dfrac{3\beta+\gamma}{(2\beta+\gamma)^2}\alpha^2$
Bertrand	$\dfrac{b}{(2b-c)^2}a^2$	$\dfrac{\beta^2}{(2\beta-\gamma)^2(\beta+\gamma)}\alpha^2$	$\dfrac{\beta(3\beta-2\gamma)}{(2\beta-\gamma)^2(\beta+\gamma)}\alpha^2$

In this context total surplus (TS) is just equal to $U(q_1, q_2)$. For future reference we give the equilibrium values of profits π, consumer surplus (CS), and total surplus for both types of competition.

Note that if q is the Cournot output and p the Bertrand price then $\pi_i^c = \beta q^2$ and $\pi_i^B = bp^2$, $i = 1, 2$, so that the profit formulae are perfectly dual. This is not the case for the other formulae. For example, (see Table 1) the dual of $(\beta+\gamma)\alpha^2/(2\beta+\gamma)^2$ would be $(b-c)a^2/(2b-c)^2$ which equals $(\beta-\gamma)^2\alpha^2/(2\beta-\gamma)^2(\beta+\gamma)$ and not $\beta^2\alpha^2/(2\beta-\gamma)^2(\beta+\gamma)$. This is because the CS and TS functions do not treat prices and quantities symmetrically.

Note that when the goods are perfect substitutes ($\beta = \gamma$) the Bertrand price and profits are zero and we have the efficient outcome (price equal marginal cost). When the goods are perfect complements the Cournot consumer surplus is zero and the Bertrand magnitudes are not defined since at the Bertrand prices the consumer demands infinite quantities.

The following proposition, the proof of which is in Singh and Vives [13], states that Bertrand competition is more efficient than Cournot competition. In all the propositions that follow we assume, unless otherwise stated, that $\beta > |\gamma|$, that is, we forget about the two extreme cases.

Proposition 1. *Consumer surplus and total surplus are larger in Bertrand than in Cournot competition except when the goods are independent, in which case they are equal. Profits are larger, equal or smaller in Cournot than in Bertrand competition according to whether the goods are substitutes, independent or complements.*

The intuition behind the proposition is simple. Firms have less capacity to raise prices above marginal cost in Bertrand competition because the perceived elasticity of demand of a firm when taking as given the price of the rival is larger than that which the same firm perceives when taking the quantity of the rival as given. The result is that in Bertrand competition and in equilibrium firms quote lower prices than the Cournot ones. This

322

is always good for consumers. For firms it is bad if the goods are substitutes since low prices mean low profits; if the goods are complements the situation is reversed, to increase profits firms have to lower prices to gain market.

4. The uncertainty model

Consider the model advanced in the last section but now with α, the demand intercept, being a random variable normally distributed with mean $\bar{\alpha}$ and variance $V(\alpha)$. Firm i receives a signal s_i which consists of α plus some noise ϵ_i, $s_i = \alpha + \epsilon_i$, $i = 1, 2$. We assume that the error terms (ϵ_1, ϵ_2) follow a bivariate normal distribution, independent of α, with zero means and covariance matrix $\left| \begin{smallmatrix} v_1 & \sigma_{12} \\ \sigma_{12} & v_2 \end{smallmatrix} \right|$, with $v_i \geq \sigma_{12} \geq 0$, $i = 1, 2$. All this is common knowledge to the firms. Given these assumptions, $E(\alpha \mid s_i) = (1 - t_i)\bar{\alpha} + t_i s_i$ and $E(s_j \mid s_i) = (1 - d_i)\bar{\alpha} + d_i s_i$, where $t_i = V(\alpha)/(V(\alpha) + v_i)$ and $d_i = (V(\alpha) + \sigma_{12})/(V(\alpha) + v_i)$, $i = 1, 2$, $i \neq j$. Note that $1 \geq d_i \geq t_i \geq 0$, so that both conditional expectations are convex combinations of $\bar{\alpha}$ and the received signal s_i. We say that signal s gives more precise information about α than signal s' if its mean squared prediction error is smaller, i.e., if $E\{\alpha - E(\alpha \mid s)\}^2 < E\{\alpha - E(\alpha \mid s')\}^2$. This is equivalent to saying that the variance of the error term of signal s is smaller than the one for s'. Therefore as v_i ranges from 0 to ∞ the signal goes from being perfectly informative to being not informative at all and at the same time t_i ranges from 1 to 0. When the information is perfect, $E(\alpha \mid s_i) = s_i$; when there is no information, $E(\alpha \mid s_i) = \bar{\alpha}$.

A strategy for a firm is a Borel measurable function that specifies an action, price or quantity, for each possible signal the firm may receive. Firms are assumed to be risk neutral. Each firm makes a conjecture about the opponent's strategy. A Bayesian Nash equilibrium[1] is then a pair of strategies and a pair of conjectures such that (a) each firm strategy is a best response to its conjecture about the behavior of the rival and (b) the conjectures are right.

Cournot equilibrium

In the Cournot game, firms set quantities and a strategy for firm i specifies a quantity for each signal the firm may receive. We show that there is a unique equilibrium with linear (affine, to be precise) strategies.[2]

---

[1] See Harsanyi [7].

[2] Note that given our normality, assumption α and the signals may take negative values. Firms are constrained to choose positive prices and quantities. For convenience we ignore this and, given the firm's strategies that we derive, we can get negative prices and

Proposition 2. *The unique Bayesian equilibrium of the Cournot game is* $(\sigma_1^*(\cdot), \sigma_2^*(\cdot))$, *where* $\sigma_i^*(s_i) = A + B_i t_i (s_i - \bar{\alpha})$ *with* $A = \bar{\alpha}/(2\beta + \gamma)$ *and* $B_i = (2\beta - \gamma d_j)/(4\beta^2 - \gamma^2 d_1 d_2)$, $i = 1, 2$, $j \neq i$.

Proof. We first show that if firm 1 uses $\sigma_1^*(s_1) = A + B_1 t_1 (s_1 - \bar{\alpha})$ the unique best response for firm 2 is to use $A + B_2 t_2 (s_2 - \bar{\alpha})$. To see this notice that the expected profit of firm 2 choosing the quantity q_2 given the signal s_2 if firm 1 uses $\sigma_1^*(s_1)$ is

$$E(\alpha - \gamma \sigma_1^*(s_1) - \beta q_2 | s_2) q_2.$$

So the optimal choice for firm 2 is

$$q_2^* = \frac{1}{2\beta} E(\alpha - \gamma \sigma_1^*(s_1) | s_2) = \frac{1}{2\beta} (E(\alpha | s_2) - \gamma E(\sigma_1^*(s_1) | s_2))$$

which, after some computations, equals $A + B_2 t_2 (s_2 - \bar{\alpha})$.

Uniqueness follows similarly as in Basar and Ho [1] or Clarke [2], using the fact that $\beta \geq |\gamma|$. ∎

Remark 4.1. Suppose $v_i = v$, $i = 1, 2$, when the firms have no information at all. For $v = \infty$, the equilibrium strategy is constant and equal to $\bar{\alpha}/(2\beta + \gamma)$, the Cournot outcome when there is no uncertainty. As the information the firms receive improves, i.e., as v declines and t goes towards one, the slope of the linear strategy increases till it reaches $1/(2\beta + \gamma)$ when $t = 1$. Then $\sigma_1^*(s_1) = s_1/(2\beta + \gamma)$, which is the full information outcome.

Remark 4.2. The expected Cournot output always equals the Cournot certainty output (with $\bar{\alpha}$). Since $\sigma_i^*(s_i) = A + B_i t_i (s_i - \bar{\alpha})$ and $E s_i = \bar{\alpha}$, $E(\sigma_i^*(s_i)) = A$, which equals $\bar{\alpha}/(2\beta + \gamma)$. Note that when $s_i = \bar{\alpha}$, $\sigma_i^*(s_i) = A$ so that equilibrium strategies always go through the point $(s_i, q_i) = (\bar{\alpha}, \bar{\alpha}/(2\beta + \gamma))$.

We would like to know how expected profits in equilibrium are affected by variations in the precision and correlation of the signals the firms receive. Expected profits in equilibria are easy to compute. $E(\pi_1 | s_1) = E((\alpha - \gamma \sigma_2^*(s_2) - \beta \sigma_1^*(s_1)) | s_1) \sigma_1^*(s_1) = [E(\alpha - \gamma \sigma_2^*(s_2) | s_1) - \beta \sigma_1^*(s_1)] \sigma_1^*(s_1)$, but $E(\alpha - \gamma \sigma_2^*(s_2) | s_1) = 2\beta \sigma_1^*(s_1)$ according to the first order conditions, therefore $E(\pi_1 | s_1) = \beta (\sigma_1^*(s_1))^2$ and $E\pi_1 = \beta E(\sigma_1^*(s_1))^2$. Substituting in

Footnote 2 *(cont.)*
outputs for certain combinations of α and the signals. The probability of such an event can be made arbitrarily small by appropriately choosing the variances of the model.

Duopoly information equilibrium

$\sigma_1^*(s_1) = A + B_1 t_1 (s_1 - \bar{\alpha})$ we get $E\pi_1 = \beta(A^2 + B_1^2 t_1 V(\alpha))$. The slope of the linear strategy $\sigma_1^*(s_1)$, $B_1 t_1$, is the channel through which changes in the precision and correlation of the signals get transmitted to expected profits.

Lemma 1. *The slope of $\sigma_i^*(\cdot)$*

    (a)   *increases with the precision of the information of firm i,*

    (b)   *decreases, is unaffected, or increases with the precision of its competitor's information and with the correlation of the signals according to whether the goods are substitutes, independent or complements.*

Proof. The slope in question is $B_1 t_1 = ((2\beta - \gamma d_2)/(4\beta^2 - \gamma^2 d_1 d_2)) t_1$. Noting that $d_i = t_i(1 + (\sigma_{12}/V(\alpha)))$ and $t_i = V(\alpha)/(V(\alpha) + v_i)$, $i = 1, 2$, and using the fact that $d_i \leq 1$, $i = 1, 2$, we get by inspection that $B_1 t_1$ decreases with v_1 and, upon differentiating, that sign $\partial B_1 t_1 / \partial v_2 = $ sign $-\gamma = $ sign $\partial B_1 t_1 / \partial \sigma_{12}$. ∎

    The intuition behind (a) is clear. As firm 1 gets better information it trusts more the signal received and responds more to divergences of s_i and $\bar{\alpha}$ (see Remark 1). This is independent of the nature of the products. To understand (b) note that the covariance between the signals is $V(\alpha) + \sigma_{12}$, which is always positive and increasing in σ_{12} since $\sigma_{12} \geq 0$. Suppose the goods are substitutes. If firm 1 observes a high signal, $s_1 > \bar{\alpha}$ (recall that the signals are positively correlated), this means that probably firm 2 has observed a high signal too. Now, firm 2, according to (a), will produce less if v_2 is high than if it is low. The optimal thing to do for firm 1 is to produce a high output since in Cournot competition with substitutes if you expect the competitor to produce low you want to produce high. Therefore $\partial B_1 t_1 / \partial v_2 > 0$ in this case. To evaluate the impact of an increased correlation in the signals we can reason similarly. If firm 1 observes a high signal, $s_1 > \bar{\alpha}$, it will produce less if σ_{12} is high than if it is low since in the former case the probability that the competitor has received a high signal too is larger and if firm 1 expects a high output of the competitor it has an incentive to reduce its own output. Therefore $\partial B_1 t_1 / \partial \sigma_{12} < 0$.

    We are now ready to state

Proposition 3. *In equilibrium, the expected profit of firm i*

    (a)   *increases with the precision of its own information,*

    (b)   *decreases, is unaffected, or increases with the precision of the competitor's information and with the correlation of the signals according to whether the goods are substitutes, independent or complements.*

Proof. Recall that $E\pi_1 = \beta(A^2 + B_1^2 t_1 V(\alpha))$, then

    (a) B_1 and t_1 decrease with v_1.
    (b)   Sign $\partial E\pi_1/\partial v_2 = $ sign $\partial B_1/\partial v_2 = $ sign γ according to Lemma 1.
    (c)   Sign $\partial E\pi_1/\partial \sigma_{12} = $ sign $\partial B_1/\partial \sigma_{12} = $ sign $-\gamma$ according to Lemma 1.

($\gamma > 0$ for substitutes and $\gamma < 0$ for complements.)   ■

Bertrand equilibrium

In the Bertrand game firms set prices and a strategy for firm i specifies a price for each signal the firm may receive. The duality argument gives us the Bertrand equilibrium strategies. Identifying α with α, β with b, γ with $-c$, and s_i with $\hat{s}_i$, where $\hat{s}_i = s_i/(\beta + \gamma)$, we get

Proposition 2a. *The unique Bayesian equilibrium of the Bertrand game is $(\tau_1^*(\cdot), \tau_2^*(\cdot))$, where $\tau_i^*(\hat{s}_i) = \hat{A} + \hat{B}_i t_i (\hat{s}_i - \bar{a})$ with $\hat{A} = \bar{a}/(2b - c)$ and $\hat{B}_i = (2b + cd_j)/(4b^2 - c^2 d_1 d_2)$, $i = 1, 2$, $j \neq i$.*

Remarks similar to Remarks 1 and 2 apply to the Bertrand case and Lemma 1 and Proposition 2 hold replacing $\sigma_i^*(\cdot)$ by $\tau_i^*(\cdot)$ and exchanging substitutes for complements.

5. The two-stage game

In Section 4 we assumed firms received signals satisfying certain properties. We provide now, along the lines of Novshek and Sonnenschein, a rationale for these signals.

Suppose firm i starts with an n_i independent observation sample $(r_{i1}, \ldots, r_{in_i})$ satisfying $r_{ik} = \alpha + u_{ik}$, where the u_{ik}'s are i.i.d. normal with mean zero and variance σ_u^2 and independent of α. Firm i decides to put $\lambda_i n_i$, $0 \leq \lambda_i \leq 1$, observations in a common pool. The signal firm 1 receives, s_1, is then the best (minimum variance unbiased) estimate of α based on $n_1 + \lambda_2 n_2$ observations, its own sample plus the observations put in the common pool by firm 2. This is just the average, $s_1 = \alpha + (1/(n_1 + \lambda_2 n_2))(\sum_{k-1}^{n_1} u_{1k} + \sum_{k=1}^{\lambda_2 n_2} u_{2k})$. With this information structure the error terms of the signals (ϵ_1, ϵ_2) follow a bivariate normal distribution with zero means and covariance matrix $\begin{vmatrix} v_1 & \sigma_{12} \\ \sigma_{12} & v_2 \end{vmatrix}$, where $v_i = \sigma_u^2/(n_i + \lambda_j n_j)$, $i = 1, 2$, $j \neq i$ and $\sigma_{12} = ((\lambda_1 n_1 + \lambda_2 n_2)/(n_1 + \lambda_2 n_2)(n_2 + \lambda_1 n_1))\sigma_u^2$. Note that

Duopoly information equilibrium

$v_i \geq \sigma_{12} \geq 0$, $i = 1, 2$. λ_i is, thus, the proportion of observations firm i puts in the common pool. $\lambda_i \in \Lambda_i$, where $\Lambda_i = \{0, 1/n_i, \ldots, (n_i - 1)/n_i, 1\}$, $i = 1, 2$. When $\lambda_1 = \lambda_2 = 0$ there is no pooling of information, $v_i = \sigma_u^2/n_i$, $i = 1, 2$, and $\sigma_{12} = 0$. When $\lambda_1 = \lambda_2 = 1$ there is complete pooling and $v_i = \sigma_{12} = \sigma_u^2/(n_1 + n_2)$, $i = 1, 2$. Information sharing has two effects: it decreases the variance of the error terms and it increases their correlation (and therefore the correlation of the signals).

Lemma 2.

    (a) v_i decreases with λ_j, $j \neq i$, and is independent of λ_i.
    (b) σ_{12} increases with λ_i if $\lambda_j < 1$, $i = 1, 2$, $j \neq i$.

Otherwise is independent of λ_i.

Proof. (a) By inspection.
    (b) $\sigma_{12} = ((\lambda_1 n_1 + \lambda_2 n_2)/(n_1 + \lambda_2 n_2)(n_2 + \lambda_1 n_1))\sigma_u^2$. Differentiating with respect to λ, one gets $\partial \sigma_{12}/\partial \lambda_1 = ((1 - \lambda_2)n_1 n_2/(n_1 + \lambda_2 n_2)(n_2 + \lambda_1 n_1)^2)\sigma_u^2$. (In fact, λ_i is discrete but this does not matter here.) ∎

Consider now a two-stage game where first firms decide how much information are they going to put in the common pool. We suppose there is an agency, a trade association, for example, that collects an $n_1 + n_2$ observation sample and that forms the signals according to the instructions of the firms, the λ_i's. At the first stage, then, firm i picks independently $\lambda_i \in \Lambda_i$ and communicates it to the agency. At the second stage, firms, knowing the selected pair (λ_1, λ_2), play the Bayesian (Cournot or Bertrand) game. For each pair (λ_1, λ_2) we have a well-defined (proper) subgame. We are interested in subgame perfect Nash equilibria of the two-stage game, where equilibrium strategies form a (Bayesian) Nash equilibrium in every subgame (see Selten [12]).

Lemma 3. *In Cournot competition with substitutes (or Bertrand with complements) expected profits of firm i decrease with λ_i. In Bertrand competition with substitutes (or Cournot with complements) expected profits of firm i increase with λ_i and with λ_j, $j \neq i$. If the goods are independent $E\pi_i$ are increasing with λ_j and unaffected by λ_i, $j \neq i$, $i = 1, 2$.*

Proof. Consider the Cournot case. Increases in λ_i give better information to firm j, $j \neq i$, and increase (maybe weakly) the correlation of the firm's signals. If the goods are substitutes, according to Proposition 3, both effects decrease $E\pi_i$. If the goods are complements both effects increase $E\pi_i$. Increases in λ_j, $j \neq i$, give better information to firm i and

327

increase (maybe weakly) the correlation of the firm's signals. If the goods are complements both effects increase $E\pi_i$. Note that if they are substitutes the second decreases $E\pi_i$ so that nothing can be said a priori except if $\lambda_i = 1$. Then the covariance of the signals cannot be increased and the first effect dominates. The Bertrand case, as usual, follows by the duality argument. ∎

According to Lemma 3 in Cournot competition with substitutes to set $\lambda_i = 0$ is a dominant strategy for firm i since $E\pi_i$ decreases with λ_i whatever the value of λ_j, $j \neq i$. Symmetrically, in Bertrand competition to put all the information in the common pool is a dominant strategy for firm i. If the goods are independent $E\pi_i$ is unaffected by λ_i, $i = 1, 2$. Therefore we have established the following proposition.

Proposition 4. *Suppose the goods are not independent. Then the two-stage game has a unique subgame perfect equilibrium in dominant strategies at the first stage. With substitutes it involves no pooling of information in Cournot competition and complete pooling in Bertrand competition. With complements the result is reversed.*

Remark 5.1. If the goods are independent any pair (λ_1, λ_2), $\lambda_i \in \Lambda_i$, $i = 1, 2$, is an equilibrium.

Remark 5.2. If the goods are perfect substitutes Proposition 4 holds for Cournot competition since in this case Lemma 3 holds as well. In Bertrand competition prices and expected profits are zero independently of the pooling decisions of the firms. Any pair (λ_1, λ_2) is an equilibrium in this case.

Remark 5.3. Note that in Bertrand competition with substitute products to pool information is a dominant strategy for firm i even if the firm has much better information than its competitor, i.e., even if n_i is much larger than n_j, $j \neq i$.

Remark 5.4. Suppose the goods are substitutes. Note that given that at the second stage a Bayesian Bertrand equilibrium is reached the firms obtain an efficient outcome by completely pooling their information since $E\pi_i$ is increasing in λ_i and λ_j, $j \neq i$, $i = 1, 2$, in this situation. When the second stage is Cournot the firms, by choosing noncooperatively not to share any information, may not reach an efficient outcome. If the products are not very good substitutes complete pooling may dominate, in profits terms, the no pooling arrangement.

328

Table 2. *Equilibrium strategies for firm* i

	NP	P
C	$\dfrac{\bar{\alpha}}{2\beta+\gamma}+\dfrac{t}{2\beta+\gamma t}(s_i-\bar{\alpha})$	$\dfrac{1}{2\beta+\gamma}(\bar{\alpha}+\bar{t}(s_i-\bar{\alpha}))$
B	$\dfrac{\bar{a}}{2b-c}+\dfrac{t}{2b-ct}(\hat{s}_i-\bar{a})$	$\dfrac{1}{2b-c}(\bar{a}+\bar{t}(\hat{s}_i-\bar{a}))$

Table 3. *Equilibrium expected profits for firm* i

	NP	P
C	$\beta\!\left(\dfrac{\bar{\alpha}^2}{(2\beta+\gamma)^2}+\dfrac{t}{(2\beta+\gamma t)^2}V(\alpha)\right)$	$\dfrac{\beta}{(2\beta+\gamma)^2}(\bar{\alpha}^2+\bar{t}V(\alpha))$
B	$b\!\left(\dfrac{\bar{a}^2}{(2b-c)^2}+\dfrac{t}{(2b-ct)^2}V(a)\right)$	$\dfrac{b}{(2b-c)^2}(\bar{a}^2+\bar{t}V(a))$

The following proposition compares the profits for the firms under the two extreme information sharing situations when each firm has a sample of size n. (For the rest of the paper we are going to restrict attention to these cases.) Let $v=\sigma_u^2/n$, $t=V(\alpha)/(V(\alpha)+v)$ and $\bar{t}=V(\alpha)/(V(\alpha)+v/2)$. When no information is pooled $v_j=v$, $i=1,2$, and $\sigma_{12}=0$ so that $t_i=d_i=t$, $i=1,2$. With complete pooling, $v_i=\sigma_{12}=v/2$, $i=1,2$, so that $d_i=1$ and $t_i=\bar{t}$, $i=1,2$.

First, we give expressions for equilibrium strategies and expected profits of the four possible combinations of Cournot C, or Bertrand B; pooling P, or not pooling NP. Using Proposition 2 and the expressions for expected profits we get Tables 2 and 3.

Let $E\pi_i^P$ and $E\pi_i^{NP}$ denote, respectively, expected profits of firm i with complete pooling and with no pooling of information.

Proposition 5. *Let $v>0$, then, in equilibrium,*

(a) *in Bertrand competition with substitute products (or in Cournot with complements), $E\pi_i^P>E\pi_i^{NP}$, $i=1,2$;*

(b) *in Cournot competition with substitutes (or in Bertrand with complements), letting $\mu=\gamma/\beta$,*

(i) *If $|\mu|\geq 2(\sqrt{2}-1)$ then $E\pi_i^{NP}>E\pi_i^P$, $i=1,2$.*
(ii) *If $2(\sqrt{2}-1)>|\mu|>\frac{2}{3}$ then $E\pi_i^P\gtrless E\pi_i^{NP}$ iff*

329

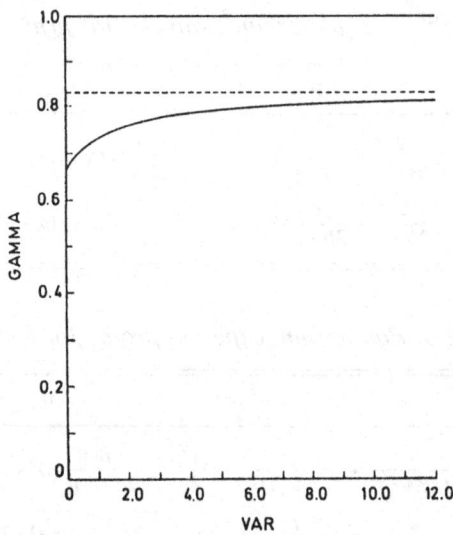

Figure 1. Cournot with substitutes. Expected profits. $E\pi_i^P$ greater (smaller) than $E\pi_i^{NP}$ below (above) the continuous line [GAMMA $\equiv \gamma/\beta$, VAR $\equiv v/V(\alpha)$].

$$\frac{v}{V(\alpha)} \underset{<}{\overset{>}{\gtrless}} \frac{4-4\mu-3\mu^2}{\mu^2+4\mu-4}, \quad i=1,2.$$

(iii) If $|\mu| \leq \frac{2}{3}$ then $E\pi_i^P > E\pi_i^{NP}$, $i=1,2$.

(See Figure 1.)

Remark 5.5. When the goods are perfect substitutes the proposition applies for the Cournot case. In the Bertrand case $E\pi_i$ are zero with pooling or no pooling.

Proof. (a) Follows from Lemma 3.

(b) We only have to compare $t/(2\beta+\gamma t)^2$ with $\bar{t}/(2\beta+\gamma)^2$ in the Cournot case and $t/(2b-ct)^2$ with $\bar{t}/(2b-c)^2$ in the Bertrand case. The second follows from the first, noting that c is negative for complements and $\gamma/\beta = c/b$. After some computations, in the Cournot case, we have that $E\pi_i^{NP} \gtreqless E\pi_i^P$ iff $3\mu^2+4\mu-4 \gtreqless (v/V(\alpha))(4-4\mu-\mu^2)$. The values $\frac{2}{3}$ and $2(\sqrt{2}-1)$ are, respectively, the unique roots in the $[0,1]$ interval of the LHS and RHS. For $\mu < \frac{2}{3}$ the LHS is negative and the RHS positive. For $2(\sqrt{2}-1) > \mu > \frac{2}{3}$ both are positive. For $\mu > 2(\sqrt{2}-1)$ the LHS is positive and the RHS negative. ∎

330

The proposition has an easy intuitive explanation. Complete pooling of information cuts the variance of the error terms of the signals the firms receive by half and correlates perfectly the strategies of the firms. In Cournot competition with substitutes the second effect is bad for expected profits, the first, the joint decrease in variance, it is easily seen to be good by differentiating $E\pi_i$ with respect to v.

Which effect dominates depends on the degree of product differentiation. If the goods are close substitutes, i.e., γ/β is close to one, the correlation effect is going to prevail since it is weighted precisely by γ/β and conversely if the goods are not good substitutes. There is also an intermediate region where it pays to pool information if the precision of the firm's information is poor enough. Note that if the goods are perfect substitutes, $\beta = \gamma = 1$, it never pays to share information. (See Figure 1.) In view of Proposition 5 we see that when the goods are not very good substitutes, in Cournot competition, the firms face a Prisoner's Dilemma type situation since not to pool any information is a dominant strategy for each firm but by sharing information the firms would increase their profits.

6. Welfare

We analyze the welfare consequences, in terms of expected consumer surplus ECS and expected total surplus ETS of two extreme situations, no sharing and complete sharing of information, when the firms have the same information to start with. Tables 4 and 5 give the equilibrium values of ECS and ETS in the four possible cases we are considering. Note that the Cournot and Bertrand expressions are not "dual." To compute them note that the expected value of any equilibrium strategy is equal to the equilibrium strategy when $\bar{\alpha}$ is known to obtain with certainty (see Remark 4.1). All the expressions decompose into two parts: one analogous to the certainty expression with $\bar{\alpha}$ (see Section 3) and another obtained by taking deviations from the mean $\bar{\alpha}$.

Before making any welfare comparisons we will see how variations in the precision of the firm's information have very different welfare effects in Cournot or Bertrand competition. Note that we consider here exogenous variations in v, i.e., variations induced not by information sharing decisions but by changes in the size of the sample firms receive (equal by assumption for both firms) or by changes in σ_u^2.

Proposition 6. *If firms pool their information, ECS and ETS increase (decrease) with the precision of the information in Cournot (Bertrand) competition. If firms do not pool their information the same holds except*

331

Table 4. Expected consumer surplus

	NP	P
C	$\dfrac{\beta+\gamma}{(2\beta+\gamma)^2}\bar{\alpha}^2 + \dfrac{\beta+\gamma t}{(2\beta+\gamma t)^2}tV(\alpha)$	$\dfrac{\beta+\gamma}{(2\beta+\gamma)^2}(\bar{\alpha}^2+\bar{t}V(\alpha))$
B	$\dfrac{\beta^2}{(2\beta-\gamma)^2(\beta+\gamma)}\bar{\alpha}^2 + \dfrac{\beta[\beta(4-3t)-\gamma t(1-t)]}{(2\beta-\gamma t)^2(\beta+\gamma t)}V(\alpha)$	$\dfrac{\beta^2\bar{\alpha}^2+[(2\beta-\gamma)^2-(\beta-\gamma)(3\beta-\gamma)\bar{t}]V(\alpha)}{(2\beta-\gamma)^2(\beta+\gamma)}$

Table 5. Expected total surplus

	NP	P
C	$\dfrac{3\beta+\gamma}{(2\beta+\gamma)^2}\bar{\alpha}^2 + \dfrac{3\beta+\gamma t}{(2\beta+\gamma t)^2}tV(\alpha)$	$\dfrac{3\beta+\gamma}{(2\beta+\gamma)^2}(\bar{\alpha}^2+\bar{t}V(\alpha))$
B	$\dfrac{\beta(3\beta-2\gamma)}{(2\beta-\gamma)^2(\beta+\gamma)}\bar{\alpha}^2 + \dfrac{\beta[\beta(4-t)-t(3-t)]}{(2\beta-\gamma t)^2(\beta+\gamma t)}V(\alpha)$	$\dfrac{\beta(3\beta-2\gamma)\bar{\alpha}^2+[(2\beta-\gamma)^2-(\beta-\gamma)^2\bar{t}]V(\alpha)}{(2\beta-\gamma)^2(\beta+\gamma)}$

when $(|\gamma|/\beta)\, t$ is greater (or equal) than $\frac{2}{3}$, then with complements ECS^{C} decreases (weakly), and with substitutes ETS^{B} increases (weakly), with the precision of the information.

Proof. In obvious notation, ECS_P^C and ETS_P^C increase and ECS_P^B and ETC_P^B decrease with $\bar{t}$ by inspection of the formulae in Tables 4 and 5. On the other hand, differentiating we get

$$\mathrm{Sign}\left\{\frac{\partial \mathrm{ECS}_{NP}^C}{\partial t}\right\} = \mathrm{Sign}\{2\beta + 3\gamma t\}$$

which is positive if $\dfrac{\gamma}{\beta}t > -\dfrac{2}{3}$ and nonnegative otherwise.

$$\mathrm{Sign}\left\{\frac{\partial \mathrm{ECS}_{NP}^B}{\partial t}\right\} = \mathrm{Sign}\{-(\beta - \gamma)(6\beta - \gamma t)\}$$

which is negative always.

$$\mathrm{Sign}\left\{\frac{\partial \mathrm{ETS}_{NP}^C}{\partial t}\right\} = \mathrm{Sign}\{6\beta + \gamma t\}$$

which is positive always.

$$\mathrm{Sign}\left\{\frac{\partial \mathrm{ETS}_{NP}^B}{\partial t}\right\} = \mathrm{Sign}\{(\beta - \gamma)(3\gamma t - 2\beta)\}$$

which is negative if $\dfrac{\gamma}{\beta}t < \dfrac{2}{3}$ and nonnegative otherwise. ∎

Remark 6.1. If the goods are perfect substitutes the proposition applies for the Cournot case. In the Bertrand case ECS and ETS, which are equal since $E\pi_i$ are zero, are not affected by the precision of the firm's information. This is clear since firms set prices equal to marginal cost anyway.

Proposition 7. *Let $\mu = \gamma/\beta$ and $\bar{\mu}$ be the unique root of $\mu^3 + \mu^2 - 8\mu + 4$ in the interval $[0,1]$ ($\bar{\mu} \approx 0.56$).*

In Cournot competition, pooling dominates no pooling in terms of ECS and ETS except maybe when the goods are complements. In that case:

(a) *If $|\mu| \geq 2(\sqrt{2}-1)$, then $\mathrm{ECS}_{NP} > \mathrm{ECS}_P$.*

(b) *If $2(\sqrt{2}-1) > |\mu| \geq \bar{\mu}$ then $\mathrm{ECS}_{NP} \gtreqless \mathrm{ECS}_P$ iff*

$$\frac{v}{V(\alpha)} \lesseqgtr \frac{4 + 8\mu + \mu^2 - \mu^3}{\mu^2 - 4\mu - 4}$$

(See Figure 2.)

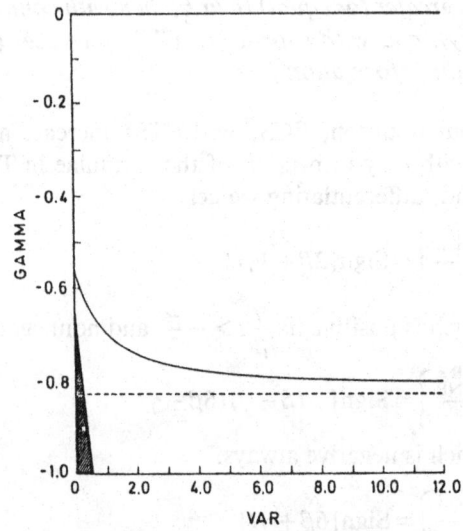

Figure 2. Cournot with complements. Expected consumer surplus. In the interior of the shaded region $\partial\text{ECS}^{NP}/\partial t > 0$. ECS^P greater (smaller) than ECS^{NP} above (below) the continuous line [GAMMA $\equiv \gamma/\beta$, VAR $\equiv v/V(\alpha)$].

In Bertrand competition, no pooling dominates pooling in terms of ECS and ETS except maybe when the goods are substitutes. In that case:

(a) *If $\mu \geq 2(\sqrt{2}-1)$ then $\text{ETS}_P > \text{ETS}_{NP}$.*
(b) *If $2(\sqrt{2}-1) > \mu \geq \bar{\mu}$, then $\text{ETS}_P \gtreqless \text{ETS}_{NP}$ iff*

$$\frac{v}{V(\alpha)} \lesseqgtr \frac{4-12\mu+9\mu^2-\mu^4}{8\mu-3\mu^2-\mu^3-4}.$$

(See Figure 3.)

Proof. Let $f_2(\mu) = 4-12\mu+9\mu^2-\mu^4$ and $f_1(\mu) = 4-8\mu+\mu^2+\mu^3$. Note that $f_2(\mu) = (1-\mu)f_1(\mu)$. It is easily seen that $\bar{\mu}$ is the unique root of f_1 in $[0,1]$ ($\bar{\mu} \approx 0.56$), so that $f_2(\bar{\mu}) = 0$. Also the unique root of $4+8\mu+\mu^2-\mu^3$ in $[-1,0]$ is $-\bar{\mu}$ since this function is equal to $f_1(-\mu)$. Let $g_2(\mu) = 8\mu-3\mu^2-\mu^3-4$ and $g_1(\mu) = \mu^2+4\mu-4$. Note that $g_2(\mu) = (1-\mu)g_1(\mu)$. The unique root of g_1 in $[0,1]$ is $2(\sqrt{2}-1)$ (which is 0.83 approximately), therefore $2(\sqrt{2}-1)$ is also a root of g_2. Now, using the formulae in Tables 4 and 5 and after some computations we obtain,

(i) $\text{ECS}_P^C \gtreqless \text{ECS}_{NP}^C$ iff $f_1(-\mu) \gtreqless (v/V(\alpha))g_1(-\mu)$. For $\mu \geq -\bar{\mu}$ the LHS is nonnegative and the RHS negative. For $-\bar{\mu} > \mu > 2(1-\sqrt{2})$ both are

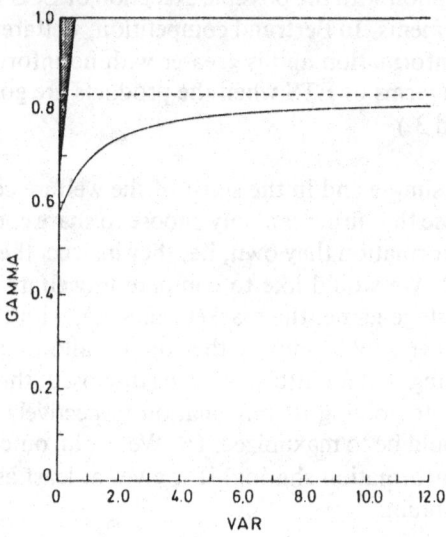

Figure 3. Bertrand with substitutes. Expected total surplus. In the interior of the shaded region $\partial \text{ETS}^{\text{NP}}/\partial t > 0$. ETS^{P} greater (smaller) than ETS^{NP} above (below) the continuous line [GAMMA $\equiv \gamma/\beta$, VAR $= v/V(\alpha)$].

negative. For $\mu \leq 2(1-\sqrt{2})$ the LHS is negative and the RHS is nonnegative.

(ii) $\text{ETS}_{\text{P}}^{\text{C}} \gtreqless \text{ETS}_{\text{NP}}^{\text{C}}$ iff $12 - 5\mu^2 - \mu^3 \gtreqless (v/V(\alpha))(3\mu^2 + 4\mu - 12)$. The LHS is always positive and the RHS is always negative. (Recall $|\mu| < 1$.)

(iii) $\text{ECS}_{\text{NP}}^{\text{B}} \gtreqless \text{ECS}_{\text{P}}^{\text{B}}$ iff $(12 + 3\mu^3 - 8\mu - 7\mu^2)(v/V(\alpha)) \gtreqless \mu^4 + 5\mu^2 + 12\mu - 6\mu^3 - 12$. The LHS is always positive and the RHS always negative. (Recall $|\mu| < 1$.)

(iv) $\text{ETS}_{\text{P}}^{\text{B}} \gtreqless \text{ETS}_{\text{NP}}^{\text{B}}$ iff $g_2(\mu)(v/V(\alpha)) \gtreqless f_2(\mu)$. For $\mu \leq \bar{\mu}$, the LHS is negative and the RHS nonnegative. For $\bar{\mu} < \mu < 2(\sqrt{2} - 1)$ both are negative. Otherwise the LHS is nonnegative and the RHS negative. (Note that $\text{ECS}_{\text{NP}}^{\text{B}} = \text{ECS}_{\text{P}}^{\text{B}}$ and $\text{ETS}_{\text{NP}}^{\text{B}} = \text{ETS}_{\text{P}}^{\text{B}}$ when $\mu = 1$.) ∎

Remark 6.2. The proposition applies when the goods are perfect substitutes ($\mu = 1$) if Cournot competition prevails. In Bertrand competition pooling makes no difference in ECS or ETS. Prices equal marginal cost and consumers get the maximum surplus they can get in either case.

Remark 6.3. The exceptions in Proposition 6 and 7 are when we consider ECS^{C} or ETS^{B}. In Cournot competition, welfare, in terms of ECS or ETS, increases with the precision of information and is greater with

335

pooling of information with the possible exception of ECS when the goods are strong complements. In Bertrand competition, welfare decreases with the precision of information and is greater with no information sharing except possibly in terms of ETS when the products are good substitutes. (See Figures 2 and 3.)

To keep things simple and in the spirit of the welfare comparisons we are making suppose that firms can only choose to share completely or not share at all the information they own, i.e. they instruct the testing agency $\lambda_i \in \{0, 1\}$, $i = 1, 2$. We would like to compare in welfare terms the outcome of the two-stage game, the market outcome, with the outcome an authority or planner could induce either by not allowing the agency to form or by requiring that all information be disclosed, thus enforcing no pooling or complete pooling of information respectively. The objective of the planner would be to maximize ETS. We say an outcome is optimal (with respect to information sharing) if it gives at least as much ETS as the planner can obtain.

Proposition 8. *If the goods are complements the market outcome is always optimal. If the goods are substitutes, in Cournot competition the market outcome is never optimal, in Bertrand competition it is optimal if the goods are close to perfect substitutes or if they are moderately substitutes and the precision of the information is low.*

Proof. For complements. In Cournot competition the market outcome involves pooling, $\lambda_i = 1$, $i = 1, 2$, and $\text{ETS}_{NP}^C < \text{ETS}_P^C$ from Proposition 7. In Bertrand, we have $\text{ETS}_{NP}^B > \text{ETS}_P^B$ and the market outcome involves no pooling, $\lambda_i = 0$, $i = 1, 2$.

For substitutes. In Cournot competition the market outcome is NP, but $\text{ETS}_{NP}^C < \text{ETS}_P^C$. In Bertrand competition the market outcome is P and $\text{ETS}_P^B > \text{ETS}_{NP}^B$ under (a) and (b) of Proposition 7. ∎

Remark 6.4. If the goods are independent there are four equilibria in the two-stage game and therefore four possible market outcomes. Discarding the nonsymmetric ones, we will have that one of the remaining is going to be optimal in each type of competition. (The pooling one in Cournot and the no pooling one in Bertrand.)

Remark 6.5. If the goods are perfect substitutes Proposition 8 holds. In Bertrand competition any pooling arrangement is self-enforcing (i.e., it can be a market outcome) and optimal since in that case ETS is constant over arrangements.

7. Efficiency and the value of information

In this section we extend Proposition 1 to the incomplete information case, confirming thus that "Bertrand competition is more efficient than Cournot competition," and we compare the private and social value of information under the two types of competition.

Proposition 9. *In welfare terms, either ECS or ETS, Bertrand is strictly better than Cournot. Furthermore, $E\pi_i^C \gtreqless E\pi_i^B$ according to whether the goods are substitutes, independent or complements. This holds comparing either the no pooling subgames or the complete pooling ones.*

Proof. First note that it is sufficient to show it when $\bar{\alpha} = 0$. If $\bar{\alpha} > 0$, then all the expressions have "certainty" terms (with $\bar{\alpha}$) which we can rank according to the certainty proposition. Let then $\bar{\alpha} = 0$. Using Tables 3–4 with $\bar{\alpha} = 0$, the relevant inequalities follow noting that $|\gamma|/\beta$, t, and $\tilde{t}$ are between zero and one. ∎

Remark 7.1. Notice that when the goods are independent and we have two monopolies expected profits are equal with price and quantity setting but, contrary to the certainty case, ECS and ETS are larger with price setting. Thus under uncertainty and incomplete information consumers and society have another reason to prefer price over quantity setting apart from the traditional one that firms have less monopoly power under Bertrand competition.

Remark 7.2. Bertrand competition is more efficient than Cournot competition (in terms of ETS) even if we look at the outcomes of the two-stage game. Take the substitutes case. With Cournot the market outcome involves no pooling and with Bertrand, pooling. From Propositions 7 and 9 we know that $\text{ETS}_P^B > \text{ETS}_P^C > \text{ETS}_{NP}^C$, so that $\text{ETS}_P^B > \text{ETS}_{NP}^C$. It may happen though that Bertrand profits be larger than the Cournot ones. From Table 3 we get $E\pi_{NP}^C = \beta((\bar{\alpha}^2/(2\beta+\gamma)^2) + (t/(2\beta+\gamma t)^2) V(\alpha))$ and $E\pi_P^B = (b/(2b-c)^2)(\bar{a}^2 + \tilde{t}V(a))$. We know that the "certainty" term (involving $\bar{\alpha}$ or $\bar{a}$) will be larger in the Cournot case, but not very much if the products are very differentiated (γ small). The other term may be larger in the Bertrand case, and make up the difference, if the information of the firms is not very precise ($v/V(\alpha)$ not close to zero), and if there is enough basic uncertainty ($V(\alpha)$ not too small relative to $\bar{\alpha}$). For example, if $\gamma = 0.1$, $\bar{\alpha} = 10$, $V(\alpha) = v = 1$, then $E\pi_P^B > E\pi_{NP}^C$. Similarly, if the goods are complements one sees immediately that $\text{ETS}_{NP}^B > \text{ETS}_P^C$ but

337

Table 6. *Private value of information
to firm* i

	P	NP
C	$\dfrac{\beta}{(2\beta+\gamma t)^2}\,tV(\alpha)$	$\dfrac{\beta}{(2\beta+\gamma)^2}\,(\tilde{t}-t)V(\alpha)$
B	$\dfrac{b}{(2b-ct)^2}\,tV(a)$	$\dfrac{b}{(2b-c)^2}\,(\tilde{t}-t)V(a)$

it may be the case that $E\pi_P^C > E\pi_{NP}^B$ for the same type of parameter configurations as above.

The value of information

Recall we are considering symmetric situations where both firms receive an n-sample. We define the private value of information to firm i, PVI, as the difference in expected profits between receiving the n-sample and getting no information at all (the other firm gets an n-sample in either case). As before let $v=\sigma_u^2/n$ and $t=V(\alpha)/(V(\alpha)+v)$. When $n_1=0$ and $n_2=n$, with no pooling $v_1=\infty$, $v_2=v$, and $\sigma_{12}=0$ so that $d_1=t_1=0$ and $d_2=t_2=t$; with pooling $v_i=\sigma_{12}=v$, $i=1,2$, so that $d_i=1$, $t_i=t$, $i=1,2$. Now, recalling that the formulae for the Cournot expected profits is $\beta(A^2+B_i^2 t_i V(\alpha))$ where $A=\bar{\alpha}/(2\beta+\gamma)$ and $B_i=(2\beta-\gamma d_j)/(4\beta^2-\gamma^2 d_1 d_2)$, $j\neq i$, and using the formulae in Table 3 we can get the PVI in the Cournot case. The Bertrand case follows by duality. Table 6 gives the results.

We define the social value of information (SVI) as the difference in ETS between the firms receiving signals of the same finite variance v and the firms receiving no information at all. Using the formulae in Table 5 and noting that when t or $\tilde{t}$ equals zero, ETS^C is just the Cournot certainty expression (with $\bar{\alpha}$) while ETS^B is the Bertrand certainty expression plus $V(\alpha)/(\beta+\gamma)$, one gets Table 7.

Proposition 10. *The social value of information is positive in Cournot and negative in Bertrand competition. The private value of information to the firms is always positive and larger or smaller in Cournot than in Bertrand competition according to whether the goods are substitutes or complements. This holds comparing either the no pooling subgames or the pooling ones and also in the two-stage game where the information sharing decision is endogenous.*

338

Duopoly information equilibrium

Table 7. *Social value of information*

	NP	P
C	$\dfrac{3\beta+\gamma t}{(2\beta+\gamma t)^2}\,tV(\alpha)$	$\dfrac{3\beta+\gamma}{(2\beta+\gamma)^2}\,\bar{t}V(\alpha)$
B	$-\dfrac{(\beta-\gamma t)(\beta-\gamma)}{(2\beta-\gamma t)^2(\beta+\gamma)}\,tV(\alpha)$	$-\dfrac{(\beta-\gamma)^2}{(2\beta-\gamma)^2(\beta+\gamma)}\,\bar{t}V(\alpha)$

Proof. From the proof of Proposition 9 it follows that

$$(\beta/(2\beta+\gamma t)^2)V(\alpha) \gtreqless (b/(2b-ct)^2)V(a)$$

if and only if $\gamma \gtreqless 0$ and

$$(\beta/(2\beta+\gamma)^2)V(\alpha) \gtreqless (b/(2b-c)^2)V(a)$$

if and only if $\gamma \gtreqless 0$, so that from Table 6 we get that $\text{PVC}^C \gtreqless \text{PVI}^B$ if and only if $\gamma \gtreqless 0$ with either pooling or not pooling of information. Now, with substitutes $\text{PVI}^C_{NP} > \text{PVI}^C_P$ since $1/(2\beta+\gamma t)^2 > 1/(2\beta+\gamma)^2$ and $t > \bar{t}-t$ and therefore $\text{PVI}^C_{NP} > \text{PVI}^B_P$. With complements we get similarly that $\text{PVI}^B_{NP} > \text{PVI}^C_P$. The inequalities for the SVI follow by inspection of Table 7. ∎

Remark 7.3. When the goods are perfect substitutes the private and social value of information is zero in Bertrand competition since prices equal marginal cost independently of the information received.

8. Concluding remarks: extensions and policy implications

Extensions

We have considered a symmetric duopoly model. In principle there should be no difficulty in relaxing the symmetry assumption (and deal with a nonsymmetric model as in Singh and Vives [13]) or the duopoly assumption and deal with more than two firms. Computations would be very cumbersome, particularly when trying to relax both at the same time.

Note that the Cournot model can be reconsidered to accommodate the case where firms are uncertain about their common marginal costs and receive signals giving information about them. We could imagine a situation where firms have a common technology with only one variable input, oil, for example, the price of which is uncertain. The variable cost of producing one unit of output m is a constant times the price of oil. Letting $\hat{\alpha} = \alpha - m$ we can use our model with $\hat{\alpha}$. The signals in this example could come from an energy forecasting agency. For the Bertrand case new computations need to be made.[3]

Finally, a word about the Normality assumption. We use it for analytical convenience although in our context it would be more natural to use a distribution with compact support. In fact the property we need to get linear (affine) equilibrium strategies is that conditional expectations be linear (affine). The Normal is the most common distribution with this property. Note that if $E(\alpha \mid s_i) = T + t s_i$, for some constants T and t, and $E s_i = \bar{\alpha}$ then necessarily $T = (1-t)\bar{\alpha}$ since $E\{E(\alpha \mid s_i)\} = \bar{\alpha}$ so that $\bar{\alpha} = T + t\bar{\alpha}$.

Policy implications

We have seen that the market outcomes and optimal outcomes (with respect to information sharing) depend crucially on the type of competition, the nature of the goods and the degree of product differentiation. This has immediate policy implications regarding information sharing. If the goods are complements the best policy is no intervention since the market outcome is already optimal. If the goods are substitutes and Cournot competition prevails, public policy should encourage information sharing. (It could do that by requiring, e.g., trade associations or testing agencies to disclose all information to the firms.) If Bertrand competition prevails and the goods are close substitutes no intervention is needed. If they are poor substitutes pooling of information should be avoided (no trade association allowed to form). In the intermediate region where the goods are moderately good substitutes if the precision of the firms' information is good enough no intervention is required, otherwise the authority should discourage the sharing of market data. Note that in this case the authority has no incentive to improve the precision of the firms' information (by subsidizing information acquisition, e.g.) since expected total surplus is decreasing with the precision of information.

We see therefore that policy prescriptions, or inferences of firm behavior, based on the Cournot model with homogenous product could be misleading when out of context. For example, if the goods are substi-

---

[3] A situation where two firms are bidding for a government contract can be thought of as a Bertrand model. If the firms have the same (unknown) costs we are in the *common value* case of the auction literature. The incentives to gather and share information in this context (see [9, 10]) contrast sharply with the results we have obtained in the paper for Bertrand competition with substitutes. I am grateful to an anonymous referee for pointing this out.

tutes observing the firms pool information in Cournot competition is not evidence that they are setting quantities collusively if the goods are not very good substitutes. In this case pooling of information increases expected profits and although a pooling agreement is not self-enforcing in our two-stage game it could be in a repeated situation. Firms would be colluding then in their market research but not in setting outputs.

References

1. T. Basar and V. C. Ho, Informational properties of the Nash solutions of two stochastic nonzero-sum games, *J. Econom. Theory* 7 (1976), 370–87.
2. R. Clarke, "Collusion and the Incentives for Information Sharing," working paper No. 8233, University of Wisconsin–Madison, 1983.
3. V. Crawford and J. Sobel, Strategic information transmission, *Econometrica* 50 (1982), 1431–51.
4. A. K. Dixit, A model of duopoly suggesting a theory of entry barriers, *Bell J. Econom.* 10 (1979), 20–32.
5. E. Gal-Or, "Information Sharing in Oligopoly," University of Pittsburgh, working paper, 1982.
6. R. Harris and T. Lewis, "Strategic Commitment under Uncertainty with Private Information," California Institute of Technology, working paper, 1982.
7. J. Harsanyi, Games with incomplete information played by Bayesian players, I, *Management Sci.* 14 (1967–78), 159–82; II, 320–34; III, 486–502.
8. H. Leland, Theory of the firm facing uncertain demand, *Amer. Econom. Rev.* 62 (1972), 278–91.
9. P. Milgrom and R. Weber, A theory of auctions and competitive bidding, *Econometrica* 50 (1982), 1089–122.
10. ———, The value of information in a sealed bid auction, *J. Math. Econom.* 10 (1982), 105–14.
11. W. Novshek and H. Sonnenschein, Fulfilled expectations Cournot duopoly with information acquisition and release, *Bell J. Econom.* 13 (1982), 214–8.
12. R. Selten, Re-examination of the perfectness concept for equilibrium points of extensive games, *Internat. J. Game Theory* 5 (1975), 25–55.
13. N. Singh and X. Vives, "Price and Quantity Competition in a Differentiated Duopoly," discussion paper, No. 154, C.S.O.I., University of Pennsylvania, 1983.

CHAPTER 14

Information transmission – Cournot and Bertrand equilibria

ESTHER GAL-OR

We examine how incentives for two duopolists to honestly share information change depending upon the nature of competition (Cournot or Bertrand) and the nature of the information structure. While in earlier papers uncertainty is about an unknown common demand intercept, in the present paper uncertainty is about unknown private costs. The different information structure reverses the incentives to share information. While with unknown common demand sharing is a dominant strategy with Bertrand competition and concealing is a dominant strategy with Cournot competition, with unknown private costs sharing is a dominant strategy with Cournot competition and concealing is a dominant strategy with Bertrand competition.

1. Introduction

We examine how incentives for two duopolists to honestly share information change depending upon the nature of competition (Cournot or Bertrand) and the nature of the information structure. In contrast to earlier papers [Gal-Or (1985), Novshek and Sonnenschein (1982) and Vives (1984)], where uncertainty is about an unknown common demand intercept, in the present paper uncertainty is about unknown private costs. With an uncertain demand each firm observes a private signal of a parameter of the model which affects everyone's payoff function in the same way. With uncertain costs each firm observes a private signal of a parameter of the model which is different for each firm. While the first environment is called a "common value" problem in the auction literature, the second environment is called a "private values" problem in the same literature.[1] We demonstrate that the different information structure considered by

Israel Institute of Technology and University of Pittsburgh.

Esther Gal-Or, "Information Transmission – Cournot and Bertrand Equilibria," *Review of Economic Studies* 53, 1, 1986, pp. 85–92.

First version received June 1984; final version accepted May 1985 (Eds.).

I am grateful to an anonymous referee whose comments led to a significant improvement in the interpretation of the results.

[1] An anonymous referee pointed out that this is the key difference between the present paper and earlier findings.

342

us, reverses the incentives to pool information. With unknown common demand, Vives demonstrates that sharing is a dominant strategy with Bertrand competition and concealing is a dominant strategy with Cournot competition. In contrast, with unknown private costs we demonstrate that sharing is a dominant strategy with Cournot competition and concealing is a dominant strategy with Bertrand competition.

The pooling of private information about unknown costs has two effects on the firm. On one hand, more accurate information about the rival's cost is available, and the strategies can be more accurately chosen. For example, when one firm observes a low signal for its unit cost and reveals it to the competitor, it reduces the likelihood that the competitor "overproduces." On the other hand, the pooling of the information reduces the correlation among the decision rules. For instance, with output levels as strategies, when one firm observes a low signal for its unit cost and reveals it to the competitor, the first firm expands output and the competitor contracts output. Increased accuracy has an unambiguous positive effect on the payoff of the firm. Reduced correlation has a positive or negative effect dependent upon the slope of the reaction functions of the firms. If they are downwards sloping (Cournot competition) reduced correlation has a positive effect, and if they are upwards sloping (Bertrand competition) reduced correlation has a negative effect. Our main result is consistent with the above discussion. More explicitly, perfect revelation is a dominant strategy at the Cournot equilibria and no revelation is a dominant strategy at the Bertrand equilibria.

It is noteworthy that reduced correlation among the decision rules happens in one model, since uncertainty is about a parameter of the model which is different for each firm. If there was a common shock which affects every firm's cost function similarly, the pooling of private information would lead to increased correlation among the decision rules. With a common shock to the costs, when one firm observes a high cost signal, both firms are more likely to face high costs. Hence when this signal is revealed, both firms reduce output. Such increased correlation among decision rules occurs also in Vives and Gal-Or when uncertainty is about an unknown common demand intercept. As an outcome the incentives to share information are opposite to the ones obtained in the present paper.

In our model, each firm produces a differentiated product and faces a stochastic technology. The random shock that determines the firm's cost function is different from the shock that determines its rival's cost. Each firm gets to observe a private signal about unit cost, chooses whether to reveal it to the other firm and how complete this revelation will be. An "outside agency" (a trade association for example) conducts the transmission of the private information. If a firm decides to partially reveal its information it reports to the agency the noise variance of its transmission. Since the messages are randomly chosen their precision (hence informative value) is reduced. The variance of the distribution measures the degree of revelation of the information. When the variance is equal to zero firms choose to truthfully report their private signals. This case represents complete information sharing. When the variance is equal to infinity firms choose arbitrarily their reported message without any relation to their private information. Hence the message has no informative value. This case represents no information sharing. When the variance is a finite positive number firms report messages that are related to their private signals, but additional noise is generated in their messages. This case represents partial information sharing. The continuous degree of sharing that is permitted in our model is an extension of the all-or-none sharing that is considered by Vives. It resembles the continuous sharing assumed in our earlier work or the work of Novshek and Sonnenschein. After the stage of information transmission each firm chooses either its level of output (at the Cournot equilibria) or its price (at the Bertrand equilibria).

The result obtained in the present paper together with earlier results indicate, that an industry will have incentives to create an "association" that collects and publicizes information, dependent upon the type of competition in the industry and the source of uncertainty in the market. If firms compete in quantity the "association" will collect and publicize information about a parameter of the model that is different for each firm, such as costs. If they compete in price it will collect and publicize information about a parameter of the model that is common to all firms, such as a common demand intercept.

To the best of our knowledge, there is only one other paper that relates to information sharing about costs (Shapiro [1984]). In contrast to the present paper, Shapiro considers only the Cournot equilibria with the all-or-none option for sharing. He demonstrates that firms are better off if both reveal information than if both conceal information about costs. Hence his result is consistent with ours. Bertrand equilibria are not considered by Shapiro.

Our paper is organized as follows: in the next section, we describe the model, in Section 3 we derive the equilibria and in Section 4 we include concluding remarks.

2. The model

A market consists of two firms each producing a differentiated product. The market demand is linear, namely

Information transmission

$$p_i = a - bq_i - dq_j, \quad a, b, d > 0; \quad b \geq d, \quad i, j = 1, 2, \quad i \neq j \tag{1}$$

where p_i is the price and q_i the amount produced of product i. Since $d > 0$ the two products are substitutes and since $b \geq d$ "cross effects" are dominated by "own effects." The closer the coefficients b and d are to each other the less differentiated the two products are. In particular, when $b = d$ the two products are homogeneous.

The technology is stochastic but it exhibits constant returns to scale, namely for a given state of nature the unit cost of production is a constant equal to c_i, $i = 1, 2$. The value of c_i is a random variable that is normally distributed with mean zero and variance σ_c. Its value is determined independent of c_j, $j \neq i$.

Before choosing its strategy each firm observes a signal for its unit cost. This signal z_i is determined as follows:

$$z_i = c_i + e_i \tag{2}$$

where $e_i \sim N(0, m)$ and e_i and c_j are independently distributed $\forall i, j$, e_i and e_j are independently distributed $i \neq j$.

According to (2) each firm observes a noisy signal for its unit cost. This signal is independently distributed of the signal observed by the other firm. Hence one firm can make no inferences about the unit cost of its competitor based upon its private information.

At the first stage of the game each firm chooses an amount of garbling to which any public report it makes is subject. The amount of garbling chosen by firm i is denoted by s_i. If $s_i = 0$, the firm perfectly reveals its private information, if $s_i = \infty$ the firm generates infinite noise in its public reports so that their information content is worthless. If $0 < s_i < \infty$ the firm *partially* reveals its private information. Since firms are required to commit themselves to a fixed amount of garbling prior to learning their signals it is crucial that the transmission of the information is conducted by an "outside agency." The agency chooses the reported message of firm i, z_i as follows:

$$\hat{z}_i = z_i + f_i, \quad \text{Cov}(f_1, f_2) = \text{Cov}(f_i, c_j) = \text{Cov}(f_i, e_j) = 0, \quad \forall i, j$$
$$f_i \sim N(0, s_i), \quad i = 1, 2. \tag{3}$$

The value of s_i is chosen and reported to the agency *prior* and independent of the actual realization of z_i. Relaxing this assumption might lead to substantial analytical complications such as the need to consider mixed garbling strategies. The assumption that the message is an unbiased estimator of the true signal is made without any loss of generality, since if messages are biased and the bias is common knowledge each firm can subtract the bias from the message delivered.

345

After selecting messages according to (3), the agency reports $\hat{z}_1$, $\hat{z}_2$, s_1 and s_2 to both firms. Hence firms get a report about the realized values of the messages and their accuracy. The reported information is subsequently used by each firm to select its strategy for the second stage of the game. The choice of strategy may depend upon the vector of observations, that becomes available after the stage of information transmission. This vector for firm i is denoted by $t_i = (z_i, \hat{z}_1, \hat{z}_2, s_1, s_2)$. Hence firm i can condition its strategy at the second stage on its private signal and the messages delivered by the agency. To summarize, the game between the firms consists of two stages. At the first stage each firm decides how noisy its message is going to be and at the second stage it chooses a decision rule conditioned upon a vector of observations that becomes available. At the second stage we consider both a game where output levels are strategies and a game where prices are strategies. We derive the Nash equilibria of both stages of the game, and investigate the incentives to share information in each case. We demonstrate that perfect revelation ($s_i = 0$) is a dominant strategy with output levels as strategies (Cournot competition), and no revelation ($s_i = \infty$) is a dominant strategy with prices as strategies (Bertrand competition). These results are opposite to the ones obtained by Vives.

3. Derivation of the equilibria

3.1 Cournot equilibria

At the Cournot equilibria the strategy of each firm consists of an amount of garbling and an output level, namely the pair $(s_i, q_i(t_i))$ where $s_i \in R^+$ and $q_i: R^3 \times (R^+)^2 \to R^+$. The payoff function of firm i is:

$$J^i(s_i, s_j, q_i(t_i), q_j(t_j)) = E\{q_i(t_i)[a - bq_i(t_i) - dq_j(t_j) - c_i]\},$$

$$i, j = 1, 2, \quad i \neq j \tag{4}$$

where E is the expected value operator. We consider only subgame perfect equilibria. Hence we have to guarantee that the strategy choice made by each firm at the beginning of the first stage remains optimal at the second stage as well. It is this subgame that we consider first. At the second stage firm i chooses $q_i(\cdot)$ to maximize

$$W^i = E_{z_j, c_i, c_j}\{q_i(t_i)[a - bq_i(t_i) - dq_j(t_j) - c_i] \mid t_i\}, \quad i, j = 1, 2; \ i \neq j. \tag{5}$$

The expected value operates on the random variables that remain unobservable at the second stage, namely z_j, c_i and c_j. In Lemma 1 we derive

346

the unique Nash equilibrium of the second stage game for given s_1 and s_2 chosen at the first stage.

Lemma 1. *For given s_1 and s_2 the following decision rules are the unique Nash equilibrium (Cournot) of the second stage subgame,*

$$q_i(t_i) = C_0^i + C_1^i \hat{z}_j + C_2^i \hat{z}_i + C_3^i z_i \qquad (6)$$

where

$$C_0^i = a/(2b+d)$$
$$C_1^i = d\sigma_c/(4b^2 - d^2)(m + \sigma_c + s_j)$$
$$C_2^i = -d^2\sigma_c/2b(4b^2 - d^2)(m + \sigma_c + s_i)$$
$$C_3^i = -\sigma_c/(m + \sigma_c)2b.$$

Proof. To maximize (5) while taking $q_j(t_j)$ as given:

$$\frac{\partial W^i}{\partial q_i} = a - dE_{z_j}(q_j(t_j) \mid t_i) - E(c_i \mid t_i) - 2bq_i(t_i) = 0$$

$$\frac{\partial^2 W^i}{\partial q_i^2} = -2b < 0.$$

Hence

$$q_i(t_i) = [a - dE_{z_j}(q_j(t_j) \mid t_i) - E(c_i \mid t_i)]/2b, \quad i,j = 1,2; \ i \neq j. \qquad (7)$$

The following posterior expected values are required in (7):

$$E(c_i \mid t_i) = E(c_i \mid z_i) = \frac{\sigma_c}{\sigma_c + m} z_i$$

$$E(q_j(t_j) \mid t_i) = C_0^j + C_1^j \hat{z}_i + C_2^j \hat{z}_j + C_3^j E(z_j \mid \hat{z}_j) \qquad (8)$$

where

$$E(z_j \mid \hat{z}_j) = \frac{(m + \sigma_c)\hat{z}_j}{m + \sigma_c + s_j}.$$

Using (8) in (7) and requiring (7) to hold for every possible t_i and t_j yields a system of eight linear equations in eight unknowns. Solving this system yields the unique solution specified in (6). According to Radner (1962) it is sufficient to restrict attention to decision rules of the generic form specified in (6) since the decision rules have to be affine in the vector of observations. ∎

It is noteworthy from (6) that without any transmission of the information $(s_1 = s_2 = \infty)$ $\text{Cov}(q_1(t_1), q_2(t_2)) = 0$ and with partial or complete transmission $\text{Cov}(q_1(t_1), q_2(t_2)) < 0$. Hence information sharing about stochastic private costs reduces the correlation between the output decisions of the firms. This is in contrast to information sharing about a stochastic common demand that increases the correlation between the decision rules. Proposition 1 follows from Lemma 1.

Proposition 1. *If $\sigma_c > 0$ (technology is stochastic) the unique Cournot equilibrium of the two stage game is $s_i = 0$ and $q_i(t_i)$ that satisfies (6).*

Proof. Substituting the decision rules derived in Lemma 1 in the payoff function (5) yields the Nash equilibrium payoffs of the second stage subgame. We denote it by $w_i(s_i, s_j, t_i)$ for firm i. The payoff of the two stage game can subsequently be computed as follows:

$$v_i(s_i, s_j) = E_{t_i}[w_i(s_i, s_j, t_i)] = bE_{t_i}[q_i(t_i)]^2$$

$$= b\frac{a^2}{(2b+d)^2} + \frac{\sigma_c^2}{(m+\sigma_c)4b^2} + \frac{d^2\sigma_c^2}{(4b^2-d^2)^2(m+\sigma_c+s_j)}$$

$$+ \frac{d^2\sigma_c^2(8b^2-d^2)}{4b^2(4b^2-d^2)^2(m+\sigma_c+s_i)}. \tag{9}$$

This is a strictly decreasing function of s_i. Hence $s_i = 0$ is a dominant strategy for each firm. ∎

According to the proof of Proposition 1 perfect revelation is a dominant strategy for each firm at the Cournot equilibria with uncertainty about private costs.[2] This is an opposite result to the one obtained by us or by Vives where the uncertainty was about the common intercept of the demand. With uncertainty about common demand there is no information sharing at the Cournot equilibria. Notice that perfect revelation is a dominant strategy even if firms know their own costs perfectly, i.e. $m = 0$.

3.2. Bertrand equilibria

At the Bertrand equilibria the strategy of each firm consists of an amount of garbling and a price. If firms choose prices p_1 p_2 the output levels are determined from (1) as follows:

---

[2] Given Nash equilibrium outputs in the second stage of the game, perfect revelation by one agent is a best response to any amount of revelation by agent 2. If the second stage component of agent 2's output is not the Nash equilibria choice, then the agent's best response is not necessarily perfect revelation.

$$q_i = \frac{a}{b+d} + \frac{dp_j - bp_i}{(b-d)(b+d)}, \quad i \neq j; \; i,j = 1,2.$$

Hence, the payoff of firm i is:

$$J^i(s_i, s_j, p_i(t_i), p_j(t_j)) = E\left\{(p_i(t_i) - c_i)\left(\frac{a}{b+d} + \frac{dp_j(t_j) - bp_i(t_i)}{(b-d)(b+d)}\right)\right\}$$

$$i \neq j; \; i,j = 1,2. \tag{10}$$

Since we only consider subgame perfect equilibria the decision rule $p_i(t_i)$ should maximize the payoff functions of the second stage game. In Lemma 2 we derive the "best response" strategies of the second stage subgame.

Lemma 2. *For given s_1 and s_2 the following decision rules are the unique Nash equilibrium (Bertrand) of the second stage subgame.*

$$p_i(t_i) = D_0^i + D_1^i \hat{z}_j + D_2^i \hat{z}_i + D_3^i z_i \tag{11}$$

where

$$D_0^i = \frac{a(b-d)}{(2b-d)}$$

$$D_1^i = \frac{db\sigma_c}{(4b^2 - d^2)(m + \sigma_c + s_j)}$$

$$D_2^i = \frac{d^2 \sigma_c}{2(4b^2 - d^2)(m + \sigma_c + s_i)}$$

$$D_3^i = \frac{\sigma_c}{2(m + \sigma_c)}.$$

Proof. Similar to the proof of Lemma 1. ∎

We use the decision rules of Lemma 2 in order to derive the Nash equilibrium payoff of the second stage game denoted by $w_i(s_i, s_j, t_i)$ where

$$w_i(s_i, s_j, t_i) = E_{z_j, c_i, c_j}\{[p_i(t_i) - c_i]^2 \mid t_i\} \cdot \frac{b}{(b-d)(b+d)}$$

$$= \{p_i^2(t_i) - 2E(c_i \mid t_i) p_i(t_i) + E(c_i^2 \mid t_i)\} \frac{b}{(b-d)(b+d)}$$

Since

$$c_i \mid z_i \sim N\left(z_i \frac{\sigma_c}{\sigma_c + m}, \frac{m\sigma_c}{m + \sigma_c}\right)$$

349

it follows that

$$E(c_i \mid z_i) = \frac{\sigma_c z_i}{m + \sigma_c} \quad \text{and} \quad \frac{(c_i - z_i \sigma_c/(\sigma_c + m))^2}{m\sigma_c/(m + \sigma_c)} \bigg|_{t_i} \sim \chi^2(1).$$

Hence

$$E(c_i^2 \mid z_i) = \frac{m\sigma_c}{m + \sigma_c} + z_i^2 \left(\frac{\sigma_c}{m + \sigma_c} \right)^2$$

and we obtain the payoff function (as a function of s_i and s_j) of both stages as follows:

$$v_i(s_i, s_j)$$

$$= E_{t_i}\{w(s_i, s_j, t_i)\}$$

$$= E_{t_i} \left\{ \left[p_i(t_i) - z_i \frac{\sigma_c}{m + \sigma_c} \right]^2 + \frac{m\sigma_c}{m + \sigma_c} \right\} \frac{b}{(b-d)(b+d)}$$

$$= \frac{b}{(b-d)(b+d)} \left\{ \frac{a^2(b-d)^2}{(2b-d)^2} + \frac{\sigma_c^2 + 4m\sigma_c}{4(m+\sigma_c)} + \frac{d^2 b^2 \sigma_c^2}{(4b^2 - d^2)^2(m+\sigma_c+s_j)} \right.$$

$$\left. - \frac{d^2 \sigma_c^2(8b^2 - 3d^2)}{4(4b^2 - d^2)(m+\sigma_c+s_i)} \right\}. \tag{12}$$

Proposition 2 follows trivially from (12).

Proposition 2. If $\sigma_c > 0$ (technology is stochastic) the unique Bertrand equilibrium of the two stage game is $s_i = \infty$ and $p_i(y_i)$ that satisfy (11).

Proof. Follows trivially from (12) since $v_i(s_i, s_j)$ is a strictly increasing function of s_i. ∎

From Proposition 2 generating infinite noise in its report is a dominant strategy for each firm.[3] Hence with uncertainties about private costs there are no incentives to share information at the Bertrand equilibria. This result holds even if firms know their costs perfectly, i.e. $m = 0$. This is in contrast to perfect revelation that arises at the Bertrand equilibria with uncertainties about common demand (Vives). The reason for the different result follows from (11). If there is no transmission of information ($s_1 = s_2 = \infty$) $\text{Cov}[(p_1(t_1) - c_1)(p_2(t_2) - c_2)] = 0$. If there is partial or complete transmission of information $\text{Cov}[(p_1(t_1) - c_1)(p_2(t_2) - c_2)] < 0$. Since the

[3] Given Nash equilibrium prices in the second stage of the game.

reaction functions are upwards sloping this reduced correlation reduces the profit of a single firm. Hence there are no incentives to transmit information to rivals. At the Bertrand equilibria with uncertainty about a common parameter, sharing leads to increased correlation and increased expected profits. Hence, in common value games sharing is a dominant strategy at the Bertrand equilibria.

4. Concluding remarks

An industry will have incentives to create an "association" that collects and publicizes information dependent upon the nature of competition in the industry and the nature of the information structure. If firms compete in quantity the "association" will collect and publicize information about a parameter of the model that is different for each firm (such as private costs). If they compete in price it will collect and publicize information about a parameter of the model that is common to all firms (such as a common demand intercept). The above conclusion is based upon the derivations in the present paper as well as earlier papers on oligopolistic information transmission.

Though not explicitly derived here or in earlier papers, our main conclusion holds also if uncertainty is about a common shock to costs or uncertainty is about different private demand intercepts. It can be demonstrated that the incentives to share information are the same with a common shock to costs as they are with a common shock to the demand intercept (common value game). Similarly, the incentives are the same with different private demand intercepts as they are with different private costs (private values game).

References

Basar, R. and Ho, Y. C. (1974), "Information Properties of the Nash Solutions of Two Stochastic Nonzero-Sum Games," *Journal of Economic Theory,* 7, 370–87.

Crawford, V. and Sobel, J. (1982), "Strategic Information Transmission," *Econometrica,* 50, 1431–51.

DeGroot, H. (1970), *Optimal Statistical Decisions* (New York: McGraw-Hill).

Gal-Or, E. (1985), "Information Sharing in Oligopoly," *Econometrica,* 53, 329–43.

Novshek, W. and Sonnenschein, H. (1982), "Fulfilled Expectation Cournot Duopoly with Information Acquisition and Release," *Bell Journal of Economics,* 13, 214–8.

Palfrey, T. (1984), "Uncertainty Resolution, Private Information Aggregation and The Cournot Competitive Limit," *Review of Economic Studies,* 52, 69–83.

Radner, R. (1962), "Team Decision Problems," *Annals of Mathematical Statistics,* 33, 857–81.

Shapiro, C. (1984), "Exchange of Cost Information in Oligopoly" (Working paper, Princeton University).

Vives, X. (1985), "Duopoly Information Equilibrium: Cournot and Bertrand," *Journal of Economic Theory,* 34, 71–94.

CHAPTER 15

Uncertainty resolution, private information aggregation, and the Cournot competitive limit

THOMAS R. PALFREY

A Cournot model of oligopoly in which otherwise identical firms have private differential information about the common cost of production and a shared (but unknown) demand curve is examined. A Bayesian equilibrium of the corresponding game of incomplete information is solved for explicitly and analyzed. In the symmetric equilibrium, different firms produce at different output levels because they have different information. Because the information individual firms have is random, total output and hence market price is also random for any finite number of firms.

The main result of the paper relates to the asymptotic properties of the equilibrium, when the number of firms becomes large. Under fairly general conditions on the joint distribution of demand and individual firms' information about demand, the random equilibrium price converges almost surely to a constant in the limit. More importantly, this price equals the perfectly competitive price. In other words, in large markets, even if no firm knows the true market demand curve and firms are not price-takers and do not use price as a signal to improve their information, the competitive price will prevail with certainty. In the limit, aggregate outcomes are as if all firms shared their private information with each other.

1. Introduction

In a stimulating paper, Wilson (1977) makes an observation about how a particular market mechanism is able to process diverse imperfect information in a very efficient way. He shows under fairly general conditions that if a number of buyers each obtain an equivalent amount of free partial information about the common value of a good which is to be sold via a first-price auction, then as the environment becomes more competitive, the price in the market will converge almost surely to the true value

Carnegie-Mellon University.

Thomas R. Palfrey, "Uncertainty Resolution, Private Information Aggregation, and the Cournot Competitive Limit," *Review of Economic Studies* 52, 1, 1985, pp. 69–83.

First version received February 1983; final version accepted July 1984 (Eds.).

The author has benefited from discussions with David Easley, Steve Matthews, and Steve Spear. Comments by two referees and Kevin Roberts were also very helpful.

of the good. The powerful feature about this result is that no participant in the market knows the true value at the time bids are submitted, no private information is transmitted between market participants, there is no pooling of information, yet incentives act on the participants in such a way that price will precisely equal value in the competitive limit. This result is extended and generalized by Milgrom (1979), who obtains necessary and sufficient conditions for convergence in probability to true value.

The question addressed in this paper is whether diverse imperfect information may be processed via other market pricing mechanisms as perfectly as it is processed in an auction. The particular environment analyzed here is one in which there are many firms each producing a homogeneous product which is then sold at a price which equates total output and demand. A common production technology and demand curve is shared by all firms.

The principal departure from classical oligopoly models in this approach is that the market participants do not have complete information about all factors affecting their ultimate profit in the market. The producing firms have identical, but unknown, constant average costs of production, c, and must produce before learning this cost and before knowing exactly what the demand function is. Each firm, however, observes a private signal which is independent of the signals observed by the other firms, conditional on the *true* demand function and actual production costs. This signal contains some information which allows firms to get a better estimate about true demand and cost than they would have had without observing the signal. This Cournot problem is posed as a game of incomplete information and the asymptotic properties of the equilibrium are examined. The behavioural assumption about firm decision-making is that they are Cournot–Bayesian–Nash players of a static oligopoly game. In this respect, the basic structure of the model is similar to the duopoly model used by Novshek and Sonnenschein (1982).

The introduction of differential information into the classic oligopoly model has a number of desirable features. The most obvious is that it relaxes the strong assumption that the common demand curve faced by firms in an industry is known perfectly and does not require all firms to have the same probabilistic beliefs about demand. Because firms make decisions based on different probabilistic beliefs, firms will not all make the same output decisions in equilibrium. Some firms appear to "guess correctly" (e.g. produce high levels when demand is high) and other firms make what appear in hindsight to be bad judgments (e.g. produce very little when demand is high). In the model here, all guesses are good guesses, given available information, but some firms are luckier than others.

The Cournot competitive limit

An alternative "reduced form" interpretation of the model is that firms have probabilistic beliefs about the decisions by other firms in the industry. With a finite number of firms, these beliefs are fulfilled in equilibrium only on average, or in a probabilistic sense. In the competitive limit, however, beliefs are non-probabilistic (i.e. degenerate distributions) and are fulfilled *exactly* in equilibrium. That is, in the limit no firm will regret (i.e. wish to change) its decision *after the fact,* given all other firms' decisions and the true state of demand.

This last feature relates to a natural question which arises in this model, and which is essentially the same question addressed by Wilson (1977) in his auction environment. As the number of firms gets large, will the market price converge precisely to the true (but unknown) cost? In the environment studied here, the answer is quite positive. The main result essentially states that if there exists a sequence of *feasible* strategies which lead to convergence, then sequences of *equilibrium* strategies will lead to convergence. In this strong sense, a competitive market reveals the true state of the world, and yields a perfectly efficient allocation. The aggregate outcomes (total industry output and price) will be as if all firms had perfect information, or, alternatively, as if all firms shared their private information with each other.

2. The model

There are n firms, indexed by $i = 1, \dots, n$ producing a homogeneous output. They have a shared linear market demand function, with inverse demand function given by $p(X) = a - bX$, where X is the total output by all firms and p is price. Firms have identical constant unit cost of production, c, which is assumed to be strictly positive. If a, b, c are known with certainty, and $a \geqq c$, then the competitive level of (total) output is $w = (a - c)/b$. It is also well known that w is the limit of the aggregate Cournot output level when the number of firms becomes large. In this paper, we assume that a and c (and hence w) are not known with certainty by all firms.

Instead, we assume that only b is known with certainty, but firms have uncertainty about a and c. The way one models firm information about demand and cost becomes crucial in a world of uncertainty like this. One could imagine, for example, that all firms know the true distribution of a and c, and act to maximize expected profits. Since in such a situation all firms have identical expectations, the competitive output would be $\bar{w} = E(a - c)/b$ and $\bar{w}$ would also be the Cournot limit. A more likely situation is that different firms have different expectations about the distribution of w, due to having different information. One might imagine this

355

different private information as being generated by some random process such as market surveys conducted independently by the firms in order to estimate a, or imperfect internal accounting procedures used to calculate c. Firms start out with the same, correct prior distribution about w, but each privately receives a noisy signal about w and this process generates n (possibly different) posterior distributions about w. With a finite number of firms it is rather difficult to define what is the competitive level of output, because all firms have private information. It would, for example, depend upon the particular draw of signals observed by the firms. One candidate definition is what could be called a "full communication" competitive level of output. That is, one could calculate the common posterior all firms would have if all signals were public information instead of private information, and define $\hat{w} = E_s(a-c)/b$ where E_s is the expectation conditional on s, the entire vector of private signals. The problem with this definition is that it presumes all signals are public rather than private. In a sense $\hat{w}$ represents the most information which could possibly be reflected in output; it is as close as possible to the full information competitive supply. This full communication output level has the following interesting property. If the random process generating signals is different for all "true" values of $(a-c)$ then the full communication competitive output level $\hat{w}$ will converge to the full information competitive supply, $(a-c)/b$. A natural question to ask is how close to this will you come in an appropriately modified version of the Cournot competitive limit when private information is not shared between firms?

The rest of this paper establishes a set of sufficient (and almost necessary) conditions for price and output in the Cournot limit with differential private information to *precisely* equal the full information competitive supply and price. That is, in the limit, price and quantity is as if private signals were public signals and all firms had no uncertainty about demand and cost. We will assume that w can take on K (finite) different values, and that there are S (finite) different signals, $v_1, \ldots, v_s$ firms can receive. We will denote by W and V the row vectors $(w_1, \ldots, w_K)$, and $(v_1, \ldots, v_s)$. The joint distribution of W and V is common knowledge and is the same for all firms. If p_{ks} represents the probability of w_k and v_s then this joint distribution is given by a $K \times S$ probability matrix $P = [p_{ks}]$. If $w = w_k$, then the conditional distribution of signals is given by

$$\left(\frac{p_{k1}}{\sum_{s=1}^{S} p_{ks}}, \ldots, \frac{p_{kS}}{\sum_{s=1}^{S} p_{ks}} \right).$$

Conditional on w_k, each firm independently draws a signal from this conditional distribution. We write these K S-vectors of probabilities as a $K \times S$ matrix

356

$$P^K = [p_{ks}^K] \quad \text{where} \quad p_{ks}^K = \frac{p_{ks}}{\sum_{l=1}^{S} p_{kl}}.$$

If any firm i receives a signal $s_i = v_s$, then from P and Bayes' rule one can calculate a Bayesian posterior probability distribution of w, given by

$$\left(\frac{p_{1s}}{\sum_{l=1}^{K} p_{ls}}, \dots, \frac{p_{Ks}}{\sum_{l=1}^{K} p_{ls}} \right).$$

There are S of these conditional (on v) distributions of w and we write these S K-vectors as a $K \times S$ matrix

$$P^S = [p_{ks}^S] \quad \text{where} \quad p_{ks}^S = \frac{p_{ks}}{\sum_{l=1}^{K} p_{ls}}.$$

Another matrix which will be useful in the analysis below is

$$\Pi = P^S P^{K'} = [\pi_{kl}],$$

where Π is $K \times K$. The typical element π_{kl} can be interpreted as an expected posterior probability of w_k conditional on $w = w_l$.

Finally, for a given sample size n, we define the random variable q_{kl}^n as the sample mean posterior probability of w_k conditional on $w = w_l$. Then $E(q_{kl}^n) = \pi_{kl}$ for all n, k, l. Again, we define the corresponding $K \times K$ matrix $Q^n = [q_{kl}^n]$.

The game of incomplete information played between the firms is defined in the usual way. A strategy of firm i in the n-firm game, $x_i^n : V \to R^+$ is a function which maps each possible signal into an output choice. It is an S-vector where the sth component $x_{is}^n = x_i^n(v_s)$ is the level of output x_i, produced by firm i if $s_i = v_s$ and there are n competing firms.[1] An equilibrium of the game with n firms is a collection of n S-vectors,

$$\Sigma^{n^*} = (x_1^{n^*}, \dots, x_n^{n^*})$$

such that for all i and s, $x_{is}^{n^*}$ maximizes expected profit for firm i conditional on $s_i = v_s$ if all other firms use strategies $(x_1^{n^*}, \dots, x_{i-1}^{n^*}, x_{i+1}^{n^*}, \dots, x_n^{n^*})$. Because of the symmetric position of firms ex ante it is natural to restrict attention to a symmetric equilibrium in which $x_1^n = \cdots = x_n^n$. We denote such a symmetric equilibrium strategy simply by x_n^*.

Since the vector of signals received by firms is a random variable, total output of the n firms is also a random variable, the distribution of which is determined by P, n, and Σ^n. We will denote total output of n firms *conditional* on $w = w_k$ by X_n^k. The vector of these K random variables

---

[1] The information structure outlined above is essentially an n-firm discrete version of the one employed by Novshek and Sonnenschein (1982) in a duopoly model which investigated the incentives to pool information.

357

will be denoted $X_n = (X_n^1, \ldots, X_n^K)$. Total output of n firms, excluding firm i, is denoted $X_n^i = (X_n^{1i}, \ldots, X_n^{Ki})$. Expected value of X_n is denoted $E_n = (E_n^1, \ldots, E_n^K)$ and expected value of X_n^i is denoted $E_n^i = (E_n^{1i}, \ldots, E_n^{Ki})$.

Before proceeding it may be useful to give an example which illustrates the above structure.

Example. Suppose $n = 2$, $b = 1$, $c = 2$ (with certainty) and a is equally likely to be either 10 (high demand) or 8 (low demand). Hence $K = 2$ and

$$w_1 = 8$$

$$w_2 = 6.$$

Let $S = 3$ and interpret these three signals as being "demand likely to be high" (v_1), "no useful additional information" (v_2), and "demand likely to be low" (v_3). One can imagine these signals as, for example, qualitative summaries from a market survey. The joint probability distribution of w and v is known to be

$$P = \begin{pmatrix} \dfrac{1}{4} & \dfrac{1}{6} & \dfrac{1}{12} \\ \dfrac{1}{12} & \dfrac{1}{6} & \dfrac{1}{4} \end{pmatrix}.$$

From P we can easily compute P^K, P^S and Π, to obtain

$$P^K = \begin{pmatrix} \dfrac{1}{2} & \dfrac{1}{3} & \dfrac{1}{6} \\ \dfrac{1}{5} & \dfrac{1}{3} & \dfrac{1}{2} \end{pmatrix} \qquad P^S = \begin{pmatrix} \dfrac{3}{4} & \dfrac{1}{2} & \dfrac{1}{4} \\ \dfrac{1}{4} & \dfrac{1}{2} & \dfrac{3}{4} \end{pmatrix} \qquad \Pi = \begin{pmatrix} \dfrac{7}{12} & \dfrac{5}{12} \\ \dfrac{5}{12} & \dfrac{7}{12} \end{pmatrix}.$$

Obviously the distribution of X_2 depends upon the strategies used by each firm, as well as P. To illustrate one possibility, suppose that both firms use the same strategy, given by

$$x_1^2(v_1) = x_2^2(v_1) = 5$$

$$x_1^2(v_2) = x_2^2(v_2) = 3 \cdot 5$$

$$x_1^2(v_3) = x_2^2(v_3) = 2.$$

Given these strategies one can compute the distributions of total output conditional on w, (X_2^1, X_2^2), by using the matrix P^K. The support of two conditional distributions of X_2 is $(4, 5 \cdot 5, 7, 8 \cdot 5, 10)$, with probabilities $(1/36, 1/9, 5/18, 1/3, 1/4)$ for X_2^1 and $(1/4, 1/3, 5/18, 1/9, 1/36)$ for X_2^2. Similarly, one can compute the conditional distributions of output excluding one firm. Since both firms use the same strategy these distributions do not depend upon which firm is excluded. The support of both of these distributions, X_2^{1i} and X_2^{2i}, is $(2, 3 \cdot 5, 5)$ with probabilities $(1/6, 1/3, 1/2)$ and $(1/2, 1/3, 1/6)$ respectively. Expectations of X_2^1, X_2^2, X_2^{1i}, and X_2^{2i} can be easily computed directly from the distributions, and are equal to 8, 6, 4, and 3, respectively.

3. Convergence theorem

Before formally stating assumptions sufficient for almost sure convergence of total output to the full information competitive output, we present a simple *necessary* condition for convergence which provides part of the basic intuition for the main result. Interestingly, it will turn out that this necessary condition is also very nearly a sufficient condition.

In order for the equilibrium total output to converge almost surely to the competitive output, clearly there must exist a sequence of arbitrary (i.e. not necessarily equilibrium) strategies such that the sequence of total outputs generated by them converges in mean to the competitive output. For given n, let $x_n = (x_{n1}, \ldots, x_{nS})$ be an arbitrary strategy which is used by all firms. Using the notation introduced earlier, expected total output when each of n firms is producing according to x_n is given by:

$E_n = nP^K x_n'$ where x_n' is the transpose[2] of x_n.

Convergence requires (at least) that

$$\lim_{n \to \infty} E_n = W$$

which can be rewritten

$$\lim_{n \to \infty} nP^K x_n = W. \tag{1}$$

If we consider the system of linear equations

$$P^K y = W \quad \text{(where } y \text{ is } S \times 1) \tag{2}$$

then a necessary *and* sufficient condition for there to exist a non-negative sequence $\{x_n\}_{n=1}^\infty$ satisfying (1) is that there exists a solution $y^* \geqq 0$ to (2). Necessity is obvious. Sufficiency is established easily by letting $x_n = y^*/n$. This is summarized below as Theorem 1.

Theorem 1. $X_n \to^{a.s.} W$ *only if* $P^k y = W$ *has a solution* $y^* \geqq 0$.

---

[2] For notational convenience, henceforth all vectors in equations are column vectors. Transposes (') will only be denoted for matrices P^K, P^S, Π, Q.

359

A number of observations can now be made. First, if there are fewer signals than states (i.e. $S < K$) then $P^K y = W$ will usually not have a solution y^* because P^K will have rank less than K. Similarly, if $S \geq K$ but some of the signals are linear combinations of other signals, then it is again possible that P^K is of insufficient rank which would violate the necessary condition. Since P^S has the same rank as P^K, the necessary condition essentially requires that the vectors of posteriors on W generated by the S different signals (i.e. the columns of P^S) must span a space of dimension no less than K. In other words, there must be enough diversity in the possible information that firms might receive.

Second, it is possible that $P^K y = W$ has solutions, but none of the solutions is non-negative. Since firms are constrained to produce non-negative output, this would prevent convergence. There are several special cases where this could happen. For example, if all entries of P^K are positive (i.e. the support of the distribution of signals conditional on w is independent of w) then all components of W need to be strictly positive. If one of the states corresponds to zero competitive output, then it is generally impossible to obtain convergence, since y^* would have to contain some negative components.

A third observation worth noting is that for a sequence of strategies $\{x_n\}_{n=2}^{\infty}$ such that

$$\lim_{n \to \infty} n x_n = y^*$$

then not only will

$$\lim_{n \to \infty} E_n = W$$

but, more important, $X_n \to W$ almost surely, since $n x_n$ is bounded.

The above necessary conditions were derived without any consideration of the strategic behaviour of firms. There is no guarantee that

$$y^* = \lim_{n \to \infty} n x_n^*,$$

where $\{x_n^*\}$ are no longer arbitrary strategies, but each x_n^* is an equilibrium to the n-firm incomplete information game. At first glance it would seem that such a coincidence would be quite unlikely. As it happens, conditions only slightly stronger than the necessary condition stated in Theorem 1 suffice. These conditions are:

Assumption A1. P has rank K.

Assumption A2. $(P^K)^{-1} W > 0$ where $(P^K)^{-1}$ is the pseudoinverse of P^K.

The Cournot competitive limit

We now proceed to state and prove the central result of the paper.

Theorem 2. *If Assumptions A1 and A2 hold, then $X_n^* \to$ ᵃ·ˢ· W, where X_n^* is the unique symmetric equilibrium aggregate output with n-firms.*

A formal proof is given in the appendix. In order to better understand the economic intuition behind the convergence result, the following informal, heuristic argument is offered. Before making this argument, it may be helpful to think of the competitive limit as being achieved partly as a result of an economic "law" of large numbers and partly as a result of a statistical law of large numbers. The economic "law" is that (at least in the environments considered here) as the number of firms goes to infinity, aggregate expected profits go to zero. We show informally below that this implies that aggregate output conditional on the true state converges in mean to the competitive level of output, as long as P has rank K. The statistical law of large numbers then enables us to strengthen the convergence in mean result to almost sure convergence, since the variance of aggregate output conditional on the true state must converge to 0. This informal proof presumes existence. The formal proof of Theorem 2 in the appendix establishes existence by actually constructing an equilibrium.

Informal proof. The following four steps provide the intuition behind the information aggregation results in Theorem 2 and (later) Theorem 3.

(a) *Expected profit, conditional on signal, converges to zero for each signal:* Suppose not. Then there is some signal, v_s, some number $\gamma > 0$, and some subsequence, $\{v_r\}_{r=1}^{\infty}$ such that, for all r, the expected profit in equilibrium to any firms receiving signal v_s when $n = v_r$ is greater than or equal to γ. To see this, note that expected profit conditional on receiving *any* signal is bounded below by 0 since a firm can always guarantee itself non-negative profit by producing 0. Given our assumptions about demand, price is bounded above by some $\bar{p}$. Hence, along the subsequence described above, each firm receiving signal v_s must be producing at least $\gamma/\bar{p}$. However, if this is true, expected aggregate output in any state of the world for which $p_{ks} > 0$, is unbounded in the limit. If so, expected profits for a firm observing v_s must be negative, a contradiction.

(b) *Conditional on any signal, the expected output of other firms converges to the conditionally expected competitive output.* Suppose not. Then for some signal and some subsequence, expected output of other firms conditional on that signal is either greater or less than the expected competitive output along that subsequence by at least some number $\delta > 0$. If less, then the same argument as in (a) will apply and a contradiction

361

is reached. If greater, then expected profits are negative for any positive output the firm produces, so that firm is clearly better off producing nothing. Thus as long as $x_n^* \gg 0$ for sufficiently large n, a contradiction is reached in this case as well. That all firms produce positive output for sufficiently large n is guaranteed by (A2).

(c) *Output converges in mean to the competitive output.* We can write (b) in our notation as:

$$\lim_{n \to \infty} (n-1) P^{S'} P^K x_n^* = P^{S'} W.$$

Because the rank of P is equal to K (A1), the rank of P^S (and Π and P^K) is also equal to K. Thus we can premultiply both sides of the above equation by $(P^S P^{S'})^{-1} P^S$, since $P^S P^{S'}$ is a square matrix of full rank (equal to K), and hence invertible. This implies:

$$\lim_{n \to \infty} (n-1) P^K x_n^* = W$$

which implies

$$\lim_{n \to \infty} P^K (n x_n^*) = W.$$

Since the left-hand side is the vector of expected outputs conditional on w, (c) is established.

(d) *Output converges almost surely to the competitive output.* From above, $n x_n^*$ is bounded. Hence the variance of expected output converges to 0. Almost sure convergence follows immediately.

Observe that in the limit equilibrium aggregate output conditional on each state is known by all firms to be precisely equal to the full information competitive output. In addition, firms' profits converge to zero in probability. Therefore, despite the firms' incomplete private information about the state of the world they know the equilibrium conditional aggregate output and profits with virtual certainty in the limit.

This knowledge is sufficient for firms to "discount" their private information appropriately in equilibrium, much as bidders in an auction discount their private information in order to avoid the winner's curse. By making these adjustments, firms are all able to earn non-negative expected profits regardless of the signal they receive. As the environment becomes more competitive, these expected profits are all going to zero. The two assumptions we made guarantee that there will be "enough" information in the signals so that this "conditional" zero-profit condition implies convergence in mean to the full information perfectly competitive output. Almost sure convergence does not require any additional assumptions.

The Cournot competitive limit

The following three examples are given to illustrate the importance of the assumptions of the model. In all examples, we let $b=1$ and cost is fixed at $c=1$. The signal space is taken to be the two element set $\{0,1\}$.

Example 1 (all assumptions of the model are satisfied):

$$a = \begin{array}{l} 3 \text{ with probability } 1/2 \\ 4 \text{ with probability } 1/2 \end{array}.$$

Thus, $w_1=2$, $w_2=3$, each with equal probability. The joint distribution of signals and demand is given by:

$$P = \begin{pmatrix} \dfrac{1}{3} & \dfrac{1}{6} \\[2mm] \dfrac{1}{6} & \dfrac{1}{3} \end{pmatrix}.$$

Hence

$$P^S = P^K = \begin{pmatrix} \dfrac{2}{3} & \dfrac{1}{3} \\[2mm] \dfrac{1}{3} & \dfrac{2}{3} \end{pmatrix}, \qquad \Pi = \begin{pmatrix} \dfrac{5}{9} & \dfrac{4}{9} \\[2mm] \dfrac{4}{9} & \dfrac{5}{9} \end{pmatrix}.$$

A general formula for equilibrium strategies is easily derived by combining equations (3) and (6) of the appendix to obtain

$$x_n^* = \tfrac{1}{2}P^{S'}\left(I - \left(\frac{2}{n-1}\Pi^{-1} + I\right)^{-1}\right)W.$$

From the parameters of the example, this gives

$$x_n^*(0) = \frac{n+41}{(n+1)(n+17)}$$

$$x_n^*(1) = \frac{4n+44}{(n+1)(n+17)}.$$

Expected total output with n firms is $nP^K x_n^*$ which equals

$$\frac{n}{n+1}\begin{pmatrix} \dfrac{2n+42}{n+17} \\[2mm] \dfrac{3n+43}{n+17} \end{pmatrix}$$

which converges to $W=\left(\tfrac{2}{3}\right)$. By the law of the large numbers, actual output converges almost surely to this also.

363

Example 2 (Assumption A1 not satisfied): Same as example 1 except

$$P = \begin{pmatrix} \dfrac{1}{4} & \dfrac{1}{4} \\[2mm] \dfrac{1}{4} & \dfrac{1}{4} \end{pmatrix}.$$

In other words, signals convey no useful information. Since π is not invertible, we cannot use (10) to solve for equilibrium strategies. Nonetheless, it is easily shown that $x_n(0) = x_n(1) = 5/2(n+1)$ is the unique symmetric equilibrium strategy. Output is a degenerate random variable with $X_n = (n/n+1)(5/2)$. Price is high when demand is high and low when demand is low, in contrast to the previous example in which price always equals 1 (cost) in the limit.

Example 3 (Assumption A2 not satisfied):

$a_1 = 1$

$a_2 = 2.$

Thus $w_1 = 0$, $w_2 = 1$, each with equal probability. The joint distribution of signals and states of demand is given by

$$P = \frac{1}{2} \begin{pmatrix} \rho & 1-\rho \\ 1-\rho & \rho \end{pmatrix}$$

where ρ is a parameter which can take on values between 1/2 and 1.

One can show that for n greater than $1 + (2/[\rho^2 - (1-\rho)^2])$ only firms who observe $s = 1$ (the "optimistic" signal) will produce. This is precisely what assumption (A2) rules out. The reason is that if $a = 1$ (low demand) profits are bounded above by 0. Hence firms who think that there is a high enough probability that the state is $a = 1$ earn negative expected profits at any positive output level they choose.

The equilibrium output of an "$s_i = 1$" firm if $n > 1 + (2/[\rho^2 - (1-\rho)^2])$ is $x_n^*(1) = \rho/(2 + [\rho^2 + (1-\rho)^2](n-1))$ and the equilibrium output of an "$s = 0$" firm if $n > 1 + (2/[\rho^2 - (1-\rho)^2])$ is $x_n^*(0) = 0$.

Since the proportion of firms receiving signal $s_i = 1$ is ρ if $a = 2$ and $(1-\rho)$ if $a = 1$, total output converges to $\rho^2/(\rho^2 + (1-\rho)^2)$ when $a = 2$ and converges to $\rho(1-\rho)/(\rho^2 + (1-\rho)^2)$ when $a = 1$. However, this is not the perfectly competitive output of 1 when $a = 2$ and 0 when $a = 1$. Competitive price is 1 in both states, but price in the Cournot limit is too high (Price $= (\rho^2 + 2(1-\rho)^2)/(\rho^2 + (1-\rho)^2) > 1$) when $a = 2$, and is too low (Price $= (1 - 3\rho(1-\rho))/(\rho^2 + (1-\rho)^2) < 1$) when $a = 1$. Also note that when information is very poor (ρ close to 1/2), output is the same in

364

both states and price is more variable ($\approx 3/2$ when $a = 2$, $\approx 1/2$ when $a = 1$). When information is very good (ρ close to 1), output is more responsive to true demand and price approaches the competitive price of 1.

The source of the problem here is that $(P^K)^{-1}W$ has one positive and one negative component for large n. Thus the non-negativity constraint is binding for firms observing the pessimistic signal. Therefore, the information contained in the pessimistic signal is not fully reflected in aggregate output since firms receiving these signals just drop out of the market.

4. Extensions

In the previous section, linear demand functions were used in order to construct the equilibrium explicitly. This simplified the limiting analysis a great deal. The intuitive proof given for Theorem 2 suggests that the main result is true in non-linear environments as well. The purpose of this section is to show that linear demand functions are not particularly special in this regard. As before, the shared inverse demand function and the common marginal cost may both be uncertain and the uncertainty need not enter additively. We represent this random inverse demand function (net of cost)[3] by $\mathcal{P}(x_1 + \cdots + x_n, a)$, where a is a random variable, taking on possible values $a_1, \dots, a_K$. Given any realization a_k, $\mathcal{P}(\cdot, a_k)$ is a known function, denoted $\mathcal{P}_k(\cdot)$. In the linear case treated before, $\mathcal{P}_k(\cdot)$ corresponds to $bw_k - b(x_1 + \cdots + x_n)$. Using the same notation as before, given signal $s_i = v_s$, a firm chooses x_{is} to maximize

$$x_{is}\left\{ \sum_{k=1}^{K} p_{ks}^S E[\mathcal{P}_k(X_n^{ki} + x_{is})] \right\}.$$

We make the following assumptions

Assumption A1'. P has rank K, $p_{ks} > 0$ for all $k = 1, \dots, K$, $s = 1, \dots, S$.

Assumption A2'. There exists $\bar{n}$ such that a symmetric equilibrium exists with

$$x_n^*(v_s) > 0 \quad \forall s, \forall n \geq \bar{n}.$$

Assumption A3. $\mathcal{P}_k''(\cdot)$ exists, $-M \leq \mathcal{P}_k'(\cdot) < 0$ on $[0, \infty]$, $\exists \bar{X} > 0$ such that $\mathcal{P}_k(\bar{X}) < 0$, for all k.

Theorem 3. *Assumptions A1', A2' and A3 imply that price converges almost surely to the competitive price, i.e. $\mathcal{P}_k(X_n^k) \to^{\text{a.s.}} 0$, for all k.*

---

[3] $\mathcal{P}$ may be interpreted as the difference between the market price and unit cost. The perfectly competitive outcome would have $\mathcal{P}_k = 0$ in every state k.

Proof. See Appendix.

While the theorem does not explicitly identify the class of demand functions and information structures which lead to convergence, it is clear that the original restrictions of linear demand and additive uncertainty were much stronger than necessary. Basically what the theorem asserts is that if there is sufficient diversity of signals, (A1'), and if in equilibrium none of the firm types (with types being determined by signals) drops out the market, (A2'), then almost sure convergence to the competitive outcomes occurs. Example 3 illustrated what happens if some types drop out of the market. In that case, A1 was satisfied, but A2 failed. Only one type produced in equilibrium. The assumption that $p_{ks} > 0$ for all k and s is inessential and is made only to simplify the proof. The third assumption guarantees that profit functions and marginal revenue functions are well-defined and bounded.

It was assumed from the start that firms were Cournot competitors. It is interesting to note that a similar convergence result should hold, albeit with slightly different assumptions about the information structure, if firms are Bertrand competitors. The Bertrand model can be interpreted as a type of auction in which firms bid a price p and receive nothing if they do not quote the lowest price, but receive the random variable $X(p)(p-c)$ if they win. Results in Wilson (1977) and Milgrom (1979) suggest that under fairly weak informational conditions the equilibrium price in the Bertrand equilibrium will converge to the competitive price.

A number of features of the model were introduced in order to make the analysis simple, and these deserve some discussion. First, the finiteness of the signal and state spaces permitted the use of elementary matrix algebra in the proofs. Finiteness of the signal space is clearly not needed, and an earlier draft of the paper allowed for fairly arbitrary signal spaces. Others [for example, Novshek and Sonnenschein (1982)] have analyzed a duopoly game with differential information in which signals are drawn from the unit interval. The results proved here can be extended to apply to environments with a continuum of signals. The choice of a finite signal space was made because it provides a clearer intuition about what is driving the results.

Second, the players in the game were assumed to be risk neutral. While this assumption may appear quite strong at first glance, it is probably not crucial to the convergence result. Since firms effectively face no risk in the limit,[4] risk aversion or risk preference should not influence behaviour.

---

[4] To clarify this, the uncertainty a firm faces about the state is not reduced as the number of firms increases, but in the limit a firm's equilibrium profit is independent of the state. (Recall that equilibrium profits converge almost surely to zero.) Hence there is no payoff-relevant uncertainty in equilibrium.

Wilson (1977) and Milgrom (1979) also find that risk attitudes play no role in their auction convergence results.

Third, it was assumed that the cost function, although uncertain, was the same for all firms. What happens when the assumption of common costs is dropped is not immediately evident. The same remark applies to dropping the assumption of a shared demand curve. Extensions of these results to oligopoly models of product differentiation would entail the relaxation of one or both of these two assumptions.

Another important question which is not dealt with in this paper is the problem of acquiring costly proprietary information. This question has been posed in the context of an auction environment by Matthews (1984), Milgrom and Weber (1980), Milgrom (1981), and Lee (1981), and in the context of an asset market by Grossman and Stiglitz (1980) and elsewhere. In this paper, as in Wilson (1977) and Milgrom (1979), the information acquisition problem is exogenous to the model. As Matthews (1984) points out, endogeneity of information acquisition when information is costly can alter the convergence property of auction mechanisms. One suspects the main result in this paper may suffer a similar weakness.

The problem of information acquisition and information sharing in a Cournot world is being examined elsewhere. Palfrey (1982), Vives (1982), Gal-Or (1983), Clarke (1982), and Novshek and Sonnenschein (1982) have some preliminary results along these lines.

5. Conclusions

An interesting consequence of the convergence theorem relates to the more general question of pricing in competitive markets under uncertainty. To the extent that the model here is a reasonable description of a perfectly competitive market, price will precisely equal marginal cost, even if individual firms face a lot of uncertainty. Price will *not* equal average (expected) marginal cost. Similarly, price and output will *not* be determined by the "average" demand curve, if demand is uncertain. Even though all individual decisions are made independently and are based on *different* posterior distributions of cost and residual demand, aggregate market outcomes are determined by true cost and true demand.

The reason that price converges to marginal cost is that the Cournot game successfully aggregates all the firms' private information. Uncertainty is resolved in the competitive limit. As noted earlier this result is very similar to the results of Wilson (1977) and Milgrom (1979) concerning the convergence properties (the competitive limit) of auction market mechanisms. Their conclusion that auction mechanisms are very efficient aggregators of diverse private information apparently applies to the

367

Cournot "mechanism" as well. The market price is the same in the limit as it would be if each firm actually observed all other firms' private information. However, an additional restriction is necessary in the Cournot game because production quantities rather than prices (or bids) are the strategic variables and these quantities are constrained to be non-negative.

The fact that diverse private information can be efficiently aggregated in these two much different settings – an auction game in one case and a Cournot production game in the other case – suggests a property which may be shared by a broader class of models of price formation under conditions of incomplete private information. In auctions and in Cournot oligopoly, market equilibrium is determined by independent, private decisions by the market participants. Price is an *outcome* of the game rather than being a parameter which participants take as given when making decisions. As a market gets large, the ex post aggregate outcomes (e.g. prices) of the game of incomplete private information approach the aggregate outcomes of the corresponding game with perfect information. The price generated in the *n*-person game is a consistent estimator of the Walrasian price.

The extent to which this is a general property shared by many competitive pricing mechanisms is an important question which deserves further study. A positive answer would imply that competitive behavior in large markets solves, to some extent, potential ex post inefficiencies stemming from uncertainty and diverse[5] private information. The conclusion would be that in large enough markets, diverse private information does not drastically alter the conclusions reached by the idealized Walrasian model of pricing in a full information world. In any case, such research will provide some guidance as to when and why differential information alone might lead to market outcomes different from those predicted by classical, perfect information, price-taking models.

Appendix

Proof of Theorem 2. The proof is constructive and has two parts. In the first part, an equilibrium sequence of aggregate outputs, X_n^*, is derived without imposing non-negativity constraints on the firms' maximization problems, and it is proved that the constructed sequence of equilibrium aggregate outputs satisfies

---

[5] This notion of diverse, of *differential,* information here is to be distinguished from *a priori asymmetry* of information in moral hazard and adverse selection problems. These remarks are not made in reference to the latter sorts of problems. Nonetheless, it is perhaps worth noting recent work by Holmstrom (1981) and others which suggests that even problems arising from a priori information asymmetries are sometimes mitigated by large numbers of agents.

$X_n^* \to \text{a.s. } W.$

In the second part, it is shown that (A2) implies $x_n^* > 0$, for sufficiently large n. Hence, given (A2), unconstrained equilibrium best responses equal non-negative-constrained best responses, for sufficiently large n.

(i) Construction of the symmetric equilibrium sequence, without constraining best responses:

If firm i observes signal $s_i = v_s$ and all other firms produce according to the strategy x_n, then firm i chooses x_{is} to maximize expected profits, conditional on having observed signal v_s. This expression is:

$$E\{x_{is}((w - X_n^i) - x_{is}) \mid s_i = v_s\} = x_{is} \sum_{k=1}^{K} p_{ks}^S(w_k - E_n^{ki} - x_{is}). \tag{3}$$

From (1), the first order necessary condition for firm i having observed $s_i = v_s$ is given by

$$x_{is} = \frac{1}{2} \sum_{k=1}^{K} p_{ks}^S(w_k - E_n^{ki}). \tag{4}$$

Since (3) is concave in x_{is}, (4) is a sufficient as well as necessary condition for x_{is} to be the unique best response if signal v_s is observed by firm i. We can write this S-vector of best responses by

$$x_i^* = \tfrac{1}{2} P^{S'}(W - E_n^i). \tag{5}$$

Since we are constructing a symmetric equilibrium (5) is the same for *all* n firms and E_n^i simply equals $(n-1)E_n/n$. Thus, we can obtain an expression for total output given any n-vector of private signals, $(s_1, \ldots, s_n)$, by summing the rows of (5) corresponding to these n signals. This yields

$$X_n = \tfrac{1}{2} Q_n'(nW - (n-1)E_n). \tag{6}$$

Taking conditional expectations of X_n gives us

$$E_n = \tfrac{1}{2} \Pi'(nW - (n-1)E_n). \tag{7}$$

The linear system defined by (7) can be rewritten as

$$\left(\frac{2}{n-1} I + \Pi'\right) E_n = \frac{n}{n-1} \Pi' W \tag{8}$$

where I is the $K \times K$ identity matrix.

Since P is rank K, Π is non-singular. Hence the inverse operator is continuous at Π, so we have

$$\lim_{n \to \infty} E_n = W.$$

Combining (6) and (7) gives

369

$$X_n = Q_n'(\Pi')^{-1}E_n.$$

By the strong law of large numbers, $Q_n \to^{\text{a.s.}} \Pi$ so that $Q_n'(\Pi')^{-1} \to^{\text{a.s.}} I$. Since $E_n \to W$ and both I and W are fixed constants, $X_n \to^{\text{a.s.}} W$.

(ii) We now prove that

$$\lim_{n \to \infty} nx_n^* = (P^K)^{-1}W > 0.$$

It then follows immediately that for sufficiently large n, $x_n^* > 0$.

From (8) we have

$$\Pi'E_n = \frac{n}{n-1}\Pi'W - \frac{2}{n-1}E_n$$

so that

$$E_n^i = W - \frac{2}{n-1}(\Pi')^{-1}E_n^i. \tag{9}$$

Since $E_n \to W$, $E_n^i \to (n-1)W/n$ and hence from (8)

$$\lim_{n \to \infty} E_n^i = \left(I - \frac{2}{n}(\Pi')^{-1}\right)W. \tag{10}$$

From (5) we can obtain

$$nx_n^* = \frac{n}{2}P^{S'}(W - E_n^i). \tag{11}$$

Substitution of (10) in (11) and taking limits gives

$$\begin{aligned}
\lim_{n \to \infty} nx_n^* &= \frac{n}{2}(P^{S'})\left(I - \left(I - \frac{2}{n}(\Pi')^{-1}\right)\right)W \\
&= (P^{S'})(\Pi')^{-1}W \\
&= (P^K)^{-1}W \\
&> 0
\end{aligned}$$

by (A2). It follows that for sufficiently large n, $x_n^* > 0$. ∎

Proof of Theorem 3. (A2') and (A3) imply that, for $n \geq \bar{n}$, equilibrium output choices lie between 0 and $\bar{X}$ for all s and satisfy the first order necessary condition below:

$$-x_{is}^* \sum_{k=1}^{K} p_{ks}^S E\{\mathcal{P}_k'(X_n^{ki} + x_{is}^*)\} = \sum_{k=1}^{K} p_{ks}^S [E\{\mathcal{P}_k(X_n^{ki} + x_{is}^*)\}]. \tag{12}$$

By (A3) we have $-M < \sum_{k=1}^{K} p_{ks}^S E\{\mathcal{P}_k'(X_n^{ki} + x_{is}^*)\} < 0$. Hence the R.H.S. of (12) is bounded above by $-Mx_{is}^*$. We next establish that, for all s, the

R.H.S. of (12) – which can be interpreted as the expected markup of price over cost if a firm receives signal s – must approach 0 as n gets large. First we show that $\lim_{n\to\infty} x_{is}^* = 0$ for all s, by the following argument. Suppose for some s $\lim_{n\to\infty} x_{is}^* \neq 0$. Since $\{x_{is}^*\}_{n=2}^{\infty}$ is a bounded nonnegative sequence, it must contain a convergent subsequence, denoted $\{x_{is}^{\nu^*}\}_{\nu=1}^{\infty}$, such that $\lim_{\nu\to\infty} x_{is}^{\nu^*} = \delta > 0$. Fix ϵ such that $0 < \epsilon < \delta$ and let $\bar{\nu}$ be such that, for all $\nu \geq \bar{\nu}$, $|x_{is}^{\nu^*} - \delta| < \epsilon$. Now let L be the smallest integer greater than or equal to $1 + \bar{X}/(\delta - \epsilon)$. Consider a firm i which observes signal v_s when there are $\nu \geq \max(\bar{\nu}, L)$ other firms (all using strategy x^{ν^*}). If L or more firms other than i also observe signal v_s then for all k price, net of cost, is less than or equal to $\mathcal{P}_k(L(\delta - \epsilon)) \leq r < 0$ where $r = \max_k [\mathcal{P}_k(\bar{X})]$. If less than L other firms observe signal v_s then clearly price, net of cost, is bounded, since $\mathcal{P}_k(0) < \infty$. Denote this bound by B. Denote by λ_k^{ν} the probability that fewer than L out of ν firms receive v_s if the true state is a_k. That is

$$\lambda_k^{\nu} = \sum_{l=1}^{L-1} \binom{\nu}{l} (p_{ks}^K)^l (1 - p_{ks}^K)^{\nu-1}, \quad k = 1, \ldots, K.$$

Hence expected price, net of cost, is bounded above by

$$\sum_{k=1}^{K} p_{ks}^s (\lambda_k^{\nu} B(0) + (1 - \lambda_k^{\nu}) r),$$

which is less than 0 for sufficiently large ν, since $\lim_{\nu\to\infty} \lambda_k^{\nu} = 0$ for all k. Therefore the firm in question has a unique best response of $x_{is} = 0$, which is a contradiction. Hence, $\lim_{n\to\infty} x_{is}^* = 0$ for all s. Consequently the R.H.S. of (12) converges to 0. Furthermore it implies that

$$\lim_{n\to\infty} E\{\mathcal{P}_k(X_n^{ki} + x_{is}^*)\} = \lim_{n\to\infty} E\{\mathcal{P}_k(X_n^k)\} \quad \text{for all } k \text{ and } s.$$

Therefore

$$\lim_{n\to\infty} \sum_{k=1}^{K} p_{ks}^S [E\{\mathcal{P}_k(X_n^k)\}] = 0 \quad \text{for all } k.$$

Taking conditional expectations gives

$$\lim_{n\to\infty} \Pi E\{\mathcal{P}_k(X_n^k)\} = 0 \quad \text{for all } k.$$

Since Π is invertible by (A1), $E\{\mathcal{P}_k(X_n^k)\} \to 0$ for all k. This implies that nx_n^* is bounded. Hence $\lim_{n\to\infty} \text{var}(X_n^k) \to 0$, and therefore $\mathcal{P}_k(X_n^k) \to^{\text{a.s.}} 0$ for all k. ∎

References

Boullion, T. and Odell, P. (1971), *Generalized Inverse Matrices* (New York, Wiley).

Clarke, R. N. (1982), "Collusion and the Incentives for Information Sharing" (Working Paper No 8203, University of Wisconsin–Madison).

Gal-Or, E. (1983), "Information Transmission and Correlated Signals" (Manuscript, University of Pittsburgh).

Grossman, S. and Stiglitz, J. (1980), "On the Impossibility of Informationally Efficient Markets," *American Economic Review* 70, 393-409.

Harsanyi, J. (1967-68), "Games with Incomplete Information Played by Bayesian Players," *Management Science* 14, 159-82, 320-34, 486-502.

Holmström, B., "Moral Hazard in Teams," *Bell Journal of Economics,* 13, 324-40.

Lee, T. (1981), "Resource Information Policy and Federal Resource Leasing" (Discussion Paper No 81-11, Department of Economics, University of California, San Diego).

Matthews, S. (1984), "Information Acquisition in Discriminatory Auctions," in M. Boyer and R. Kihlstrom (eds.). *Bayesian Models in Economic Theory* (Elsevier).

Milgrom, P. (1979), "A Convergence Theorem for Competitive Bidding with Differential Information," *Econometrica* 47, 679-88.

———, (1981), "Rational Expectations, Information Acquisition, and Competitive Bidding," *Econometrica,* 49, 921-43.

Milgrom, P. and Weber, R. (1982), "A Theory of Auctions and Competitive Bidding," *Econometrica* 50, 1089-122.

Novshek, W. and Sonnenschein, H. (1982), "Fulfilled Expectations Cournot Duopoly with Information Acquisition and Release," *Bell Journal of Economics* 13, 214-8.

Palfrey, T. (1982), "Risk Advantages and Information Acquisition," *Bell Journal of Economics,* 13, 219-24.

Vives, X. (1982), "Duopoly Information Equilibrium: Cournot and Bertrand," *Journal of Economic Theory* (forthcoming).

Wilson, R. B. (1977), "A Bidding Model of Perfect Competition," *Review of Economic Studies* 44, 511-8.

CHAPTER 16

Losses from horizontal merger: the effects of an exogenous change in industry structure on Cournot–Nash equilibrium

STEPHEN W. SALANT, SHELDON SWITZER, AND ROBERT J. REYNOLDS

The consequences of a horizontal merger are typically studied by treating the merger as an exogenous change in market structure that displaces the initial Cournot equilibrium. In the new equilibrium the merged firm is assumed to behave like a multiplant Cournot player engaged in a noncooperative game against other sellers. The purpose of this article is to evaluate an unnoticed comparative-static implication of this approach: some exogenous mergers may reduce the endogenous joint profits of the firms that are assumed to collude. Cournot's original example is used to illustrate this and other bizarre results that can occur in the Cournot framework if the market structure is treated as exogenous.

I. Introduction

In the Cournot [1838] solution to the oligopoly problem, each firm's output choice is profit-maximizing given the outputs of the other firms. The Cournot approach is conventionally extended to industries with merged firms and cartels by treating each merged entity as a collective of plants under the control of a particular player in a noncooperative game. The payoff to each coalition is the sum of the profits that accrue to each of its members. For each exogenous specification of market structure (partition of plants into coalitions), outputs, profits, and market prices are endogenously determined.

The purpose of this article is to explore and evaluate an unnoticed comparative-static implication of such Cournot models: some exogenous mergers *may reduce* the endogenous joint profits of the firms that are assumed to collude. Similar results arise using other solution concepts [Cave, 1980]. In the Cournot case losses from horizontal merger may seem surprising, since the merged firm always has the option of producing exactly as its components did in the premerger equilibrium. But such

Stephen W. Salant, Sheldon Switzer, and Robert J. Reynolds, "Losses from Horizontal Merger: the Effects of an Exogenous Change in Industry Structure on Cournot–Nash Equilibrium," *The Quarterly Journal of Economics* 98, 2, 1983, pp. 185–99. © 1983 by the President and Fellows of Harvard College. Reprinted by permission of John Wiley & Sons, Inc.

STEPHEN W. SALANT, SHELDON SWITZER, ROBERT J. REYNOLDS

a situation is not an equilibrium following the merger, since – *given* unchanged outputs of the other players – the merged firm would then have an incentive to alter its production (i.e., to reduce it).

In the next section we raise the possibility diagrammatically that some exogenous mergers may be unprofitable. Section III then establishes that this outcome can in fact arise by examining Cournot's original example where identical firms with constant unit costs of production sell a homogeneous product to consumers with a linear demand curve. The section also establishes a number of other bizarre comparative-static results for this example. At the conclusion of the section, the example is modified to show that exogenous mergers can still cause losses even when the merger creates such large efficiency gains through scale economies that it would be socially advantageous.

We wish to emphasize at the outset that Cournot's example is chosen merely as the simplest in which to display various puzzling phenomena. In particular, the loss-from-merger result *can also arise* in more complex Nash equilibrium models – with differentiated products, dynamics, increasing marginal costs, and so forth. Indeed, we first observed losses from merger in a dynamic oil model where each Cournot player chooses a time-dated vector of extraction (subject to capacity and exhaustion constraints) and incurs marginal costs that are increasing functions of the rate of extraction. The parameters used in this computerized model [Salant, 1981 and 1982] were not intended to generate peculiar behavior, but rather to approximate the current world oil market. Nor does the loss-from-merger result arise because of the partial-equilibrium nature of the analysis. In an independent analysis using a general-equilibrium framework, Okuno et al. [1980, p. 29] display an example with the same characteristic.

Section IV discusses the significance of our paradoxical comparative-static results for attempts to build a theory of horizontal mergers. Should the Cournot–Nash equilibrium concept – and indeed any solution concept where an exogenous merger can cause a loss – be discarded? Few solution concepts would survive such a test. Or should the decision to merge be endogenized as a move in a larger game? This latter approach is exciting because it would permit *predictions* about which mergers are contained in the set of equilibria and which mergers will never occur. Antitrust authorities need not concern themselves with blocking mergers outside the equilibrium set, since market forces would prevent their occurrence; for the same reason, the government could not cause such mergers to occur (without using supplementary incentives) even if they would be socially desirable. Finally, such models may ultimately help us understand the evolution of industry structure over time as coalitions form and regroup.

374

Losses from horizontal merger

To illustrate how the decision to merge can be endogenized as a move in a larger game, a simple model is outlined with a single stage of coalition formation. In this model all of the mergers in the equilibrium set are profitable, thus eliminating the paradoxes that arise when mergers are treated as exogenous. Furthermore, among the equilibria are not only merger to monopoly but also less complete mergers. Such a characteristic seems important in a model of horizontal mergers; otherwise, its predictions will conflict with the structure of every industry in existence that is not a complete monopoly. The simple model outlined in Section IV is provided only as an illustration of a promising approach. A more complex but realistic model using this same approach is under construction.

II. The potential loss from horizontal mergers

Consider a Cournot equilibrium in which each firm in an industry operates independently. This can be compared with the Cournot equilibrium in which a subset of the firms merge, while the other firms remain independent. Such a comparison can be used to examine those cases in which the joint profits of the merged firms would be *smaller* than the sum of their profits prior to merger. It is convenient to refer to the subset of firms that will participate in the proposed merger as "insiders" and those firms that will continue to behave independently after the merger as "outsiders." We shall make use of Figures 1 and 2. To simplify these figures, we have drawn the functions in each as linear; however, no result depends on the linearity of our drawing. Denote by $R_O(Q)$ the total amount that noncooperating outsiders would produce for any given aggregate production (Q) by insiders. $R_O(Q)$ can easily be computed by deducting the given aggregate production by insiders (Q) from the consumer demand curve, computing the Nash equilibrium among the noncooperating outsiders relative to this residual demand curve, and adding up the equilibrium production at each outsider firm. Denote by $R_I^{NC}(q)$ the total amount that the noncooperating insiders would produce (prior to merger) for any given aggregate production (q) by outsiders. $R_I^{NC}(q)$ can easily be computed by deducting from the consumer demand curve the given aggregate production by the outsiders (q), computing the Nash equilibrium among the noncooperating insiders relative to this residual demand curve, and adding up the equilibrium production at each insider firm. We can then use these curves to determine outputs prior to the merger. In Figure 1, a Nash equilibrium occurs at A, where the reaction functions of the outsiders (R_O) and the noncolluding insiders (R_I^{NC}) intersect. Outsiders produce the horizontal component of A (q_{NC}) in aggregate and insiders produce

375

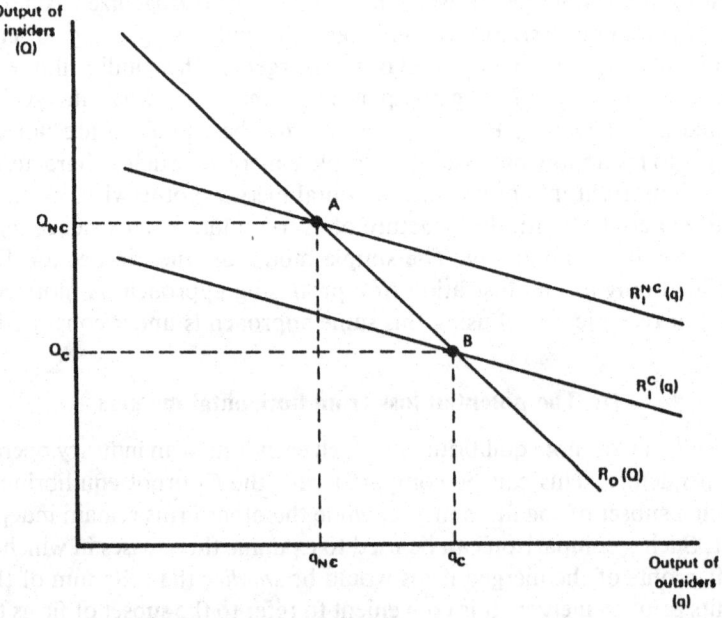

Figure 1. Production responses from merger.

the vertical component (Q_{NC}). An exogenous merger will displace the equilibrium. Graphically, it will cause some of these curves to shift. Since the response of the noncolluding outsiders to the aggregate supply of the insiders does not depend on whether that supply was produced by a merged firm or a set of noncolluding firms, R_O does not shift. In contrast, the reaction function of the insiders will shift when the insiders merge. Denote by $R_I^C(q)$ the production of the insiders after the merger, given outsider production q. Then, $R_I^C(q) < R_I^{NC}(q)$. For any given output by outsiders, insiders will contract their aggregate output when they merge because they will then internalize the inframarginal losses that they impart to each other.

We conclude, therefore, that a merger causes the equilibrium output of the insiders to contract and the output of the outsiders to expand. To determine its effects on profits, we examine Figure 2. Denote the sum of the profits of the insiders prior to and following the merger, respectively, as $\Pi_I^{NC}(q)$ and $\Pi_I^C(q)$. For any given level of production by outsiders, the aggregate profits of the insiders can only increase (since they can always run their plants so as to mimic the premerger equilibrium). Hence

376

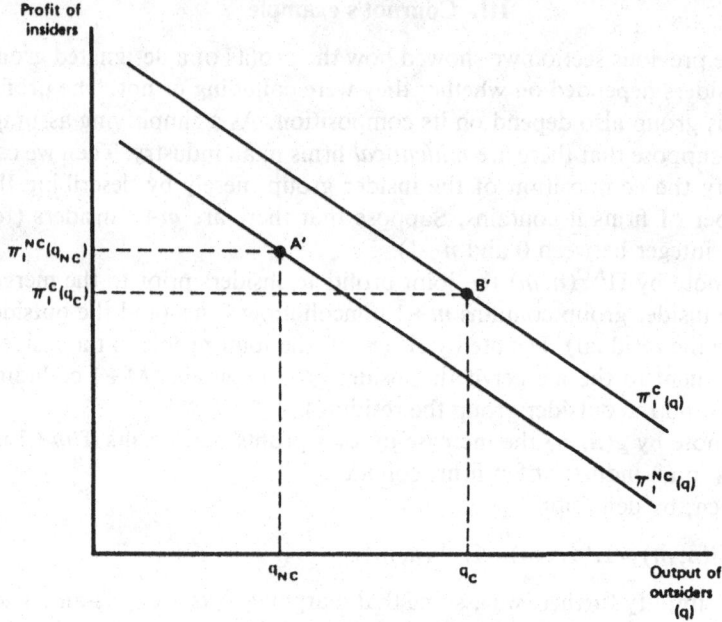

Figure 2. Profit consequences of merger.

Π_I^C lies above Π_I^{NC}. But as the outputs of the outsiders increase, the profits of the insiders decrease. Hence the *possibility* arises that the increase in production by outsiders following the merger will reduce insider profits by more than the increase in profits that would have occurred had outsider production remained constant. This possibility is illustrated in Figure 2, where the profits following the merger (the vertical component of B') are smaller than the profits prior to the merger (the vertical component of A'). Thus, it is the output expansion of the outsider firms that can in principle cause a reduction in profits for the merging firms.[1]

Of course, the model has more structure than we have considered. Hence, conceivably the possibility illustrated in Figure 2 can never occur. To demonstrate that the possibility can indeed arise, we need look no further than Cournot's classic example.

---

[1] It should be noted, however, that industry profits will always increase in response to the merger. If the merger is unprofitable, the profits of the noncolluding firms will have increased by more than the loss in the profits of the insiders.

STEPHEN W. SALANT, SHELDON SWITZER, ROBERT J. REYNOLDS

III. Cournot's example

In the previous section we showed how the profits of a designated group of insiders depended on whether they were colluding or not. The profits of this group also depend on its composition. As a simplifying assumption, suppose that there are n *identical* firms in an industry. Then we can specify the composition of the insider group merely by describing the number of firms it contains. Suppose that there are $m+1$ insiders (for m an integer between 0 and $n-1$).

Denote by $\Pi^{NC}(n, m)$ the joint profits to insiders prior to the merger if the insider group contains $m+1$ noncolluding firms (and the outsider group the residual). Denote by $\Pi^C(n, m)$ the joint profits to the insiders subsequent to the merger if the insider group contains $M+1$ colluding firms (and the outsider group the residual).

Denote by $g(n, m)$ the increase in joint profits that results if $m+1$ insiders in an industry of n firms collude.

Then, by definition,

$$g(n, m) = \Pi^C(n, m) - \Pi^{NC}(n, m).$$

To simplify further, we assume that marginal costs are constant. Then if each firm in an x-firm equilibrium earned $\Pi(x)$,

$$\Pi^{NC}(n, m) = (m+1)\Pi(n); \tag{1}$$

$$\Pi^C(n, m) = \Pi(n-m); \tag{2}$$

and

$$g(n, m) = \Pi(n-m) - (m+1)\Pi(n). \tag{3}$$

Equation (1) follows from the assumption that all firms are identical. Hence prior to the merger, the $m+1$ insiders earn jointly $m+1$ times as much as the typical firm in the n-firm equilibrium. Equation (2) depends, in addition, on the assumption of constant marginal costs. Because of this assumption the insiders – once they have merged – behave exactly like any of the other firms in an $n-m$ firm symmetric equilibrium. Equation (3) follows by substitution.

In Cournot's example with constant marginal costs (α) and linear[2] demand ($P = \beta - \Sigma_{i=1}^n Q_i$), it is straightforward to calculate $\Pi(n)$:

$$\Pi(n) = ([\beta - \alpha]/[n+1])^2. \tag{4}$$

---

[2] Since any linear demand curve can be expressed in this form if the output units are defined appropriately, the assumption of a unitary slope is unrestrictive.

To verify this, we first deduce the output of each firm in an n-firm symmetric Cournot equilibrium and then calculate the resulting profit per firm as a function of n. Firm j maximizes profits by setting Q_j to solve

$$\max_{Q_j \geq 0} Q_j \left[\beta - Q_j - \sum_{i \neq j} Q_i - \alpha \right].$$

If optimal production by firm j is positive, then $\beta - \sum_{i \neq j} Q_i - \alpha - 2Q_j = 0$. In a symmetric Nash equilibrium, the output of each firm in the industry will be identical so that $Q_i = Q_j = Q$. Therefore, $Q = [\beta - \alpha]/[n+1]$. Since $\Pi(n) = (P - \alpha)Q$, we can substitute the equilibrium output per firm and verify equation (4):

$$\Pi(n) = (\beta - nQ - \alpha)Q$$

$$= ([\beta - \alpha]/[n+1])^2.$$

The change in insider profits due to merger (equation (3)) can, therefore, be reexpressed as

$$g(n, m) = \left(\frac{\beta - \alpha}{n - m + 1} \right)^2 - (m+1) \left(\frac{\beta - \alpha}{n+1} \right)^2$$

$$= (\beta - \alpha)^2 \{ (n - m + 1)^{-2} - (m+1)(n+1)^{-2} \}. \tag{3'}$$

For any specified number of firms (n) in the premerger equilibrium, equation (3') can be used to determine whether collusion by $m+1$ insiders would be profitable. Losses from merger occur if and only if $g < 0$. In Figure 3 we plot $\Pi^C(n, m)$, $\pi^{NC}(n, m)$ and $g(n, m)$ against m (for a fixed n). The $g(n, m)$ function can be used to deduce several noteworthy properties of this example (for $n \geq 2$).

A. If there is no merger, there will be neither gain nor loss. Trivially, if a single insider is joined by no others in a merger, then its profits will be unchanged $g(n, 0) = 0$, for $n = 2, 3, \ldots$. The profit of the firm will be $\Pi(n)$ both before and after this degenerate merger.

B. Merger by a larger number of firms *may* cause a loss to the colluding firms. This result follows,[3] since

$$\left. \frac{\partial g(n, m)}{\partial m} \right|_{m=0} < 0.$$

Indeed, over a range of m, losses from merger are *larger* the greater the number of firms in the coalition. For example, if $n = 12$, a merger by

---

[3] $\dfrac{\partial g(n, m)}{\partial m} = (B - \alpha)^2 [2(1 + n - m)^{-3} - (1+n)^{-2}].$

379

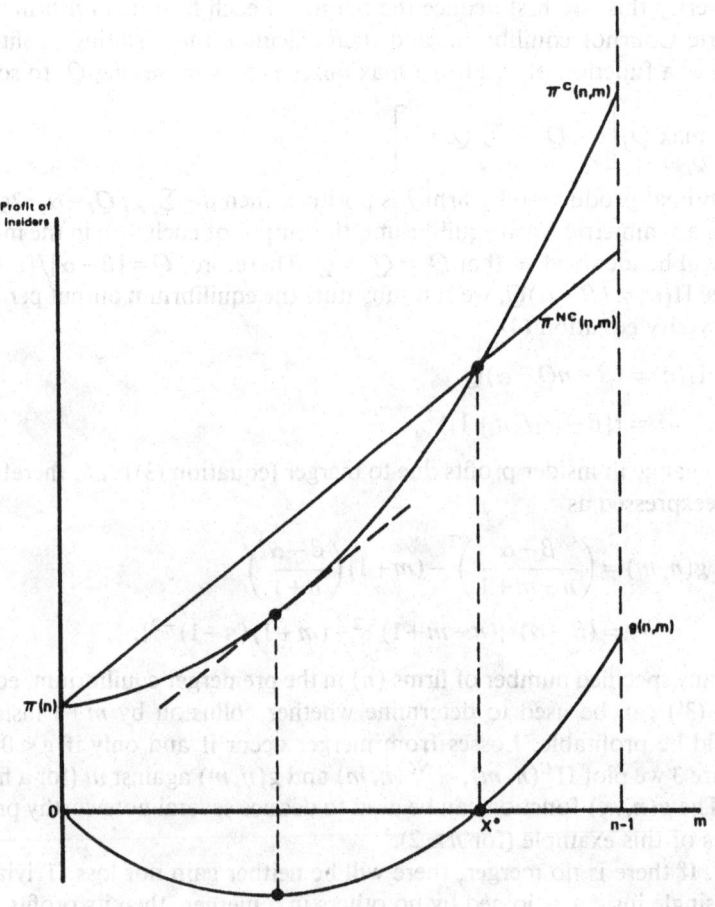

Figure 3. Unprofitable merger.

seven firms ($m = 6$) generates even larger losses than a merger by any smaller number of firms.[4]

C. Merger to monopoly is always profitable. When all the firms in an n-firm equilibrium collude, so that there are no outsiders, profits must increase, since joint profits will then be maximized. Formally, $g(n, n-1) > 0$, for $n = 2, 3, \dots$.

---

[4] To illustrate, when there are twelve firms in the premerger equilibrium ($n = 12$), a merger by seven firms ($m = 6$) will generate larger losses to the insiders than the losses that would be incurred by three merging firms. For $m = 6$, $g(n, m)/(B - \alpha)^2 = -0.021$, while for $m = 2$, $g(n, m)/(B - \alpha)^2 = -0.010$. Indeed, the loss is more than twice as large.

D. For any given number of firms in the premerger equilibrium, if a merger by a specified number of firms causes losses (respectively, gains), a merger by a smaller (larger) number of firms will cause losses (gains). We have noted that $g(n, 0) = 0$, $\partial g(n, 0)/\partial m < 0$, and $g(n, n-1) > 0$, from properties A, B, and C, respectively. Since $g(\cdot, \cdot)$ is continuous in its second argument, there must exist at least one root $x^* > 0$ such that $g(n, x^*) = 0$. Furthermore, since $g(n, x)$ is strictly convex[5] in its second argument, $g(n, x) < 0$ for $x^* > x > 0$. Similarly, $g(n, x) > 0$ for $x > x^*$.

E. For *any* n, it is sufficient for a merger to be unprofitable that less than 80 percent of the firms collude. Consider the gain-from-merger function $g(n, m)$ defined above. Let $x^*(n) + 1$ be the (unique) number of firms in the coalition that will lead to neither gains nor losses for an industry with n firms in the premerger equilibrium. Let $\alpha + (m+1)/n$ be the number of insiders as a proportion of all the firms in the industry. Then a merger causes neither losses nor gains if $\hat{\alpha} = [x^*(n)+1]/n$. This break-even fraction $\hat{\alpha}$ reaches its minimum value of 0.8 when $n = 5$. In other words, the break-even value for all other industry sizes *exceeds* 80 percent.[6] The result, therefore, follows from property D. To illustrate, note that if $n = 3$, a merger by a pair of firms is unprofitable; and if $n = 4$, a merger by either two or three firms is unprofitable.

F. If any given fraction α (< 1) of an industry is assumed to merge, there is an industry size (n) large enough for this merger to cause losses. Let R be the ratio of the postmerger profits of the insiders to their premerger profits. That is, $R = \Pi^C(n, m)/\Pi^{NC}(n, m) = \Pi^C(n, \alpha n - 1)/\Pi^{NC}(n, \alpha n - 1)$, where $\alpha = (m+1)/n$. If $R < 1$ for a merger by a proportion α of an industry of size n, then such a merger would be unprofitable. The proposition

[5] $\dfrac{\partial^2 g(n, m)}{\partial m^2} = (B-\alpha)^2[6(1+n-m)^{-4}] > 0.$

[6] $g(n, \alpha n - 1) = (B-\alpha)^2 \left(\dfrac{(1+n)^2 - \alpha n(2+n-\alpha n)^2}{(2+n-\alpha n)^2(1+n)^2} \right),$

where $g(n, \alpha n - 1) = 0$ when the numerator (N) of the bracketed term equals zero: $N = (1+n)^2 - \alpha n(2+n-\alpha n)^2 = 0$. This equation is a cubic in α and has three roots:

$$\alpha_1 = \frac{1}{n}, \quad \alpha_2 = \frac{(2n+3)-\sqrt{4n+5}}{2n}, \quad \text{and} \quad \alpha_3 = \frac{(2n+3)+\sqrt{4n+5}}{2n}.$$

The third root exceeds unity and is inadmissible; the first is the root associated with the degenerate merger. The second is the root of interest – that is, $\hat{\alpha} = \alpha_2$ – and is itself a function of n:

$$\frac{d\hat{\alpha}}{dn} = \frac{(2n+5)(4n+5)^{1/2} - 3(4n+5)}{2n^2(4n+5)};$$

$$\frac{d^2\hat{\alpha}}{dn^2} = \frac{6(4n+5) - (2n+10)(4n+5)^{1/2} - (4n^2+10n)(4n+5)^{-1/2}}{2n^3(4n+5)}.$$

Thus, $\hat{\alpha}(n)$ reaches a relative minimum at $n = 5$ and a relative maximum at $n = -1$. Hence for $n \geq 1$, $\hat{\alpha}(n) \geq \hat{\alpha}(5) = 0.8$.

follows by noting that (for any $\alpha < 1$) $R \to 0$ as $n \to \infty$.[7] For example, even when 98 percent of the firms in an industry merge, there exists an industry size large enough for this "virtual" monopolization to cause a loss.

G. Mergers that create efficiency gains through scale economies can still cause losses. Suppose, in our example, that a merger of two firms resulted in a loss of L. If instead each firm had positive fixed costs but the same constant marginal costs as before, the postmerger equilibrium would be unchanged, but the entire output of the merged firm would be produced by a single plant – the plant with the lower fixed cost. As long as the fixed cost of each plant was less than L, the fixed cost saved by shutting down the highest cost plant would be too small to make the exogenous merger profitable.

H. A merger that provides efficiency gains may be socially beneficial even if it is privately injurious to the merging parties. Consider a merger that results in a loss to insiders. Since the merger results in a price increase, it also injures consumers. Nonetheless, in some cases, those producers not party to the merger gain so much that these other losses are outweighed. We define any situation where the sum of consumer and producer surpluses increases as an improvement in social welfare. To see how such a case can be constructed, consider again the Cournot example. In the absence of fixed costs, the gain to the merging firms is $g(n, m)$, defined in equation (3'). It was shown that $g(n, m)$ is zero for $m = 0$, is a strictly convex function of m, and initially decreases in m. Similarly, we can write the gain in *social* welfare when $m + 1$ firms out of n firms merge as $S(n, m)$, where

$$S(n, m) = (B - \alpha)^2 \left\{ \frac{n-m}{1+n-m} - \frac{n}{1+n} - \frac{1}{2} \left(\frac{n-m}{1+n-m} \right)^2 + \frac{1}{2} \left(\frac{n}{1+n} \right)^2 \right\}.$$

It can be verified that $S(n, m)$ is zero for $m = 0$, is a strictly concave function of m, and initially decreases in m – but at a *slower* rate than $g(n, m)$. It follows, therefore, that for small m the social loss is smaller than the loss to the merging parties. Now, if each firm has a fixed cost of F, the social gain from a merger by $m + 1$ firms is $\hat{S}(n, m)$, where $\hat{S}(n, m) = S(n, m) + mF$. Similarly, the gain to the merging firms is $\hat{g}(n, m)$, where $\hat{g}(n, m) = g(n, m) + mF$. That is, both the merging parties and society benefit by the same amount when the m plants are shut down following

[7] $R = \dfrac{(n+1)^2}{(m+1)(n-m+1)^2} = \dfrac{(n+1)^2}{\alpha n(n-\alpha n+2)^2}$.
For any $\alpha < 1$, $\lim_{n \to \infty} R = 0$.

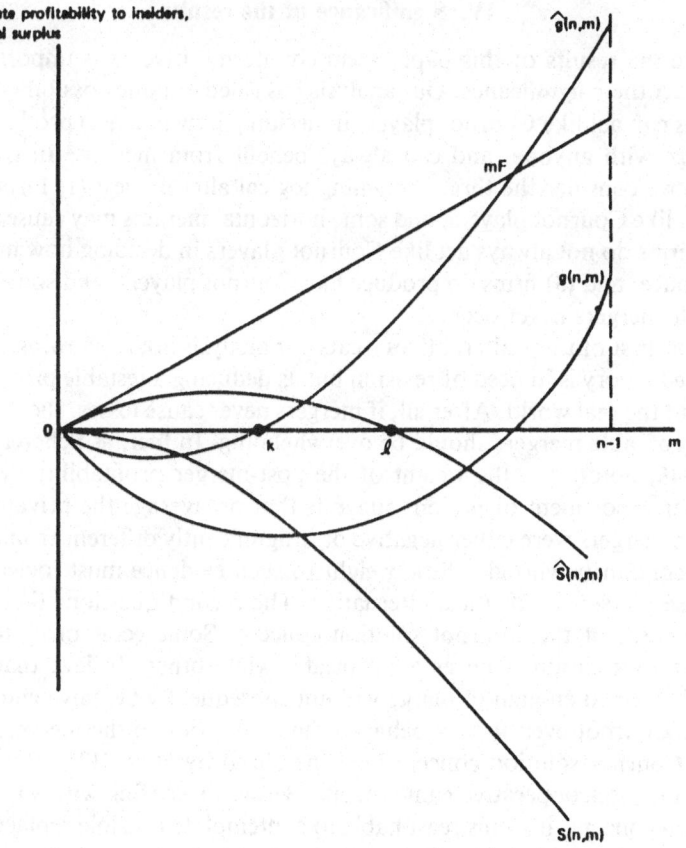

Figure 4. Unprofitable merger may be socially desirable.

the merger. Since the social loss was smaller than the loss to these firms, it is possible to select F so that $\hat{S}(n, m) > 0 > \hat{g}(n, m)$. We illustrate this in Figure 4, where $S(n, m)$, $g(n, m)$, $\hat{S}(n, m)$, and $\hat{g}(n, m)$ are plotted against m (holding n fixed). Denote the merger size that results in zero social gain (respectively, zero private gain to the merging parties) as l (as k). For $m > l$, mergers cause private gains ($\hat{g} > 0$) but social losses ($\hat{S} < 0$). Such mergers are presumably ones antitrust authorities should discourage. For $k < m < l$, mergers create both private and social gains. For $m < k$, however, mergers would create social benefits but would injure the merging parties. Such mergers are presumably ones antitrust authorities would like to occur.

383

IV. Significance of the results

Since the results of this paper seem counterintuitive, it is important to ponder their significance. Our analysis has ruled out one possibility – that firms can act like Cournot players in deciding how much to produce, can merge with anyone, and can always benefit from merger.[8] In this section we consider the three remaining logical alternatives: (1) Firms produce like Cournot players, and some horizontal mergers may cause losses; (2) firms do not always act like Cournot players in deciding how much to produce; and (3) firms do produce like Cournot players, and some specifiable mergers never occur.

The first of these alternatives treats our analysis not as showing that received theory is in need of revision but as deducing a testable proposition about the real world. After all, if mergers never cause losses, the evidence of profitable mergers should be overwhelming. In fact, as Scherer [1980, p. 546] notes, "...the weight of the post-merger profitability evidence for an assortment of nations suggests that on average the private gains from mergers were either negative or insignificantly different from zero."

Economists who give little weight to such evidence must logically espouse the second or third alternative. The second questions the appropriateness of the Cournot solution concept. Some economists feel the Cournot solution is never appropriate, while others believe that firms sophisticated enough to merge will not subsequently be naive enough to play Cournot even if they behaved that way prior to the merger.[9] Now the Cournot solution concept (as generalized by Nash [1951]) underlies most of noncooperative game theory. Before dispensing with so serviceable a concept, it seems reasonable to contemplate possible replacements and to ask on what foundation, if not the Nash–Cournot solution, is a theory of mergers to be based? In response to our earlier draft, Cave [1980] has shown that exogenous mergers may cause losses under a large variety of cooperative and noncooperative solution concepts including Nash noncooperative equilibrium, Nash (trembling hand) perfect equi-

---

[8] The assertion in the text is true if the interaction among the firms occurs in a single period. It might be possible, however, that exogenous mergers will always be profitable if the interaction among firms has no definite horizon. For it seems possible that each outsider firm would be reluctant to expand output in a period by so much that the merger would be unprofitable for fear the merger would be dissolved, leaving each outsider firm with less profits in every period thereafter. We wish to thank the referee for pointing out the possible implications of this repeated game.

[9] If this latter view is correct, it would have an important implication. The behavior of a multiplant player in an oligopolistic industry could not be predicted without knowing the historical circumstances under which the many plants came to be operated by that player.

Losses from horizontal merger

librium, strong equilibrium, Nash–Harsanyi bargaining with either fixed or variable threats, and the Shapley value. Moreover, Aumann [1973] discovered that mergers may be disadvantageous using the core solution.[10] If every solution concept which implies that exogenous mergers may cause losses is to be shunned, there remain few candidates on which to base a theory of mergers, and these seem inappropriate on other grounds. Under such circumstances – *and without the necessary empirical information to choose among solution concepts* – it seems imprudent to reject any solution concept simply because it predicts that exogenous mergers can generate losses.

Instead, it may be more useful to extend the existing Cournot theory so as to *endogenize* the merger decision. The new theory would then *predict* that specific mergers – being disadvantageous – would not occur in equilibrium. This underlies the third alternative mentioned above.

To illustrate, we sketch a simple model where firms decide whether or not to merge and how much to produce. The model uses the Nash–Cournot solution concept and treats the merger decision as a move in an enlarged noncooperative game.[11] In equilibrium, no merger causes a loss.

The players in our illustrative game are the n independent firms. Each player's strategy consists of a partition of the firms in the industry into coalitions and an output proposal for each firm in the coalition to which the particular player belongs. Each player's payoff depends on the strategies of the n players. If players pick different partitions, the unmerged "status-quo" profits result. If all players pick the same partition, each firm shares equally in the profits of the coalition to which he belongs. The profits result from each firm producing the mean of what is proposed for him by all participants in his coalition.[12]

---

[10] Okuno, Postlewaite, and Roberts [1980] have independently shown that exogenous mergers may cause losses, using a Nash noncooperative solution to a Shapley–Shubik exchange game with a continuum of traders. Their article provides a useful review of the literature on disadvantageous coalitions, which grew out of Aumann's work.

[11] For a related approach see Selten [1973].

[12] An alternative specification may seem more plausible and will generate the identical set of equilibria. Suppose that a strategy for each player consists of a description of whom he would like to collude with and the proposed total output of that coalition. That is, the player specifies nothing about mergers to which he is not a party, nor does he propose how the total output is to be produced within his own coalition. Given the strategies of the players, the payoffs are determined as follows. If any player proposes a coalition whose other members do not propose that same coalition, no mergers occur, and the status quo profits result. If there is agreement about coalitions, each player gets an equal share of the profits of the coalition to which he belongs. Profits of any particular coalition depend on market price (a decreasing function of the sum of average joint output proposals of each coalition), and on the average proposed output of the particular coalition, and on the cost of producing the average proposed output in the cheapest way. In equilibrium, given the proposals of the other players, none of the n firms has

385

STEPHEN W. SALANT, SHELDON SWITZER, ROBERT J. REYNOLDS

It should be evident that no Nash equilibrium in this game can be disadvantageous, since any player can always propose a different partition than the other players and thereby obtain the status quo profit. This makes valid our intuition that (in equilibrium) firms cannot do worse than they did prior to merger, since they can always replicate what they did earlier. In addition, every advantageous merger in the game where industry structure is exogenous can be supported as a Nash equilibrium in the extended game. This follows, since each firm perceives itself to control the outputs of every member of its own coalition and gets a given fraction of the coalition profits; it therefore will make the same choices as the multiplant Cournot player in the game with the market structure exogenous. Finally, no extraneous equilibria have been introduced by enlarging the game, since any equilibrium in the extended game must also be an equilibrium in the game with exogenous market structure. An analysis of this as well as more realistic but complex games where mergers are endogenized is reported in Cave and Salant [1981].

We conclude by noting the implications for policy by recognizing that the merger decision is endogenous. In any model with endogenous mergers, the only mergers the private market will let stand are those in the equilibrium set.[13] Socially injurious mergers that are not in the set of equilibria need not be guarded against, since they are disadvantageous and will not occur. Socially beneficial mergers that, although they create efficiency gains,[14] are not in the set of equilibria cannot be achieved (without using supplementary incentives) for the same reason.

References

Aumann, Robert, "Disadvantageous Monopolies," *Journal of Economic Theory,* VI (1973), 1–11.
Cave, Jonathan, "Losses Due to Merger," Federal Trade Commission working paper, 1980.

Footnote 12 *(cont.)*
any incentive to alter the average proposed output of his own coalition, although he perceives himself able to do so by altering his own proposal for its total output.
[13] The reader should note that the decision to spin-off from a parent corporation or to defect from a cartel is simply the reverse of the merger decision. Hence our analysis has implications for these issues. Consider, for example, the question of cartel stability. All cartels contain at least one destabilizing force, since each member can benefit from cheating given an unchanged price or unchanged outputs of other producers. But if the other cartel members would be injured by the defection, they may make attempts to deter it. Such attempts, if successful, impart stability to the cartel. In contrast, if circumstances prevail where a merger would be disadvantageous, the defection may be beneficial to *every* member of the cartel. In that case, the cartel is unstable, and the defection is assured.
[14] See the end of Section III.

Cave, Jonathan, and Stephen Salant, "Towards a Theory of Mergers," mimeo (1981).

Cournot, Augustin, *Researches into the Mathematical Principles of Wealth* (1838), translated by Nathaniel T. Bacon (New York, NY: Macmillan, 1897).

Nash, John, "Non-Cooperative Games," *Annals of Mathematics,* LIV (March 1951), 286–95.

Okuno, Masahiro, Andrew Postlewaite, and John Roberts, "Oligopoly and Competition in Large Markets," *American Economic Review,* LXX (March 1980), 22–31.

Salant, Stephen W., *Imperfect Competition in the World Oil Market* (Lexington, MA: Lexington Books, 1981).

——, "Imperfect Competition in the International Energy Market: A Computerized Nash–Cournot Model," *Operations Research,* XXX, No. 2 (March–April 1982), 252–80.

Scherer, F. M., *Industrial Market Structure and Economic Performance,* 2nd ed. (Chicago, IL: Rand McNally, 1980).

Selten, Reinhard, "A Simple Model of Imperfect Competition Where 4 Are Few and 6 Are Many," *International Journal of Game Theory,* II, No. 3 (1973), 141–201.

EXPLAINING OBSERVED BEHAVIOR

CHAPTER 17

Delegation and the theory of the firm

JOHN VICKERS

> The use of thugs or sadists for the collection of extortion or the guarding
> of prisoners, or the conspicuous delegation of authority to a military com-
> mander of known motivation, exemplifies a common means of making
> credible a response pattern that the original source of decision might have
> been thought to shrink from or to find profitless, once the threat had failed.
>
> Schelling (1960, pp. 142–3).

If control of my decisions is in the hands of an agent whose preferences
are different from my own, I may nevertheless prefer the results to those
that would come about if I took my own decisions. This has some interesting implications for the theory of the firm. For example, in markets
where firms are interdependent, it is *not* necessarily true that maximum
profits are earned by firms whose objective is profit-maximization.

This can be seen in a simple example of entry deterrence. Firm A is deciding whether or not to enter a market currently monopolized by firm B.
If A enters, B (or rather its managers) must decide whether to respond
aggressively or in an accommodating fashion. Entry is profitable for A if
and only if B does not fight. Faced with the fact of entry, it is more profitable for B to accommodate than to fight, but B's profits are greater still
if there is no entry. Consider how the game would unfold in each of the
following circumstances (which are assumed to be common knowledge):

(I) B's managers are always concerned to maximize profits;
(II) B's managers are principally concerned to maintain their domi-
      nance over the market: considerations of profit are secondary.

In case (I) it is clear that entry will take place and will be accommodated.
If B's managers were to fight entry, they would be failing to maximize

This paper is based on a chapter of my M.Phil. thesis, "Strategic Competition and the Theory of Market Structure," Oxford University (1983).
John Vickers, "Delegation and the Theory of the Firm," *Economic Journal Supplement*
95, 1984, pp. 138–47.
I am very grateful to Partha Dasgupta, Dieter Helm, Colin Mayer, Jim Mirrlees, Ray Rees,
two referees and especially to George Yarrow [who has also explored this subject: see
Yarrow (forthcoming) Chapter 4] for their helpful comments and suggestions.

profits in the circumstances then prevailing. Relying on this fact, A will enter the market. In case (II), however, entry will be deterred, because A knows that B's managers would fight entry. Thus the known presence of managers of type (II) – whose objective is *not* principally to maximize profits – has the effect of earning greater profits for B than would be the case if B's managers had profit-maximization as their objective.

This example highlights an important distinction between two senses of an expression of the form "x is a u-maximizer." In the following this shall be taken to mean that x's disposition, intention or objective is the maximization of u. And the expression "x maximizes u" shall be used to describe the consequences, effects or results that x tends to bring about. With this terminology it is not nonsense to say that u-maximizers do not necessarily maximize u.

Such a statement may nevertheless appear to be applicable only in special cases – such as the entry deterrence example. But this is not so. Indeed, in games it is almost always the case that u-maximizers do not maximize u. The reason is essentially that the outcome of the game depends on the objectives of all the players. In fact the question of strategic delegation is equivalent to questions of strategic voting and incentive compatibility.

The next section addresses the issue of strategic delegation in terms of a framework borrowed from the literature on incentive compatibility. This enables one to see in what sense delegation is almost always advantageous; and a relationship between delegation and Stackelberg leadership becomes clear. In Section II these claims are illustrated by examining delegation in the context of the familiar model of Cournot oligopoly.

In Section III it is suggested that these results on delegation have a bearing on some issues in the theory of the firm. First, the separation of the ownership and control of a firm may be a good thing for the owners, because non-profit-maximizing managers may earn higher profits than would profit-maximizers. Second, this affects the validity of "natural selection" arguments of the sort advanced by Friedman (1953) and others to justify the hypothesis that firms are (as if) profit-maximizers: if profit-maximizers do not earn maximum profits then such arguments fail. Third, reasons of strategic delegation may influence the design of managerial incentive schemes, perhaps helping to explain why they are sometimes based on relative, rather than absolute, performance. Fourth, the horizontal organization of a firm (e.g. into separate divisions) can be seen as a form of delegation that may have strategic advantages in relation to other firms. Fifth, vertical arrangements – such as those between a manufacturer and distributor – can be viewed within the perspective of strategic delegation. By not integrating his operations, the manufacturer effectively delegates some decisions to an agent with incentives different from his own. Vertical restraints imposed by the manufacturer further influence those incentives. These examples are intended only as illustrations of the ways in which the strategic advantages of delegation might be enjoyed by firms.

I. Delegation and incentive compatibility

The aim is to show that it is only for a particular class of games that a principal would give to an agent acting on his behalf an incentive structure the same as his own. Because this problem is equivalent to the problem of the truthful revelation of preferences, about which much is known, we can employ recent work on incentive compatibility; this section borrows particularly from d'Aspremont and Gérard-Varet (1980), to which the reader is referred for a more rigorous treatment.

An important issue in the literature on incentive compatibility is the question of whether allocation mechanisms can be designed in such a way that each individual is willing to reveal truthfully his private information (e.g. his preferences). An allocation mechanism is a rule that specifies the outcome or allocation as a function of the signals sent by individuals in the preceding communication game.

In the context of delegation, the analogue of the communication game will be called the *agent appointment game,* and the analogue of the allocation mechanism will be called the *outcome function.* This is assumed to determine the outcome of the *game between agents* as a function of the agents chosen by the principals in the preceding agent appointment game. The outcome function is regarded as being given exogenously – by game theoretic considerations (such as Nash equilibrium). The case in which a principal appoints an agent with an incentive structure the same as his own (or, equivalently, acts on his own behalf) is analogous to the truthful revelation of private information.

The game between agents is the n-person game in normal form denoted

$$\Gamma(\mathbf{a}) = \{[X_i, U_i(\cdot; a_i)]; \ i = 1, \ldots, n\}$$

where $\mathbf{a} = (a_1, \ldots, a_n)$ is the vector of agent types, X_i is the strategy space of the agent chosen by principal i, and U_i is his utility function. U_i is a function of the strategy n-tuple $x \in X$ (the Cartesian product of the X_i) and the agent type a_i.

The game between agents is preceded by the agent appointment game, which is denoted

$$G(z) = (\{A_i, U_i[z(\cdot); \alpha_i]\}; \ i = 1, \ldots, n).$$

JOHN VICKERS

Here A_i is the space of agent types from which principal i chooses. Principal i is himself of type $\alpha_i \in A_i$. The function z specifies the outcome $z(\mathbf{a})$ of the game between agents as a function of the vector of agent types chosen. [For simplicity it is assumed that a principal's payoff depends only upon the outcome $z(\mathbf{a})$ and his own type α_i; it does not depend directly upon the type of agent he chooses. This corresponds roughly to the idea that agents of different types are equally costly to employ.] We say that the agent appointment game $G(z)$ is *incentive compatible for principal i* if it is optimal for i to choose the agent of his own type, i.e. α_i, given that others do likewise, i.e. given that j chooses α_j for all $j \neq i$. (This notion of incentive compatibility is not as demanding as that which requires α_i to be a dominant strategy, i.e. optimal *whatever* the other principals do. Only if α_i is a dominant strategy would principal i *never* wish to delegate.)

We wish to find conditions on the game $\Gamma(\alpha)$ that characterize incentive compatibility in the game $G(z)$. In other words, what must be true of the game between agents in which principals choose agents of their own type in order for the principals to find it optimal to do just that? The required condition is a generalization of Stackelberg's equilibrium concept for duopoly. We say that $x \in X$ is a *Stackelberg point for agent i* in $\Gamma(\mathbf{a})$ if x is on the other players' joint reaction function and is at least as good for i as any point on the other players' joint reaction function in the game $\Gamma(\mathbf{a})$. (The other players' joint reaction function is the set of points such that all players other than i are making best replies to their rivals' strategies.)

Whether or not the agent appointment game $G(z)$ is incentive compatible depends on the outcome function z and the richness of the sets A_i. Several results are stated in d'Aspremont and Gérard-Varet, of which we shall mention just one [see their Theorem 2.3; see also Dasgupta et al. (1979, Theorem 7.3)]. We say that z is a *Nash outcome function* (undominated) if, for all $\mathbf{a}$, $z(\mathbf{a})$ is a Nash equilibrium in $\Gamma(\mathbf{a})$ (which is dominated by no other Nash equilibrium). Incentive compatibility can now be characterized.

Proposition. Assume that z is an undominated Nash outcome function and that for all i there is some $a_i \in A_i$ such that $z(\alpha_i, ..., \alpha_{i-1}, \alpha_i, \alpha_{i+1}, ..., \alpha_n)$ is a Stackelberg point for i in $\Gamma(\alpha)$. Then, $G(z)$ is incentive incompatible for all principals i if and only if $z(\alpha)$ is a Stackelberg point for all i in $\Gamma(\alpha)$.

Essentially the condition says that i can shift his best reply function so that some Stackelberg point for i can be obtained as a Nash equilibrium.

394

Much weaker conditions can be stated which ensure that $G(z)$ is not incentive compatible for i. Indeed, in more fully specified contexts it is 'almost always' the case (in a sense that can be made precise) that $G(z)$ is not incentive compatible for principal i.

The purpose of this section has been to demonstrate the link between the questions of delegation and incentive compatibility, and to characterize the conditions under which strategic delegation is advantageous in terms of the Stackelberg property. The next section illustrates these themes.

II. An example

It is commonly contended that the interests of those who take the decisions in large firms are advanced by high sales rather than purely by profits. In this section we postulate a very simple managerial utility function which is a combination of profits and sales volume. We consider the case of fixed numbers oligopoly, where there are constant unit costs common to each firm, and where the industry faces a linear demand curve. This enables us clearly to illustrate the claims made in the previous section.

We assume that there are n firms in the industry and that the objective of the managers of firm i is to maximize

$$M_i = \pi_i + \theta_i q_i \tag{1}$$

where

$$\pi_i = p(Q)q_i - cq_i \tag{2}$$

and $Q = \sum q_i$. Combining (1) and (2) we have

$$M_i = p(Q)q_i - (c - \theta_i)q_i. \tag{3}$$

It can be seen immediately that M_i is the same as the objective function of a profit-maximizing firm with unit costs of $c - \theta_i$.

We assume that the rules of the game – or the outcome function – are Nash–Cournot. Suppose that $p(Q) = A - Q$. Then in equilibrium we have

$$q_i^* = (p^* - c + \theta_i) \tag{4}$$

$$p^* = (A + nc - \sum \theta_j)/(n+1) \tag{5}$$

$$M_i^* = (q_i^*)^2. \tag{6}$$

(It is assumed that $p^* > c - \theta_i$ for all i.)

Since $\pi_i = M_i - \theta_i q_i$ it follows that

$$\pi_i = (A - c - \sum \theta_j)[A - c + (n+1)\theta_i - \sum \theta_j]/(n+1)^2. \tag{7}$$

The level of θ_i which maximizes π_i^* given θ_j for $j \neq i$ is

$$\hat{\theta}_i = (n-1)\left(A - c - \sum_{j \neq i} \theta_j\right)\Big/ 2n. \tag{8}$$

This shows that the θ-setting game is not incentive compatible if $n > 1$, because it cannot be the case that $\hat{\theta}_i = 0$ for all i. The Nash equilibrium of the θ-setting game is symmetric with

$$\hat{\theta} = (n-1)(A-c)/(n^2+1). \tag{9}$$

Correspondingly we have

$$\hat{q} = n(a-c)/(n^2+1) \tag{10}$$

$$\hat{p} = (A + n^2 c)/(n^2+1) \tag{11}$$

$$\hat{\pi} = n(A-c)^2/(n^2+1)^2. \tag{12}$$

Compared with the case in which all firms are managed by profit-maximizers, output per firm is higher, price is lower and profits are lower.

It is easy to check that a profit-maximizing firm facing $n-1$ rivals all with $\theta_j = \hat{\theta}$ would choose $q = \hat{q}$ if it could commit its output prior to the other firms making their output decisions – i.e. if it were Stackelberg leader. Moreover, the $n-1$ rivals would each choose an output of $\hat{q}$ at the symmetric Nash equilibrium of the subgame following the move of the Stackelberg leader.

Note that for $n > 1$, $\hat{\theta}$ is decreasing and goes to zero in the limit. So, in this example, the extent of deviation from profit-maximization at the symmetric equilibrium vanishes as competition grows.

Now briefly consider the case in which $\theta_j = 0$ for $j = 2, \ldots, n$. That is, all firms but one are profit-maximizers. From (8) it can be seen that

$$\hat{\theta}_1 = (n-1)(A-c)/2n \tag{13}$$

in which case

$$\pi_1 = (A-c)^2/4n = n\pi_j; \quad j = 2, \ldots, n. \tag{14}$$

This shows rather vividly the extent to which non-profit-maximizers can surpass profit-maximizers in terms of profits. Indeed, here the non-profit-maximizer earns greater profits than those of his rivals added together, no matter how many rivals there are.

The example can be modified to illustrate the remarks in the introduction about entry deterrence. Let the model be as before, except that entry involves payment of a sunk cost F^2. Suppose that firm 1 is already in the market and that its managers maximize $\pi_1 + \theta q_1$. Suppose that firm 2, a profit-maximizer, is contemplating entry. Entry is profitable only if

$$\theta < A - c - 3F. \tag{15}$$

If (15) does not hold, then entry is deterred because firm 1 is not a profit-maximizer. Firm 1's profits are higher in this case than if it had been a profit-maximizer not deterring entry provided that

$$[(A-c)^2-\theta^2]/4 > (A-c)^2/9. \tag{16}$$

Therefore entry deterrence by non-profit-maximizers can be profitable if

$$A-c > 3F > (A-c)\left(1-\frac{\sqrt{5}}{3}\right). \tag{17}$$

Thus the point does not hinge on very special parameter values.

Throughout this section it has been supposed that managers maximize a linear combination of profits and sales volume. This assumption was made only to keep the illustration simple. Very similar results are obtained if managers maximize a combination of profits and revenue, for example. Alternatively one can suppose that managers maximize some function of the profits of the various firms.

As an illustration of this final point, suppose that the utility of the managers of firm 1 depends on the *relative* profitability of firm 1, as follows:

$$M_1 = \pi_1 - \frac{\beta}{n-1} \sum_{j=2}^{n} \pi_j. \tag{18}$$

For simplicity, let all the other firms be profit-maximizers. Then at the Nash equilibrium of the quantity-setting game between firms

$$\pi_1 = \left(\frac{A-c}{\beta+n+1}\right)^2 (1+\beta). \tag{19}$$

This is maximized when $\beta = n-1$, or, in other words, when the managers of the firm 1 maximize the profits of their own firm minus those of all other firms. This suggests that a firm's *absolute* performance may benefit from its managers' objective being *relative* performance, a point which is pursued in the next section.

III. Implications for the theory of the firm

The fact that delegation can have strategic advantages has a bearing on several issues in the theory of the firm. As Schelling (p. 29) notes, "The principle applies in distinguishing...the management from the board of directors." In more general terms, the separation of ownership from control in the large corporation may in some cases be no bad thing for the owners. Indeed the separation may be in some cases essential for the credibility of some threats, promises and commitments. Several theories of the firm postulate that the interests of managers – their incomes, status, power, security, etc. lie partly with sales and growth rather than purely with profits [see e.g. Hay and Morris (1979, Chapter 8)]. In the example in the previous section it was shown how the presence of managers who place some emphasis on sales can enhance profits. Of course nothing general follows directly from this, but perhaps the example is suggestive.

Natural selection

Schelling's observation about delegation has a bearing on the validity of natural selection arguments[1] which employ a kind of "economic Darwinism" to justify the hypothesis

that under a wide range of circumstances individual firms behave *as if* they were seeking rationally to maximize their expected returns and had full knowledge of the data needed to succeed in this attempt; *as if*, that is, they knew the relevant cost and demand functions, calculated marginal cost and marginal revenue from all actions open to them, and pushed each line of action to the point at which the relevant marginal cost and marginal revenue were equal. (Friedman [1953, p. 21])

Friedman's phrase *"seeking* rationally to maximize" indicates that he is speaking of profit maximization as an objective, and not just in terms of results. His reference to equating marginal cost and marginal revenue suggests that he has in mind straightforward profit maximization, involving decisions about quantity, for example. (Contrast this with the example in the previous section, where the managers that made the greatest profits did not operate where MC = MR.) Finally, the reference to marginal revenue, rather than price, suggests that Friedman's argument is intended to apply not only to perfectly competitive markets. Friedman continues:

Let the apparent immediate determinate of business behaviour be anything at all – habitual reaction, random chance or whatnot. Whenever this determinant happens to lead to behaviour consistent with rational and informed maximization of returns, the business will prosper and acquire resources with which to expand; whenever it does not, the business will tend to lose resources and can be kept in existence only by the addition of resources from outside. The process of "natural selection" thus helps to validate the hypothesis [see above] – or, rather, given natural selection, acceptance of the hypothesis can be based largely on the judgement that it summarizes appropriately the conditions for survival.

[1] The classic articles are Alchian (1950) and Friedman (1953). The remarks here apply mainly to Friedman's formulation of the argument. His argument has of course been criticized on many grounds – see, for example, Winter (1964).

Delegation and the theory of the firm

But even if it were true that the only survivors of the economic struggle were the firms that made the greatest profits, it would not follow that they were profit-maximizers in the sense of having profit-maximization as their objective, or behaving as such. Thus there is a critical ambiguity in Friedman's phrase "maximization of returns." We have argued that such a phrase has two meanings – referring to results and to objectives – which can come apart when there is interdependence between firms (irrespective of the number of firms: see equation (14) above). Friedman, however, appears to switch from one meaning to the other for his argument to go through. In short, if strategic interactions imply that the direct pursuit of profit does not lead to maximum profits, then forces of natural selection might see the demise of the profit-maximizer rather than his ultimate survival.

Managerial incentives

In a number of recent papers [including Lazear and Rosen (1981), Holmstrom (1982), and Nalebuff and Stiglitz (1983)] it has been shown that incentive schemes based on relative performances can be superior to individualistic incentive schemes. This literature has generally focused on the case of one principal with many agents in an uncertain environment where agents' effort levels are not observable by the principal. If the uncertainties facing different agents are correlated to some degree, then relative performance contains useful additional information about effort rates. This is exploited by incentive schemes based on relative performance, with desirable consequences for efficiency and flexibility.

The argument set out earlier in this paper points to another, independent reason for incentive schemes based on relative performance, namely strategic advantage. This was illustrated by the simple example at the end of the previous section, in which it was advantageous to have managers with the objective of maximizing the profits of their own firm minus those of their rivals. In setting with many interdependent principal-agent pairs, payment according to relative performance may therefore have strategic, as well as informational, advantages.

Horizontal integration

A curious feature of Cournot oligopoly models is that horizontal merger is often disadvantageous to the merging parties. Salant et al. (1983, p. 193) show that in the linear Cournot oligopoly model it is sufficient for a merger to be unprofitable that less than 80% of the firms collude. For example, in the model in the previous section with all firms profit-maximizing and $n = 3$, if two firms merge, their joint profits fall from $(A-c)^2/8$ to $(A-c)^2/9$. Salant et al. note that "the decision to spin-off from a parent corporation or to defect from a cartel is simply the reverse of the merger decision" (p. 199, footnote 13). The same is true if the parent company is organized into several divisions – say one for each brand of product – with the management of each division aiming to maximize the profits of the brand, rather than those of the parent company. In this case it is true not only that divisional managers, to whom decision-making power is delegated, have objectives different from the parent, but also that they have inconsistent objectives: manager x is concerned with the profitability of brand x, whereas manager y is out to maximize the profits of rival brand y. Such an arrangement may nevertheless have merit from the point of view of the parent, because it has the strategic effect of curbing the output of rival firms.

Vertical integration and restraints

The theme of much work on vertical integration is that "integration harmonizes interests" [Williamson (1971, p. 117), and see Williamson (1975)]. The question then arises of why vertical integration does not proceed further: for example, why does a manufacturer not integrate with the distributor of his products? Williamson (1975, Chapter 7) answers this question in terms of the increasing distortion associated with transactions as the firm grows or becomes more complex. In short, there is inefficiency in transactions which mitigates against integration.

Moreover, if Schelling's ideas on delegation apply here, there may also be good strategic reasons for non-integration. Strategic delegation involves a suitable divergence of interests, rather than a harmony of interests. In this light, consider vertical restraints between a manufacturer and distributor or retailer, such as franchise fees and quantity forcing (i.e. a requirement that the distributor sell a minimum quantity of the manufacturer's product). In a recent paper, Mathewson and Winter (1983) have regarded vertical restraints as devices to bring distributors' actions into line with the manufacturer's interests. Their framework has one principal and many agents, and the argument is essentially that vertical restraints serve to correct externalities (*a*) between manufacturer and distributors, and (*b*) between the distributors themselves. However, in an oligopolistic setting, there is also interdependence between rival manufacturers, which vertical restraints might influence.

For example, the Cournot model in Section II could be interpreted as follows. Think of M_i in equation (3) as the gross profit of distributor i,

Delegation and the theory of the firm

who is supplied by manufacturer i at a wholesale price of $c - \theta_i$, where c is the unit manufacturing cost. Suppose for simplicity that a franchise fee is charged so that the joint profits of distributor i and manufacturer i are enjoyed by the manufacturer, except for a fixed fee to the distributor. Then optimal wholesale prices are found from equation (8) above. The case of a vertically integrated firm corresponds to $\theta_i = 0$, and so the model illustrates the strategic advantage to be had from non-integration. Of course, the example is extremely stylized, but it shows that the argument has coherence at least in a particular case.

References

Alchian A. A. (1950). "Uncertainty, evolution, and economic theory." *Journal of Political Economy,* vol. 58, pp. 211–21.

Dasgupta, P., Hammond, P. and Maskin, E. (1979). "The implementation of social choice rules: some general results on incentive compatibility." *Review of Economic Studies,* vol. 46, pp. 185–216.

d'Aspremont, C. and Gérard-Varet, L.-A. (1980). "Stackelberg-solvable games and pre-play communication." *Journal of Economic Theory,* vol. 23, pp. 201–17.

Friedman, M. (1953). "The methodology of positive economics" in *Essays in Positive Economics.* Chicago: Chicago University Press.

Hay, D. A. and Morris, D. J. (1979). *Industrial Economics.* Oxford: Oxford University Press.

Holmstrom, B. (1982). "Moral hazard in teams." *Bell Journal of Economics,* vol. 12, pp. 324–40.

Lazear, E. P. and Rosen, S. (1981). "Rank-order tournaments as optimum labour contracts." *Journal of Political Economy,* vol. 89, pp. 841–64.

Mathewson, G. F. and Winter, R. A. (1983). "An economic theory of vertical restraints," working paper, University of Toronto.

Nalebuff, B. J. and Stiglitz, J. E. (1983). "Information, competition, and markets." *American Economic Review Papers and Proceedings,* vol. 73, pp. 278–83.

Salant, S., Switzer, S. and Reynolds, R. (1983). "Losses due to merger: the effects of an exogenous change in industry structure on Cournot Nash equilibrium." *Quarterly Journal of Economics,* vol. 98, pp. 185–99.

Schelling, T. C. (1960). *The Strategy of Conflict.* Harvard University Press.

Williamson, O. E. (1971). "The vertical integration of production: market failure considerations," *American Economic Review Papers and Proceedings,* vol. 61, pp. 112–23.

———, (1975). *Markets and Hierarchies.* New York: Free Press.

Winter, S. G. (1964). "Economic natural selection and the theory of the firm." *Yale Economic Essays,* vol. 4 (Spring), pp. 225–72.

Yarrow, G. K., *Economic Theories of Business Strategies.* Oxford: Oxford University Press (forthcoming).

CHAPTER 18

A study of cartel stability: the Joint Executive Committee, 1880–1886

ROBERT H. PORTER

This article employs weekly time series data on the Joint Executive Committee railroad cartel from 1880 to 1886 to test empirically the proposition that observed prices reflected switches from collusive to noncooperative behavior. An equilibrium model of dynamic oligopoly with asymmetric firms, together with explicit functional form assumptions about costs and demand, determines the estimating equations and stochastic structure of the econometric model. The hypothesis that no switch took place, so that price and quantity movements were solely attributable to exogenous shifts in the demand and cost functions, is then tested against this alternative and rejected.

1. Introduction

Industrial organization economists have recognized for some time that the problem of distinguishing empirically between collusive and noncooperative behavior, in the absence of a "smoking gun," is a difficult one. This article exploits the model proposed in Green and Porter (1984). They consider an explicitly dynamic model in which the firms of an industry are faced with the problem of detecting and deterring cheating on an agreement. In particular, they assume that firms set their own production level and observe the market price, but do not know the quantity produced by any other firm. Firms' output is assumed to be of homogeneous quality, so they face a common market price. If the market demand curve has a stochastic component, an unexpectedly low price may signal either deviations from collusive output levels or a "downward" demand shock.

University of Minnesota and Bell Laboratories.
Robert H. Porter, "A Study of Cartel Stability: the Joint Executive Committee, 1880–1886," *Bell Journal of Economics* 14, 2, 1983, pp. 301–14.
I have benefited from the comments of Tim Bresnahan, Ed Green, Lung-Fei Lee, Richard Quandt, the referees, and the Editorial Board, as well as from the expert research assistance of Rick Hoffbeck and the financial support of a Sloan Foundation Grant to the University of Minnesota Economics Department. I am also indebted to Tom Ulen, who made this data set available to me. An earlier version of this article was presented at the NBER Conference on "The Econometrics of Market Models with Imperfect Competition" at Northwestern University, November 1981.

Study of cartel stability

Under these circumstances participating firms can deter deviations from collusive output levels by threatening to produce at Cournot quantities for a period of fixed duration whenever they observe market price below some trigger price. A firm which considers a secret expansion of output above the collusive level must trade off immediate profit gains with the increased probability that the market price will fall below the trigger price, thereby increasing the likelihood of lower profits when the industry reverts to Cournot output levels. Green and Porter offer an explanation that what looks like collusive behavior at a point in time is actually the noncooperative outcome of a regularly repeated market game. For small enough discount rates, an output vector which yields profits in excess of the Cournot vector can be supported as a noncooperative equilibrium. Thus the results of Friedman (1977) and Telser (1972) extend to uncertain environments. In equilibrium, firms maximize expected discounted profits by producing at collusive output levels, so that any price wars which are observed should occur after unexpected drops in demand, rather than after actual cheating by member firms. Thus price wars can be the occasional equilibrium outcome of a dynamic noncooperative market game.

There are many such equilibria, as a number of output vectors can be supported by appropriately chosen (trigger price, punishment period length) pairs as noncooperative equilibria. However, such a cartel may be expected to select an enforcement mechanism which maximizes expected discounted profits, subject to the constraint that producing at collusive levels is individually rational. In equilibrium, the marginal gains from cheating in cooperative periods must be exactly offset by the marginal losses implicit in the increased probability of an industry reversion to Cournot behavior. The marginal gains from cheating increase as output in cooperative periods decreases towards perfectly collusive levels, so expected marginal losses must be increased by increasing the trigger price or the length of reversionary episodes. Expected discounted industry profits will be maximized at output levels in cooperative periods which exceed those which maximize single-period expected joint net returns, as long as the variance of the demand shock is positive (Porter, 1983).

This article adopts econometric techniques which employ aggregate time series price and quantity data for a particular industry, and which are designed to detect the behavioral switches implied by such an enforcement mechanism. I exploit the fact that there will be periodic switches or reversions between the Cournot and collusive output levels when such a noncooperative equilibrium exists. These reversions serve to identify periods of collusive behavior in a simultaneous equation switching regressions model. There is no explicit test of whether this sort of enforcement mechanism is employed. Instead, the econometric model is designed to

403

test whether significant switches in supplier behavior occurred, and to identify the periods in which they took place. One can then determine whether the pattern of these switches is consistent with an equilibrium of the Green and Porter model. Thus the theoretical model is exploited to the extent that it predicts that such switches will occur, and that they should follow a certain pattern. (Of course, this sort of outcome may also arise if there are external supply shocks which are not observed by the econometrician. I can only state whether the econometric results are consistent with the theoretical model.) The model also predicts that optimally selected output levels in cooperative periods will exceed those which would maximize static joint net returns. The econometric model allows me to determine whether this is in fact the case.

2. The Joint Executive Committee

This section contains a description of the Joint Executive Committee, henceforth referred to as the JEC, with emphasis on the period from 1880 to 1886. Readers who are interested in a more complete history should refer to MacAvoy (1965) and Ulen (1978). Much of the material in this section is drawn from these studies.

The JEC was a cartel which controlled eastbound freight shipments from Chicago to the Atlantic seaboard in the 1880s. It was formed in April 1879 by an agreement of the railroads involved in the market. The firms involved publicly acknowledged this agreement, as it preceded the passage of the Sherman Act (1890) and the formation of the Interstate Commerce Commission (1887). A separate agreement was reached for westbound shipments on the same railroad lines, primarily because of the essential physical differences of the products being transported.

The internal enforcement mechanism adopted by the JEC was a variant of a trigger price strategy. According to Ulen, there were several instances in which the cartel thought that cheating had occurred, cut prices for a time, and then returned to the collusive price.

Through-shipments of grain accounted for 73% of all dead freight tonnage handled by the JEC. The railroads also handled eastbound shipments of flour and provisions, but the prices charged for transporting these commodities were tied to the grain rate. None of these commodities is easily perishable, so speed of delivery was probably not an important factor by which firms could have differentiated their products. Furthermore, while different railroads shipped grain to different port cities, most of the wheat handled by the cartel was subsequently exported overseas, and the rates charged by different firms adjusted to compensate for differences in ocean shipping rates. Thus, the assumption that a homogeneous good was sold seems to have been approximately satisfied, and attention can be focused on the movement of grain with little loss of generality.

Price, rather than quantity, has typically been thought to be the strategic variable of firms in the rail-freight industry. In particular, the specification of Green and Porter (1984) that industry conduct during reversionary periods was Cournot might be considered unrealistic. Econometrically, it is not very difficult to modify the model so that firms revert from collusive to Bertrand behavior (as they would if they were price setters). If firms are price setters, then the inference problem they face in detecting cheating is quite similar to that originally posed by Stigler (1964). In the case of the JEC, the cartel agreement took the form of market share allotments rather than absolute amounts of quantities shipped. Firms set their rates individually, and the JEC office took weekly accounts so that each railroad could see the total amount transported. Total demand was quite variable, and the actual market share of any particular firm depended on both the prices charged by all the firms and unpredictable stochastic forces. Thus, the problem faced by the members of the JEC seems to be comparable to that posed by Green and Porter. Indeed, Brock and Scheinkman (1981) have shown that noncooperative equilibria with similar properties exist in supergames involving price-setting firms which face capacity constraints.

In their model Green and Porter explicitly rule out the possibility of entry into the market. In the case of the JEC, entry occurred twice between 1880 and 1886. It appears that the cartel passively accepted the entrants, allocated them market shares, and thereby allowed the collusive agreement to continue. The reason for this is undoubtedly that when a firm entered the rail freight industry in the late Nineteenth Century, it faced a "no-exit" constraint. To put it briefly, bankrupt railroads were relieved by the courts of most of their fixed costs and instructed to cut prices to increase business (Ulen, 1978, pp. 70–4). As a result, I deal with the actual entry which occurred during the sample period by appropriately modifying the nature of collusive and noncooperative outcomes, before and after entry, with the expectation that, *ceteris paribus,* reversionary periods should not have been precipitated by entry. Of course, entry to the industry may have increased the likelihood of future price wars.

Lake steamers and sailships were the principal source of competition for the railroads, but at no point did they enter into an agreement with the JEC. The predictable fluctuations in demand that resulted from the annual opening and closing of the Great Lakes to shipping did not disrupt industry conduct. Rather, rates adjusted systematically with the lake navigation season.

Therefore, the conduct of the JEC from 1880 to 1886 is largely consistent with the collusive equilibrium described by Green and Porter, as price wars were caused by unpredictable disturbances, rather than by entry or predictable fluctuations in demand.

3. The econometric model

This section is concerned with the possibility of estimating a model of the Nash equilibrium proposed by Green and Porter, suitably altered to reflect the structure of the JEC, by using time series data on price and aggregate output levels. A simultaneous equation switching regression model is proposed, in which the parameters of the demand and cost functions are estimated, and in which the regime classification is unknown.

Denote the market price in period t by p_t. Then the total quantity demanded is assumed to be a loglinear function of price,

$$\log Q_t = \alpha_0 + \alpha_1 \log p_t + \alpha_2 L_t + U_{1t}, \tag{1}$$

where L_t is a dummy variable equal to one if the Great Lakes were open to navigation, and $\{U_{11}, U_{12}, \ldots, U_{1T}\}$ is a sequence of independently distributed normal variables with zero mean and variance σ_1^2. Here α_1 is the price elasticity of demand, and presumably negative. Also α_2 should be negative, reflecting a decrease in demand when the lake steamers were operating.

The N active firms in the industry are assumed to be asymmetric, in that they each face a different cost function. The cost of producing output q_{it} for firm i in period t is given by

$$C_i(q_{it}) = a_i q_{it}^\delta + F_i, \quad \text{for } i = 1, \ldots, N,$$

where δ, the (constant) elasticity of variable costs with respect to output, must exceed one if an equilibrium is to exist. Here a_i is a firm-specific shift parameter, and F_i the fixed cost faced by firm i. These fixed costs are assumed to be small enough that firms have positive discounted expected profits in equilibrium.

Since the products provided by these firms are of approximately homogeneous quality, all firms will charge equal prices in equilibrium. The actions of firms under different behavioral assumptions can then be summarized by

$$p_t(1 + \theta_{it}/\alpha_1) = MC_i(q_{it}) \quad \text{for } i = 1, \ldots, N,$$

where MC_i is the marginal cost function of firm i. If firms choose price noncooperatively in each period, they price at marginal cost as Bertrand predicted, and so θ_{it} equals zero for all i and t. If instead they maximize

406

joint profits, θ_{it} equals one for all i and t. If firms produce at Cournot output levels, θ_{it} equals $s_{it} = q_{it}/Q_t$, the market share of firm i in period t.

For estimation purposes, I employ aggregate data. The individual supply equations are weighted by market shares in time t, s_{it}, and added up. Then we get the industry supply relationship

$$p_t(1+\theta_t/\alpha_1) = \Sigma_i s_{it} MC_i(q_{it}),$$

where $\theta_t = \Sigma_i s_{it} \theta_{it}$.

It can be shown that, given these functional forms for the market demand and cost functions, the market share of firm i in period t will be

$$s_{it} = \frac{a_i^{1/(1-\delta)}}{\Sigma_j a_j^{1/(1-\delta)}} \equiv s_i$$

in each of the three cases above. Thus the market share of each firm will be constant over time and invariant across changes in industry conduct. Note that the higher the value of the firm-specific variable cost shift parameter, a_i, the lower is the market share of firm i.

The supply relationship can now be written as

$$p_t(1+\theta_t/\alpha_1) = DQ_t^{\delta-1},$$

where

$$D = \delta(\Sigma_i a_i^{1/1-\delta})^{1-\delta}.$$

Note that D depends only on the parameters of the cost functions of the firms. Here θ equals zero, H, or 1 for Bertrand, Cournot, or perfectly collusive firms, respectively. H is the Herfindahl index, $H = \Sigma_i s_i^2$, and is invariant across time, as long as the number of firms remains unchanged. Suppose I_t is an indicator variable which equals one when the industry is in a cooperative regime and equals zero when the industry witnesses a reversionary episode. Then the supply relationship of the industry is given by

$$\log p_t = \beta_0 + \beta_1 \log Q_t + \beta_2 S_t + \beta_3 I_t + U_{2t}. \tag{2}$$

If reversionary periods are Bertrand, $\beta_0 = \log D$ and $\beta_1 = \delta - 1$. Since δ is assumed to be greater than one, β_1 should be positive. Here S_t is a vector of structural dummies which reflect entry and acquisitions in the industry. Recall that, for the JEC, entry does not seem to have caused reversions to noncooperative behavior. Then entry should not result in a regime change, only a shift in the parameter D. Also, $\{U_{21}, \ldots, U_{2T}\}$ is assumed to be a sequence of independent normal variables, with mean zero, variance σ_2^2, and $\text{Cov}(U_{1t}, U_{2t}) = \sigma_{12}$.

If firms behaved in cooperative periods to maximize single-period expected joint net returns, then β_3 would equal $\log(\alpha_1/(1+\alpha_1))$. However, as I discussed in the introduction, if a cartel selects an optimal trigger price strategy, output in cooperative periods will exceed perfectly collusive levels. While the industry structure described in this article differs from that of Green and Porter, there is some reason to suspect that the same sort of equilibrium will result. To repeat, the larger the profits in cooperative periods, the greater the marginal benefit to secretly cutting price. Then cheating will be deterred only if reversionary periods are of greater length, or more likely to occur. An optimal enforcement mechanism will trade off short-run profits for increased future cartel stability. Thus the value of β_3 will not be restricted, but instead estimated independently. Since market price should be higher in cooperative periods, β_3 should be positive but less than $\log(\alpha_1/(1+\alpha_1))$.

If the sequence $\{I_1, \ldots, I_T\}$ is known, then the estimation of the parameters of the demand and supply functions is straightforward, as two-stage least squares can be employed to obtain consistent estimates. If instead I_t is unknown, but assumed to be governed by the Bernoulli distribution

$$I_t = \begin{cases} 1 \text{ with probability } \lambda \\ 0 \text{ with probability } 1-\lambda, \end{cases} \tag{3}$$

then we have a simultaneous equations switching regression problem, where the "switch" is reflected solely by the constant term in the supply function. The parameters of the demand and supply functions, as well as the switch probability λ, can be estimated by appropriately generalizing a technique first proposed by Kiefer (1980), which adapts the E-M algorithm to models of this sort.

We can summarize equations (1) and (2) by writing

$$By_t = \Gamma X_t + \Delta I_t + U_t, \tag{4}$$

where

$$y_t = \begin{pmatrix} \log Q_t \\ \log p_t \end{pmatrix}, \quad X_t = \begin{pmatrix} 1 \\ L_t \\ S_t \end{pmatrix}, \quad U_t = \begin{pmatrix} U_{1t} \\ U_{2t} \end{pmatrix}$$

and where

$$B = \begin{pmatrix} 1 & -\alpha_1 \\ -\beta_1 & 1 \end{pmatrix}, \quad \Delta = \begin{pmatrix} 0 \\ \beta_3 \end{pmatrix}, \quad \text{and} \quad \Gamma = \begin{pmatrix} \alpha_0 & \alpha_2 & 0 \\ \beta_0 & 0 & \beta_2 \end{pmatrix}.$$

Here U_t is identically and independently distributed $N(0, \Sigma)$, where

$$\Sigma = \begin{pmatrix} \sigma_1^2 & \sigma_{12} \\ \sigma_{12} & \sigma_2^2 \end{pmatrix}.$$

The probability density function of y_t, given I_t, is then

408

Study of cartel stability

$$h(y_t \mid I_t) = (2\pi)^{-1} |\Sigma|^{-1/2} \|B\|$$
$$\times \exp\{-\tfrac{1}{2}(By_t - \Gamma X_t - \Delta I_t)'\Sigma^{-1}(By_t - \Gamma X_t + \Delta I_t)\},$$

and the likelihood function, if there are T observations, is

$$L(I_1, \dots, I_T) = \prod_{t=1}^{T} h(y_t \mid I_t).$$

If the $\{I_t\}$ sequence is known, then we can obtain estimates of B, Γ, Δ, and Σ by maximizing $L(I_1, \dots, I_T)$. When the $\{I_t\}$ series is unknown and governed by equation (3), then the probability density function of y_t is given by

$$f(y_t) = (2\pi)^{-1} |\Sigma|^{-1/2} \|B\|$$
$$\times [\lambda \exp\{-\tfrac{1}{2}(By_t - \Gamma X_t - \Delta)'\Sigma^{-1}(By_t - \Gamma X_t - \Delta)\}$$
$$+ (1-\lambda) \exp\{-\tfrac{1}{2}(By_t - \Gamma X_t)'\Sigma^{-1}(By_t + \Gamma X_t)\}]$$

and the likelihood function by

$$L = \prod_{t=1}^{T} f(y_t). \tag{5}$$

Given an initial estimate of the regime classification sequence, say $\{w_1^0, \dots, w_T^0\}$, where w_t^0 is an estimate of $\Pr\{I_t = 1\}$, we can obtain an initial estimate of λ by using

$$\lambda^0 = \Sigma_t w_t^0 / T,$$

and initial estimates of Δ, Σ, B, and Γ by maximizing $L(w_1^0, \dots, w_T^0)$. Denote these estimates by $\Omega^0 = (\Delta^0, \Sigma^0, B^0, I^0)$. Kiefer's algorithm then updates the w_t^0 series by Bayes' rule, so that

$$w_t^1 = \Pr\{I_t = 1 \mid y_t, X_t, \Omega^0, \lambda^0\}$$
$$= \frac{\lambda^0 h(y_t \mid X_t, \Omega^0, I_t = 1)}{\lambda^0 h(y_t \mid X_t, \Omega^0, I_t = 1) + (1-\lambda^0) h(y_t \mid X_t, \Omega^0, I_t = 0)}.$$

Given the new regime classification series $\{w_1^1, \dots, w_T^1\}$, new estimates of $(\Delta, \Sigma, B, \Gamma)$, say Ω^1, can be obtained by maximizing $L(w_1^1, \dots, w_T^1)$ with respect to Ω. Our new estimates of λ will be $\lambda^1 = \Sigma_t w_t^1 / T$. This iterative procedure is continued until convergence occurs, say at $(\hat{w}_1, \dots, \hat{w}_T)$, $\hat{\lambda} = \Sigma_t \hat{w}_t / T$, and $\hat{\Omega}$. The stopping criterion was that the correlation between the estimated w_t sequences of two successive iterations exceed .999. As Kiefer shows, $\hat{\lambda}$ and $\hat{\Omega}$ will be the maximum likelihood estimates of λ and Ω. Thus $\hat{\lambda}$ and $\hat{\Omega}$ maximize the likelihood function L of equation (5). (This is generally true for the E-M algorithm.)

Once estimation is completed, the sample can be classified into collusive and reversionary periods. Lee and Porter (1984) show that if $\hat{w}_t$ exceeds .5, period t should be classified as collusive. This rule minimizes the total probability of misclassification in the sample. Thus, $(\hat{w}_1, \ldots, \hat{w}_T)$ generates the classification series $\hat{I}_t$, where

$$\hat{I}_t = 1 \quad \text{if} \quad \hat{w}_t > .5$$
$$= 0 \quad \text{otherwise.}$$

The Kiefer estimation scheme does not constrain the estimated $\hat{I}_t$ series to follow any particular process. If trigger price strategies of the sort described by Green and Porter actually occur, then the $\hat{I}_t$ sequence should follow a Markov process of order equal to the length of reversionary periods. Rather than attempt to estimate subject to a constraint of this sort, which would be relatively difficult, I have chosen to employ Kiefer's technique. (Note also that one would expect the duration of reversionary episodes to vary within the sample, as firms solve a new constrained-optimization problem in response to entry.) Green and Porter (1984) show that, when the number of reversionary episodes is small relative to the sample size (as is the case for the JEC data), the bias which arises from treating the endogenous Markov process as exogenous will plausibly be slight.

To see how sensitive the estimation scheme is to the specified functional forms, I also estimated the model with a linear specification of equation (4), that is, where $y'_t = [Q_t, p_t]$. These results were not significantly different from those reported in this article, and are documented in Porter (1982).

4. The data

A principal function of the JEC was information gathering and dissemination to member firms. Weekly accounts were kept to keep members abreast of developments in the industry. In this section, I document the data set which is employed in this study, and mention some of its features. A list of variables is contained in Table 1. Some summary statistics are provided in Table 2.

The quantity variable, TQG is the total tonnage of grain shipped by JEC members. It varied dramatically over the sample period, but does not appear to follow any significant trend.

The price variable, GR, is somewhat suspect. The JEC polled member firms and provided an index of prices charged. There is some reason to expect that secret price cuts would not be reflected by this index, since there is a moral hazard problem in reporting actual prices. Therefore,

Study of cartel stability

Table 1. *List of variables*

GR	grain rate, in dollars per 100 lbs.
TQG	total quantity of grain shipped, in tons.
LAKES	dummy variable: $=1$ if Great Lakes were open to navigation; $=0$ otherwise.
PO	cheating dummy variable: $=1$ if colluding reported by *Railway Review;* $=0$ otherwise.
PN	estimated cheating dummy variable.
DM1	$=1$ from week 28 in 1880 to week 10 in 1883; $=0$ otherwise; reflecting entry by the Grand Trunk Railway.
DM2	$=1$ from week 11 to week 25 in 1883; $=0$ otherwise; reflecting an addition to New York Central.
DM3	$=1$ from week 26 in 1883 to week 11 in 1886; $=0$ otherwise; reflecting entry by the Chicago and Atlantic.
DM4	$=1$ from week 12 to week 16 in 1886; $=0$ otherwise; reflecting departure of the Chicago and Atlantic from the JEC.

The sample is from week 1 in 1880 to week 16 in 1886.

any price wars precipitated by secret price cutting may have been recorded with a lag. On the other hand, the existence of this sort of information structure is necessary if an enforcement mechanism involving reversions to noncooperative behavior, or price wars, is to be witnessed. It is of crucial importance that firms monitor some variable (in this case their own market share) which imperfectly reflects the actions of other firms. Here firms knew what prices they charged their own customers, but the *GR* series would not be of much use in determining whether other firms were secretly cutting price.

While the *LAKES* variable documents when the JEC faced its main source of competition, it would be preferable if the prices charged by the lake steamers has also been used in the econometric work. Unfortunately, this series was not available.

The *PO* series equals one unless the *Railway Review,* a trade magazine, reported that a price war was occurring. This series concurred with the reports of the *Chicago Tribune* and other accounts in this period. The *PN* series is the $\hat{I}_t$ sequence, the estimated classification index which indicates whether industry conduct in period t is cooperative, and which should mirror the *PO* series if the latter is at all accurate. One reason for estimating a *PN* series is that *PO*, reported by Ulen (1978), conflicts sharply with an index of cartel adherence created by MacAvoy (1965).

411

Table 2. *Summary statistics*

Variable	Mean	Standard deviation	Minimum value	Maximum value
GR	.2465	.06653	.125	.40
TQG	25384	11632	4810	76407
LAKES	.5732	.4954	0	1
PO	.6189	.4864	0	1

The various *DM* dummy variables proxy structural change caused by entry, departures from the JEC, or additions to existing networks. [In 1886, the Chicago and Atlantic temporarily left the JEC because of a dispute with the railroad which provided them access to the eastern seaboard. This railroad (the Erie) was not a JEC member.] In each case, these changes are presumed to result in a once-and-for-all shift in the constant term of the supply relationship, which is consistent with the algebra of the previous section.

Finally, I also employed dummy variables to capture seasonal aspects of market demand supply. Each year was segmented into thirteen four-week segments, and so twelve "monthly" dummies entered both the demand and the supply equations.

One assumption of the econometric model of the previous section is that the output share of JEC members are relatively stable across episodes of reversionary conduct. These shares are allowed to vary when structural change occurs. There are five distinct periods in the sample, as reflected by the *DM* variables. *DM1* and *DM3* correspond to the longest periods (281 of 328 sample points), and all reversionary episodes occurred during these intervals. Within these intervals, the average sum (across firms) of squared deviations from allocated market shares was roughly the same in cooperative and reversionary periods. Thus, the assumption of approximately constant market shares seems reasonable, between times of structural change. (This is also borne out by data on the Herfindahl index.) While MacAvoy's (1965) results indicate significant fluctuations from trend shares, he does not examine deviations from allotted shares.

5. Results and interpretation

This section contains an interpretive discussion of the econometric results. The regression coefficients obtained when two-stage least squares are applied to the system of equations (4), taking the *PO* series to be an

Table 3. *Estimation results**

Variable	Two stage least squares (employing *PO*)		Maximum likelihood (yielding *PN*)**	
	Demand	Supply	Demand	Supply
C	9.169 (.184)	−3.944 (1.760)	9.090 (.149)	−2.416 (.710)
LAKES	−.437 (.120)		−.430 (.120)	
GR	−.742 (.121)		−.800 (.091)	
DM1		−.201 (.055)		−.165 (.024)
DM2		−.172 (.080)		−.209 (.036)
DM3		−.322 (.064)		−.284 (.027)
DM4		−.208 (.170)		−.298 (.073)
PO/PN		.382 (.059)		.545 (.032)
TQG		.251 (.171)		.090 (.068)
R^2	.312	.320	.307	.863
s	.398	.243	.399	.109

*Monthly dummy variables are employed. To econo-
mize on space, their estimated coefficients are not reported. Estimated standard errors are in parentheses.
**PN is the regime classification series $(\hat{I}, ..., \hat{I}_T)$. The
coefficient attributed to *PN* is the estimate of β_3.

accurate classification of regimes, are displayed in the left-hand columns
of Table 3. Both single equation R^2 statistics and standard errors of the
regression are displayed. Generally speaking, all variables have coefficients of the anticipated sign significantly different from zero, but the
"fits" are not particularly good.

In the demand equation the predicted quantity is much lower when
the lakes were open. The price elasticity is negative and less than one in
absolute value. Thus, the marginal revenue associated with the industry

413

demand curve is negative. This fact is not consistent with single-period profit maximization, which stipulates that industry marginal revenue equal a weighted average of the marginal costs of individual firms, a positive number.

The supply equation is also sensible. Price was significantly higher in cooperative periods. The predicted price of suppliers is an increasing function of quantity shipped, but the elasticity is of minor magnitude and only significantly different from zero at a 15% significance level. Given the presumed cost and demand functions, this might be taken as evidence of weak diseconomies of scale, at least locally. (Of course, these diseconomies might be offset by large fixed costs.) The coefficients of the structural dummies are also reasonable. Entry led to a fall in market price, ceteris paribus, as the coefficient of *DM1* is negative, and that of *DM3* is less than that of *DM2*.

The right-hand columns of Table 3 display the results of applying Kiefer's iterative technique. (This algorithm converged to these estimates from several disparate starting points.) The coefficient attributed to *PN* is the estimate of β_3, i.e., the difference between the intercept of the supply relationship in cooperative and noncooperative periods. The obvious difference between the results of Table 3 is that measures of goodness of fit of the supply equation are dramatically better for the E-M algorithm.

For practical purposes, the demand equations of Table 3 are identical. Again, the demand curve is inelastic. The real differences are reflected in the supply relationships. The coefficient attributed to the *PN* series, β_3, is larger and with about half the standard error. If we assume that $\beta_3 = -\log(1 + \theta/\alpha_1)$ for some constant θ, then the value of θ implied by the estimates of β_3 and α_1 is .336. This is roughly consistent with Cournot behavior in cooperative periods. The witnessing of approximately Cournot behavior is by itself of no special significance. What matters is that cooperative period prices exceed those implied by competitive price setting, but are less than those consistent with static joint profit maximizing, as predicted by Porter (1983).

If we set all explanatory variables equal to their sample mean, with the exception of the *LAKES* and *PN* dummy variables, then the maximum likelihood estimates displayed in Table 3 imply the reduced-form estimates shown in Table 4. Thus, in equilibrium, price was 66% higher in cooperative periods, and quantity 33% lower. Similarly, price was 4.5% lower when the lakes were open, and quantity 33% lower. The total revenue figure is twenty times the product of *GR* and *TQG*, and so in dollars (20 × $ per 100 lbs. × tons). Thus, the cartel as a whole could expect to earn 11% higher revenues in cooperative periods, a difference of about $11,000 per week. (Recall that these are 1880 dollars.) This is the revenue

Table 4. *Price, quantity, and total revenue for different values of LAKES and PN**

Price	LAKES	
	0	1
PN 0	.1673	.1612
1	.2780	.2679

Quantity	LAKES	
	0	1
PN 0	38680	25904
1	25775	17261

Total Revenue**	LAKES	
	0	1
PN 0	129423	83514
1	143309	92484

*Computed from the reduced form of the maximum likelihood estimates of Table 3, with all other explanatory variables set at their sample means.
**Total Revenue = 20 (Price × Quantity), to yield dollars per week.

earned on grain shipments, which represented between 70 and 80% of total revenues from eastbound freight shipments by the JEC. Finally, revenues were about 35% lower when the lakes were navigable.

The *PO* and *PN* series are depicted, together with *GR*, in Figure 1, which shows when noncooperative episodes were predicted by the two series. Both series are similar to the extent that noncooperative periods averaged about 10 weeks in duration, and primarily occurred in 1881, 1884, and 1885. In several instances, *PO* reflects a price war before *PN*, and both switch back to unity together, which is consistent with *GR* not picking up secret price cuts. For either series, a regression of price war length on the realization of the demand equation residual error term in the period before the beginning of the episode had little predictive power. Of course, the demand equation is marred by a missing variable problem (namely, the price charged by lake steamers), so there is not much reason to think that the demand residuals would accurately reflect unexpected

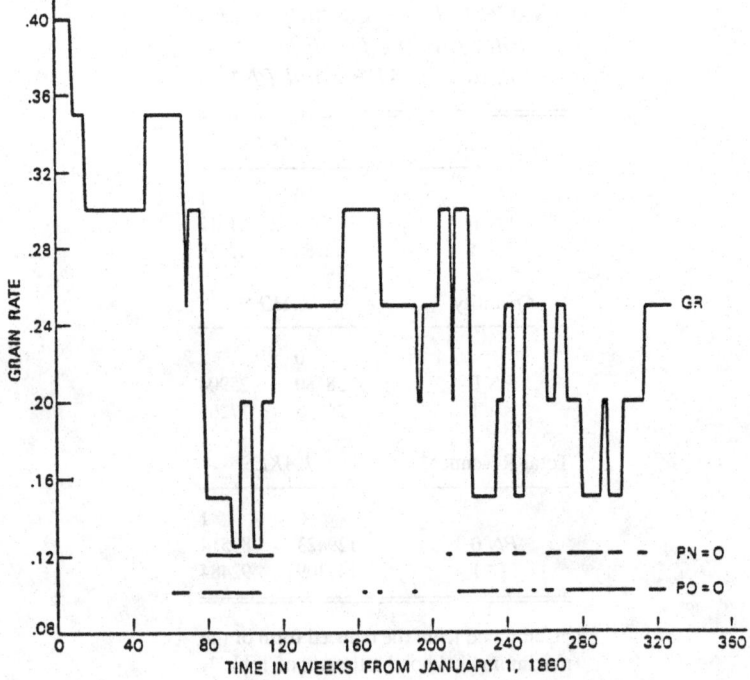

Figure 1. Plot of *GR, PO, PN* as a function of time.

disturbances. (Some people have suggested that optimal price war length might depend on the magnitude of the demand shock.) More important, since JEC firms were price setters, price wars may not have necessarily been triggered by adverse demand shocks. As predicted by Stigler (1964), unpredictable fluctuations in market shares were probably more decisive. In this sample, price wars (as measured by either *PO* or *PN*) were not preceded by large negative demand residuals.

The 1881 and 1884 incidents both began about 40 weeks after the entry of the Grand Trunk and the Chicago and Atlantic, respectively. While entry may not have immediately caused reversion to noncooperative behavior, it is quite plausible that it increased the probability of its incidence in the future, as cartel enforcement problems typically increase with the number of participating firms. In the sample, reversions were more frequent when the number of firms increased. (They were also shorter, on average.)

416

Table 5. *Index of cartel nonadherence*[1]

Year	MacAvoy[2]	Reported[3]	Estimated[4]
1880	26	0.00	0.00
1881	14	0.67	0.44
1882	18	0.06	0.21
1883	6	0.10	0.00
1884	16	0.58	0.40
1885	10	0.77	0.67
1886[5]	15	0.50	0.06

[1] Columns 1 and 2 are taken from Ulen (1978, p. 336).

[2] The number of months, summed over all cartel members, for which the difference between the actual market share and "trend" share of tonnage was greater than the standard error from the "trend" share regression of each member road. The greater this number of months, the less stable the cartel is likely to be.

[3] For year i, this index if $\Sigma(1 - PO(t))/52$, where the summation is over t in year i.

[4] This index is $\Sigma(1 - \hat{I}_t)/52$, summing over t in year i.

[5] PO and PN only exist for the first 16 weeks, so the denominator of the indices is 16 rather than 52.

The PO series collected by Ulen (1978) differs markedly from an index of cartel nonadherence created by MacAvoy (1965). These series, as well as PN, are summarized in Table 5. The "Reported" and "Estimated" columns show the fraction of weeks in each year in which PO and PN were equal to zero, respectively. Since the PN series was in no way constrained to resemble PO, it is evident that PN supports the documentation of the *Railway Review* and *Chicago Tribune*, rather than MacAvoy's results.

To conclude this section, I consider the statistical evidence that switches actually occurred and were significant. First, the coefficient of PO and that attributed to PN are significantly greater than zero, so that periods of cooperation involved a significantly higher price.

Likelihood ratio tests can be used to determine whether structural change has in fact occurred. The natural null hypothesis to be tested is that only cooperative or noncooperative behavior is observed, but not both. These are the respective implications of the equilibria described by Friedman (1977) and Telser (1972), or of a Nash open-loop strategy equilibrium. The value of the likelihood function, given the Kiefer estimation technique, can be compared to that when L is maximized subject to the constraint that $\Delta = 0$.

Suppose that L_1 is the maximized value of the log likelihood function for the specification of Table 3 when Kiefer's technique is used, and $(\hat{B}_1, \hat{\Sigma}_1)$ the corresponding estimates of (B, Σ). Further, suppose that L_0 is the maximized value of the log likelihood function for this specification when Δ equals zero, and that $(\hat{B}_0, \hat{\Sigma}_0)$ are the estimates of (B, Σ). Then

$$L_1 - L_0 = (\log\|\hat{B}_1\| - \tfrac{1}{2}\log|\hat{\Sigma}_1|) - (\log\|\hat{B}_0\| - \tfrac{1}{2}\log|\hat{\Sigma}_0|).$$

Under the null hypothesis that no regime change is observed, $2T(L_1 - L_0)$ has a chi-squared distribution with one degree of freedom. For the JEC sample, $2T(L_1 - L_0)$ is 554.1. Thus I can overwhelmingly reject the hypothesis that no switch occurred, given the specifications adopted. Price and quantity changes cannot be attributed solely to exogenous changes in demand and structural conditions. The similarity of the estimated *PN* series and the *PO* series indicate that some price changes can be attributed to periods of noncooperative behavior, and that the incidence of alleged switches in behavior cannot be explained by missing data problems.

The conclusions of this section are quite robust, as they are obtained under a variety of different specifications and functional forms.

6. Summary

The econometric evidence presented in the previous section indicates that reversions to noncooperative behavior did occur in the JEC, with a significant decrease in market price in these periods. The econometric results indicating that these episodes were concentrated in 1881, 1884, and 1885 are in keeping with the behavior of the JEC that was reported at that time. The question remaining, however, is what the causes of these reversions were.

Traditionally, breakdowns in cartel discipline have been attributed to demand slumps, both within the JEC as well as in other cartels. What distinguishes the theoretical model of Green and Porter (1984) from other theories of cartel stability is that reversionary episodes, or price wars, are caused by an unanticipated change in demand, in this case reflected by an unusually low market share for at least one firm, rather than by a prolonged drop in total market demand. Trying to determine which model best describes the observed behavior of the JEC from 1880 to 1886 is not an easy task, but I can refer to two pieces of evidence which may support the Green and Porter paradigm. First, the reduced-form estimates predict that price was lower and quantity higher in reversionary periods, ceteris paribus. Of course, this could merely reflect the fact that

418

Table 6. *Annual eastbound shipment of wheat*
from Chicago by lake and rail*

	Lake		Rail		
Year	Total	Percentage	Total	Percentage	Total Shipments
1880	16.69	77.9	4.728	22.1	21.42
1881	7.688	50.0	7.680	50.0	15.37
1882	14.94	86.2	2.389	13.8	17.33
1883	7.067	73.2	2.590	26.8	9.66
1884	11.52	66.0	5.928	34.0	17.45
1885	5.436	51.5	5.116	48.5	10.55
1886	10.51	82.6	2.209	17.4	12.72

*In millions of bushels.

demand was quite elastic with respect to price changes, a fact at least partially refuted by the estimated price elasticity of demand. Second, one can look at total grain shipments from Chicago to see what fraction is accounted for by the JEC. Annual data showing the amount of grain shipped by lake steamers versus railroads are presented in Table 6. Of the years in the sample, 1880 is a boom year, which would account for the unusually high prices charged then. Of the remaining years, the annual variation in total shipments is not correlated with measures of cartel nonadherence. The distinguishing feature of the "breakdown" years of 1881, 1884, and 1885 is the much higher market share captured by the JEC as a whole in the intermodal competition to ship wheat. This is an indication that JEC price wars were not concurrent with lake steamer price wars, and also that JEC price wars did not always occur in years when total demand was unusually low. Thus, while some observers have claimed that price wars will be triggered by the unexpected tapering off of demand, which is consistent with the paradigm of Green and Porter, the JEC seems to be a case where this was not necessarily true of periods in which demand was low *per se*. Further support of this contention is that the *PO* and *PN* series are not systematically related to the opening or closing of the lake steamer shipping season. Finally, the fact that the frequency of reversionary periods increased as the number of market participants increased is consistent with a story of dynamic cartel enforcement mechanisms, especially since the "no-exit" constraint faced by railroads deterred predatory reactions to entry.

References

Brock, W. A. and Scheinkman, J. A. "Price-Setting Supergames with Capacity Constraints." SSRI Paper No. 8130, University of Wisconsin–Madison, 1981.

Friedman, J. W. *Oligopoly and the Theory of Games*. Amsterdam: North-Holland, 1977.

Green, E. J. and Porter, R. H. "Noncooperative Collusion under Imperfect Price Information." *Econometrica*, Vol. 52 (January 1984).

Kiefer, N. M. "A Note on Switching Regressions and Logistic Discrimination." *Econometrica*, Vol. 48 (May 1980), pp. 1065–9.

Lee, L. F. and Porter, R. H. "Switching Regression Models with Imperfect Sample Separation Information – with an Application on Cartel Stability." *Econometrica*, Vol. 52 (January 1984).

MacAvoy, P. W. *The Economic Effects of Regulation*. Cambridge: M.I.T. Press, 1965.

Porter, R. H. "A Study of Cartel Stability: The Joint Executive Committee, 1880–1886." C.E.R. Discussion Paper No. 82-158, University of Minnesota, 1982.

———, "Optimal Cartel Trigger Price Strategies." *Journal of Economic Theory*, Vol. 29 (April 1983), pp. 313–38.

Stigler, G. J. "A Theory of Oligopoly." *Journal of Political Economy*, Vol. 72 (February 1964), pp. 44–61.

Telser, L. G. *Competition, Collusion, and Game Theory*. Chicago: Aldine-Atherton, 1972.

Ulen, T. S. *Cartels and Regulation*. Unpublished Ph.D. dissertation, Stanford University, 1978.

CHAPTER 19

Oligopoly and financial structure: the limited liability effect

JAMES A. BRANDER AND TRACY R. LEWIS

We argue that product markets and financial markets have important linkages. Assuming an oligopoly in which financial and output decisions follow in sequence, we show that limited liability may commit a leveraged firm to a more aggressive output stance. Because firms will have incentives to use financial structure to influence the output market, this demonstrates a new determinant of the debt-equity ratio.

The literature on financial structure and the literature on oligopoly have at least one common feature: they both place relatively little emphasis on the strategic relationships between financial decisions and output market decisions. In financial theory, the product market is typically assumed to offer an exogenous random return which is unaffected by the debt-equity positions of the firms in the market. Correspondingly, in the economic analysis of oligopoly, the firm's obligations to debt holders and the possibility of financial distress are usually ignored in modeling the strategic interaction between producers in the output market.

This approach of focusing separately on financial and output decisions is clearly useful in understanding certain aspects of both financial structure and strategic output market behavior. It seems equally clear, however, that there are important linkages between financial and output decisions.

The choice of financial structure can affect output markets in the following way, which we refer to as the limited liability effect of debt financing. As firms take on more debt, they will have an incentive to pursue output

Faculty of Commerce and Business Administration, University of British Columbia, Vancouver, B.C. V6T 1Y8, Canada, and Department of Economics, University of California, Davis, CA 95616, respectively. In writing and revising this paper we have incurred substantial debts (without offering equity participation) to several people. We are grateful to three anonymous referees, and also thank Ron Giammarino, Robbie Jones, and Barbara Spencer for helpful comments. In addition we have received help from other colleagues at UBC in both Finance and Economics, and have benefited from presenting the paper in seminars at the Rand Corporation, UC–Berkeley, the University of Regina, the University of Saskatchewan, and the University of Southern California.
James A. Brander and Tracy R. Lewis, "Oligopoly and Financial Structure: The Limited Liability Effect," *American Economic Review* 76, 5, 1986, pp. 956–70.

421

strategies that raise returns in good states and lower returns in bad states. The basic point is that shareholders will ignore reductions in returns in bankrupt states, since bondholders become the residual claimants. As debt levels change, the distribution of returns to shareholders over the different states changes, which in turn changes the output strategy favored by shareholders.[1]

A second possible linkage between output and financial markets is the strategic bankruptcy effect. Any one firm's susceptibility to financial distress depends on its financial structure, and its fortunes will usually improve if one or more of its rivals can be driven into financial distress. Therefore, firms might make output market decisions that raise the chances of driving their rivals into insolvency. Since the possibility of financial distress for each firm is contingent on its financial structure, this is a second channel for finances to affect output markets.

In this paper we examine the relationship between financial and output decisions in a formal structure capturing essential aspects of both modern financial and oligopoly theory. Our model focuses on the "limited liability" effect of debt financing. The strategic bankruptcy effects of financial decisions are analyzed in our companion paper (1985). The analysis we offer here illustrates two important points. First, output market behavior will, in general, be affected by financial structure. Second, foresighted firms will anticipate output market consequences of financial decisions; therefore, output market conditions will influence financial decisions.

In the analysis to follow, we deliberately abstract from the physical capital investment decision by assuming that the firm's capital stock is fixed (at least temporarily). We adopt this approach so as to isolate the linkage between the firm's financial position and its behavior in the output market. If physical investment was allowed to vary endogenously with the firm's financial position, certain readily identifiable effects of financial decisions on output behavior would emerge. First, firms would have an incentive to undertake capital investments that lower the marginal cost of production in output markets so as to commit themselves to more aggressive positions in the output market. (This effect has been investigated by Avinash Dixit, 1980; Curtis Eaton and Richard Lipsey, 1980; and Brander and Barbara Spencer, 1983; among others.)

In addition, as emphasized by Michael Jensen and William Meckling and Stewart Myers (1977), the firm's debt-equity mix would affect the

---

[1] The idea that limited liability creates a conflict of interest between bondholders and equity holders is described in Michael Jensen and William Meckling (1976) and in Stewart Myers (1977), and has been examined by Jeremy Bulow and John Shoven (1978), Jerry Green and Shoven (1983), and Varouj Aivazian and Jeffrey Callen (1980). These studies do not, however, explicitly consider the output market, which is the focus of this paper.

optimal investment strategy. A referee suggested that heavily leveraged firms might lower their level of physical capital investments in order to minimize the salvageable assets that would be lost to debtholders in the event of bankruptcy. This would in turn affect costs and the output market in the obvious way. These are interesting issues, but they are logically separate from the effects we identify; accordingly we abstract from the investment decision by assuming it is made before the debt-equity mix is determined. Output adjustments are therefore to be thought of as resulting from changes in variable inputs.

The basic model we investigate is a two-stage sequential duopoly game. In stage 1, the two firms decide upon financial structure. In stage 2, they select output levels taking as given the financial composition determined in stage 1. The equilibrium concept is the sequentially rational Nash equilibrium in debt levels and output levels. In other words, the second-stage outcome is a Cournot equilibrium in output which is correctly anticipated by the firms when choosing debt levels in the first stage.[2]

The output decisions of firms are made before the realization of a random variable reflecting variations in demand or costs. Once profits are determined, firms are obliged to pay debt claims out of operating profits, if possible. If profits are insufficient to meet debt obligations, the firm goes bankrupt and its assets are turned over to the bondholders. This simplified depiction of the relation between financial distress and output markets is not universally descriptive, but it does yield a tractable model that can be readily compared with similar models of output market rivalry in the oligopoly literature where financial structure is ignored.

Before proceeding it is important to place our analysis in context in both the financial and oligopoly literatures. A large part of the literature on financial structure can be regarded as a response to Franco Modigliani and Merton Miller (1958), who assert that, under certain conditions, the value of the firm is independent of financial structure. Our paper falls in the class of exceptions to the Modigliani–Miller Theorem. Following Alan Kraus and Robert Litzenberger (1973), among others, we appeal to a background of imperfect markets to allow departures from the Modigliani–Miller world. The exact nature of the market imperfections should become clear as we proceed. The standard treatment of choice of financial structure, as presented in Kraus and Litzenberger, involves a tradeoff

---

[2] In our context, sequential rationality is equivalent to what Reinhardt Selten (1975) has referred to as subgame perfection. The most important implication of subgame perfection is that players are restricted to credible threats: players cannot have equilibrium strategies that would call for them to carry out actions that would be against their best interests at the time the action is to be taken. This basic idea goes back at least to Thomas Schelling (1956).

between financial distress costs and the tax advantages of debt. Our model, which abstracts from both bankruptcy costs and taxes, points to the interaction between output and financial markets as a determinant of financial structure.

Of the existing published literature in financial theory, our paper is closest in spirit to Sheridan Titman (1984) in which financial structure influences potential profits for suppliers of a durable good. Titman argues that low levels of debt constitute a commitment by a producer to stay in the market, which raises the value of the durable good because it means that the firm will be available to service the good in the future. (This effect operates as long as each firm has some advantage over rivals in servicing its own products.) In our model, financial structure serves as a commitment to a particular output strategy,[3] and is therefore related to the recent literature on commitment in oligopoly theory, in which physical capital, location, product choice, or R&D choices constitute a first stage which influences the Nash equilibrium in the subsequent output market. Standard references in this literature include Eaton–Lipsey and Dixit.[4] The equal opportunity duopoly structure we use is similar in form to Brander–Spencer.

An outline of the paper follows. Section I sets out the basic model. Section II is devoted to the output market equilibrium and, in particular, shows the dependence of output equilibrium on financial structure and compares the output equilibrium in the (base) case, in which equity holders control the firm, with the case in which debtholders control the firm. Section III examines the selection of debt levels and describes how output market considerations influence capital structure. Section IV contains concluding remarks and discusses extensions to the paper.

I. The model

Firms 1 and 2 are rivals in an output market where they produce competing products q_1 and q_2, respectively. For concreteness, we assume there is Cournot quantity competition in the output market. Other forms of market rivalry involving advertising, R&D, or Bertrand price competition could be analyzed just as well using our model. The operating profit

---

[3] We would also like to mention a Ph.D. thesis by Vojislav Maksimovic (1986) and a discussion paper by Franklin Allen (1985) which address the same fundamental issue as this paper: the strategic relationship between oligopoly and financial markets. Maksimovic represents simultaneous development of a modeling approach that is similar in some respects to ours and establishes some of the same insights. It also examines some interesting repeated game extensions of the basic model.

[4] See Eaton and Mukesh Eswaran (1984) for a very helpful synopsis of the strategic commitment paradigm applied to industrial organization.

for firm i, which is defined as the difference between revenue and variable cost, is denoted by $R^i(q_i, q_j, z_i)$. The random variable z_i reflects the effects of an uncertain environment on the fortunes of firm i. It is assumed to be distributed over the interval $[\underline{z}, \overline{z}]$ according to density function $f(z_i)$. For simplicity we assume that z_i and z_j are independent and identically distributed.

We assume that R^i satisfies the usual properties: $R_{ii}^i < 0$, $R_j^i < 0$, and $R_{ij}^i < 0$ (where subscripts denote partial derivatives). We adopt the convention that high values of z_i lead to higher operating profits: $R_z^i > 0$, meaning that higher realizations of z_i correspond to better states of the world. The effect of z_i on marginal profit turns out to be very important in our analysis. We consider two possibilities.

(i) $R_{iz}^i > 0$. This corresponds to a situation where marginal profits are higher in better states of the world. This would arise, for example, if higher realizations of z corresponded to downward shifts of the marginal cost schedule, or to upward shifts in the marginal revenue schedule facing the firm. We take this to be the normal case.

(ii) $R_{iz}^i < 0$. This means that good states of the world are correlated with low marginal returns to extra sales. This case seems less likely to arise but it is possible.[5]

Another argument for considering the $R_{iz}^i < 0$ case arises when we assume that firms engage in other forms of competition besides quantity or price competition. For example, suppose that firms primarily compete through advertising, as is the case in some retail markets.[6] Let q_i be firm i's expenditure on advertising and assume that higher realizations of z_i correspond to cases where market demand is high. It seems plausible that, in some cases, when conditions are good, there might be little need for advertising, whereas advertising would be more effective in increasing sales in a market with sagging demand. In this case we would find that marginal returns from advertising, R_i^i, are inversely related to the state of nature, z_i, leading to the case $R_{iz}^i < 0$.

An alternative way of thinking of the sign condition on R_{iz}^i is to view q_i and z_i as separate "inputs" which go into making profits. The case $R_{iz}^i > 0$, which is the standard case under quantity competition, means

[5] A rather contrived example can be constructed as follows. Suppose that firms i and j each have fixed production capacity k, and that they are rivals in a domestic market where they produce q_i and q_j, respectively, but they also sell their remaining outputs $k - q_i$ and $k - q_j$ in separated foreign markets where they do not compete with each other and where price is given by $p^i + z_i$. In this case, higher values of z_i are certainly good for the firm, but correspond to lower levels of marginal profit in the home market.

[6] See Richard Schmalensee (1976) for an analysis of oligopoly markets where firms compete in advertising. One could turn our model into a model of advertising by taking output as exogenously fixed, and interpreting q_i as advertising expenditure.

that the two inputs are complementary, while the other case is the case of substitute inputs.

The financial structure of the firm is summarized by the variable D_i, which represents the debt obligation of firm i. As indicated in the introduction, we assume that the capital investment is made before the financing mix is decided upon. Choosing the debt level, with the total financing requirement fixed, would then fix the equity financing level by default. This interpretation is not necessary, however, and the firm could just as easily be viewed as giving the borrowed money directly to shareholders. Debt levels, in turn, are assumed to be chosen before output decisions are decided upon and are taken as given when output levels are chosen. Output decisions are then made before the uncertainty over demand or cost is resolved. It is not essential that there be no uncertainty resolved before output decisions are made. What is important is that there be some residual uncertainty left to be resolved after output decisions are made. Certainly this is true of most industries.

After production occurs and the uncertainty regarding firms' profits is settled, the firm is obliged to pay creditors D_i out of current profits. If the firm is unable to meet its debt obligations, its creditors are paid whatever operating profits are available.[7]

Given debt levels (D_1, D_2), the firm is assumed to choose output levels with the objective of maximizing the expected value of the firm to the shareholders.[8] This is what an owner-manager would choose to do, and is certainly what wealth-maximizing shareholders would want the firm to do. The value to the shareholders is referred to as the equity value and is represented by the letter V:

$$V^i(q_i, q_j : \cdot) = \int_{\hat{z}_i}^{\bar{z}} (R^i(q_i, q_j, z_i) - D_i) f(z_i) \, dz_i, \tag{1}$$

where $\hat{z}_i$ is defined by

$$R^i(q_i, q_j, \hat{z}_i) - D_i = 0, \tag{2}$$

assuming $\underline{z} < \hat{z}_i < \bar{z}$. When $z_i = \hat{z}_i$, firm i can just meet its debt obligations with nothing left over. The expression in (1) represents expected current-period profits net of debt obligations in good $(z_i \geq \hat{z}_i)$ states of the world. In bad states $(z_i < \hat{z}_i)$, the firm earns zero as all of its earnings are paid to

---

[7] For simplicity we assume that the asset value of the firm is zero, as if assets are completely used up in the production of output. Creditors can, therefore, collect only current operating profits if the firm becomes insolvent.

[8] The interesting possibilities that the rival firms may somehow be connected through interlocking directorships, or that they are both owned by a common group of shareholders are not considered here.

Oligopoly and financial structure

debtholders. (Note that we are assuming that shareholders of the firm are risk neutral with respect to the firm's returns and therefore have their interests served by maximization of expected equity value.)

Expression (2) shows the implicit dependence of $\hat{z}_i$ on D_i, q_i, and q_j. As this relationship is important in establishing the principal results of the paper, it is useful to report the following derivatives:

$$d\hat{z}_i/dD_i = 1/R_z^i(\hat{z}_i) > 0 \tag{3a}$$

$$d\hat{z}_i/dD_j = 0 \tag{3b}$$

$$d\hat{z}_i/dq_i = -R_i^i(\hat{z}_i)/R_z^i(\hat{z}_i) \tag{3c}$$

$$d\hat{z}_i/dq_j = -R_j^i(\hat{z}_i)/R_z^i(\hat{z}_i) > 0. \tag{3d}$$

The natural assumption, abstracting from agency problems between managers and shareholders, is that managers maximize equity value in this stage of the game when debt levels are taken as given. Later in the paper we examine the earlier decision of how much debt the firm should take on. At this earlier stage, managers are assumed to maximize total value. Once the debtholders are captive, however, the managers have no subsequent incentive to act in the debtholders' interests. For purposes of comparison it is, nevertheless, useful to consider the problem of maximizing the debt value of the firm in the output phase, as if debtholders were running the firm. In this case, the maximand, denoted $W^i(q_i, q_j; \cdot)$, is given by

$$W^i(q_i, q_j; \cdot) = \int_{\underline{z}}^{\hat{z}_i} R^i(q_i, q_j, z_i) f(z_i) \, dz_i + D_i(1 - F(\hat{z}_i)). \tag{4}$$

(We are assuming that $\underline{z}$, the lowest possible value of z_i, generates positive operating profits for all relevant values of the choice variables. This is a convenient but inessential assumption.) The first term in (4) represents the operating profit of the firm in states of the world when this profit is insufficient to completely cover debt obligations. The second term represents those states of the world in which the creditors of the firm are paid in full.

The model presented here is the simplest model we could develop to explore possible connections between financial decisions and oligopolistic output markets. Generalizations to include more firms, other forms of market rivalry, and correlated random disturbances yield the same qualitative results.

II. Output market equilibrium

This section examines how the limited liability aspects of financial leverage affect the strategic output decisions by firms. Taking existing debt

427

levels D_1 and D_2 as predetermined, the management of each firm chooses output to maximize either V or W, depending on whether it acts in the interest of shareholders or debtholders.

A. Equity value maximization

We take the case of equity value maximization as our standard case. Assuming an interior solution, the choice of output for firm i is obtained by setting the derivative of (1) with respect to q_i equal to zero:[9]

$$V_i^i = \int_{\hat{z}_i}^{z_i} R_i^i(q_i, q_j, z_i) f(z_i) \, dz_i.$$ (5)

The second-order condition is

$$V_{ii}^i < 0.$$ (6)

The Nash output (or Cournot) equilibrium is obtained from the simultaneous solution of (5) for $i, j = 1, 2$. In addition we also require that

$$V_{ij}^i < 0,$$ (7)

$$V_{ii}^i V_{jj}^j - V_{ij}^i V_{ji}^j > 0,$$ (8)

which are standard conditions in Cournot-type models. Equation (8) is equivalent (given second-order conditions) to reaction functions being downward sloping. It tends to hold if expected marginal revenue declines when the output of the other firm rises. Equation (8), if it holds everywhere, implies uniqueness of the equilibrium and reaction function stability. It is well-known that even in the simplest Cournot models, conditions analogous to (7) and (8) can be violated by feasible demand and cost structures, and that is certainly true here. One case in which these conditions do hold, however, is if z_i is uniformly distributed, demand is linear, and marginal cost is constant.

While this paper focuses nearly exclusively on the Cournot duopoly market structure, the first central insight we offer applies quite generally. This central insight is that higher debt levels tend, in the standard case ($R_{iz}^i > 0$), to increase a firm's desired output. The intuition is as follows.

In bad states of the world, the firm's profits are insufficient to meet its debts. The equity holders' claims on the firm go to zero, and the debtholders become the residual claimants on the firm's profits. In other words, limited liability implies that debtholders become residual claimants in bad states: specifically, when $z_i \leq \hat{z}_i$. Equity holders are residual claimants in good states of the world, as illustrated in Figure 1.

---

[9] Besides the expression in (5), the derivative of V^i with respect to q_i also includes another term, $-(d\hat{z}_i/dq_i)(R^i(\hat{z}_i) - D_i)$, which vanishes by (2).

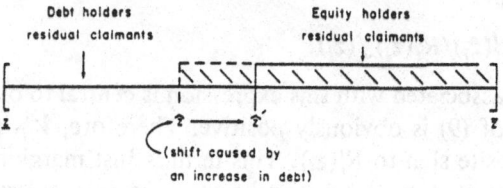

Figure 1. Division of state space into debt-relevant and equity-relevant regions.

An increase in debt causes $\hat{z}_i$ to rise, meaning that the range of states over which the firm becomes bankrupt is expanded. In particular, with $R_{iz}^i > 0$, it is states with low marginal returns to output that are moved from the region in which equity holders are residual claimants to the bankrupt region, where debtholders are the residual claimants. In other words, these low marginal profit states are no longer relevant to equity holders and equity holders would therefore want output to rise. Thus an increase in debt tends to make equilibrium output rise.

A football team that is behind late in the game will take chances that it would not normally take. The reasoning is that bad realizations are irrelevant, for the worst the team can do is lose, and it will do that anyway if it does not take chances. The more the team is behind, the more aggressive it will become. Our firm, representing equity holders, reacts in the same way. As debt rises, low marginal value states become irrelevant, for in those states the firm is turned over to the debtholders, and the equity holders get zero in any case. Since the firm restricts attention to higher marginal profit states, it adopts a more aggressive stance. (Note that the reasoning is precisely reversed if $R_{iz}^i < 0$.)

Presenting this intuition rigorously requires a slightly different treatment for each different market structure. The case of monopoly is easiest. The monopoly case is obtained by letting $q_j = 0$ in expression (5) and by assuming that q_j remains at zero throughout the comparative static exercise. Total differentiation of (5) with respect to q_i and D_i then yields the comparative static formula:

$$dq/dD = -V_{iD}^i / V_{ii}^i.$$

The denominator is negative by second-order condition (6), which means that dq/dD has the same sign as V_{iD}^i: Output rises with debt if increases in debt cause marginal expected profits to rise.

The expression for V_{iD}^i is given by

$$V_{iD}^i = -R_i^i(\hat{z}_i)d\hat{z}_i/dD,$$

429

or, using (3a),

$$V_{iD}^i = -R_i^i(\hat{z}_i)/R_z^i(\hat{z}_i)\,f(\hat{z}_i). \qquad (9)$$

The intuition associated with this expression is central to our paper. The denominator of (9) is obviously positive. Therefore, V_{iD}^i (and dq/dD) have the opposite sign to $R_i^i(\hat{z}_i)$. This term is just marginal profit evaluated at the worst state of nature relevant to equity holders. With R_i^i increasing in z, it follows that R_i^i evaluated at $\hat{z}$ must be negative, since a weighted average of R_i^i over $\hat{z}$ and strictly better states is zero from first-order condition (5). Expression (9) implies that V_{iD}^i and, therefore, dq/dD must be positive in this case. The point is that $\hat{z}$ is precisely the marginal state that is being removed from consideration (by equity holders) as D rises. Consequently, the associated value of marginal profit, $R_i^i(\hat{z})$, is also thrown out of the marginal calculation determining output. Since this is the lowest value of marginal profit, optimal output must rise.

This discussion proves that output is rising in debt (for $R_{iz}^i > 0$) in the case of monopoly. This can also be proven for perfect competition and for other market structures as well. For reasons to be discussed later, it turns out that the cases of perfect competition and monopoly are not very interesting when the full two-stage game is considered. The duopoly case is interesting in the full game. We return to the duopoly case now. Occasionally in what follows it will be helpful to examine circumstances in which the firms are symmetric in the sense that $D_1 = D_2 = D$ and operating profits R^i and R^j are identical functions.[10] In this case, given (8), the Nash equilibrium in outputs will be symmetric and unique. Proposition 1 is a formal statement, for the symmetric duopoly case, of the result just described for monopoly.

Proposition 1. *Assume firms 1 and 2 are symmetric. Then the Nash equilibrium output level $q = q_i = q_j$ is increasing in the debt level $D = D_i = D_j$ when $R_{iz}^i > 0$ and decreasing when $R_{iz}^i < 0$.*

For this and all subsequent proofs, we present the analysis only for the $R_{iz}^i > 0$ case, as the other case follows easily in a similar manner.

Proof $(R_{iz}^i > 0)$: The comparative static effect of an increase in the common debt level, D, is determined by totally differentiating first-order condition (5) $(V_i^i = 0)$ with respect to q_i, q_j, and D. Normally one would

---

[10] The symmetric case is also of empirical interest. Michael Bradley, Gregg Jarrell, and E. Han Kim (1984) present evidence that firms within the same industry tend to choose similar financial structures.

have to differentiate both first-order conditions (for i and j) and solve the resulting simultaneous system for comparative static effects dq_i/dD and dq_j/dD. Here, however, we can exploit the symmetry of the model and totally differentiate just one of the first-order conditions, incorporating the constraint that $dq_i = dq_j = dq$. This yields

$$V_{ii}^i dq + V_{ij}^i dq + V_{iD}^i dD = 0.$$

Solving for dq/dD then yields

$$dq/dD = -V_{iD}^i/(V_{ii}^i + V_{ij}^i). \tag{10}$$

The denominator in (10) is negative by (6) and (7). Just as for the monopoly case, V_{iD}^i is given by

$$V_{iD}^i = -R_i^i(\hat{z}_i)/R_z^i(\hat{z}_i) f(\hat{z}_i), \tag{11}$$

and, since R_i^i is increasing in z, $R_i^i(\hat{z}_i)$ must be negative [once again using (5)], implying that the expression in (11) is positive. Combining this with (10) yields

$$dq/dD > 0, \tag{12}$$

as was to be shown. ∎

Two important corollaries follow directly from Proposition 1.[11]

Corollary 1. *Assume firms 1 and 2 are symmetric. A completely equity-financed industry* $(D=0)$ *will produce a lower output than the corresponding leveraged industry* $(D>0)$ *when* $R_{iz}^i > 0$. *If* $R_{iz}^i < 0$, *the equity-financed industry will produce more than the leveraged industry.*

Corollary 2. *A necessary and sufficient condition for financial structure to have no effect on the output market is* $R_{iz}^i = 0$ *for* $i = 1, 2$.

The intuition underlying Proposition 1 and Corollary 1 is just as described in the monopoly case, and is not offset by the interaction between firms.

It has been noted by several authors, particularly Jensen–Meckling and Myers (1977), that if investments are chosen after financial structure is set (in contrast to the assumption of fixed capital maintained in our paper), then increasing the debt level should cause equity holders to undertake

---

[11] The statement of Proposition 1, and Corollaries 1 and 2 are strictly correct provided $\hat{z}_i > \underline{z}$ whenever $D_i > 0$. For simplicity we assume this to be the case in all that follows. If $z_i \leq \underline{z}$ for some range of positive debt levels, then the output of firm i would remain unchanged over that range.

more risky investments, since they can declare bankruptcy in bad states of the world, while earning high rates of return in good states.[12] Our results concerning the output decision are conceptually similar. The normal case, $R_{iz}^i > 0$, corresponds to a situation in which increasing output increases the variance in the firm's profit stream because the marginal returns from extra production are positively correlated with the overall fortunes of the firm: the firm benefits most from increased production in good states of nature, and is harmed most by overproduction in bad states of nature. Thus increasing output is, in our model, analogous to a risky investment in the Myers framework in that it tends to be more attractive to shareholders when the firm is partially debt financed. When $R_{iz}^i < 0$, increasing output is risk reducing. A debt-financed firm will, in this case, reduce output, as it has less need to avoid risk because it can declare bankruptcy in bad states of the world.

Corollary 2 confirms the assertion set out in the introduction that one cannot legitimately treat the financial and real sides separately, except in special cases. Our next result indicates the strategic commitment aspects of financial decisions on the firms' behavior in the output market.

Proposition 2. *Given $R_{iz}^i > 0$, a unilateral increase in firm i's debt, D_i, causes an increase in q_i and a decrease in q_j. If $R_{iz}^i < 0$, then $dq_i/dD_i < 0$ and $dq_j/dD_i > 0$.*

Proof $(R_{iz}^i > 0)$: The method of proof is to totally differentiate first-order conditions (5) to generate the following system:

$$V_{ii}^i dq_i + V_{ij}^i dq_j + V_{iD_i}^i dD_i = 0, \tag{13}$$

$$V_{ji}^j dq_i + V_{jj}^j dq_j + V_{jD_i}^j dD_i = 0. \tag{14}$$

The first point to note is that V_j^j does not depend on D_i. Putting (13) and (14) in matrix form and using Cramer's rule to solve for comparative static effects dq_i/dD_i and dq_j/dD_i yields

$$dq_i/dD_i = -V_{iD_i}^i V_{jj}^j/B \tag{15}$$

$$dq_j/dD_i = V_{iD_i}^i V_{ji}^j/B, \tag{16}$$

where $B = V_{ii}^i V_{jj}^j - V_{ij}^i V_{ji}^j > 0$ from (8). Since B is positive, while $V_{jj}^j < 0$ by (6) and $V_{ji}^j < 0$ by (7), all that is needed is to sign $V_{iD_i}^i$.

$$V_{iD_i}^i = -R_i^i(\hat{z}_i) f(\hat{z}_i) d\hat{z}_i/dD_i$$

$$= -R_i^i(\hat{z}_i)/R_{z_i}^i f(\hat{z}_i), \tag{17}$$

---

[12] See also D. Galai and R. W. Masulus (1976) and Joseph Stiglitz and Andrew Weiss (1983) for related consideration of conflict of interest issues.

Oligopoly and financial structure

by (3a). Notice that (17) is identical to (11) which we have already established is strictly positive in the proof of Proposition 1. It follows, therefore, that

$$dq_i/dD_i > 0; \qquad dq_j/dD_i < 0, \tag{18}$$

which completes the proof. ∎

Proposition 2 represents the key insight to be brought out in this analysis. Notice that first-order condition (5) is the reaction function for firm i in implicit form indicating firm i's optimal output as a function of q_j, the output of its rival. The position of firm i's reaction function in output space depends on the debt level of firm i. In particular, with $R^i_{iz} > 0$, higher levels of debt, D_i, make it optimal for firm i to produce more in response to any output from its rival, firm j. As explained earlier in connection with Figure 1, an increase in a firm's own debt level removes states of low marginal return from the region in which equity holders are residual claimants. This translates into a higher desired output level for any given output level chosen by a rival: in other words, as illustrated in Figure 2a the reaction function is shifted out. In effect, with $R^i_{iz} > 0$, debt financing serves to commit the firm to an aggressive stance in the output market.

B. Debt value maximization

The idea that managers of a firm might be controlled by debtholders cannot be taken as a serious representation of many North American firms, but it may have some empirical significance.[13] What we wish to do here is compare the objectives of debtholders with those of the equity holders.

Proceeding as before, we characterize the Nash equilibrium in the output market, where now firms act to maximize their debt value as given by (4). The Nash equilibrium output levels are given by the simultaneous solution to

$$W^i_i = \int_{\underline{z}}^{\hat{z}_i} R^i_i(q_i, q_j, z_i) f(z_i)\, dz_i = 0, \tag{19}$$

for $i = 1, 2$.[14] In addition to (19) we require

$$W^i_{ii} < 0, \tag{20}$$

$$W^i_{ij} < 0, \tag{21}$$

[13] For example, in some situations, control by debtholders, especially banks, might be a precondition for obtaining financing.
[14] Besides the term in (19), W^i_i also contains the term $(d\hat{z}_i/dq_i)(R^i(\hat{z}) - D_i)$, which is zero by (2).

433

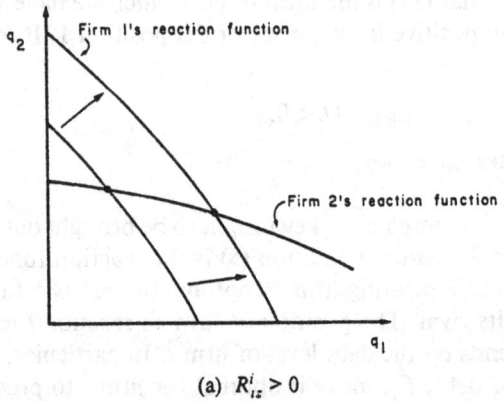

(a) $R^i_{iz} > 0$

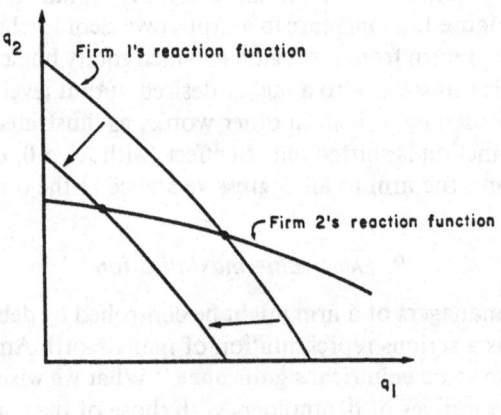

(b) $R^i_{iz} < 0$

Figure 2.

$$W^i_{ii}W^j_{jj} - W^i_{ij}W^j_{ji} > 0. \tag{22}$$

These conditions carry the same interpretation as (6)–(8) for the case of equity maximization. According to Proposition 1, equity-managed firms tend to produce a level of output above the level that maximizes overall firm value (debt value plus equity value). As noted by a referee, it follows almost directly that a firm managed by debtholders would choose an output level below the output maximizing level. We state this result without proof[15] as Proposition 3.

[15] A rigorous proof of Proposition 3 is contained in an earlier version of our paper available as UBC Economics Discussion Paper 85-10, or from the authors.

Oligopoly and financial structure

Proposition 3. *Assume firms 1 and 2 are symmetric and $D_1 = D_2 > 0$. Equilibrium output under equity value maximization is greater than (less than) equilibrium output under debt value maximization when $R^i_{iz} > 0$ ($R^i_{iz} < 0$).*

The results of Proposition 3 indicate the conflict of interest that exists between bondholders and equity holders in the firm. The different preferences of debt and equity holders for output levels are easily explained by noting that equity holders are residual claimants in some states, while debtholders are residual claimants in other states, as illustrated in Figure 1. When $R^i_{iz} > 0$, equity holders prefer larger output levels than do debtholders, because the equity holders are the residual claimants in states of nature when marginal returns are high. Debtholders become the residual claimants in those states when the firm cannot cover its debt obligation, which happen to be states in which the marginal returns to extra output are very low.

Rather clearly, if $R^i_{iz} < 0$, so that high marginal returns to output are associated with bad states of the world in which the debtholders are residual claimants, the results is reversed. In such a case, debtholders would prefer higher output levels than equity holders.

An interesting implication of the forgoing discussion is that when $R^i_{iz} > 0$, equity holders in the industry might well be better off if firms in the industry were controlled by bondholders. The reason for this is that equity-managed firms will tend to produce more than the joint profit-maximizing output. If the firms could agree to act as a cartel, they could increase combined profits. Transferring ownership to debtholders would cause the firms to move toward the cartel output level. Of course, no single firm would by itself have an incentive to transfer control, for if one firm did and the other did not, the firm controlled by the debtholders would do even worse than at the original equilibrium. In effect equity-controlled leveraged firms suffer a magnified version of the usual "prisoner's dilemma" aspect of oligopolistic rivalry, with the amount of magnification increasing with leverage.

It is intuitively reasonable that in the standard case ($R^i_{iz} > 0$), debtholders would prefer lower output levels than equity holders. What is perhaps more surprising is that debtholders, like equity holders, will in this case increase their desired output level as debt levels increase. In general comparative static effects for equity-controlled industries and debt-controlled industries are qualitatively identical.

Proposition 4. *A debt-controlled industry has the following comparative static properties:* (a) *If firms are symmetric, equilibrium output is* *increasing in the common debt level D for $R^i_{iz} > 0$, and it is decreasing in D for $R^i_{iz} < 0$. (b) With $R^i_{iz} > 0$, a unilateral increase in the debt of firm i, D_i, causes an increase in the output of firm i and a decrease in the output of firm j. If $R^i_{iz} < 0$, the signs are reversed.*

Proof. Proofs are obtained by totally differentiating first-order conditions (19) with respect to output levels and debt levels and, solving for the comparative static effects, then using (20), (21), and (22), along with (3) to obtain signs. The details of the proofs are not reported here as they are virtually identical to the details in the proofs of Propositions 1 and 2. ∎

Although these results may seem counterintuitive at first glance, the interpretations are straightforward. Consider the $R^i_{iz} > 0$ case. Looking at Figure 1 it is clear that an increase in debt levels raises the critical value of z_i at which bankruptcy occurs. Debtholders become the residual claimants over a wider range of states of the world, as higher levels of z are added to this range. Because $R^i_{iz} > 0$, the expected marginal profit of extra output goes up in the range relevant to debtholders. Therefore, on the margin it is profitable for the debtholders to increase output. As pointed out by a referee, in the limit, as the debt level becomes so large that debtholders become residual claimants in all states of the world, the firm will be managed just as if the firm were completely equity financed. Part b of Proposition 4 is explained by the same phenomenon that underlies the behavior of equity holders. For example, when $R^i_{iz} > 0$, a unilateral increase in leverage shifts the firm's reaction function outwards, increasing its equilibrium output and lowering the output of its rival.

III. Selection of debt levels

The preceding sections have examined the dependence of industry output levels on debt structure, treating debt as a predetermined or exogenous variable. In this section we describe the determinants of the debt structure. The existing literature on capital structure examines several important factors influencing the amount of debt chosen. The most standard treatment involves trading off the tax advantages of debt against bankruptcy costs in determining the optimal debt-equity position (as in Kraus and Litzenberger). Also, some analysts have stressed the use of capital structure to signal information about the firm to investors.[16] In this section we abstract from these well-understood determinants of financial

---

[16] Standard references on the use of capital structure to convey information include Stephen Ross (1977), Hayne Leland and D. Pyle (1977), and Robert Heinkel (1982).

structure and focus instead on an additional motive for holding (or not holding) debt that derives from the strategic commitment aspects of leverage in relation to output markets.

In what follows we assume that the manager of the firm is free to choose whatever output level he desires after debt is issued. In particular, bond convenants, which would restrict the manager's strategy decisions, are not considered. Bond convenants and other precommitment devices might, of course, be used for strategic purposes, but here we focus exclusively on strategic commitment through financial structure.

The equilibrium concept we use for the selection of debt levels is the Nash equilibrium in debt levels, subject to the constraint that firms and bondholders correctly anticipate the resolution of the Nash equilibrium in the output market. The equilibrium is, therefore, sequentially rational. More specifically, firms and investors understand that equilibrium output levels are determined by debt levels as implied by the simultaneous solution to first-order conditions (5). We denote the functional dependence of output levels on debt levels as follows: $q_i = q_i(\mathbf{D})$, where $\mathbf{D} = (D_1, D_2)$.

The objective of the firm's owners when making the debt decision is to maximize the total value of the firm, which is the sum of the equity value V^i and the debt value W^i. The basic point is that if potential debtholders are foresighted, then owners of the firm can sell bonds which promise to pay D_i only for their true value, taking into the account the possibility of bankruptcy. This true value is W^i. Hence the total value of the firm, denoted by Y^i is

$$Y^i(q_i(\mathbf{D}), q_j(\mathbf{D}), \mathbf{D}) = \int_{\underline{z}}^{\hat{z}_i} R^i(q_i(\mathbf{D}), q_j(\mathbf{D})) f(z_i) \, dz_i$$

$$+ \int_{\hat{z}_i}^{\bar{z}} R^i(q_i(\mathbf{D}), q_j(\mathbf{D})) f(z_i) \, dz_i. \tag{23}$$

This expression is obtained by adding (1) and (4) and noting that

$$\int_{\hat{z}_i}^{\bar{z}} D_i f(z_i) \, dz_i = D_i(1 - F(\hat{z}_i)),$$

leaving the two terms shown in (23). This combined value is, as one would expect, the expected value of operating profits over all states of the world. Because we abstract from bankruptcy costs and from the tax advantages of debt, issuing debt is strictly a break-even transaction for the firm, except for the fact that equilibrium output levels will depend on debt levels. If, by way of contrast, planned output levels were exogenously fixed (by, for example, quota allocations) then issuing debt would be purely neutral, having no effect on total value, Y^i, as in a Modigliani–Miller world.

However, q_i and q_j are written as functions of **D**, the industry debt structure, to indicate that output levels are in fact functions of the debt levels. A particular debt structure for the industry is a commitment to a particular output structure.

The marginal effect of an increase in D_i on the value of firm i is given by

$$Y_{Di}^i = \left[\int_{\hat{z}}^{\bar{z}} R_i^i(z_i) f(z_i)\, dz_i \right] dq_i/dD_i + \left[\int_{\underline{z}}^{\hat{z}} R_i^i(z_i) f(z_i)\, dz_i \right] dq_i/dD_i$$

$$+ \left[\int_{\underline{z}}^{\hat{z}} R_j^i(z_i) f(z_i)\, dz_i + \int_{\hat{z}}^{\bar{z}} R_j^i(z_i) f(z_i)\, dz_i \right] dq_j/dD_i. \tag{24}$$

The first term is zero by (5). The second term measures the effect of an induced change on q_i on the debt value of the firm. Notice that when $R_{iz}^i > 0$, (5) implies that $R_i^i(z_i) < 0$ for all $z_i \le \hat{z}_i$, reflecting the fact that equity holders will choose higher output levels than debtholders would like. A similar argument serves to establish that $R_i^i > 0$ for all $z \le \hat{z}$ whenever $R_{iz}^i < 0$. Taken together these two conditions imply

$$\int_{\underline{z}}^{\hat{z}} R_i^i(z_i) f(z_i)\, dz_i \lessgtr 0 \quad \text{if } R_{iz}^i \gtrless 0. \tag{25}$$

Using Proposition 2 ($dq_i/dD_i \gtrless$ if $R_{iz}^i \gtrless 0$), combined with (25), allows us to sign the second term in (24):

$$\left[\int_{\underline{z}}^{\hat{z}} R_i^i(z_i) f(z_i) \right] dq_i/dD_i < 0. \tag{26}$$

This term indicates that the induced change in output caused by taking on more debt exacerbates the conflict of interest between debt and equity holders and lowers the debt value of the firm. The third and final term of expression (24) represents the strategic effect of debt. A higher debt level for firm i induces a change in the equilibrium output of firm j. Specifically, if $R_{iz}^i > 0$, a higher level of debt for firm i implies lower output for firm j. This effect, taken by itself, raises both the debt value and the equity value of firm i because $R_j^i < 0$. A lowered output by firm j is unambiguously good for firm i.

Thus there are two conflicting effects of increasing debt on the value of the firm. Extra debt worsens the conflict of interest between debt and equity holders, tending to lower the value of the firm, as reflected in (26). In addition, however, extra debt has the value-increasing strategic effect we have just described. Despite these partially offsetting effects of debt, we are able to prove that the strategic effect dominates for sufficiently small levels of debt, insuring an interior ($D^i > 0$) solution to the firm's value maximization problem. Specifically, if $D_i = 0$ there is no conflict between bondholders and equity holders (there are no bondholders) implying that the second term of (24) is zero.[17] The first term is of course equal to zero, while the third term remains strictly positive implying that $Y_{D_i}^i$ is strictly positive at $D_i = 0$.

The other case, $R_{iz}^i > 0$, has strikingly different implications. In this case, dq_j/dD_i is positive, which implies that increases in D_i will cause the rival firm to increase output, which in turn lowers profits for firm i. Therefore the third term of (24) is strictly negative. Expression (24) as a whole is strictly negative at all feasible (nonnegative) levels for debt and we obtain a corner solution at $D^i = 0$. These results are expressed in Proposition 5.

Proposition 5. *Industry debt levels will be strictly positive if $R_{iz}^i > 0$. If $R_{iz}^i < 0$, firms will be entirely equity financed.*

Proposition 5, together with Proposition 1, implies that if firms hold any debt, they will produce more output than in the traditional industrial organization version of oligopoly, in which firms are assumed to be 100 percent equity financed.

The intuition underlying Proposition 5 is derived from our earlier results in Propositions 2 and 3. When marginal returns from output are positively correlated with the state of the world ($R_{iz}^i > 0$), Proposition 2 indicates that taking on more debt confers a strategic advantage of the firm, in that it causes the rival's equilibrium output to fall. This strategic benefit from debt financing must be traded off against the resulting decrease in the debt value of the firm as debt increases [as indicated by expression (24)]. We have shown that the strategic effect must dominate for sufficiently low debt levels, leading to an internal solution for the debt-equity ratio. In the case in which good states of the world are correlated with low marginal returns to output, debt has only value-reducing effects. The strategic effect of debt causes rival output to rise, and the conflict of interest between debtholders and equity holders remains. A corner solution with no debt is the solution in this case.

It also follows from the discussion above that a monopolist or a perfectly competitive firm would choose a corner solution with no debt. In either case, the strategic effect of debt financing is not relevant and firms would have no reason, in our model, to use debt. Therefore, strategic commitment through financial structure does not apply to monopoly and perfect competition in the same way that it applies to oligopoly.

---

[17] Strictly speaking $\hat{z} = z$ in this situation, rendering the integral equal to zero.

Proposition 5 should be interpreted with some care, since it is derived from a model in which certain empirically important determinants of financial structure, such as taxes, are explicitly ignored. Our analysis isolates the strategic output market effects as an influence on financial structure.

Our final result makes the point that, at least in the symmetric case, equilibrium debt levels do not maximize value for the firms taken together. While this is not surprising, given that firms behave noncooperatively in financial markets, it does suggest certain collusive financing arrangements that firms might profitably engage in.

Proposition 6. *Under symmetric conditions the value of the industry,* $Y^1(\mathbf{D}) + Y^2(\mathbf{D}) = 2Y(\mathbf{D})$, *is not maximized in equilibrium. In particular,* $dY(\mathbf{D})/dD < 0$ *if* $R^i_{iz} > 0$, *and* $dY(\mathbf{D})/dD > 0$ *if* $R^i_{iz} < 0$.

Proof $(R^i_{iz} > 0)$: If (6) and (8) hold globally, then in the special case where $D_i = 0$, $\hat{z} = \bar{z}$, and $q_i = q_j = q$, then (6) and (8) imply

$$\int_{\underline{z}}^{\bar{z}} R^i(q, q, z_i) f(z_i) \, dz_i \tag{27}$$

is strictly concave in q. Proposition 6 then follows directly from the fact that completely equity-financed firms fail to maximize joint profits because of excess production. This tendency on the part of firms to overproduce is exacerbated as they take on debt.

The basic point of Proposition 6 is straightforward. A noncooperative oligopoly produces more output than a profit-maximizing cartel or monopoly would. When $R^i_{iz} > 0$, increases in debt beyond zero cause output to rise still further: the use of debt lowers profits. In other words, debt is actually procompetitive. An interesting observation is that standard Cournot oligopoly corresponds exactly to the case of complete equity financing. Ignoring the interaction between financial and output markets causes the competitiveness of such oligopolies to be understated.

This structure also suggests that central control of financing arrangements might be an attractive collusive practice. If credit markets for a particular industry are quite concentrated, then lenders would have incentives to act as facilitating agents for collusion.

IV. Concluding remarks

This paper makes the basic point that product market decisions and financial decisions will normally be related. We have analyzed this relationship for a particular industry structure in which financial decisions

440

and product market decisions follow in sequence. In this situation, the limited liability provisions of debt financing imply that changes in financial structure alter the distribution of returns between debt and equity holders, and therefore change the output strategy favored by equity holders.

Because financial structure influences the output market equilibrium, foresighted owners of the firms will have incentives to use financial structure precisely so as to influence the output market in their favor. Given the behavior of the rival firm, a firm which ignored the strategic effect of financial decisions would have lower total value than a firm which took advantage of these effects.[18] These strategic uses of financial structure are purely predatory, and the net effect when both firms use them is that both firms are worse off. In our model, symmetric firms use financial structure as a commitment variable to influence the output market equilibrium. The symmetry is, however, not fundamental. One could examine an asymmetric market in which, for example, an incumbent firm used financial structure to preempt possible entry by a rival, just as capital or *R&D* can be used to deter entry.

Our analysis abstracts from empirically important aspects of the financial structure decision. In any empirical work one would certainly have to incorporate the tax advantages of debt, and the possibility of bankruptcy costs. In addition, the so-called agency aspects of financial structure could be very important. Specifically, if the firm is run not by shareholders but by imperfectly monitored managers, then very different results could emerge. Managers, presumably, would be very concerned about losing their jobs, especially if the outside world cannot tell whether a bankrupt firm has suffered bad luck or bad management. If so, then high debt levels might normally make the management of a firm extremely cautious and might tend to reduce industry output, in contrast to certain results in our model.

The analysis by Michael Bradley et al. and others indicates that there are systematic differences across industries and similarities within industries with respect to financial structure. Our analysis suggests that these variations in financial structure might be explained by industry-specific factors. For example, the mode of competition within an industry: price competition, quantity competition, *R&D* races, competitive advertising, and so on, would all have significant and different implications for financial

---

[18] The difference between our analysis and the analysis of conflict of interest in Myers (1977) is that here the returns themselves are endogenous. The endogeneity of the returns arises because the returns depend on a choice variable, output. If returns were purely exogenous, as in Myers, the creation of a conflict of interest between bondholders and debtholders could only lower the value of the firm unless there were some other advantage to debt, such as a tax advantage.

structure. In addition, as shown in our model, the pattern of random returns (as reflected, for example, by the sign of R_{iz}^i) is likely to have an effect on financial structure.

Another implication of our analysis is that the institutional structure of credit markets can have an important impact on the economic performance of output markets. In our model, we identify an opportunity for credit institutions with monopoly power to act as a facilitating agent for collusion in the output market, but this is only one of several possible links. Finally, our model suggests that the public finance aspects of interest deductibility might well include the output effect that is induced by the resulting higher debt levels.

The overall point that we wish to emphasize is that opening the linkage between financial markets and the "real" side of firms' decisions for analysis suggests a number of possibly important and certainly interesting economic consequences, of which our model provides some examples.

References

Aivazian, Varouj A. and Callen, Jeffrey L., "Corporate Leverage and Growth: The Game Theoretic Issues," *Journal of Financial Economics,* December 1980, 8, 379–99.

Allen, Franklin, "Capital Structure and Imperfect Competition in Product Markets," Discussion Paper, University of Pennsylvania, 1985.

Altman, Edward I., "An Empirical Investigation of the Bankruptcy Cost Question," *Journal of Finance,* September 1984, 39, 1067–89.

Bradley, Michael, Jarrell, Gregg A. and Kim, E. Han, "On the Existence of an Optimal Capital Structure: Theory and Evidence," *Journal of Finance,* July 1984, 39, 857–80.

Brander, James A. and Lewis, Tracy R., "Bankruptcy Costs and the Theory of Oligopoly," mimeo., University of British Columbia, 1985.

Brander, James A. and Spencer, Barbara J., "Strategic Commitment with R&D: The Symmetric Case," *Bell Journal of Economics,* Spring 1983, 14, 225–335.

Bulow, Jeremy and Shoven, John, "The Bankruptcy Decision," *Bell Journal of Economics,* Autumn 1978, 9, 437–56.

Dixit, Avinash, "The Role of Investment in Entry Deterrence," *Economic Journal,* March 1980, 90, 95–106.

Eaton, B. Curtis and Eswaren, Mukesh, "Asymmetric Equilibria and Strategic Behaviour in Oligopolistic Markets: A Synthesis," Discussion Paper No. 84-19, University of British Columbia, 1984.

Eaton, B. Curtis and Lipsey, Richard, "The Durability of Capital as a Barrier to Entry," *Bell Journal of Economics,* Autumn 1980, 11, 721–29.

Galai, D. and Masulis, R. W., "The Option Pricing Model and the Risk Factor of Stock," *Journal of Financial Economics,* January/March 1976, 3, 53–82.

Giammarino, Ronald M., "On the Significance of Financial Distress to the Theory of Optimal Capital Structure," unpublished doctoral dissertation, Queen's University, 1984.

Green, Jerry and Shoven, John, "The Effects of Financing Opportunities and Bankruptcy on Entrepreneurial Risk Bearing," in J. Ronen, ed., *Entrepreneurship,* Lexington: Lexington Books, 1983.

Heinkel, Robert, "A Theory of Capital Structure Relevance Under Imperfect Information," *Journal of Finance,* December 1982, 37, 1141-50.

Jensen, M. and Meckling, W., "Theory of the Firm: Managerial Behavior, Agency Costs, and Capital Structure," *Journal of Financial Economics,* October 1976, 3, 305-60.

Kraus, Alan and Litzenberger, Robert H., "A State-Preference Model of Optimal Financial Leverage," *Journal of Finance,* September 1973, 33, 911-22.

Leland, Hayne and Pyle D., "Information Asymmetries, Financial Structure and Financial Intermediation," *Journal of Finance,* May 1977, 32, 371-87.

Maksimovic, Vojislav, "Optimal Capital Structure in Oligopolies," unpublished doctoral dissertation, Harvard University, 1986.

Modigliani, Franco and Miller, Merton, "The Cost of Capital, Corporation Finance, and the Theory of Investment," *American Economic Review,* June 1958, 48, 261-97.

———, "Corporate Income Taxes and the Cost of Capital: A Correction," *American Economic Review,* June 1963, 53, 433-43.

Myers, Stewart C., "Determination of Corporate Borrowing," *Journal of Financial Economics,* December 1977, 4, 147-75.

———, "The Capital Structure Puzzle," *Journal of Finance,* July 1984, 39, 575-92.

Ross, Stephen, "The Determinants of Financial Structure: The Incentive-Signalling Approach," *Bell Journal of Economics,* Spring 1977, 8, 23-40.

Schelling, Thomas, "An Essay on Bargaining," *American Economic Review,* June 1956, 46, 557-83.

Schmalensee, Richard, "A Model of Promotional Competition in Oligopoly," *Review of Economic Studies,* November 1976, 43, 493-507.

Selten, R., "Reexamination of the Perfectness Concept for Equilibrium Points in Extensive Games," *International Journal of Game Theory,* 1975, 4, 25-55.

Stiglitz, Joseph and Weiss, Andrew, "Credit Rationing in Markets with Imperfect Information," *American Economic Review,* June 1983, 73, 393-410.

Titman, Sheridan, "The Effect of Capital Structure on a Firm's Liquidation Decision," *Journal of Financial Economics,* March 1984, 13, 137-51.